ABRAHAM
LINCOLN
A Press Portrait

THE NORTH'S CIVIL WAR SERIES
Paul A. Cimbala, series editor

ABRAHAM LINCOLN

A Press Portrait

His Life and Times
from the Original Newspaper Documents
of the Union, the Confederacy,
and Europe

by

HERBERT MITGANG

FORDHAM UNIVERSITY PRESS
NEW YORK
2000

Copyright © 1956, 1962, 1971, 2000 by Herbert Mitgang
All rights reserved
LC 00-028415
ISBN 0-8232-2061-3 (hardcover)
ISBN 0-8232-2062-1 (paperback)
ISSN 1089-8719
The North's Civil War, no 15

Library of Congress Cataloging-in-Publication Data

Abraham Lincoln, a press portrait : his life and times from the original newspaper documents of the Union, the Confederacy, and Europe / edited by Herbert Mitgang.
   p.   cm.—(The North's Civil War ; no. 15)
   Originally published: Chicago : Quadrangle Books, 1971. With new introd.
Includes index.
   ISBN 0-8232-2061-3—ISBN 0-8232-2062-1 (pbk.)
   1. Lincoln, Abraham, 1809–1865. 2. Lincoln, Abraham, 1809–1865—Relations with journalists. 3. Presidents—United States—Biography. 4. United States—Politics and government—1845–1861—Sources. 5. United States—Politics and government—1861–1865—Sources. 6. Press and politics—United States—History—19th century—Sources. I. Mitgang, Herbert. II. Series.
E457.15.M5   2000
973.7′092—dc21
[B]   00-028415

To Shirley Mitgang

Contents

Introduction to the 2000 Edition

Whenever I'm in Springfield to visit Lincoln's hometown and pursue the latest discoveries about his life, family, legal career, and presidency, I head for a newsstand and pick up a copy of the *Sangamo Journal* and the *State Register*. I like to see what both Simeon Francis's pro-Lincoln paper and what the pro-Douglas paper—which Stephen Douglas himself established—have to say. It makes for a neat political balance. The *Journal* spoke for the Whigs and later the Republicans, the *Register* for the Democrats.

Then, once again, comes a shock: I'm dreaming in the wrong century. The two independent newspapers no longer exist, except as one merged publication, the *State-Journal Register*, with an out-of-town ownership. Nothing unusual about that in the broad field of communications in the new century. The same can be said for other newspapers—not to mention the television networks and conglomerated book and magazine publishers—all over the United States. In Lincoln's time, for example, New York City had ten daily newspapers; today, it has only one broadsheet, *The New York Times*, and a couple of warring tabloids.

In a lecture delivered to his neighbors in Springfield long before he became known nationally, Lincoln said: "At length printing came. It gave ten thousand copies of any written matter quite as cheaply as ten were given before; and consequently a thousand minds were brought into the field where was but one before. This was a great gain—and history shows a great change corresponding to it—in point of time. I will venture to consider it the true termination of that period called the 'dark ages.' "

In a talk delivered in Columbus a year before his nomination, Lincoln said: "Public opinion in this country is everything." He realized that voters could be convinced at that time in only two ways—by voice (as in the Lincoln–Douglas debates) and by the press. The unamplified voice and the newspapers had at least one virtue: you could not punch up the worldwide web on a computer and get a busy signal.

Before pollsters, exit polls, ghostwriters, and spinmeisters, Lincoln recognized that the free press could lead to an educated public. With some noble exceptions, news is more partisan and limited these days but without being as independent. Like McDonald's hamburgers, some cynical journalists call the bland reports "McNews." Or, if really boring, "McSnooze."

Nobody could be bored reading the old *Register* and *Journal*. Early in Lincoln's career, the *Register* reprimanded him for his humor, calling it "assumed clownishness." In the mid-twentieth century, similar criticism was leveled against Gov. Adlai E. Stevenson of Illinois when he ran for president in 1952 and 1956 and was branded an "egghead" who talked over the heads of the people—a falsehood that insulted the intelligence of many American voters.

The *Register* called Lincoln "the ineffable despot, who, by some inscrutable dispensation of providence, presides over the destinies of this vast republic." When Lincoln ran for a second term, the *Register* said, "The doom of Lincoln and Black Republicanism is sealed. Corruption and the bayonet are incompetent to save them." The *Journal* responded by calling Charles Lanphier, the *Register*'s editor, "the agent of Jeff Davis who presides over the Copperhead sheet in this city."

It was raw stuff but enlightening and, in retrospect, fun to read.

By a little stretch of the imagination, it's possible to say that Lincoln was once a newspaper "publisher" himself. He actually owned his own newspaper briefly—a little-known chapter in his career, and one that he deliberately concealed from the public. It was the German-language Illinois *Staats-Anzeiger*. Under a secret contract drawn by Lincoln himself in 1859—while he was busy lining up support for the Republican nomination for president—any time that Theodore Canisius, the owner of the paper, failed to espouse the Republican line, Lincoln could reclaim its type and press. (The document of ownership gave the price as $400.) The paper, of course, was designed to convince German voters to toe the party line. Both parties to the deal held up their ends of the bargain. Before his inauguration, Lincoln sold back the paper to Canisius. Once in office, Lincoln paid off the support by naming Canisius the American consul in Vienna.

It's interesting to note that—a century before A. J. Liebling, the *New Yorker* press critic, said it cynically—Lincoln was aware that "freedom of the press is guaranteed only to those who own one."

So it went from city to city with the outspoken party press. The *Chicago Tribune* was for Lincoln; the *Chicago Times* against; the *Cincinnati Daily*

Commercial was for; the *Cincinnati Enquirer* against. The *Louisville Journal* had been one of Lincoln's favorite newspapers—"He studied and paid for it when he had not money enough to dress decently," said James Quay Howard, who interviewed many of Lincoln's old friends. The Louisville paper played it down the middle for a Kentucky boy, saying, "We do not concur with him in some of his views, but there is much good in Abraham's bosom."

Most of the secessionist papers were vitriolic about the "Black Republican" in the White House. But the Upper South had a newspaper in Knoxville with a memorable logotype: *Brownlow's Whig and Rebel Ventilator*. It was edited by Parson Brownlow, who was a great supporter of President Lincoln and his wartime aims.

Lincoln was devoted to newspapers. With no harm done to the newsprint, he read the big city papers from all over the country before delivering them when he was the New Salem postmaster. Moreover, he served as a newspaper agent, collecting money from subscribers, a little-known fact that can be found in the *Sangamo Journal* of October 31, 1835. On page 1 there's a notice from Simeon Francis dunning his subscribers. In the statewide list appears the name A. Lincoln, Esq., as the agent for New Salem. Then as now, the practice of double-dipping by an officeholder was not unheard-of.

While serving as a representative in the Illinois General Assembly, Lincoln reported the doings of the state legislature for the *Sangamo Journal*. That was one way to make sure the news came out right—his way. Today he would be called a "stringer," writing for space rates. Did Lincoln try to manipulate the press? Not quite; he just wanted the reports to come out accurately—that is, *his* way. But then so did the other side in those times of a frankly partisan press.

President Lincoln did not forget his old friend from the *Sangamo Journal*. In 1864 Lincoln appointed Simeon Francis an Army paymaster, a job he held until 1870. From the White House, Lincoln wrote: "The *Journal* paper was always my friend; and, of course its editors the same."

I'm delighted to see that the *State Journal-Register* still carries those words today.

In this respect, I must mention that *The New York Times*, where I hung my hat for many years as a writer and editor, received a similar communication from President Lincoln. But I'm glad that I wasn't around as a correspondent for *The Times* when Lincoln wrote to Henry J. Raymond, the New York paper's editor-publisher, complaining about one of his reporters: "What a very mad man your correspondent, Smedley, is. What does he think of a man who makes charges against another which he does not know to be true, and could easily learn to be false?"

Nevertheless, on May 24, 1864, President Lincoln wrote to Secretary of War Stanton: "*The Times*, I believe, is always true to the Union, and therefore should be treated at least as well as any." Lincoln wrote those words as an endorsement on a letter from *The Times* Washington bureau, enclosing a pass to the Army of the Potomac. Stanton declined to endorse it, saying no passes would be issued unless approved by General Grant or General Meade.

No hard feelings, not with a friend in the press. A few weeks later, Raymond served as chairman of the platform committee that nominated Lincoln for a second term while, at the same time, he edited the influential New York newspaper. That kind of open partisanship would never happen today—not even for an overnight stay by a publisher in the Lincoln bedroom.

When Lincoln gave his Cooper Union talk, he composed his handwritten words so carefully that he went to the *Tribune* office that night to check the page proofs. (It's too bad that a printer tossed the speech into the wastebasket afterward.) Those words sent his ideas soaring across the country. Together with the widely circulated photograph that Mathew Brady took at his studio on lower Broadway, the Cooper Union speech—so Lincoln later said—helped to make him president.

New York was home to the powerful group of editors known as the "newspaper generals"—Henry J. Raymond of *The Times*, Horace Greeley of *The Tribune*, William Cullen Bryant of *The Post*, James Gordon Bennett of *The Herald*. The troublemaking Democratic congressman Benjamin Wood owned the *Daily News*. What they all had in common was that, much to their chagrin, *they* were not president of the United States. That did not prevent them from telling Lincoln how to run the Army of the Potomac and the endangered Union.

The *Herald* led in name-calling. Of a pro-Lincoln meeting in wartime, Bennett said, "It was a gathering of ghouls, vultures, hyenas, and other feeders of carrion. The great ghoul of Washington [Lincoln] authorized the meeting and the little ghouls and vultures conducted it."

The most telling communication of all was written by Lincoln himself to Greeley, whose *chutzpah* was unexcelled. Just before the Preliminary Emancipation Proclamation, Greeley wrote an open letter to Lincoln, demanding that slaves of rebels coming within Union lines be freed. We all know of Lincoln's memorable response. But what I would like to emphasize is this: It was the finest example of his constitutionalism, political acumen, logical thinking, and, especially, his straightforward writing style: "My paramount object in this struggle is to save the Union, and is not either to save or to destroy slavery. If I could save the Union without freeing *any* slave, I would do it, and if I could save it by freeing *all* the slaves, I would do it, and if I could save it by freeing some and leaving others alone, I would also do that." And then he concluded: "I have here stated my purpose according to my view of *official* duty; and I intend no modification of my oft-expressed *personal* wish that all men everywhere could be free."

Here was the Jeffersonian Lincoln, speaking for the ages. In our textbooks, we tend to divide American history into presidential and military time frames. Yet I am always surprised when I realize that, for seventeen years, Lincoln and Jefferson were alive at the same time. It is little wonder that Lincoln's fundamental ideas were rooted in the Declaration of Independence and the Constitution.

In his response to Greeley, Lincoln called him "an old friend whose heart I have always supposed to be right." Nevertheless, Lincoln trumped the *Tribune* editor by making sure that *his* answer appeared in an open reply in the Washington *National Intelligencer.* As he had done during his youth in Springfield, he was still using the press as a forum in Washington.

I like what Lincoln told his cabinet, behind closed doors, about Greeley in the summer of 1864: "Greeley is an old shoe—good for nothing now, whatever he had been. In early life, and with few mechanics and but little means in the West, we used to make our shoes last a great while with much mending, and sometimes when far gone, we found the leather so rotten the stitches would not hold. Greeley is so rotten that nothing can be done with him. He is not truthful; the stitches all tear out."

Lincoln was what today we would call a "newspaper junkie." As president, Lincoln sometimes would step outside the White House and ask a startled passerby to send the corner newsboys up the street to his front door. I like that image; it's one of the legends that I believe is true.

As a lawyer, Lincoln knew the importance of keeping the record straight even if the newspapers were less than honest in their sensational reporting. He recognized that the newspapers were party organs, with little pretense of objectivity, yet with outspoken editors who allowed themselves fiery editorializing—in the South as well as the North. During the Lincoln–Douglas debates (I like the fact that the contestants and the press called them "joint discussions" rather than debates), every nuance was watched and reported.

Whenever possible, Lincoln corrected the galleys of his speeches before they were put into permanent print in the papers. The one-sided reporting of the *Chicago Tribune* and the *Chicago Times* showed in their reporting of the debates. They interjected applause and hits for their candidates.

Here are some of the headlines in the anti-Lincoln *Chicago Times* after the first "joint discussion" in Ottawa:

LINCOLN BREAKS DOWN

LINCOLN'S HEART FAILS HIM!

LINCOLN'S LEGS FAIL HIM!

LINCOLN'S ARMS FAIL HIM!

LINCOLN FAILS ALL OVER!!

THE PEOPLE REFUSE TO SUPPORT HIM!

THE PEOPLE LAUGH AT HIM!

DOUGLAS THE CHAMPION OF THE PEOPLE!

DOUGLAS SKINS THE "LIVING DOG"

The air of hostility hanging over the debates and the "phonographic" (that is, shorthand) reporters who covered it brought outcries from Lincoln's friends. The *Chicago Times* blamed its fake reporting on the fact that "Lincoln cannot speak five grammatical sentences in succession."

How did Lincoln handle the partisan press? Before the senatorial contest and presidential nomination, Lincoln sent many "confidential" communications to newspaper editors to make sure that his views were represented accurately.

It was not calling the president a lunatic and warmonger that got certain Northern newspapers into trouble but, instead, what the Union generals considered a fifth column—a stab in the back of their own lines by certain newspapers. *The Crisis*, a Democratic paper in Columbus, called Lincoln "a half-witted usurper." Other Copperhead papers branded him a "monster," but they were not suppressed, although individual generals made an effort to censor them.

Lincoln explained his attitude toward such personal attacks in a communication in the middle of the war, when victory was not at all certain, to Gen. John M. Schofield:

> You will only arrest individuals, and suppress assemblies, or newspapers, when they may be working palpable injury to the Military in your charge, and in no other case will you interfere with the expression of opinion in any form, or allow it to be interfered with violently by others.
>
> In this, you have a discretion to exercise with great caution, calmness, and forbearance.

Actually, Lincoln himself ordered the suspension of only one newspaper— *The New York World.* He did so not because it was the leader of the radical opposition to his conduct of the presidency but because it ran an inflammatory faked proclamation in his name. *The World* was ruled by Mayor Fernando Wood of New York and August Belmont, an influential banker, who is better known to daily-double fans today for the racetrack bearing his name. Its editor-in-chief was Manton Marble, who was described by other journalists as "a mercenary scribbler, who has no scruple in admitting that he wrote for pay, and for the party that pays the most."

The heart of the fake proclamation called for a day of fasting and prayer and for a draft of 400,000 men into the Army. The proclamation sounded like a Copperhead plot to set off a new draft riot in New York. It bore the signature of President Lincoln and Secretary of State Seward. The fake set off alarm bells in Washington and among the troops in the field when its falsity was revealed. In his constitutional role as commander in chief, Lincoln then ordered Gen. John A. Dix, who commanded the Army of the East, to shut down *The World* and the *Journal of Commerce*, which had also run the fake proclamation.

Lincoln gave these reasons:

> Whereas there has been wickedly and traitorously printed and published . . . a false and spurious proclamation purporting to be signed by the President and to be countersigned by the Secretary of State, which publication is of a treasonable nature, designed to give aid and comfort to the enemies of the United States and to the rebels now at war against the government and their aiders and abettors, you are therefore commanded forthwith to arrest and imprison the editors, proprietors and publishers of the aforesaid newspapers . . . and you will hold the persons so arrested in close custody until they can be brought to trial before a military commission for their offense. You will also take possession by military force of the printing establishment of *The New York World* and *Journal of Commerce* and prohibit any further publication.

Several days after the arrests of the two newspapermen who had written the fake proclamation, the War Department allowed the newspapers to resume publishing.

Far more controversial, of course, was Lincoln's suspension of the writ of habeas corpus and his exercise of martial law. Actually, he was on stronger grounds in suspending the writ because the Union was dealing with an insurrection, and as Lincoln said, he was obliged to see that the laws were faithfully executed. Against this reasoning for the writ stood the First Amendment as a bulwark for the press. Ever the constitutionalist, Lincoln was not suspending newspaper opinions; he was suspending treasonous acts.

As president, Lincoln sent letters to journalists that were usually friendly but sometimes brutally frank. To Bennett of the *New York Herald*, he wrote: "The Administration will not discriminate against the *Herald*, especially while it sustains us so generously, and the cause of the country as ably as it has been doing." But a different tone was reserved for Nathaniel Paschall, editor of the *Missouri Republican*, who received this "private and confidential" letter—filled with more Lincolnian honey than vinegar: "Please pardon me for suggesting that if the papers, like yours, which heretofore have persistently garbled, and misrepresented what I have said, will now fully and fairly place it before their readers, there can be no further misunderstanding. I beg you to believe me sincere when I declare that I do not say this in a spirit of complaint or resentment; but that I urge it as the true cure for any real uneasiness in the country."

I believe that there are perils for historians and journalists today who try to draw exact parallels between Lincoln's time and ours. We must always remember that there was a war on; at first, enemy artillery was almost within reach of the capital. Lincoln was not exaggerating when he bid farewell to his Springfield neighbors at the railway station before going to Washington, never to return alive, that he "faced a task greater than that which rested upon Washington."

When he was criticized for not caving in to the enemy within, Commander in Chief Lincoln said, "I think the time is not unlikely to come when I shall be blamed for having made too few arrests rather than too many."

Of all the American journalists covering the war and White House, one stood out as the favorite of President and Mary Lincoln. He was Noah Brooks, a California newspaperman for the *Sacramento Union*. He used a pseudonym—Castine—after the name of his hometown in Maine. Brooks saw the president several times a week; he was destined to become one of his secretaries.

Lincoln once told Brooks: "You speak of Lincoln stories. I don't think that is the correct phrase. I don't make the stories mine by telling them. I am only a retail dealer."

Of the foreign correspondents who covered Lincoln, one stood out as a keen observer who went against the hostile views of the powerful *London Times*. He was Edward Dicey, a young British writer for *The Spectator* and *Macmillan's* magazine. This is how he reported Lincoln after a visit: "Lincoln spoke but little, and seemed to prefer others talking to him instead. But when he did speak, his remarks were shrewd and sensible. Although in his badly fitting suit of black, he did not have the appearance of a gentleman, still there is about him something more important, a complete absence of pretension, and an evident desire to be courteous to everybody, which is the essence, if not the outward form of high breeding."

After the assassination, Dicey wrote an article summing up Lincoln's greatness: "I do not believe the late president was a man of genius. His record is grand and noble enough without our needing to attribute to him qualities he did not possess. His name will, if I mistake not, be cherished by the American people. History, I think, will say that our own days produced a yet nobler representative of American courage, and honesty, and self-sacrifice, in the person of Abraham Lincoln."

HERBERT MITGANG

Sources
and Publications

The original sources of this material are derived from newspaper morgues, public and private libraries, historical societies, and university collections from Maine to California. In Castine, Maine, for example, I spoke to friends and examined the papers of Noah Brooks, who was Lincoln's favorite Washington correspondent (and has the final article in this book). Many librarians in towns small and large cooperated cheerfully; they are our overlooked scholars.

The Illinois State Historical Library and the New York Public Library's various departments and rooms were major sources. The new interpretations here are mine, of course. They are based in part on three visits I made to the Illinois prairie country, going over lands Lincoln surveyed, sitting in old courthouses where he practiced, studying original sites where he debated. James T. Hickey, curator of the Lincoln collection at the State Historical Library, and Max Goodsill of Knox College, Galesburg, guided me in these areas. James N. Adams, in charge of the library's newspaper room, made possible parts of the early chapters of this book because of his meticulous indexing of the Springfield press. The late state historian Harry E. Pratt, Marion D. Pratt, and Margaret A. Flint all helped. A study of the bulletins from the present state historian, Clyde Walton, was enlightening.

The New York Public Library's newspaper annex, now in the West Forties near the Hudson River, was an indispensable source of original and microfilmed material. It was then located in mid-Manhattan's sewing-machine district, of all places. But Lincoln is where you find him. The newspaper annex is a curious place frequented by seedy historians and scholarly horse-players who show up before the daily double to study the back numbers of racing's *Morning Telegraph*. Perhaps the historian–horse-player combination is not so curious at that. There is a kinship between them: both chart past performances in order to handicap the present.

Scores of other libraries contributed hints, leads, and publications—

too many to list for proper credit. The major large-city newspapers that published during Lincoln's time are fairly good sources of comment on their own friendship with Lincoln, usually only a little exaggerated. Scholars pursuing particular details about an event or a person mentioned are advised to try newspapers (if in existence) or state historical libraries. The best sources of information in the Lincoln field are the Library of Congress, the Illinois State Historical Library, the Chicago Historical Society, and the New York Public Library. Several other libraries of Americana as represented in the press are particularly strong on the mid-nineteenth century.

I pay special tribute to the memory of Carl Sandburg. During long talks and walks in Springfield, Galesburg, Gettysburg, New York City, and Flat Rock, North Carolina, he enriched his own great Lincoln biography for me with comments about Lincoln's complex "velvet and steel" nature—and generously shared his own instincts about life with a groping scholar and newspaperman. And finally, I acknowledge the devoted aid of my wife, Shirley Mitgang, in preparing and shaping the scattered material for book publication.

The following newspapers and magazines have at least one entry and sometimes (the *New York Tribune* and *Springfield Journal*) more than twenty-five. They are listed here to indicate the range of opinion in this press biography and to guide scholars in exploring the publications of Lincoln's time.

NEWSPAPERS

California: *Daily Alta California*, San Francisco.
Connecticut: *Hartford Press; Norwich Courier.*
Illinois: *Sangamo Journal* and *Illinois Journal; Illinois State Register; Chicago Tribune; Chicago Times; Chicago Press; Chicago Journal; Alton Telegraph; Illinois Gazette; Rockford Forum; Belleville Advocate; Peoria Transcript; Peoria Democrat Press; Quincy Whig; Danville Sun; Fulton Telegraph; Galesburg Democrat; Menard Index.*
Indiana: *Evansville Journal.*
Kansas: *Palermo Leader; Lawrence Republican.*
Kentucky: *Paris Citizen; Frankfort Commonwealth; Louisville Journal.*
Louisiana: *New Orleans Delta; New Orleans Bee; Daily Picayune.*
Maine: *Bangor Democrat.*

Sources and Publications

Maryland: *Baltimore American; Kent News; The South; Baltimore Patriot.*

Massachusetts: *Boston Daily Advertiser; Lowell Journal; Boston Atlas; Boston Journal.*

Missouri: *St. Louis New Era; St. Louis Democrat; St. Louis Republican.*

New York: *New-York Times; New York Tribune; New York Herald; New York World; New York Daybook; New York News; New York Post; Abend Zeitung.*

Ohio: *Cincinnati Commercial; Cincinnati Enquirer; Columbus Crisis.*

Pennsylvania: *Reading Journal; Lancaster Herald; Chester County Times; Philadelphia Journal.*

South Carolina: *Charleston Mercury.*

Tennessee: *Brownlow's Knoxville Whig and Rebel Ventilator.*

Texas: *Houston Telegraph; Dallas Herald.*

Virginia: *Richmond Whig; Richmond Dispatch; Richmond Sentinel; Southern Illustrated News; Petersburg Express.*

Washington, D.C.: *National Intelligencer; Daily Chronicle.*

Wisconsin: *Galesville Transcript.*

England: *London Critic; London Times; Punch; Spectator; Morning Post.*

France: *La Patrie; Le Siècle.*

Italy: *Gazetta di Firenze; Milan Perseverance.*

MAGAZINES

Atlantic Monthly; Harper's Weekly; Harper's Monthly; Home Journal; Littell's Living Age; Vanity Fair; Watchman & Reflector.

Introduction

Abraham Lincoln entered public life nearly a century and a half ago —long before the selling of cosmeticized Presidents in televised packages —when the force of a man's mind and the power of his lungs still counted.

The story of Lincoln's life can be newly discovered in the raw language of the newspapers and broadsides that reported his personal growth and career. The press of his time was a direct, unpolled reflection of the shades and fervor of clashing public ideologies. In taking the measure of a man and his philosophy, one can always apply modern yardsticks and meanings. The scholar, however, finds authenticity refreshing and turns to original sources and contemporary documents.

In recent years, Lincoln's life has been reinterpreted many times for political purposes; much chicken in Republican box lunches has been larded with fat-cat credos that Lincoln himself would have found hard to swallow. He has been updated continuously, with interpretations as far removed from his principles as those attributed to him by the Copperhead and fire-eating Southern publications during his years as the sixteenth President. The most outrageous distortions of all have claimed that Lincoln was really a racist who favored slavery. It is essential, therefore, to examine not simply a sentence here and there, or a campaign speech, but the long, straight line of his life as he lived it—and as it was revealed by the press to the American people.

"Please pardon me for suggesting that if the papers, like yours, which heretofore have persistently garbled and misrepresented what I have said, will now fully and fairly place it before their readers, there can be no further misunderstanding," Lincoln wrote to the editor of the *Missouri Republican*.

From his first days in New Salem, Lincoln was aware of the press as a forum for aiding or misrepresenting a candidate's cause. As a young postmaster he read the newspapers from different parts of the country that came to his surprisingly well-educated, even sophisticated Illinois village. He relied on reporters, editors, and publishers throughout his political journey. Often, to make or refute a point, he took quill in hand and wrote a letter to the editor. Perhaps his most telling statement of policy during the Civil War appeared in the form of "A Letter from the President," dated August 22, 1862. Though addressed to Horace Greeley of the *New York Tribune*, it was planted in the Washington *National Intelligencer*. The letter was picked up by all newspapers, North and South, read for its nuances, pondered. It included these telling words about the Lincoln administration's wartime priorities and the President's personal inclinations:

"I would save the Union. I would save it the shortest way under the Constitution. . . . If I could save the Union without freeing any slave I would do it; and if I could save it by freeing all the slaves I would do it; and if I could save it by freeing some and leaving others alone, I would also do that. . . . I have here stated my purpose according to my view of *official* duty; and I intend no modification of my oft-expressed *personal* wish that all men everywhere could be free."

Next to his own, the words which help to illuminate Lincoln for the latest generation are those written by reportorial and editorial opinion-makers. The journals of his time, with few second thoughts or concessions to propriety, presented history in the rough. Their reports of what Lincoln said and how he acted supplemented what he actually did at high moments of his inscribed life. The editorial comments—advice and contempt, petulance and acrimony—are among the most violent bestowed upon an American President in peace and war. In this book no attempt is made to conceal nugatory reports or slanderous opinions. The words are set forth undiluted, as they appeared then and were read by, among others, Mr. Lincoln himself.

When he was a representative in the Illinois General Assembly in the 1830's, Lincoln personally reported the doings of the legislature for the *Sangamo Journal*, Springfield's Whig paper. He had worked for the newspaper as an agent, signing up subscribers; often he hung around the newspaper shop. Sometimes, just for the hell of it, Lincoln wrote letters to the editor under assumed names. One such letter brought Lincoln to duel-point with a gentleman he ridiculed. This serio-comic incident in 1842, when the youthful legislator was unmarried, is reported in detail here for the first time, as he and his friends and neighbors read of it in the local papers. Asked about the weapons that might be used in the near-challenge, Lincoln suggested, "How about cow dung at five paces?" Later, seeking higher office, he preferred to forget the whole thing—the silliest incident in his life.

Not only did Lincoln know and make friends with newspapermen; for a time he owned his own newspaper, the Illinois *Staats-Anzeiger*.

Introduction

Under a contract dated May 30, 1859, between Abraham Lincoln and Theodore Canisius, any time this paper failed to espouse the Republican line, Lincoln could reclaim its type and press. (Lincoln drew up the contract himself.) Before his inauguration, he sold the paper back to Canisius, who later was appointed American consul in Vienna.

As a rising politician on the prairie, Lincoln made the newspaper his stump. For newspapers in those days, far more than today, were news themselves. "At length printing came. It gave ten thousand copies of any written matter quite as cheaply as ten were given before; and consequently a thousand minds were brought into the field where was but one before. This was a great gain—and history shows a great change corresponding to it—in point of time. I will venture to consider it the true termination of that period called the Dark Ages." So Lincoln spoke in a lecture on Washington's Birthday, 1859, in recognition of the crucial role played by the emerging press of the period. A year before, at the time of his debates with Douglas up and down Illinois, he had carefully corrected the galleys of his speeches printed in the press, preparing them for permanent publication.

The bigwigs of the press and of politics in Lincoln's time were often one and the same. In New York alone, Henry J. Raymond was not only editor of the *New-York Times;* he was also lieutenant governor of the state, a key figure at conventions, and the chairman of the Republican National Committee during Lincoln's reelection campaign in 1864. Horace Greeley of the *New York Tribune* sized up Lincoln in 1847 as a representative in the Thirtieth Congress, and served as a major force when the Republican party was created in 1856, the year Lincoln received a solid preliminary vote for the vice-presidential nomination on the Fremont ticket. William Cullen Bryant of the *New York Evening Post* was a poet and important editorial voice. The troublemaking Democratic Congressman Benjamin Wood owned the *Daily News* in New York. In the South, R. B. Rhett, Jr., editor of the *Charleston Mercury*, was a prime example of a politician who used the press as his platform. It was Rhett's father, with the *Mercury* as his cutting weapon, who led the voices for secession.

The story of Lincoln's life as told through the eyes of the contemporary press properly begins in Springfield. "The *Journal* paper was always my friend; and, of course its editors the same." With these words in 1864 Lincoln showed his friendship for the Springfield *Sangamo Journal* (later the *Illinois Journal*), his home-town supporter. Here in 1832 Lincoln first announced his candidacy for the Illinois Assembly—the first time he was seen and heard by the reading public. When Lincoln went off to the Black Hawk Indian War in 1832, the paper pointed out that he was on active service. Consistently, to the end of his life, the *Journal* reported favorably on Lincoln's fortunes—sometimes with an assist from Lincoln himself in the "communications" column.

At the same time the Democratic newspaper in Springfield, the *Illinois State Register*, took Lincoln to task throughout his career. The *Register* declared that Lincoln was a joker instead of a thinker and not to be taken seriously; this claim was made often in the western press. The *Register* chided Lincoln for what it called his "assumed clownishness"— and the criticism was taken to heart. In the course of the Lincoln-Douglas debates, the *Register* and the *Journal* lined up behind their own party men. Applause and three-times-three hurrahs depended on which paper one read.

So with the other cities. The *Chicago Tribune* was for Lincoln, the *Chicago Times* against him; the *Cincinnati Daily Commercial* for, the *Cincinnati Enquirer* against. Whenever possible, comments from both sides are given in this book, which includes publications, both Union and Confederate, from twenty states and the District of Columbia.

Most Southern newspapers were vitriolic during the war, but there were indications from time to time that the maligned "Black Republican in the White House" was on the South's conscience. Before the elections the *Louisville Journal* played it down the middle for a Kentucky boy: "Several papers in the Northwest are strongly recommending the Hon. Abraham Lincoln for the Presidency. We do not concur with him in some of his views, but there is much good in Abraham's bosom." The Kentucky newspaper had been one of Lincoln's favorites; he subscribed to it when, according to friends, he did not have enough money to dress decently. Journalism was outspoken and individual in all sections of the country. The remarkable logotype of Parson Brownlow's paper in Knoxville said it plainly: *Brownlow's Whig and Rebel Ventilator*.

Papers in the Far West and Southwest covered the war almost as closely. The *Sacramento Union*, powerful in California, was lucky to have one of the best Washington correspondents, Noah Brooks, whose pen name, "Castine," came from his Maine birthplace. Brooks wrote a colorful series of letters sympathetic to the Union cause and to Lincoln, who offered him the post of private secretary a few months before the assassination. The most shocking lines after that event appeared in the *Tri-Weekly Telegraph*, Houston: "From now until God's judgment day, the minds of men will not cease to thrill at the killing of Abraham Lincoln."

Magazines and literary periodicals, especially those centered in Boston, stimulated the abolitionist movement. Among those represented here is the *Atlantic Monthly*, "a magazine of Literature, Art, and Politics," from which came Ralph Waldo Emerson's estimate of the Emancipation Proclamation. Mrs. Harriet Beecher Stowe's appraisal of Lincoln is reprinted from that pocket-sized periodical *Littell's Living Age*, which appealed to many female readers. *Harper's Monthly* and *Frank Leslie's Illustrated Newspaper*, *Vanity Fair* and the *Southern Illustrated News* of Richmond, among other publications, reported and sometimes distorted the progress of the war as well as the wartime President.

At the time of our Second American Revolution, Europe had its troubles too. England shook in the aftermath of the Crimean War; in France the Second Republic devolved into the Second Empire; Garibaldi and his Thousand ran through the streets of Palermo to resurrect and unify Italy. The haughty attitude of *The Times* of London was copied and reprinted on the continent; vicious anti-Lincoln cartoons in *Punch* by John Tenniel (who later repented and illustrated *Alice in Wonderland*) were touched up and reprinted in the Confederate publications. By contrast, Edward Dicey, an astute English writer for *The Spectator* and *Macmillan's* magazine, observed Washington, the Northern states, Congress, and Lincoln sympathetically. "History will say that our own days," Dicey wrote, "produced a yet nobler representative of American courage, and honesty, and self-sacrifice in the person of Abraham Lincoln."

What is intended in this book is an illumination from unretouched facts, crude ideas, words, and interpretations in the original on the theory that the closer one gets to firsthand reports the truer will emerge the Lincoln personality and the forces around him. There are no changes in the material, no summaries or digests. Some extraneous and repetitive matter (often caused by exigencies of narrow news columns) has been omitted. The typograpical style has not been tampered with, which accounts for some of the peculiar punctuation but also helps to retain the flavor of American journalism and the more polished prose of British publications in the middle of the last century.

Against the background of these reports and opinions, the Lincoln disclosed by a hundred publications opened anew here—by friendly contemporaries and virulent enemies in the North, South, and in Europe —is all the more impressive. He is a human Lincoln, capable of steadfast principle yet compromise, of underlying morality yet compassion. The character of Lincoln emerges as the greatest single gain of the Civil War— and a symbol of decency and conscience for Americans today.

HERBERT MITGANG

ABRAHAM
LINCOLN
A Press Portrait

Chapter 1

The Young Lincoln

MARCH 1832–AUGUST 1846

Leaving his boyhood behind him in Kentucky and Indiana, the young Lincoln arrived in New Salem, Sangamon County, Illinois, in the summer of 1831. He was twenty-two. Prophetically, an election was going on and because he could make "a few rabbit tracks" with the pen, he became voting clerk. Less than a year later, he was in politics.

A self-announced candidate for election to the State Legislature, he had declared himself and then volunteered in the militia for the Black Hawk Indian uprising. His unit was officially designated "Captain Abraham Lincoln's Company of the First Regiment of the Brigade of Mounted Volunteers." He won military election as a company leader; after his military discharge as a private (his own company had disbanded and he had re-enlisted), he returned to New Salem to face the voters. Running as a Whig in a Democratic-dominated state, he was defeated. However, he received almost a unanimous vote in his own precinct of New Salem, 227 votes against 3.

Lincoln revealed himself—and was so seen by the public, who were to judge him many times later—for the first time in the *Sangamo Journal*, Springfield. From its first issue on Nov. 10, 1831, the editors spoke for the Whigs and became close personal and political friends of Lincoln. The Journal was published "every Thursday evening, office in the new brick building, fronting on the Public Square, north-west of the Court House, Up Stairs." Here Lincoln came to converse with the editor, Simeon Francis, who ran a big slogan on his little paper: "Not the glory of Caesar, but the Welfare of Rome." The Sangamo Journal (so called after the river and county of Sangamon) later became

3

the Illinois Journal. It remained Lincoln's home-town paper and forum all through his political youth and maturity.

When Lincoln ran for his first office, in a typical issue of the early 1830's he could read such stories in the Springfield paper as "An Adventure in the South Seas," reprinted from Blackwood's Magazine; a reminiscing article on the Battle of Waterloo called "The Fate of Ney"; a news report on the cholera epidemic in Paris, many local notices and frontier stories—this being the West—on Indian massacres in Illinois.

Lincoln's announcement for office made a point of improving the navigation on the Sangamon. Springfield and the county were thinking in terms of commerce. In the early months of 1832 the small steamer Talisman had made its way up the Sangamon and the excitement it caused was on the mind of the electorate.

And so on page 2, columns three and four, of the Sangamo Journal for March 15, 1832, from New Salem there was a communication from a newcomer, "Your friend and fellow-citizen, A. LINCOLN."

COMMUNICATION
To the People of Sangamo County

FELLOW CITIZENS: Having become a candidate for the honorable office of one of your representatives in the next General Assembly of this state, in accordance with an established custom, and the principles of true republicanism, it becomes my duty to make known to you—the people whom I propose to represent—my sentiments with regard to local affairs.

Time and experience have verified to a demonstration, the public utility of internal improvements. That the poorest and most thinly populated countries would be greatly benefitted by the opening of good roads, and in the clearing of navigable streams within their limits, is what no person will deny. But yet it is folly to undertake works of this or any other kind, without first knowing that we are able to finish them—as half finished work generally proves to be labor lost. There cannot justly be any objection to having rail roads and canals, any more than to other good things, provided they cost nothing. The only objection is to paying for them; and the objection to paying arises from the want of ability to pay.

With respect to the county of Sangamo, some more easy means of communication than we now possess, for the purpose of facilitating the task of exporting the surplus products of its fertile soil, and importing necessary articles from abroad, are indispensably necessary. A meeting has been held of the citizens of Jacksonville, and the adjacent country, for the purpose of deliberating and enquiring into the expediency of constructing a rail road from some eligible point on the Illinois River, through the town of Jacksonville, in Morgan county, to the town of Springfield, in Sangamo county. This is, indeed, a very desirable object. No other improvement that reason will justify us in hoping for, can equal in utility the rail road. It is a never failing source of communication, between places of business remotely situated from each other. Upon the rail road the regular progress of commercial intercourse is not interrupted by either high or low water, or freezing weather, which are the principal difficulties that render our future hopes of water communication precarious and uncertain. Yet, however, desirable an object the construction of a rail road through our country may be; however high our imaginations may be heated at thoughts of it—there is always a heart appalling shock accompanying the account of its cost, which forces us to shrink from our pleasing anticipations. The probable cost of this contemplated rail road is estimated at $290,000;—the bare statement of which, in my opinion, is sufficient to justify the belief, that the improvement of Sangamo river is an object much better suited to our infant resources.

Respecting this view, I think I may say, without the fear of being contradicted, that its navigation may be rendered completely practicable, as high as the mouth of the South Fork, or probably higher, to vessels of from 25 to 30 tons burthen, for at least one half of all common years, and to vessels of much greater burthen a part of that time. From my peculiar circumstances, it is probable that for the last twelve months I have given as particular attention to the stage of the water in this river, as any other person in the country. In the month of March, 1831, in company with others, I commenced the building of a flat boat on the Sangamo, and finished and took her out in the course of the spring. Since that time, I have been concerned in the mill at New Salem. These circumstances are sufficient evidence, that I have not been very inattentive to the stages of the water.—The time at which we crossed the mill dam, being in the last days of April, the water was lower than it had been since the breaking of winter in February, or than it was for several weeks after. The principal difficulties we encountered in descending the river, were from the drifted timber, which obstructions all know is not difficult to be removed. Knowing almost precisely the height of water at that time, I believe I am safe in saying that it has as often been higher as lower since.

From this view of the subject, it appears that my calculations with regard to the navigation of the Sangamo, cannot be unfounded in reason; but whatever may be its natural advantages, certain it is, that it never can be practically useful to any great extent, without being greatly improved by art. The drifted timber, as I have before mentioned, is the most formidable barrier to this object. Of all parts of this river, none will require so much labor in proportion, to make it navigable, as the last thirty or thirty-five miles; and going with the meanderings of the channel, when we are this distance above its mouth, we are only between twelve and eighteen miles above Beardstown, in something near a straight direction; and this route is upon such low ground as to retain water in many places during the season, and in all parts such as to draw two-thirds or three-fourths of the river water at all high stages.

This route is upon prairie land the whole distance;—so that it appears to me, by removing the turf, a sufficient width and damming up the old channel, the whole river in a short time would wash its way through, thereby curtailing the distance, and increasing the velocity of the current very considerably, while there would be no timber upon the banks to obstruct its navigation in future; and being nearly straight, the timber which might float in at the head, would be apt to go clear through. There are also many places above this where the river, in its zig zag course, forms such complete peninsulas, as to be easier cut through at the necks than to remove the obstructions from the bends—which if done, would also lessen the distance.

What the cost of this work would be, I am unable to say. It is probable, however, it would not be greater than is common to streams of the same length. Finally, I believe the improvement of the Sangamo river, to be vastly important and highly desirable to the people of this county; and if elected, any measure in the legislature having this for its object, which may appear judicious, will meet my approbation, and shall receive my support.

It appears that the practice of loaning money at exorbitant rates of interest, has already been opened as a field for discussion; so I suppose I may enter upon it without claiming the honor, or risking the danger, which may await its first explorer. It seems as though we are never to have an end to this baneful and corroding system, acting almost as prejudicial to the general interests of the community as a direct tax of several thousand dollars annually laid on each county, for the benefit of a few individuals only, unless there be a law made setting a limit to the rates of usury. A law for this purpose, I am of opinion, may be made, without materially injuring any class of people. In cases of extreme necessity there could always be means found to cheat the law, while in all other cases it would have its intended effect. I would not favor the passage of a law upon this subject, which might be very easily evaded. Let it be such that the labor and difficulty of evading it, could only be justified in cases of the greatest necessity.

Upon the subject of education, not presuming to dictate any plan or system respecting it, I can only say that I view it as the most important subject which we as a people can be engaged in. That every man may receive at least, a moderate education, and thereby be enabled to read the histories of his own and other countries, by which he may duly appreciate the value of our free institutions, appears to be an object of vital importance, even on this account alone, to say nothing of the advantages and satisfaction to be derived from all being able to read the scriptures and other works, both of a religious and moral nature, for themselves. For my part, I desire to see the time when education, and by its means, morality, sobriety, enterprise and industry, shall become much more general than at present, and should be gratified to have it in my power to contribute something to the advancement of any measure which might have a tendency to accelerate the happy period.

With regard to existing laws, some alterations are thought to be necessary. Many respectable men have suggested that our estray laws— the law respecting the issuing of executions, the road law, and some others, are deficient in their present form, and require alterations. But considering the great probability that the framers of those laws were wiser than myself, I should prefer meddling with them, unless they were first attacked by others, in which case I should feel it both a privilege and a duty to take that stand, which in my view, might tend most to the advancement of justice.

But, Fellow-Citizens, I shall conclude.—Considering the great degree of modesty which should always attend youth, it is probable I have already been more presuming than becomes me. However, upon the subjects of which I have treated, I have spoken as I thought. I may be wrong in regard to any or all of them; but holding it a sound maxim, that it is better to be only sometimes right, than at all times wrong, so soon as I discover my opinions to be erroneous, I shall be ready to renounce them.

Every man is said to have his peculiar ambition. Whether it be true or not, I can say for one that I have no other so great as that of being truly esteemed of my fellow men, by rendering myself worthy of their esteem. How far I shall succeed in gratifying this ambition, is yet to be developed. I am young and unknown to many of you. I was born and have ever remained in the most humble walks of life. I have no wealthy or popular relations to recommend me. My case is thrown exclusively upon the independent voters of this county, and if elected they will have conferred a favor upon me, for which I shall be unremitting in my labors to compensate. But if the good people in their wisdom shall see fit to keep me in the back ground, I have been too familiar with disappointments to be very much chagrined.

Your friend and fellow-citizen,

A. LINCOLN.

New Salem, March 9, 1832.

Lincoln, after serving as postmaster of New Salem, by virtue of his good local showing in 1832 ran again for the General Assembly in 1834. This time he made it. After his term was over, he did surveying and continued his studies in the law. Then in 1836 he stood for re-election as a Representative. The talk at the time was of free Negroes voting and the white man's franchise regardless of property. It was, too, a year of a Presidential election. The Hugh L. White referred to in Lincoln's communication was a Whig aspirant from Tennessee. Lincoln and the Whigs won the county—though Martin Van Buren, the Democratic candidate, won nationally—in the election referred to in this letter to the Sangamo Journal, June 18, 1836.

NEW SALEM, June 13, 1836.

To the Editor of the Journal:

In your paper of last Saturday, I see a communication over the signature of "Many Voters," in which the candidates who are announced in the Journal, are called upon to "show their hands." Agreed. Here's mine!

I go for all sharing the privileges of the government, who assist in bearing its burthens. Consequently I go for admitting all whites to the right of suffrage, who pay taxes or bear arms, (by no means excluding females.)

If elected, I shall consider the whole people of Sangamon my constituents, as well those that oppose, as those that support me.

While acting as their representative, I shall be governed by their will, on all subjects upon which I have the means of knowing what their will is; and upon all others, I shall do what my own judgment teaches me will best advance their interests. Whether elected or not, I go for distributing the proceeds of the sales of the public lands to the several states, to enable our state, in common with others, to dig canals and construct rail roads, without borrowing money and paying interest on it.

If alive on the first Monday in November, I shall vote for Hugh L. White for President. Very respectfully,

A. LINCOLN.

In the pre-election heat of the combined local and national campaign of 1836, Lincoln was out on the stump. He spoke in Springfield, canvassing with Democrats, and after the speech referred to here, reportedly was carried on his friends' shoulders from the courthouse. A gentleman signing himself "Up to the Hub," of obvious Whig persuasion, was carried away in another manner when he heard Lincoln speak. "A girl might be born and become a mother before the Van Buren men will forget Mr. Lincoln," said "Hub" in a memorable expression at the end of his letter to the Sangamo Journal of July 16, 1836.

To the Editor of the Journal:

As an accidental visitor at the Court House on Monday last, I take the liberty of making a few comments,

When I entered, Mr. [Ninian W.] Edwards had just risen. The force of his argument, substantiated as it was by the evidence before him, which he occasionally quoted to the people, exhibited to them the course pursued by Mr. Van Buren, so far as the course of this trackless candidate can be traced. He disclaimed any intention of raising up the demon of party spirit among us, but since the attack had come from the opposite party, accusing him and his party of being White, nay federal candidates, he took the liberty of showing that he was not a federalist, and succeeded to the satisfaction of all present. The deep earnestness of Mr. Edward's manner, which truth and conscious rectitude in the cause he supports never fails to inspire, when promulgating doctrines that cannot be refuted, coming as they did from an honest heart, had a most powerful effect upon honest men.

Dr. Early followed Mr. Edwards. This gentleman, accustomed to hold out promises to the dying, attempted to sustain his sinking and dying cause, by pronouncing all that Mr. Edwards had said, *false.* The doctor seemed to be aware that broad assertions would not do for an enlightened people, against positive proof. He then attempted to direct the attention of the people from the main question by stating, "that one of the principal writers on the question of free negro suffrage, here, would sooner see his daughter married to a negro than a poor white man." A Johnson or Anti-

Van Buren man might prefer such an alliance, but it will not answer to tell such a story to the people of Illinois, who are as free as the breezes that blow over our prairies. No, he may tell it to them—he may scatter it far and wide from the pulpit and the stump, and they will not believe him. It will only recoil upon him whose head was so ingenious and whose heart was so base as to fabricate such a story. Towards the close of Dr. E's. speech, I left the Court House. . . .

Next came Mr. Calhoun. He was more honest than the doctor, and admitted that Van Buren had voted to extend the right of suffrage to free negroes—and attempted to excuse him because Gen. Jackson had done the same—a truth untold in history and unheard of in song or story, and begged the people to forgive Van Buren because Jackson had erred.—As well might Mr. Calhoun oppose his bare assertion to the written history of our country as to say, that he who is about to retire to the Hermitage, covered with civil and military honors, having filled the measure of his country's glory, did not oppose his bare breast to a British foe, as to make the people believe, upon his assertion, unsupported by history, that Gen. Jackson voted to extend the right of suffrage to free negroes. Knowing Mr. Calhoun to have been heretofore bitterly opposed to Gen. Jackson— having never voted for him—I was not surprised that such a charge should come from him. I am aware that Gen. Jackson may have committed errors—that is the lot of all mortals—but I cannot listen with patience when I hear him charged with more than erring nature is heir to.

☞ Does not the blood of every former supporter of Jackson boil, when he hears the fair fame of the old hero tarnished! And for what? To support the sinking cause of Martin Van Buren! . . .

Mr. Lincoln succeeded Mr. Calhoun. At first he appeared embarrassed, and his air was such as modest merit always lends to one who speaks of his own acts. He claimed only so much credit as belonged to one of the members of the last Legislature, for getting the State out of debt. He next came to Mr. Calhoun and the land bill. At one fell stroke, he broke the ice upon which we have seen Mr. Calhoun standing, and left him to contend with the chilling waters and merciless waves. His speech became more fluent, and his manner more easy as he progressed. In these degenerate days it seems to be the fashion of the day for all parties to admire even the frailities of the administration. The Van Buren men, particularly, are even taking shelter like ghosts under the rotten bones and tombstones of the dead acts of the administration. Mr. Lincoln, however, lifted the lid, and exposed to the eye the wretched condition of some of the acts of the Van Buren party. A girl might be born and become a mother before the Van Buren men will forget Mr. Lincoln. From beginning to end Mr. Lincoln was frequently interrupted by loud bursts of applause from a generous people.

Mr. Quinton next spoke. He said he had been a Jackson man since 1824, voted for him and had he had all the votes in the state in his belly, would have given them to him—made some remarks about Mr. Lincoln, which he immediately took back, and strange to tell, closed without saying, I am, gentleman, a whole-hog Jeffersonian Jackson Democratic Van Buren Republican according to the Jeffersonian School. UP TO THE HUB.

One of the issues facing Representative Lincoln was that of the State Bank, which the Democrats wanted to investigate. Lincoln, Whig floor leader, was on the Committee on Finance. In a speech in the Assembly against what he called the "mobocratic spirit," he said that "by injuring the credit of the Bank, you will depreciate the value of its paper in the hands of the honest and unsuspecting farmer and mechanic." Editor Francis, in a brief editorial in the Sangamo Journal of Jan. 28, 1837, reminded readers of Lincoln's Kentucky origins.

Mr. Lincoln's remarks on Mr. Linder's Bank resolution, in this paper, are quite to the point. Our friend carries the true Kentucky rifle, and when he fires seldom fails of sending the shot home.

Routine politicking, meetings, speeches, toasts, back-slapping—these were the activities of Representative Lincoln, already an important legislator at the age of twenty-eight in 1837. Sangamon County's seven Representatives and two Senators, known as the "Long Nine" because of their height, managed to get the state capital moved from Vandalia to Springfield, their county. Much log-rolling had been done by Lincoln and his colleagues to pull this off. The occasion arose for windbag celebrating, of toasting and being toasted, as reported in the Sangamo Journal, Aug. 12, 1837.

COMMUNICATIONS

ATHENS, August 3, 1837

The Citizens of this place and vicinity, to-day gave a public dinner to the Delegation from this County, as a demonstration of approbation of their course in the Legislature. We have to regret that it was not in the power of Mr. Fletcher or Col. Dawson to attend. Mr. J. D. Allen acted as

Marshal of the day, assisted by Messrs. Hurt and Grosh as Deputy Marshals. Wm. P. Brown, Esq. presided at the table as President. The Springfield Band kindly volunteered their services on the occasion. At one o'clock about one hundred and fifty gentlemen sat down to an excellent dinner, prepared by Mr. Anderson. After the cloth was removed, the following toasts were disposed of.

REGULAR TOASTS

1. The United States. 'Our country and whole country.'
2. The State of Illinois. Possessed of a fertile soil and salubrious climate, surrounded by navigable rivers and lakes, we look forward to the brilliant destiny that awaits her, with a confidence undisturbed by the present disastrous condition of our beloved country.
3. The County of Sangamon. One of the brightest stars in the galaxy which constitute our State. Let her be now and forever one and inseparable.
4. The recent session of our State Legislature. Its members have performed their duty promptly. Well done good and faithful servants.
5. The Internal Improvement system—As we have embarked in it, let it be energetically prosecuted. Its results will be felt in the rapid accumulation of wealth and population, and their inseparable concomitants the advancement of education and the developement of the great natural wealth of the State.
6. Illinois State rights and States men.—May all parties unite in advancing the former and sustaining the latter.
7. The United States Bank and State Bank of Illinois. Their 'rags' are good in Athens.
8. John T. Stuart—the voters of the 3d Congressional district appreciate his talents and worth, and will by a triumphant majority next August elect him to represent them in the Congress of the United States.

VOLUNTEERS

By J. K. Hurt. The 'long nine of old Sangamon.' In the language of Gen. Ewing, 'nine intellectual and physical giants.'—By a long pull, a strong pull and a pull altogether, they located the seat of government at Springfield. . . .

By G. Elkin. A Capitol gained, and not a foot of territory lost.

By W. B. Brown. The long nine of Sangamon. Deservedly popular and influential as members of our Legislature, fearless, talented and upright, they nobly maintained the interests of their constituents, raised the character of our county, and reflected honor upon our State. May they, like Crocket, go ahead.

By John B. Taylor. Illinois, a free State, governed by a judicious legislation, inhabited by an enlightened and free people. Their motto is 'Agriculture, Commerce and Manufactures.'

By H. C. Rogers. Our delegation of the last General Assembly. Their valuable services merit of their constituents the highest praise. May they be remembered should they offer their services again to the citizens of Sangamon.

Messrs. Herndon and Fletcher, the people's choice. They will glory in sustaining them, while they continue to serve them faithfully. . . .

By R. L. Wilson. The citizens of Athens. Hospitable, patriotic and intelligent. May it continue the second town in numerical strength in the Key Stone county.

E. D. Baker.—The people's choice. They will glory in sustaining him while he serves them faithfully.

A. Lincoln.—He has fulfilled the expectations of his friends and disappointed the hopes of his enemies.

By I. G. Hunter. Maj. E. D. Baker—He received a dish thoroughly minced from Mr. Lincoln and baked it until it was thoroughly done! done! Thanks to Major Baker.

By J. D. Allen. N. W. Edwards—A good scion of a noble stock.

A. G. Herndon—Much better than we expected. Must go again.

A. Lincoln—One of nature's nobility.

Robert L. Wilson—A true representative of Sangamon County and an honest man.

Col. John Dawson.—A true friend of Democratic principles, and a faithful servant of the people.

Hon. Dan Stone.—The citizens of Sangamon will not forget their absent friend.

By H. C. Rogers. Our Systems of Internal Improvement and Education. Both eminently calculated to elevate the character, promote the happiness, and wealth of the citizens of our State. We wish them the greatest possible success.

Col. Wm. F. Elkin.—His merits silence his enemies.

By A. Lincoln. Sangamon county will ever be true to her best interests and never more so than in reciprocating the good feelings of the citizens of Athens and neighborhood.

By A. G. Herndon. Athens: May she continue to increase in population until she ranks with the first towns of the State.

The Springfield Band. Our thanks are due them for their attendance on the present occasion. They merit the greatest praise and commendation.

By Thomas C. Elkin. Education—the pillar which upholds the temple of liberty. Immortality to those who have reared it in Illinois.

Numerous other volunteers were presented, but copies of them were not obtained. The company separated in good time, and nothing occurred to mar the pleasures of the day.

In the editorial opinion of the Illinois State Register, Lincoln and his "Springfield Junto" were guilty of handpicking candidates in the local race for Representative. There was a background to the accusation. The Register, founded by William Walters, assisted by Charles H. Lanphier who later became editor, was Democratic. Lincoln was trying to swing public printing over to the Sangamo Journal; The Register had been designated the official paper by the State Government. Hence this editorial in the Register of Nov. 23, 1839.

DICTATION OF THE "SPRINGFIELD JUNTO"

When it was known that there was to be a special election for a member of the Legislature, several Whigs of Menard county met together to consult upon the propriety of running a candidate from that county. The names of Bowling Green, Josiah B. Smith, and John Bennett, were spoken of, and as the Whigs of Petersburg were not able to determine which should be run, the whole matter was referred to three members of the "SPRINGFIELD JUNTO." Mr. LINCOLN, one of the three, with his two associates, DECLARED AT ONCE THAT JOHN BENNETT SHOULD RUN, and accordingly had him announced as a candidate, in the Journal.

The people of Sangamon will thus see the manner in which this JUNTO DISPOSE OF THEIR BUSINESS; and tell them who they shall, and who they shall not vote for. Would Mr. Lincoln be likely to urge a candidate upon the people, unless he were well assured that he would, if elected, go the whole hog with the Springfield Junto members. The independent Whigs of Sangamon are enraged at this DICTATION, and many of them who are determined not to submit to be led by the "SPRINGFIELD JUNTO" have brought out SAMUEL WYCKOFF, and will vote for him for Representative. Although Esquire WYCKOFF is opposed to us in politics, we are satisfied that, if he should be elected, he will sustain the interests of the Farmers of Sangamon in opposition to the DICTATION OF THE SPRINGFIELD JUNTO.

Lincoln became fair game for the Democratic Register of Springfield. In November of 1839, Lincoln was speaking as a candidate for Presidential elector. A rival—to be heard from again—emerged as spokesman for the Democrats: Stephen Arnold Douglas. There was more to it. Lincoln's law partner, John T. Stuart, had defeated Douglas for Congress the year before. The partnership was political as well. Lincoln kept Stuart informed of activities in Springfield, writing that "The Democratic giant is here; but he is not now worth talking about." These were warm-ups for debates to come nearly two decades hence. This from the Register of Nov. 23, 1839.

The Mr. Lincoln of Wednesday night, was not the Mr. Lincoln of Tuesday. He could only meet the arguments of Mr. Douglass [sic], by relating stale anecdotes and old stories, and left the stump literally whipped off of it, even in the estimation of his own friends.

On Thursday evening, Mr. Wiley and Mr. Baker spoke. We have not time to do justice to the remarks of the former, who in a modest and quiet speech, threw more light on the subject by the facts which he produced than any speaker who preceded him. He enlightened his audience. His remarks will be like "bread scattered upon the waters," which will be gathered after many days.

We view the situation of Mr. Walker, Mr. Lincoln, and their Federal colleagues, as peculiarly unfortunate. If they are asked who they intend to vote for (if elected) for President, they cannot answer. If they are asked whether they are in favor of Mr. Clay's project of a U.S. Bank, they are dumb. When they are called upon for *their* measure for collecting and disbursing the public money, they have none to give. In short, they have no measures, no principles, to advance. The people are left to grope in the dark, amidst the phantoms raised by these Federal orators. Their ground is opposition—opposition to the Administration; and when reminded that the great BANK, under whose banner they have been fighting for eight years, is broken down, and utterly insolvent, they seek to disown their great paper champion.

Under such disadvantages, it is not wonderful that Mr. Walker, and Mr. Lincoln, two of the Federal candidates for Electors, should have got used up on the occasion alluded to. The men are smart enough, but the cause they have espoused is rotten to the core.

Lincoln had to debate not only Douglas but Douglas's spokesman, the Illinois State Register. This editorial was in reply to Lincoln's explanation of his involvement with the "Springfield Junto" in the selection of a Whig candidate from Sangamon County for the General Assembly. Here was the genesis of accusations and refutations about the accuracy of political reporting that plagued Lincoln and Douglas all during their Illinois debates. From the Register, Nov. 23, 1839.

MR. LINCOLN AND THE REGISTER

On last Wednesday night, Mr. Lincoln, in the course of his reply to Mr. Douglass, travelled out of his way to attack the veracity of the editors of this paper. Under the rule agreed upon by a committee, governing the discussion, Mr. Lincoln could not be replied to by either of the editors of this paper. This Mr. Lincoln knew, and he has lowered himself in our estimation by his conduct on that occasion. He asserted that *he did not advise to the running of John Bennett* for the Legislature, but was in favour of Bowling Green; and that the editors of the Register had *lied* in making such a statement. Mr. L. said further that we had *no authority* for making the statement; and that having no authority, even if we had published the truth, we were still *liars!*

Such was the language of the man selected by the Whig party to be an elector of the high office of President of the United States—language made at a time when he was shielded from being met in reply by regulations publicly proclaimed in the presence of Mr. Lincoln at the opening of the evening's discussion.

To the indecorous language of Mr. Lincoln, we make *no reply*. We meet his assertions, however, by *re-publishing* the following letter, which will be found in the Register of Nov. 2:

"PETERSBURG, Oct. 26, 1839
"Dear Sir: On Wednesday night last there was a "caucus" held by the "Whigs" in town. At that meeting Bowling Green, John Bennett and Josiah B. Smith were mentioned for candidates, and the matter was to be submitted to A. Lincoln, Judge Logan and E. D. Baker for their decision who should run, which was done, and resulted in the nomination of John Bennett, who is a staunch

"Nullifier." He has cursed almost every thing that was not as he is on that subject. He is also a thorough "Aristocrat," a man that is a strong advocate for taking the election of Justices and Constables from the people."

The above letter was written by a highly respectable citizen of Petersburg, the original of which is now laying before us on our table. Two weeks elapsed after its publication, during which time *no reply* was made to it by Mr. Lincoln, or by any other of the parties, nor by the editor of the Sangamo Journal. The *silence* of Mr. Lincoln and his associates for two successive weeks, gave us a right to assume the contents of the letter as *true*, and we accordingly did so in an editorial article published in the last Register.

Before and since the appearance of the last Register, we have heard several of the friends of Mr. Lincoln admit, *on the streets*, that Mr. Lincoln, Judge Logan, and Mr. Baker, *did* decide that JOHN BENNETT, should be run for Representative, and they undertook to justify this party arrangement and denounce every other Whig candidate.

We have only one word to add to Mr. Lincoln. He will now see that we *had* authority for the statement made by us—such authority as Mr. Lincoln will not dispute. That he did not see it, is *his own fault*, because it was published *three weeks ago*, and ought to have been replied to long since, if he intended to reply to it at all.His allowing two weeks to pass by, with the accusation resting on him, and making no effort to relieve himself from it, gave to the public a right to look upon the accusation as true.

Lincoln's platform style was taking shape. The storytelling and intimacy were resented by rivals as a diversion from the so-called real issues. Humor was not supposed to enter politics; it was suspect then as now. In the editorial Lincoln's argument was for the United States Bank. This famous comment on Lincoln's oratory appeared in the Illinois State Register, Nov. 23, 1839.

Mr. Lincoln's argument was truly ingenious. He has, however, a sort of *assumed clownishness* in his manner which does not become him, and which does not truly belong to him. It *is* assumed—assumed for effect. Mr. Lincoln will sometimes make his language correspond with this clownish manner, and he can thus frequently raise a loud laugh among his Whig hearers; but this entire game of buffoonery convinces the *mind* of no man, and is utterly lost on the majority of his audience. We seriously advise Mr. Lincoln to correct this clownish fault before it grows upon him.

Lincoln did heavy campaigning for the 1840 election. He took on Douglas all over Illinois. The Democrats were dubbed "locofocos," after the new friction matches. Wm. Henry Harrison led the Whig ticket and "Ab'm Lincoln, of Sangamon" ran for one of his electors. The Whigs won in Sangamon County and nationally but lost in Illinois. The legislature to which Lincoln was re-elected for a fourth term was strongly Democratic. The name-calling of the violent campaign is illustrated in this defense of Lincoln and others in the Sangamo Journal of May 8, 1840.

COMMUNICATIONS

THE BLOWER BLOWED

In looking over the columns of the State Register of the 17th ult. [*April 1840*] (a thing which I but seldom do) my eye was arrested by an article headed "FEDERAL BLOW," a new glance satisfied me that it was the miserable effort of a miserable scribbler to effect some miserable object he hardly knew what. I was not long in making the discovery that it was mainly intended as a burlesque on the Harrison meeting, held at this place [Carlinville] on the 6th ult., and an attack upon persons who had taken part in that meeting.

Without preface or apology, I will proceed to bestow upon the several parts of that article, such notice as they best deserve.

It is begun with this language: "The tories of Macoupin county organized their meeting by appointing one of their *old distanced nags,* Col. [James C.] Anderson, President, and adopting several false resolution[s]." What can the *fellow* mean by calling Col. Anderson "one of the old distanced nags?" Col. A. is now for the first time before the people of Macoupin county a candidate for the State Legislature, with almost certain prospect of success. How then can he be called "a distanced nag?" This *behind the tree* warrior, like the party under whose banner he is fighting, sees and beholds with terror, and dread consternation that the *sceptre* is departing from hands that have wielded it but too long, and views with anxious eye and feelings of deepest hate, each one who might become ensign, or armor bearer, to him, into whose hands the wisdom and prudence of an intelligent and sovereign people, shall next confide the reins of Government: hence the desponding like, and the desperate use

[of] words and means however insignificant the former, or unavailing the latter, if but to gratify a vengeful feeling. . . .

But I stop not here; there are other portions of this "Federal Blow" which demand some attention; and whilst my gloves are off and my hand in, I may as well adopt the motto "carry the war to the knife and the knife to the hilt," and handle him with a kind of backwoods courtesy that will teach him the wholesome advice contained in the Eleventh Commandment. Now, if this blowmelug, who seems laboring under some great mental derangement, and which I am clearly of opinion owes its origin to an advanced stage of the *big-head*, the most dangerous of all diseases had confined his observations to things passing in his own native element, and among his comrades, I should not have troubled him with this replication; but he had the impudence to come in the house and note what was passing there, and felt no doubt that he would do injustice to his manly talents, if he did not bestow some compliment upon what he called the "severe harangue" and "scientific eloquence" of a "certain Mr. County Clerk," and but for his foolery and his falsehoods would not have been exposed by me. But I leave this Clerk to look to himself with this assurance, that who attacks him once will not desire to do so twice. A certain Mr. H. (whose name if not suppressed would have been Holton,) was also severely brushed by his racy quill. This gentleman in a short though pithy speech, clearly exposed the doctrines and mal-administration of the party in power, and rip[p]ed out the very bowels of loco focoism. No wonder he should be called a "creole looking creature" by the tenacious adherent of a desperate cause.

Mr. Lincoln is next brought upon the carpet under the name and title of "the Lion of the tribe—of Springfield importation," and "judging" say[s] he "from outward appearance originally from Liberia." This is the unkindest cut of all, and comes with a bad grace from a member of the party whose very head and leader this same Mr. L. clearly showed in his speech to be clothed with the sable furs of Guinea—whose breath smells rank with devotion to the cause of Africa's sons—and whose very trail might be followed by scattered bunches of *Nigger wool*. It would be useless to speak of his conclusive arguments and the able and forcible manner in which he treated the several branches of National politics. Upon the whole, his speech was a sound and sensible one—did much honor to himself and great justice to the cause. Its effects will be felt and long remembered in Macoupin county. It was amusing to see (as Mr. L. proceeded, aptly portraying the meanderings and political somersets [sic] of Mr. Van Buren, reading from Mr. V. B.'s own biography and quoting by memorandum the journals of Congress and of the New York Legislature) the Hectors of the party, the very pillars of the administration in this county with stretched necks and lengthened faces demanding the dates and pages with a vengeance—which were promptly given. At the close of Mr. L.'s speech a Van Buren gentleman of the legal profession who sometimes sports on the political arena stept forward and demanded to be heard, (which he did after the close of the meeting) and held forth for some time in a warm and boisterous manner, without any other seeming object than to deny what had been said on the other side. Mr. Lincoln was then invited to remain in town and see himself *used up* the next day. He accepted the invitation and remained. At the designated hour the next day, the wood and the lamp were ready but the high priest came not to the sacrifice. At length the gentleman who had given the challenge appeared and gave notice that there would be no debate unless Mr. Lincoln would get the people together, which he refused as it did not come within the purview of the challenge; and thus the farce ended.

J. A. CHESTNUT.

One of the funniest incidents in Representative Lincoln's life took place during his fourth term in the General Assembly. The legislature was dominated by the Democrats and the Whigs (the Federal members referred to) fought them with every parliamentary device— and some that were not in the book. Sometimes the doors had to be locked to keep the forum from disappearing. This did not stop Lincoln and his ephemeral colleagues. How Lincoln outwitted the Democrats is described in this serious account—humorous in spite of itself— from the Illinois State Register, Dec. 11, 1840.

CONSPIRACY OF THE FEDERAL MEMBERS OF THE LEGISLATURE TO REVOLUTIONIZE THE STATE GOVERNMENT

Both Houses of the Illinois Legislature presented, on Saturday last [Dec. 5, 1840], a most extraordinary spectacle. We can recollect nothing which bears so striking a resemblance to it, as the scenes at Harrisburg during the Ritner usurpation. In both cases it was an attempt at Revolution—an attempt to destroy the Legislative branch of our Republican system of Government.

Both Houses had, on Saturday evening [morning], passed a joint resolution to adjourn *sine die* at the close of the day's sitting, for the purpose of meeting on Monday morning agreeably to the Constitution which prescribes "the first Monday in December next ensuing the election of members" as a day on which "the General Assembly *shall* meet." Neither resolution had, however, passed *both* Houses during the morning session. In the afternoon they re-assembled at 3 o'clock, but *no quorum* appeared in either House. In the Senate a quorum shortly after appeared, and the Lt. Governor [Stinson H. Anderson] put the question on the resolution from the House to adjourn *sine die*, but *no quorum* voted. Just as the question was put, Mr. [Edward D.] Baker and a few other whig members withdrew from the Senate, purposely leaving it without a quorum.—The door keeper was immediately sent to procure the attendance of absent members, but the members refused to obey the summons, and the Senate was left without a quorum during the remainder of the day.

The House of Representatives met at 3 o'clock. The resolution from the Senate to adjourn *sine die* was taken up, and the vote being taken but 57 members answered to their names, (no quorum) there being but ten whig members in the House. The door keeper was despatched after the absentees, but returned without a member; those he had seen refusing to obey his summons. This fact was reported to the House by the Speaker, who then read from the Chair the provisions of the Constitution in such cases as follows:

SEC. 7. Art. II.—Last clause.—"Two-thirds of each House shall constitute a quorum, but a smaller number may adjourn from day to day and compel the attendance of absent members."

The doors of the House were locked to prevent the egress of members, and the door keeper was again despatched to "compel" the attendance of the absentees, but he again returned bringing with him only Mr [William B.] ARCHER of Clark. Sixty-one members were necessary to constitute a quorum, and the House was still *three* short of that number. The door keeper was again despatched for members, but those he saw refused to attend; CYRUS EDWARDS, of Madison, was found by the door keeper in the store of Ninian Edwards, Esq.—The door keeper desired him to attend, but Mr Edwards refused unless the door keeper could show a warrant to compel his attendance. The door keeper (Mr [William C.] Murphy) then produced his warrant; but Mr Edwards stepped back, and with his cane under his arm and his right hand upon it, told Mr Murphy that if he took him, *it would be at his peril!*

By this time it was growing towards night, and the House had remained in session two hours without a quorum. The greatest excitement prevailed. Mr [Ebenezer] Peck, Mr [John A.] McClernand, and Mr

[Wickliffe] Kitchell, successively addressed the House, strongly urging upon that body not to give up, until they had put down what, it was now evident to every man, was a deliberate *conspiracy*, formed by the whig leaders to destroy the deliberations and action of the Legislature. A last attempt was now made to procure a quorum. Finding it vain to obtain the attendance of a whig absentee, the sick Democratic members were sent for. Mr [John M.] Kell[e]y, Mr [Peter] Green, of Clay, and Mr [John] Dougherty, some of them from their beds, attended the House, and after candle-light 61 members being present (just a quorum) the question was taken on the resolution and PASSED, yeas 46, nays 15.

A laughable circumstance took place while the yeas and nays were being called on the passage of the resolution. Mr. LINCOLN, of Sangamon, who was present during the whole scene, and who appeared to enjoy the embarrassment of the House, suddenly looked very grave after the Speaker announced that a quorum was present.—The conspiracy having failed, Mr. Lincoln came under great excitement, and having attempted and failed to get out at the door, very unceremoniously *raised the window and jumped out,* followed by one or two other members. This gymnastic performance of Mr Lincoln and his flying brethren, did not occur until *after they had voted!* and consequently the House did not interfere with their extraordinary feat. We have not learned whether these flying members got hurt in their adventure, and we think it probable that at least one of them come [sic] off without damage, as it was noticed that his *legs* reached nearly from the window to the ground! By his extraordinary performance on the occasion, Mr Lincoln will doubtless become as famous as Mr Speaker Penrose at Harrisburg, which redoubted champion jumped out of the window during the late buck shot war in Pennsylvania!

We learn that a resolution will probably be introduced into the House this week to inquire into the expediency of raising the State House *one story higher,* in order to have the House set in the *third story!* so as to prevent members from *jumping out of the windows!* If such a resolution passes, Mr Lincoln will in future have *to climb down the spout!*

During the whole of the extraordinary scene we have related, we stood inside near the door of the House, and was [sic] an eye witness to it. We noticed Mr Baker, of the Senate, in the House, talking in an undertone to one or two of the few whig members of the House who remained at their posts.—Mr Baker seemed to be the moving spirit in the conspiracy. Absent himself from where his duty required him to be, it seemed to be his object to persuade others to follow his example. Fallen himself, he would drag others down.

The reader, by this time, is probably anxious to know the cause of this revolutionary conduct on the part of the whig members of the Legislature. The resolution to adjourn *sine die*, and open a new session on Monday, was a proposition in itself quite harmless; but the effect of it would be, as the whigs supposed, to force the banks to resume specie payments on Monday [Dec. 7], as the law of last session authorises them to suspend only till the close of the next ensuing session of the General Assembly. Thus the object of this attempt on the part of the Whigs, to destroy the action of the Legislative branch of the Government, was to prevent the Banks from resuming specie payments on the opening of the new session on Monday!

To what a humiliating condition are we brought as a people! To serve the Banks, Whig members absent themselves from their places in the Legislature in order to leave both Houses without a constitutional quorum: thus in effect prostrating the Legislature to benefit the Banks. So far as the State Bank is concerned, she had informed the Legislature that she was ready at any moment to resume specie payments: and in fact she did resume, on Monday last, the payment of all her obligations in specie, with the intention, we learn, of permanently doing so. Is it possible that the constituents of these whig members will justify this attempt to subvert the Legislature? Where will all this end? If members are justified, on one pretence, in leaving the General Assembly without a quorum, are they not on any other? And would not the constant repetition of such conduct, virtually destroy the Legislative branch of our Republican Government? The whig members of our Legislature have incurred a fearful responsibility before the people. If their conduct is sustained by that people, we may bid farewell to our boasted liberties, for only the *name* of them will remain to us. Destroy the Legislature, and what is left? ANARCHY! which may lead to Monarchy! In the present instance, the Legislature was saved by the firmness of the Democratic members, to whom too much praise cannot be awarded.

During the legislative session, a special committee was appointed to investigate the "very large expenditure of public printing." Its chairman was the Democrat Lyman Trumbull and Lincoln—who caused the committee to come into existence, with a view to embarrassing Editor Walters of the Register, the official paper, and thus perhaps help his friend Francis of the Journal—served on the committee. Nothing came of the investigation. The "indisposition" mentioned here referred to Lincoln's melancholy—he himself called it his "most dis-

creditable exhibition of myself in the way of hypochondriasm"—over *the broken engagement to Mary Todd. This from the Illinois State Register, Jan. 29, 1841.*

The editor of the [Sangamo] Journal is in a bad humor at his defeat for public printer, and continues to trouble his readers with his doleful complaints. We are very sorry for him. Perhaps he may have better luck next time. We will take the liberty of reminding him of the following good old maxims, which we have no doubt will be a source of comfort to him under the mortifying circumstances in which he is placed:

"There is many a slip between the cup and the lip."

"Be not too certain of catching the bird, even after you put the salt on his tail!"

We were a good deal amused at reading the last Journal. The editor pronounces the report of the Investigating committee on the subject of public printing "a white-washing report," and in the very next paragraph declares that it proves all he has asserted! ! ! This shows the editor of the Journal to be a prevaricating hypocrite. How can it be a white-washing report if it proves all the falsehoods the Journal has published on this subject. The editor next attempts to make his readers believe that Mr. LINCOLN dissents from the report, and accuses Mr. Cavarly with stating an untruth to the House when that gentleman said "it was the report of THE committee: I see no *minority* report." Does Simeon Francis suppose that *his* word will stand a moment against that of Judge Cavarly? There was not then, nor is there now, a minority report. The records of the House show this. Mr. Lincoln has recovered from his indisposition, and has attended the House for more than a week past during which time he made no minority report; although he attended every meeting of the committee of Investigation. Now, we ask any man of either political party, whether Mr. LINCOLN is a man who would have refused to speak out, if he had had any thing to tell?

The editor of the Journal flounders in this matter. Conscious that he has failed in his base and malicious attempt to fasten his charge of corruption on the public printer, he continues his quibbles and insinuations, and refuses to publish the result of the investigation which he was instrumental in procuring, which was conducted by his friend Mr. Lincoln, and in which the editor took part himself as a witness. This proves the editor of the Journal to be as dishonest as he is hypocritical and malicious.

The new charge which the editor makes, that "HE KNOWS Mr. Lamblin, of Wheeling, offered to furnish us with State paper for $7.50 a ream," is FALSE. Why did not the editor mention this before the committee of Investigation? No offer of the kind was made by any one previous to the purchase of paper for the State. If it had been made, it would have been promptly accepted, we have no doubt with the concurrence of the Secretary of State. But we can waste no more words in reference to this subject on the miserable caitiff who controls the leading organ of the Whigs.

The public will notice that the whole pack of Whig correspondents, who frequent the lobbies, hired to write slander for the federal papers, have followed the lead of the *slut-dog* who conducts the Journal. Without even examining what the report contains, these libellers pronounce it a *white-washing* report. Surely the standing of Mr. LINCOLN, Mr. ORMSBEE, and Mr. TRUMBULL, is sufficient of itself to refute so base and malignant a charge against them, without a word further being said in their defence.

"Mr. Lincoln begged leave to tell an anecdote"—this was a familiar phrase in the record of the Illinois legislature. This one Lincoln was to tell more than once later in Washington. The Sangamo Journal of March 5, 1841, reported it this way.

[HOUSE OF REPRESENTATIVES, Feb. 26, 1841]

Mr. LINCOLN offered an amendment, allowing the State to pay in Bonds at par for all work hereafter done [on the Illinois and Michigan Canal], and to issue therefor $3,000,000 bonds.

Mr. [William H.] BISSELL moved to strike out 3 and insert $1,500,-000. Mr. LINCOLN accepted the amendment.

Messrs. Lincoln and [Abram R.] Dodge supported the bill and Mr. [Joseph W.] Ormsbee and [Wickliff] Kitchell opposed it.

Mr. KITCHELL was surprised at the course of the gentleman from Sangamon (Mr. Lincoln). We were already prostrated by debt, and that gentleman thought it would be for the interest of the State to go still deeper. Mr. K. said it reminded him of an anecdote, which he would relate. A drunkard in Arkansas took so much of the *cretur*, that he lost his reason and remained for some time in a state of insensibility. His wife tried every experiment to cure him; but it was of no avail, until a neighbor came to the house and recommended some *brandy toddy*. The insensible man rose at the word *toddy*, and said "that is the stuff." It was so with the gentleman from Sangamon—more debt would be for the better.

Mr. LINCOLN replied. He begged leave to tell an anecdote. The gentleman's course the past winter reminded him of an eccentric old bachelor who lived in the Hoosier State. Like the gentleman from Montgomery [Kitchell], he was very famous for seeing *big bugaboos* in every thing. He lived with an older brother, and one day he went out hunting. His brother heard him firing back of the field, and went out to see what was the matter. He found him loading and firing as fast as possible in[to] the top of a tree.

Not being able to discover any thing in the tree, he asked him what he was firing at. He replied a squirrel—and kept on firing. His brother believing there was some humbug about the matter, examined his person, and found on one of his eyelashes a *big louse* crawling about. It is so with the gentleman from Montgomery. He imagined he could see squirrels every day, when they were nothing but *lice.*

[The House was convulsed with laughter.]

"Abram" Lincoln (a mispelling that pursued him into the White House) was first mentioned as a possible candidate for Governor of Illinois when he was only thirty-two years old, though already a fourth-term legislator. The idea was broached by the Fulton Telegraph, Illinois, and reprinted in the Sangamo Journal, Oct. 15, 1841, with a cautious editorial postscript probably approved before publication by Mr. Lincoln.

From the Fulton Telegraph
GUBERNATORIAL STATE CONVENTION

The question of a convention of delegates from the several counties of the State, to nominate candidates for Governor and Lieutenant Governor, has been broached by some of the whig papers, and we, though the humblest member of the family, would give our opinion.

The Alton Telegraph seems rather inclined to have all agree to the support of its candidate, (Gov. Duncan,) without a convention. We are partly of his opinion. That is, if all would agree to our nomination, and we see no difficulty in it, we should not wish for a convention. We are decidedly of the opinion that among the whigs of Old Fulton, (and they are as numerous as those of most other counties, though they have been in a minority,) Abram Lincoln, of Sangamon, would be as acceptable a candidate for Governor as could be started. And unless the friends of the other candidates can relinquish their preference and agree on him, we are for a convention. Personally or politically, we have nothing to say against the other candidates. Col. Davidson we think cannot receive the strength of the north on account of the canal question. Gen. Duncan has had the honor being once Governor, and we are at a loss to know what superior claims he has to further patronage. But we have many reasons to urge why we think the great talents, services and high standing of Mr. Lincoln should bring our friends to the decision of taking him up as a candidate for Governor, but we have not room for them now, and shall defer them to a future period.

The "Fulton Telegraph" pays a just compliment to Mr. LINCOLN. His "talents and services" endear him to the whig party; but we do not believe that he desires the nomination. He has already made great sacrifices in sustaining his party principles; and before his political friends ask him to make additional sacrifices, the subject should be well considered. The office of Governor, which would of necessity interfere with the practice of his profession, would poorly compensate him for the loss of four years of the best portion of his life. These remarks, however, are not authorized by him—though they accord with the feelings of many of his immediate friends.

Lincoln came close to fighting a duel. Several satirical letters signed "Rebecca" appeared in the Sangamo Journal, written by Mary Todd and her friend Julia Jayne. The object of the ridicule was James Shields, Democratic state auditor and friend of Stephen Douglas. He was attacked for his manners and bearing as well as the troubled state of fiscal affairs in Springfield. Lincoln added fuel to the fire by writing a letter to the editor from the mythical "Lost Townships," dated Aug. 27, 1842, which was a mixture of nonsense and accusation against Shields. A friend of Shields demanded to know who wrote the anonymous letters. Shields threw out a challenge to Lincoln, who took responsibility for all the letters. Lincoln specified cavalry broadswords of the largest size. The place, beyond the reach of Illinois law, was to be within three miles of Alton on the Missouri side of the Mississippi River. The public first learned about it from an editorial in the Alton Telegraph and Democratic Review of Oct. 1, 1842, in which Alton is indignant that a duel came so near "our city."

OUR CITY

Was the theatre of an unusual scene of excitement during the last week, arising from a visit of two distinguished gentlemen of the city of Springfield, who, it was understood, had come here with a view of crossing the river to answer the "requisitions of the code of honor," by brutally attempting to assassinate each other in cold blood.

We recur to this matter with pain and the deepest regret. Both are, and have been, for a long time, our personal friends. Both we have ever esteemed in all the private relations of life, and consequently regret that what we consider an imperative sense of duty we owe to the public, compels us to recur to the disgraceful and unfortunate occurrence at all. We, however, consider that these gentlemen have both violated the laws of the country, and insist that neither their influence, their respectability nor their private worth, should save them from being made amenable to those laws they have violated. Both of them are lawyers—both have been Legislators of this State, and aided in the construction of laws for the protection of society—both exercise no small influence in community—all of which, in our estimation, aggravates instead of mitigating their offense. Why, therefore, they should be permitted to escape punishment, while a friendless, penniless, and obscure person, for a much less offense, is hurried to the cells of our county jail, forced through a trial, with scarcely the forms of law, and finally immured within the dreary walls of a Penitentiary, we are at a loss to conjecture. It is a partial and disreputable administration of justice, which, though in accordance with the spirit of the age, we must solemnly protest against. Wealth, influence, and rank, can trample upon the laws with impunity; while poverty is scarcely permitted to utter a word in its defense if charged with crime in our miscalled temples of justice.

Among the catalogue of crime that disgraces the land, we look upon none to be more aggravated and less excusable than that of dueling. It is the calmest, most deliberate, and malicious species of murder—a relict of the most cruel barbarism that ever disgraced the darkest periods of the world—and one which every principle of religion, virtue and good order, loudly demands should be put a stop to. This can be done only by a firm and unwavering enforcement of the law, in regard to dueling, towards all those who so far forget the obligations they are under to society and the laws which protect them, as to violate its provisions. And until this is done, until the civil authorities have the moral courage to discharge their duty and enforce the law in this respect, we may frequently expect to witness the same disgraceful scenes that were acted in our city last week.

Upon a former occasion, when under somewhat similar circumstances our city was visited, we called upon the Attorney General to enforce the law, and bring the offenders to justice. Bills of indictment were preferred against the guilty; but there the matter was permitted to rest unnoticed and unexamined. The offenders in this instance, as in the former, committed the violation of the law in Springfield; and we again call upon Mr. Attorney General Lamborn, to exercise a little of that zeal which he is continually putting in requisition against less favored but no less guilty offenders, and bring ALL who have been concerned in the late attempt at assassination to justice. Unless he does it, he will prove himself unworthy the high trust that has been reposed in him.

How the affair finally terminated, not having taken the trouble to inquire, we are unable to say. The friends of Mr. SHIELDS and Mr. LINCOLN claim it to have been settled upon terms alike honorable to both, notwithstanding the hundred rumours—many of which border upon the ridiculous—that are in circulation. We are rejoiced that both were permitted to return to the bosom of their friends and trust that they will now consider, if they did not do it before, that rushing unprepared upon the untried scenes of Eternity, is a step too fearful in its consequences to be undertaken without preparation.

We are astonished to hear that large numbers of our citizens crossed the river, to witness a scene of cold-blooded assassination between two of their fellow-beings. It was no less disgraceful than the conduct of those who were to have been the actors in the drama. Hereafter, we hope the citizens of Springfield will select some other point to make public their intention of crossing the Mississippi to take each other's life than Alton. Such visits cannot but be attended not only with regret, but with unwelcome feelings: and the fewer we have, the better.

We should have alluded to this matter last week but for our absence at Court.

The dueling business (wrote Lincoln to his friend Josh Speed) still rages in Springfield. Now the news spread all over the capital. The seconds began to make charges and countercharges. The serious turned comic-opera. Shields challenged Bill Butler, one of the "Long Nine," who together with Elias Merryman was one of Lincoln's seconds. Then John Whiteside, Shields's second, considered himself insulted by Dr. Merryman. So Lincoln became Merryman's second. The first ver-

sions of the story of the original duel challenge between Lincoln and Shields began to appear. Note the reference to "Captain Lincoln," a reminder of the Black Hawk war service. From the Sangamo Journal, Oct. 7, 1842—and there was still more to come.

COMMUNICATION

SPRINGFIELD, OCT. 3, 1842.

To the Editor of the Sangamo Journal:

SIR—To proven: misrepresentation of the recent affair between Messrs. Shields and Lincoln, I think it proper, to give a brief narrative of the facts of the case, as they came within my knowledge; for the truth of which I hold myself responsible, and request you to give the same publication. An offensive article, in relation to Mr. Shields, appeared in the Sangamon Journal of the 2d September last, and on demanding the name of the author, Mr. Lincoln was given up by the Editor. Mr. Shields previous to this demand, made his arrangements to go to Quincy on public business; and before his return, Mr. Lincoln had left for Tremont to attend the Court, with the intention, as we learned, of remaining on the circuit several weeks. Mr. Shields, on his return, requested me to accompany him to Tremont; and on arriving there, we found that Dr. Merryman and Mr. Butler had passed us in the night, and got there before us—we arrived in Tremont, on the 17th ult., and Mr. Shields addressed a note to Mr. Lincoln immediately, informing him, that he was given up as the author of some articles, that appeared in the Sangamon Journal, (one more over the same signature having made its appearance at this time,) and requesting him, to retract the offensive allusions, contained in said articles in relation to his private character. Mr. Shields handed this note to me to deliver to Mr. Lincoln, and directed me, at the same time, not to enter into any verbal communication, or be the bearer of any verbal explanation, as such were always liable to misapprehension. This note was delivered by me to Mr. Lincoln, stating, at the same time, that I would call at his convenience for an answer. Mr. Lincoln, in the evening of the same day, handed me a letter addressed to Mr. Shields. In this he gave or offered no explanation; but stated therein, that he could not submit to answer further, on the ground that Mr. Shields's note contained an assumption of facts, and also a menace. Mr. Shields then addressed him another note, in which he disavowed all intention to menace, and requested to know, whether he, (Mr. Lincoln,) was the author of either of the articles, which appeared in the Journal, headed lost *Townships*, and signed

Rebecca; and if so, he repeated his request, of a retraction of the offensive matter, in relation to his private character; if not, his denial would be held sufficient. This letter was returned to Mr. Shields unanswered, with a verbal statement "that there could be no further negociation between them, until the first note was withdrawn." Mr. Shields thereupon sent a note, designating me as his friend, to which Mr. Lincoln replied, by designating Dr. Merryman. These three last notes passed on Monday morning the 19th. Dr. Merryman handed me Mr. Lincoln's last note when by ourselves, I remarked to Dr. Merryman that the matter was now submitted to us, and that I would propose, that he and myself, should pledge our words of honor to each other, to try to agree upon terms of amicable arrangement; and compel our principals to accept of them;—to this he readily assented, and we shook hands upon the pledge. It was then mutually agreed, that we should adjourn to Springfield, and there procrastinate the matter, for the purpose of effecting the secret arrangement between him and myself. All this I kept concealed from Mr. Shields—our horse had got a little lame in going to Tremont, and Dr. Merryman invited me to take a seat in his buggy—I accepted the invitation the more readily, as I thought that leaving Mr. Shields in Tremont, until his horse would be in better condition to travel, would facilitate the private agreement between Dr. Merryman and myself. I travelled to Springfield part of the way with him, and part with Mr. Lincoln, but nothing passed between us on the journey, in relation to the matter in hand; we arrived in Springfield on Monday night; about noon on Tuesday, to my astonishment, a proposition was made, to meet in Missouri, within three miles of Alton, on the next Thursday! The weapons, Cavalry broad swords of the largest size. The parties, to stand on each side of a barrier, and to be confined to a limited space—as I had not been consulted at all on the subject, and considering the private understanding between Dr. Merryman and myself, and it being known, that Mr. Shields was left at Tremont, such a proposition took me by surprise, however, being determined, not to violate the laws of the State, I declined agreeing upon the terms until we should meet in Missouri. Immediately after, I called upon Dr. Merryman, and withdrew the pledge of honor between him and myself, in relation to a secret arrangement. I started after this to meet Mr. Shields, and met him about twenty miles from Springfield. It was late on Tuesday night when we both reached the city, and learned that Dr. Merryman had left for Missouri, Mr. Lincoln having left before the proposition was made, as Dr. Merryman had himself informed me. The time and place made it necessary to start at once. We left Springfield at 11 o'clock on

Tuesday night, travelled all night, and arrived in Hillsboro' on Wednesday morning, where we took in Gen. Ewing—from there we went to Alton, where we arrived on Thursday; and as the proposition required three friends on each side, I was joined by Gen. Ewing and Dr. Hope, as the friends of Mr. Shields—we then crossed to Missouri, where a proposition was made by Gen. Hardin and Dr. English, (who had arrived there in the meantime as mutual friends) to refer the matter, to I think, four friends, for a settlement. This I believe Mr. Shields would refuse and declined seeing him, but Dr. Hope who conferred with him upon the subject, returned and stated, that Mr. Shields declined settling the matter through any other, than the friends he had selected, to stand by him on that occasion. The friends of both the parties, finally agreed to withdraw the papers (temporarily) to give the friends of Mr. Lincoln an opportunity to explain. Whereupon the friends of Mr. Lincoln, to-wit: Messrs. Merryman, Bledsoe and Butler, made a full and satisfactory explanation, in relation to the article which appeared, in the Sangamon Journal of the 2d; the only one written by him. This was all done without the knowledge or consent of Mr. Shields; and he refused to accede to it, until Dr. Hope, Gen. Ewing and myself, declared the apology sufficient, and that we could not sustain him in going further. I think it necessary to state further, that no explanation or apology, had been previously offered, on the part of Mr. Lincoln, to Mr. Shields; and that none was ever communicated by me to him; nor was any ever offered to me, unless a paper read to me by Dr. Merryman, after he had handed me the broadsword proposition on Tuesday. I heard so little of the reading of the paper, that I do not know fully what it purported to be, and I was the less inclined to enquire, as Mr. Lincoln was then gone to Missouri, and Mr. Shields not yet arrived from Tremont. In fact, I could not entertain any offer of the kind, unless upon my own responsibility, and that, I was not disposed to do, after what had already transpired.

I make this statement, as I am about to be absent for some time, and I think it due to all concerned, to give a true version of the matter before I leave.

Your obedient servant,
JOHN D. WHITESIDE

To the Public

SPRINGFIELD, 5th Oct., '42

I met Gen. Whiteside on Monday evening last at the American house, for the purpose of arranging a difficulty between Messrs. Butler and Shields. Gen. Whiteside refused to proceed to the adjustment of the affair in this State upon the grounds that it would render him amenable to its laws. The interview then terminated. Early the next morning I received the following note from him:

6 o'clock, A.M: 4th Oct. '42

Dr. Merryman:

    The proposition you handed me about 9 o'clock last night I indignantly refused to entertain. I had waited all day for an answer, and none was given until late at night, while my principal was attending a social party. The matter is referred to me by Mr. Shields, and to you by Mr. Butler, and we are bound to conduct it as gentlemen.

    I told you upon a former occasion, that nothing could be finally arranged until we should leave the State; that as citizens, we must respect its laws. I called at your boarding house at 10 o'clock last night, and found the house shut up. Now I take occasion to tell you that your weapons and distance will be accepted. This is your right, and I insist on mine; therefore, I designate Missouri, within a mile of Jefferson Barracks. The designation of place is as much my right as it is yours, and I shall not allow you to dictate the whole of the preliminaries. For this I am responsible, and not my principal. I therefore insist upon you as a gentleman to recognize this as my right, and if a gentleman, you will do it. You and I can agree upon the time, but you cannot dictate it. I propose next Friday 3 o'clock P.M.

Your obedient servant,
JOHN D. WHITESIDE.

To this I replied as follows:

SPRINGFIELD, 8 o'clock, A.M.
Tuesday, 4th Oct., 1842.

    SIR—I regret that the arrogant, dictatorial, rude, and ungentlemanly character of your note of 6 o'clock this morning, precludes the possibility of my communicating any further on the subject to which it alludes.

Respectfully,
E. H. MERRYMAN.

Gen. JOHN D. WHITESIDE.

This he refused to receive; and after tak[ing] a copy, he returned it to me. Sometime afterwards, the note below was handed me by Col. Shields.

33

SPRINGFIELD, 10 o'clock, Oct. 4th, '42.

DR. E. H. MERRYMAN:

SIR—From the tenor of your last note to me, by the hand of Capt. Lincoln, I have to request that you will meet me at the Planter's House, in the city of St. Louis, on Friday next, where you will hear from me further.

Your Ob't. Serv't,

JOHN D. WHITESIDE.

I then made this enquiry:

SPRINGFIELD, 3½ o'clock, Oct. 4th, '42.

Gen. JOHN D. WHITESIDE:

SIR—Your note of 10 o'clock to day, has been received. I wish to know, Sir, if you intend that note as a challenge; if so, my FRIEND will wait upon you with the CONDITIONS of our meeting.

Respectfully,

E. H. MERRYMAN.

To this I received the following answer:

SPRINGFIELD, 4 o'clock. Oct. 4th, '42.

DR. E. H. MERRYMAN:

SIR—I acknowledge the receipt of your 2d note by Capt. Lincoln, and will say in reply that you shall have a note of the character you allude to when we meet in the Planter's House, on Friday next in St. Louis.

Your obedient servant,

JOHN D. WHITESIDE.

I then sent him the annexed note by Mr. Lincoln:

SPRINGFIELD, 7 o'clock, P.M. 4th Oct. '42.

GEN. JOHN D. WHITESIDE:

SIR—I still deny your right to name time and place, for the adjustment of the difficulty between us; nevertheless, as I cannot well spare time, I am willing to meet you at the time you mentioned, at the most suitable point out of the State. That being Louisiana, Missouri. I hereby promise to see you there on Friday next.

Respectfully,

E. H. MERRYMAN.

This he refused to receive. Below is Mr. Lincoln's statement of what passed between him and Gen. Whiteside.

Upon presenting this note to Gen. Whiteside, and stating verbally that it was an agreement to meet him at the time he mentioned, at Louisiana, Missouri, he replied:—

"Lincoln, I can not accept any thing from him now. I have business at St. Louis: and it is as near as Louisiana.

A. LINCOLN.

I then requested Mr. Lincoln to deliver him the following verbal message:

> Dr. Merryman requests me, as he understands you are going away, to give you notice, that he will publish the correspondence which has passed between you and him, with such comments as he shall think proper.

> Upon making the above statement verbally to Gen. Whiteside, he replied—"I am going away when it suits my convenience; but I expect Dr. Merryman, as an honorable man, to meet me at St. Louis. We then shall be untrammeled by the laws of this State."

A. LINCOLN.

The above is a correct statement of the correspondence and facts, in relation to which the community can form their own judgment.

E. H. MERRYMAN.

The duel story ended, appropriately, with a story. Afterwards they told of Lincoln, asked what his weapons would be in a challenge, suggesting, "How about cow-dung at five paces?" The full account of the original abortive duel finally came out in the published correspondence of the affair as it was seen, read and pondered by the citizens of Springfield. From the Sangamo Journal, Oct. 14, 1842.

COMMUNICATION

SPRINGFIELD, Oct. 8, 1842.

Editors of the Journal:

GENT.—By your paper of Friday, I discover that Gen. Whiteside has published his version of the late affair between Messrs. Shields and Lincoln. I now bespeak a hearing of my version of the same affair, which shall be true, and full, as to all material facts.

On Friday evening, the 16th of September, I learned that Mr. Shields and Gen. Whiteside had started in pursuit of Mr. Lincoln, who was at Tremont, attending court. I knew that Mr. Lincoln was wholly unpracticed, both as to the diplomacy and weapons commonly employed in similar affairs; and I felt it my duty, as a friend, to be with him, and, so far as in my power, to prevent any advantage being taken of him as to either his honor or his life. Accordingly Mr. Butler and myself started, passed Shields and Whiteside in the night, and arrived at Tremont ahead of them, on Saturday morning. I told Mr. Lincoln what was brewing, and asked him what course he proposed to himself. He stated that he was wholly opposed to duelling, and would do any thing to avoid it that might not degrade him in the estimation of himself and friends; but if such degradation or a fight, were the only alternative, he would fight.

In the afternoon Shields and Whiteside arrived, and very soon the former sent to Mr. Lincoln by the latter, the following note or letter.

TREMONT, Sept. 17th. 1842.

A. Lincoln, Esq.

I regret that my absence on public business compelled me to postpone a matter of private consideration a little longer than I could have desired. It will only be necessary, however, to account for it by informing you that I have been to Quincy on business that would not admit of delay. I will now state briefly the reasons of my troubling you with this communication, the disagreeable nature of which I regret—as I had hoped to avoid any difficulty with any one in Springfield, while residing there, by endeavoring to conduct myself in such a way amongst both my political friends and opponents, as to escape the necessity of any. While thus abstaining from giving provocation, I have become the object of slander, vituperation and personal abuse, which were I capable of submitting to, I would prove myself worthy of the whole of it.

In two or three of the last numbers of the Sangamo Journal, articles of the most personal nature and calculated to degrade me, have made their appearance. On enquiring I was informed by the editor of that paper, through the medium of my friend, Gen. Whiteside, that you are the author of those articles. This information satisfies me that I have become by some means or other, the object of your secret hostility. I will not take the trouble of enquiring into the reason of all this, but I will take the liberty of requiring a full, positive and absolute retraction of all offensive allusions used by you in these communications, in relation to my private character and standing as a man, as an apology for the insults conveyed in them.

This may prevent consequences which no one will regret more than myself.

Your ob't serv't,
JAS. SHIELDS.

[Copy.]

About sun-set Gen. Whiteside called again, and received from Mr. Lincoln the following answer to Mr. Shields' note.

TREMONT, Sept. 17th. 1842.

Jas. Shields, Esq.

Your note of to-day was handed me by Gen. Whiteside. In that note you say you have been informed, through the medium of the editor of the Journal, that I am the author of certain articles in that paper which you deem personally abusive of you: and without stopping to enquire whether I really am the author, or to point out what is offensive in them, you demand an unqualified retraction of all that is offensive; and then proceed to hint at consequences.

Now, sir, there is in this so much assumption of facts, and so much of menace as to consequences, that I cannot submit to answer that note any farther than I have, and to add, that the consequence to which I suppose you allude, would be matter of as great regret to me as it possibly could to you.   Respectfully,

A. LINCOLN.

In about an hour Gen. Whiteside called again with another note from Mr. Shields; but after conferring with Mr. Butler for a long time, say two or three hours, returned without presenting the note to Mr. Lincoln. This was in consequence of an assurance from Mr. Butler that Mr. Lincoln could not receive any communication from Mr. Shields unless it were a withdrawal of his first note or a challenge. Mr. Butler further stated to Gen. Whiteside that on the withdrawal of the first note and a proper and gentlemanly request for an explanation, he had no doubt one would be given. Gen. Whiteside admitted that that was the course Mr. Shields ought to pursue, but deplored that his furious and intractable temper prevented his having any influence with him to that end. Gen. W. then requested us to wait with him until Monday morning, that he might endeavor to bring Mr. Shields to reason.

On Monday morning he called and presented Mr. Lincoln the same note as Mr. Butler says he had brought on Saturday evening. It was as follows:

TREMONT, Sept. 17th. 1842.

A. Lincoln, Esq.

In your reply to my note of this date, you intimate that I assume facts, and menace consequences, and that you cannot submit to answer it further. As now, sir, you desire it, I will be a little more particular. The editor of the Sangamo Journal gave me to understand that you are the author of an article which appeared I think in that paper of the 2d Sept. inst, headed the Lost Townships, and signed Rebecca or Becca. I would therefore take the liberty of asking whether you are the author of said article or any other over the same signature, which has appeared in any of the late numbers of that paper. If so, I repeat my request of an absolute retraction of all offensive allusion contained therein in relation to my private character and standing. If you are not the author of any of the articles, your denial will be sufficient. I will say further, it is not my intention to menace, but to do myself justice.

Your obd't serv't,
JAS. SHIELDS.

[Copy.]

This Mr. Lincoln perused, and returned to Gen. Whiteside, telling him verbally, that he did not think it consistent with his honor to negociate for peace with Mr. Shields, unless Mr. Shields would withdraw his former offensive letter.

In a very short time Gen. Whiteside called with a note from Mr. Shields designating Gen. Whiteside as his friend, to which Mr. Lincoln instantly replied designating me as his. On meeting Gen. Whiteside he proposed that we should pledge our honor to each other that we would endeavor to settle the matter amicably, to which I agreed, and stated to him the only conditions on which it could be so settled, viz. the withdrawal of Mr. Shields' first note, which he appeared to think reasonable, and regretted that the note had been written,—saying, however, that he had endeavored to prevail on Mr. Shields to write a milder one, but had not succeeded. He added, too, that I must promise not to mention it as, he would not dare to let Mr. Shields know that he was negociating peace, for said he—"He would challenge me next, and as soon cut my throat as not." Not willing that he should suppose my principal less dangerous than his own, I promised not to mention our pacific intentions to Mr. Lincoln or any other person, and we started for Springfield forthwith.

We all, except Mr. Shields, arrived in Springfield late at night on Monday. We discovered that the affair had, somehow, got great publicity in Springfield, and that an arrest was probable. To prevent this, it was agreed by Mr. Lincoln and myself that he should leave early on Tuesday morning.—Accordingly he prepared the following instructions for my guide, on a suggestion from Mr. Butler, that he had reason to believe that an attempt would be made by the opposite party to have the matter accommodated.

In case: Whiteside shall signify a wish to adjust this affair without further difficulty, let him know that if the present papers be withdrawn, and a note from Mr. Shields asking to know if I am the author of the articles of which he complains, and asking that I shall make him gentlemanly satisfaction, if I am the author, and this without menace, or dictation as to what that satisfaction shall be, a pledge is made that the following answer shall be given:

"I did write the 'Lost Township' letter which appeared in the Journal of the 2nd. Inst. but had no participation, in any form, in any other article alluding to you. I wrote that, wholly for political effect. I had no intention of injuring your personal or private character or standing as a man or a gentleman; and I did not then think, and do not now think that that article, could produce or has produced that effect against you, and had I anticipated such an effect I would have forborne to write it. And I will add, that your conduct towards me, so far as I knew, had always been gentlemanly; and that I had no personal pique against you, and no cause for any."

If this should be done, I leave it with you to arrange what shall & what shall not be published.

If nothing like this is done—the preliminaries of the fight are to be—

1st. Weapons—Cavalry broad swords of the largest size, precisely equal in all respects—and such as now used by the cavalry company at Jacksonville.

2nd. Position—A plank ten feet long, & from nine to twelve inches broad to be firmly fixed on edge, on the ground, as the line between us which neither is to pass his foot over upon forfeit of his life. Next a line drawn on the ground on either side of said plank & paralel with it, each at the distance of the whole length of the sword and three feet additional from the plank; and the passing of his own such line by either party during the fight shall be deemed a surrender of the contest.

3. Time—On thursday evening at five o'clock if you can get it so; but in no case to be at a greater distance of time than friday evening at five o'clock.

4th. Place—Within three miles of Alton on the opposite side of the river, the particular spot to be agreed on by you.

Any preliminary details coming within the above rules, you are at liberty to make at your discretion; but you are in no case to swerve from these rules, or to pass beyond their limits.["]

In the course of the forenoon I met Gen. Whiteside, and he again intimated a wish to adjust the matter amicably. I then read to him Mr. Lincoln's instructions to an adjustment, and the terms of the hostile meeting, if there must be one, both at the same time.

He replied that it was useless to talk of an adjustment, if it could only be effected by the *withdrawal* of Mr. Shields' paper, for such withdrawal Mr. Shields would never consent to. Adding, that he would as soon think of asking Mr. Shields to "butt his brains out against a brick wall as to withdraw that paper." He proceeded—"I see but one course—that is a desperate remedy—'tis to tell them if they will not make the matter up they must fight us." I replied that if he chose to fight Mr. Shields to compel him to do right, he might do so; but as for Mr. Lincoln, he was on the defensive, and I believed in the right, and I should do nothing to compel him to do wrong.—Such withdrawal having been made indispensable by Mr. Lincoln I cut the matter short as to an adjustment, and proposed to Gen. Whiteside to accept the terms of the fight, which he refused to do until Mr. Shields arrival in town, but agreed, verbally, that Mr. Lincoln's friends should procure the broadswords and take them to the ground. In the afternoon he came to me saying that some persons were swearing out affidavits to have us arrested, and that he intended to meet Mr. Shields immediately and proceed to the place designated, lamenting, however, that I would not delay the time that he might procure the interference of Gov. Ford and Gen. Ewing, to mollify Mr. Shields. I told him that an accommodation except upon the terms I mentioned, was out of the question—that to delay the meeting was to facilitate our arrest, and as I was determined not to be arrested I should leave town in fifteen minutes. I then pressed his acceptance of the preliminaries, which he disclaimed upon the ground that it would interfere with his oath of office as Fund Commissioner. I then, with two other friends, went to Jacksonville, where we joined Mr. Lincoln about 11 o'clock on Tuesday night. Wednesday morning we procured the broadswords and proceeded to Alton, where we arrived about 11 A.M. on Thursday. The other party were in town before us. We crossed the river and they soon followed. Shortly after Gen. Hardin and Dr. English presented to Gen. Whiteside and myself the following note:

ALTON, Sept. 22, 1842

Messrs. Whiteside and Merryman:
   As the mutual personal friends of Messrs. Shields and Lincoln, but without authority from either, we earnestly desire to see a reconciliation of the misunderstanding which exists between them.

Such difficulties should always be arranged amicably if it is possible to do so, with honor to both parties.

Believing ourselves, that such an arrangement can possibly be effected, we respectfully but earnestly submit the following proposition for your consideration:

Let the whole difficulty be submitted to four or more gentlemen, to be selected by yourselves, who shall consider the affair, and report thereupon for your consideration.

JOHN J. HARDIN,
R. W. ENGLISH.

To this proposition Gen. Whiteside agreed; I declined doing so without consulting Mr. Lincoln. Mr. Lincoln remarked that as they had accepted the proposition, he would do so, but directed that his friends should make no terms except those first proposed. Whether the adjustment was finally made upon these very terms, and no other, let the following documents attest:—

MISSOURI, Sept. 22, 1842.
Gentlemen:

All papers in relation to the matter in controversy between Mr. Shields and Mr. Lincoln, having been withdrawn by the friends of the parties concerned, the friends of Mr. Shields ask the friends of Mr. Lincoln to explain all offensive matter in the articles which appeared in the Sangamo Journal of the 2d, 9th and 16th of September, under the signature of Rebecca, and headed "Lost Township."

It is due to Gen. Hardin and Mr. English to state that their interference was of the most courteous and gentlemanly character.

JOHN D. WHITESIDE,
WM. LEE D. EWING,
T. M. HOPE.

MISSOURI, Sept. 22, 1842.
Gentlemen:

All papers in relation to the matter in controversy between Mr. Lincoln and Mr. Shields having been withdrawn by the friends of the parties concerned, we, the undersigned, friends of Mr. Lincoln, in accordance with your request, that explanation of Mr. Lincoln's publication in relation to Mr. Shields in the Sangamo Journal of the 2d, 9th and 16th of Sept., be made, take pleasure in saying that altho' Mr. Lincoln was the writer of the article signed Rebecca in the Journal of the 2d, and that only, yet he had no intention of injuring the personal or private character or standing of Mr. Shields as a gentleman or a man, and that Mr. Lincoln did not think, nor does he now think that said article could produce such an effect, and had Mr. Lincoln anticipated such an effect, he would have forborne to write it—we will further state that said article was written solely for political effect, and not to gratify any personal pique against Mr. Shields, for he had none, and knew of no cause for any. It is due to Gen. Hardin and Mr. English to say that their interference was of the most courteous and gentlemanly character.

E. H. MERRYMAN,

A. T. BLEDSOE,

WM. BUTLER.

Let it be observed now that Mr. Shields' friends, after agreeing to the arbitrament of four disinterested gentlemen, declined the contract, saying that Mr. Shields wished his own friends to act for him. They then proposed that we should explain without any withdrawal of papers—this was promptly and firmly refused, and Gen. Whiteside himself pronounced the papers withdrawn. They then produced a note requesting us to "*disavow*" all offensive intentions in the publications, &c, &c. This we declined answering and only responded to the above request for an explanation.

These are the material facts in relation to the matter, and I think present the case in a very different light from the garbled and curtailed statement of Gen. Whiteside. Why he made that statement I know not, unless he wished to detract from the honor of Mr. Lincoln. This was ungenerous, more particularly as he on the ground requested us not to make in our explanation, any quotations from the "Rebecca papers"—also not to make *public the terms of reconciliation*, and to unite with them in defending the honorable character of the adjustment.

Gen. W. in his publication says—"The friends of both parties agreed to withdraw the papers (temporarily) to give the friends of Mr. Lincoln an opportunity to explain." This I deny. I say the papers were withdrawn to enable Mr. Shields' friends to *ask* an explanation; and I appeal to the documents for proof of my position.

By looking over these documents, it will be seen, that Mr. Shields had not before asked for an *explanation*, but had all the time been dictatorily insisting on a *retraction*.

Gen. Whiteside, in his communication, brings to light much of Mr. Shields' manifestations of bravery behind the scenes. I can do nothing of the kind for Mr. Lincoln. He took his stand when I first met him at Tremont; and maintained it *calmly* to the last, without difficulty or difference between himself and his friends.

I cannot close this article, lengthy as it is, without testifying to the honorable and gentlemanly conduct of Gen. Ewing and Dr. Hope, nor indeed can I say that I saw anything objectionable in the course of Gen. Whiteside up to the time of his communication. This is so replete with prevarication and misrepresentation, that I cannot accord to the General that candor which I once supposed him to possess. He complains that I did not procrastinate time according to agreement. He forgets that by his own act he cut me off from that chance in inducing me, by promise, not to communicate our secret contract to Mr. Lincoln. Moreover I could see no consistency in wishing for an extension of time at that stage of the affair, when in the outset they were in so precipitate a hurry, that they could not wait three days for Mr. Lincoln to return from Tremont, but must hasten there, apparently with the intention of bringing the matter to a speedy issue. He complains, too, that after inviting him to take a seat in my buggy, I then took a different route than arranged. Absurd. The valorous gentleman suggests that he beguiled the tedium of the journey by recounting to me his exploits in a well-fought battle; dangers on "the battlefield," in which I don't believe he ever participated,— doubtless with a view to induce a salutary effect on my nerves, and impress me with a proper notion of his propensities.

One more main point of his argument and I have done. The General seems to be troubled with a convenient shortness of memory on some occasions. He does not remember that any explanations were offered at any time unless it were a paper read with a "broad-sword proposition" was tendered when his mind was so confused by the precipated clatter of broad-swords, or *something else*, that he did "not know fully what it purported to be." The truth is, that by unwillingly refraining from mentioning it to his principal, he placed himself in a dilemma, which he is now endeavoring to shuffle out of. By his inefficiency and want of knowledge of those laws which govern gentlemen in matters of this kind, he has done great harm to his principal, a gentleman who I believe ready at all times to vindicate his honor manfully, but who has been unfortunate in his selection of his friend, and this fault he is now trying to wipe out by doing an act of still greater injustice to Mr. Lincoln.

E. H. MERRYMAN.

Another Presidential election was in the offing, and Lincoln again was canvassing for the party, for the losing cause of Henry Clay. Lincoln was still the "great Goliath of the Springfield Junto." His debating opponent, the Illinois Democratic elector John Calhoun, had once been Lincoln's chief surveyor in the mid-1830's. This name-calling report differed from that of the friendly Sangamo Journal which said: "The efforts of Mr. Lincoln were distinguished for ability, and in all candor we must say, that we did not discover a single position raised by Mr. Calhoun, that he did not entirely demolish." Not so, in the Democratic Illinois State Register, March 22–29, 1844.

POLITICAL DISCUSSION

March 22, 1844.

This being the first week of our Circuit Court, the public speakers, of both parties, devote the evening hours, to the discussion of the great questions involved in the coming Presidential election.

On Monday evening [March 18, 1844] Judge [Alfred W.] CAVARLY (one of the democratic electors) delivered an able and interesting address. Mr. C. in the course of his argument, quoted from a speech of Mr. [John T.] Stuart, made in Congress, an admission that the consumer of imported articles paid the duty or tax, which was concealed in the retail price of the goods. This so disturbed Mr. Lincoln, that he promised to forfeit his "ears" and his "legs" if he did not demonstrate, that protected articles have been cheaper since the late Tariff than before. To our surprise, Judge [Stephen T.] Logan, endorsed Lincoln's promise.

Will Mr. Lincoln or Judge Logan, say they believe that the late Tariff law was the cause of the diminution in the price of manufactured articles last spring? We think not.

On Tuesday evening, Judge [William C.] BROWN, (whig elector) replied to Mr. Cavarly.

On Wednesday evening, Mr. [John] Calhoun, (Democratic elector,) developed the hidden mysteries of the Tariff, and leading measures of the whigs, to the public gaze. So completely did he expose modern whiggery and its anti-republican measures, that [Edward D.] Baker himself turned pale, and Lincoln trembled at the thought of loosing [sic] his legs and his ears.

THE DEMOCRACY OF SANGAMON BUCKELING [sic] ON THEIR ARMOR

March 29, 1844.

The recent discussion in this city, has done much to encourage democrats—and more to expose coon whiggery. Mr. Calhoun has demolished Lincoln, the great Goliath of the Junto—legs and all. Scarcely a grease spot has been left. Lincoln's defence of the coon tariff, was like a shrewd lawyer's defence of a horse thief, or a highway robber—quibble, quibble, quibble. His *"probabilities"* and *"possibilities,"* is perfect moonshine, furnishing ample light to exhibit the utter weakness of his cause; and were an insult to the reflecting faculties of the shool-boy [sic].

POLITICAL DISCUSSION IN THIS CITY

March 29, 1844.

I shall content myself by presenting a synopsis of Mr. Calhoun's leading arguments with Mr. Lincoln's "sneers" at them.

Mr. Calhoun proved beyond all cavil that in its operation the entire burden [of the tariff] fell on the consumer, yet Mr. Lincoln had the hardihood to assert that it might *probably* fall upon the manufacturer, after Mr. Calhoun had shown that it *positively* fell upon the consumer. Will Mr. L. tell us who paid the duty on Dr. Shields' knives? But this being a fact which he *dare not* deny and *cannot* controvert, he passes over with a *"sneer!"*

As to the second: Notwithstanding that it is so superlatively foolish, and carries with its own refutation, Mr. Lincoln had the presumption to insult the understandings of his hearers, by re-asserting that such was the case [that goods were cheaper because of the tariff].

Probably his *pack-horse* may believe this. The "shingle clappers" by whom he was surrounded, no doubt, received it with implicit faith and credit; but what must have been Mr. Lincoln's opinion of the intelligence of his auditory if he expected them to swallow that?

Mr. Lincoln very candidly acknowledged his inability to prove that the tariff had anything to do with the *late* low prices throughout this country and Europe.

I defy Mr. L. or any man living to prove that the relation of cause and effect subsists between [the tariff and the price of goods].

Whiggery may well exclaim—save me from my friends! A more complete and perfect *expose* of the iniquity and absurdity of the tariff system, could not be desired than was unwittingly furnished by Mr. Lincoln himself. It stands very much in need of another advocate to protect it from Mr. L's defence.

Now Lincoln sought a seat in the United States House of Representatives. An election was coming up in August, 1846, and he began to line up the newspapers in the Seventh Illinois District. "I want you to let nothing prevent your getting an article in your paper of this week," wrote Lincoln to one Whig editor. The idea was to obtain the Whig nomination for himself under the "rotation" system and stymie the re-election bid of John J. Hardin. Hence two reports such as this, from the Sangamo Journal of Feb. 5, 1846.

At a meeting of the whigs of Athens precinct, in Sangamon county, held at the school house in Athens, on the 31st of January, 1846, JAMES K. HURT, Esq. was called to the chair, and J. H. SHEPHERD, appointed Secretary. After the object of the meeting had been briefly explained by the chair, J. H. Shepherd offered the following preamble and resolutions, which were adopted by acclamation—

Whereas the time for selecting a whig candidate for Congress for this District at the next election is approaching; and whereas our present Representative, Hon. E. D. Baker, recognizing the principle of 'rotation in office,' has generously declined a re-election—Therefore,

Resolved, That we recommend to our fellow whigs of this District our friend of 'long standing' and tried faith, A. LINCOLN, Esq. as most deserving the nomination at this time.

Resolved, That in this expression of preference we intend no disparagement to others that have been, or may be, spoken of as candidates, but simply that in integrity and ability, we regard him the equal of any, while on the balance sheet between services rendered, and favors received, we regard his claim as superior to any. . . .

PUBLIC MEETING

At a meeting of the Whigs of Menard county, held pursuant to a previous call at Petersburgh [sic], on the 12th of February, A.D. 1846,

The following Preamble and Resolutions were adopted unanimously.

Whereas, the time is approaching for the nomination of a Whig candidate for Congress in this district, and inasmuch as we regard office, as a trust reposed in, and an honor conferred on men, for their talents, integrity, and devotedness to the interests of their country, therefore

Resolved, That we recommend to our whig friends throughout the district, ABRAHAM LINCOLN, Esq., as most deserving the nomination.

Resolved, That in thus expressing our preference, we mean no disparagement to any who now are, or hereafter may become candidates, but simply, that in integrity and talent we consider him equal to any, whilst in the scale of services rendered and favors received, we consider his claims as superior to all.

Resolved, That our delegates be instructed to give their votes in said Convention for Abraham Lincoln, Esq. . . .

Lincoln was nominated by acclamation for the U.S. Congressional seat. Hardin had withdrawn and the field cleared. The election was coming up in August. As in the earlier Lincoln campaigns for the State legislature, it was time for William Walters, editor and publisher of the Illinois State Register, to strew the path with nettles, which he did on May 8, 1846.

A. LINCOLN, Esq. has been nominated by the Petersburg (Whig) Convention for Congress; only one half the Counties in the District represented, or thereabouts. Is Lincoln for 54 40, or is he for "compromising" away our Oregon territory to England, as his brother Whigs in Congress, along with the "nullifiers," as the Journal calls them, appear to be determuned on? This, the People ought to know, before they vote next August. No shuffling, Mr. Lincoln! Come out, square!

Chapter 2

Congressman Lincoln

AUGUST 1846–OCTOBER 1854

After August 3, 1846, he was Congressman Lincoln. His next office would be President. It had been touchy getting the Congressional nomination in the first place; the campaign itself was rough as bark. Lincoln had written one of his many letters marked confidential to a friend in Cass County: "Now if you should hear anyone say that Lincoln don't want to go to Congress, I wish you as a personal friend of mine, would tell him you have reason to believe he is mistaken. The truth is, I would like to go very much."

Lincoln's opponent was Peter Cartwright, Democrat and Methodist circuit-rider. Brother Cartwright's campaign was aimed at both Lincoln and the Devil: sometimes on the stump he tried to prove they were the same fellow. The accusation was made that Lincoln was irreverent, that he didn't belong to any church. This issue of religion was to come up when he ran for President, too. Lincoln indicated that religion was personal, not political. And once bluntly: "When any church will inscribe over its altar, as its sole qualification for membership, the Savior's condensed statement of the substance of both law and Gospel, 'Thou shalt love the Lord thy God with all thy heart, and with all thy soul and thy neighbor as thyself,' that church will I join with all my heart and all my soul."

On election day Lincoln received 6,340 votes, Cartwright 4,829, Walcott (Abolitionist) 249. He was in, but the wild accusations by the circuit-rider still remained to be answered. This Lincoln did by having the following campaign handbill reprinted by Allen N. Ford, editor, in the Illinois Gazette, of Lacon, on Aug. 15, 1846.

TO THE VOTERS OF THE SEVENTH CONGRESSIONAL DISTRICT.

Fellow-citizens:

A charge having got into circulation in some of the neighborhoods of this district, in substance that I am an open scoffer at Christianity, I have by the advice of some friends concluded to notice the subject in this form. That I am not a member of any Christian church, is true; but I have never denied the truth of the Scriptures; and I have never spoken with intentional disrespect of religion in general, or of any denomination of Christians in particular. It is true that in early life I was inclined to believe in what I understand is called the "Doctrine of Necessity"—that is, that the human mind is impelled to action, or held in rest by some power, over which the mind itself has no control; and I have sometimes (with one, two or three, but never publicly) tried to maintain this opinion in argument. The habit of arguing thus however, I have entirely left off for more than five years. And I add here, I have always understood this same opinion to be held by several of the Christian denominations. The foregoing is the whole truth, briefly stated, in relation to myself, upon this subject.

I do not think I could myself, be brought to support a man for office, whom I knew to be an open enemy of, and scoffer at, religion. Leaving the higher matter of eternal consequences, between him and his Maker, I still do not think any man has the right thus to insult the feelings, and injure the morals, of the community in which he may live. If, then, I was guilty of such conduct, I should blame no man who should condemn me for it; but I do blame those, whoever they may be, who falsely put such a charge in circulation against me.

July 31, 1846.

A. LINCOLN.

Before leaving for Washington, Lincoln attended the big 1847 Harbor and River Convention in Chicago. This national convention was run by the Whigs, who came out strongly in favor of improvements. Horace Greeley of the New York Tribune was there and wrote his first comment about Lincoln—more to come—for New York readers: "In the afternoon Hon. Abraham Lincoln, a tall specimen of an Illinoisan, just elected to Congress from the only Whig district in the state, was called out, and spoke briefly and happily." This is how the Chicago Daily Journal, July 6, 1847, predicted Lincoln's future.

FIFTH OF JULY

THE CONVENTION—THE PAGEANT.

A great, a glorious day has gone down—a day which children's children will remember, when the actors that took part, and the hands that indited are cold and motionless; as a day when party predilections were obliterated; when sectional interests were forgotten; when from eighteen free and independent Sovereignities, men came up to the achievement of a noble work, united their voices in one grand harmony, for the promotion of an object demanded alike by the most enlightened self interest, the most liberal view, and indeed by common humanity.

[A description of the convention followed.]

The several propositions were adopted with great unanimity.

On motion the States were called alphabetically, and requested to select one of their number, as a committee to nominate officers for the permanent organization of the Convention.

The following States answered, and named committee as follows:

Connecticut—John A. Rockwell,
Florida—John G. Camp,
Georgia—Thomas Butler King,
Indiana—S. C. Sample,
Illinois—A. Lincoln,
Iowa—N. L. Stout,
Maine—M. A. Chandler,
Massachusetts—Artemas Lee,
Michigan—John Biddle,
South Carolina—J. L. H. Cross,
Missouri—Albert Jackson,
New Hampshire—F. S. Fish,
New Jersey—Hon. L. Kirkpatrick,
New York—Hon. J. C. Spencer,
Ohio—Hon. R. C. Schenk,
Pennsylvania—A. G. Ralston,
Rhode Island—E. C. Graves,
Wisconsin—Marshall M. Strong.

On motion, the Convention adjourned until four o'clock, P.M.

––––––––

We are happy to see the Hon. ABRAM LINCON in attendance upon the Convention, the only Whig representative to Congress from this State. This is his first visit to the Commercial emporium of the State, and we have no doubt his visit will impress him more deeply if possible with the importance, and inspire a higher zeal for the great interest of River and Harbor improvements. We expect much from him as a representative in Congress, and we have no doubt our expectations will be more than realized, for never was reliance placed in a nobler heart, and a sounder judgment. We know the banner he bears, will never be soiled.

This was the XXXth Congress Lincoln entered in 1847: a home of giants, like Webster and Calhoun, and a breeding ground for men who would emerge during the Civil War, like Andrew Johnson and Jefferson Davis. Lincoln was insignificant, only in "the early prime of manhood," in the phrase used at the end of this size-up of the new members by "H.G."—Greeley in the New York Tribune of Dec. 11, 1847.

THE NEW CONGRESS
Editorial Correspondence

WASHINGTON, Thursday eve. Dec. 9, 1847.

The XXXth Congress has terminated the daily sessions of its first week—and quite satisfactorily. The American Senate always has been, and I trust always will be, a dignified and orderly body, although an individual of contrary habits and impulses may occasionally straggle into it; but the House too generally resembles a menagerie shaken up by an earthquake.—I have watched the new House anxiously this week, and I think it a decided improvement on its immediate predecessor—in intellect, in character and in manners. That there are rowdies among its members is quite likely, but I hope no determined brawlers nor confirmed drunkards, such as have made themselves disgustingly conspicuous on its floor in former years. As yet, there has been no striking exhibition of personal acrimony, and no remarkable display of superlative egotism. The Speaker is the very man for his place—courteous, dignified, able, prompt, commanding, and so manifestly anxious to do his duty faithfully and treat every Member with impartial kindness, that his success in filling that arduous and difficult post cannot be doubtful. Every Member must feel a personal interest in sustaining him. There will of course be stormy times in the House; but I confidently believe it will be more decorous and orderly in the main than any of its last five predecessors.

The Senate has greatly changed since I first looked upon it, not many years ago. Mr. WEBSTER is not yet here; while Messrs. FORSYTH, WHITE,

POINDEXTER, LEIGH, RIVES, WOODBURY, EVANS, SOUTHARD, EWING, TALL-
MADGE, WRIGHT, SIMMONS, &c, &c and, 'noblest Roman of them all,'
HENRY CLAY, have vacated its seats—most of them forever. There are
still left of the old magnates, WEBSTER and CLAYTON, CALHOUN and
BENTON, MANGUM and CRITTENDEN, DAVIS and BERRIEN, while the recent accessions of R. JOHNSON, DIX, CAMERON, CASS, HANNEGAN and
above all of CORWIN, have been calculated to sustain the justly high character of this illustrious body. Still, I think, few will contend that the
Senate of 1847 is equal to that of '34 or '41.

Of the new accessions, however, several have brought to the Senate
eminent talents and enviable reputations. Many of them have served
with credit in the House as well as in the Legislatures of their several
States. Of these are JOHN P. HALE of N.H. (from whose energetic character and independent position I hope much good.) JOHN BELL of Tenn.
(detained at home, I regret to say, by illness,) JEFFERSON DAVIS of Miss.
JOSEPH H. UNDERWOOD of Ky. R. M. T. HUNTER of Va. and S. A. DOUG-
LASS of Ill. Two others have been Governors of their several states—ROGER
S. BALDWIN of Conn. and ALPHEUS FELCH of Michigan.—Messrs. CLARKE
of R.I. DOWNS of Lou and FOOTE of Miss. have acquired distinction in the
Legislatures of their several States. MASON of Va. has been in the House,
though not distinguished there; and I believe Messrs. BRADBURY of Me.
and SPRUANCE of Del. have served in the Legislatures of their States,
though of this I have no clear recollection.

—The new House has a large proportion of new Members, as each
House is apt to have. Of these Gen. JAMES WILSON of N.H. is known
through the Free States as a most effective public speaker, has served with
distinction in the Legislature, and will take a high rank here. From our
own State, Messrs. WILLIAM DUER of Oswego, JOHN M. HOLLEY of
Wayne (alas that his health should be so broken!) D. D. ST. JOHN of Sul-
livan and N. K. HALL of Erie, have served with credit in our State Assembly—the two first-named with distinction. Mr. F. A. TALLMADGE
was four years in the State Senate and Mr. DUDLEY MARVIN was in Congress some 30 years ago. I believe most of our other 'new men' are making
'their first appearance on any stage.' So of the New-Jersey men, of whom
one at least—Mr. D. S. GREGORY—will signalize his term by as much useful work as little useless talk as any other Member. Pennsylvania, Maryland, Virginia and North Carolina, have each an unusual proportion of
new Members, but I scarcely know any of them yet; and so of Ohio and
Kentucky. . . .

The West has sent us some 'new men,' who in due time will make themselves heard. Among these on the Whig side are ABRAHAM LINCOLN of Ill. WILLIAM P. HASKILL of Tenn, GEORGE G. DUNN and ELISHA EMBREE of Ind. and PATRICK W. TOMPKINS of Miss.—all (I think) Clay Electors and effective canvassers in '44; all in the early prime of manhood; heretofore State Legislators and men of sterling qualities, to whom the floor of Congress (no matter if they never make Speeches) affords liberal opportunities of usefulness. I must here close this hurried survey.

H. G.

[Horace Greeley]

Lincoln made his first important speech in the House of Representatives on January 12, 1848—a speech questioning the Polk Administration's justifications behind the war with Mexico. The Whig line, which Lincoln expounded, was that the war was "unnecessarily and unconstitutionally commenced by the President." In a series of resolutions Lincoln demanded to know the exact "spot" where American blood was first shed and if that "spot" was American territory. The "spot resolutions," as they came to be known, got Lincoln into hot water with some of his friends who considered them unpatriotic. The Rockford Forum, Illinois, Jan. 19, 1848, agreed with the Baltimore Patriot. So did the Missouri Republican, quoted in the Illinois Journal (formerly the Sangamo Journal, Springfield) of Feb. 3, 1848. Both pro-Lincoln reports follow.

MR. LINCOLN'S RESOLUTIONS.—Mr. Lincoln, the Whig member from this State, has introduced a series of resolutions into the House of Representatives upon the subject of the war, which among the multitude that have been offered, are spoken of as being direct to the point.

"Potomac," the correspondent of the Baltimore Patriot thus speaks of Mr. L.: "The resolutions of Mr. Lincoln, of Illinois, submitted to the House to-day, will attract attention from the fact that they stick to the spot in Mexico, where the first blood of the war was shed, with all the tightness that characterized the fabled shirt of the fabled Nessus! Evidently there is music in that very tall, Mr. Lincoln."

From the Missouri Republican

WASHINGTON, D.C., Jan. 12, 1848.

In the House, to-day, the Hon. Abraham Lincoln of the Springfield district, Illinois, and the only Whig member from that State, addressed the Committee of the Whole. The subject was the reference of the President's message, and he defined his position on the war, and took up the question of the Rio Grande. His speech was one of great power, and replete with the strongest and most conclusive arguments. He commanded the attention of the House, which none but a strong man can do; and this speech, together with a happy and effectual off-hand speech he made the other day on the subject of the controversy between the Postmaster General and the Baltimore and Richmond Railroad Company, placed him in the very first rank in the House. This, however, is no more than what his friends, who knew him, expected, and the people of his district, and, indeed, of the State, may well feel proud of such a representative.

The opposition press in Illinois began to attack Lincoln for his stand on the Mexican War, with the Democratic Illinois State Register leading the pack. "Spotty" Lincoln was villified—they asked what would the "gallant heroes" of the war think of him? The Register, on Jan. 21 and again on Jan. 28, 1848, spoke out.

Among those who voted that the war is unconstitutional, was Mr. LINCOLN, the member from this district—a district which has sent one thousand gallant soldiers to the war, who immortalized themselves and our state upon the glorious battle-fields of Buena Vista and Cerro Gordo. What will these gallant heroes say when they learn that their representative has declared in the national councils that the cause in which they suffered and braved everything, was "unconstitutional" "unnecessary," and consequently infamous and wicked?

We have not patience, if we had the space, to dwell longer this week upon the revolting and disgraceful proceedings of the entire body in Congress. Thank God, there is a party strong enough to defend the national honor and save the American name from the foul disgrace which these moral traitors think to fasten upon it forever.

"Out damned SPOT!"

Mr. LINCOLN, the member in Congress from this district, has made his *debut* in Congress by a speech in opposition to the war policy of the administration. We have not received a copy of this speech yet, therefore we are not yet informed whether Mr. L. took ground against the war *in toto* or not, but as his name is recorded among the infamous 85, who voted that the war was "unconstitutional and unnecessary," we presume that he backed his vote in his speech.

*Because the "spot resolutions" would affect his political future,
Lincoln's partisans were agitated. Lincoln wrote from Washington
to his law partner, William Herndon, "if you misunderstand, I fear
our other good friends will also. . . . I will stake my life, that if you
had been in my place, you would have voted just as I did." The Belleville Advocate, Illinois, March 2, 1848, reported the anti-Lincoln feeling.*

No state has more reason to be proud of the prompt manner in
which her citizens rushed to the battlefield, at the call of their country
and their gallantry during the conflict. Her representatives in Congress
are equally distinguished for their patriotic support of the war—all of
those representatives, save one, Mr. Lincoln, the Whig member. His
course in denouncing his country, has called forth a stern rebuke from
many of his constituents, and will be more signally condemned.

At a meeting, without distinction of party, held in Clark County,
Ill., the following resolution was adopted:—

RESOLVED, That Abe Lincoln, the author of the "spotty" resolutions
in Congress, against his own country, may they long be remembered by
his constituents, but may they cease to remember him, except to rebuke
him. They have done much for him, but he has done nothing for them,
save, the stain he inflicted on their proud name of patriotism and glory,
in the part they have taken in their country's cause.

During the canvas he pledged himself to sustain the war. The Washington correspondent of the Illinois State Register, thus alludes to the
reception given his speech in Congress:—But what measure of indignation will not Illinois award his Toryism?

By reference to the debates published in the Union, you will perceive
that Mr. Lincoln has been handled most severely by several members. I
was present a few days ago, and heard Mr. Jamison of Missouri, allude
to the course taken by Mr. Lincoln, and in a most scorching manner, commented upon the speech of the successor of Hardin, and Baker. I think
that Mr. Lincoln will find that he had better remained quiet. He will
doubtless regret that he voted that Hardin, Zabriskei, Houghton, Furgu-
son, Robbins, Woodward, Bartleson, Atherton, Rountree, Street, Davis,
Price, Fletcher, Kelley, Cowardan, Murphey, and others fell while leading the brave Illinoisans to ROBBERY AND DISHONOUR. He will regret that he
has, by his vote, stigmatized the brave men of the State, with having left
the ploughshear and pen, to take the sword "IN AID OF A WAR OF RAPINE

AND MURDER." He will regret possibly that he has thrown upon the escutcheon of Illinois the stain of having sent six thousand men to Mexico, to record their infamy and shame in the blood of poor, innocent, unoffending people, whose only crime was weakness. He will regret that he has declared by his vote that the "God in Heaven has forgotten to defend the weak and innocent, and permitted the strong hand of murderers and demons from hell to kill men, women and children, and lay waste and pillage the land of the just."

Another precinct was heard from in the anti-Lincoln chorus of opposition to his Mexican War stand. He was a one-term "Ranchero Spotty" and "Benedict Arnold." From the Illinois State Register, March 10, 1848.

MORGAN COUNTY

At a meeting of the citizens of Appolonia precinct, convened at the house of James Brian, the 1st of March, the following resolutions were unanimously adopted by the entire meeting: . . .

5. That as citizens of the seventh congressional district of Illinois we can but express the deep mortification inflicted upon us by our representative in Congress in his base, dastardly and treasonable assault upon President Polk, in his disgraceful speech on the present war, and in the resolutions offered by him against his own government, in flagrant violation of all expectation here, and direct opposition to the views of a majority of our congressional electors. That this district has been often afflicted with inefficient *per diem* men, or unfortunate representation, but never until now has it known disgrace, so black, so mortifying, so unanswerable. Such insulting opprobrium cast upon our citizens and soldiers, such black odium and infamy heaped upon the living brave and illustrious dead can but excite the indignation of every true Illinoian, the disgust of republicans and the condemnation of men. Therefore henceforth will the Benedict Arnold of our district be known here only as the Ranchero Spotty of one term.

The political nature of the anti-Lincoln censure was underlined by the Illinois Journal, Springfield (it had changed its name from the Sangamo Journal in September, 1847), which declared it outright locofocoism. The Journal, March 16, 1848.

We learn from the [Illinois State] Register that the democracy of Appalonia precinct in Morgan county, in meeting, complimented Mr. Lincoln, by passing a resolution of censure. We see nothing new or remarkable in this. When has locofocoism in Appalonia precinct done otherwise than denounce Mr. Lincoln? When has it ever refused to adopted [sic] any set of resolutions that its leader required them to adopt?

These Appalonian loco focos, at the recent Constitutional Election, voted unanimously in favor of sustaining the old system of life offices, four dollars a day for Representatives, State Banks and corrupt legislation. The censure of such a coterie will not be very sensibly felt by Mr. Lincoln.

Months afterward the Democratic politicians in Illinois were still trying to make capital of the "spot resolutions." Major Richardson was an Illinois Congressman. This comment is from the Peoria Democratic Press, May 17, 1848.

MAJ. WM. A. RICHARDSON

The brilliant conduct of this tried soldier on the bloody field of Buena Vista, has only been equalled by his devotion to the interests of his constituents. Since he took his seat in Congress, no member has attended more strictly to the duties of his office than the Major has, and upon all the leading measures that come before that body, he assumes the most elevated position and sustains with nerve and resolution what he conceives to be the true interests of his country—and we feel assured that so far as his course has come to the knowledge of his constituents, it has received their hearty approval. The high and patriotic ground he took upon the war question is alone sufficient to render him a favorite of the people of this gallant State.

The contrast between his course and that of "SPOTTY LINCOLN," exhibits more than anything else, the wide difference between the sentiments advocated by the democratic party and those which are clung to by the enemies of the country—and whilst Maj. Richardson will be remembered in the grateful hearts of his countrymen, the miserable man of "Spots" will pass unnoticed save in the execration that his treason will bring upon his name. The views and acts of the former were the "embodiment" of patriotism, whilst those of the latter displayed the treason of an ARNOLD, and all the "bloody-hands and hospital grave" disposition of a CORWIN. Maj. Richardson will live in the affections of the people ever after death. Lincoln will be "dead whilst among the living."

Greeley's paper began to take notice of the tall man from Illinois. Lincoln went with the Illinois delegation to the Whig National Convention in Philadelphia early in June, 1848. Upon his return to Washington he made a speech in Congress on internal improvements. The issue of slavery was before the House, too. From the New York Tribune, June 22, 1848.

THINGS IN WASHINGTON

Debate in the House. . . .
Correspondence of *The Tribune*

WASHINGTON, Tuesday, June 20.

The Civil and Diplomatic bill being before the House in the Committee of the Whole, sundry speeches were let off, having of course no relation to the subject. Mr. LINCOLN of Ill. made a very sensible speech upon the question of Internal Improvements. He evidently understood the subject, and, better still, succeeded in making the House understand it. Tall men come from Illinois. JOHN WENTWORTH and LINCOLN are both men of mighty stature, and their intellectual endowments correspond with their physical.

Mr. LINCOLN was succeeded by Mr. WICK of Ind.—a wick without oil. He spoke to the dough-faces, of whom he is a great part. Rather, he spoke not, but read. He did not dare to trust his voice to the inspiration of the moment, but thought to hide his blushes beneath or behind foolscap. He can make an improvement upon his mode of delivery—let the town-crier read his words. All well-disposed citizens would then disperse, quicker than at the reading of the riot-act.

Mr. HUDSON of Mass. followed in an able, dispassionate, well-reasoned speech, upon the question of Slavery. He advanced no extreme opinions, he defended no insane conduct. His speech was eminently practical and conciliatory. Loco-Foco LAHM, who hoped to entrap him, took nothing by his motion. He inquired of Mr. HUDSON if, entertaining the sentiments he uttered in regard to Slavery, he could nevertheless support Gen. TAYLOR? Mr. HUDSON calmly replied that he drew a distinction between persons who, having been born in the South, educated and reared in the belief that there was no moral wrong in Slavery, consistently supported the institution, and another class who, having been born and brought up at the North, never had aught but free influences around them, never respired but free air, never commerced with but free men, and yet, to gain party ends of personal aggrandisement, toadied, flattered and cringed to the South. The application of his answer could not be mistaken. He, with all other honest men of the North, could support an honorable slave-holder rather than a parasitical servile. . . .

In the 1848 national election Lincoln again took the stump, this time for the Whig candidacy of Zachary Taylor. In Congress he made a speech against Taylor's Democratic opponent, Lewis Cass, ridiculing the latter's war record and his own: "By the way, Mr. Speaker, did you know I am a military hero? Yes sir; in the days of the Black Hawk War, I fought, bled, and came away. If he saw any live, fighting Indians, it was more than I did; but I had a good many bloody struggles with the mosquitoes." Then Lincoln went on a speaking tour of New England, pointing out on the platform that the Whigs and Free-Soilers were both against the extension of slavery. He mingled with the New England abolitionists, making important contacts. This is how he was received in Worcester, Mass., as told in the Boston Daily Advertiser, Sept. 14, 1848.

THE WORCESTER CONVENTION
From our own Correspondent

WORCESTER, Sept. 12, 1848. }
Tuesday, 11 o'clock, P.M. }

The Whig State Convention for the nomination of Governor and Lieutenant Governor, and Presidential Electors, is to be held here tomorrow. Many of the delegates are already present, and are attended by staunch Whigs from all parts of the State. The best possible spirit prevails, and there is every indication of a renewed triumph for the Whig party in November next.

So many Whigs from all parts of the Commonwealth are here, that a meeting has been held this evening, to enable them to consult with and encourage each other, and compare notes about the past, present and future. It was full and enthusiastic, and gives good promise of success to come.

The meeting was called to order at half past seven o'clock, by Hon. IRA BARTON, Chairman of the Whig Club of Worcester, who, with a pleasant remark about the merging of the Whig Club of the city into a meeting of the Whigs of the State,—nominated Mr. ENSIGN H. KELLOGG of Pittsfield, as Chairman of the meeting, and this nomination was accepted by acclamation. . . .

When Mr. John Quincy Adams told Mr. Hudson, the representative from Worcester, that he believed Gen. Taylor would do more than any other man to prevent the extension of slavery, it might well be believed that he was looking forward to exactly such a state of things as now existed.

Mr. Kellogg then referred to the position and claims of Mr. Van Buren, and asked, pertinently and forcibly, whether we were to take a single and sudden assertion, and declaration of principle, as an answer to all the evidence of his former life and action, and a reason to suppose that his principles and character were changed.

Mr. Kellogg then introduced to the meeting the Hon. ABRAM LINCOLN, whig member of Congress from Illinois, a representative of *free soil*.

Mr. LINCOLN has a very tall and thin figure, with an intellectual face, showing a searching mind, and a cool judgment. He spoke in a clear and cool, and very eloquent manner, for an hour and a half, carrying the audience with him in his able arguments and brilliant illustrations,—only interrupted by warm and frequent applause. He began by expressing a real feeling of modesty in addressing an audience "this side of the mountains," a part of the country where, in the opinion of the people of his section, everybody was supposed to be instructed and wise. But he had devoted his attention to the question of the coming Presidential election, and was not unwilling to exchange with all whom he might meet the ideas to which he had arrived.

He then began to show the fallacy of some of the arguments against Gen. Taylor, making his chief theme the fashionable statement of all those who oppose him, ("the old Locofocos as well as the new") that he *has no principles*, and that the whig party have abandoned their principles by adopting him as their candidate. He maintained that Gen. Taylor occupied a high and unexceptionable whig ground, and took for his first instance and proof of this his statement in the Allison letter—with regard to the Bank, Tariff, Rivers and Harbors, &c.—that the will of the people should produce its own results, without Executive influence. The principle that the people should do what—under the constitution—they please, is a whig principle. All that Gen. Taylor does is not only to consent, but to appeal to the people to judge and act for themselves. And this was no new doctrine for Whigs. It was the "platform" on which they had fought all their battles, the resistance of Executive influence, and the principle of enabling the people to frame the government according to their will. Gen. Taylor consents to be the candidate, and to assist the people to do what they think to be their duty, and think to be best in their natural affairs, but because *he don't want to tell what we ought to do,* he is accused of having no principles. The Whigs here maintained for years that neither the influence, the duress, or the prohibition of the Executive should control the legitimately expressed will of the people; and now that on that very ground, Gen. Taylor says that he should use the power given him by the people to do, to the best of his judgment, the will of the people, he is accused of want of principle, and of inconsistency in position.

Mr. Lincoln proceeded to examine the absurdity of an attempt to make a platform or creed for a national party, to *all* parts of which *all* must consent and agree, when it was clearly the intention and the true philosophy of our government, that in Congress all opinions and principles should be represented, and that when the wisdom of all had been compared and united, the will of the majority should be carried out. On this ground he conceived (and the audience seemed to go with him) that General Taylor held correct, sound republican principles.

Mr. Lincoln then passed to the subject of slavery in the States, saying that the people of Illinois agreed entirely, with the people of Massachusetts on this subject, except perhaps that they did not keep so constantly thinking about it. All agreed that slavery was an evil, but that we were not responsible for it and cannot affect it in States of this Union where we do not live. But, the question of the *extension* of slavery to new territories of this country, is a part of our responsibility and care, and is under our control. In opposition to this Mr. L. believed that the self named "Free Soil" party, was far behind the Whigs. Both parties opposed the extension. As he understood it the new party had no principle except this opposition. If their platform held any other, it was in such a general way that it was like the pair of pantaloons the Yankee pedler offered for sale, "large enough for any man, small enough for any boy." They therefore had taken a position calculated to break down their single important declared object. They were working for the election of either Gen. Cass or Gen. Taylor.

The Speaker then went on to show, clearly and eloquently, the danger of extension of slavery, likely to result from the election of General Cass. To unite with those who annexed the new territory to prevent the extension of slavery in that territory seemed to him to be in the highest degree absurd and ridiculous. Suppose these gentlemen succeed in electing Mr. Van Buren, they had no specific means to *prevent* the extension of slavery to New Mexico and California, and Gen. Taylor, he confidently believed, would not encourage it, and would not prohibit its restriction. But if Gen. Cass was elected, he felt certain that the plans of farther extension of territory would be encouraged, and those of the extension of slavery would meet no check.

The "Free Soil" men in claiming that name indirectly attempted a deception, by implying that Whigs were *not* Free Soil men. In declaring that they would "do their duty and leave the consequences to God," merely gave an excuse for taking a course that they were not able to maintain by a fair and full argument. To make this declaration did not show what their duty was. If it did we should have no use for judgment, we might as well be made without intellect, and when divine or human law does not clearly point out what *is* our duty, we have no means of finding out what it is by using our most intelligent judgment of the consequences. If there were divine law, or human law for voting for Martin Van Buren, or if a fair examination of the consequences and first reasoning would show that voting for him would bring about the ends they pretended to wish—then he would give up the argument. But since there was no fixed law on the subject, and since the whole probable result of their action would be an assistance in electing Gen. Cass, he must say that they were behind the Whigs in their advocacy of the freedom of the soil.

Mr. Lincoln proceeded to rally the Buffalo Convention for forbearing to say anything—after all the previous declarations of those members who were formerly Whigs—on the subject of the Mexican war, because the Van Burens had been known to have supported it. He declared that of all the parties asking the confidence of the country, this new one had *less* of principle than any other.

He wondered whether it was still the opinion of these Free Soil gentlemen, as declared in the "whereas" at Buffalo, that the whig and democratic parties were both entirely dissolved and absorbed into their own body. Had the Vermont election given them any light? They had calculated on making as great an impression in that State as in any part of the Union, and there their attempts had been wholly ineffectual. Their failure there was a greater success than they would find in any other part of the Union.

Mr. Lincoln went on to say that he honestly believed that all those who wished to keep up the character of the Union; who did not believe in enlarging our field, but in keeping our fences where they are and cultivating our present possession, making it a garden, improving the morals and education of the people; devoting the administration to this purpose; all real Whigs, friends of good honest government;—the race was ours. He had opportunities of hearing from almost every part of the Union from reliable sources, and had not heard of a country in which we had not received accessions from other parties. If the true Whigs come forward and join these new friends, they need not have a doubt. We had a candidate whose personal character and principles he had already described, whom he could not eulogize if he would. Gen. Taylor had been constantly, perserveringly, quietly standing up, *doing his duty*, and asking no praise or reward for it. He was and must be just the man to whom the interests, principles and prosperity of the country might be safely intrusted. He had never failed in anything he had undertaken, although many of his duties had been considered almost impossible.

Mr. Lincoln then went into a terse though rapid review of the origin of the Mexican war and the connection of the administration and of General Taylor with it, from which he deduced a strong appeal to the Whigs present to do their duty in the support of General Taylor, and closed with the warmest aspirations for and confidence in a deserved success.

At the close of this truly masterly and convincing speech, the audience gave three enthusiastic cheers for Illinois, and three more for the eloquent Whig member from that State.

News of Lincoln's swing through New England traveled slowly westward. The Worcester speech impressed the Whigs in Illinois and Missouri and the Illinois Journal of Oct. 3, 1848, always on the alert for favorable news to reprint about the Springfield Representative, copied this from the St. Louis New Era.

The St. Louis New Era says:—"The speech of the Hon. A. Lincoln, of Illinois, in Worcester, Mass., at the Whig Convention, is said to have been one of the ablest efforts of a political character ever heard in that place. A number of Free Soil Whigs who were tinctured with the Van Buren mania, abandoned all such suicidal efforts, and publicly pledged themselves to stand by the nominations made at the Philadelphia Convention."

Lincoln's reception in New England continued to be enthusiastic. In Lowell, Mass., he spoke before a group of "sterling Whigs." One report said that "Hon. Abram Lincoln addressed the assembly in a masterly and convincing manner, frequently interrupted by bursts of warm applause." This report is from the Lowell Journal and Courier, Sept. 18, 1848.

WHIG MEETING

The sterling Whigs of Lowell came together last Saturday evening, at the City Hall. The meeting was called to order by the Chairman of the Whig Central Committee, Hon. Linus Child; Homer Bartlett, Esq., was chosen chairman, and A. Gilman, Sec'y. After a few animating remarks from the Chairman, he introduced George Woodman, Esq., of Boston, who made a very pertinent and witty off-hand speech, which was frequently interrupted by the spontaneous plaudits of the audience. At the close of his speech, Mr. Woodman introduced the Hon. Abraham Lincoln, of Illinois. It would be doing injustice to his speech to endeavor to give a sketch of it. It was replete with good sense, sound reasoning, and irresistable argument, and spoken with that perfect command of manner and matter which so eminently distinguishes the Western orators. He disabused the public of the erroneous suppositions that Taylor was not a Whig; that Van Buren was anything more than a thorough Locofoco, on all subjects other than Free Territory, and hardly safe on that—and showed up, in a masterly manner, the inconsistency and folly of those Whigs, who, being drawn off from the true and oldest free soil organization known among the parties of the Union, would now lend their influence and votes to help Mr Van Buren into the Presidential chair.— His speech was interrupted by the cheers of the audience, ev[in]cing the truth of the great supposition that the dead can speek.

At the close of the speech, the Secretary, by request, read the letter of Gen. Taylor to Capt. Alison, which had just been received, in which he says, "From the beginning till now, I have declared myself to be a Whig, on all proper occasions."

Lincoln and Seward occupied the platform in Boston, where the rising young Congressman from Illinois wound up his New England speaking tour. His speaking style impressed the cultivated Boston Whigs. One reported: "The chief charm of his address lay in the homely way he made his points. For plain pungency of humor, it would have been difficult to surpass his speech." Importantly, Lincoln and Seward had a chance to speak privately about the need to give more attention to the slavery question. The Boston Atlas, on Sept. 23 and 25, 1848, reported the reception in "this good Whig city."

65

GREAT WHIG TAYLOR MEETING IN BOSTON

Speeches of Gov. Seward of N.Y. and Hon. Mr. Lincoln of Illinois.

The Tremont Temple was filled last night in every part, by the Whigs of Boston, to listen to speeches from Governor Seward, of New York, and Hon. Abram Lincoln, of Illinois.

At half-past 7 o'clock, the meeting was called to order by WILLIAM HAYDEN, Esq., and, on motion, Hon. GEORGE LUNT was chosen Chairman; and EZRA LINCOLN, JR., Secretary. Both Mr. Hayden and Mr. Lunt made remarks—brief, but pointed, which were well received. Mr. Lunt concluded by introducing to the audience Ex-Governor Seward, of New York, who was received as he came forward with the most enthusiastic applause. After the cheering had subsided, Mr. Seward addressed the meeting substantially as follows:

In the darkest hour of the Roman Republic, when Caesar, flushed with victory, sought to crush the liberties of Germany, Pompey was with other legions in Africa. Some of the people were in favor of declaring for Caesar—others again for Pompey. Cicero said:—"He knew whom he ought to avoid, but had some hesitation whom he ought to follow."

Such is the position or had been the position of some of the Whigs, and such is the question which they are called upon to decide. The Philadelphia Convention had placed before the Whigs of the country, the names of General ZACHARY TAYLOR and MILLARD FILLMORE, (immense applause), and invited them to follow and support them. The Baltimore Convention had nominated Lewis Cass. We have our choice, and we know whom we should avoid, even though some may hesitate whom to follow. I have determined myself whom I ought to follow, and have come before you to express very briefly the reasons which influence my choice. [Mr. Seward continued at some length.]

Mr. Lincoln, of Illinois, next came forward, and was received with great applause. He spoke about an hour, and made a powerful and convincing speech, which was cheered to the echo. We have notes of his speech, but the crowded state of our columns, and the lateness of the hour at which the meeting adjourned, preclude the possibility of doing anything like justice to Mr. Lincoln's speech today.

Mr. Lincoln concluded at half past ten o'clock. The audience then gave three hearty cheers for "Old Zack," three more for Governor

Seward, and three more for Mr. Lincoln, and then adjourned; and thus ended one of the best meetings ever held in this good Whig city.

———

Sept. 25, 1848

NORFOLK COUNTY.

Our correspondent "Hancock" closed his letter from Dedham as the delegation from Roxbury was marching to the hall where Mr. Lincoln was to speak. We learn that the hall was well filled, and that Hon. James Richardson, president of the Dedham Whig Club, presided, and after a few brief and appropriate remarks, introduced Hon. Mr. Lincoln, of Illinois, who addressed the assembly for an hour, in a very agreeable and entertaining manner. After which the meeting adjourned, and the Dedham Whig Club, accompanied by the delegation from the Taylor Whig Club of Roxbury, with the Dorchester Band, escorted Mr. Lincoln to the cars; an engagement at Cambridge prevented him from remaining longer.

———

HON. ABRAHAM LINCOLN.—In answer to the many applications which we daily receive from different parts of the State, for this gentleman to speak, we have to say that he left Boston on Saturday morning, on his way home to Illinois.

Near the close of his Congressional term Lincoln made one more important talk: on Jan. 10, 1849, he proposed that no person should be held in slavery within the District of Columbia. Then Stephen Logan, running for Lincoln's seat in Congress, lost; Lincoln stumped for Logan, but the opposition kept throwing up his Mexican War stand. After a losing bid for the Commissionership of the General Land Office, Lincoln returned to practice law in Springfield. Some Whigs thanked him for his Congressional service, as noted in the Illinois Journal, Aug. 1, 1850.

WHIG CONVENTION IN MENARD COUNTY

At a Convention of the Whigs of Menard county, at Petersburgh [Petersburg], July 20, 1850, for the purpose of electing delegates to send to the Pekin Convention 1st Monday in August next, to put in nomination a candidate for Congress; Doct. F. Regnier was called to the chair, and D. A. Brown, Secretary. Martin S. Morris, M. C. Dawson and J. M. Robinson were elected Delegates.

The following resolutions were offered by M. S. Morris, and unanimously adopted by the Convention—

Resolved, That it is with most profound regret we have heard of the death of our Illustrious Chief Magistrate Gen. Zachary Taylor.

Resolved, That we have full confidence in his successor, the Hon. Millard Fillmore.

Resolved, That our thanks are due to our late talented whig representative, the Hon. A. Lincoln, for the able and faithful manner in which he discharged his duty as representative in Congress.

Resolved, That the Hon. Richard Yates, of Jacksonville, is the choice of this meeting as our candidate for Congress. . . .

Lincoln concentrated on his law practice in the early 1850's. The people of Illinois saw him following the court on the circuits. In later years he was to say, "How many times I have laughed at your telling me plainly that I was too lazy to be anything but a lawyer." These were the family years, the quiet years politically. But they were coming to an end. Strongly responsible was Senator Stephen A. Douglas, who in 1854 introduced a bill that would repeal the Missouri Compromise of 1820 prohibiting slavery's extension. No office, no campaign was involved. Lincoln spoke out on principle. Lincoln wrote this editorial himself for the Illinois Journal of Sept. 11, 1854.

THE 14TH SECTION

September 11, 1854.

The following is the 14th section of the Kansas-Nebraska law. It repeals the Missouri Compromise; and then puts in a declaration that is not intended by this repeal to legislate slavery in or exclude it therefrom, the territory.

"Sec. 14. That the Constitution, and all the laws of the United States which are not locally inapplicable, shall have the same force and effect within said territory of Nebraska as elsewhere in the United States, except the 8th section of the act preparatory to the admission of Missouri into the Union, approved March sixth, eighteen hundred and twenty, which being inconsistent with the principles of nonintervention by Congress with slavery in the states and territories as recognized by the legislation of eighteen hundred and fifty, commonly called the compromise measures, is hereby declared inoperative and void; it being the true intent and meaning of this act not to legislate slavery into any territory or state, nor to exclude it therefrom, but to leave the people thereof perfectly free to form and regulate their domestic institutions in their own way, subject only to the Constitution of the United States: Provided, that nothing herein contained shall be construed to revive or put in force any law or regulation which may have existed prior to the act of sixth of March, eighteen hundred and twenty, either protecting, establishing, prohibiting, or abolishing slavery."

The state of the case in a few words, is this: The Missouri Compromise excluded slavery from the Kansas-Nebraska territory. The repeal opened the territories to slavery. If there is any meaning to the declaration in the 14th section, that it does not mean to legislate slavery into the territories, it is this: that it does not require slaves to be sent there. The Kansas and Nebraska territories are now as open to slavery as Mississippi or Arkansas were when they were territories.

To illustrate the case: Abraham Lincoln has a fine meadow, containing beautiful springs of water, and well fenced, which John Calhoun had agreed with Abraham (originally owning the land in common) should be his, and the agreement had been consummated in the most solemn manner, regarded by both as sacred. John Calhoun, however, in the course of time, had become owner of an extensive herd of cattle—the prairie grass had become dried up and there was no convenient water to be had. John Calhoun then looks with a longing eye on Lincoln's meadow, and goes to it and throws down the fences, and exposes it to the ravages of his starving and famishing cattle. "You rascal," says Lincoln, "What have you done? What do you do this for?" "Oh," replies Calhoun, "everything is right, I have taken down your fence; but nothing more. It is my true intent and meaning not to drive my cattle into your meadow, nor to exclude them therefrom, but to leave them perfectly free to form their own notions of the feed, and to direct their movements in their own way!"

Now would not the man who committed this outrage be deemed both a knave and a fool,—a knave in removing the restrictive fence, which he had solemnly pledged himself to sustain;—and a fool in supposing that there could be one man found in the country to believe that he had not pulled down the fence for the purpose of opening the meadow for his cattle?

Without his consent, Lincoln was placed on the ballot for the Illinois General Assembly—where he had been a legislator twenty years before 1854. He and Mrs. Lincoln tried to have his name taken off the ballot; it is possible he let it stay on, doing nothing in his own behalf, in order to strengthen the Whig ticket. He was elected—and refused to accept the office, formally declining in a letter to the county clerk of Sangamon. Lincoln was after bigger game—the United States Senate seat. The Quincy Whig, quoted in the Illinois Journal of Sept. 15, 1854, spoke up for Lincoln for the office he didn't seek yet won.

Hon. Stephen T. Logan and Abraham Lincoln are announced in the Springfield (Ill.) Journal as candidates for the General Assembly from Sangamon county, subject to the decision of a convention, should one be held.

Most noble men are they—worthy to represent intelligent and bold, free-spoken freemen.—It is a pity—a wonderous pity—that Hon. A. Lincoln does not fill the seat now held by Stephen A. Douglas. It would be infinitely better for the rights and interests of the great West, as it would have been far better for the peace, harmony and fraternity of the North and South, and the stability of our glorious Union.—Quincy [Ill.] Whig.

The rivals of old—Lincoln and Douglas, citizen and Senator, Whig and Democrat—had found a new issue: the extension of slavery. And their newspaper advocates of those first days in Springfield—the Whig Journal and the Democratic Register—came out swinging. The Illinois State Journal of Oct. 5, 1854, commented on how Lincoln scattered Douglas's arguments to the wind.

HON. A. LINCOLN'S SPEECH

Agreeably to previous notice, circulated in the morning by hand bill, Hon. A. Lincoln delivered a speech yesterday at the State House, in the Hall of Representatives, in reply to the speech of Senator Douglas, of the preceding day. Mr. L. commenced at 2 o'clock, P.M., and spoke above three hours, to a very large, intelligent and attentive audience. Judge Douglas had been invited by Mr. Lincoln to be present and to reply to Mr. Lincoln's remarks, if he should think proper to do so. And Judge Douglas was present, and heard Mr. Lincoln throughout.

Mr. Lincoln was frequently and warmly applauded. It was judged a proud day for all who love free principles and the unstained republicanism of our revolutionary days. Mr. Lincoln's argument was clear and logical, his arrangement of facts methodical, his deductions self-evident, and his applications striking and most effective. We venture to say that Judge Douglas never in the Senate Chamber or before the people, listened to just such a powerful analysis of his Nebraska sophisms, or saw such a remorseless tearing of his flimsy arguments and scattering them to the winds, as he endured yesterday from Mr. Lincoln.

Such a speech would have to be read entire to be appreciated, so compact was it, and interlocked in all its parts. We do nothing but sketch its course.

Senator Douglas "pounded him [Lincoln] to pumice with his terrible war club of retort and argument." At least, that was the version of the Springfield debate on the Nebraska bill by the Democratic organ, the Illinois State Register, Oct. 6, 1854.

"BEHOLD, HOW BRIGHTLY BREAKS THE MORNING!"

On Wednesday afternoon a large audience assembled in the representatives' hall, to hear a speech from Mr. Lincoln, in opposition to Judge Douglas and the Nebraska bill. Judge Douglas was present, and from an understanding that he would reply to Mr. Lincoln, expectation was on tiptoe. Mr. Lincoln had been selected as the Goliah of the anti-Nebraska black republican fusionists. He had been nosing for weeks in the state library, and pumping his brains and his imagination for points and arguments with which to demolish the champion of popular sovereignty. It is our duty to record the result of his wonderful labors and exertions. He commenced by a number of jokes and witticisms, the character of which will be understood by all who know him, by simply saying they were *Lincolnisms*. He declared that he was a national man—that he was for letting the institution of slavery alone when it existed in the states —that he was for sustaining the fugitive slave law—that there was a clear grant of power in the constitution to enable the south to recover their fugitive slaves, and he was for an efficient law to effect the object intended. He then branched off upon the ordinance of 1787, and worked his way down to the Kansas and Nebraska act. Leaving out the declarations we have spoken of, his speech was one that would have come from Giddings or Sumner, and that class of abolitionists, with more grace than from any men we know of. He quoted the speech of Judge Douglas in 1849, and endeavored to show that he stood now where Judge D. stood then. He attempted to show that the Kansas-Nebraska bill was inconsistent with the legislation of 1850, and maintained that it was as much the duty of congress to prohibit slavery in the territories as to prohibit the slave trade—made what some of his hearers seemed to consider good hits, and called forth the cheers of his friends. He spoke for nearly three hours and a half, and concluded at about half past five o'clock.

Judge Douglas then took the stand and commenced his vindication. At the first pass at his opponent he gored and tossed him upon the horns of a dilemma, while the thunders of the applauding multitude shook the state house from turret top to foundation stone. He proceeded, point by point, to meet the argument of his adversary, and repel his assaults and inuendoes in such a triumphant manner that the people could not be restrained.—Though Judge Douglas desired that they would not applaud, and his hearers seemed desirous to conform to his wishes, yet such was the feeling of enthusiasm that it had to have vent. We have witnessed many an outburst of approbation from political gatherings, but never, in our time, have we seen such a deep, heartfelt and heart-reaching concurrence in the sentiments of a public speaker. It could no more be repressed than can the eruption of the volcano when the pent up fires have acquired their fullest fever. But Judge Douglas proceeded. He showed them that when he came into public life, he found the Missouri line of 36 deg. 30 min., upon the statute books—that although he never did think the principle of a geographical line a sound one, yet he was willing to adopt it in extending it indefinitely westward, as we might acquire territory—and consequently proposed and supported it in its application to Texas, and the territory acquired from Mexico, until he was driven from it by the Wilmot provisoists, among whom was Lincoln himself—that his speech in 1849 was made in defence of his action in favor of the line of 36 deg. 30 min., in preference to supporting the Wilmot proviso—that he was always willing to abide by that line, until he was overdone and instructed by the legislature to oppose it. And now, when he had again conformed his action to the legislative will of his own state, and to his own sentiments of just legislation, he was accused of being a traitor for doing what his accusers had compelled him to do. As well, said he, might a man meet me on the highway, and with a loaded pistol demand and rob me of my money, and then turn round and taunt me for having delivered it up.

. . . He went over every one of Mr. Lincoln's points, and when he concluded, there was nothing left of his arguments—as we heard it remarked, he seemed not content to butcher his antagonist with tomahawk and scalping knife, but he pounded him to pumice with his terrible war club of retort and argument. Even Lincoln's friends gave it up that he was numbered with the slain. We learn that some gentleman proposed to call the coroner to inquire as to the cause of his death. We hope that the effect of this discussion will be to make Mr. Lincoln a wiser man, and will teach him that no talent he may possess, no industry he may see, no art he can invent, can stay the power of truth that supports the friends of the Nebraska measure. It might as well be expected to crush the Rocky Mountains with a snow flake as to put down the principle of popular sovereignty, sustained and advocated by such a man as Stephen A. Douglas.

The debates on the extension of slavery moved beyond Springfield. Speeches were made in a number of towns. Lincoln was observed as the most effective speaker in the state against Douglas and the "Nebraska swindle." There were portents of his future and a look back by the Chicago Journal, as reprinted in the Illinois Journal of Nov. 3, 1854.

MR. LINCOLN

Mr. Lincoln recently made a speech on the Nebraska swindle in Chicago. The Chicago Journal thus remarks of him and his speech:

"Mr. Lincoln has seen something of life—not in the common acceptation of the phrase but in reality. Born of parents who could only give him faith in rectitude and virtue, he has become what he is through the trials of poverty and by the sweat of his brow. How he guided a flatboat over the Ohio, or how he afterwards had his last article of property consisting of a chain and compass, sold under the sheriff's hammer, are matters of small interest now. How he became the most powerful speaker and one of the ablest lawyers in the West are of more moment. That he is such cannot be denied by those who have heard him on great occasions. He rises in might as the occasion rises in importance before him. His speech of last evening was as thorough an exposition of the Nebraska iniquity as has ever been made, and his eloquence greatly impressed all his hearers, but it was manifest as he frequently remarked that "he could not help feeling foolish in answering arguments which were no arguments at all." He could not help feeling silly in beating the air before an intelligent audience. It is a fruitless job to pound dry sand under the delusion that it is a rock.—The laborer may get his eyes full, but the sand is just as sandy as it was before."

Lincoln was back in politics. The term of Senator James Shields was expiring—the same Shields of the "Rebecca" letters, of the dueling incident a dozen years ago—and Lincoln began to line up support. "I have really got it into my head to try to be United States Senator," he wrote to one competitor for the seat. Through double-dealing by Governor Joel Matteson of Illinois, Lincoln lost in the vote among the legislators; he threw his votes to the victorious Lyman Trumbull, who was an anti-Nebraska bolter from the Democratic party. The Illinois Gazette of Lacon came out for Lincoln and the Illinois Journal reprinted the editorial, Dec. 14, 1854, before the election in February, 1855.

ELECTION OF SENATOR.—Among the many duties imposed upon our General Assembly elect, will be the election of a U.S. Senator to fill the vacancy occasioned by the expiration of GEN. SHIELDS' term on the 4th of March next.

As we have an anti-Nebraska Legislature, the election of a man of like political character to supply said vacancy, follows as a matter of course. This the people will expect. Now, who is the lucky man to be, is the question just at this time. Some have named one and some another; we are for HON. ABRAM LINCOLN, most decidedly; regarding him as the best and most available candidate for that office in the State. Mr. LINCOLN has been long in public life—a Representative in Congress and frequently in our General Assembly; and would have figured more largely as a public man had he been of the dominant party. He possesses all the solidity and splendor of talent—that comprehensiveness of intellect and coolness of judgment, which would ever characterize members of the American Senate. If elected to that honorable office, he will a[c]quit himself satisfactorily and reflect credit upon the State.—Lacon [Illinois] Gazette.

And Lincoln's name—including the confounded "Abram"—came into the open for still another office—that of Governor. He did not make the run. *The Illinois Journal of Jan. 5, 1856, reported the preference. It looked as if Lincoln was in politics for good.*

FOR GOVERNOR.—The Danville Sun, in speaking of the several gentlemen spoken of for Governor, expresses its preference for the Hon. ABRAM LINCOLN, of this city. It insures old Vermillion [sic] for him by a large majority.

Chapter 3

The Great Debater

OCTOBER 1854–NOVEMBER 1858

The birth of the Republican party and the renascence of Abraham Lincoln in the tumult of American politics coincided. The party came into existence in Illinois on May 29, 1856. On that day Lincoln delivered his famous "lost speech" to the convention at Bloomington. The meeting began as a convention of all opponents of the extension of slavery: Anti-Nebraska Democrats, Free-Soilers, Abolitionists, Know-Nothings and Whigs. It adopted a platform with strong anti-Nebraska planks; then and there the Republican party in Illinois was born.

Lincoln, in response to calls, got up to speak. It was close to an abolitionist speech; probably the strongest public utterance against slavery by Lincoln. "This thing of slavery is more powerful than its supporters," Lincoln said, in the reconstructed reports. "It debauches even our greatest men. Monstrous crimes are committed in its name. In a despotism one might not wonder to see slavery advance steadily and remorselessly into new dominions; but is it not wonderful, is it not even alarming, to see its steady advance in a land dedicated to the proposition that 'all men are created equal'?"

William Herndon, of Lincoln and Herndon, said it was the greatest speech of Lincoln's life. Heretofore, Herndon said later, Lincoln had simply argued the slavery question on grounds of policy—never reaching the question of the radical and eternal right. Now he was newly baptized. "If Mr. Lincoln was six feet, four inches high usually, at Bloomington that day he was seven feet, and inspired at that. From that day to the day of his death he stood firm in the right."

At Bloomington that day were several important editors. This is how John L. Scripps of the Chicago Press saw Lincoln, as described in the Illinois Journal on June 3, 1856.

HON. A. LINCOLN

During the recent session of the State anti-Nebraska Convention, the Hon. A. Lincoln of this city made one of the most powerful and convincing speeches which we have ever heard. The editor of the Chicago Press [John L. Scripps], thus characterizes it:

["]Abram Lincoln of Springfield was next called out, and made the speech of the occasion. Never has it been our fortune to listen to a more eloquent and masterly presentation of a subject. I shall not mar any of its fine proportions of brilliant passages by attempting even a synopsis of it. Mr. Lincoln must write it out and let it go before all the people. For an hour and a half he held the assemblage spell-bound by the power of his argument, the intense irony of his invective, and the deep earnestness and fervid brilliancy of his eloquence. When he concluded, the audience sprang to their feet, and cheer after cheer told how deeply their hearts had been touched, and their souls warmed up to a generous enthusiasm.["]

At the first Republican National Convention in June, 1856, John C. Fremont was nominated for President. Lincoln received 110 votes against Wm. L. Dayton's 259 in an informal ballot for the Vice Presidency. When Lincoln heard of this, he said, "I reckon that ain't me; there's another great man in Massachusetts named Lincoln." Here, too, he was called "Abraham Sinclair." This is how the New York Tribune reported the convention on June 20, 1856.

THE PEOPLES' CONVENTION.

———

From Our Own Reporters

WM. L. DAYTON FOR VICE-PRESIDENT.

LAST DAY.

PHILADELPHIA, Thursday, June 19—10 A.M.
The Convention reassembled—the President, Col. LANE of Indiana, in the Chair. The proceedings were opened by a prayer by the Rev. Mr. LEVY.

Mr. LEIGH of New-Jersey offered the following resolution:

Resolved, That a National Convention of young men in favor of free speech, free soil, free Kansas and Fremont for President, be held during the month of September, in the City of New York, under the call of the National Republican Convention.

Mr. WHELPLEY of New-Jersey said that he arose to nominate a man for candidate for the Vice-Presidency who in the House of Representatives steadfastly opposed the passage of the Compromise measures in 1850, and was stricken down for that act and for the advocacy of the very principles which we advocate here [Cheers]. He referred to WILLIAM L. DAYTON of New Jersey [Loud cheers].

Mr. FISHER of Penn. said he took the liberty to nominate a man whose name would be a tower of strength in Pennsylvania—David Wilmot of Penn. [Loud cheers].

Mr. ALLISON of Penn. presented the resolutions which had been adopted by the Republican State Convention. Mr. Allison said he had been requested to nominate as a candidate for the Vice-Presidency Abraham Lincoln of Ill. [Cheers]. He knew him to be the prince of good fellows, and an old-line Whig [Cheers].

Col. W. B. ARCHER of Ill. said he was acquainted with Mr. Lincoln, and had known him over thirty years. He was a native of Kentucky, and had always been a Clay Whig and a firm friend of this Republic. He had no fear of the North of Illinois, but the South was inhabited by emigrants from Kentucky and Tennessee, but with Lincoln on the ticket Illinois would be safe for Fremont, [cheers], and he believed it would be safe without him, [loud cheers and laughter], but doubly safe with him.

Judge SPAULDING of Ohio—Can Mr. Lincoln fight?

Col. ARCHER (jumping at least eighteen inches from the floor, and gesturing emphatically with his arms, YES, SIR. *He is a son of Kentucky* [Loud and prolonged laughter and cheers].

Mr. JAY of New-Jersey said he was an Old Line Democrat, and had always been until that party had sunk the name underneath the feet of the slave power [Cheers]. He should have voted for Franklin Pierce if he had had then a vote, and as it was he worked for him, and he was ashamed of it. As they had nominated an Old Line Democrat for President, Democrat as he (Mr. Jay) was, he thought they should now vote for an Old Line Whig for Vice-President. He therefore seconded the nomination of Wm. L. Dayton of New-Jersey (cheers), who had been sacrificed by the "Hemlock" Democracy of New Jersey for his opposition to the Fugitive Slave Bill. With the name of W. L. Dayton attached to that of John C. Fremont, success was certain [Cheers].

Judge PALMER of Illinois said he, too, was an Old Line Democrat, and he did vote for Frank Pierce [Laughter]. But he was sorry for it. He arose here to speak of the policy of nominating Abraham Lincoln of Illionis [Cheers]. He had met Mr. Lincoln—no, he meant rather that when Mr. Lincoln was about in political contests, he (Mr. Palmer) generally dodged (Laughter). But if this Convention nominated Mr. Dayton of New Jersey, Illinois was there [Cheers]. If the candidate was to be the distinguished gentleman of Pennsylvania they would support him [Loud cheers]. He intended to name his next boy David Wilmot [Prolonged laughter and cheers]. But if they wanted ten thousand additional votes in Illinois give them Abraham Lincoln. He believed they could beat the Democracy without him, but they wanted to do it easily [Loud cheers].

Mr ELLIOT of Massachusetts read the following dispatch which was received with loud cheers:

"In Massachusetts great rejoicing. Have good Committee. Give us a good Vice President. Clear the track!"

The Convention then went into an informal ballot for Vice-President, with the following result: [Dayton, 259; Lincoln, 110]. . . .

The formal ballot was then taken. All the votes were given for William L. Dayton, except eight from Connecticut, four for Banks and four for Lincoln; nineteen from New York, fourteen for Lincoln, three for Sumner, one for King and one for Ford; and four from Pennsylvania, two for Lincoln, one for John Allison and one for Dr. Elder.

After the vote of Delaware was declared, Judge PALMER of Illinois said: In behalf of the delegation of the State of Illinois I return thanks to such members of this Convention as have honored the favorite of our State with their vote. Illinois asks nothing for herself in this contest. She is devoted—and I trust that the result of the next election will prove that she is devoted—to the great cause that has brought us together [Cheers]. She knew that in Abraham Lincoln we had a soldier tried and true. We offered him to the Republican party of the United States for the position that we have indicated, but we are content to prefer harmony and union to the success even of our cherished favorite. Therefore, we say to those of our friends who have honored us, we commend them to withdraw the votes thus cast for Mr. Lincoln, and give them that direction that will make the vote unanimous and harmonious for Wm. L. Dayton [Loud applause].

The formal ballot was then proceeded with, every vote being cast for Dayton. When Kansas was called, a voice arose: "Kansas will follow manifest destiny" [Enthusiastic applause]. . . .

A GENTLEMAN moved that the vote be made unanimous.

The CHAIRMAN said there was no need of that; the vote was unanimous [Immense cheering and three cheers for William L. Dayton].

The PRESIDENT announced that the Hon. Mr. Van Dyke would now address the Convention.

Mr. VAN DYKE appeared upon the stand and said:

Gentlemen of the Convention: It seems eminently appropriate that something should be said on the present occasion by New Jersey. The duty of performing this has been unfortunately, I think, imposed upon me. But I shall not attempt to make a regular speech, but will make a few remarks in a very plain way. New-Jersey, I think, should be heard for two reasons. You will bear in mind that a majority of the votes given originally from New Jersey were given for Judge M'Lean of Ohio. I heard it said during the progress of the canvass, that unless Judge M'Lean should be the nominee New Jersey would probably bolt. I would like to know who has uttered that slander [Loud cheers]. . . . Gentlemen, we were perfectly willing not only to go, but to go with perfect alacrity, if we could not get Judge M'Lean, for John C. Fremont of California [cheers]—the man who has traced the paths of the buffalo through the windings and gorges of the Rocky Mountains, who has grappled with the grizzly bear upon their snow-capped summits—the man who has planted the standard of the United States in the golden regions of California—the man who through toil, trial, suffering, danger, hunger and snow, has done all these things, and, with the capacity of Caesar himself, that has gained such magnificent results, and who, withal, is so capable of giving us magnificent accounts of them [enthusiastic cheers]—a man, gentlemen, whose fame is already too large for this continent—a man, around whose brow are clustering the laurels and the honors of scientific establishments beyond the Atlantic wave—a man who has traced, not only with his own eye and his own thought the vast extent of country in the West, and surveyed the whole of it, but has put it down on the map so that every school-boy and school-girl can see and examine it [Cheers]. Gentlemen, the State of New-Jersey is willing to go for this man; and with John C. Fremont and William L. Dayton upon our ticket [loud cheers], we will awaken every mountain echo in New-Jersey from the New-York line to the jumping-off place at Cape May [Prolonged cheers]. . . . Gentlemen, I have another duty to perform, and it is to return my thanks for the very handsome manner in which Illinois has yielded her preferences [loud cheers] to New-Jersey's favorite son. Gentlemen from Illinois, it was my pleasure to know right well the long "Sucker" you presented. I knew Abraham Sinclair in Congress well, and for months I sat by his side. I knew him all through, and knew him to be a first-rate man in every respect; and if it had not been the will and pleasure of the Convention to have selected William L. Dayton, I know with what perfect alacrity I would have gone for him. I know we of New-Jersey would have all gone for him if New-Jersey had been called upon to make another sacrifice, and I know that none would have more readily consented to the sacrifice than the victim himself [Loud cheers]. I thank you, therefore, gentlemen from Illinois, for the graceful manner in which you yielded your own preferences and unanimously voted for Mr. Dayton of New-Jersey [Cheers]. Gentlemen of this Convention, we are embarked in a great cause. You know my own affinities have always been with the Whig party, and those who know me well enough, know I am ready to abandon every single one, so far as this issue is concerned, to secure the success of Republican principles, and I will not abandon it while a plank remains of the Republican ship [Cheers]. We have embarked on this Republican ship, and that ship is not to be surrendered under any circumstances. If the storms do overwhelm us and we are unable to navigate the troubled sea, rather than desert, let us go down with her [Cheers]. Before we will abandon this glorious ship in which we have embarked, we will nail our colors to the mast, spread every sail, and give her to the God of the storm, of the lightning and the gale [Prolonged cheers].

Whatever Lincoln said was news now to the important New York press. They began to print his speeches in full. The Supreme Court's decision in the Dred Scott case prompted first a talk by Senator Douglas and two weeks later a reply by Lincoln. The Springfield correspondence of the New York Tribune, July 6, 1857.

LINCOLN'S REPLY TO DOUGLAS.

Correspondence of The N.Y. Tribune.

SPRINGFIELD, Ill., June 30, 1857.

We of the West are certainly a progressive people. I used to think this a peculiar characteristic of "Yankees," but my opinion is somewhat modified on that subject.

While there is a lull in the political horizon generally, here in Illinois the elements seem to have been awakened from their repose. The immediate cause of this was a recent speech of Mr. Douglas in this city, of the import of which the readers of THE TRIBUNE are already informed. I herewith send you a brief synopsis of a speech in reply, made by the Hon. Abraham Lincoln of this city.

The Hon. Mr. Lincoln began by briefly stating the object of his speech. It was because Douglas had recently made an address in the same place, in which he attempted to controvert opinions which he (Mr. L.) thought were right, and to assail (politically) the men who entertained those opinions. He began with Utah, and showed most conclusively that Douglas had not only backed down from his doctrine of popular sovereignty, but that it was only a deceitful pretense from the beginning.

The Nebraska act itself forced Governors and Secretaries and Judges on the people of the Territories without their consent or choice. Douglas evaded the only question the Republicans had ever pressed upon the Democracy in regard to Utah, which was "if the people of Utah shall peacefully form a State Constitution tolerating polygamy; will the Democracy admit them into the Union?" Was it not a part of the Douglas' "sacred right of self-government" for the people to have it, or rather to keep it, if they choose? These questions Douglas had never answered.

In regard to Kansas Mr. L. said, the substance of the speech of Douglas on that subject was an effort to put the Free-State men in the wrong for not voting at the election of Delegates to the constitutional Convention, and then he (Mr. L.) fully vindicated the course they had pursued. He alluded to the recent election in that Territory, and showed it to have been an exquisite farce, said he was watching with interest to see what figure the "Free-State Democrats" cut in the concern. Of course they would do their duty, and of course they would not vote for Slave-State candidates. At the same time he whispered his suspicions that there were no such beings in Kansas as "Free-State Democrats," and if there should be found one such, he thought it would be well to stuff and preserve his skin as a specimen of a species of the genus Democrat soon to be extinct.

Next, the Dred Scott decision receives attention. He declared that he believed as much as Douglas in obedience to and respect for the judicial department of Government; but he knew that the court which made the decision referred to had often overruled its own decisions, and he meant to do what he could to have it do so in this instance. No "*resistance*" was offered. This decision was wanting in any claim to public confidence, and it is not "*resistance*," it is not factious, or even disrespectful, to treat it as not having quite established a settled doctrine for the land. The Dred Scott decision was in part at least based upon historical facts, which were not really true; among others the assumption by Chief Justice Taney that the public estimate of the black man is more favorable now than it was in the days of the Revolution, is a mistake. In some particulars the condition of the race has been ameliorated; but, as a whole, in this country the change between then and now is decidedly the other way; and their ultimate destiny has never appeared so utterly hopeless as in the last three or four years. In two of the five States—New-Jersey and North Carolina—that then gave the negro the right of voting, that right has since been taken away; and in a third, New-York, it has been greatly abriged, while it has not been extended, as far as I know, to a single additional State, though the number of States has more than doubled. In those days Legislatures held the unquestioned power to abolish Slavery in their respective States; but now it is becoming quite fashionable for State Constitutions to withhold that power from the Legislatures. In those days, by common consent the spread of the black man's bondage to new countries was prohibited; but now, Congress decides that it will not continue the prohibition, and the Supreme Court decides that it could not if it would. In those days, our Declaration of Independence was held sacred by all, and thought to include all; but now, to aid in making the bondage of the negro universal and eternal, it is sneered at and construed, and hawked at and torn, till, if its framers could rise from their graves, they could not at all recognize it. All the powers of earth are after him. Mammon is after him; ambition follows, and philosophy follows, and the Theology of the day is fast joining the cry. They have him in his prison house; they have searched his person, and left no prying instrument with him. One after another they have closed the heavy iron doors upon him, and now they have him, as it were, bolted in with a lock of a hundred keys, which can never be unlocked without the concurrence of every key. The keys are in the hands of a hundred different men, and they are scattered to a hundred different and distinct places; and they stand musing as to what invention, in all the dominions of mind and matter, can be produced to make the impossibility of his escape more complete than it is.

Mr. L. next refuted the charge made by Douglas that the Republicans were laboring for the amalgamation of the races, and showed that Slavery, not Freedom, tended to amalgamation.

There are some other points in Mr. Lincoln's address which I should like to notice if I had time, but my communication will be too lengthy. It is sufficient to say, that it was a masterly effort, and a complete refutation of the sophistries of Douglas, and was listened to with deep interest by a large and respectable audience assembled in Representatives' Hall. Mr. Lincoln is too well known in Illinois to need a word of commendation; but it may be interesting to Republicans at a distance to be informed that there is not a man in this State whose opinions on political subjects command more universal respect by all classes of men, than his. The party may well be proud of such an advocate.

But it is not often that we have such a feast of fat things as has been provided for us of late. On the Monday evening following the speech of Mr. Lincoln, the Hon. Mr. Trumbull accepted an invitation which he had previously received by a delegation of our most respectable citizens who waited on him in a body, at the residence of a friend whom he was visiting.

It is refreshing to us, who have borne the disgrace of being misrepresented in the United States Senate by such a political gamester as Stephen A. Douglas, to know that the odium is in a measure relieved by the presence in that body of the Hon. Lyman Trumbull. A man who has sense enough to know the right, and the moral courage, ability and independence to maintain it. . . .

Correspondence of the Chicago Tribune.

SPRINGFIELD, Ill., June 27, 1857.

The Hon. Ab. Lincoln opened his great speech here a few minutes after eight o'clock p. m., in the hall of the House of Representatives. His speech was an answer to Senator Douglas. The hall was filled comfortably full, and the intense interest with which Republicans, the Bogus Democracy and others listened to every sentence—every word—testifies to the abiding interest felt in the subject and to the power of logical truths—truths welded together by the powers of logic. There was no rant —no fustian—no bombast, but there was something in it of more force and power than these; the heart felt, and he gave utterance to the heart inspirations, clothed in the eternal maxims of the purest reason. Mr. Lincoln divided his subject into three heads.

1. He addressed the people for about half an hour on the affairs of Kansas, stating that nothing but bold wicked despotism ruled or reigned there since it was organized into a Territory. "Well might Mr. Douglas slip slyly over this part of his case, as if he heard nothing of Kansas. Let him but look over into the western horizon and see the heavens lit up by the glories of Squatter Sovereignty, which Douglas had so backed down

from. Look, Douglas, and see yonder people fleeing—see the full columns of brave men stopped—see the press and the type flying into the river!—and tell me what does this? It is your Squatter Sovereignty, and you have now backed down from the principle. The people there cannot vote, and you ought to know it if you do not."

2. He then took up Mormon Utah, and dwelt about as long on this head as he did on Kansas, stating as a reason that, as Douglas had not made these the heads of his speech, he would not. Lincoln said Douglas had alleged that the Mormons were in rebellion against the Government and law:

"The Mormons ought to obey the law, as all good citizens do and should. They burned up the records of Utah; but let me ask Douglas one question: The Mormons desired to live without law, without records, without courts; and I thought the sacred right of Squatter Sovereignty secured to every people the right of the people to live as they pleased. Now, why deprive them of this fundamental right? That is the question. 'Why your present backing down?' This thing of Squatter Sovereignty was never anything but a humbug, generated in the marshes and pools of South Carolina, and used as a pretext to run and pour slaves out all over the land, as hot lava is belched from the crater of the fire-mountain. It stinks of fraud."

3. Mr. Lincoln then took up the Dred Scott case, and handled it as only Lincoln can. Douglas had said that the glorious, immortal fathers of 1776 could not be defended from the charge of asses and liars, when they said in the Declaration of American Independence that all men are created equal, unless it should be limited to Englishmen in terms, and not generally to all men. Mr. Lincoln analyzed it—dissected Douglas's idea, and held up to the gaze of the crowd the skeleton Douglas would have. He made that presented by Douglas grin and menace tyranny, despotism, divine right of kings, aristocracy, and us, whipped and chained slaves. "What," said Mr. Lincoln, "would become of that noble band of liberty-loving, philosophical, patient and patriotic Germans? what of the energetic, law and order Englishmen, the genuine, country-loving Scotchmen, the Frenchmen—the world, if Mr. Douglas's idea were to prevail, that the Declaration is not true? Away, away, away! with the cursed thought! It dissembles, it cheats, and leads downward, dragging the nation in chains after it."

I do not pretend to give his exact words, but I give you the substance —the essence, and I cannot in a letter do more. Mr. Lincoln then from this noble defense and vindication of the Fathers of 1776, of Washington, Henry, Franklin, Jefferson, and others—came to Douglas's pet idea of Amalgamation. He is better posted in facts than Douglas is; he showed that some 50,000 colored freemen lived in the North; but they were made up before they came North, and he also showed that some 300,000 or 400,-000 mulattoes lived in the South, where they are manufactured to order—that is, where the owners and fathers copulate with slave women, stealing the virtue God gave every woman as a jewel of innocence and purity. This is done against the will of the woman, or degradation springing out of Slavery has taught them vice. Keep the free white race and the Negro slave separate and apart in the new Territories and no amalgamation can take place, but let them run over the whole land as slaves with the horrors of Slavery, and then amalgamation will prove rank, and God will sweep us with a brush of fire from this solid globe.

All over Illinois, Lincoln was heard as the dominant voice of the Republican party in the West. Between speeches he carried on his law practice. The Southern Illinoisan editorial on how Lincoln took the "little giant" to task was reprinted in the Illinois Journal, July 16, 1857.

ABE LINCOLN'S SPEECH
From the Southern Illinoisan.

We this week spread this able and masterly refutation of Douglas' slanders against the Republican party before our readers. Its exposition of the flimsy and false ground assumed by Judge Douglas, and the fullness and exactness of its conclusions, expressed so plainly, must strike the mind of every man of common sense forcibly.

Mr. Lincoln takes the "little giant" to task in admirable style, pulling his empty argument asunder, piece by piece, and exposing the falsity of his positions in all their "naked deformity," leaving him, as it were, like the ghostly trunk of some forest monster, which, after having underwent the fury of the storm, is left, standing alone, bereft of every outward vestige which once served to indicate its power and beauty.

Let every man desiring to keep posted up with the politics of the day read Abe Lincoln's speech. Read it carefully, and see how completely he riddles the weak and untenable assertions advanced by Stephen A. Douglas, the great mogul of modern Democracy and squatter sovereignty demagogue.

A battle royal loomed ahead. There was no question that Lincoln would face Douglas for the Senate seat in November, 1858. Lincoln the storyteller became the subject of friend and foe in the Illinois press, to prove or disprove his qualifications. The Illinois Journal of Feb. 26, 1858, reprinted with delight this story—it referred to Lincoln as "the one who is to be elected to the U.S. Senate next winter as Douglas' successor"—from two Democratic papers.

THE GREAT CONGRESSIONAL FIGHT

The [Illinois State] Register of yesterday copies from the Peoria Transcript the following good story, by one of our distinguished fellow townsmen, "the one who is to be elected to the U.S. Senate next winter, as Douglas' successor." Read it and laugh:

When the news of the late great battle in Congress reached Springfield, a coterie of congenial spirits assembled in the Governor's room at the State House, for the purpose of talking the matter over. After it had been pretty thoroughly canvassed, and just as a portion of the company were about to retire, a well known ex-Congressman—the one who is to be elected to the U.S. Senate next winter as Douglas' successor—dropped in. Of course every man in the crowd desired to know *his* opinion, for he always has an original way of illustrating it.

"Well, ———." said Gov. B.[issell], as the gentleman addressed familiarly doubled himself into a vacant chair, "what is your opinion of the knock down in Congress? We have just been talking it over a little."

"It reminds me," said ———, "of a case I once had up at Bloomington."

"Let's hear it!" all said.

"Two old farmers living in the vicinity of Bloomington, had, from time immemorial, been at loggerheads. They could never agree, except to disagree; wouldn't build division fences; and, in short, were everlastingly quarreling. One day, one of them got over on the land of the other; the parties met, and a regular pitched battle between them was the consequence. The one who came out second best sued the other for assault and battery, and I was sent for to come up and defend the suit.

"Among the witnesses for the plaintiff was a remarkably talkative old fellow, who was disposed to magnify the importance of the affair to my client's disadvantage. It came my turn to question him:

"Witness," said I, "you say you saw this fight."

"Yes, stranger; I reckon I did."

"Was it much of a fight?" said I.

"I'll be darned if it wasn't, stranger; a right smart fight."

"How much ground did the combatants cover?"

"About an acre, stranger."

"About an acre," I repeated, musingly.

"Well, now, witness, just tell me, *wasn't that just about the smallest crop of a fight off of an acre of ground that ever you heard of?*"

"That's so, stranger; *I'll be gol darned if it wasn't!*"

"The jury," added ———, giving his legs an additional twist, after the crowd had finished laughing at the application of the anecdote—"the jury fined my client just ten cents!"

If there is a better illustration of the result of the memorable conflict in Congress than the case above, we should like to hear of it. In order to be appreciated, however, one should hear ——— tell it. No man can "get off" a thing of the kind with more comical effect.

> "*Abraham Lincoln is the first and only choice of the Republicans of Illinois for the United States Senate.*" *This resolution was passed at the Republican Convention in Springfield on June 16, 1858. The deprecating remarks of the Douglas organ, the Illinois State Register of June 17, 1858, played down what Lincoln said there, calling the events "of modified black republican stripe."*

THE REPUBLICAN CONVENTION

The Republican convention, or mass meeting, for the nomination of treasurer and school superintendent, was held at the state house yesterday. The attendance was large, the northern counties sending an excess of delegates to make up for the sparse representation from other sections. The gathering was a reflex of the party's strength in the state—all at one end, though the republican state committee's call was for a convention based upon population, and not upon republican votes. The committee's liberality to Egypt in this regard was meagerly responded to, however. As a mass meeting it was a numerous gathering, comprising most of the republican leaders and managers in the state; not including [John] Wentworth, however, though announced yesterday as present by the [Illinois] *Journal*, with the names of numerous others alleged to be present as delegates, but who were not here.

During the sitting of the convention much windy declamation was perpetrated, in which the shrieking efforts of the campaign of '56 were repeated, clearly exhibiting the intention of the assemblage to block out a programme for a canvass based solely upon slavery agitation. This was the beginning, middle and ending of all their harangues, the speakers all the while claiming especially to speak for white men as against negroes! . . .

In another column of to-day's paper we give a synopsis of the proceedings, omitting the resolutions adopted, which we will give hereafter. They are of modified black republican stripe, in some respects, evidently drawn with intent to cover up the salient points of the creed, but in fact evidently covering the same old federal ground of the right of congress to rule, whether reflecting the popular will or not.

Mr. Lincoln is recommended for senator, and however unusual such an issue may be, it is now plainly and squarely one before the people of the state for United States senator—Stephen A. Douglas on the one side and Abraham Lincoln on the other. The democracy of the one against the black republican principles of the other. For one we accept the issue in this shape and shall so fight the battle—popular sovereignty against congressional sovereignty—democracy against federalism. But of these resolutions more hereafter.

The republicans have now presented their list and will go to work vigorously to secure a victory. They will spare no pains or labor to achieve it, and they should be met on the part of democrats with equal vigor and determination. Let every precinct, county and congressional district be thoroughly organized. Let the issue be fairly and fully presented to the people of the state, and there cannot be a doubt of the election of the democratic state ticket, a democratic legislature and a democratic United States senator.

The memorable address at the Republican nomination convention in Springfield came to be known as the "House Divided" speech. Lincoln—over the opposition of his advisers—came right out with it: " 'A house divided against itself cannot stand.' I believe this government cannot endure, permanently half-slave and half-free. I do not expect the Union to be dissolved—I do not expect the house to fall—but I do expect it will cease to be divided. It will become all one thing, or all the other." Joseph Medill's and Charles Ray's Chicago Tribune, on June 19, 1858, gave Lincoln prominence and support.

MR. LINCOLN'S SPEECH

We publish this morning the logical and masterly argument delivered by Hon. ABRAHAM LINCOLN before the Republican State Convention at Springfield, on Wednesday evening last. We can say nothing better of it than to commend it to the careful perusal of every citizen of Illinois, Republican or Democrat. It is a powerful summing up of the issues before the people—clear, concise, argumentative, unimpassioned and courteous. So far as Mr. LINCOLN is concerned, this speech may be taken as the ground-work of the campaign. We shall take our course; other Republicans will take theirs. Mr. LINCOLN's is already taken and we leave it to speak for itself—assured that it will meet the approbation of every right minded man in the State, as an able, honorable and statesmanlike effort. Particularly would we commend it for its dignified and gentlemanly bearing towards Mr. DOUGLAS. In the campaign of 1854, in which Mr. LINCOLN was very active and conspicuous, we thought he strained a point in his ever courteous treatment of the author of the Nebraska bill. But we gladly record the fact that the same spirit of kindness is in store for the Illinois Senator from the man whom the Republicans have chosen to stand in the fore front of the battle now. Let each present the issue of the contest according to the best of his ability and integrity, without personality, without [more] allusion to the past than is absolutely necessary to make of its connection with the present, and we shall have, no doubt, of the verdict of the people, *Let the right prevail.*

The positions taken by Mr. LINCOLN, to which we would especially invite the attention of our readers, are these:—

1. The doctrine of Squatter Sovereignty, embodied in the Nebraska Bill, and the Dred Scot decision of the Supreme Court, are so admirably matched as to afford ground for the presumption they were each prepared for the other—the object being, first, to make slavery possible in the free Territories, and second, to make it possible in the free States.

2. The doctrine of Squatter Sovereignty, reduced to its minimum, is that one man may make a slave of another in a free Territory, and no third man, either in or out of the Territory, shall object.

3. A little quarrel or a great one, as people view it, has sprung up between Senator Douglas and the President. But the difference between them is a question of *fact*—not of *principle*. Mr. Douglas holds that the Lecompton Constitution was not the will of the people of Kansas. The President holds that it was. Both agree that it ought to be. On this question of fact merely, hangs the whole strife. So far as the argument is concerned, we must say that Judge Douglas has altogether the advantage of his adversary. But Judge Douglas has not said, does not say, that there is a particle of principle involved in the case. The most that can be said for him is, that he is opposed to the Lecompton Constitution because he

thinks it is *not* the will of the people. On neither of those points did the Republican party ever differ from him.

4. Mr. DOUGLAS takes especial pains to say that he cares not whether slavery is voted up or voted down. Republicans *do* care. They would vastly prefer that it should be voted down. If we exercise the charity to think that Mr. DOUGLAS would *personally* prefer to have it voted down, he is left on a worse horn of the dilemma, viz: he would have the people of the country and the policy of the Government placated to a condition of total indifference whether slavery is voted up or down in all our territories—a condition which he himself would repudiate and scorn as an individual!

5. In the Dred Scot decision which Mr. DOUGLAS took on an early occasion to endorse, it is declared that a negro brought into a free State, for the convenience of his master, may be again declared a slave by any Court outside of that free State—which his master can subsequently force him into. That which may apply to one slave may apply to a thousand. Thus the only present difficulty in the way of holding slaves in Illinois is the uncertainty of getting them back into Missouri or Kentucky in case they choose to assert their freedom.

6. Again; the Dred Scot decision denies the power of a Territory, through its Legislature, to abolish or inhibit slavery. But it leaves the political exigencies in the future. This is a niche in which a future decision will rest as cozily as did the original Dred Scott dictum in the niche left by the "great principle of the Nebraska bill." The Nebraska bill asserted, in a vague way, the right of the people to form and regulate their domestic institutions, but omitted to give the people power to prevent the introduction of slavery in their Territorial condition. Judge TANEY filled up the interstice by saying they could not. Now *he* leaves a little room for future filling; and the omission may be supplied by deciding that *States* have no power to prevent the introduction of slavery within their sovereignty—provided it shall seem likely such a decision could be maintained after it is pronounced.

These are the main faults of Mr. LINCOLN's argument, and we believe they are unanswerable.

Lincoln's enemy—it was more than opposition—was the Chicago Daily Times, edited during the debates by James W. Sheahan. It brought up an old charge: Lincoln's "spot resolutions" when he was a Representative during the Mexican War were unpatriotic. The Chicago Times erred in stating that Lincoln failed to vote supplies for the volunteers. *Lincoln attributed this mistake to a mix-up and to the "blind rage of The Times to assail me." Lincoln, the "living dog," is compared with Douglas, of "world-wide distinction," in the Chicago Times, June 23, 1858.*

"HAPPY COMPARISONS"

A Republican editor writing from the Springfield Republican Convention to his own paper, described the speech of the Hon. A. Lincoln as abounding in strong arguments, great research, and "happy comparisons." We know Mr. Lincoln personally, and have no disposition to say one word having the slightest approach to disrespect, but as he has set himself before the people of Illinois as the competitor of Senator Douglas, and has not only invited, but actually made comparisons between himself and his opponent, we feel warranted in taking notice of what he has said in this particular.

There are a number of Republicans (as well as several Republican newspapers) who think that in a struggle for the defence of the State, and of the Constitution, and of the North, good sense would dictate that a Senator who can command support and power with the entire people of the Union, would be of more service than a mere individual whose influence would be confined to his own person, and whose power would be exhausted by the casting of his own vote. Mr. Lincoln, in his speech, after pointing out to the Republicans of Illinois the reasons why he, Lincoln, should be elected, turns to the question of whether he or Mr. Douglas would prove the most serviceable representative in the councils of the nation, and he says: (we give the extract, *italics and all*, just as we find it published in the Springfield *Journal:*)

"There are those who denounce us *openly* to their *own* friends, and yet whisper us *softly*, that Senator Douglas is the *aptest* instrument there is, with which to effect that object. They do *not* tell us, nor has *he* told us, that he *wishes* any such object to be effected. They wish us to *infer* all, from the facts, that he now has a little quarrel with the present head of the dynasty; and that he has regularly voted with us, on a single point, upon which, he and we, have never differed.

"They remind us that *he* is a very *great* man, and that the largest of us are very small ones. Let this be granted. But "a living dog is better than a dead lion." Judge Douglas, if not a *dead* lion for *this* work, is at least a *caged* and *toothless* one. How can he oppose the advances of slavery? He don't care anything about it. His avowed mission is impressing the "public heart" to care nothing about it."

Mr Lincoln thinks proper to speak of his competitor as a "*dead lion*," and to hold himself up to the people of Illinois as a "*living dog*." We have no right to question Mr. Lincoln's estimation of himself; he has applied it to himself, and has, to give it stronger significance, italicised the expression in his printed speech.

We think that for a "dead lion," or even a "caged and *toothless*" one, Senator Douglas possesses and displays considerable vitality. To kill a dead lion, all the "living dogs" of Illinois have been let loose with sharpened fangs. To fight a "toothless" lion all the living dogs from Cairo to Chicago have been lashed and whipped into the hunt. And yet there is not a "living dog" in the entire pack that does not tremble and quake, lest that dead and toothless animal, even in death, may rise and put him in jeopardy. Was the lion who stood in the pathway of Lecomptonism dead when he bid the entire power and patronage of the Government defiance, and forbid the consumation of that iniquity? Was that the voice of a dead lion, which has been heard in the mountains and valleys of Pennsylvania, upon the streams of Ohio, all over the prairies of the Northwest, and even now finds a responsive echo throughout the State of Virginia? Was that the struggle of a dead lion which forced a proud and overbearing majority in both houses of Congress, backed by all the power and appliances of the Federal Government, to abandon after a four months' struggle, their infamous measure, and send the Lecompton Constitution back to Kansas to be buried beyond all hope of resurrection by the people of that Territory? If that was the power of a dead lion, we would like to know whether there is a "living dog" in Illinois who could have done the same deed? Suppose that Douglas had not been in the Senate, and his place had been occupied by a "living dog" in the person of Abram Lincoln, would Lecompton have been delayed one hour in its triumphant passage?

Who else than Douglas could have arrested that measure when he did, and as he did? A new and popular Administration just entering into office, a large Administration majority in both branches of Congress, the entire patronage of the Government undisposed of, and yet a man arose up there and bid that majority and that Administration to stop in the prosecution of an unjust measure. Call you, Mr. Lincoln, the man who did that successfully a dead lion—a toothless animal? And pray, when do you ever expect to be able, in the Senate or out of it, anywhere, at home or abroad, to approach in power and influence that achievement of a dead lion? In that hour, of what avail would have been the barking of a "living dog?"

We remember that on one occasion, some years ago, a bill was pending in the House of Representatives at Washington for the purchase of medicines and the employment of nurses to attend the sick and dying American soldiers in the hospitals and camps of hot and burning Mexico, when our suffering soldiers—the volunteers of Illinois and of Indiana—the men who at Buena Vista had followed Hardin and Bissell, and who through the desert had accompanied Shields and Foreman—were crying out in their fever for cooling drinks and kind hands to minister to their dying wants; we know that when the bill to purchase these medicines, and furnish necessaries for the American soldiers who were sick and dying was pending, a "living dog" reared his ungainly person in the national councils, and in a yelping, barking tone, refused them succor! Let them die—let them die, the men of Illinois, who fought over and rescued the dead body of Hardin, who echoed back the cheering call of Bissell, of Richardson, of Moore, of Harris, let them die. I, a "living dog" from the State of Illinois, refuse to send these men food, clothing, or medicine. I, Abram Lincoln, of Sangamon county, refuse to vote one dollar to feed, cloth, or minister to the wants of the sick and dying volunteers from my own State, who are suffering in Mexico. Let them die like dogs! Let them die for want of medicine! Let the fever-parched lips of my Illinois neighbors crack in painful agony—not one drop of cooling liquid shall soothe them if I can help it. What if they have served their country; what if they have encountered and beaten back an enemy thrice their own number; what if they do lie on damp grounds by night, and march in blistering sunlight by day; what if they have proved, every man of them, to be a LION in his country's cause, I, Abram Lincoln, am a living dog and "a living dog is better than a dead lion."

Oh, Mr. Lincoln, the living dog at that day tried his powers with the man who is now styled a "dead lion;" you then refused succours to your countrymen in Mexico, but the "living dog" was powerless even for evil. The money was voted, and the living dog skulked back into obscurity. Was not that a deed worthy of "a living dog;" would not even a dead lion be ashamed that his memory should be stained by the record of such an act?

Democrats of Illinois, Republicans of Illinois! the man who styles himself a "living dog" asks you to support him for the United States

Senate. The man who aspires to be your representative in the Senate, who offers himself to fill the place heretofore filled with such world-wide distinction by Douglas, tells you that he will go there as a living dog. He has been in Congress before, but who is there outside of the old settlers of Illinois has any recollection of his service there? What did he do? What did he say? What act is there which has rendered his service or his presence there memorable? Who is there in Illinois or in the Union that can remember any act or speech (other than the one we have mentioned) by Lincoln in the Congress of the United States. He asks you to send him there because he is better than a dead lion. But is the lion dead? Why the hostile array then that has been prepared to kill the lion who is already dead?

People of Illinois Mr. Lincoln has stated the issue—"a living dog" or a "lion" not dead, nor wounded, nor toothless, nor caged, but free, bold, firm, strong, and more powerful than ever. Choose you, as your representative, the man who claims no higher rank than that of a "living dog," or the man who has exercised, and forever will exercise a controlling power over the legislation of his country.

The New York press covered the Illinois Senatorial campaign—and its behavior strongly concerned Lincoln and his cohorts. "What does the New-York Tribune mean by its constant eulogizing, and admiring, and magnifying of Douglas? Does it, in this, speak the sentiments of the Republicans at Washington?" This, from Lincoln to Senator Lyman Trumbull. In a New York Tribune report, June 26, 1858, Lincoln and Douglas were compared.

ILLINOIS

SKETCH OF THE HON. ABRAHAM LINCOLN.
Correspondence of The N.Y. Tribune.

COLLINSVILLE, Ill., June 15, 1858.
The decided expressions of the Republican Convention of this State in favor of Abraham Lincoln for Senator, in the place now held by Judge Douglas, will give interest to anything throwing light upon the character and abilities of Mr. Lincoln, especially to those who are not acquainted with him. As he has served only one term in the Lower House of Congress, and that so long ago as 1846–8, there must be many who would like to know how he will be likely to fill the place of the now so

notorious—I might say distinguished—Douglas. Is he a match for his "illustrious predecessor?"

The style of the two men is quite different. Lincoln is colloquial, affable, good-natured, almost jolly. He states the case at issue with so much easy good humor and fairness that his opponents are almost persuaded he is not an opponent at all. As he proceeds with the argument, he grants the opposition almost all they claim. In a doubtful case he asks them, if present, to state their choice in a dilemma, and so he proceeds, weaving his argument of indisputable facts and principles, until, before you are aware of it, he has linked his granted premise to his conclusion with hooks of steel. There is no faulty link in the chain, and none open enough to get a wedge into. All this time you have scarcely suspected him of any set purpose. He was simply talking about things as they are, in a pleasant, after-dinner mood. Sometimes, for a single sentence, he might seem to warm into eloquence, but it seemed only the leading of the subject, and not from any purpose to make a speech. If you differ with him in regard to any fact, he is quite willing you should have it your own way. If he makes use of a point which is in dispute, he says he "thinks" it is so, but he does not build his argument upon it.

If Douglas were equally careful to take his positions rightly and espouse only a good cause, he would be a stronger man. But Lincoln has the strength which attaches to sound moral feeling and a just cause; and his temperate mode of argumentation will well befit the Senate, though he does not on the stump affect the dignity which the "distinguished Senator" naturally wears. I may add that Lincoln, being a Southern man by birth and education, is one of that sort of Republicans who cannot be seduced from their convictions.

But I am forgetting myself, which was chiefly to relate an incident showing the two men in contact and somewhat in comparison. I think it has never been in print.

It was in the Fall of 1854, when the Nebraska bill was a fresh topic. Lincoln was speaking to some two thousand persons in the State House at Springfield. Douglas sat on the Clerk's platform, just under the Speaker's stand. In his introduction, Lincoln complimented his distinguished friend; said he himself had not been in public life as he had; and if he should, on that account, mistake any fact, he would be very much obliged to his friend the Judge, if he would correct him. Judge Douglas rose with a good deal of Senatorial dignity, and said that it was not always agreeable to a speaker to be interrupted in the course of his remarks, and therefore, if he should have anything to say, he would wait until Mr.

Lincoln was done. For some reason, he did not keep to his purpose, but quite frequently rose to put in a word when he seemed to think his case required immediate attention. One of these passages—and it was pretty nearly a sample of the rest—was in this wise: Lincoln had been giving a history of the legislation of the Federal Government on the subject of Slavery, and referring to the opinions held by public men, and had come down to the Nicholson letter, wherein the denial of the power of Congress to prohibit Slavery in the Territories was first presented to the public. Said he, "I don't know what my friend the Judge thinks" (and he looked down upon him with a smile half playful, half rogueish), "but really it seems to me that *that* was the origin of the Nebraska bill." This stroke at the Senator's laurels in the matter of the "great principle," created a good deal of laughter and some applause, which brought the Judge to his feet. Shaking back his heavy hair, and looking much like a roused lion, he said, in his peculiarly heavy voice which he uses with so much effect when he wishes to be impressive, "No, Sir! I will tell you what was the origin of the Nebraska bill. It was this, Sir! God created man, and placed before him both good and evil, and left him free to choose for himself. That was the origin of the Nebraska bill." As he said this, Lincoln looked the picture of good nature and patience. As Douglas concluded, the smile which lurked in the corners of Lincoln's mouth parted his lips, and he replied, "Well, then, I think it is a great honor to Judge Douglas that he *was the first man to discover that fact*." This brought down the house, of course, but I could not perceive that the Judge appreciated the fun in the least.

I quote from memory and do not undertake, of course, to be verbally correct. My version may serve for a slight glimpse of the man. You, Mr. Editor, will not have forgotten his record on the Wilmot Proviso. He never faltered then nor since, nor need there be any conjectures about his course in the Senate, as there must be in any event concerning a distinguished individual, whom some Republicans ever have thought might possibly be chosen. Lincoln, in the Senate, will be the right man in the right place.   W.

"Somebody named Lincoln"—at age forty-nine, on the eve of the great debates, such was the fame in most of the Southern press of the man from Illinois, who in two and a half years would be elected President. (Note how closely the malignity of this report from the New Orleans Delta resembles that of the anti-Lincoln Chicago Times.) Reprinted in the Chicago Tribune, July 5, 1858.

NEW ORLEANS DELTA ON THE ILLINOIS
REPUBLICAN CONVENTION
From the New Orleans Delta.

GRAND CONVOCATION OF FANATICS.—The Black Republicans of Illinois lately assembled in Grand Council in Springfield. The nomination of a State ticket drew together as precious set of pestilent fanatics and demagogues as can be found outside of New England.

Somebody named Lincoln, who in the eyes of his friends is an unshorn Sampson of Free-soilism, was the favorite of the Convention for United States Senator, in place of Douglas. This Lincoln made a speech in which he hit the "Little Giant" some terrible blows, then proceeded to demolish the Democracy, and obliterate Slavery. As everybody was a Lincolnite, the proceedings of the Convention began with Lincoln and ended with Lincoln. The go-between nomination for State candidates seemed to be of nominal importance.

The Chicago TRIBUNE, the "honest Iago" of a journal which supported Lane in Kansas, though knowing him to be one of the greatest knaves in the Union, grows jubilant over the doings of this convention—claps its hands, stamps its feet, and cries out,

> "Sound the loud timbrel over Egypt's dark sea,
> Jehovah has triumphed; his people are free."

Here is blasphemy for you! Cromwell is said to have labelled his cannon with the scriptural words: "Lord, open thou our mouths, and we will show forth thy praise!" But the canting Puritan would yield the palm of impiety to the man of the *Tribune*, who proclaims that the negro-stealers of Illinois are the people of Jehovah, and that in the unanimity which marked the proceedings of this Black Republican Convention, Jehovah has triumphed. Garrison and Abby Folsom must look to their laurels.

Some of the speeches delivered in this Convention are exceedingly rich specimens of Western eloquence, and while they provoke a smile, it is well enough to remember that the sentiments uttered by these speakers show an unalterable hostility to Slavery, and a determination to drive the knife into the lungs of the South.

The "Hon. Mr. Sweet" made a sugary speech, which pleased the palate of the Black Republicans amazingly. Sweet upon the Free soilers, sour upon the "negro-drivers," and severe upon the Democracy, his remarks were received with rapturous applause. . . .

It is quite evident that the Black Republicans of Illinois are making a united effort to sweep the State at the approaching election. Indeed, everywhere in the West, the anti-Slavery leaders survey the field, raise themselves in their stirrups, and swing high the black banner, confident of success in the great battle of 1860.

The Douglas Senatorial campaign began formally in Chicago, July 9, 1858, when he made a speech attacking Lincoln's "House Divided" speech. In legalistic fashion, suggesting some guidance from Lincoln, the voice of Republicanism in Illinois set out the difference between what was said and how it was distorted. From the Chicago Tribune, July 12, 1858.

THE LATEST DOUGLASISM ON RECORD

We say it to the credit of Democratic politicians, that it has not often been our duty to expose so small a quibble or so glaring a misstatement as the following, which fell from Mr. DOUGLAS' mouth on Friday evening. It must be recorded to the honor of LEIB and the imperishable renown of KISSANE, that neither of these exponents of the Cincinnati Platform ever mumbled such childishness or flew so straight in the face of facts, in the presence of an audience speaking the English language. We experience the sensation of foolishness in telling our readers that the remarks which follow on the right hand column, are a falsehood. The urchin who could not discern it would be properly turned out of school for a dunce. Mr. DOUGLAS should make one more such effort and then follow the fortunes of his ex-lieutenant in Nebraska.

We refer to his statement of Mr. LINCOLN's position as laid down in the late Springfield speech of the latter on a subject which will more clearly appear by a comparison of the following extracts from the speeches of the two gentlemen:

MR. LINCOLN'S POSITION AS MR. LINCOLN STATED IT.	MR. LINCOLN'S POSITION AS MR. DOUGLAS STATED IT.
"We are now far into the fifth year since a policy was initiated with the avowed object and confident promise of putting an end to slavery agitation. Under the	"In the first place he (Mr. Lincoln) sets out in his speech to say, quoting from Scripture, that "A house divided against itself cannot stand;" that the American

operation of that policy that agitation has not only not ceased, but has constantly augmented. In my opinion, it will not cease until a crisis shall have been reached and passed. "A house divided against itself cannot stand." I believe this Government cannot endure permanently, half Slave and half Free. I do not expect the Union to be dissolved—I do not expect the house to fall—but I do expect it will cease to be divided. It will become all one thing or all the other. Either the opponents of Slavery will arrest the further spread of it, and place it where the public mind shall rest in the belief, that it is in the course of ultimate extinction; or its advocates will push it forward till it shall become alike lawful in all the States—old as well as new, North as well as South."

Government divided into an equal number of Free and Slave States, cannot stand. That they should all be the one or all the other. In other words, he asserts as a fundamental principle of this Government, that there must be uniformity in the laws—local laws and domestic institutions of each and all the States of this Union. He therefore invites all the non-slaveholding States to band together, organize as one body, and make war upon slavery in Kentucky, upon slavery in Virginia, upon slavery in the Carolinas, upon slavery in all the slaveholding States of the Union, and to persevere in that war until it shall be exterminated. He then invites the slave-holding States to band together as a unit, and make aggressive war upon the Free States of this Union, with a view to establish slavery in Illinois, New York, and New England—in every Free State of the Union—and keep up that warfare until it shall be firmly established in their limits. He advocates boldly and clearly a war of sections—a war of the North against the South—of the Free States against the Slave States—a war of extermination to be continued relentlessly until the one or the other shall be universal, and all the States shall either become free or become slave."

We remarked that we felt foolish in showing the falsity of Mr. Douglas' rendering of his antagonist's English. If the good sense of our readers will permit we will say however, that Mr. Lincoln's remarks brought down to their smallest compass, were these: "I believe that the two principles now struggling for supremacy on this Continent—freedom and slavery—are so antagonistic, so irreconcilable, that their present strife *will not terminate* until one has subdued the other." Mr. DOUGLAS' translation, or as our German friends would very properly say "upsetting," of this remark, reduced in like manner, is as follows: "Mr. LINCOLN says a house divided against itself cannot stand. 'He therefore *invites*' each section of the Union to arm itself with powder and ball and march against, and extinguish the institutions of the other." If we may reduce it to another degree of compactness, it is this: Mr. LINCOLN believes that there is now a struggle, and that it will continue till a certain result is reached; but Mr. DOUGLAS says that Mr. LINCOLN *calls* upon the participants in the struggle to throw down the slow weapon of the ballot box and *precipitate the result by the sword!*

What shall we say of the nonsense of such logic as this? It is a Douglasism! That describes it better than a whole dictionary. But what shall we infer from this manner of treating an opponent's argument? Simply this:

1. That Mr. LINCOLN's speech is unanswerable. Mr. DOUGLAS had laid himself out to demolish his rival's work. He has had a printed copy of his speech for a fortnight. He has tried every expedient known to logic, sophistry or demagogism, to overthrow its premises and bring to naught its conclusions. And here is the childish result of his efforts! A very little giant indeed, if this be a sample of his performances.

2. That falsehood, and not truth, is to be the cue of the campaign on the part of Mr. DOUGLAS and his allies. The low prevarication which we have exposed, is but a specimen brick of his whole harangue. The specious twaddle about Popular Sovereignty—the right of the people of a Territory to do something when they are becoming a State, which they can never do before that period—is another. The *involuted* sophism—a wheel within a wheel—by which he conveys the idea that this Popular Sovereignty, this new principle conferring the right of regulating the relations of husband and wife, parent and child, etc., should of course give the right of regulating the relations of master and servant—is another. Whence, sir, comes any master or any servant to be brought into your reckoning? Upon what principle has one man the original, primary right to call another his servant? Are you prepared to say the Almighty established *this* "relation," as he established that of husband and wife, parent and child? Your logic leads you to that assumption, and no other. And yet you dare not say so for your life—or your office, which is the

same thing. Yet another internal deceit, like a minnow inside a fish swallowed by a whale, and we have done. After asserting that Popular Sovereignty confers upon the people of a Territory the right of regulating the relations of husband and wife, etc., and should therefore confer the right of regulating those of master and servant—what next? Precisely this: *that it* DOES NOT *confer the right of regulating the relations of master and servant upon the people of a Territory,* but while investing (or rather, not molesting) them in the right of regulating those other relations, *it especially prevents them from touching these* until they have reached the sovereignty of a State. Slavery exists in Kansas and Nebraska to-day—and why? Because the people have Popular Sovereignty enough to regulate the relations of husband and wife, *but not enough to regulate those of master and servant!* O, for another pennyworth of Popular Sovereignty, with DOUGLAS to measure it out!

His Mexican War voting record in Congress kept tugging at Lincoln's sleeve. Joseph Medill, one of the publishers of the pro-Lincoln Chicago Tribune, asked Lincoln privately to set the record straight. Lincoln replied, "I was in Congress but a single term. I was a candidate when the Mexican War broke out—and I then took the ground, which I never varied from, that the administration had done wrong in getting us into the war, but that the officers and soldiers who went to the field must be supplied and sustained at all events." Thereafter, the Chicago Press and Tribune (so called because the Press and Tribune were merged in 1858) ran the facts of Lincoln's record. Reprinted in the Illinois State Journal, Springfield, July 16, 1858.

MR. LINCOLN ON THE MEXICAN WAR

The [Chicago] *Times* has not yet retracted the charge that Mr. Lincoln voted against sending supplies to the American army in Mexico, although the utter falsity of the statement has been again and again demonstrated, and even the *State Register,* from very shame, is compelled to admit that its co-worker in slavery propagandism has brought a charge against Mr. Lincoln which is directly contradicted by that gentleman's Congressional record. We stated some time ago that the *Times* would stick to the lie. Its antecedents warranted the statement, and the result shows that it is consistent with itself. Such readers as have access only to the *Times,* will, of course, accept as the truth its falsification of Mr. Lincoln's Congressional course—as they will believe a good many other things which never had existence outside that laboratory of lies. But fortunately for the truth, that class of readers is small, and is not likely ever to be any larger. If any one of them, by accident, or otherwise, should come into possession of a copy of this paper, we ask him to read the extract from a speech of Mr. Lincoln, made in Congress, July 27th, 1848, which we publish in another column. That extract, while it puts anew the brand of falsehood upon the charge of the *Times*, also states very clearly the light in which the Whig party regarded the Mexican war, as well as the patriotic considerations which induced them to send their best men to suffer from the hardships and risk the perils of the campaign, and to steadily vote in Congress for such supplies of men and money as the exigencies of affairs required. It is only necessary to read it to see where Mr. Lincoln stood, and to appreciate fully the intense meanness which prompted the *Times* to falsify his position, and the intenser meanness which induces it not to retract its calumnies.

Lincoln—by plan and coincidence—happened to follow Douglas in speaking engagements in July, 1858. Then Lincoln decided to appear on the platform with Douglas simultaneously—"to divide time, and address the same audiences during the present canvass." Douglas, after some bargaining over terms, agreed to debate in seven Illinois districts—Ottawa, Freeport, Jonesboro, Charleston, Galesburg, Quincy, Alton. The Chicago Times, meanwhile, accused Lincoln of riding Douglas's coattails on July 30, 1858.

AN AUDIENCE WANTED

It was Japhet, we believe, whose adventures in search of his father, furnished the novelist with the plot of a popular romance. There are but few of our readers who have not known, or at least heard of physicians unable, even in the midst of sickness, to obtain patients, lawyers unable to obtain clients, and actors unable to draw houses. But we venture to say that never before was there heard of in any political canvass in Illinois, of a candidate unable to obtain an audience to hear him! But such is the fact. Abe Lincoln, the candidate of all the Republicans, wants an audience. He came up to Chicago, and, taking advantage of the enthusiasm of Douglas' reception, made a speech here; he went to Bloomington, and, at the Douglas meeting, advertised himself for a future occasion; at Springfield he distributed handbills at the Douglas meeting imploring the people to hear him. The Springfield attempt was a failure. He came to

Chicago, and declared it impossible for him to get the people to turn out to hear him, and then it was resolved to try and get him a chance to speak to the crowds drawn out to meet and welcome Douglas. That proposition was partially declined and another substituted; but yet the cringing, crawling creature is hanging at the outskirts of Douglas' meetings, begging the people to come and hear him. At Clinton he rose up at the Democratic meeting, and announced his intention to speak at night, but only 250 persons could be induced to attend his meeting.

He went yesterday to Monticello in Douglas' train; poor, desperate creature, he wants an audience; poor, unhappy mortal, the people won't turn out to hear him, and he must do something, even if that something is mean, sneaking, and disreputable!

We have a suggestion to make to Mr. Judd [Norman B. Judd, chairman of the Republican State Central Committee]—the next friend of Lincoln. There are two very good circuses and menageries traveling through the State; these exhibitions always draw good crowds at country towns. Mr. Judd, in behalf of his candidate, at a reasonable expense, might make arrangements with the managers of these exhibitions to include a speech from Lincoln in their performances. In this way Lincoln could get good audiences, and his friends be relieved from the mortification they all feel at his present humiliating position.

William Cullen Bryant, editor of the New York Post, sent Chester P. Dewey to Illinois to cover the debates. This is how the candidates were sized up by the Post on Aug. 16, 1858, several days before the formal debates commenced.

August 16, 1858

CHICAGO, August 13—The interest in politics increases here at the campaign (for U. S. Senator) progresses. Illinois is regarded as the battleground of the year, and the results of this contest are held to be of the highest importance to the welfare of the country and the success of the great contending parties. The Republican Convention of June 16, after placing a state ticket in nomination, named as its choice for United States senator to succeed Mr. Douglas, Mr. Lincoln, of Springfield. This expression met at once the approval of the Republicans of the state.

Mr. Lincoln was regarded as the man for the place. A native of Kentucky, where he belonged to the class of "poor whites," he came early to Illinois. Poor, unfriended, uneducated, a day-laborer, he has distanced all these disadvantages, and in the profession of the law has risen steadily to a competence, and the position of an intelligent, shrewd and well-balanced man.

Familiarly known as "Long Abe," he is a popular speaker, and a cautious, thoughtful politician, capable of taking a high position as a statesman and legislator. His nomination was proof that the Republicans of Illinois were determined in their hostility to Mr. Douglas, and that no latter-day conversion of his, however luminous it might appear to some eastern eyes, could blind them to the fact that in him were embodied the false and fatal principles against which they were organized. They had grown mighty in their opposition to Douglas, and in his defeat they were certain of an enlarged and a well-established party.

The people of Illinois felt certain that they knew best the sentiment of their state, and they repudiated the counsels of those who suggested that Douglas was a good-enough Republican, and that he might be used to break down the democratic party here and in the northwest. The present attitude of Mr. Douglas, so entirely consistent with his antecedents, is good evidence that the Republicans in Illinois did well to condemn the time-serving and dangerous suggestions that emanated from Washington and New York and which had voice in many influential journals in the East.

Mr. Douglas, in all his speeches, claims to be a democrat, and demands the support of democrats in his assault upon Republicanism. The "Little Giant" is changed in no respect; and as the canvass grows warmer, the breech widens, and his actual position becomes more clearly defined. He is of other material, altogether, than that which makes Republicanism. He is still an out-and-out pro-slavery man. In one of his recent speeches he stopped to read the dispatch announcing Blair's defeat in St. Louis, as the over-throw of "negro equality" and all that sort of stuff that forms the staple of democratic rhetoric.

Douglas is working like a lion. He is stumping the state, everywhere present and everywhere appealing to his old lieges to stand by him. Never did feudal baron fight more desperately against the common superior of himself and his retainers.

Lincoln, too, is actively engaged. His senatorial nomination has sent him to the field, and he is working with an energy and zeal which counter-balance the spirit and dogged resolution of his opponent. Lincoln is battling for the right and Douglas is desperately struggling to save himself from utter political ruin. He is losing strength daily, while Lincoln is surely gaining upon him.

At the first joint debate in Ottawa twelve thousand people stood in the summer sun for three hours and listened. Horace White, covering for the pro-Lincoln Chicago *Tribune*, said, "The Ottawa debate gave great satisfaction to our side. Mr. Lincoln, we thought, had the better of the argument, and we all came away encouraged. But the Douglas men were encouraged also. In his concluding half hour, Douglas spoke with great rapidity and animation, and yet with perfect distinctness, and his supporters cheered him wildly." How the anti-Lincoln Chicago *Times* saw it, Aug. 22, 1858, follows.

THE CAMPAIGN

DOUGLAS AMONG THE PEOPLE

Joint Discussion at Ottawa!

LINCOLN BREAKS DOWN.

ENTHUSIASM OF THE PEOPLE!

THE BATTLE FOUGHT AND WON.

Lincoln's Heart Fails Him!
Lincoln's Legs Fail Him!
Lincoln's Tongue Fails Him!
Lincoln's Arms Fail Him!
LINCOLN FAILS ALL OVER!!

The People Refuse to Support Him!
The People Laugh at Him!

DOUGLAS THE CHAMPION OF THE PEOPLE!

Douglas Skins the "Living Dog."

THE "DEAD LION" FRIGHTENS THE CANINE.
Douglas "Trotting" Lincoln Out.

DOUGLAS "CONCLUDES" ON ABE.

On Saturday, the first of the series of joint discussions between Lincoln and Douglas took place at Ottawa. Below we publish a full report of the speeches.

At an early hour Ottawa was alive with people. From daylight till three o'clock in the afternoon the crowds came in, by train, by canal-boat, and by wagon, carriage, buggy, and on horseback. Morris, Joliet, and all the towns on the railroad, above and below Ottawa, sent up their delegates. Lincoln on Friday night left Peoria, and passed up the road to Morris, where he staid over, in order that he might have the appearance of being escorted to Ottawa by the crowds who filled the special train on Saturday morning. Douglas left Peru in the morning in a carriage, escorted by a large delegation on horseback, and in vehicles. The procession as it passed along the road received new accessions at every cross-road and stopping place, and when it reached Ottawa it was nearly a mile in length. As it passed through the streets the people from the sidewalks, from windows, piazzas, house-tops, and every available standing point, cheered and welcomed him. Upon his arrival at the Geiger House he was welcomed by Wm. H. H. Cushman, in the following remarks:

[A brief speech of welcome was delivered]

Mr. Douglas responded in a few appropriate remarks, and throughout the entire proceedings was cheered most enthusiastically.

At two o'clock the multitude gathered in the public square, the sun shining down with great intensity, and the few trees affording but little shade. It would seem that the most exposed part of the City was selected for the speaking. After a long delay, the discussion was opened by Judge Douglas, who spoke as follows:

[The text of Judge Douglas's and Mr. Lincoln's talks followed]

When Douglas had concluded the shouts were tremendous: his excoriation of Lincoln was so severe, that the Republicans hung their heads in shame. The Democrats, however, were loud in their vociferation. About two-thirds of the meeting at once surrounded Douglas, and with music, cheers, and every demonstration of enthusiastic admiration they escorted him to his quarters at the hotel, where for several minutes they made the welkin ring with their cheers, and applause.

Lincoln in the meantime seemed to have been paralyzed. He stood upon the stage looking wildly at the people as they surrounded the triumphant Douglas, and, with mouth wide open, he could not find a friend to say one word to him in his distress. It was a delicate point for Republicans who had witnessed his utter defeat, and who knew how severely he felt it, to offer him condolence, or bid him hope for better success again. The only thing they could say was that Lincoln ought not to travel round with Douglas, and had better not meet him any more. When Douglas and the Democrats had left the square, Lincoln essayed to descend from the stage, but his limbs refused to do their office. During Douglas' last speech Lincoln had suffered severely; alternately burning with fever, and then suddenly chilled with shame, his respiratory organs had become obstructed, his limbs got cold, and he was unable to walk. In this extremity, the Republican Marshal called half a dozen men, who, lifting Lincoln in their arms, carried him along. By some mismanagement the men selected for this office happened to be very short in stature, and the consequence was, that while Lincoln's head and shoulders towered above theirs, his feet dragged on the ground. Such an exhibition as the "toting" of Lincoln from the square to his lodgings was never seen at Ottawa before. It was one of the richest farces we have ever witnessed, and provoked the laughter of all, Democrats and Republicans, who happened to see it.

Hostile handling of the Ottawa debate and the "phonographic" (shorthand) reporters who covered it brought outcries from Lincoln's friends. The Chicago Times Aug. 25, 1858, blamed it all on the fact that "Lincoln cannot speak five grammatical sentences in succession."

LINCOLN'S SPEECH

We delayed the issue of our Sunday morning's paper some hours in order that we might publish in full the speeches of Lincoln and Douglas, at Ottawa. We had two phonographic reporters there to report those speeches. One of them (Mr. Sheridan) we have known personally for years, and know him to be one of the most accomplished phonographers in the United States Senate. The other (Mr. Binmore) is reputed to be a most excellent reporter, and having had occasion to mark the manner in which he has on several occasions executed his duty, we are satisfied that he is not only a competent but a most faithful reporter. These two gentlemen reported the two speeches, and they, shortly after their arrival in Chicago from Ottawa, commenced transcribing the speeches from their notes. We published both speeches as they were furnished us by the reporters.

The Chicago *Tribune* and the Chicago *Journal*, both charge that we mutilated Mr. Lincoln's speech; and the *Tribune* goes further and alleges that Senator Douglas in person changed, mutilated, and falsified the report of Lincoln's speech as published in this paper. We have to say to these gentlemen, each and every one of them who will assume responsibility for the charge, that the statement is a falsehood, a falsehood utterly malicious, because known to be untrue. We brand the author of the statement, and we care not who he be, as a liar—In applying that epithet, we do it meaning it in the fullest extent of the term, and those to whom it is applicable can find us at our office.

Any one who has ever heard Lincoln speak, or who is acquainted with his style of speaking, must know that he cannot speak five grammatical sentences in succession. In his speeches he admits his own want of education, and his inability to speak correctly. We published Mr. Lincoln's speech exactly as it was delivered, except whenever it was possible, without destroying the sense, the proof-reader and the reporter corrected his wanton violations of the rules of grammar. The report of his speech in the *Tribune* differs from ours, but that is not our fault. We published what he said, and did not endeavor to polish up sentences by remodeling them, or put in whole paragraphs of which Lincoln's tongue was innocent. We know, and all the world knows, that in the *Tribune* office is employed the man who wrote Junius' letters. Because this man chose to make for Lincoln a speech that he never uttered, because this man chose to write a speech, couched in language to which Lincoln is an utter stranger, it is not just to charge us with crime for publishing what Lincoln did say.

We repeat, that Lincoln's speech, as published in the TIMES, is as it was transcribed by the reporter, and is positively the speech he delivered. We never touched a line of the manuscript of Lincoln's speech. And, we repeat again, that whichever one of the editors of that paper who holds himself responsible for the charge that Lincoln's speech was altered, changed, or modified by any person connected with this office, or by Judge Douglas, is hereby, in as pointed a manner as if it was uttered to his face, branded as a falsifier. Let the scoundrel take it up if he dare.

What the New York press editorialized about the Illinois Senatorial race could mean votes. Lincoln said, "If the [New York] Tribune continues to din [Douglas's] praises into the ears of its five or ten thousand Republican readers in Illinois, it is more than can be hoped that all will stand firm." Horace Greeley, strangely, inclined toward Douglas in '58. Language like this, from the New York Tribune of Aug. 26, 1858, worried Lincoln.

Perhaps no local contest in this country ever excited so general or so profound an interest as that now waging in Illinois, with Senator Douglas, the Federal Administration, and the Republican party headed by Messrs. Lincoln and Trumbull as the combatants. Apart from the eminent ability and ardent passions of Mr. Douglas, which must always excite attention to any struggle in which he may be engaged, his position as the object of Executive animosity and the uncertain character of his future relations to the Democratic party, draw toward him a degree of sympathy even from many who have been wont to regard him with very different feelings. It is true that this sympathy is diminished by the manner in which he has chosen to conduct the canvass, which reminds us more of the wild and unscrupulous athlete of his earlier days than of the noble displays of last Winter, when he stood forth in the Senate Chamber as the champion of popular rights against Executive usurpation, without the need of employing any other weapons than those of truth, and of a logic none the less conclusive because it was altogether honest.

As our readers are already aware, one of the features of this remarkable contest is a series of public meetings in different parts of the State, where Mr. Douglas and Mr. Lincoln successively address the people—a mode of discussing political questions which might well be more generally adopted. The first of these meetings was held at Ottawa on Saturday, the 21st inst., and we publish on another page a full report of the speeches on both sides. Of the two, all partiality being left out of the question, we think Mr. Lincoln has decidedly the advantage. Not only are his doctrines better and truer than those of his antagonist, but he states them with more propriety and cogency, and with an infinitely better temper. More than this, in this discussion Mr. Douglas was betrayed into what was perhaps a fault as well as a blunder; at any rate, it was a blunder of a very gross character. He cited certain resolutions, which he alleged were adopted as the platform of the Illinois State Convention of 1854, and these alleged resolutions he made the text of a large portion of his speech. But it appears that no such resolutions were ever offered at any Republican State Convention in Illinois, or adopted by any such Convention. *The Press and Tribune* of Chicago charges that Mr. Douglas was aware of this, and that he committed an intentional fraud in producing the resolutions as he did. They were, it seems, really adopted at a small local meeting in Kane County; and yet the Senator brought them forward as the platform of a State Convention. Our Chicago cotemporary will have it that Mr. Douglas did this for effect at the moment, well knowing that the imposition must be exposed in due time. This is hardly credible; but there is no doubt that such a misrepresentation is, at least, a blunder, which must ultimately prove injurious to the party by which it is committed.

But it is not merely as a passage at arms between two eminent masters of the art of intellectual attack and defense that this discussion is worthy of study. It touches some of the most vital principles of our political system, and no man can carefully peruse it without some benefit, whatever his convictions as to the questions at issue between the disputants.

One of the important opinion makers in slave-holding Kentucky was controversial George D. Prentice, editor of the Louisville Journal, one of the publications Lincoln clipped and studied for many years. Regarding Lincoln speeches during the debates the Journal said, "Let no one omit to read them. They are searching, scathing, stunning. They belong to what some one has graphically styled the tomahawking species." When the Louisville Journal leaned toward Lincoln editorially, the Springfield Journal of Aug. 30, 1858, reprinted the favorable sentiments.

A SIGNIFICANT ARTICLE—THE LOUISVILLE JOURNAL OUT FOR LINCOLN

Some time since the [Springfield, Ill.] Register paraded with much gusto, an article from the Louisville [Kentucky] Journal, complimenting Mr. Douglas for his anti-Lecomptonism. The Register argued from it that the Louisville Journal, Mr. Crittenden, Mr. Bell and other leaders of the American party were in favor of Mr. Douglas' election.—If that ever was so, Mr. Douglas' late speech in which he fully indorses all the enormities of Niggerism and Dred Scottism, have opened their eyes and disabused their minds. Finding that he has gone back to his wallowing in the dirty mire of Locofocoism, they have dropped him "like a hot potato." In the Louisville Journal of the 24th [August] after giving a decided expression in opposition to Douglas, it makes the following indorsement of Mr. Lincoln:

The pretensions of Mr. Lincoln are of a very different order. He is unquestionably a very talented man, able to cope with any Democrat he may meet in the Senate. If we are correctly informed, he has always been eminently conservative and was a most thorough Whig till the breaking up of that party. But the union of the opposition is a national necessity which greatly outweighs any single man's pretensions. Mr. L's talents, character, and position will give him much influence, if he chooses to exercise it, in bringing about that union.—Will he so use his influence? If the opposition should unite and nominate a slave-holding American, like Crittenden or Bell, or a slave-holding Whig, like Rives, of Virginia, or Graham of North Carolina, will Mr. Lincoln support the nomination? If he will thus promise, we do not see how Americans and Whigs can withhold from him a zealous support. We had supposed him to be an impracticable abolitionist or something near it from the representation of his views made by Douglas in his Chicago speech; but after reading the speech of Lincoln at Chicago and Springfield, we find he has been most grossly misrepresented by Douglas. He merely insists that slavery shall be confined in its present Territorial limits, a theory, which although wrong, is of no practical import, as climate will effectually do that without the aid of law. He fully concedes the right of each State to regulate slavery for itself, and denounces the idea of any aggression upon slaveholders within the States. If the Democracy is to be defeated and another party placed in power, as every opposition man hopes, the policy of electing a Senator who will sustain that other party is too obvious to need comment.

The second joint debate at Freeport, far in the northwestern corner of Illinois, took place before 15,000 people who stood in "weather chilly and damp." The Chicago Times said there was a leak in the roof of the platform where they spoke and it seemed confined to the spot where Lincoln stood, "his boots glistening with the dampness." The Chicago Tribune's Joseph Medill said that Lincoln, over the opposition of some of his friends, asked Douglas that day: "Can the people of a United States Territory, in any lawful way, against the wish of any citizen of the United States, exclude slavery from its limits prior to the formation of a State constitution?" This is how the Illinois State Journal, Springfield, on Aug. 30, 1858, reported the Freeport debate.

Correspondence of the Illinois State Journal

THE GREAT DEBATE
AT FREEPORT
BETWEEN LINCOLN AND DOUGLAS

Immense Concourse of People.

Douglas "trotted through" and "brought to his milk."

FREEPORT, *Stephenson County,*
August, 27 1858.

Eds. Journal:—This has been a grand day for Lincoln and a glorious one for the Republican cause. The great discussion between Lincoln and Douglas has resulted in the overwhelming discomfiture of the "little giant." He was completely wiped out and annihilated. To use his own choice vernacular, he was thoroughly "trotted through." Lincoln "brought him to his milk" in a most triumphant manner.

I have not time before the mail closes to go into the details of the discussion but the crowd was immense numbering altogether upwards of twenty thousand, and four fifths of them good and staunch Lincoln men. They came in their might from all the surrounding counties. Carroll county mustered several thousand strong. Joe Daviess sent over nine car loads including the Lincoln club of Galena. Large delegations came in from Rockford and other points, and all with their banners and bands and music.

Douglas arrived the night before the discussion but met with a poor reception. Lincoln came in on the morning train from Amboy at 10 o'clock. Full five thousand strong received him at the depot and escorted him to the hotel where he made a short speech which set the crowd in a blaze of enthusiasm. He was several times afterwards called out by the various delegations, who as they arrived, paraded in quest of his quarters to pay their respects to him.

At two o'clock P.M. he was wheeled to the place appointed for the speaking in a cannestoga wagon, drawn by six white horses. A tremendous hurrah went up as the crowd joined in the procession and march, the music playing and the flags and banners waving in all directions. Douglas was to have been driven out in a splendid six horse coach, but when he saw Lincoln's equipments, he backed out of the arrangement.

What shall I say of the speaking? Lincoln made a most powerful speech, and charged home upon Douglas with a vengeance which was perfectly overwhelming. There was no escape from the coils which Lincoln wound around him, and his speech in reply was without spirit, without power and labored throughout. His platitudes about amalgamation and nigger equality—his only political stock in trade—were too old, too stupid to be listened to with patience. Lincoln's half hour rejoinder was admirable, and clinched the argument of the first speech so that Douglas fairly squirmed under the infliction. At the close, cheer after cheer for Lincoln rent the air in prolonged shouts. The whole crowd seemed, with one voice, to join in the enthusiasm for "Old Abe," while Douglas crawled off to his quarters like a whipped spaniel.

At night, and now while I write, a tremendous meeting is being held in front of the Hotel, and Lovejoy is making a speech every word of which brings the blood from the negroites. The Douglas followers tried to get up a meeting at the Court House, but failed. I close as I commenced, by saying this has been a grand day for Lincoln and a glorious one for the cause.—It is thought that Douglas, sick of his seven appointments, will decline to meet Lincoln in any further debate. If he will only keep on the track, every meeting will make hundreds of votes for us.

On the question of slavery in a United States Territory, which Lincoln propounded to Douglas in the Freeport debate, a Southern view of the crucial issue appeared in the Louisville Journal, reprinted in the Chicago Tribune of Sept. 4, 1858.

THE LOUISVILLE JOURNAL ON DOUGLAS AND LINCOLN—OPINION OF THE HOME ORGAN OF HENRY CLAY

The Louisville *Journal* has received Douglas' Freeport speech, and to the Senator's new averment that slavery may be kept out of the Territories by the refusal of the local legislatures to pass police laws for its protection, in spite of the authoritative mandate of the Constitution and the Supreme Court, thus replies:

Mr. Lincoln, though doubtless far from approving this answer, will probably deem it more satisfactory than Senator Douglas's Southern Democratic friends are likely to think it. We ask these gentlemen, plainly, what they *do* think of it. Is it good Southern doctrine? Is it good law? Is it statesmanlike? Is it even in conformity with that system of public ethics which obtains among nations tolerably civilized? Saying nothing of historic prestige—spawn of Senator Douglas's own brain as it is—is it comparable, in honesty, or dignity, or expediency, or any other quality which might palliate or redeem a grave error, to Mr. Lincoln's position on the same question? Most certainly it is not. A more silly, disgusting exhibition of ignorance and duplicity was never made by a man of respectable pretensions. According to Senator Douglas, the Territorial Legislatures, though prohibited by the Constitution from abolishing slavery within their respective jurisdictions, may lawfully abstain from enforcing the rights of slaveholders, and so extinguish the institution by voluntary neglect. In other words, Senator Douglas contends that the Territorial Legislatures may lawfully evade the Constitution by deliberately omitting to protect the rights which it establishes. He holds that the people of the Territories may lawfully abolish slavery indirectly, though the Constitution forbids them to abolish or prohibit it directly. It is impossible to conceive of squatter sovereignty in a more contemptible shape than this. It is the scurviest possible form of the scurviest of all possible heresies. A refinement, moreover, is added to the enormity of the fact that the Dred Scott decision, to which Senator Douglas constantly parades his allegiance, expressly precludes the whole thing. The opinion of the Court in that case denies the right of the Territorial Legislatures to refuse protection to slavery as distinctly as it denies their right to abolish or prohibit it. "And if the Constitution," says the Court, "recognizes the right of property of the master in a slave, and makes no distinction between that description of property and other property owned by a citizen, no tribunal, acting under the authority of the United States, whether *LEGISLATIVE, Executive or Judicial, has a right to draw such a distinction, or DENY to it the benefit of the provisions and guarantees which have been provided for the protection of private property against the encroachments of the Government.*" The doctrine finds as little warrant in the late famous opinion of the Supreme Court as in law or morals or the dictates of a fair and wise statesmanship. It has no basis either in reason or authority. It is utterly and astoundingly false. No friend to the constitutional rights of the South or to manly public dealing can or will tolerate it for an instant. It is a most vile and miserable and unmitigable heresy. Senator Douglas, in publicly espousing it, goes several lengths beyond the most intense and passionate Republican in the whole North. He rushes in where Mr. Lincoln and his colleagues scorn to tread.

Mr. Lincoln's position on this point has the merit of openness if not justness. Indeed, as compared with that of his adroit but short-sighted and unscrupulous antagonist, it possesses merits considerably more substantial than simple frankness. While taking sound national ground on every other important point of the "vexed question," Mr. Lincoln avows his belief "in the right and duty of Congress to prohibit slavery in all the United States Territories." We consider this an error, involving, theoretically at least, very grievous injustice to the citizens of the slaveholding States. It is undoubtedly a serious error, regarded in itself. Yet every impartial mind must perceive and admit that it is the pink of truth and justice compared with the wretched doctrine announced by Senator Douglas. In the name of common sense and common fairness, if slavery is to be prohibited or abolished in the Territories by any legislative tribunal, let it be done by one in which the whole nation is represented, and not by one composed of the representatives of the first stragglers from some over-burdened city or restless border State who happen to squat on the public domain. If slavery is to be prohibited in the Territories by legislation at all, let it be done by the people of the United States, and not by the first handful of nomadic settlers in the Territories themselves. If we must have any sovereignty in the case, apart from the Constitution, give us the sovereignty of the American people, not squatter sovereignty in its most detestable and unwarrantable shape. Senator Douglas, as we have seen, gives us the latter—Mr. Lincoln the former. Between the two, no intelligent, discerning patriot can hesitate a moment. Mr. Lincoln's position, aside from its virtually speculative cast, is infinitely less unfriendly to the constitutional rights and just interests of the South. When, furthermore, we reflect that the Supreme Court has pronounced this identical position unconstitutional, and would infallibly nullify any Congressional legislation in pursuance of it, the practical consequence of Mr. Lincoln's error vanishes into all but nothing. It becomes a harmless crotchet—a political dream. But if it were as vital as it is lifeless, it would be immeasurably less pernicious than the reckless and shameless heresy of Douglas. It would be difficult, in fact, to imagine a doctrine on the subject that would not be. Abolitionism itself, as respects the Territories, has never, in its highest fury, assumed such radical and scandalous ground as Senator Douglas took in his Freeport speech. Garrison, with all his fanatical and demoniacal hatred of slavery, has never in his whole life uttered an opinion at once so insulting and injurious to the South. The force of unscrupulous Northern demagogism seems spent in this last expedient o fthe unscrupulous little demagogue of Illinois.

This is a Southern view of the matter at issue; but it is out-spoken honest and significant of more to follow. The [Louisville] *Journal* concludes its lengthy article on the Illinois canvass as follows:

We can hardly be mistaken in thinking that this somewhat unexpected development will strike our political friends in Illinois as something more than significant. We shall be mistaken if they do not consider it decisive, and promptly throw aside whatever imperfect, half-formed sympathies with Senator Douglas they may have hitherto entertained. Such sympathies, if they exist, or have existed, must now be curdled into the sourest aversion and disgust.

"Abraham, of Sangamon," in this vicious and fantastic editorial in the Chicago Times, is compared to Titus Oates, the English imposter who fomented agitation against an alleged Popish Plot whereby Roman Catholics were pledged to massacre Protestants and burn London. Lord Macauley's description of Oates—"his forehead low as that of a baboon"—is applied to Lincoln. From the Chicago Times, Sept. 2, 1858.

THE MODERN OATES

In the year 1678 the island of Great Britain was the scene of vast confusion, strife, bloodshed and murder. A man who had neither position, character, or respect for truth, who had been, by public consent, consigned to a social as well as political condition appropriate to his merits, rose up, and by an appeal to the lower and baser passions and prejudices of the people, made himself the lion of a few years, and was the instrument, during that time, of the judicial murder of some of the purest as well as most exalted men of that age. The name of this man was Titus Oates, and the reader of English history will search in vain for his equal in all that was mendacious, avaricious, and infamous. The days in which he lived, and in which he deceived and misled the hearts and the power of a whole people, were days of unusual excitement. Men in those days lived in fear and trembling, not knowing when they retired at night who would be in power when the next day dawned; and Oates, taking advantage of the feverish excitement of the age, put into practice a system of defamation which in this year 1858, has been taken up by men in Illinois, not like Oates for the purpose of sacrificing life, but for none the less malicious and corrupt object of destroying character, breaking down reputation, and elevating themselves to power and to place. The Oates of 1678 took advantage of an excitement in religious matters to proclaim the wonderful discovery of a number of terrible "conspiracies," and in all these conspiracies he swore were concerned all the men high and low who he thought stood in the way of his own dishonorable ends, or whose downfall would prove gratifying to the low besotted minds of the revengeful and fanatical.

In Abraham Lincoln we have an Oates of the present day: he comes before the people, book in hand, proclaiming that he has discovered divers extraordinary "conspiracies," having for their object the demoralization of the government; the destruction of the Constitution; the subversion of the freedom of the people; the enslaving of thousands of freemen; the overthrow of the State governments and their utter extinction under the feet of arbitrary federal power; the prostitution of the army and navy to enforce obedience to the mandates of the slave driver, and the merciless sacrifice of the lives of men, women and children upon the once happy fields of the National Territories. We have not enumerated one-tenth of the awful things contemplated to be accomplished by the "conspirators," whose horrid designs have been brought to light by Abraham, of Sangamon. Our readers have heard and have read his disclosures; they rival those of Oates; nothing in all that Oates discovered was more horrible or treasonable than that discovered by Lincoln; the most material difference is that while Oates charged his "conspirators," among other crimes, with a design upon the life of the King, Lincoln charges his "conspirators" not only with a design upon the lives of unoffending, peaceable people, but with having instigated, set on foot, and consummated the brutal murder of men, the terrible and horrifying violation of women, the slaughter of helpless babes, and the wanton destruction of property—all in Kansas!

The actions of the two men, Oates and Lincoln, correspond in other particulars. Oates had been a clergyman, enjoying the respect and confidence of the people and of his superiors, but because of his mis-conduct in office, he had been ejected and had become an outcast. Lincoln was once elected to Congress, but by his treasonable speeches, his unpatriotic course, his general betrayal of the rights and honor of his country— his immediate constituents sickened of him, and before his time had half expired elected a Democrat to fill the place he had disgraced. Macaulay, speaking of Oates' discoveries of conspiracies, says—"the public mind was so sore and excitable that these lies readily found credit with the vulgar." Oates soon became a hero. . . .

Early last spring, Lincoln, ambitious to emerge from the political obscurity into which he had been sunk by his former conduct in public life, made a speech in Madison county, in which he hinted at various "conspiracies" which he would be too happy to disclose if a proper consideration was offered. At the Republican State convention, in June last, that consideration was offered, he was nominated for the Senate, and hardly had the applause that followed that nomination died away, when he took the witness stand, and repeated his foul charges of "conspiracy." He accused Douglas, Buchanan, Toucey, Floyd, Cass, Cobb, Brown,

Black, and Thompson, Taney, Daniel, Grier, Wayne, Catron, Campbell, and Nelson, Pierce, Marcy, Guthrie, Davis, Cushing, Dobbin, McClelland, and Campbell, with having villanously entered into a conspiracy to overturn the Constitution of the United States, force African slavery into every State in the Union, and curse the people of all the States with all the powers of a brutal and tyrannical despotism. We need not repeat the thousand details of this fictitious story, nor how the conspirators are identified with and made responsible for all the outrages and villanies, real and imaginary, which have been located in Kansas. The object of Mr. Lincoln, like that of Oates, was to impose upon the vulgar, and the leading Republicans, like the magistrates of England, believe, or pretend to believe, his fictions. The charge of conspiracy is the whole stock in trade of the arrant adventurer. He seeks notoriety and position, and to hide his own former ingnominious course behind the portentous cloud of some mysterious conspiracy. As Oates, the outcast and disgraced clergyman, was forgotten in the Patriot, who disclosed conspiracies and denounced the conspirators, so Lincoln, the repudiated and scorned ex-Congressman, hopes to rise into notorious consequence by exposing conspiracies and denouncing conspirators. Though Oates' stories were all eventually proven to be false, and he was punished therefor still, for the time, they served his purpose, and by them he accomplished his ends, and Lincoln, hoping a like success, cares very little for the universal condemnanation which he knows will fall upon him in the future, provided, like Oates, he can swim at once into power and enjoy the ill-gotten proceeds of his infamous defamation.

As Oates had his imitators, so has Lincoln! While Lincoln was belaboring his sides, and making the prairies wild with his wretched distortions of grammar in talking about conspiracies and conspirators, one Lyman Trumbull, envious of that notoriety which Lincoln enjoyed and which to use Macaulay's words, "has for low and bad minds all the attractions of glory," also rose up, and he, too, had further and fouler and more wicked conspiracies to expose, and by a strange coincidence, the same men whom Lincoln had denounced as conspirators, were also denounced by Trumbull; and as Oates and Carstairs were followed by one "Bedloe, a noted swindler," so were Lincoln and Trumbull followed by Carpenter; and as the brothels of London poured out their hundreds of false witnesses against the alleged conspirators of 1678, so the Federal offices of Illinois in 1858 have poured out their false witnesses, all striving and laboring to out do the original discoverer in the infamy of their accusations and the shamelessness of their falsehoods. Everywhere, all over the State, the men who mistake notorirty [sic] for honor, are belching forth their accusations of conspiracy; nay, in imitation of the villain who testified that he stood behind a door and heard the Queen of England consent to the assassination of her husband, Lyman Trumbull swears that he stood inside the Senate Chamber and saw the conspirators perform an act of treason, and he heard one of them confess it was the result of a "conspiracy," yet for two years this immaculate witness, this wretched imitator of the followers of Oates kept the knowledge of the fact to himself, and did not dare to make it public until he feared Lincoln would enjoy all the infamous notoriety attaching to his false testimony of "conspiracies." These men seek to destroy their opponents by this worn-out, absurd, and flimsiest of all flimsy accusations—conspiracy. It is the burden of all their harangues. Lincoln, Neagle, Trumbull, Carpenter, Lovejoy and Fitch—all talk about conspiracies and conspirators, and like Oates and his followers, each endeavors to excel his companions in the malignity as well as falsehood of his allegations.

We have styled Lincoln the Oates of the day. Who that has ever seen Lincoln will not realize the following description of Oates, which we quote from Macaulay: "his legs uneven as those of a badger, his forehead low as that of a baboon, his purple cheeks, and his monstrous length of chin had been familiar to all who frequented the courts of law." We intend no personal disrespect to Mr. Lincoln by quoting the description, but as he has resorted for his own personal ends to the measures rendered infamous in past days by the villain Oates, we have thought that our review of his conduct would be more complete by giving a description of the personal appearance of the man he had chosen to imitate.

We cannot close without reminding our readers that after enjoying a feast such as vampyres might be supposed to delight in, Oates and all his imitators met gloomy, horrible ends—scorned and despised while living, reviled and made infamous in history. They lived long enough to see their falsehoods exposed, and to taste those pains which an outraged public opinion visited upon their iniquities. A like fate awaits the witnesses of the present day—the "conspiracies" have been proved to be works of imagination, and the witnesses who have sought to blacken and destroy the honor and reputation of others, are already beginning to feel that deep horror and detestation which the people of Illinois entertain for the false and malicious accuser, the mean and disreputable slanderer and villifier of men who have, and will forever enjoy, the esteem and admiration of the nation.

This dispute over what was said and reported continued throughout the debates. The fourth, at Charleston, caused diverse opinions on Lincoln and Negro equality. Interestingly, the Illinois State Journal, Sept. 28, 1858, uses the phrase "eminent conservatism" to describe Lincoln's speeches.

HOW THEY LIE!

In the [Springfield] *Register* of yesterday we find dished up in characteristic hobgoblin style a chapter setting forth what that sheet calls Mr. Lincoln's negro equality proclivities. The following is a paragraph:

> The immortal Lincoln, *having launched forth upon the doctrine of equality,* renders it necessary to call in all the diversified talent in the country to establish the same.

In the Chicago *Times*, Douglas' Northern organ, in its issue of the 24th [September] takes the other *chute* and dishes up a chapter proving that Lincoln believes just the reverse of the above. It asks—

> What said Lincoln at Charlestown? Why, that the negro was created by the Almighty *the inferior and subordinate of the white man;* that he should not be made even a voter in Illinois; that he ought to be kept in the condition of subordination and *servitude* so long as he shall wear a black face!—*Chicago Times 24th.*

The *Register* and the *Times* will observe that there is a barefaced and emphatic lie out between them—a lie which honest journalists would not be guilty of.

The object of these contradictory electioneering falsehoods against Mr. Lincoln is very apparent. The *Times* seeks to divert votes from Mr. Lincoln in the northern part of the State, by making it appear that he is an ultra pro-slaveryist, while the *Register* attempts a similar game here in the center by its senseless twaddle about "negro equality."

The mendacity and meanness of Mr. Douglas' two hand organs as above exhibited is loathsome to all honest men. So far from its accomplishing what was intended, it will only disgust decent Democrats with their party and make votes for Lincoln, whose eminent conservatism is known to all who have read his speeches.

The fifth debate took place on the Knox College campus in Galesburg. This is how they saw the candidates and the pageantry of the day, as described by Jason Sherman, editor of the Free Democrat, Galesburg, Oct. 8, 1858.

"Great out pouring of people. Twenty thousand persons present."

The expectations of all parties were far surpassed in the results of Thursday. The crowd was immense notwithstanding the remarkable heavy rains of the day previous, and the sudden change during the night to a fierce blowing, cutting wind, which lasted during the whole day, ripping and tearing banners and sending signs pell mell all over the town.

At early dawn our gunners announced the opening day and at an early hour the people began to pour in from every direction in wagons, on horseback and on foot.

ARRIVAL OF DOUGLAS

At about ten o'clock the Burlington train arrived with Mr. Douglas and a large delegation of both Douglas and Lincoln men from the West.

Mr. Douglas was escorted to the Bancroft house when a portion of the students from Lombard presented him with a beautiful banner. A well prepared, but somewhat fulsome address was made on its delivery by George Elwell, who was followed by two young ladies, each with a symbolic address, the whole of which we could not catch.

Mr. Douglas responded with great felicity and his friends were well satisfied with their part in the performance. The banner was a "true circle" of silk, with a beautifully embroidered wreath within which was inscribed: "Presented to Stephen A. Douglas by the students of Lombard College." The speaker said the circle was emblematic of Mr. Douglas' course. So it was, in a different sense than that meant by them.

Mr. Douglas was then escorted to the Bonny House, where a large multitude of all parties gathered to see and shake hands with him.

DELEGATION MEETS LINCOLN

At twelve o'clock the republicans with the military went to meet Lincoln, who was to come in with the Knoxville delegation. Hard by two they reached the place of rendezvous, when the delegation came along "mammoth" would not describe it. It was like one of Sylvanus Cobb's tales, of monstrous length and "to be continued."

Lincoln was escorted to the house of Henry R. Sanderson, when a reception speech was made by T. G. Frost, and the most beautiful banner of the day prepared by the ladies of Galesburg, was presented by Miss Ada Hurd. It was an American shield handsomely embroidered. Upon one side was the inscription: "Presented to the Hon. A. Lincoln by the Republican Ladies of Galesburg, Oct. 7th, 1858." On the reverse was the Declaration of Independence upon a scroll executed with a pen by a Mr. Clark of Peoria. Miss Hurd, who is of a queenly appearance, rode up at the head of a troop of equestrians and receiving the banner from the attendant presented it in a very neat and well spoken address. Mr. Lincoln's remarks in reply were very happy. It was the most beautiful ceremony of the day.

A banner was also presented Mr. Lincoln by the students of Lombard University.

THOUSANDS FROM ABROAD

By this time the delegations of both parties began to come in strong. Mercer turned a large delegation for Douglas as well as a large one for Lincoln; but Wataga, Henderson and the adjoining villages bore off the palm for numbers, their delegation alone being over half a mile in length.

Monmouth sent up a rousing delegation for Lincoln. Someone down there is great for crayon sketches, as the banners of this delegation were of the most amusing kind:

First, came one inscribed The Monmouth Glee Club.

Second, a crayon sketch of Douglas and Toombs modifying, in which Douglas with pen in hand is erasing the clause referring the Kansas Constitution back to the people.

Third, a representation of Jim Davidson, his head just stricken from his shoulders. In a scroll Jim learns that it is one hundred eighty-four miles to Monmouth.

Fourth, "Doug at Freeport," "my platform," in which Douglas stands "reversed" upon the Dred Scott platform, one leg of which is giving out beneath.

Fifth, "Coming from Egypt," in which Douglas, roaring with rage, is being punched up with Lincoln's cane.

Other banners in that delegation we have not time to notice.

Of the notable banners in the procession we observed the following: A representation of the capitol and over the door Douglas' complaint (he's got my place). Douglas is turning away, while Lincoln is coming in.

A representation of a two-donkey act, or Douglas attempting to ride "Popular Sovereignty" and "Dred Scott." His straddle is remarkable but not equal to the task, as both animals, kicking up their heels, send him a-sprawling.

"Knox College goes for Lincoln" stretched across the south front and on the north end of the college building: We will subdue Stephen A. Douglas.

"Abe Lincoln, the Champion of Freedom." Upon this banner was also a portrait of Long Abe.

MEETINGS IN THE EVENING

In the evening Hon Archibald Williams of Quincy addressed the republicans at Dunn's hall, in a speech of great power. It was one of the most telling of the campaign. As a by-stander remarked: "There are more brains in his skillet than all the rest put together."

He was followed by Captain Prentiss of the same place in a brilliant effort.

The Monmouth Republican Glee Club enlivened the evening with some of the most laughable songs, ground out by one of their number, who gets them up to suit the time. One was written after the speeches of the day were over, and portrayed the manner in which Lincoln shaved Douglas in the most side-splitting style.

The club is said to be making more republicans in the country than all the stumpers put together. [Judge Douglas' speech followed]

The candidates faced each other for the last time in the middle of October, 1858, at Alton. Lincoln summed up his seven debates in these words: "I have said and I repeat it here, that if there be a man amongst us who does not think that the institution of slavery is wrong in any one of the aspects of which I have spoken, he is misplaced and ought not to be with us. . . . That is the real issue. That is the issue that will continue in this country when these poor tongues of Judge Douglas and myself shall be silent. It is the eternal struggle between these two principles—right and wrong—throughout the world. . . . No matter in what shape it comes, whether from the mouth of a king who seeks to bestride the people of his own nation and live by the fruit of their labor, or from one race of men as an apology for enslaving another race, it is the same tyrannical principle." The reverberations of these words echoed across the land. In Concord, New Hampshire,

Lincoln was heard—as noted on Election Day, Nov. 2, 1858, in the Illinois Journal, Springfield.

MR. LINCOLN—WHAT IS THOUGHT
OF HIM ABROAD

In the last number of the Concord (N.H.) *Independent Democrat,* we find a graphic and unbiassed resume of the late contest in this State. We extract from it the following handsome compliment to the Hon. ABRAHAM LINCOLN:

> As an outsider, with many personal sympathies for Douglas, we have carefully read the reports of the speeches of these chosen champions of "Douglas Democracy" and Republicanism. And we are compelled to the conclusion that in Abraham Lincoln, Stephen A. Douglas finds his equal and his superior, as a skillful debater and as an orator. If Douglas has fulfilled the expectations of his friends and excited their enthusiasm, Lincoln has excited an equal enthusiasm among the Republicans and displayed a degree of ability far exceeding the most sanguine expectations of those who expected most of him. His meetings have every where been thronged by immense audiences whose enthusiasm has been almost unbounded. From being regarded, as he was at the outset of the campaign, the equal of Douglas and the standard bearer of the Republican army, he is now looked upon as the "embodiment" of the whole contest. And whatever shall be the result of the election, which takes place in Illinois next Tuesday, Abraham Lincoln will emerge from the smoke of the battle covered with honors.

In reference to the result of the battle, the *Democrat* makes the following remarks:

> What the result will be, it is useless to predict. The "National Democracy" are evidently nowhere except in the Post Offices and other receptacles of desperate spoilsmen. The rank and file of the party are with Douglas. The contest is between the Republicans and the Douglasites, and one of these parties must win the field. The Republicans are active, and confident of success. They feel sure of electing their State ticket. But, owing to an iniquitous apportionment by which the Northern half of the State is shorn of almost half its proper strength, the Legislature is far from being sure for the Republicans. We shall not be surprised should Douglas succeed

in securing a majority friendly to his re-election. Should Douglas succeed he will be thereby the installed chief of a "faction" in the Democratic party. Should he fail, it is difficult to see how he can rise again very soon. In either event Slave Democracy will be damaged, and Republican principles be strengthened. In either event, Illinois is severed from her ancient alliance with the South, and may hereafter be counted on, as immovably committed to Republican Freedom.

"Lincoln is beaten." He received more votes of the people than Douglas. But because of the districting and holdover Senators, Douglas was elected, 54 to 41, on the first ballot of the Illinois legislature. Lincoln's strong friend, the Chicago Tribune, Nov. 10, 1858, saw a new standard of Republicanism emerging from defeat, with Lincoln as spokesman.

ABRAHAM LINCOLN

Mr. Lincoln is beaten. Though Presidential management and the treachery of pretended friends may prevent Mr. Douglas' return, Mr. Lincoln cannot succeed. We know of no better time than the present to congratulate him on the memorable and brilliant canvass that he has made. He has fully vindicated the partialities of his friends, and has richly earned, though he has not achieved, success.

He has created for himself a national reputation that is both envied and deserved; and though he should hereafter fill no official station, he has done in the cause of Truth and Justice, what will aways entitle him to the gratitude of his party and to the admiration of all who respect the high moral qualities and the keen, comprehensive, and sound intellectual gifts that he has displayed. No man could have done more. His speeches will become landmarks in our political history; and we are sure that when the public mind is more fully aroused to the importance of the themes which he has so admirably discussed, the popular verdict will place him a long way in advance of the more fortunate champion by whom he has been overthrown.

The Republicans owe him much for his truthfulness, his courage, his self-command, and his consistency; but the weight of their debt is chiefly in this: that, under no temptation, no apprehension of defeat, in compliance with no solicitation, has he let down our standard in the least. That God-given and glorious principle which is the head and front of Republicanism, "All men are created equal, and are entitled to life, liberty and the pursuit of happiness," he has steadily upheld, defended, illustrated and applied in every speech which he has made. Men of his own faith may have differed with him when measures only were discussed; but the foundation of all—the principle which comprehends all—he has fought for with a zeal and courage that never flagged or quailed. In that was the pith and marrow of the contest.

Mr. Lincoln, at Springfield at peace with himself because he has been true to his convictions, enjoying the confidence and unfeigned respect of his peers, is more to be envied than Mr. Douglas in the Senate! Long live Honest Old Abe!

Chapter 4

A National Man

NOVEMBER 1858–MAY 1860

From his defeat in the Senatorial campaign of '58, Lincoln emerged as a man of national importance. The highest office he had held was United States Representative, and that for only a term which could in fairness be called undistinguished. But the debates with Senator Douglas, an important leader of the Democratic party, had received national attention. They focused on the issue of the extension of slavery and of the "institution" itself, factors which went to the heart of the rapidly expanding economy of the country and the morality of its people. Lincoln had articulated the thoughts of the many elements making up the Republican party.

The people in the nation could ponder the words spoken by Douglas during the sixth debate at Quincy: "Let each state mind its own business and let its neighbors alone! If we will stand by that principle, then Mr. Lincoln will find that this great republic can exist forever divided into free and slave states." The question of rights had been debated three quarters of a century, from the days of Jefferson and Adams, and Lincoln had put it in plain words for his time: "The Democracy of today hold the liberty of one man to be absolutely nothing, when in conflict with another man's right of property. Republicans, on the contrary, are for both the man and the dollar; but in cases of conflict, the man before the dollar." Such reasoning could not be ignored, only postponed.

The opinion makers were thinking ahead to '60. The man credited as the first to put it in writing before the people was Jeriah Bonham, editor of the *Illinois Gazette*, Lacon, Ill. He had heard Lincoln on the stump as a Clay elector in '44 and heard him again at Peoria in '54 speaking against the repeal of the Missouri Compromise. Hastily penning his ideas as his newspaper went to press, Bonham wrote the first "Lincoln for President" editorial for the Nov. 4, 1858, issue.

ABRAHAM LINCOLN FOR PRESIDENT IN 1860

The contest just closed, and the glorious result of yesterday's election, showing by the popular vote that Illinois is redeemed from Democratic domination . . . although the Legislature will be Democratic by reason of the unfair apportionment of the state . . . by a former Democratic Legislature, in gerrymandering the state, . . . thus insuring the election of Democrats to the Legislature and thwarting the will of the people, by securing the reelection to the Senate . . . of Stephen A. Douglas to misrepresent them for six years more from the 4th of March next, instead of Abraham Lincoln, the orator and statesman, whom the popular voice has declared should be entitled to that high office.

To him, the Republican standard-bearer, their chosen leader in the brilliant and glorious contest just closed, we are indebted for this glorious result.

The masterly manner in which he conducted the canvass, both in the joint discussions with Douglas, and his grand speeches made to the people in all parts of the state, has attracted the attention of the whole country and the world to the man that gave utterance to the sublimest truths yet enunciated, as principles now adopted as the future platform of the Republican party, and marks him as the leading statesman of the age, possessing the confidence of the people in his flexible honesty, and his fitness to lead the people in yet other contests, in which the field will be the nation, and his leadership to conduct the hosts of freedom to victory in 1860. What man now fills the full measure of public expectation as the statesman of to-day and of the near future, as does Abraham Lincoln? And in writing our own preference for him, we believe we but express the wish of a large majority of the people that he should be the standard-bearer of the Republican party for the Presidency in 1860.

We know there are other great names that will be presented for this great honor—names that have a proud prominence before the American people—but in statesmanship Lincoln is the peer of the greatest of them.

There are McLean, Seward, Chase, Bates, Cameron, and possibly others who will be presented before the convention meets, and their friends will urge their claims with all the pertinacity that devoted friendship and political interests may dictate, and their claims as available candidates will be fully canvassed. And possibly they possess all these in an eminent degree; but Abraham Lincoln more so, both as to eminent statesmanship and also availability. . . .

In the next campaign of 1860 the issues are already sharply defined. These will be, as they have been in our state canvass, slavery and slavery extension on the one hand, and freedom and free territory on the other. Douglas will lead the cohorts of slavery. Lincoln should lead the hosts of freedom in this "irrepressible conflict." Who has earned the proud position as well as he? as he is in himself the embodiment and exponent of our free institutions. These two men have fought the battles over the plains of Illinois. What so proper as their being the champions of the two principles on the national field?

The attitude of Greeley of the New York Tribune was respectful of Lincoln the defeated candidate—plus the usual advice on what Lincoln might have done. Lincoln had shown great patience and respect during the campaign, saying at one point, "Greeley denies that he directly is taking part in favor of Douglas, and I believe him. Still his feeling constantly manifests itself in his paper, which, being so extensively read in Illinois, is, and will continue to be, a drag upon us." From the New York Tribune, Nov. 17, 1858.

The Republicans of Illinois fought their late battle under serious disadvantages. In the first place, they knew, and the whole State knew, that a majority of the Republicans of other States believed it would have been wiser not to contest the return of those Members of Congress who had from first to last opposed the Lecompton imposture, as every Democrat from Illinois did. Though the knowledge of this fact did not shake their purpose, it could not fail to relax in some degree their energies. They must have felt the want of a hearty and perfect sympathy on the part of their brethren outside of their borders. The "floating vote"— that is, the vote of that considerable number who have no decided, no settled convictions with respect to the great question of the day— would naturally go against them. To have polled so large a vote, and secured such a majority under the circumstances, are achievements of which the Republicans of Illinois may well be proud. The Legislature is against them, as the U. S. Senate will be, with five to four of the Representatives in Congress, but the popular verdict, the popular intelligence, are clearly on their side. The Future is theirs.

It is but natural and just that they should regard with proud affection and gratitude their standard-bearer in the late contest, ABRAHAM LINCOLN. Though their triumph does not enure to his benefit, does not secure him the post which they had assigned him, it was undoubtedly won in good part by his abilities and his exertions. [*Chicago Tribune editorial, "Mr. Lincoln is beaten . . . ," of Nov. 10, 1858, followed. It appears at the end of the previous chapter.—Editor*]

—This is mainly just. Mr. Lincoln's campaign speeches were of a very high order. They were pungent without bitterness and powerful without harshness. The brief address at Springfield in which he opened the canvass is a model of compactness, lucidity and logic. As a condensed statement of the issues which divide the Republicans from the Democrats of our day, it has rarely or never been exceeded. And, throughout the weary months of almost daily discussion or canvassing which followed, Mr. Lincoln's speeches justified the confidence and admiration of his supporters. *The Chicago Times* made its worst mistake in endeavoring to disparage those speeches and representing their author as unqualified to enter the lists with such an antagonist as Douglas.

And yet—since nothing human is quite perfect—we found or fancied in the tenor of Mr. Lincoln's speeches too little attention to the single point on which Mr. Douglas is strong with the unreflecting and undiscerning. We allude of course to "Popular Sovereignty"—the assumption that the inhabitants of a Territory have a natural right to establish as well as to prohibit slaveholding on the soil of that Territory. This assumption is plausible, and naturally commends itself to the thoughtless many who regard slaveholding as a question of convenience and profit merely—an affair of latitude and temperature—having no moral character whatever. "What can be fairer," they triumphantly ask, "than to let each territory decide for itself whether to uphold or reject Slavery?"

To which we make answer:

I. It is decidedly, manifestly fairer to let each person decide for himself, not merely whether to hold slaves or not hold them, but also whether to be a slave or not be one. This is genuine Popular Sovereignty, and Individual Sovereignty as well.

II. In case it were right for a community to decide by a vote whether it should be slaveholding or non-slaveholding, then the class or race who are to be slaves, if there be such, ought clearly to be allowed an equal vote with others. To let A. decide whether B. shall be a slave or not, is not genuine Popular Sovereignty. Mr. Lincoln tersely said at Springfield that the Douglas doctrine of Popular Sovereignty amounted to this—If A. chooses to make B. his slave, C. shall not interfere. But it is really worse than this. It amounts fully to this: A, B. and C. vote to decide whether D, E, F. and G. shall be slaves or freemen; and two of them voting for Slavery to one against it, Slavery is by that vote established. But we say Not so! Let us take the votes of D, E, F, and G, also, and, if they vote (as we know they will) not to be slaves, then Slavery is voted down. Mr. Douglas's Nebraska bill contradicts Mr. Douglas's vaunted principle of Popular Sovereignty, by making one class arbiters of the destiny of another.

III. If the People of a Territory are by vote to establish or reject Slavery, there must be a *time* for so doing. When shall it be? The Cincinnati Platform very clearly fixes the time for taking such vote, *at the formation of a State Constitution*. This demolishes at a blow the phantom of "Popular Sovereignty," as applied to the Territories. It leaves them, at least with regard to Slavery, dependents or wards of the Federal Government, to be allowed to vote when they come of age, and not till then. The Douglas query, "Why should not the People of a Territory freely accept or reject Slavery, as well as those of a State?" is thus blown back into his face. *The Cincinnati Platform* concedes them no such right, and Mr. Douglas ostentatiously plants himself on that Platform.

IV. Suppose it were conceded that a Territory might freely accept or reject Slavery, when should it be at liberty to exercise that power? May the first ten settlers, by a majority vote, establish or exclude Slavery? If not the first ten, may the first twenty? thirty? fifty? one hundred? five hundred? or any other definite number? May the first Territorial Legislature decide this momentous question? If not this, which one? May the decision of this year be upset by a popular vote next year? If not, how then? *And what shall be the law of the Territories respecting Slavery* UNTIL *such decision shall have been made?*

V. How is Popular Sovereignty (of the Douglas stripe) in the Territories to be harmonized with the Dred Scott decision? Or, if you like it better this way, how much room is left for Popular Sovereignty after accepting and indorsing that decision?

—Such are a few of the points we should have pressed, the questions we should have insisted on, had we stood in Mr. Lincoln's place through the late canvass—pressed them not once only, nor casually and incidentally, but in every discussion and every speech, until all but the most besotted partisans should have been made to see that the vaunted doctrine of "Popular Sovereignty," regarded as a solution of the problem of Slavery in the Territories under the Democratic Platform, is an "airy nothing," a juggle, a phantasy, a gross delusion. Mr. Lincoln's speeches were doubtless more attractive to their hearers, far more readable by others, than they would have been had he devoted them mainly to the demolition of Mr. Douglas's castle; yet we believe they might have been rendered more effective by a rigid adherence to the Napoleonic rule of warfare— to be the stronger if possible on the point where the fortune of the day is to be decided, even at the cost of being deplorably weaker, if needful, everywhere else. While we think no man could have upborne the Republican standard more gallantly than Mr. Lincoln has done, it seems to us possible to have done so more skillfully—therefore more effectively. If this criticism seems unkind, we shall regret the misapprehension, not the frankness which impelled it.

Lincoln was a voice heard in the Territory of Kansas as well as in the Empire State. It was the issue of slavery in Kansas which had spurred Lincoln to action against Douglas. "If we lose Kansas to freedom, an example will be set which will prove fatal to freedom in the end," Lincoln had said in 1856 at Bloomington. Now a partisan in Kansas, the Palermo Leader, spoke for him, as reprinted in the Illinois State Journal, Nov. 27, 1858.

The Palermo (Kansas) Leader says:
"For Abraham Lincoln we have full sympathy. By the force of his indomitable intellect, with the support of sound, consistent principles, he has attacked the stronghold of the giant and taken it—he has met the giant in single combat and thrown him. We say thrown him, for whether Stephen A. Douglas has secured his election to the United States Senate by fair means or by foul means, or not, it has been from no confidence of the people of Illinois in the uprightness of his aims, and the man of the opposition has changed the current. If elected by fair means, a sympathy for the good he once did—not for what he is to-day—has determined it. If elected by foul means, an imported vote and Egyptian darkness explain it all."

In Pennsylvania, it was recalled that Lincoln had been a prominent candidate for the Vice Presidency at the Philadelphia Convention in 1856—they saw him now with a reputation "as extensive as the country itself." The Chicago Tribune on Dec. 16, 1858, reprinted the Reading Journal, Pa.

THE REPUBLICANS OF ILLINOIS—
ABRAHAM LINCOLN

From the Reading (Pa.) Journal.

The smoke of the battle has at length cleared away, and we are enabled to ascertain the exact condition of things in this State (Illinois). The Republicans have borne aloft their banner in triumph, and with all the free States (except California,) they are now enrolled on the side of the people, prepared to fight manfully in their behalf. When the first intelligence of the result came over the wires, it was loudly proclaimed that with the success of Douglas the popular vote was largely with his party, and subsequently that he had triumphed over both the Republican party and that of the General Administration. A slight alteration of the figures, however, puts this matter in a different light. It is now ascertained that on the *Congressional ticket*, the Republicans have a majority of the popular vote, over both branches of the Democratic party, (whilst Douglas is in a minority of 9,116 votes,) and that had it not been for the pelting storm with which the Northern part of the State was visited on the day of the election, that majority would have been increased by thousands. . . .

One word in regard to their standard-bearer in this exciting canvass. Though unsuccessful, Mr. Lincoln has made for himself a reputation as a great statesman and popular debater, as extensive as the country itself, whilst his earnest devotion to principle must have won the respect and admiration of the most determined opponents. His name, we perceive, has been mentioned in various parts of the country, in connection with the highest post in the gift of the people. A prominent candidate for the Vice Presidency before the Philadelphia Convention in 1856, it is only needed that, at the proper time, his friends should present an unbroken front for the ablest statesman of the West, and the East will delight to honor the man whose integrity and adherence to principle are as proverbial as his mental endowments have been rendered conspicuous in the brilliant canvass through which he has now just passed.

Three cheers for the Republicans of Illinois, and three times three for their gallant leader.

Republicans all over the West invited Lincoln to their States to speak. In September, 1859, he went to Ohio, where Salmon P. Chase was considered the favorite son candidate for the Republican Presidential nomination the following year. An election was set in Ohio in the fall and since the Democrats had obtained Senator Douglas to speak, the Republicans called on Lincoln. In Cincinnati the battle lines were drawn in the press as in Chicago during the great debates. The Toledo Blade announced that "the able and distinguished champion of Republicanism" was on the way. This is how the pro-Lincoln Daily Commercial of Cincinnati reported his reception on Sept. 17, 1859.

The Hon. ABE LINCOLN, of Illinois, is expected here this evening, and will be received with becoming pomp and circumstance. His political friends propose, we believe, to make his reception equal to that given the Little Giant by the ever faithful Democracy. As we are in the way of lionizing the politicians of Illinois, we see no reason why Mr. LINCOLN should not have as big a turn out as DOUGLAS. He is a very able man, and a droll one, full of facts and a sort of odd wit that takes the crowds immensely. He speaks to-night at Fifth street market place, and will be well worth hearing.

The friends of Senator DOUGLAS are disposed to deny that he is a minority Senator. It is indisputably true, however—that is, it can't be honestly disputed, for the figures show the fact—that the members of the Legislature of Illinois who last winter voted for the Hon. ABRAM LINCOLN for the position of Senator of the United States, received more votes than the members who voted for Mr. Douglas. This has been attributed with some plausibility to the opposition of the Administration to Mr. Douglas. It is our opinion, however, that next to his own extraordinary exertions, and the fact that at that time he occupied a position that commanded the regard of independend men, Senator Douglas owes his late re-election to the Senate to the hostility of the Administration, and the ineffable meanness of the tools of Mr. BUCHANAN in Illinois. Under all the circumstances, however, if the State had been fairly districted, the Hon. Abram Lincoln would have been returned to the Senate of the United States.

SPEECH OF HON. ABR'M LINCOLN
ON THE
EAST PORTICO OF THE CAPITOL, AT
COLUMBUS YESTERDAY

At 3 P.M. yesterday, "Old Abe" Lincoln, as he is called in Illinois, addressed the people assembled from all the countryside at Columbus.

A National Man NOVEMBER 1858–MAY 1860

Abram Lincoln is a dark complexioned man, of a very tall figure, and so exceedingly "well preserved" that he would not be taken for more than thirty eight, though he is rising of fifty years of age. His countenance should be called a very good one; his features are strongly marked, and his general bearing reminds one of Governor Jones, of Tennessee, more, perhaps, than of any other living political celebrity. We don't know his lineage, but he is evidently of the Kentucky "race" of men, and a fine type of that race.

He commenced by remarking that this was the first time he had spoken in Ohio—and he must not forget that this people were accustomed to the intellectural presence and stately eloquence of Senator Chase, the dramatic oratory of Corwin, and the eloquence of other of her favored sons.

He would introduce his speech by reading an introduction prepared for him in advance by the Ohio Statesman of this morning, which said:

"Mr. Lincoln is the man who in the debate with Senator Douglas last year in Illinois, declared himself in favor of negro suffrage."
Mr. Lincoln read from his Ottawa speech—the first pitched battle with Douglas—in which he met the column, in his own State. The extract read was a felicitously constructed argument in favor of the *rights* of all men of whatever height, color or age, without insisting upon the necessity or the propriety of marrying the people whose inaliable rights he declared. He was now fifty years of age and he had never had a black person for a slave nor yet for a wife. When Judge Douglas first insinuated this charge of forming an amalgamation he (Lincoln) had shown that the bleaching process was confined to those States where the institution of Slavery was recognized by law, and where the virtue of the female was as much at the disposal of the master as was her body. He presumed Col. Manypenny, of the Statesman, was an honest man, (groans) and he gave him this public refutation of his charge that he might correct it in his paper before the lapse of time should induce uncharitable people to pronounce the editor of the Statesman a calumniating liar. (Cheers.)

The opposition in Ohio saw Lincoln as an example of the "Western man" but without the profundity of Douglas. These reports are from the pro-Douglas, Democratic Cincinnati Enquirer, published between Sept. 16 and 20, 1859. (The first anecdote about Lincoln, interestingly, was recalled and brought up to date nearly a hundred years afterward by defeated Democratic Presidential candidate Adlai Stevenson after the 1952 election.)

HOW ABE LINCOLN FELT WHEN
ON THE SCAFFOLD

A good anecdote is told of LINCOLN, the Black- Republican Senator of Illinois, who is invited here by his political brethren to make them a speech in opposition to that lately given us by the Little Giant. LINCOLN, like the little bull who stood on the railway track and tried to butt at the engine, and was afterward gathered up along the road in the mixed-up shape of sausage-meat, in "dabs"—as PAT said, when he saw the collision, "Be Jasus, ye've courage, but d——n yer judgment!"—has probably forgotten that the locomotive ran over him in Illinois, and that only a few of his fragments have yet been found. But the anecdote: After fiercely contesting the election with DOUGLAS, and affecting confidence that he would have a Legislature favorable to his election over his formidable competitor, that body met, and the result was considerably against him. A gentleman, when the election was announced, queried with LINCOLN how he felt? Said ABE: "Well, I feel just like the boy who stubbed his toe—too d——d badly hurt to laugh, and to d——d proud to cry!"

ABE will stub his toe here if he comes.

THE LINCOLN MEETING LAST EVENING

The Opposition have been making great preparations all the week to draw together a meeting that would rival that which turned out to greet Senator DOUGLAS on Friday, 9th inst. They sent to Illinois and procured Mr. LINCOLN, DOUGLAS' unsuccessful competitor for the United States Senate, in the hope that his fame, linked as it is with Mr. DOUGLAS, would draw out the masses.

They gave notice of the meeting in all the city journals for a week, and had large bill-posters out for several days. They appointed it in Fifth-street Market-space, on Saturday night, which is the best place and the best night in the week to draw out a large crowd. They fired every cannon in the streets and discharged fireworks from the speaker's stand. Notwithstanding all this work, aided by a fine night, the meeting was not one-quarter as large as that of Mr. DOUGLAS, who came here on short notice, on a different night from that which he had appointed.

We were not disappointed, however, in the comparative smallness of the Opposition gathering. They have not a man in their ranks who begins to possess the celebrity and popularity of Judge Douglas at this time. No man in the Union can draw such immense crowds, by the force of his name and character, as Senator Douglas. Mr. Lincoln, although a man of some ability, is not a very pleasing or impressive speaker, and we think disappointed the expectations of his friends.

AN ADMISSION OF LINCOLN

Lincoln, in his speech to the Republicans last evening, insisted that Senator Douglas was a better and more judicious friend to the South than were the Southern statesmen themselves; he was quite as pro-slavery as the most extreme and ultra Southern men. Those at the South who are abusing Douglas will please make a note of this admission of Lincoln.

THE HARBINGER OF DEFEAT
TO THE REPUBLICANS

If we had any doubts before they are not put at rest by the appearance of Abe Lincoln, who is the harbinger of ill luck to his party, that the Republicans will be defeated on the second Tuesday of October.

RECEPTION OF HON. ABE LINCOLN—HIS ADDRESS
IN FIFTH-STREET MARKET-SPACE
LAST EVENING

Hon. Abe Lincoln, chiefly known here as Douglas' opponent for the Senate in the recent extraordinary campaign in Illinois, arrived in the city at seven o'clock last evening, and was received at the Cincinnati, Hamilton and Dayton Railroad Depot by a number of Republicans, who cheered him loudly and fired a cannon frequently, and then escorted him to the Burnet House, where he shook many hands, and took his tea in very great haste.

At a quarter after eight o'clock he was driven to Fifth-street Market-space in a carriage, accompanied by a number of persons on horseback (many others following on the sidewalks,) arrangements having been made for him to speak from the portico of E. & D. Kinsey's store and dwelling. Quite a crowd was assembled on the square, where bonfires were blazing, rockets whizzing, cannon firing and every effort making to give a show of enthusiasm to the scene. . . .

The President, Benjamin Eggleston, introduced Hon. Abe Lincoln as "the distinguished statesman, the expounder of the Constitution, the opponent of squatter sovereignty and the friend of freedom," when the latter personage went forward and was received with cheers.

MR. LINCOLN'S APPEARANCE AND MANNER.

Hon. Mr. Lincoln is a tall, dark-visaged, angular, awkward, positive-looking sort of individual, with character written in his face and energy expressed in his every movement. He has the appearance of what is called in the North-east a Western man—one who, without education or early advantages, has risen by his own exertions from an humble origin. Indeed, in this respect he resembles Douglas, to whom, however, in largeness of thought, profundity of penetration and excellence of judgment, he is greatly inferior.

Mr. Lincoln was, we believe, originally a flatboatman, and one perceives in him the traces of his early life and profession. He makes no pretension to oratory or the graces of diction, but goes directly to his point, whatever it may be, bent upon uttering his thought, regardless of elegance or even system, as best he can. With orthoepy he evidently has little acquaintance, pronouncing words in a manner that puzzles the ear sometimes to determine whether he is speaking his own or a foreign tongue.

MR. LINCOLN'S ADDRESS.

Calling the crowd by the name of fellow-citizens of Ohio, he said that that was the first time in his life he had appeared before an audience in so large a city, and that therefore he felt somewhat embarrassed.

He had found, however, when one was embarrassed, that the best way to proceed was to go on without thinking what one was to say or do, and he would adopt the method in that instance. [the speech followed]

MR. LINCOLN AND HIS SPEECH

The Honorable ABRAHAM LINCOLN, of Illinois, was in this city on Saturday evening last, and delivered a speech to a large and—conventionally at least—respectable audience. Mr. LINCOLN was received on his arrival at the depot by quite a concourse of our fellow-citizens, anxious to gain a view of so distinguished a personage, was waited upon at the Burnet House—in the words of the *Gazette*—by "some few persons, who desired to show him by personal visit that respect which his honesty and talent has procured for him at home and wherever his name is known," and was welcomed by the expenditure of about the usual quantity of brazen music and villainous saltpeter.

A "verbatim report" of the speech of Mr. LINCOLN was given by our enterprising neighbor of the *Gazette*, in their yesterday's impression. Mr. LINCOLN—so we are informed by the editor of that journal—"is deficient in clap-trap, but *excels in logic and honesty;* and herein" —our contemporary continues—"he differs from Judge DOUGLAS." We thank him for his indorsement.

We have glanced over the speech of Mr. LINCOLN in the *Gazette*. We do not say that we have read it: it is not worth reading. It contains nothing that is calculated to make any man wiser, or more learned; to make him a better citizen or a better man; to give him any insight into the character of the Government, or into his duty as a part of the governing power. It is, in a single expressive word, trash—trash from beginning to end; trash without one solitary oasis to relieve the dreary waste that begins with its nearest and ends with its furthest boundary.

Among public addresses from the stump, the speech of Mr. LINCOLN belongs to the lowest order. It is not the speech of a statesman; it is not the speech of a politician; it is not even the speech of a fair partisan. It is the speech of a pettifogging demagogue, devoted to an uncandid and one-sided discussion of the real or presumed party and doctrinal status of a third person. It is not a business for the display of either logic or honesty, and, therefore—we beg pardon of our cotemporary for disagreeing with him—there is no appearance of those qualities.

We do not propose to review the speech of Mr. LINCOLN. Indeed, there is nothing to review. Its material is the ordinary slip-slop of the Republican party press, interlarded with profane ejaculations, hyperbolical expressions and staring comparisons, to fit it for delivery to a mixed audience. Mr. LINCOLN was a candidate against Mr. DOUGLAS for a seat in the Senate of the United States; and, after a severe contest, was defeated. Upon this fact stands his reputation—all that he ever had; and out of this fact grows his political character. He is the symbol of private and party enmity to the Senator of Illinois, accidentally endowed with voice and personality—owing his entire significance to that antagonism. Without DOUGLAS LINCOLN would be nothing; and this he virtually admits by being nothing but anti-Douglas. At once a parasite and enemy, he labors insanely to destroy that upon which depends his own existence. The speech of Mr. Lincoln was well received. His audience was in excellent humor with itself and with its orator. His remarks were interrupted—as appears by the report—by frequent laughter and applause. One of Mr. Lincoln's strongest points is his propensity to misstate the positions and exaggerate the remarks of his antagonist, in the indulgence of which we observe he was so happy as to bring down the crowd on several occasions. When he told his hearers that "Douglas' popular sovereignty, as a principle, is simply this: 'If one man chooses to make a slave of another man, neither that other man nor any body else has a right to object,'" he was answered with "cheers and laughter." It was undoubtedly received as an excellent joke. As a truth it would not have been at all laughable; we must, therefore, take the applause as a tribute paid to the author's wit at the expense of his credit for veracity. His speech was full of jokes of a similar character—well calculated to reduce to less than nothing the reputation of their utterer as a man of truth and candor. Indeed, it appears that the crowd was not long in finding out its man; for the rambling dialogue between the orator and his hearers into which the speech degenerated indicated well enough the respect in which he had come to be holden, who was not too proud to stand up and utter palpable lies for their amusement.

We do not know but, in what we have said above, we have committed a radical error. We may have brought the address of Mr. Lincoln to a standard for which it was not intended. We have spoken of the gentleman from Illinois as the Hon. Abraham Lincoln: we remember now that by his admirers he is known as Abe and Old Abe Lincoln. Nay, so was he advertised and puffed and placarded around this city during last week: Old Abe was coming—rough old customer—great blackguard—tremendous on the stump—says just what he pleases—be after little Dug with a sharp stick. The idea was that to a good deal of native rudeness and vulgarity of character the aforesaid Abe had added something by assiduous practice—that in choosing among the various known modes to attain unsound popularity, he had chosen the habits of the boor and the vocabulary of the ruffian as best adapted at once to his taste and his capacity; and that he had, to a more than ordinary extent, succeeded in making himself the thing he desired.

Now, we will confess that if this is Mr. Lincoln, the speech was perfectly in character. Every thing is as it should have been; the audience applauded in the right places, and every feature of the transaction was in proper keeping with every other. The orator did as he was expected to do. The crowd was pleased because it got what it expected. It was not the statesman but the mountebank that was wanted. The mountebank came; and the honors were easy.

Lincoln's swing through Ohio was news to Washington, which followed the canvass closely because of the significance of the election there. When the Ohio voters went to the polls the month after Lincoln and Douglas spoke in the State, this time the Republicans won handily. The National Intelligencer of Washington, D.C., was reprinted in the Illinois State Journal, Sept. 28, 1859.

MR. LINCOLN'S CINCINNATI SPEECH

The *National Intelligencer* of the 22nd [September] publishes the Hon. Abraham Lincoln's speech, delivered at Cincinnati on the 17th, and says of it—"Readers of all shades of opinions will peruse with interest the speech, on the topics of the day, made on the 16th at Cincinnati by the Hon. Mr. Lincoln, of Illinois, who so arduously stumped his State last autum[n] as the Republican antagonist of Senator Douglas. Indeed, in his speech, which we now present, the orator handles the honorable Senator's doctrines without gloves."

After the Ohio Republican victory, Lincoln moved to the forefront among candidates for the party nomination scheduled in the spring of 1860. Ever alert to items in the friendly press for the hometown man, the Illinois State Journal of Springfield, first on Oct. 18, 1859, then on Nov. 23, 1859, found publications in Pennsylvania and Connecticut mentioning Lincoln for high office.

A PRESIDENTIAL TICKET

The Lancaster [Pa.] *Examiner and Herald*, the well known old time Whig organ, comes out for Simon Cameron, of Pennsylvania, for President and Abraham Lincoln, of Illinois, for Vice President. It remarks that it is essential to the success of the Republican party in 1860, that they carry Pennsylvania and Illinois, and it thinks with this ticket that our triumph is certain. We think this ticket would suit the Republicans of Illinois better if the names were transposed.

CONNECTICUT FOR MR. LINCOLN

The Norwich [Conn.] Courier, one of the ablest journals in Connecticut, speaks of a strong feeling in that section in favor of the Hon. Abraham Lincoln, of Illinois, for the Presidency or Vice Presidency.

In the same spirit, George D. Prentice, editor of the influential Louisville Journal, Kentucky, noted the Lincoln boom. From the Illinois State Journal, Jan. 18, 1860.

PRENTICE ON LINCOLN.— The Louisville [Ky.] Journal is responsible for the following: "Several papers in the Northwest are strongly recommending the Hon. Abraham Lincoln for the Presidency. We do not concur with him in some of his views, but there is much good in Abraham's bosom."

Now Lincoln's friends in Springfield could speak out, especially after the studied manner in which the Illinois State Journal encouraged the Lincoln for President movement. Lincoln himself in the months before the convention was keeping up a correspondence with important Republican leaders, being careful not to encourage or discourage favorite son candidates from other states nor to tie himself up. This editorial is from the Illinois State Journal, Jan. 14, 1860.

MR. LINCOLN AND THE PRESIDENCY

It will be seen by the proceedings in another place that the Republican Club of this city has organized itself into a "Lincoln Club," and intend to use all honorable means to secure the nomination of that distinguished Illinoisan as the Republican candidate for President at the approaching National Convention. We doubt not that as the favorite son of Illinois, the suggestion of "Old Abe's" name for the Presidency will meet with a loud and cordial response throughout the State and the entire Northwest. Already, in all directions, the public press are making him their first choice for the nomination.

As a matter of national policy, we believe that the next President of the United States should come from the Western States, and no state is more deserving of the honor of sending forth the Republican champion for that high office than that one which has been the great political battle ground of the country for the last four years. When ABRAHAM LINCOLN entered that battle ground, the members were against him; when the memorable campaign of 1858 was ended, nothing but an unfair apportionment of the members of the Illinois Legislature gave success to his rival in that body, while "Popular Sovereignty," the voice of the people, had pronounced in his favor.

ABRAHAM LINCOLN has arrived at that period of life when man's mental and physical powers and faculties are in their prime. God gave him a mind of unusual strength, and time and labor and study have made him one of the great men of the land. The purity of his patriotism, his incorruptible integrity and his ability to sustain himself and the country in any position in which he may be placed, no one who knows him can for a moment doubt. The people of Illinois are justified in their determination to place the name of their distinguished citizen before the country for the highest honors in the nation's gift. They do it because they know him; because they have confidence in him as a man for the times; because with him in the Presidential chair, the rights of the people of all the States will be secured, respected and maintained; because he interprets the constitution as did our fathers who made it and illustrated it in their acts; because he is a conservative National Republican.

The Great West will give a telling vote at the next Presidential election, and the candidacy of ABRAHAM LINCOLN will secure that vote for the Republicans beyond controversy. With him as our standard bearer, we are sure of all the Northwestern States, except Missouri, and the Republicans of other States could not cast their votes for a worthier, an abler, or more available man. The enthusiasm which his name excites all over the country, since his powerful and most eloquent vindication of the great Republican cause in the late contest in this State, shows that he has become the Nation's man and a tower of strength to the party whose leader he is now regarded.

The Republicans of Illinois will sustain and support, with their full strength, the Presidential nominee of the Chicago Convention, whoever he may be; but they respectfully, yet earnestly, call upon the Republicans of the Union to weigh the claims, estimate the qualifications and availability, and consider the fitness and propriety of giving the nomination to ABRAHAM LINCOLN of Illinois.

An important Presidential campaign biography was first printed in, of all places, the Chester County Times, Chester, Pa., on Feb. 11, 1860. This was how much of the country first saw Lincoln personally. These were the circumstances: Jesse W. Fell, a Bloomington friend of

Lincoln's, asked him to write a biography of himself for use in the Eastern press. Lincoln complied with a statement of less than seven hundred words, saying: "Herewith is a little sketch, as you requested. There is not much of it, for the reason, I suppose, that there is not much of me. If anything be made out of it, I wish it to be modest, and not to go beyond the material. If it were thought necessary to incorporate anything from any of my speeches, I suppose there would be no objection. Of course it must not appear to have been written by myself." Fell sent a sketch to Joseph J. Lewis of West Chester, Pa., who made it into a lengthy biography. Then papers all over the country, including the Chicago Press and Tribune in Lincoln's own state, reprinted it.

For the Chester County Times
ABRAHAM LINCOLN

Among the distinguished men who, by their patriotism and eloquence, have assisted to create and sustain the party of constitutional freedom which now predominates in most of the free States, there is no one who has a firmer hold on the confidence and affections of the people of the Great West, or is more an object of their enthusiastic admiration, than Abraham Lincoln of Springfield, Illinois. No traveller that visits the valley of the Mississippi, north of the Ohio, can fail to be impressed with the unrivalled popularity of that eminent Republican chief throughout that whole region: and it is impossible to doubt that he will be vigorously pressed upon the Chicago Convention, by the representatives of a large and earnest constituency, as a proper standard bearer of our great national party in the impending struggle for the Presidency. In consequence of the position he occupies in the regards of our western brethren, as a champion of the Republican faith, I have been interested to inquire into the incidents of his life and the prominent traits of his character. I now furnish you with the result of my inquiries, though they have been attended with but moderate success, and have elicited much less than I reasonably hoped to obtain.

Abraham Lincoln is a native of Hardin county, Kentucky. He was born on the twelfth day of February, 1809. His parents were both born in Virginia, and were certainly not of the first families. His paternal grandfather, Abraham Lincoln, emigrated from Rockingham county, Virginia, to Kentucky, about 1781 or 2, where a year or two later he was killed by Indians, not in battle, but by stealth, while he was laboring to open a farm in the forest. His ancestors, who were responsible members of the Society of Friends, went to Virginia from Berks county, Pennsylvania. Descendants of the same stock still reside in the eastern parts of this State. Mr. Lincoln's father, at the death of his father, was but six years of age, and he grew up literally without education. He removed from Kentucky to what is now Spencer county, Indiana, in 1816. The family reached their new home about the time the State was admitted into the Union. The region in which they settled was rude and wild, and they endured, for some years, the hard experience of a frontier life, in which the struggle with nature for existence and security is to be maintained only by constant vigilance and efforts. Bears, wolves and other noxious animals still infested the woods, and young Lincoln acquired more skill in the use of the rifle than knowledge of books. There were institutions here and there known by the flattering denomination of "schools," but no qualification was required of a teacher beyond "readin', writin' and cypherin'," as the vernacular phrase ran, as far as the rule of three. If a straggler supposed to understand Latin happened to sojourn in the neighborhood, he was looked upon as a wizard, and regarded with an awe suited to so mysterious a character. Hard work and plenty of it was the order of the day, varied, indeed, by an occasional bear hunt, a not infrequent deer chase, or other wild sport. Of course when young Lincoln came of age he was not a scholar. He could read and write and had some knowledge of arithmetic, but that was about all; and, as yet, he had but little ambition to know more of what was to be found in books. His attainments otherwise were not to be despised. He had grown to be six feet four inches in stature, was active and athletic, could wield the axe, direct the plough or use the rifle as well as the best of his compeers, and was fully up to all the mysteries of the woods, to the deeper mysteries of prairie farming, and fully inured by hardship and toil. Since he arrived at age he had not been at school. Whatever his requirements are, they have been picked up from time to time as opportunity occurred or as the pressure of some exigency demanded.

At twenty-one he removed to Illinois and passed the first year in Macon County, in active labor on a farm. Then he got to New Salem, at that time in Sangamon, now in Menard county, where he remained about a year, as a sort of clerk in a store. Then came the Black Hawk war. A company of volunteers was raised in New Salem and the surrounding country, and young Lincoln was elected captain—a success which, as he has often said, gave him more pleasure than any he has since enjoyed.

He served with credit during the campaign, and became popular. On his return in the fall of 1832, he was a candidate for the legislature, and ran, but was beaten. This was the only time that he has ever failed of an election by the people when he has sought their suffrages. The next and three succeeding biennial elections he was elected to the legislature and served with distinguished reputation in that body. While a member of the legislature he first gave indications of his superior powers as a debater, and he increased, by frequent practice, his natural facility for public speaking. His latent ambition was excited by success and he improved industriously the opportunities that offered of self cultivation. From the position of a subaltern in the ranks of the Whig party, a position which was appropriately assigned him by his unaffected modesty and humble pretensions, he soon became recognized and acknowledged as a champion and a leader, and his unvarying courtesy, good nature and genial manners, united with a certain lofty disinterestedness, and generous abnegation of self, made him a universal favorite.

During his legislative period he studied law, and, removing to Springfield, he opened an office and engaged actively in practice. Business flowed in upon him, and he rose rapidly to distinction in his profession. He displayed remarkable ability as an advocate in jury trials, and many of his law arguments were masterpieces of logical reasoning. There was no refined artificiality in his forensic efforts. They all bore the stamp of masculine common sense; and he had a natural, easy mode of illustration, that made the most abstruse subjects appear plain. His success at the bar, however, did not withdraw his attention from politics. For many years he was the "wheel horse" of the Whig party in Illinois, and was on the electoral ticket in several Presidential campaigns. At such times he canvassed the States with his usual vigor and ability. He was an ardent friend of Henry Clay and exerted himself powerfully in his behalf in 1844, traversing the entire State of Illinois, and addressing public meetings daily until near the close of the campaign, when, becoming convinced that his labors in that field would be unavailing, he crossed over into Indiana, and continued his efforts up to the day of the election. The contest of that year in Illinois was mainly on the question of the tariff. Mr. Lincoln, on the Whig side, and John Calhoun, on the Democratic side, were the heads of the opposing electoral tickets. Calhoun, late of Nebraska, now dead, was then in full vigor of his really great powers, and was accounted the ablest debater of his party. They stumped the State together, or nearly so, making speeches usually on alternate days at each place and each addressing large audiences at great length, sometimes four hours together. Mr. Lincoln, in these elaborate speeches, evinced a thorough mastery of the principles of political economy which underlie the tariff question, and presented arguments in favor of the protective policy with a power and conclusiveness rarely equalled, and at the same time in a manner so lucid and familiar and so well interspersed with happy illustrations and apposite anecdotes as to secure the delighted attention of his auditory.

Mr. Lincoln has been a consistent and earnest tariff man from the first hour of his entering public life. He is such from principle, and from a deeply rooted conviction of the wisdom of the protective policy; and whatever influence he may hereafter exert upon the government will be in favor of that policy.

In 1848, he was elected to Congress and served out his term; and he would have been reelected had he not declined to be a candidate. As to the character of his services, in that body, my information does not enable me to speak particularly.

In the National Convention of 1848, of which he was a member, he advocated the nomination of Gen. Taylor, and sustained the nomination by an active and energetic canvass of his own State. In 1852 he was equally efficient in his efforts for Gen. Scott, and was considered by the Whigs of Illinois and of the Northwest as one of their ablest and wisest leaders.

From 1849 to 1854, Mr. Lincoln was engaged assiduously in the practice of his profession, and being deeply immersed in business, was beginning to lose his interest in politics, when the scheming ambition and grovelling selfishness of an unscrupulous aspirant to the Presidency brought about the repeal of the Missouri Compromise. That act of baseness and perfidy aroused the sleeping lion and he prepared for new efforts. He threw himself at once into the contest that followed and fought the battle of freedom on the ground of his former conflicts in Illinois with more than his accustomed energy and zeal. He fully appreciated the importance of the slavery issue, and felt the force of the moral causes that must influence the question, and he never failed to appeal to the moral sentiment of the people in aid of the argument drawn from political sources, and to illuminate his theme with the lofty inspirations of an eloquence, pleading for the rights of humanity.—A revolution swept the State. For the first time a majority of the legislature of Illinois was opposed to the Democratic administration of the federal government. They were not, however, all free-soilers in principle. A small body of Anti-Nebraska Democrats held the balance of power. This circumstance gave occasion for a striking exhibition of Mr. Lincoln's habitual magnanimity.

A United States Senator was to be elected in place of Gen. Shields, who had yielded to the influence of his less scrupulous colleague and, against his own better judgment, had voted for the Kansas–Nebraska act. Mr. Lincoln was the admitted leader of the opposition and was universally regarded as their candidate for Senator. Governor Matteson was the candidate of the Nebraska Democrats and Lyman Trumbull of the handful of Anti-Nebraska Democrats in the legislature. The election came on, and a number of ballots were taken, the almost united opposition voting steadily for Lincoln, but a few Anti-Nebraska Democrats for Trumbull. Mr. Lincoln became apprehensive that those men would vote for and elect Matteson, and to prevent such a consummation he went personally to his friends and by strong persuasion induced them to vote for Trumbull. He thus secured, by an act of generous self-sacrifice, a triumph for the cause of right, and an advocate of it on the floor of the Senate, not inferior in earnest zeal for the principles of republicanism to any member of that body. It was not without difficulty, however, that this object was accomplished. The opposition throughout the State had with great unanimity looked to Mr. Lincoln to represent Illinois in the Senate, and it was with great reluctance that their representatives in the legislature could be induced to disappoint their constituents by giving their votes to another.

From his thorough conviction of the growing magnitude of the slave question and of the need of a strong effort to preserve the territories to freedom, Mr. Lincoln was among the first to join in the formation of the Republican party, although the public opinion around him was strongly adverse to that movement. He exerted himself for the organization of the Republican forces in Illinois, and attended the first Republican convention held in the State. That was at Bloomington in May, 1856. His speech in that convention was of surprising power and eloquence, and produced great effect. In the contest of that year Mr. Lincoln was at the head of the Illinois electoral ticket, and labored earnestly, though vainly, to wrest that State from the grasp of the pro-slavery democracy, with "the walking magazine of mischief," as Douglas has been appropriately termed at its head.

When the campaign of 1858 was about to open the voice of the Republican party of Illinois was so unanimous and enthusiastic in his favor as the successor of Judge Douglas, that in a full State convention of over five hundred delegates the unusual step was taken of nominating him for that office by acclamation. The enthusiasm of the delegates in convention extended to their constituents. The party went into the contest with the name of Lincoln on all their banners, instituted Lincoln clubs, wore Lincoln badges, and held Lincoln meetings at almost every school-house in the State. The respective parties were marshaled under leaders, who were fitting representatives of the principles of each. Lincoln, the consistent advocate of institutional government, cognizant of indefeasible rights, and animated and controlled by a sense of human responsibility independent of conventional rules placed himself upon the battlements of the constitution, and summoned to his side the friends of law, order and humanity. Douglas, in the spirit of a system which assigns all power to a majority and flatters the people in the concrete, while it cheats the individual of all security for his personal rights, appealed to popular prejudice and to the antipathies of race. The one held slavery to be an institution in conflict with the principles of free government, wholly de-pendent upon positive law, and never to be extended where it could be legitimately prohibited; while the other averred that the despostic will of any majority, though of a community existing only in a state of pupilage under the guardianship of federal authority ought to be competent to establish it without question by that authority and without regard to moral considerations. The contest excited intense interest and was main-tained with infinite spirit. Lincoln, after vainly attempting to draw his wary opponent into a joint canvass of the entire State, met him in seven great debates in as many Congressional Districts, and in the opinion of every candid judge fairly overthrew him in argument on all controverted points. The result was that though a majority of the popular vote was ob-tained by Lincoln, Douglas obtained by the instrumentality of an old and grossly unequal apportionment of the districts a majority of the Rep-resentatives and thus secured his re-election to the United States Senate.

Since that great contest, Mr. Lincoln has repeatedly given his power-ful aid, in support of the Republican cause in other States, as in Ohio, Wisconsin and Kansas during the present year, and, in every instance, he has been received with enthusiasm by the people, evincive of the hold he has on the popular heart. Wherever he speaks he draws together large crowds of interested listeners upon whom he never fails to make a marked impression. Though a ready and fluent speaker, he avoids declamation, and is never betrayed into mere word-painting which his good taste ha-bitually rejects. He abhors emptiness as heartily as did the great Webster in his prime, and employs as the vehicle of his thoughts a style of singu-lar clearness and simplicity. In his statement of facts he is scrupulously accurate, and to every opportunity he exhibits the utmost fairness, candor and liberality, retorting no abuse, but preserving an unfailing courtesy even under the severest provocation. His manner is earnest, his arguments close and logical and he reaches his conclusions by a process that seems to render those conclusions inevitable. Whether you agree with him or not you cannot listen to him without being satisfied of his sincerity, and that his object is not victory but truth.

In private life Mr. Lincoln is a strictly moral and temperate man, of frank and engaging manners, of kind and genial nature, unaffectedly modest, social in disposition, ready in conversation, and passing easily from grave to gay and from gay to grave, according to the humor of the hour or the requirements of the occasion, a firm friend and yet not implacable to an enemy, a consistant politician, a good citizen and an honest patriot.

The boom was on. The Republican nominating convention was to meet in Chicago in May. Lincoln in the few remaining months was busy assuring his friends what his position was on various issues. The Chicago Tribune, so faithful to Lincoln during the debates, wrote out its reasons for his nomination on Feb. 16, 1860.

THE PRESIDENCY—ABRAHAM LINCOLN

Of three or four States which are believed to constitute the debatable ground in the next Presidential campaign, and whose electoral votes will determine the result, Illinois is universally conceded to be one. It appears to be a foregone conclusion that the nomination of the Chicago Convention will be conferred upon no one who does not unite in himself the essential of requisite qualification, devotion to the distinctive principles of the Republican party, and availability in the States alluded to above.

We have no hesitation in saying that as respects the first two essentials, Abraham Lincoln, of Illinois, is the peer of any man yet named in connection with the Republican nominations, while in regard to availability, we believe him to be more certain to carry Illinois and Indiana than any one else, and his political antecedents are such as to commend him heartily to the support of Pennsylvania and New Jersey.

Mr. Lincoln would now be in the seat occupied by Mr. Douglas in the U. S. Senate, but for the gross unfairness of the apportionment of our legislative representation. In his contest with Mr. Douglas in 1858, less than two hundred additional votes in close districts would have secured his triumph, bad as the apportionment was. At the same election the Republicans achieved a victory on their State officers—the vote of the latter being about equal to the aggregate vote of the Douglasites and

A National Man NOVEMBER 1858–MAY 1860

Democrats. On the popular vote in the three Northern Congressional districts there was a Republican loss of several thousand growing out of the belief that Judge Douglas had permanently broken with the Democratic party, and the persistent manner in which Eastern Republicans and newspapers advocated his election. With Mr. Lincoln as our candidate for the Presidency, not only would all these votes be recovered, but greater or less inroads would be made in the ranks of the Democracy, and the State be secured beyond any possible contingency.

But the popularity of Mr. Lincoln is not confined to Illinois or to the Northwestern States. His memorable canvass with Mr. Douglas in 1858, gave Republicans throughout the Union an opportunity of becoming familiar with his admirable personal qualities, his entire devotion to the distinctive principles of the party, his rare abilities, and his broad, statesmanlike views of national political questions. We briefly sum up some of the elements of his popularity and strength:

1st. A gentleman of unimpeachable purity of private life. His good name is not soiled by a single act, political, social, moral or religious, that we or his friends need blush to own as his. In all his relations to his fellows he has not yet been guilty of that thing upon which an enemy can place his finger and say, "this is dishonest," or "this is mean." Herein he is the peer of the most unspotted man in the Republic—the living likeness, full length size, of the best of the eminent characters who laid the foundation of the government.

2d. A man of, at once, great breadth and great acuteness of intellect. Not learned, in a bookish sense, but master of great fundamental principles, and of that kind of ability which applies them to crises and events. The masterly canvass which he made with Douglas, and his later speeches in Ohio, mark him as one of the ablest political thinkers of his day.

3d. Right on the record. An Old Line Whig of the Henry Clay school, originally, he came early into the Republican movement in which he has since been so conspicuous. He has that radicalism which a keen insight into the meaning of the anti-slavery conflict is sure to give; but, coupled with it, that constitutional conservatism which could never fail in proper respect for existing institutions and laws, and which would never precipitate or sanction innovations more destructive than the abuses that they seek to correct. Right on the question of Slavery, on the Homestead question, on all the issues which divide the parties; needing no tinkering to make him acceptable to Pennsylvania and New Jersey—candidate of the party which in itself is an embodiment of the principles and measures necessary for the perpetuity of the Union and the preservation of our free institutions—he would enter the field acceptable to the Opposition of all shades of opinion, harmonizing all interests, conciliating all jarring elements—the master of the position, a guarantor of success.

4th. A man of executive capacity. Never garrulous, never promising what he cannot perform, never doing anything for show or effect, laboriously attentive to detail, industrious and conscientious, he would see to it that no want of promptness, attention, or industry on his part should defeat the reforms in the administration of national affairs which Republicanism is pledged to inaugurate.

These are some of the reasons why we favor the nomination of Mr. Lincoln for the first place on the National Republican ticket. We do not know, however, that he has any aspirations for the position. While others are intriguing and trading, he is at his professional work, content to be let alone. But he is no doubt at the disposal of his friends; and we feel very confident that Illinois will present his name to the Chicago Convention, as the man, above all others, who will be most likely to lead the Republican party on to a glorious victory, and whose administration of the National Government would recall the best days of the Republic. Should the Convention give him this position, then the honor which he has not sought, but which his admirers have hoped he might attain, will, like ripe fruit, fall into his hands. Abraham Lincoln will never be President by virtue of intrigue and bargain.

When Lincoln received an invitation from the Young Men's Republican Union to speak in New York, he accepted. This was to be the Cooper Union speech, a high point in the nominating buildup because, among other reasons, it was in the State of William Seward, Lincoln's principal rival for the Republican nomination. After showing the draft of his speech to Joseph Medill and Charles H. Ray, editors of the Chicago Press and Tribune, Lincoln departed for New York. On the day he arrived, Saturday, Feb. 25, 1860, the New York Tribune ran this notice and biography.

ABRAHAM LINCOLN of Illinois will, for the first time, speak in this Emporium, at Cooper Institute, on Monday evening. He will speak in exposition and defense of the Republican faith; and we urge earnest Republicans to induce their friends and neighbors of adverse views to accompany them to this lecture. The Association which has taken the responsibility of drawing Mr. Lincoln from his Western home and business, to give our citizens this gratification and the Republican cause this aid, have deserved well of their compatriots, and we shall wisely encourage them to similar efforts in future.

ABRAHAM LINCOLN was born in Hardin County, Kentucky, Feb. 12, 1809, and is of course 51 years old. His parents were of Quaker stock, that migrated from Pennsylvania to Virginia, whence his grandfather removed in 1781–2 to Kentucky, and was there surprised and killed by Indians while at work on his clearing. Like most pioneers, he left his family poor; and his son also died prematurely, leaving a widow and several children, of whom Abraham was then six years old. The family removed soon after to Southern Indiana, where Abraham grew to the stature of six feet and some inches, but enjoyed scarcely better facilities for schooling than in Kentucky. Probably six months in all of the rudest sort of schooling comprehends the whole of his technical education. But hard work and plenty of it, the rugged experiences of aspiring poverty, the wild sports and rude games of a newly and thinly peopled forest region —the education born of the log-cabin, the rifle, the ax, and the plow— made him the man he has since proved himself.

At 21, he pushed further West into Illinois, which has for the last thirty years been his home, living always near and for some years past in Springfield, the State Capital. He worked on a farm as hired man his first year in Illinois; the next year he was a clerk in a store; then volunteered for the Black Hawk war, and was chosen a captain by his company; the next year was an unsuccessful candidate for the Legislature; was chosen the next, and served four sessions with eminent usefulness and steadily increasing reputation; studied law, meantime, and took his place at the bar; was early recognized as a most effective and convincing advocate before the People of Whig principles and the Protective policy, and of their illustrious embodiment, Henry Clay; was a Whig candidate for Elector in nearly or quite every Presidential contest from 1836 to 1852, inclusive; was chosen to the XXXth Congress from the Central District of Illinois in 1846, and served to its close, but was not a candidate for re-election; and in 1849 measurably withdrew from politics and devoted himself to his practice, until the Nebraska Iniquity of 1854 called him again into the political arena. He was the candidate of the Whigs for U. S. Senator before the Legislature chosen that year; but they were not a majority of the body; so he declined and urged his friends to support Judge Trumbull, the candidate of the anti-Nebraska Democrats, who was thus elected. Mr. Lincoln's name headed the Fremont Electoral Ticket of Illinois in 1856.

In 1858, he was unanimously designated by the Republican State

Convention to succeed Mr. Douglas in the Senate, and thereupon canvassed the State against Mr. D. with remarkable ability. Mr. Douglas secured a majority of the Legislature and was elected, but Mr. Lincoln had the larger popular vote.

—Such is ABRAHAM LINCOLN of Illinois—emphatically a man of the People, a champion of Free Labor, of diversified and prosperous Industry, and of that policy which leads through peaceful progress to universal intelligence, virtue and freedom. The distinguishing characteristics of his political addresses are clearness and candor of statement, a chivalrous courtesy to opponents, and a broad genial humor. Let us crowd the Cooper Institute to hear him on Monday night.

William Cullen Bryant, poet and editor of the New York Evening Post, introduced Lincoln to the audience: "I have only, my friends, to pronounce the name of Abraham Lincoln of Illinois [loud cheering], I have only to pronounce his name to secure your profoundest attention." Some 1,500 people in the Cooper Institute had paid twenty-five cents to hear him. Bryant was there not only as one of the sponsors of Lincoln's visit but as a reporter of the event for his Evening Post of Feb. 28, 1860.

[By William Cullen Bryant]

February 28, 1860

When we have such a speech as that of Abraham Lincoln, of Illinois, delivered at the Cooper Institute last evening to a crowded, deeply interested and enthusiastic audience, we are tempted to wish that our columns were indefinitely elastic.

We have made room for Mr. Lincoln's speech notwithstanding the pressure of other matters, and our readers will see that it was well worthy of the deep attention with which it was heard. That part of it in which the speaker places the Republican party on the very ground occupied by the framers of our constitution and fathers of our republic, strikes us as particularly forcible.

In this great controversy the Republicans are the real conservative party. They simply adhere to a policy which had its origin with George Washington of Virginia, Benjamin Franklin of Pennsylvania, Abraham Baldwin of Georgia, Alexander Hamilton of New York, and other men from other states worthy to be named with them.

It is remarkable how perfectly all the eminent statesmen of that age were agreed upon the great question of slavery in the territories. They never thought of erecting the slaveholding class into an oligarchy which was to control the political administration of the country, dictate to the judiciary, and invade and occupy the new regions possessed by the confederation. They regarded it—and this fully appears from authentic and undisputed records—by a consent next to unanimous, as a class which was never to exist beyond the limits of the old thirteen states.

At that time the slave holders were content to await, within the limits they occupied, the hour, which Washington, himself one of their number, benevolent and liberal-minded as he was, hoped was not far distant, when our republic should present to the world the spectacle of "a confederacy of free states."

All the clamor about northern aggression, all the menaces of a dissolution of the Union, have only this grievance as their cause, that we think as Washington thought, hope as he hoped, and act as he acted; and they have only this object in view—to force us from the course he approved and which our conscience approves still, and to compel us to adopt a new policy, new measures, new views of the meaning of the constitution, opening the gates of the territories of the barbarian institution which our fathers intended should wither into decrepitude, and pass to its dissolution within its original limits.

All this may not be new, but it is most logically and convincingly stated in the speech—and it is wonderful how much a truth gains by a certain mastery of clear and impressive statement. But the consequences to which Mr. Lincoln follows out the demands of these arrogant innovators give an air of novelty to the closing part of his argument.

What they require of us is not only a surrender of our long-cherished notions of constitutional rights, inherited from our ancestors and theirs; not only a renunciation of the freedom of speech, but a hypocritical confession of doctrines which revolt both our understanding and our conscience, a confession extorted by the argument of the highwayman, the threat of violence and murder. There is to be no peace with the South till the slaveholders shall have forced us to say that slavery is right—not merely to admit it by silence, but to shout the accursed doctrine with all the strength of our lungs.

With the renunciation of the creed of liberty must come the reconsideration and rejection of our free constitutions. Every one of the constitutions of the free states puts the stigma of public abhorrence upon slavery, and is an offense and an insult to the slaveholder. They who cannot submit to allow the natural lawfulness of slavery to be questioned in public debate, or in the discussions of the press, certainly will not tolerate the more solemn declaration of the right of all men to freedom embodied and proclaimed in the state constitutions of the North and West. One by one these state constitutions must be given up, torn in pieces, and trampled under foot at the bidding of the preachers of the new political gospel.

At Cooper Union Lincoln said: "Neither let us be slandered from our duty by false accusations against us, nor frightened from it by menaces of destruction to the government nor of dungeons to ourselves. Let us have faith that right makes might, and in that faith, let us, to the end, dare to do our duty as we understand it." Henry J. Raymond's New York Times was succinct: "There was a very large meeting of Republicans at Cooper Institute last night to listen to that noted political exhorter and prairie orator, Abe Lincoln. The speaker, as soon as he appeared on the platform, was vehemently cheered, and during the delivery of his address frequently applauded." Nothing more. After the speech Lincoln went to the New York Tribune office to look over the proofs. This Tribune editorial appeared on Feb. 28, 1860.

The Speech of ABRAHAM LINCOLN at the Cooper Institute last evening was one of the happiest and most convincing political arguments ever made in this City, and was addressed to a crowded and most appreciating audience. Since the days of Clay and Webster, no man has spoken to a larger assemblage of the intellect and mental culture of our City. Mr. Lincoln is one of Nature's orators, using his rare powers solely and effectively to elucidate and to convince, though their inevitable effect is to delight and electrify as well. We present herewith a very full and accurate report of this Speech; yet the tones, the gestures, the kindling eye and the mirth-provoking look, defy the reporter's skill. The vast assemblage frequently rang with cheers and shouts of applause, which were prolonged and intensified at the close. No man ever before made such an impression on his first appeal to a New-York audience.

Mr. Lincoln speaks for the Republican cause tonight at Providence, R.I., and it is hoped that he will find time to speak once or more in Connecticut before he sets his face homeward.

We shall soon issue his Speech of last night in pamphlet form for cheap circulation.

After Cooper Union Lincoln spoke in New England cities—as in 1848 when he campaigned for Taylor. He made several local references to the strike of Massachusetts shoemakers that was in progress early in March, 1860. The Hartford Press, Connecticut, said that "Mr. Lincoln thanked God that we have a system of labor where there can be a strike. Whatever the pressures there is a point where the workman may stop." The Hartford Press reported Lincoln's visit on March 6, 1860.

REPUBLICAN MASS MEETING AT THE CITY HALL!
SPEECH BY HON. ABRAHAM LINCOLN!

GREAT ENTHUSIASM!

Popular Sovereignty, or the "Don't Care" Policy, Exposed.

The City Hall was full last night, pressed down, shaken together and running over—and hundreds came and went unable to get within hearing distance. Punctually at 7½ o'clock, Hon. Abraham Lincoln of Illinois made his appearance, and after the rousing cheers were ended was introduced to the audience by Geo. G. Sill, Esq., president of the Republican Club, and received again with cheers.

With a very brief introduction he went straight at his subject. Slavery is the great political question of the nation. Though all desire its settlement, it still remains the all-pervading question of the day. It has been so especially for the past six years. . . .

Mr. Lincoln then took up the Massachusetts shoemaker's strike, treating it in a humorous and philosophical manner, and exposing to ridicule the foolish pretence of Senator Douglas—that the strike arose from "this unfortunate sectional warfare." Mr. Lincoln thanked God that we have a system of labor where there can be a strike. Whatever the pressure, there is a point where the workman may stop. (Applause and cheers for free labor.)

He didn't pretend to be familiar with the subject of the shoe strike —probably knew as little about it as Senator Douglas himself. This strike has occurred as the Senator says, or it has not. Shall we stop making war upon the South? We never have made war upon them. If any one has, better go and hang himself and save Virginia the trouble. If you give up your convictions and call slavery right as they do, you let slavery in upon you—instead of white laborers who can strike, you'll soon have black laborers who can't strike.

I have heard that in consequence of this "sectional warfare," as Douglas calls it, Senator Mason of Va. had appeared in a suit of homespun. Now up in New Hampshire, the woolen and cotton mills are all busy, and there is no strike—they are busy making the very goods Senator Mason has quit buying! To carry out his idea, he ought to go barefoot! If that's the plan, they should begin at the foundation, and adopt the well-known "Georgia costume" of a shirt-collar and pair of spurs! ("Irrepressible" laughter and applause.)

It reminded him of the man who had a poor old lean, bony spavined horse, with swelled legs. He was asked what he was going to do with such a miserable beast—the poor creature would die. "Do?" said he, "I'm going to fat him up; don't you see that I have got him real fat as high as the knees?" (Roars of laughter.) Well, they've got the Union dissolved up to the ankle, but no farther! (Applause and laughter.). . .

The speech went home to the hearts of all who heard it. Near a thousand formed in procession, and headed by the Hartford Cornet Band, escorted the Orator of the West to the residence of Mayor Allyn, and he bade them good night.

The eager crowd cheered Mr. Lincoln, cheered Gov. Buckingham, cheered the "Old Fremont Camp" and the new one that is to be, and cheered for Buckingham and Victory, and insisted upon one or two short talks. Geo. S. Gilman requested all who would work with all their might for Liberty, from now until election, to say "Aye." The response was tremendous.

Now all eyes were on the Chicago convention. Back home in Illinois after the successful Eastern tour, Lincoln could read with satisfaction an editorial reporting his trip favorably and advocating his cause for the Presidential nomination. All the more gratifying that the editorial appeared in the Menard Index (reprinted, March 28, 1860, in the Illinois State Journal), of Petersburg, a short distance from New Salem, where once in 1832 he had written a letter to the editor of the Sangamo Journal announcing his candidacy for the Illinois legislature and then gone off to the Black Hawk war.

(*From the Menard Index*)
MR. LINCOLN IN THE EAST

Mr. Lincoln's recent tour through the eastern States has given him a wonderful popularity there. From every place where he has spoken he has received the most flattering encomiums. The enthusiasm which his presence raised in the east is an earnest of that which would be excited by his nomination for the Presidency. There seems to be a strong feeling in favor of nominating Mr. Lincoln in case Douglas is the Democratic candidate; it being generally conceded that he is the strongest candidate against Douglas. We believe the same thing is true against any possible nominee, and that he should be nominated in any event. Considering the matter in a local point of view, we look upon the nomination of Mr. Lincoln as securing the State of Illinois to the Republicans for the future, so long as the issues remain the same that they are now. He will most surely carry the State, and with him the State ticket will be elected, the Legislature secured and Senator Trumbull re-elected to his seat in the Senate. While we intend to accomplish this result anyhow, we can in no way be so sure of doing it as by having our ticket headed by Abraham Lincoln for President. In view of the importance of this election to the future supremacy of the Republican party in thus State; we hold that every friend of the party in this State should use every effort to accomplish Mr. Lincoln's nomination.

Chapter 5

Lincoln for President

MAY 1860–MARCH 1861

Two weeks before the Republican party convention at the Wigwam in Chicago, Lincoln wrote to Senator Lyman Trumbull: "As you request, I will be entirely frank. The taste is in my mouth a little; and this, no doubt, disqualifies me, to some extent, to form correct opinions." Lincoln spent the time planning strategy with advisers and managers and trying to allay doubts by replying to letters from Republicans in other states on various issues. This would be the culmination of six years of debates and speeches on the question that was tearing the country apart.

The day before the convention opened, Murat Halstead, the correspondent of the Cincinnati Commercial, reported that "The city of Chicago is attending to this convention in magnificent style. It is a great place for large hotels, and all have their capacity for accommodation tested. The great feature is the Wigwam erected within the past month, expressly for use of the convention, by the Republicans at Chicago, at a cost of seven thousand dollars. It is a small edition of the New York Crystal Palace." The colors of different candidates came out; the Seward men wore badges of silk with his likeness and name. The next day the astute Halstead reported: "The current of the universal twaddle this morning is that 'Old Abe' will be the nominee."

But it did not seem that way in the general view of the convention because the candidacy of Seward seemed so well organized. Thurlow Weed, editor of the Albany Evening Journal, headed the Seward forces. He was to say later, "there can be no doubt that the nomination which was made is regarded as the very next choice of the Republicans *of New York. No other man, beside their own favorite, so well represents the party in the great struggle now going on as Abraham Lincoln."*

And on the day before the convention, delegates could pick up the *Chicago Press and Tribune, May 15, 1860,* and receive some timely advice if in doubt.

THE WINNING MAN—ABRAHAM LINCOLN

In presenting ABRAHAM LINCOLN to the National Republican Convention, as a candidate for the Presidency, we are actuated not by our great love and esteem for the man, by any open or secret hostility to any other of the eminent gentlemen named for that high office, nor by a feeling of State pride or Western sectionalism, but by a profound and well-matured conviction that his unexceptionable record, his position between the extremes of opinion in the party, his spotless character as a citizen, and his acknowledged ability as a statesman, will, in the approaching canvass, give him an advantage before the people which no other candidate can claim. We are not disposed to deny that Mr. SEWARD, is, the question of availability being set aside, the first choice of perhaps a majority of the rank and file of the party; that Gen. CAMERON has claims upon Pennsylvania which his friends will not willingly have overlooked; that the statesman-like qualities, inflexible honesty and marked executive ability of SALMON P. CHASE entitle him to a high place in Republican esteem; that Mr. BATES' pure life and noble aims justly command the confidence of troops of friends; that the chivalric WADE has extorted the admiration of the North and West; that FESSENDEN, for his gallant service must be gratefuly remembered; and that JOHN McLEAN, whose life is without a stain, and whose love of country has never been challenged, must be remembered as a strong and unexceptional man. But Illinois claims that Mr. LINCOLN, though without the ripe experience of SEWARD, the age and maturity of BATES and McLEAN, or the fire of FESSENDEN and WADE, has that rare and happy combination of qualities which, *as a candidate,* enables him to outrank either.

I. By his own motion, he is not a candidate. He has never sought, directly or indirectly, for the first or second place on the ticket. The movement in his favor is spontaneous. It has sprung up suddenly and with great strength, its roots being in the conviction that he is the man to reconcile all differences in our ranks, to conciliate all the now jarring elements, and to lead forward to certain victory. Having never entered into the field, he has put forth no personal effort for success, and he has never made, even by implication, a pledge of any sort by which his action, if he is President, will be influenced for any man, any measure, any policy. He will enter upon the contest with no clogs, no embarrassment; and this fact is a guaranty of a glorious triumph.

II. In all the fundamentals of Republicanism, he is radical up to the limit to which the party, with due respect for the rights of the South, proposes to go. But nature has given him that wise conservatism which has made his action and his expressed opinions so conform to the most mature sentiment of the country on this question of slavery, that no living man can put his finger on one of his speeches or any one of his public acts as a State legislator or as a member of Congress, to which valid objection can be raised. His avoidance of extremes has not been the result of ambition which measures words or regulates acts, but the natural consequence of an equable nature and in mental constitution that is never off its balance. While no one doubts the strength of his attachments to the Republican cause, or doubts that he is a representative man, all who know him see that he occupies the happy mean between that alleged radicalism which binds the older Anti-Slavery men to Mr. Seward, and that conservatism which dictates the support of Judge Bates. Seward men, Bates men, Cameron men and Chase men can all accept him as their second choice, and be sure that in him they have the nearest approach to what they most admire in their respective favorites, which any possible compromise will enable them to obtain.

III. Mr. LINCOLN has no new record to make. Originally a Whig, though early a recruit of the great Republican party, he has nothing to explain for the satisfaction of New Jersey, Pennsylvania or the West. His opinions and votes on the Tariff will be acceptable to all sections except the extreme South, where Republicanism expects no support. Committed within proper limitations, set up by economy and constitutional obligation, to the improvement of rivers and harbors, to that most beneficent measure, the Homestead bill, and to the speedy construction of the Pacific Railroad, he need write no letters to soften down old asperities, growing out of these questions, which must inevitably play their part in the canvass before us. He is all that Pennsylvania and the West have a right to demand.

IV. He is a Southern man by birth and education, who has never departed from the principles which he learned from the statesmen of the period in which he first saw the light. A Kentuckian, animated by the hopes that bring the Kentucky delegation here, a Western man, to whom sectionalism is unknown, he is that candidate around whom all opponents of the extension of Human Slavery, North and South, can rally.

V. Mr. LINCOLN is a man of the people. For his position, he is not indebted to family influence, the partiality of friends or the arts of the politician. All his early life a laborer in the field, in the saw-mill, as a boatman on the Wabash, Ohio, and Mississippi, as a farmer in Illinois, he has that sympathy with the men who toil and vote that will make him strong. Later, a valiant soldier in the Black Hawk war, a student in a law office, bending his great powers to overcome the defects of early training; then a legislator, and at last a brilliant advocate, in the highest courts, and a popular leader in the great movement of the age, there is enough of romance and poetry in his life to fill all the land with shouting and song. Honest Old Abe! Himself an outgrowth of free institutions, he would die in the effort to preserve to others, unimpaired, the inestimable blessings by which he has been made a man.

VI. Without a stain of Know-Nothingism on his skirts, he is acceptable to the mass of the American party who, this year, will be compelled to choose between the candidate of Chicago and the nominee of Baltimore. The experience of two years has proved their error and his wisdom. They want the chance to retrieve the blunders of the past. Endeared by his manly defence of the principles of the Declaration of Independence to the citizens of foreign birth, he could command the warm support of every one of them from whom, in any contingency, a Republican vote can be expected.

VII. Mr. LINCOLN is an honest man. We know that the adage "Praise overmuch is censure in disguise" is true; and we know, too, that it is the disgrace of the age that in the popular mind, politics and chicane, office and faithlessness, go hand in hand. We run great risk, then, in saying of Mr. Lincoln what truth inexorably demands,—that in his life of 51 years, there is no act of a public or private character, of which his most malignant enemy can say, "this is dishonest," "this is mean." With his record, partizanship has done its worst, and the result we have stated. His escutcheon is without a blemish.

VIII. After saying so much, we need not add that Mr. LINCOLN can be elected, if placed before the people with the approbation of the Convention to meet to-morrow. In New England, where Republicanism pure and simple is demanded, and where he has lately electrified the people by his eloquence, his name would be a tower of strength. New York, who clings with an ardent embrace to that great statesman, her first choice, would not refuse to adopt Mr. LINCOLN as a standard bearer worthy of the holy cause. Pennsylvania, satisfied with his views in regard to the present necessity of fostering domestic interests, and the constitutional moderation of his opinions upon slavery, would come heartily into his support. The West is the child of the East, and aside from her local pride in one of the noblest of her sons, she would not fail by her plaudits to exalt and intensify the enthusiasm which the nomination of Honest Old Abe would be sure to excite. The West has no rivalry with the East, except in the patriotic endeavor to do the most for the Republican cause. Ohio, Indiana, Illinois, Iowa, Minnesota and Wisconsin desire no triumph in the East does not share—no victory over which the East may not honestly exult. In a contest for Lincoln, they would fight with zeal and hope that has never animated the Republic hosts.

We present our candidate, then, not as the rival of this man or that, not because the West has claims which she must urge; not because of a distinctive policy which she would see enforced; not because he is the first choice of a majority; but because he is that honest man, that representative Republican, that people's candidate, whose life, position, record, are so many guarantys of success—because he is that patriot in whose hands the interests of the government may be safely confided. Nominated, he would, we believe, be triumphantly elected; but if another, in the wisdom of the Convention, is preferred, we can pledge him to labor, as honest and effective as any that he ever done for himself, for the man of the Convention's choice.

During the convention Lincoln remained at home in Springfield. "I am a little too much a candidate to stay home and not quite enough a candidate to go," he had decided. But his managers were busy at Lincoln headquarters in the Tremont House, nailing down delegations. The New York Tribune's Greeley filed a late dispatch before the balloting began: "My conclusion, from all that I can gather, tonight, is that the opposition to Gov. Seward cannot concentrate on any candidate, and that he will be nominated." What did happen is described in the New York Times, May 19, 1860.

PROCEEDINGS OF THE CONVENTION
From the Associated Press

CHICAGO, Friday, May 18.
The Wigwam was closely packed for a full hour before the Convention assembled this morning. The interest in the proceedings appears on

the increase as the time for ballotting approaches. A crowd, numbered by thousands, has been outside the building since 9 o'clock, anxiously awaiting intelligence from the inside. Arrangements have been made for passing the result of the ballots up from the platform to the roof of the building and through the sky-light—men being stationed above to convey speedily the intelligence to the multitude in the streets.

A large procession was formed by the various delegations to march to the Hall, preceded by bands of music, New York being by far the most numerous.

As the delegates entered on the platform, the several distinguished men were greeted with rounds of applause by the audience.

The opening prayer was delivered by Rev. Mr. GREEN, of the Tabernacle Baptist Church.

Three or four meetings were held at a distance outside, and during the silence of the prayer in the Convention the roars and shouts of these meetings could be distinctly heard in the Wigwam.

The President, on opening the proceedings, begged the audience to refrain as much as possible from applause, and to preserve as far as consistent the decorum and dignity of the meeting.

The President announced an invitation for an excursion over the Chicago and Galena Railroad; also, a communication from the workingmen of Brooklyn, Williamsburgh and Greenpoint, New York, in favor of bestowing the Government lands on actual settlers, and for arresting the further sale of the public lands.

Both communications were ordered to be entered on the record.

The President announced the motion pending to be, to take a ballot for a candidate for President of the United States. . . .

WM. M. EVARTS rose and said: I beg leave to offer the name of WM. H. SEWARD as a candidate before this Convention for the nomination of President of the United States.

This nomination was received with loud and long continued applause.

Mr. JUDD, of Illinois, rose and said: Mr. President, I beg leave to offer as a candidate before this Convention for President of the United States the name of ABRAM LINCOLN, of Illinois.

The crowded audience greeted this nomination with perfectly deafening applause, the shouts swelling into a perfect roar, and being continued for several minutes, the wildest excitement and enthusiasm prevailing. At the close of the applause some hisses were heard, but the pressure for LINCOLN was tremendous.

Mr. DUDLEY, of New Jersey, persented the name of WM. E. DAYTON. [Light applause.]

Gov. REEDER, of Pennsylvania—The State of Pennsylvania desires to present as her candidate the name of SIMON CAMERON. [Applause.]

Mr. CARTER, of Ohio, put forward the name of SALMON P. CHASE, of Ohio. [Loud applause.]

Mr. SMITH, of Maryland—I am instructed by the State of Indiana to second the motion of ABRAM LINCOLN. [Another outburst of enthusiastic applause from the body of the hall, mingled with some hisses.]

FRANCIS P. BLAIR, of Missouri, nominated EDWARD BATES, of Missouri. [Applause.]

Mr. BLAIR, of Michigan, said on the part of Michigan—I desire to say that the Republicans of that State second the nomination of WM. H. SEWARD for the Presidency.

Tremendous applause followed this speech, thousands of those present rising and waving their hats and handkerchiefs, and swelling the applause to a thundering roar through several minutes. This was followed by some hisses and loud applause for LINCOLN, when the friends of SEWARD again rallied, determined not to be put down in applause by the friends of LINCOLN. At this second trial of the lungs, however, it was evident that the crowd was more divided than at first appeared, and the Lincoln men apparently had the majority.

TOM CORWIN, of Ohio, nominated JOHN MCLEAN, of Ohio, for the Presidency. [Loud applause.]

CARL SCHURZ, of Wisconsin, on the part of his State, here rose and seconded the nomination of WM. H. SEWARD.

Upon this another scene of the greatest enthusiasm and tumultuous excitement ensued.

Mr. NORTH, of Minnesota, also seconded, on the part of Minnesota, the nomination of Mr. SEWARD. [Tremendous applause.]

Mr. WILSON, of Kansas—The delegates and people of Kansas second the nomination. [Renewed cheers.]

Mr. DELANO, of Ohio—On the part of a large number of people of Ohio, I desire to second the nomination of the man who can split rails and maul Democrats, ABRAM LINCOLN. [Rounds of applause by Lincoln men.]

A Delegate from Iowa also seconded the nomination of Mr. LINCOLN, on the part of that State, amid renewed excitement and applause.

A VOICE—ABE LINCOLN has it by the sound now. Let us ballot. Cheers and hisses.

Judge LOGAN, of Illinois—Mr. President, in order or out of order, I propose this Convention and audience give three cheers for the man who is evidently their nominee.

Hisses and cries of "No," "No," "Call the roll."

The PRESIDENT—If the Convention will get over this irrepressible excitement, the roll will be called.

After some further excitement, the calling of the roll commenced, the applause at the different announcements being with difficulty checked.

When Maryland was called, the Chairman of the delegation cast the vote of the State for BATES, two Delegates claiming their right to individual votes.

After some discussion, the Convention rejected the votes as cast by the Chairman, and received the votes of the Delegates separately.

FIRST BALLOT.

The first ballot resulted as follows:

FOR MR. SEWARD.

Maine	10	N. Hampshire	1	Massachu'ts	21
New-York	70	Pennsylvania	1½	Maryland	3
Virginia	8	Kentucky	5	Michigan	12
Texas	4	Wisconsin	10	Iowa	2
California	8	Minnesota	8	Kansas	6
Nebraska	2	Dis. of Col.	2		

Total 173½

FOR MR. LINCOLN

Maine	6	N. Hampshire	7	Massach'sts	4
Connecticut	2	Pennsylvania	4	Virginia	11
Kentucky	6	Ohio	8	Indiana	26
Illinois	22	Iowa	2	Nebraska	1

Total 102

Whole number of votes 465
Necessary to a choice 233

SECOND BALLOT.

The second ballot was then taken.

FOR MR. LINCOLN

N. Hampshire .	9	Vermont	10	R. Island	3
Pennsylvania ..	48	Delaware	6	Kentucky	9
Ohio	14	Iowa	5		

Total 181

FOR MR. SEWARD.

Massachusetts .	22	New-Jersey ...	4	Pennsyl'va ...	2½
Kentucky	7	Texas	6	Nebraska	3

Total 181½

THIRD BALLOT.

The third ballot was taken amidst excitement, and cries of "the ballot." Intense feeling existed during the ballot, each vote being awaited in breathless silence and expectancy.

FOR MR. LINCOLN

Massachusetts .	8	Rhode-Island .	5	New-Jersey ...	8
Penn. (appl.) ..	52	Maryland	9	Kentucky	13
Ohio, (appl.) ..	29	Oregon	4		

This gave LINCOLN 230½ votes, or within 1½ of a nomination.

Mr. ANDREWS, of Massachusetts, then rose and corrected the vote of Massachusetts, by changing four votes and giving them to LINCOLN, thus nominating him by 2½ majority.

The Convention immediately became wildly excited.

A large portion of the delegates who had kept tally, at once said the struggle was decided, and half the Convention rose cheering, shouting, and waving hats.

The audience took up the cheers, and the confusion became deafening.

State after State rose, striving to change their votes to the winning candidate, but the noise and enthusiasm rendered it impossible for the delegates to make themselves heard.

Mr. McCRILLIS, of Maine, making himself heard, said that the young giant of the West is now of age. Maine now casts for him her 16 votes.

Mr. ANDREWS, of Massachusetts, changed the vote of that State, giving 18 to Mr. LINCOLN and 8 to Mr. SEWARD.

Intelligence of the nomination was now conveyed to the men on the roof of the building, who immediately made the outside multitude aware of the result. The first roar of the cannon soon mingled itself with the cheers of the people, and at the same moment a man appeared in the hall bringing a large painting of Mr. LINCOLN. The scene at this time beggars description—11,000 inside and 20,000 or 30,000 outside were yelling and shouting at once. Two cannon sent forth roar after roar in quick succession. Delegates tore up the sticks and boards bearing the names of the several States and waved them aloft over their heads, and the vast mulititude before the platform were waving their hats and handkerchiefs. The whole scene was one of the wildest enthusiasm.

WM. M. EVARTS, of New-York, having obtained a hearing, said: Mr. Chairman, can New-York have the silence of the Convention? [Cries, "Yes! yes!"] I ask if the vote has yet been announced. [Cries, "Not yet."] Then, Sir, I wait to be in order.

Mr. BROWN, of Missouri, desired to change 18 votes of Missouri for the gallant son of the West, ABRAM LINCOLN. Iowa, Connecticut, Kentucky and Minnesota also changed their votes. The result of the third ballot was then announced:

Whole number of votes cast 466
Necessary to a choice 234
Mr. Abram Lincoln received 354
     And was declared duly nominated.

The States still voting for SEWARD were Massachusetts, 8; New-York, 70; New-Jersey, 5; Pennsylvania, ½; Maryland, 2; Michigan, 12; Wisconsin, 10; California, 3. Total, 110½.

Mr. DAYTON received one vote from New-Jersey, and McLEAN half a vote from Pennsylvania.

The result was received with renewed applause.

When silence was restored, WM. M. EVARTS came forward on the Secretary's table and spoke as follows:

Mr. CHAIRMAN, GENTLEMEN OF THE NATIONAL CONVENTION: The State of New-York, by a full delegation, wishing complete unanimity in purpose at home, came to this Convention and presented its choice—one of its citizens who had served the State from boyhood up, and labored for it and loved it. We came here a great State, with, as we thought, a great statesman, [applause,] and our love of the great Republic from which we are all delegates. The great Republic of the American Union, and our love for the great Republican Party of the Union, and our love of our Statesman and candidate, made us think we did our duty to the country, and the whole country, in expressing our preference and love for him. [Applause.] But, gentlemen, it was from Gov. SEWARD that most of us learned to love Republican principles and the Republican Party. [Cheers.] His fidelity to the country, the Constitution and the laws—his fidelity to the party and the principle that majorities govern—his interest in the advancement of our party to its victory, that our country may rise to its true glory, induce me to declare that I speak his sentiments, as I do the united opinion of our delegation, when I move, Sir, as I do now, that the nomination of ABRAM LINCOLN, of Illinois, as the Republican candidate for the suffrages of the whole country, for the office of Chief Magistrate of the American Union, be made unanimous. [Applause, and three cheers for New-York.]

A life-size portrait of ABRAM LINCOLN was here exhibited from the platform amidst renewed cheers.

Mr. ANDREWS, of Massachusetts, on the part of the united delegation of that State, seconded the motion of the gentleman of New-York, that the nomination be made unanimous. After declaring the devotion of Massachusetts to the principles of freedom and equality, he extolled Gov. SEWARD as a statesman and patriot, and pledged the State to roll up over 100,000 majority, and give the 18 (13?) electoral votes to the candidates.

Eloquent speeches, indorsing the nominee, were also made by CARL SCHURZ, F. P. BLAIR, of Missouri, and Mr. BROWNING, of Illinois—all of which breathed a spirit of confidence and enthusiasm.

At the close, three hearty cheers were given for New-York, and the nomination of Mr. LINCOLN was made unanimous.

With loud cheers for LINCOLN, the Convention adjourned till 5 o'clock.

The wind-up of the convention at the Wigwam, the excitement of Lincoln supporters, the disappointment of Seward men, the "wild whooping of the boys" for the man "whose neighbors named him 'honest' " is described by Murat Halstead in the Daily Commercial, Cincinnati, May 21, 1860.

CONCLUSION OF PROCEEDINGS AT CHICAGO

The scenes of the Convention.

After a rather dull speech from Mr. Browning, of Illinois, responding in behalf of Lincoln, the nomination was made unanimous, and the Convention adjourned for dinner. The town was full of the news of Lincoln's nomination, and could hardly contain itself. There were bands of music playing, and processions marching, and joyous cries heard on every hand, from the army of trumpeters for Lincoln, of Illinois, and the thousands who are always enthusiastic on the winning side. But hundreds of men who had been in the wigwam were so prostrated by the excitement they had endured, and their exertions in shrieking for Seward or Lincoln, that they were hardly able to walk to their hotels. There were men who had not tasted liquor, who staggered about like drunkards, unable to manage themselves. The Seward men were terribly stricken down. They were mortified beyond all expression, and walked thoughtfully and silently away from the slaughter house, more ashamed than embittered. They acquiesced in the nomination, but did not pretend to be pleased with it; and the tone of their conversations, as to the prospect of electing the candidate, was not hopeful. It was their funeral, and they would not make merry.

A Lincoln man who could hardly believe that the "Old Abe" of his adoration was really the Republican nominee for the Presidency, took a chair at the dinner table at the Tremont House, and began talking to those around him, with none of whom he was acquainted, of the greatness of the events of the day. One of his expressions was, "Talk of your money and bring on your bullies with you!—the immortal principles of the everlasting people are with Abe Lincoln, of the people, by——." "Abe Lincoln has no money, and no bullies, but he has the people by——." A servant approached the eloquent patriot and asked what he would have to eat. Being thus recalled to temporal things he glared scornfully at the servant and roared out, "Go to the devil—what do I want to eat for? Abe Lincoln is nominated, G—— d—— it; and I'm going to live on air—the air of Liberty by——." But in a moment he inquired for the bill of fare, and then ordered "a great deal of everything"—saying if he must eat he might as well eat "the whole bill." He swore he felt as if he could "devour and digest an Illinoi prairie." And this was one of thousands.

The great agony was now over. The nomination of Vice-President was not particularly exciting. Cassius M. Clay was the only competitor of Hamlin, who made any show in the race; and the outside pressure was for him. At one time a thousand voices called "Clay!" Clay!" to the Convention. If the multitude could have had their way, Mr. Clay would have been put on the ticket by acclamation. But it was stated that Mr. Hamlin was a good friend of Mr. Seward. He was geographically distant from Lincoln and was once a Democrat. It was deemed judicious to pretend to patronize the Democratic element, and thus conciliate those who were calling the Convention an "old Whig concern." They need not have been afraid, however, of having it called an old Whig affair, for it was not "eminently respectable," nor distinguished for its "dignity and decorum." On the other hand, the satanic element was very strongly developed. After the nominations, there were the usual stump speeches, and complimentary resolutions, and the valedictory from the Chairman, and the "three times three" upon adjournment.

The city was wild with delight. The "Old Abe" men formed processions, and bore rails through the streets. Torrents of liquor were poured down the hoarse throats of the multitude. A hundred guns were fired from the top of the Tremont House. The Chicago Press and Tribune office was illuminated.—That paper says:

"On each side of the counting room door stood a rail—out of the three thousand split by "honest Old Abe" thirty years ago on the Sangamon river bottoms. On the inside were two more, brilliantly hung with tapers."

I left the city on the night train on the Fort Wayne and Chicago Road. The train consisted of eleven cars, every seat being full and people standing in the aisles and corners. I never before saw a company of persons so exhausted as they were. The Lincoln men were not able to respond to the cheers which went up along the road for "old Abe." At every station where there was a village, until two o'clock, there were tar barrels burning, drums beating, boys carrying rails; and guns, great and small, banging away. The weary passengers were allowed no rest, but plagued by the thundering jar of cannon, the clamor of drums, the glare of bonfires, and the whild whooping of the boys, who were delighted with the idea of a candidate for the Presidency who thirty years ago had split rails on the Sangamon river—classic stream now and forevermore—and whose neighbors name him "honest."

M. H.

[Murat Halstead.]

A rather imaginative though somewhat naïve special-dispatch to the New York Times was filed at the conclusion of the convention— including the misnomer "Abram" for the man who that day was nominated for President. Henry Raymond of The Times had been for Seward; Greeley of The Tribune for Bates. This report was written by Joseph Howard, Jr., in The Times of May 19, 1860.

FROM CHICAGO

THE REPUBLICAN TICKET FOR 1860

Abram Lincoln, of Illinois, Nominated
for President.

The Late Senatorial Contest in Illinois to be Re-
Fought on a Wider Field.

Hannibal Hamlin, of Maine, the Candidate
for Vice-President.

Disappointment of the Friends of
Mr. Seward.

INTENSE EXCITEMENT AND ENTHUSIASM

Reception of the Nominations in this City.

How They are Hailed Throughout the
North.

Special Dispatch to the New-York Times

CHICAGO, Friday, May 18.

The work of the Convention is ended. The youngster who, with ragged trousers, used barefoot to drive his father's oxen and spend his days in splitting rails, has risen to high eminence, and ABRAM LINCOLN, of Illinois, is declared its candidate for President by the National Republican Party.

The result was effected by the change of votes in the Pennsylvania, New-Jersey, Vermont, and Massachusetts Delegations.

Mr. SEWARD's friends assert indignantly, and with a great deal of feeling, that they were grossly deceived and betrayed. The recusants endeavored to mollify New-York by offering her the Vice-Presidency, and agreeing to support any man she might name, but they declined the position, though they remain firm in the ranks, having moved to make LINCOLN's nomination unanimous. Mr. SEWARD's friends feel greatly chagrined and disappointed.

Western pride is gratified by this nomination, which plainly indicates the departure of political supremacy from the Atlantic States. The prominent candidates for Vice-Presidency were MESSRS. HICKMAN, BANKS, CLAY and REEDER. Pennsylvania desired HICKMAN. New-York, in order to resent the conduct of Pennsylvania, Massachusetts and Kentucky, favored Mr. HAMLIN, of Maine; and on the second ballot, cast her whole strength for him, and it was owing to this, and the desire to conciliate New-York, that his nomination was so promptly secured.

Immense enthusiasm exists, and everything here would seem to indicate a spirited and successful canvass. The city is alive with processions, meetings, music and noisy demonstrations. One hundred guns were fired this evening.

The Convention was the most enthusiastic ever known in the country, and if one were to judge from appearances here, the ticket will sweep the country.

Great inquiry has been made this afternoon into the history of Mr. LINCOLN. The only evidence that he has a history as yet discovered, is that he had a stump canvass with Mr. DOUGLASS, in which he was beaten. He is not very strong at the West, but is unassailable in his private character.

Many of the delegates went home this evening by the 9 o'clock train. Others leave in the morning.

A grand excursion is planned to Rock Island and Davenport, and another to Milwaukee and Madison, and still another over the Illinois Central, over the prairies. These will detain a great many of the delegates and the editorial fraternity.

The Wigwam is as full as ever—filled now by thousands of original LINCOLN men, who they "always knew" would be nominated, and who first suggested his name, who are shouting themselves hoarse over the nomination. "What was it WEBSTER said when TAYLOR was nominated?" ask the opponents of LINCOLN. "What was the result of the election?" retort LINCOLN's friends.

Thirty-three guns were fired from the top of the Tremont House.

The dinner referred to in Tuesday evening's dispatch was a private one, and I regret that inaccurate reading of it should have misrepresented the position of the delegation as regards Mr. GREELEY. His right to act as he deemed best politically, was not denied, and consequently there was no defence of his career needed.

Massachusetts delegates, with their brass band, are parading the streets, calling at the various headquarters of the other delegations, serenading and bidding them farewell. "Hurrah for LINCOLN and HAMLIN —Illinois and Maine!" is the universal shout, and sympathy for the bottom dog is the all-pervading sentiment.

The "Wide-Awakes," numbering about two thousand men, accompanied by thousands of citizens, have a grand torch-light procession. The German Republican Club has another. The office of the *Press and Tribune* is brilliantly illuminated, and has a large transparency over the door saying, "For President, Honest Old ABE." A bonfire thirty feet in circumference burns in front of the Tremont House, and illumines the city for miles around. The city is one blaze of illumination. Hotels, stores and private residences, shining with hundreds of patriotic dips. ENOUGH.

HOWARD.

[Joseph Howard, Jr.]

The eyes of the country now moved from Chicago to Springfield. To George Ashmun, President of the Republican National Convention, Lincoln wrote, "Deeply, and even painfully sensible of the great responsibility which is inseparable from that honor—a responsibility which I could almost wish had fallen upon some one of the more eminent and experienced statesmen whose distinguished names were before the Convention, I shall, by your leave, consider more fully the resolutions of the Convention." The nation sought personal details of the Westerner, and John L. Scripps in the Chicago Tribune of May 23, 1860, supplied them (Lincoln read the editorial before it was published). Interestingly, a sentence in this editorial—the one where Lincoln says, "They shan't do it, d-n 'em!"—was cut out of a future campaign pamphlet based on this Scripps statement.

LINCOLN AS HE IS

Ten thousand inquiries will be made as to the looks, the habits, tastes and other characteristics of Honest Old Abe. We anticipate a few of them.

Mr. Lincoln stands six feet and four inches high in his stockings. His frame is not muscular, but gaunt and wiry; his arms are long, but not unreasonably so for a person of his height; his lower limbs are not disproportioned to his body. In walking, his gait though firm is never brisk. He steps slowly and deliberately, almost always with his head inclined forward and his hands clasped behind his back.

In matters of dress he is by no means precise. Always clean, he is never fashionable; he is careless but not slovenly. In manner he is remarkably cordial, and at the same time, simple. His politeness is always sincere but never elaborate and oppressive. A warm shake of the hand and a warmer smile of recognition are his methods of greeting his friends.

At rest, his features though those of a man of mark, are not such as belong to a handsome man; but when his fine dark gray eyes are lighted up by any emotion, and his features begin their play, he would be chosen from among a crowd as one who had in him not only the kindly sentiments which women love, but the heavier metal of which full grown men and Presidents are made. His hair is black, and though thin is wiry. His head sits well on his shoulders, but beyond that it defies description. It nearer resembles that of Clay than that of Webster; but is unlike either. It is very large and, phrenologically, well proportioned, betokening power in all its developments. A slightly Roman nose, a widecut mouth and a dark complexion, with the appearance of having been weather-beaten, completes the description.

In his personal habits, Mr. Lincoln is as simple as a child. He loves a good dinner and eats with the appetite which goes with a great brain; but his food is plain and nutritious. He never drinks intoxicating liquors of any sort, not even a glass of wine. He is not addicted to tobacco, in any of its shapes. He never was accused of a licentious act in all his life. He never uses profane language. A friend says that once, when in a towering rage in consequence of the efforts of certain parties to perpetrate a fraud on the State, he was heard to say "They shan't do it, d—n 'em!" but beyond an expression of that kind, his bitterest feelings never carry him. He never gambles; we doubt if he ever indulges in any games of chance.

He is particularly cautious about incurring pecuniary obligations for any purpose whatever, and in debt, he is never content until the score is discharged. We presume he owes no man a dollar. He never speculates. The rage for sudden acquisition of wealth never took hold of him. His gains from his profession have been moderate, but sufficient for his purposes. While others have dreamed of gold, he has been in pursuit of knowledge. In all his dealings he has the reputation of being generous but exact, and above all, religiously honest. He would be a bold man who would say that Abraham Lincoln ever wronged any one out of a cent, or ever spent a dollar that he had not honestly earned. His struggles in early life have made him careful of money; but his generosity with his own is proverbial.

He is a regular attendant upon religious worship, and though not a communicant, is a pew-holder and liberal supporter of the Presbyterian Church in Springfield, to which Mrs. Lincoln belongs. He is a scrupulous teller of the truth—too exact in his notions to suit the atmosphere of Washington as it now is. His enemies may say that he tells Black Republican lies; but no man ever charged that, in a professional capacity, or as a citizen dealing with his neighbors, he would depart from the Scriptural command.

At home he lives like a gentleman of modest means and simple tastes. A good sized house of wood, simply but tastefully furnished; surrounded by trees and flowers, is his own, and there he lives, at peace with himself, the idol of his family, and for his honesty, ability and patriotism, the admiration of his countrymen.

If Mr. Lincoln is elected President, he will carry but little that is ornamental to the White House. The country must accept his sincerity, his ability and his honesty, in the mould in which they are cast. He will not be able to make as polite a bow as Frank Pierce, but he will not commence anew the agitation of the Slavery question by recommending to Congress any Kansas-Nebraska bills. He may not preside at the Presidential dinners with the ease and grace which distinguish the "venerable public functionary," Mr. Buchanan; but he will not create the necessity for a Covode Committee [John Covode, Republican Congressman, was chairman of a house committee investigating charges against Buchanan] and the disgraceful revelations of Cornelius Wendell [a Congressional printer, who testified before a Senate Committee about sums exacted from him by Democrats]. He will take to the Presidential chair just the qualities which the country now demands to save it from impending destruction—ability that no man can question, firmness that nothing can overbear, honesty that never has been impeached, and patriotism that never despairs.

The opposition and friendly press began to debate Lincoln's background and qualifications. In this New York Tribune editorial replying to the Democratic Philadelphia Journal (which was suppressed in 1863), Greeley recalls that his opposition to Lincoln in the Senatorial contest in 1858 helped to defeat the man he now praised. At this post-nomination time, too, a public battle took place between Greeley and Raymond of the Times, who blamed Greeley for sabotaging the Seward cause. This Tribune editorial appeared May 24, 1860.

MR. LINCOLN'S ABILITIES

The following article from The Philadelphia Evening Journal sums up so completely all that has been put forth in disparagement of Mr. Lincoln's qualifications for the Presidency, that we print it entire, in order that our readers may have the whole case before them. Hear The Journal:

WHY SHOULD LINCOLN BE PRESIDENT.— It is very evident that the "Republican" newspapers are hard put to it for something to say in favor of Mr. Lincoln. His record as a statesman is a blank. He has done nothing whatever in any executive, judicial, or legislative capacity, that should entitle him to public respect. There is not in all the history of his life any exhibition of intellectual ability and attainments fitting him for the high and responsible post in the Government for which he has been nominated. When in Congress, from 1847 to 1849, he was not only not distinguished by any display of parliamentary talent, or by any special service, but those who sat in the same Congress find it difficult to remember that any such person as Abraham Lincoln occupied a seat on the floor. His contest in 1858 with Mr. Douglas for the election as United States Senator from Illinois is the beginning of his fame, and while he showed in that controversy the rough strength of a practiced stump speaker, and the pluck of a champion who enters the ring with a crowd of sturdy backers, he exceeded even Seward in the extravagance of his views respecting the Slavery question, while his coarse language, his illiterate style, and his vulgar and vituperative personalities in debate, contrast very strongly the elegant and classical oratory of the eminent Senator from New-York. But the party organs think Lincoln is a capital man for a political canvass, because, forsooth, he was once a flat-boatman and a rail-splitter. Now, we have great and sincere respect for what are denominated self-made men—for men who, springing from an obscure condition, and struggling against adverse circumstances in early life, manage, by the force of natural character and heroic efforts, to rise to honorable independence and distinction. We do not deny to Mr. Lincoln the merit of having made good use of his opportunities and means, and we should like to see him enjoy all the just rewards of his manly industry and self-reliance and self improvement. But there is a proper measure of desert in these cases, which should not be disregarded. It does not by any means follow that because an individual who, beginning life as a flat-boatman and wood-chopper, raises himself to the position of a respectable County Court lawyer and a ready stump speaker, is therefore qualified to be President of the United States. There is no fitness or proportion between the two things—between the measure of merit or title and the high and arduous trust to be conferred. It is much more wise and logical to put the proposition thus—if a man is, in all essential respects, eminently fitted for the Presidential office, the fact that he was once a boatman and a mauler of rails, is greatly to his credit; but it will not do to say that he is qualified to be and deserves to be President, because, as a boy, he split logs and steered a "broadhorn" on the Mississippi. But the "Republican" newspaper organs must accept the postulate in the latter form, in order to suit the case of their candidate; and we shall doubtless be asked to adopt it as a safe and judicious rule for the election of men to the highest posts in the Government. But will the people be cheated by such clap-trap? We think not.

—Let us turn now to the other side, and, having considered both, we shall be able to form a pretty accurate judgment on the matter at issue. Ponder, then, these undeniable facts:

1. Mr. Lincoln was born in the very humblest walks of life, and was left in extreme poverty by the death of his father when he was but six years of age. He never enjoyed the advantage of wealthy or powerful relatives. He had very little schooling of any kind—none but in the rudest log cabins of the frontier forests. He has had no special good luck, and, since he ceased to be very poor, has lived on his own moderate earnings, never having known what it is to be rich. And yet this man has just been nominated for President over the heads of several concededly, eminently able and worthy men who were his competitors. Is there not in these facts a solid basis for the presumption that he is a man of unusual ability?

2. His life-battle has been fought under many extraneous disadvantages. The State wherein all his years of manhood have transpired has been steadily opposed to him in politics. It was overwhelmingly for Jackson; he was against him. It resisted the Harrison tornado, which swept all beside of the Free West—all but his and one other (New-Hampshire) of the Free States—all but seven States in the entire Union. It steadily

opposed Clay and Taylor, whom he as steadily supported. It never elected a United States Senator opposed to what is called Democracy until 1854–5; and then Mr. Lincoln was the first choice of nine-tenths of the Opposition; but he and these nine-tenths were Whigs, while the residue were anti-Nebraska Democrats, who disliked to vote for a Whig, and presented Judge Trumbull; so the Whigs—at Mr. Lincoln's earnest entreaty—went over to Judge T. and elected him. Is it likely that the Whigs would have unanimously selected an inferior man to send, on their very first chance, to the Senate, over the heads of such men as O. H. Browning, Jackson Grimshaw, Richard Yates, S. T. Logan, and many other steadfast champions of their cause, who certainly are *not* inferior men? What would have been their motive for so perverse a choice?

3. Mr. Lincoln's rise has been gradual and steady. At twenty-three years of age, having volunteered for the Black Hawk war, he was chosen captain of his company. Having been previously a flat-boat man, a rail-splitter, a farm-hand and a store-clerk, he became next a land-surveyor, and followed this vocation till the grand crash of 1837 temporarily destroyed it, when his instruments were sold away from him on execution. He was soon after, at about 30 years of age, chosen to the Legislature, and rechosen thrice in succession. While thus living on the pittance paid to a legislator (the age of Gridiron Railroads and such like having not then dawned on a benighted world) he studied law, and was admitted to the bar. In 1844—when 35 years of age, and quite a novice in his profession—he was chosen to head the Clay Electoral Ticket, and in that capacity to canvass the State, which he did most thoroughly and effectively. And his work was so well done that we believe he has been at the head, formerly of the Whig, latterly of the Republican ticket, at every subsequent Presidential election. He certainly headed the Republican Electoral Ticket in 1856. When was it ever before imagined or pretended that inferior men, especially when rudely educated, are habitually chosen for such positions?

4. Mr. Lincoln was a candidate for Congress (House) in 1846, and was the only Whig (out of seven) elected from the State. His majority was 1,511—the largest, we are confident, ever given in that District to any candidate opposed to what is called Democracy. It is much larger than any other of which we have a record. The same District gave Mr. Clay but 914 majority in '44, and Gen. Taylor but 1,501 majority on a vastly heavier vote in '48. Gen. Taylor's vote was swelled by the great number of volunteers residing in the District who had served under him in the Mexican war. Mr. Logan (Whig) was *beaten* for Congress this year—Col. Harris

(Dem.) carrying the District by 106 majority over him. And in 1850 Mr. Yates (now Republican candidate for Governor) only won it back by 754 majority—not half that cast in '46 for Mr. Lincoln.

5. Since '46, Mr. Lincoln has not been a candidate before the People for any office but that of Elector of President. But in 1858 the Republican State Convention unanimously designated him as their representative man to stump the State against Stephen A. Douglas. They knew that the struggle would be a desperate one—that they must put their very best foot foremost. If they had had a champion whom they supposed abler and worthier than Mr. Lincoln, they would have chosen that champion for this arduous service. They had nearly all heard Lincoln and their other speakers, and ought to have known by this time who was their best man; yet they chose Abraham Lincoln. If they don't know who is their best man, should not missionaries be sent out to teach them?

6. Mr. Lincoln went into this canvass under most discouraging auspices. Many leading Republicans out of the State thought the opposition to Mr. Douglas impolitic and mistaken. We certainly thought so; and, though we said little on the point, our very silence was damaging in a State where more people read this paper than any other. It has been a hundred times asserted that THE TRIBUNE "defeated Lincoln." But there were other outside influences, as adverse and at least equally potent. In 1856, the State polled 37,444 American or Whig votes for Fillmore. Many of these were cast by natives of Kentucky; all by men who love and confide in John J. Crittenden. In the thickest of the fray, a letter from Mr. Crittenden was published, advising them to favor Mr. Douglas's reëlection. Undoubtedly, this had an overruling influence with thousands. Yet, after Messrs. Lincoln and Douglas had thoroughly canvassed the State, the People voted, with the following result:

		Fremont	Fillmore	Buchanan
Total vote in '56		96,189	37,444	105,348
		Lincoln	Lecompton	Douglas
Total vote in '58		125,275	5,071	121,190
L's gain on '56	29,086	Douglas's do		15,742

Lincoln's net gain, 14,344

Or, give Douglas the entire Lecompton vote in addition to his own, and Lincoln still gains on him 9,273.

—Bear in mind that this was a contest in which the sympathies of men indifferent to party were almost wholly with Douglas, wherein many Republicans supported him throughout, wherein Crittenden summoned the Americans to his aid, and wherein he stood boldly on the ground of Popular Sovereignty, with the prestige of having just before defeated the infamous Lecompton bill. All things considered, we recall nothing in the history of political campaiging more creditable to a canvasser than this vote is to Lincoln.

—We have thus dwelt throughout on facts of public record or of universal notoriety. The Speeches made to the same audiences in that canvass by Messrs. Lincoln and Douglas were collected and printed by the Republicans of Ohio for cheap and general dissemination, long before they dreamed that Mr. Lincoln would be the Republican candidate for President. We had sold hundreds of them at our counter, as we had thousands of Mr. Lincoln's Speech in this City, before the meeting of the Chicago Convention; we expect to sell thousands of the former and tens of thousands of the latter forthwith. Every reader can herein see just what manner of man Mr. Lincoln is, and how he bears himself when confronted with one of the very best and most effective popular canvassers in the Democratic ranks. If Mr. Lincoln is weak, or ill informed, or anywise deficient, this protracted Discussion with Douglas must show it. Will *The Journal* aid us in giving it the widest possible circulation?

—Of Mr. Lincoln's merits as "a flat-boatman and mauler of rails," we have little to say. We are no judge of flat-boat navigation; but the rails made by Lincoln thirty years ago, which we saw in Chicago, seemed a very fair article. Let us put these entirely out of the account, and judge Mr. Lincoln solely by his intellectual and political record as a public man. If the facts do not prove him very different from what *The Journal* represents him, the American People will so decide. We fearlessly await their verdict.

In Springfield Lincoln's longtime friend, the Illinois Journal, delighted to observe the split in the Democratic ranks and the weakened position of Stephen Douglas. They also found much to laugh over in comments on the "distinguished Sucker" (an affectionate term for an Illinoisian), and how to pronounce his name. From the Illinois Journal, May 31, 1860. The final anecdote—known to every schoolboy —appeared on June 2, 1860.

HUMORS OF THE CAMPAIGN

The Illinois *Republican* contains the following obituary notice of a once popular animal:

DIED.—At Charlestown, South Carolina, on the 3d inst., the old and well-known horse Democracy.

The above named horse was sired by Thos. Jefferson and dam(n)ed by Stephen A. Douglas.

The following, which occurred in Washington a few days after the nominations at Baltimore, will serve to show how that nomination is looked upon by the "live men" of the South American party:

A prominent Southern Opposition member of Congress met one of the returning delegates from that Baltimore Convention. "Well," said he, "who did you nominate?" "We nominated Bell and Everett." "What! Bell and Everett?" "Yes." "Why didn't you nominate Choate?" "Choate! why, he is dead!" "Oh, I know it; but he hasn't been dead a very long time."

FAITH AND WORKS.—An ardent young Republican rushed into the *Herald* office in Cleveland last Monday, and handed Benedict a manuscript which read thus:

Two things are necessary to salvation, viz.: *Faith* and *Works*. In Abraham we have *Faith*, and in Hannibal, *Works*. The country is saved.

The young man fainted.

The Detroit *Advertiser* gives the first joke of the campaign in that section. A Republican was hailed by a Douglas man on the receipt of the news of the nomination of Abraham Lincoln, with the question:

"Hillo! what do you think *now?*"

"Think? what do I think?" was the ready reply. "I think you had better embrace the only opportunity you'*ll* ever have of getting into '*Abraham's bosom*,' and join the Republicans at once."

PROPER PRONOUNCIATION OF LINCOLN.—The nomination of Abraham Lincoln, as the Republican candidate for President, has raised the question of its proper pronounciation—many contending that it should be pronounced according to its liberal orthography—*Lincollen*. All the best authorities, however, agree in pronouncing it as they do out West—*Linken*. Below we give three leading authorities on the subject:

Link-on—Lippencott's Gazetteer.

Link-un—Webster's Unabridged.

Ling-kun—Worcester's New Dictionary.

In Illinois, where everybody claims the privilege of familiarity with

"Old Abe," they have somewhat improved on the above, and speak of the distinguished Sucker as "*Old Abe Linkem.*"

"HURRAH FOR LICKEM AND HANGEM!"—A gentleman of this place was reading the *Gazette* on the day it was issued, containing the announcement of the nominations at Chicago, when a little boy, about ten years of age, inquired of him, "Who's nominated?" The gentleman informed him that it was Lincoln of Illinois and Hamlin of Maine. The boy started off, and shouted at the top of his voice, "Hurrah for Lickem and Hangem!" Not so bad a misnomer after all.—*Cor. Cin. Gaz.*

TIT FOR TAT.—The Bell and Everett organ in this city a day or two ago published the following: "Why is it impossible for 'Abe' Lincoln to attain the Presidential chair? Because he lacks an *l* of being *able.*" If you come to that, why is it impossible that Bell should ever attain the Presidential chair? Ans.—Because he lacks an *a* of being *abel.* So far as joking is concerned, we consider both attempts exercrable, but this ringing the changes upon names is a game that two can play at.—*Boston Journal.*

WHAT PRENTICE THINKS OF OLD ABE.—The Republican organs, by common consent, designate their candidate for the Presidency as "Honest Old Abe." We are by no means disposed to deny his right to the designation. We know him personally, and however strongly we may condemn some of the doctrines to which he is committed, we have at no time seen reason to doubt his honesty. We believe that he has the good of his country at heart. Thus much we take pleasure in saying in his behalf.—*Louisville Journal.*

☞ The St. Louis Evening *News* says: "There is an upheaving all through the land, just now, in behalf of Douglas."

Spewing him out are they?

LINCOLN'S CONSCIENTIOUSNESS IN BOYHOOD

We have heard, says the Evansville (Ind.) Journal, the following anecdote related of the People's candidate for the Presidency, which shows the love of knowledge, the industry, the conscientiousness and the integrity of the subject of this sketch:

It is well known that he lived in Spencer county, above here in Indiana, in his young days. He was a hard-working lad, and very eager in his thirst for knowledge. A man named Crawford owned a copy of "Weem's Life of Washington"—the only one in the whole neighborhood.

Young Lincoln borrowed that interesting book, (not having money to spare to buy one,) and while reading it, by a slight negligence left it in a window, when a rainstorm came up and wet the book so as to ruin it. Young Lincoln felt very badly, but like an honest boy he went to Mr. Crawford with the ruined book, acknowledged his accountability for its destruction, and his willingness to make due compensation. He said he had no money, but would work out the value of the book.

The owner of the book said to him, "Well, Abe, being as it's you, I won't be hard on you. If you will come over and pull fodder for two days, I'll let you off."

Abe went over accordingly, and pulled fodder the requisite time; and so tall and handy a lad was he, that Crawford required him to pull the fodder off of the tallest stalks, while he took the shortest ones himself.

The story is told with much gusto by one of our prominent citizens, who used to know Abe Lincoln in his younger days in Spencer county, and who now—since the once humble lad has become the choice of a great party for the highest office in the world,—regards him with strong affection, and supports him with enthusiasm.

Long memories lived in Illinois. In Springfield they remembered two Representatives from the county of Sangamon, Dan Stone and A. Lincoln, way back in 1837, protesting against pro-slavery resolutions. Lincoln, at the age of 28, standing on principle against the Southern sympathizers in the Illinois General Assembly. Here was the consistent record of a quarter of a century, in spite of Lincoln's conciliatory language, of opposition to human enslavement. The Illinois Journal, June 2, 1860.

MR. LINCOLN'S POLITICAL OPINIONS

In looking back over Mr. Lincoln's political record it is a gratifying fact to discover that he has ever been consistent, with himself in his views and opinions on the great questions which have so long been under discussion before the American people. A firm and unflinching Whig during the lifetime of that good old-party and ever one of its most uncompromising defenders, we still find him, as the Republican Standard bearer for the Presidency, promulgating the same doctrines he did then and fighting for the supremacy of the same great principles of Government. In 1836–7 Mr. Lincoln was one of the Representatives in the Legislature from

Sangamon County and during the session, as usual, resolutions taking an extreme Southern view on the subject of Democratic slavery were brought forward, discussed and finally adopted. Mr. Lincoln refused to vote for them but took advantage of the Constitutional privilege allowing any two members to enter their protest upon the Journals of the House to give his views on the subject, in the form of a protest. The paper is worthy of being produced at the present time and we give it, as follows:

March 3d, 1837.
The following protest was presented to the House, which was read and ordered to be spread on the journals, to-wit:

"Resolutions upon the subject of domestic slavery having passed both branches of the General Assembly at its present session, the undersigned hereby protest against the passage of the same.

They believe that the institution of slavery is founded on both injustice and bad policy; but that the promulgation of abolition doctrines tends rather to increase than abate its evils.

They believe that the Congress of the United States has no power, under the Constitution, to interfere with the institution of slavery in the different States.

They believe that the Congress of the United States has the power, under the Constitution, to abolish slavery in the District of Columbia; but that that power ought not to be exercised unless at the request of the people of said District.

The difference between these opinions and those contained in the said resolutions, is their reason for entering this protest."

DAN STONE,
A. LINCOLN,
Representatives from the county of Sangamon.

Ten years after this time Mr. Lincoln was a member of Congress from this District, and we still find him enunciating the same conservative and conciliatory views. Aside from his speeches, which we have no room now to quote from, he matured and proposed to bring forward in Congress "a bill to abolish slavery in the District of Columbia, *by consent of the free white people of said District and with compensation to owners.*" The bill was first proposed as a substitute for a resolution of Mr. Gott, of Conn., and afterwards as an independent measure. . . .

Ten years after this in 1858, we find Mr. Lincoln and Mr. Douglas pittied together, before the people for the U.S. Senatorship; and we still see Mr. Lincoln maintaining and defending the same opinions which he

avowed in 1837 and 1848. At the Freeport debate in response to inter-
rogatories from Mr. Douglas, he declared among other things, that he
"did not stand pledged to the abolition of slavery in the District of
Columbia." But said he:—

> In relation to that, I have my mind very distinctly made up. I
> should be exceedingly glad to see Slavery abolished in the District
> of Columbia. I believe that Congress possesses the constitutional
> power to abolish it. Yet as a member of Congress, I should not, with
> my present views, be in favor of endeavoring to abolish Slavery in
> the District of Columbia, unless it would be upon these conditions:
> First that the abolition should be gradual; second, that it should be
> on a vote of the majority of qualified voters in the District; and
> third, that compensation should be made to unwilling owners. With
> these three conditions, I confess I would be exceedingly glad to see
> Congress abolish Slavery in the District of Columbia, and in the
> language of Henry Clay, "sweep from our Capitol that foul blot
> upon our 'nation.'"

We do not wish to be understood as seeking to convey the impression that wise men never change their opinions or that political consistency is always indicative of a great statesman, but we think it difficult to
find a political record running through twenty years, which has been so
decided and yet so uniform and so consistent as that of Mr. Lincoln
upon the great questions of the day. The same opinions which he held to
and maintained when he was first elected to the Legislature, he has continued to hold to and defend up to the present time. While old parties
have gone down and new ones have arisen; while old political landmarks
have been swept away and new creeds have appeared; while other public
men, his cotemporaries and rivals, have changed and been transformed
so that it is no longer possible to identify them, Mr. Lincoln still stands
by the matured and well considered views which he formed in early manhood. He studied "the question of the proper division of local from
Federal authority from the fathers of the Constitution and the framers
of the Government under which we live," and he still believes they
"understood this question just as well and even better than we do now."

The Southern press, between the time of the nomination and
inauguration, admitted grudgingly that the Republican candidate had
qualifications to arouse the sympathy of voters. The Kentucky papers

pointed with pride (albeit between the lines) to the fact that Lincoln was born there. The New Orleans Bee found him popular among the burly sons of the West. From reprints in the Illinois Journal, June 2, 13 and 14, 1860.

From the Paris [Ky.] Citizen, Southern Opposition

SOUTHERN TRIBUTE TO MR. LINCOLN HERE.

Mr. Lincoln, though a decided Republican, and a complete exponent of the purposes and spirit of the party, is not the object of those popular prejudices that attach to Mr. Seward, his strongest competitor for the nomination. He is a man of ability, not equal to Mr. Seward in culture or in his experience of public affairs, but is considered by many as his equal in natural force of intellect. We heard one of the discussions between him and Douglas in the famous campaign of 1858, and we certainly regarded him as a full match, at least, for that distinguished politician. There are some things in the personal character and career of Mr. Lincoln, which will give him great popularity, if they do not excite enthusiasm among the people. Born of humble parentage, and passing the years of his childhood, youth and early manhood amid the hardships of the backwoods of Kentucky, Indiana and Illinois, acquiring an education by his own labors as best he could, and gradually working his way to distinction, his life has been one well calculated to excite the admiration and sympathy of voters, most of whom are themselves working men. When to this is added the purity of his private life, the general recognition of which has given him, in his own State, the sobriquet of "Honest Old Abe," we are compelled to admit that the Chicago Convention has nominated the very hardest man to beat it could possibly have given us.

The question now is, "How is this ticket to be beaten?" We confess that in the divided, distracted and chaotic condition of all other parties, the problem is extremely difficult of solution.

WHAT THE SOUTH THINKS.—The New Orleans Bee says of the Chicago platform, that the Convention has "promulgated a programme of principles which, with few exceptions, would apply quite as readily to one portion of the country as another." It continues:

"The Black Republicans denounce forays like that of John Brown in emphatic language, disclaim the slightest intention of interfering with the institutions of the South, and confine the assertion of their peculiar tenets to the denial of the duty of Congress to protect slavery, and to the expression of an opinion in favor of the immediate admission of Kansas into the Union:"

In regard to the candidate, the *Bee* thinks "that the Republicans have furnished a signal manifestation of their determination to avoid extremes;" and it says of Mr. Lincoln: "He is a man of agreeable manners, a ready and forcible speaker, self-made and self-taught, and personally popular among the burly sons of the West."

LINCOLN'S BIRTH PLACE.—A letter from Louisville states that in Kentucky Abraham Lincoln personally is spoken well of by all. "As an individual, he is liked for his honesty and sincerity, his Democratic habits and manners, and his Henry Clay type of character. A Kentuckian from Nelson county tells me that Lincoln stock in that vicinity is first-rate, and that the old farmers who knew and loved Abe's father, and remember Abe when an infant and a poor orphan boy, talk as if they have half a notion to vote for the worthy and now so distinguished man. Though biographers say he was born in Hardin, the Nelson folks, whose county adjoins Hardin and Washington, insist he first saw the light of day from the top of "Possum Ridge," in Washington, near the Washington and Nelson border line; and Washingtonians confirm it. I don't know who is correct. It may be the honor of Abe Lincoln's birth place will, after a while, be as much disputed by some counties of Kentucky as is that of Gen. Jackson's by some States of our Union.

Hundreds of poems were to be written by skilled and unskilled but sincere men, all mentioning Lincoln. This, from the Chicago Press and Tribune, was picked up by the Illinois Journal, July 2, 1860.

POETRY

From the Press and Tribune

"RIGHTEOUS ABE-L."

By M. C. SPAULDING.

When old Tom Jefferson was here
Teaching his maxims to the world,

He uttered one we hold most dear—
One which at tyrant's thrones he hurled,

"In choosing men select the best
Your neighborhood affords,
And to your crop apply the test
That marks *good* fruit from gourds.

"Let them be men whose faithfulness
You've *tried*, and therefore *know*,
Whose every virtue all confess
Pure white as driven snow.

"Their honesty being well known,
Ability comes next;
If this you find maturely grown,
You'll no more be perplexed.

Had old Tom lived until to-day,
To vote for President,
"That maxim's 'true as truth,' " he'd say,
"LINCOLN's the man I meant.

"For I have found him honest, Abe-L,
Righteous as he of yore,
I'll warrant he will do as *well*
As Abraham, and more.

EVANSTON, ILL.

From abroad, especially England, much misunderstanding of Lincoln and his manner and meaning was due to appear. This analysis, moderate in tone, found its way into the Illinois Journal of Aug. 16, 1860.

The London *Critic* reviews the speeches of Abraham Lincoln. In the course of its article occurs the following passage: "It is from the speeches which Mr. Lincoln has from time to time delivered in opposition to Mr. Douglas, that we gather some idea of his mental qualifications. We collect from the speeches of Mr. Lincoln that he has a mind rather of the straightforward than of the subtle order; that he rather seizes upon great and prominent facts and argues them to plain conclusions, than builds up elegant but fragile theories upon the treacherous basis of fanciful speculation; that he is earnest more than passionate, and commanding more than persuasive. Indeed, every one of his speeches which we have read, bears upon the face of it evidence that he is 'Honest Old Abe.' "

Lincoln led to something sinister called Lincolnism—that all men of all races are equal by nature, and ought to be equal in government. This was considered a fallacious fundamental idea of Lincoln Republicanism by Lumsden, Kendall & Co., editors and proprietors, The Daily Picayune, New Orleans, Aug. 18, 1860, a newspaper suppressed after the capture of New Orleans.

LINCOLN DELUSIONS

The Republican paper in Chicago was lately pressed by one of its cotemporaries with the question, "Does it dare propose to let loose four millions and a half of black slaves to vagabondize over the country and mingle on equal terms with the free white men of Illinois?"

His answer is a political curiosity.

In the first place, he unconsciously expresses his disgust at the idea of harboring the liberated slaves in Illinois, by protesting it to be a "cruel and wicked imposition" on the credulity of the North, invented to chill and curdle their sympathy for the slave, to say that the North will be deluged by them in the event of emancipation. It is a "dishonest device" of slaveholders "to convert Northern men into doughfaces."

Northern Abolitionists, therefore, desire to have nothing to do with the freed negro. They want to emancipate him, but he must keep away from them. It "curdles" their blood with disgust to have it imagined that the blacks, for whose liberation they are pleading, shall come among themselves to sit down, as equals, alongside of their clamorous friends. Their gorge rises at the thought that their own garments should even be soiled by contact with their disenthralled brethren.

The Press accordingly proceeds to combat this apprehension by averring that there is no fear that emancipation in the South will bring any free Negro into the North. He encourages the Abolitionists with the confident opinion that "if all the slaves in the South were granted their freedom to-morow it is doubtful whether an omnibus load of them would cross the line of Mason and Dixon."

He attempts to cheer them up with the assurance that, on the contrary, instead of a rush of freed negroes North, three hundred thousand free negroes from the North would migrate South, and join themselves to their kindred races in these States, to enjoy the ease and comfort they are all going to enjoy as free men in the Southern States. The North will have less than before, it will get rid of its own nuisances by turning them upon us.

Northern Abolitionism defends itself to the instincts of the white races by pretending that the emancipation of four millions of slaves, which it expects to be kept in the South, is also an economical way of getting rid of three hundred thousand of those whose way of using their freedom makes them offensive to the North.

It is hardly worth the while to argue against such inconsistent trash. It is intended to quiet for a while the natural alarm of reflecting men at the North, against the effects upon themselves of the realization of the fundamental idea of Lincoln Republicanism—that all men of all races are equal by nature, and ought to be equal in government. But the plea, demonstrable as it is to be fallacious in theory, overlooks the very important practical fact that the condition of the liberated slave, his residence in any Southern community, or the admission thereto of any more African blood, depend on the Legislatures of the several Southern States. The Northern man who shrinks from contact in his own person with this back element, will receive with many suspicions those wild speculations on the possibility that a Jamaica can be established in every Southern State, from which the North will obtain nothing but advantage. Emancipation, by the act of all the Southern States, is a monstrous impossibility. Emancipation by the border States, whenever that shall come, will be accompanied necessarily by the deportation of the freed, and preceded by the removal of the bulk of the slaves South. Does it enter into the head of any man of sane mind that the Southern slaveholding States would permit the introduction of that liberated class at all, and that they would not legislate against it in the most rigid form? It is true that Illinois might also legislate to keep them out of her borders. That is the principle of a good deal of her legislation, and the avowals of repugnance now before us to the association threatened by this immigration, would foreshadow some still more severe police provisions, in order to prevent the incoming of liberated slaves into Illinois. But what, their humane men will ask, is to become of the wretched victims of their officious intervention? Excluded from the South by the law of a stern political duty and social necessity; proscribed by the sentiment of the North, in derision of its own theories of equality; and what sort of philanthrophy is that which, wrapping itself up in a stoical security, afar off, labors to turn a class of helpless creatures out of their comfortable homes, and at the same time, closes the door of their only place of refuge against them.

These are phases of the electioneering talk of Lincolnism, in the North, which it deeply interests the people of the South to know.

Mr. Lincoln sat home, a custom of Presidential candidates, between nomination and Election Day. He watched the political picture closely and was in steady communication with his lieutenants of the press, men such as Joseph Medill of the Chicago Tribune. Visitors poured into Springfield, some from the South. Mr. Lincoln's talks with some Southern gentlemen are the subject of a letter to the Baltimore Patriot, explained in the Illinois Journal, Sept. 26, 1860.

MR. LINCOLN AT HOME

We take the following extract of a letter written from this city to the Baltimore *Patriot*, one of the leading Bell papers of the South:

"Some of the most interesting interviews which Mr. Lincoln has had, has been with extreme Southern gentlemen, who came full of prejudices against him, but who left satisfied with his loyalty to all the constitutional rights of the South. I could tell you of some most interesting cases, but it is enough to know that the general sentiment of all Southern men who have conversed with him is the same as that publicly expressed by Mr. Goggin, of Virginia, Mr. Perry, of South Carolina, Mr. McRae, of North Carolina, and many others, who have not hesitated to avow their intention of accepting Mr. Lincoln's election, and holding him to the constitutional discharge of the Presidential office.

"You know Mr. Crittenden and Mr. Breckinridge and Mr. Bell, personally, and intimately, I believe, and I am sure you would be satisfied with the election to the Presidency of either of these gentlemen, in a personal point of view, and apart from Mr. Breckinridge's being a Democrat. If you know Mr. Lincoln, [we do,] I do not see how you can fail to recognize in him all the high and lofty qualities personally of the gentlemen just named. He is a Kentuckian, and we shall have a Henry Clay administration at his hands. That is enough for me.

"I notice you concede the election of Mr. Lincoln. You do no more than acknowledge, in advance, the self-evident culmination of the campaign. That Mr. Lincoln should be your second choice, after Mr. Bell, seeing that both of them were old Clay men, is to your credit. Nobody, who has ever known the *Patriot*, would expect it to become a tender to Democracy in any form. I rejoice that you have held firm to the old faith. The old Clay guard of Illinois know how to estimate your constant fidelity to principles. You are not alone amongst the old Clay men of the South. I could give you the names of Southern men you little dream of, who occupy precisely your position, and who will never countenance the restoration of Democracy to power again, by any act of theirs. You do but justice to Mr. Bell when you oppose all colitions with Democracy."

The foreign voter was important and the way the wind blew in the foreign-language press was observed by the Lincoln camp. Lincoln himself had, since May 30, 1859, controlled the Illinois Staats-Anzeiger —his contract of ownership said the paper had to be Republican politically. Before leaving Springfield he transferred the paper back to Theodore Canisius. The following article, commenting on the Abend Zeitung, was first reprinted in the New York Post, then in the Illinois Journal, Sept. 26, 1860.

THE WAY THE REPUBLICANS SUFFER FROM FUSION

The *Abend Zeitung*, a New York German paper, speaking of the disgust occasioned among the German Democrats by the fusion schemes of their leaders, says: "As Scroggs, Dodge and thousands of other Americans will vote for Lincoln, not because he is an 'American,' but in order to express their disapprobation of the unscrupulous sale of their party by its leaders, so thousands of German Democrats will vote for him, and for similar reasons. The other day a 'Democratic Lincoln Club' was formed in one of the upper wards of this city, consisting of forty German citizens, who formally declared their intention of voting for Old Abe, instead of going it blind for the confusion ticket. We might mention other similar cases. Scarcely a single German Republican ward meeting is held at which a number of Democrats do not have themselves enrolled in the list of Republican voters. In 1856 barely one-half or two-fifths of the naturalized Germans cast their votes for Fremont, but in 1860 from two-thirds to three-fourths—in number from eight to nine thousand—of the German voters will cast their suffrages for Lincoln. Fremont's entire vote in the city was less than eighteen thousand; Lincoln's will not be less than thirty-five thousand."—*New York Post.*

Lincoln received the campaign name "rail splitter" when his cousin John Hanks showed up at the Illinois Republican convention with "two rails from a lot of 3,000 made in 1830 by Thos. Hanks and Abe Lincoln." Thenceforth Lincoln was the rail candidate. How this struck the opposition and the real issues of the election were explained in the New York Tribune, Oct. 23, 1860.

BRADY ON RAIL-SPLITTING

Mr. James T. Brady, Breckinridge candidate for Governor of our State, made a speech at Binghamton last Thursday, in the course of which he is reported by *The Times* as talking thus:

"He spoke of Mr. Lincoln as one who did not owe his nomination to the fact that he had split rails in early life, or hairs on entering the legal profession, as some satirists of that fraternity alleged. He was a gentleman of intellect, a lawyer of ability, and a gentleman against the purity of whose character no individual or journal had made a suggestion. . . . Mr. Brady referred to Mr. Greeley of THE TRIBUNE, for having called him to account as if he had spoken disrespectfully of manual laborers. Industry of all kinds is of course honorable, but the men who appealed to workingmen to give their support to a candidate, and proclaim him specially worthy of elevation because he had toiled more with his hands than his brains, were practicing arts of the demagogue, which the workers themselves could not but condemn. The humblest toiler in our land, bereft wholly of education, looked with reverence on intellectual superiority or culture, and hoped and strove, out of the means obtained from his labor, to place some favorite son or relative in a higher social position than he himself occupied, and qualify him for the stations to which mental discipline was indispensable. The rail splitting, therefore, might as well be omitted in advocating the claims of one who left the ranks of the laborer to enter the brotherhood of lawyers."

—Let us try once more—for we are long-suffering and anxious to be understood—to bring this matter of rail-splitting to the level of the capacity of Mr. Brady and of *The Times*, which has hitherto indulged in a strain of remark similar to the above.

It is undeniably true that splitting rails never qualified a man for the Presidency—so let *that* point be deemed settled. Many a man has split more rails—perhaps better ones—than Abraham Lincoln, who never will be President, and never ought to be. Nor does any one, as Mr. Brady mistakenly supposes, consider a candidate "specially worthy of elevation because he had toiled more with his hands than his brains." So let *that* man of straw be wantonly buffeted no more.

But we are engaged in a great political controversy, whereof the relative justice, fitness, and beneficence of the antagonistic systems of Free and Slave Labor are the real foundation. Messrs. Bell and Breckinridge believe Slavery essentially and eternally right—a proper and just relation through which service may be exacted and labor constrained. Mr. Douglas has—not once merely, but at least a hundred times—proclaimed his conviction that Slavery is, if not absolutely and universally right, at least right within certain latitudes and under certain conditions of soil, climate, and other industrial aptitudes. "As between the white man and the negro, I stand for the white man; as between the negro and the crocodile, I go for the negro," is the favorite form of expression through which Mr. Douglas enunciates his conviction that Slavery ought to exist in the Sugar and Cotton growing regions. A hundred times has he asserted that Slavery is morally right wherever it is economically expedient; and that it is thus expedient wherever a fervid sun renders man averse to labor. Repeatedly has he scouted the assumption that the Northern States abolished Slavery because they deemed it unjust, or for any other reason than that they found it unprofitable. Hence, he logically proclaims his perfect indifference as to Slavery's being "voted up or voted down" in any Territory or in any State.

The Republicans, on the contrary, hold Slavery to be essentially wrong, unjust, pernicious, and therefore resist its extention into, establishment by, or recognition as already legally existing in, any of the Territories which are destined to become States of our Union. They seek to destroy it in the germ, so that it shall not establish itself in the now embryo but soon to be sovereign States, now subject to National control and plastic to National influences, but which, once admitted as States, will be thereafter subject only to the legally declared will of their own citizens respectively. . . .

ABRAHAM LINCOLN illustrates our position and enforces our argument. His career proves our doctrine sound. He is Republicanism embodied and exemplified. Born in the very humblest White stratum of society, reared in poverty, earning his own livelihood from a tender age by the rudest and least recompensed labor, soon aiding to support his widowed mother and her younger children, picking up his education as he might by the evening firelight of rude log cabins, clearing off primeval forests, splitting rails at so much per thousand, running a flat-boat, and so working his way gradually upward to knowledge, capacity, esteem, influence, competence, until he stands to-day the all but elected President of this great, free People—his life is an invincible attestation of the superiority of Free Society, as his election will be its crowning triumph. That he split rails is of itself nothing; that a man who at twenty was splitting rails for a bare living is at fifty the chosen head of the greatest and most intelligent party in the land, soon to be the Head also of the Nation —this is much, is everything. PENNSYLVANIA sees it—so does INDIANA; why cannot Mr. Brady?

On Election Day, November 6, they saw Lincoln go to his office, then across the street to the Sangamon County Court House, and return to the borrowed Governor's room at the State House. They who looked saw him go to the telegraph office to get the latest returns. And across the country, as the dispatches went out from Springfield, recording the candidate's every move, this is how they saw him. The New York Tribune, Nov. 10, 1860, datelined Election Day. Note the use of the word "irrepressible" near the end of this report—the clever word of the day which was a take-off on the "irrepressible conflict."

FROM THE HOME OF MR. LINCOLN

ELECTION DAY AT SPRINGFIELD
From Our Special Correspondent

SPRINGFIELD, Ill., Tuesday Nov. 6, 1860.
Until to-day, the day of election, the political excitement has not been so great in this city as might have been supposed, in view of the residence here of the most prominent of the Presidential candidates. During last week, and even so late as yesterday, the preparations for this day's work were carried on with a quiet and systematic regularity, rather than with the unbounded extravagance often of late displayed further East. But, yesterday afternoon and evening, indications of a warmer and more eager feeling appeared. In the State-House square, in the Post-Office, and upon the corners of the streets, there were many busy little gatherings of anxious debaters, all looking forward with hopes more or less ardent, to

the impending local contest—for the question as to all results beyond the immediate precincts was put by as sufficiently well settled. It was at the Post-Office, too, the evening before election, that I caught my first accidental glimpse of Mr. Lincoln. He was standing alone before his box, "in hight somewhat less than a steeple" (as the Republican Glee-Clubs sing it out here), waiting for the distribution of the mail. His rather remarkable elevation above the rest of his fellow-citizens was, indeed, the only evidence just then of his identity, for it was too dark to distinguish features, and he took no part in the numerous discussions near at hand. Upon the assortment of the mail he fell to work very vigorously at an enormous mass of letters, newspapers, and documents of doubtful aspect —powerful applications, perhaps—a quantity almost too great for one man to carry away, to say nothing of reading afterward. The energy and perseverance with which Mr. Lincoln gave himself up to the task of transferring this huge pile of communications from their official repository to his own arms, was admirable to witness. Some friends approached and asked him, "how he could stand the pressure," to which he answered that he should endeavor to sustain himself until Tuesday night, at least. There was then in the way of light conversation, a little curiosity expressed as to his vote on the following day, which Mr. Lincoln promptly gratified, by declaring, without reserve, that he should vote for Yates (the Republican candidate for Governor of Illinois). This did not seem to satisfy the questioner, who explained that he was more particularly curious to know how Mr. Lincoln would vote on the Presidential question. "How vote?" said Mr. Lincoln, "well, undoubtedly like an Ohio elector of which I will tell you—by ballot;" after which, he related some droll anecdote, and walked away, bearing up bravely under his heavy accumulation of correspondence, and leaving his hearers all laughing.

But to-day tranquillity forsook Springfield. Sunrise was announced by discharges of cannon, which were continued until the morning was well on its way. Then the out-door tumult was supplied by bands of music, which, in wagons, were drawn about the city to stir whatever sluggish spirits there might be among the populace, and waken all slumbering resolutions. The voices of men, assembling at the polls, were also heard in good-natured clamor. The voting began early, and for a while appeared all to the advantage of the Republicans; but the influence of the imported "residents," of whom great numbers were on hand, was presently shown. In order to maintain their majority in the State Legislature, and thus to secure the election of an Opposition Senator in place of Trumbull, the Democrats had given especial attention to such counties as they considered it possible, by any expedients, for them to carry. Sangamon County is one of these, and here, accordingly, their efforts were in a degree concentrated. The easy condition of qualification as a voter in any county—provided the required year's residence in the State is assured—naturally produced a sudden and disagreeable, though not unexpected amplification of the ordinary population. But still, although there was probably not the best feeling on either side, the election progressed with as little turbulence as ever elections are troubled with.

During the greater part of the day Mr. Lincoln remained in the Governor's room, at the State-House—which he has occupied for the past few months—quietly overlooking the outside proceedings at the Court-House, which stands just opposite to his window, and receiving and entertaining such visitors as called upon him. These were both numerous and various—representing, perhaps, as many tempers and as many nationalities as could easily be brought together at the West. He was seated most of the time —rising only now and then at the entrance of some new visiting delegation—in an arm chair of liberal proportions, in which he seemed exceedingly composed and comfortable, but which he hardly appeared to fill to anything like repletion. Nobody expects to find Mr. Lincoln a portly man, but at first sight his slenderness strikes one as even beyond what had been expected. His great hight (extent, they jocularly call it here) adds to this effect. It is in more ways than one that he stands far above the rest of the people round about. On the whole, until he is more familiarly seen, it is not the exterior of Mr. Lincoln that attracts; but, instead, his winning manner, his ready good humor, and his unaffected kindness and gentleness toward all who approach him. His affability appears to have no limit as to persons. All share it. Next to this, his most marked characteristic is the steady earnestness with which he considers and reviews all subjects that are brought before him. His attention and his animation are the same, whatever may be the immediate topic. In conversation he always leads, not from any endeavor of his own, but because the right is at once and naturally yielded to him by all listeners. He must be a clever talker who would keep even with him. His manner in speaking is somewhat different from what his appearance would suggest, for while his movements and gestures are quick, and the play of his gestures is always lively, his utterance is peculiarly assured and emphatic. His bearing altogether is very striking. The cultivation of personal graces has probably no charm for him, but the graces of his nature are such as never need elaboration. There is something beyond all art in the frank and honest sunshine of his countenance, so full of fine expression. Mr. Lincoln's age, I believe, is fifty-one, but he certainly has no appearance of being so old. His hair is black, lightly touched with gray, and his eye is brighter than that of many of his juniors.

Among his callers in the morning were some rough-jacketed constituents who, having voted for him, and expressed a wish to look at their man, came in timidly, were kindly received, and, after a dumb sitting of a quarter of an hour, went away, thoroughly satisfied in every manner. There were two or three strangers from New-York, of whom Mr. Lincoln thought they ought better to be at home voting. In many cases it seemed as if he would be quite justified in letting out symptoms of being bored, but these never escaped him. On the contrary, he was ever ready to meet the fancies of his guests, in whatever direction they might lead him. Somebody signified deep interest in the subject of rail-splitting, and sought explanations, which Mr. Lincoln gave with great minuteness and simplicity, and quite as earnestly as, a minute before, he had discussed the attitude of the State of New-York, showing how the operation was performed "in his time," and contrasting it with the more modern method of dividing logs, which he admitted to be an improvement.

Since every Republican vote in the county was needed, as likely to affect the result in the State Legislature, Mr. Lincoln had determined not to withhold his, but had intended to wait until toward evening, before going to the polls, in order to avoid, as much as possible, encountering a crowd. At about 3 o'clock, however, he was informed that the way was as clear as it probably would be at any time, and he decided to go over at once. He started, just a moment after receiving a cheering dispatch from Simeon Draper of New-York, accompanied by a number of his more intimate friends. After he had gone a little way, an old gentleman who was with him intimated that he would, after all, prefer to remain in the Governor's room, and look out upon the scene from the window. So Mr. Lincoln went back with him, put him in a favorable position for seeing all that was to pass, and then started out again.

On his way across to the Court-House, Mr. Lincoln was not observed; but as soon as he stood upon the sidewalk, and advanced to the steps, he was recognized, and welcomed with such a cheer as no man ever received who has not the hearts as well as the voices of his people. Every vestige of party feeling seemed to be suddenly abandoned. Even the distributors of the Douglas tickets shouted and swung their hats as wildly as the rest. Mr. Lincoln walked leisurely through the hall and up the stairway, followed by as many of the multitude as could get near him, and, on entering the voting-room, was hailed with a burst of enthusiasm which almost extinguished the remembrance of that which he had just received below. There, too, there was no sign of political feeling. I saw a spry old party, with his hand full of Democratic documents, forget his special function so far as to prance upon a railing, and to take the lead in an infinite series of Lincoln cheers. The object of all this irrepressible delight took it as calmly as he could, and, urging his way to the voting table, deposited the straight Republican ticket, with only the omission of his own name from the heading of the honorable list, which he himself removed. After thus serving his friends, and leaving his own name to look out for itself without any help from him, he turned toward the door again, and endeavored to pass out. It would have seemed impossible for greater enthusiasm to be now shown than was before displayed, but the crowd certainly tried their best at it. Then Mr. Lincoln took off his hat and smiled all around upon them; and when he smiles heartily there is something in it good to see. So his neighbors thought, too, for a number came about him to shake him by the hand and have a few words with him as he moved along. But this was soon over, and he was suffered to return to his more quiet quarters at the State-House, from which—so quickly it had all passed—he had not probably been absent more than five minutes. And, after getting back, he turned to the entertainment of his visitors as unconcernedly as if he had not just received a demonstration which anybody might well take a little time to think of and be proud over.

The afternoon went on uneventfully, and at evening, when the polls closed, there was still doubt as to the result in this particular neighborhood. As I close, late in the evening, this uncertainty is not removed, although it now seems to be taken for granted that the Republicans have not suffered. The city is resting and preparing for public demonstrations to-morrow, and Mr. Lincoln, almost alone, is sitting snugly in the telegraph office, where Mr. Wilson, model of telegraph superintendents, has provided for his speedy receipt of all news that shall arrive.

> While the citizens of Sangamon County went to the polls, the *Illinois State Register*—Lincoln's ancient Democratic foe in Springfield —talked of how the Senate would "convict Abraham Lincoln and dismiss him from office," if he acted unconstitutionally. *The Register, Nov. 7, 1860.*

THE QUESTION OF DISUNION

At the hour we write these lines, the American people, in all parts of the United States, are exercising their constitutional privilege of electing a president and vice-president of the United States for the next four years. Before our readers will have glanced at this column, they will have scanned the election returns, and will in all probability, know who have been chosen for those two offices. If the state of New York decides against Lincoln, his election will be an impossibility—he will be outside the canvass, forever. If New York shall decide for him, then he will be elected president of the United States for four years from the 4th of March next. The election of Mr. Lincoln will be a national calamity, a calamity that will do more to destroy the comity that ought to exist between the states, and to destroy the affection that should be entertained by the people of all sections for their fellow countrymen.

But, much as we may deplore the election of Lincoln, because of its calamitous consequences, we choose to put on record now, before the result of the election is declared, that under no circumstances, can disunion be the remedy or redress for the unfortunate choice. Mr. Lincoln may obtain a majority of the election college, and yet receive less than one-third of the popular vote, yet he will nevertheless be constitutionally elected. Douglas may obtain a larger popular vote than Lincoln, and may not get one electoral vote, yet, there being no violation of the constitution involved in it, it is one of the things to which Mr. Douglas and his millions of friends will have, as legal citizens, to submit. It has been proposed by those who seek a disruption of the Union, that in case Mr. Lincoln shall be elected president the southern states shall withdraw from the Union; and active measures having for their purpose that secession, to be consummated upon the contingency of Lincoln's election, have been taken by several southern states. We wish to place on record now, that in our judgment the unanimous voice of the democrats of Illinois will be that such secession, being an act not within the constitutional power of any state, will become rebellion and treason on the part of every individual who by any overt act seeks to overthrow the constitutional authority of the federal government in any one of the states. And, being the act of individuals, each and every person who may attempt it, should be seized and punished just as any other rebel or traitor would be seized or punished. We of course, mean these remarks to apply to secession or disunion because of Lincoln's election.

There is another class who propose to "submit" to the election of Lincoln, but who propose to secede when he shall attempt to do, or shall do, any unconstitutional act. We do not see that this proposed secession has any higher or more commendatory sanction in law or morals than that which is contingent upon Lincoln's election. The constitution provides a remedy for all wrongs that may be committed under its forms. If Mr. Lincoln shall in any manner exceed his authority, or violate the constitution, that constitution itself provides the remedy for the wrong. In article 2, sec. 4, the constitution provides: "The president, vice president, and all civil officers of the United States, shall be removed from office, on impeachment for, and conviction of treason, bribery, or other high crimes and misdemeanors.". . .

The fear that the Senate will not convict a President for official crime, has we know been strengthened in the public mind by the fact that the execrable old despot, who has, to the shame of his country four months longer to act as President, has never been displaced, but has had a senate ready and too willing to execute his will. But the expression of public sentiment, and its direct application to all those who have been the supple tools of his tyranny, cannot fail to have a wholesome effect upon the next senate. We do not despair therefore of the senate; we believe that in a clear case of the unconstitutional exercise of power by the president, the senate would, upon a constitutional form of trial convict Abraham Lincoln and dismiss him from office. But, whether the senate would or would not do its duty, the constitution has provided that form and that remedy, and until that remedy has been tested and proved a failure, we cannot but say that secession and rebellion are to be treated as secession and rebellion, and participants in them are to be treated as traitors deserve to be treated.

Should Mr. Lincoln be elected, great as the calamity will prove to be, still we think it is the duty of every democrat to give to his administration (not his party) every aid and support that the government can constitutionally demand of citizens, and if in the exercise of his high duties, the arm of treason be raised, it will be the duty of every democrat, when called upon, to aid the government in all constitutional measures to put down the treason, punish the traitors, and protect the American Union.

The longtime Lincoln supporter—the Illinois State Journal— announced the Republican victory, and immediately took the Springfield Register to task for its gloomy outlook. This rather optimistic editorial appeared Nov. 8, 1860.

MR. LINCOLN'S ELECTION

The election of Mr. Lincoln will be a national calamity, a calamity that will do more to destroy the comity that ought to exist between the States, and to destroy the affection that should be entertained by the people of all sections for their fellow country-men.—*Register.*

The comity referred to by the *Register* was destroyed by Stephen A. Douglas, when his "ruthless hand" broke down the Missouri Compromise. The affection which ought to exist between the different States has not been known, since the unfortunate hour when he introduced into the United States Senate, the Kansas-Nebraska bill, that Pandora's box of all the evils which now afflict the country. Mr. Lincoln's election so far from being a "national calamity" will do more than anything else, to bring peace back to the country and restore that affection which heretofore was entertained "by the people of all sections for their fellow countrymen." The people are tired of the wranglings and agitations in which the Democracy have so needlessly embroiled the nation, and they have elected Mr. Lincoln for the express purpose of ending them; and such will be the end, aim and effect of his administration.

In New York City, James Gordon Bennett's Herald—which had told all sorts of anti-Lincoln tales during the campaign—sent a reporter into the streets to catch the reactions of the electorate to a Republican President. Tammany wasn't so happy; the prophecy at the end about Lincoln removing every Irishman from the New York police force was, to be sure, unrealized. The New York Herald, Nov. 8, 1860.

THE DAY AFTER THE BATTLE

The heat of the contest is over, and the victor has been proclaimed. The sun shone as brightly yesterday as of yore, notwithstanding the threatened disruption of things terrestrial. As far as New York was concerned, the business people had resumed their occupations; carts and wagons were driven through the crowded streets; hackmen were on their stands, ready to take up—and take in—a fare if they had the chance; workmen and mechanics pursued their daily business, at least such as had not received too many wounds in the head by means of the political pocket pistol, the whiskey bottle. In fact, everything had resumed its wonted appearance.

THE STOCK MARKET AND NEIGHBORHOOD.

There were a few local peculiarities—things incidental upon the close of a struggle—a kind of debris that remained—which may need a few words to describe. As the money market had been so fearfully affected by the approaching combat, it was natural that anxious persons should look in that direction to see if it was in any serious degree affected. But nothing was materially disturbed. Stocks, as in all such excitements, were feverish, but no danger was feared. The "animals" of the brokers' menagerie were quiet and calm, and made no savage roaring and growling, as has been the case during the past few weeks. The long—and to strangers mysterious— passage way that runs from No. 53 Beaver street along the backs of the houses and finds an exit near the corner of Exchange place, and through which passage the *habitués* of that money-broking—and at the same time occasionally heart-breaking—locality are constantly to be seen making their "entrances and exits," was as busy as ever, though there would be an occasional small gathering of the "fraternity" there, who would discuss the events of the previous day; but after a few minutes' conversation one would break away with "Oh! damn it, let it go; its all over now, so let it rest." One other would, perhaps, remark that, "Lincoln's election would reduce stocks;" but he would be answered with "Deuce a bit! They always fluctuate for a few weeks on either side of an election, and they will do so now. It's all right!" The following colloquy took place in that very passage:—

"Halloa, Tom, and ha'nt we had a fine victory?"

"What do you call a victory?"

"Why, the election of Lincoln."

"You outrageous old turncoat! Why, on Monday you went for the fusion as hard as any man, and now you claim Lincoln's election as a victory. Get out!"

"And quite right, too. Haven't I always been an old fashion whig? And what are Lincoln's principles but whigish? Therefore, as I am a whig, why the election of one with my ideas must be a victory. There, now!"

"Oh, get out! Just like you all. By the 4th of March there will not be a fusion man on the street, but they will all have turned as black in their principles as they are in their legs."

"That's treason," said No. 1, with a laugh, and they separated.

TAMMANY HALL AND NEIGHBORHOOD.

At Tammany Hall everything looked mean and dull. There was not a single cheerful face in the barroom. One man had settled himself down into a chair, and had contracted upon his brow one of the most outrageous furrows that could be imagined. He kept his gaze constantly on the window, and if a citizen chanced to address him, let him look out for his nose, for the snap that would be made at it would almost take it off. Others would be silently reading the returns, and when they came to the name of any place that should have given Tammany a majority, and found it either reduced or turned upon the "other tack," they would utter a *sotto voce* expletive that would fully express their bitter feelings.

In front of Crook & Duff's there would be an occasional gathering of a few choice individuals, but after a short stay, away they would go. One gentleman asserted that "he would give the city a week to see the result; but, in his opinion, the Union was virtually dissolved." For the greater part, all the persons that could be beguiled into conversation were now for Lincoln, and notwithstanding the large majority of the city on Tuesday, yesterday scarcely showed a fusion man in any of the thoroughfares.

THE CITY HALL.

The City Hall was deserted. The few democrats who made their appearance walked in with a long but resigned countenance. When they spoke they did so good humoredly, and expressed their conviction that "the best man was elected." Some seemed to think that "if any trouble broke out in the South it would be principally of a commercial character and not warlike." The courts may be said to have been idle; and, as regarded election day, the persons around the Hall asserted that they never had seen such a quiet Presidential election. One respectable gentleman, who had witnessed six of them, besides all the minor ones, said the "quietness of the thing was unprecedented.". . .

BROADWAY AND THE HEADQUARTERS.

Along Broadway business went on as usual, excepting around the headquarters of the different political parties. At the Bell-Everett quarters a small party were engaged on the stairs leading to their rooms debating the cause of the defeat. In the rooms above some few "Minute Men" were rather excitely speaking of the contest, when one said:—"If it had not been for the farmers with their muddy faces and still muddier brains we should have gained the day." "Never mind," said another; "the victory in the Ninth ward will make up for all."

At the republican headquarters the Wide Awakes indulged in a little bit of humor yesterday morning to the annoyance of their opponents. They had a large card hung up in front of the building, and on the pasteboard was the following:—

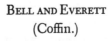

BELL AND EVERETT
(Coffin.)

TO THE MEMORY OF DEPARTED WORTH.

Of course it amused the passers by; but it was rather too bad "to hit a fellow when he was down," at least so said one of them. After dinner the late edition of the HERALD was brought in, and one of the party began reading the returns therefrom, and as every victory was read off the cheers were loud and prolonged. The Albany returns met with a very hearty reception. There was a general surprise among the republicans that the Ninth ward had gone so opposite to the usual course, and many said they would have to inquire into the matter.

A procession of Hibernians, with green sashes, passed across Broadway yesterday afternoon, preceded by a band playing dead march music. "There goes the funeral of poor Old Tammany," said a wag, as he passed by; "he is off to Greenwood."

At the various hotels on Broadway, couples and small groups were to be seen conversing one with the other. The smiling faces of the one side and the elongated countenances of the other at once told which were of the victorious party.

THE FIFTH WARD HOTEL.

At the Fifth Ward Hotel they seemed to have some consolation in the fact that Wood had beaten Williamson, some asserting that as the Congress was "composed mainly of democrats, old Uncle Abe, honest or not, would not have much power to act or veto."

Salt river tickets were in active circulation, and political medals and photographs were much reduced in price—the unsuccessful candidates selling only for two cents, while Lincoln was worth six cents.

THE HERALD OFFICE.

In front of the HERALD office a great excitement existed in consequence of the demand for papers. It was not only in that part of the city, but all over it, that the excitement prevailed, and the HERALD in many places realized three times its regular price, notwithstanding we printed over one hundred and five thousand copies. Several of the newsboys tried to palm off old copies of other journals upon the anxious multitude; but all around the office refused them, preferring to wait until the issue of the later edition with the full returns.

In the cars there was an occasional excitement, and in one of these vehicles the cheers for Lincoln were vociferous. One man, who had, or fancied he had, been insulted by an Irish policeman, proclaimed loudly that "he was glad that Lincoln was elected, as he would soon remove every Irishman from the force."

In Missouri the oddly named St. Louis Democrat (it was a Republican newspaper) traced the election of Lincoln to events which brought the Republican President back to the political arena—the extension of slavery in the territories, in 1854. The Missouri interpretation was reprinted in the Illinois Journal, Nov. 8, 1860.

"VICTORY! PEACE!!"

The St. Louis Democrat heralds the election of Mr. Lincoln to the Presidency in the following eloquent pean of "victory and peace:"

The seven years' war is at last ended, by the election of Abraham Lincoln as Chief Magistrate of the Republic. Let the nation rejoice at this glorious event. Let a choral shout of exultation rise from the soul of the people, at this, their great victory, over the enemies of freedom and the upholders and champions of wrong. The joy is too great for verbal expansions; the vista opened is too radiant and boundless for description.

For nearly seven years the two principles have fought for the possession of the broad outlying Territories—the one entering the arena like a naked man, the other armed to the teeth—and Freedom, such is the Godlike force that dwells in it, has prevailed. Slavery, shorn of its prestige, and baffled in all its cunning arts and desperate expedients, retires within its ancient limits like an invading army beaten back.

Thus is the glorious truth emphasized again, that right at last makes might. Thus have American institutions re-instated themselves in the affections and admirations of the world. The Sovereignty of the people rising in awful majesty has overwhelmed the minions of oligarchical tyranny and slavery propagandism. The fiat has gone forth which transfers the sceptre from the nerveless grasp of recreant and degenerate Democracy to another power, in the person of Abraham Lincoln. That dethroned and discrowned dynasty will never again betray the rights which it was appointed to guard and vindicate. The line fitly ends with James Buchanan.

Will any faction in the country dare to raise a rebel howl against the sovereignty of the nation, as exercised in the election of Lincoln? We hope not, for if any faction should, swift ruin would fall upon it like a thunderbolt. The duty of all loyal men, now that the contest is over, is to rally round the nation's choice, and give effect to the nation's will. The distinctive party appellations should no longer be heard; all mere party strife should be suspended until the enemies of the Union, if they dare proceed to overt acts, are compelled to submit to the laws. Treason should be extinguished before party controversies are revived. But it is our firm belief, that never was the country less liable to be subjected to the desolating curse of civil war. Peace will follow our victory. The President elect is a wise, temperate, conservative, patriotic statesman, whose noble ambition it will be to demean himself in his high office for the good of all; not to make himself the leader of a crusade against one section of the country. It is, therefore the duty of all men who are not disloyal to the institutions under which they live, and faithless to the Constitution which they have sworn to maintain—it is their duty to give his Administration a fair trial before condemning him. He is the nation's choice, and no anointed king since the days of David could claim a diviner right to rule than he. But who can realize the full meaning of his election? The United States, under the policy which he is commissioned to inaugerate, will enter on a new career—a career which will be attended with a wondrous material development and the elevation of the public mind to higher and nobler reaches—a career which shall restore the country to the path of true progress and put an end to the sectional jealousies and antipathies which have grown rank under Democratic misrule.

The results of the election came in: Lincoln received 1,866,452 votes, his three opponents 2,815,617. Lincoln had the majority in the Electoral College. This is how Lincoln received news of the victory. The New York Tribune, Nov. 12, 1860.

FROM THE HOME OF MR. LINCOLN

HOW MR. LINCOLN RECEIVED THE ELECTION NEWS

From Our Special Correspondent

SPRINGFIELD, Ill., Nov. 7, 1860.

About 9 o'clock last evening, when the returns began to tap in at the telegraph office, Mr. Lincoln, who had been notified beforehand, went over from the State-House with a few friends, established himself comfortably near the instruments, and put himself into easy communication with the operators. The first fragments of intelligence were caught by the Superintendent as they ticked off at the tables, and, even before they could be recorded, were eagerly repeated and welcomed by all, for they came from the best counties in Illinois, and were full of good cheer. Excepting Mr. Lincoln, whose interest was not so actively manifested, everybody present showed great excitement over each fresh bit of news, and so, for a while, the Superintendent, Mr. Wilson, continued announcing all details as they came in. But presently this was dropped, and during a quarter of an hour hardly any sound was heard, excepting the rapid clickings of the rival instruments, and the restless movements of the few most anxious among the party of gentleman who hovered affectionately near the mysterious tables, as if discovering a certain satisfaction in carefully following the course of the machinery, however unintelligible its whispering might be to them. Mr. Lincoln sat or reclined upon a sofa, while his companions mostly stood clustering around him. At length full sheets of returns were transcribed, and were taken apart, and read aloud by Mr. Wilson—the listeners allowing no particle of good news to go by without their quick congratulations. The first sheets were covered with minutes of county and town elections in Illinois, which, with of course slight variations at certain points, were all pleasant to hear about. As the evening advanced, other excitements were afforded by batches of private messages which came rushing in, mostly addressed to Mr. Lincoln, but in some cases to Senator Trumbull, who had joined the company a little after the time of assembling. For these messages an active watch soon began to be kept, and the moment that one was lifted from the table, it would be clutched by some of the ardent news-seekers, and sometimes, in the hurry and scramble, would be read by almost every person present before it reached him for whom it was intended. Whenever the information was of peculiarly gratifying character, as it often was, the documents would be taken out by some thoughtful friend of the populace outside, and read aloud in the State-House, or elsewhere, to large crowds which had met and were enjoying celebrations on the strength of their own convictions that the expected news would be sure to justify them. Occasionally, a line or two would come with so much force of encouragement as to set the little group beside itself with elation. A confident declaration from Gen. S. Cameron, promising abundance of good things from Pennsylvania, produced a sensation that quite took away the composure of the telegraph manipulators; and some superb items which came just after from Simeon

Draper, setting aside all possibility of doubt as to New-York, aroused demonstrations still more gleeful. There was just one person, however, who accepted everything with almost an immovable tranquility. Not that Mr. Lincoln undertook to conceal in the slightest degree the keen interest he felt in every new development; but, while he seemed to absorb it all with great satisfaction, the intelligence moved him to less energetic display of gratification than the others indulged in. He appeared, indeed, to be as fully alive to the smaller interests of some local districts, in which the fortunes of his friends were concerned, as to the wider and more universally important regions; and, in fact, his only departure from perfect quiet throughout the night was on hearing, just before he withdrew, of the complete success of the Republican ticket in his own precinct.

Matters went on in the same way until midnight, when the returns from Democratic States began to push in. Mr. Lincoln raised himself to listen to the Missouri news, saying that "we should now get a few licks back," but very soon seemed surprised and pleased, as the rest also were, to find that the "licks" were by no means altogether of unrelieved severity. From the Southern States the current now began to flow steadily, and as the repetitions became a little monotonous, and as all this intelligence simply followed a foregone conclusion, Mr. Lincoln and the party went over at half-past twelve o'clock to a little gathering in a hall at the other side of the State-House, which had been arranged and prepared by the ladies of Springfield in anticipation of a long and weary night for their brothers, husbands, and so forth. The feminine exitement in Springfield during this campaign has been most ardent and most uninterrupted, at least on the Republican side; and the inspiring devotion with which the gentler duties of this particular occasion were fulfilled, was of an order to fill a stranger with profoundest regrets that all his political ways of life were not turned toward Springfield. With a vivid sense of the peculiar necessities of the hour, all lighter graces and charms were held in subjection, and rigid attention to the claims of appetite was invited—nay, exhorted, and sometimes imperiously commanded. It appeared to be a distinct article in the creed of the fair entertainers that their mission, as true Republican wives and sisters, was poorly carried through until oceans of coffee and continents of food—with lesser lakes of other fluid, and sundry islands of confection—had been put in the way of each male that fell within their custody; and the unaffected sorrow which they could not conceal, when satiety was sometimes forced to resist their generous advances, was enough to cause a general submission to absolute gluttony, for the sake of relieving the poignancy of their sufferings. It is difficult to express the utter abandonment of hospitality with which these ladies honored all, even the least of their guests; but how can I attempt to describe the manner in which they surrounded, and took possession of, and clung to Mr. Lincoln, when he appeared among them? I can only say that that rare possibility—the last extremity of feminine enthusiasm—was here overwhelmingly illustrated. He was smiled at in the best Republican smiles, and sung at in vigorous Republican choruses, and led by Republican allurements to a snug Republican seat in a corner, not too far from Mrs. Lincoln (who had been present during most of the evening), where prolonged trials of his powers of refusal immediately beset him. The only shade of grief among the fair assemblage—and perhaps I forgot to mention that it really was very fair—arose from a consciousness that Mr. Lincoln could not be expected to comfort himself with all the fine Republican coffee, and all the excellent eatables that remained. After a half hour of solicitous attention here—the first public testimonial of delight over his success—he returned to the telegraph office, where he remained until half past 1 o'clock, at which hour enough was known to set aside all manner of doubt as to the grand result. Just before he withdrew, a messenger brought in the returns of the city, from which it was evident that the entire Republican ticket had been carried here—a matter about which Mr. Lincoln had said he "did not feel quite easy," in view of the Democratic antecedents of the locality, and the expected importations of voters. Upon this Mr. Lincoln for the first and only time departed from his composure, and manifested his pleasure by a sudden exuberant utterance—neither a cheer nor a crow, but something partaking of the nature of each. And then, laughing contentedly, he said good night to the little company, and presently the wearied operators were left alone to their then only half-finished tasks.

The city was alive and animated throughout the night. The meetings at the State-House were not adjourned until dawn, and the popular feeling became so uncontrollable at about four in the morning that there was nothing to satisfy it but to bring out the big gun and make it thunder rejoicings for the crowd. A part of Springfield was consequently in somewhat shattered condition of nerve this morning, though still ready for any emergency of cheering or hand-shaking that might occur. Mr. Lincoln was up early, and at his accustomed station in the Governor's room, where multitudes of citizens thronged all the morning to shower congratulations upon him. Certainly well pleased, he received all as placidly as ever, and entertained all with the old freedom and good humor. The conversation would touch on rail-splitting. Everybody seems to have his special inquiry on that point. Undoubtedly it will have to follow "the weather," as a favorite popular topic for the next four years at the White House. Of course Mr. Lincoln doesn't seek it, but neither does he shun it. A pair of new steel wedges for separating logs, of more improved pattern were lying on his table. "Are *those* the wedges, Sir?" asked a curious visitor. "These, Sir," said Mr. Lincoln, "are the identical wedges—that were sent to me about a week ago."

This afternoon a vast number of strangers has poured into the city from various parts of the State, to share in the anticipated jubilee.

A new correspondent for the New York Herald, Henry Villard, came out to Springfield to cover Lincoln and found "motley" visitors: "Everybody that lives in this vicinity or passes through this place goes to take a look at Old Abe. Muddy boots and hickory shirts are just as frequent as broadcloth, fine linen, etc. The ladies, however, are usually dressed up in their very best, although they cannot hope to make an impression on old married Lincoln." And the special correspondent of the New York Tribune wondered, "Possibly it is to be hereafter a leaf of history, that he is now recording—who can tell?" From the Tribune of Nov. 14, 1860.

FROM THE HOME OF LINCOLN

From Our Special Correspondent

SPRINGFIELD, Ill., Thursday, Nov. 8, 1860.

Mr. Lincoln's regular habits are not in the slightest degree changed since the assurance of his election to the Presidency. Without showing anything like indifference to his new honors, he bears them so quietly and easily as to clearly prove that the dignity of his high office will not weigh at all oppressively upon him. Some of his friends here appear to be greatly rejoiced at his unvarying calmness after his triumph, as if any other condition were to be expected of such a man. Mr. Lincoln is no more unduly elated by his success than he would have been unduly depressed in case of defeat. He is precisely the same man as before—open and generous in his personal communications with all who approach him, though reticent enough, for the present, as regards his political intentions. With his neighbors he is on the same hearty terms as ever. Last evening, in order to learn the latest intelligence from the doubtful counties of his own State, he went from his own room in the State-House over to the Representatives' Hall, where a meeting of four or five hundred citizens and strangers had assembled to hear the returns read. He was, as soon as discovered, seized upon, and led to the platform, where he was installed in the Speaker's chair, and guarded on all sides to prevent any sudden escape—a movement which naturally aroused fresh enthusiasm. Mr. Lincoln himself read a few of the returns, as they were brought in, and then, after listening to a few capital off-hand speeches made by delegates from various districts, insisted upon being relieved, and withdrew, first nominating a chairman to take his place, and assume "all his duties."

To-day Mr. Lincoln's room has been more than usually thronged with visitors from all quarters. There have been a few even from New-York and Pennsylvania, and one or two who, with ludicrous independence, have taken pains to assert their political hostility in the same breath with their personal regard. Mr. Lincoln receives all with equal urbanity. He sits or stands among his guests, throwing out hearty Western welcomes, asking and answering questions, joking, and endeavoring to make matters every way comfortable to all present. If a bashful stranger appears, manifesting a little awe at the sudden contact with the new President, Mr. Lincoln is likely to give him a word or two of particular attention, and pretty nearly sure to soon set him at his ease. Occasionally he excuses himself to the company, and sits for a little while at a corner table with his private secretary, dictating or making drafts of correspondence, and then everybody looks wistfully around, as if ready to sacrifice anything for the sake of knowing the purport of the few lines which that steady hand is rapidly ciphering. It may be a matter of great significance, or it may be a simple response to some friendly congratulation. Possibly it is to be hereafter a leaf of history, that he is now recording—who can tell? Nobody but himself, certainly, and you may be sure he will not. So the visitors give their silent consideration, for the time, to the surroundings of the room. There is not a great deal to excite interest. One table is covered with law books, and another is littered with newspapers enough to supply a country journalist with items for a year. Heaps and hills of newspapers, a few opened, the greater part still unfolded. If you take the wrappers from a few of these neglected sheets, you will find, within, whole columns of fervid eloquence, sonorous with big capitals, and bursting with hot Republican sentiment, all carefully marked and underlined, the sooner to catch the attention of the great chief. Alas for the little ambitions of the village editors. They have sent the cherished begettings of their brains to an oblivion too deep and to crowded for any chance of rescuing. Upon the same table, hidden beneath the newspaper avalanche, is a scrap-book, in which are collected the reports of the Lincoln and Douglas debates of 1858, cut from the journals in which they first appeared. Excellent reading they are, too, better than the elaborately prepared volume, for they give what that lacks, vivid pictures of the effects produced upon the listeners, their cries of applause, their laughter, their indignation at some stately piece of Little Gigantic insolence, and their occasional wild enthusiasm at some overwhelming master-stroke of the Republican orator. These reports come warm and alive to the reader; in the volume they are a little colder, though doubtless quite as nutritious. There are also some books of miscellaneous character, presents to Mr. Lincoln, and there are a pair of first-class improved wedges, for splitting logs, which everybody persists in looking upon as relics of Mr. Lincoln's early life, but which really were sent to him only about a fortnight ago, together with a fine ax, upon which, cut into the steel, is this inscription:

> Presented to
> HON. ABRAHAM LINCOLN,
> By WILLIAM BRADY
> Of Mount Joy,
> Lancaster County, Pa.
>
> ———
>
> Free Labor and Free Men,
> The Hope of Our Country.

No other word or message accompanied this gift, and, indeed, hardly anything more was needed. Over the table a neat wooden chain is hanging, another present, which was carved by an old Wisconsin farmer out of a rail—not, however, a Lincoln rail, as everybody is disposed to think. In all other respects the room is very simple in appearance, and offers no special charm or attraction to the curious.

The only serious point discussed to-day in Mr. Lincoln's room was the chance of a majority in the State Legislature. Senator Trumbull's prospects brightened in the afternoon, and there was great satisfaction over them, in which Mr. Lincoln was as earnest as if his own immediate interests were concerned. There were some questions as to annunciations of intention, by speech or by letter, which Mr. Lincoln answered by saying that at present he had no intention whatever of making any public declaration—a statement which he afterward once or twice repeated.

Texas newspapers, from the election to the assassination, were among the most vituperative in the South. The Dallas Herald—which was to say of Lincoln's death, "God Almighty ordered this event or it could never have taken place"—called for action against Lincoln now. From the Dallas Herald, Nov. 14, 1860.

THE ELECTION OF LINCOLN

The evil days, so dreaded by our forefathers and the early defenders of the Constitution, are upon us. We need not disguise the fact from ourselves, our friends, or our country. These days of dominant Republicanism, which, years ago, the best men of the Confederacy looked upon as the dies irae—the day of visitation and of wrath, are no less dangerous —no brighter or more hopeful now, than in our earlier purity.—The pure hearts of our distinguished Statesmen, who, years ago, saw the cloud no bigger than a man's hand, who prophesied evil to the country from this speck on the political horizon,—those pure hearts, we say, would now tremble at the accumulation of iniquity laid up against this aggressive party, its slow and steady accretions, until the last straw has broken the camel's back, and an outraged and forbearing people stand up in their majesty, and say—"thus far, and no farther!"

But, we would ask, are these really evil days—are these the dark days when no man can work—are these the days of our sure visitation? Speaking for Texas, we would say they are not; they are the dark hours that usher in the brighter morn, if we, as a firm united people, stand true to ourselves, our honor, and our country. The dark days of the Revolution were the prelude to the brilliant future, and the sufferings of our people were the pangs of travail to the birth of a mighty nation. We do not despair: troubles may arise and, for a time, darken the cloud that hangs o'er us; prudence and untiring vigilance will be called into active requisition, and the wisdom of our people urgently demanded. When the people act as one man, we fear not for the result, nor dread the gilded bait that may be held out to the South to appease her wrath. Action, prompt and determined action, is all we need. But if we stand with stolid indifference or abject submission, then will we be like the maiden Andromeda, chained to the rock to be devoured at leisure by the monster of the sea. We emphatically state that we are no submissionist, nor do we believe that one twentieth of our people are. We make these remarks more to define our own position than to promulgate any new doctrine. The times call for a clear and unequivocal expression, for or against submission; and it is the duty of all men to speak out.

———

☞ To those submissionists who ask if the mere election of Lincoln would be just grounds for resistance *now*, we would say, the evil that can be remedied to-day, should not be suffered to increase for years, until the whole body politic becomes diseased. If we honestly believe and fully understand the principles of the Republican party to be aggressive upon the South, and subversive of the intent and meaning of the Constitution, why should we wait until the party is safely intrenched in power and fortified with all the appliances of governmental patronage, before a blow is struck. Is there a man in Texas so insane as to believe that the policy of the Republicans will be less objectionable four years hence than at present? Will they come down voluntarily from their strong position, —will they be weaker four years hence than they are at this day? If the submissionists mean to resist at some future day, waiting for the overt act, we say they have committed that act already in electing a sectional President, who has said that he hates slavery as much as any abolitionist, and that it must be extinguished.—They have had Moses and the Prophets, and yet they hardened their hearts against us, nor will they do us justice even should one rise from the dead. The South must stand firm now, or forever after this hold her peace. "Procrastination is the thief of time"; and if we fail to assert and demand our rights, it were better that a mill-stone were hanged about our necks and all of us thrown into the sea.

The Northern European press, taking a leaf from the powerful London Times, generally was hostile to Lincoln. From England a proclamation was to come from Queen Victoria in a half-year, taking notice of the hostilities between the United States of America and "certain states styling themselves the Confederate States of America." This implied recognition and the "royal determination to maintain a strict and impartial neutrality" was not looked upon favorably in the North. The London Times, which would reflect a more positive anti-Lincoln stand later, in an editorial of Nov. 20, 1860, was quite dispassionate.

The event which has occupied the attention of the United States for the last four years has at length come to pass, and virtually, although not as yet legally, Mr. LINCOLN has been elected the President, and Mr.

HAMLYN the Vice-President, of the great American Confederacy. The event had been long foreseen, and will surprise nobody who has paid the least attention to American politics. It is the natural reaction against the outrages and excesses of 1855 and 1856, the protest of the freeest and best educated part of the American people against the acts of high-handed violence and oppression which preceded the advent of Mr. BUCHANAN to power. If the South has at length found that it is not omnipotent in the councils of the country, that unpleasant discovery is owing to the foolish and intemperate use which the South has made of its prosperity. While demanding the most implicit respect for its own opinions, the South has been even ostentatious in proclaiming a bitter and cynical contempt for the opinions and the feelings of others. Slavery has been defended as the normal and perfect state of human society, and the North has been bitterly taunted with its honest industry, and the coarseness of manners which the fastidious Southern planter traces to that cause. While claiming for itself the monopoly of the government of the United States, the South has constantly held the language of disaffection, and the United States have been ruled by a party which was perpetually talking of disuniting them. So far from wondering that these things should have produced the result we have just witnessed, it has long appeared to us impossible that they should not. Mankind, if ruled at all, must be ruled either by force or persuasion. The South could not employ the former, and have long substituted the language of provocation and defiance for the latter. But these and many other circumstances, while they fully account for the change which has taken place, tend very considerably to diminish its significance. Had the South been always reasonable and conciliatory, we must have regarded the election of Mr. LINCOLN as evidence of an intolerance of the very institution of Slavery which might portend results fatal to the stability of the Union; but the South has really taken so much pains to bring the present result to pass that it has no right to be surprised at its own success.

The causes to which the election of a Republican President is owing are chiefly interesting to us so far as they afford us any guidance in estimating the effect such a change will produce on the foreign policy of the Union. The first impression may be that a President agreeing with the general sentiment of this country on the subject of Slavery would be more likely to preserve amicable relations between the two countries than a President in avowed opposition to European notions on this important point. It is thus that the POPE and Cardinals argue, that if the PALMERSTON Ministry were to be overthrown in England its policy would be reversed by its successors. Both ideas appear to us equally fallacious. The days are gone by when the policy of a great and civilized nation can be altered by the change of a Prime Minister, and the President of the United States is in some respects little more and in others not so much. The Chinese gain nothing by the accession to office of their earnest advocates of 1857; nor, we suspect, will the change in the American Government produce any particular advantage to England. We are not likely to see a President of the United States who will seriously compromise the relations between England and the Union, nor yet a President who will resist the temptation of making a little capital for his party among the Irish and the Republican emigrants from Europe, by embarking in small quarrels and showing a certain amount of petty hostility. We do not expect that, so far as our own affairs are concerned, we have changed Presidents for the better; nor, on the other hand, do we fear that the change will be for the worse. That it is no longer generally popular in the United States to be on ill terms with Great Britain has been abundantly proved by the generous and hospitable reception of the Prince of WALES. This good feeling and our own good intentions are a sufficient guarantee for peace and good understanding, and for us the questions involved in the triumph of either contending party are comparatively of little moment. It is very fortunate that it should be so. It is very fortunate that we have in the good feeling and common interest of the two nations a guarantee much stronger than the caprice of Ministers or Presidents. For ourselves, then, as far as the immediate interest of this country is concerned, we regard the accession to power of the Republican President without any very strong feeling of triumph. We have lived on good terms with his Democratic predecessor; we do not doubt that we shall be able to maintain the same relations with the new Chief of the State.

But, although this may be all very plain and easy to us, there is a considerable number of persons in America to whom, apart from mere political considerations, the change of Presidents is not a matter of indifference. First, there are all the *employés*, from the Secretaries of State down to the sorters of letters and tide-waiters. The vote that has substituted a Republican for a Democrat at the White-house is to them, and each of them, a sentence of ruthless and indiscriminate proscription. There is no need to affix the lists of the proscribed in public places, after the fashion of the cynical SYLLA. The proscription is exactly coincident with the number of placeholders. We cannot expect that any argument will reconcile these martyrs to their doom. Then there are the slave-owners themselves, whose acute sensibilities on the subject of their "peculiar domestic institution," whose hatred of the North, and whose fears of the masses of barbarism by which they have surrounded themselves, have led them very much to over-estimate the real importance of the change. There can be no slave so stupid and ignorant as not to know that the blow which his master has been talking of and fearing so long has fallen at last, and who will not derive from it a far greater degree of confidence than it ought really to inspire. The reign of terror now prevailing in Texas is a sufficient proof of the existence of this spirit of exaggeration, and it may, perhaps, operate to call forth from the slaves some manifestation of feeling, which can have no other result than to rivet fetters already too severe. We may surmise that the disgraceful traffic in slaves, sure, sooner or later, to follow the institution of slavery itself, will be kept under with a vigorous hand. We may expect to find the Supreme Court of the United States restored, if not to impartiality, to something more like a balance of opinion by the appointment of eminent Republican lawyers, and we may expect to find in the administration of the Territories a spirit which will render the repetition of scenes like those of Kansas impossible.

We know not that the friends of the Negro have much more to expect from the new President. His powers are very limited, and will be confined within a space much narrower than their strictly legal extent by the same necessity which has made Mr. BUCHANAN abstain from any attempt on Cuba, and tolerate the anarchy and even the aggressions of unhappy Mexico. For the safety of the Union itself we confess we have no fear. Of course, it will take some time before men can cool down from the bluster which has been so profusely used for electioneering purposes to the language of moderation and truth. Some men have said these things so often that they are ashamed to show how little they believe them, and some so often that they have really learnt to believe them themselves. But when the cooler heads of the South begin to consider how imaginary is the injury which they have sustained, how vast are the interests involved, how heavy would be the cost, how considerable the danger, of disunion, and how impossible it would be for the Southern States to maintain in the face of the world the strong position they now hold as members of the great American Confederacy, we suspect that the South will think better of it, and turn its activity into the more practical channel of providing Mr. LINCOLN with a Democratic successor in 1864.

The state of Florida was heard from: Lincoln becoming the symbol of the Union. From the Illinois Journal, Dec. 11, 1860.

Charleston, [S.C.] Dec. 9. . . .

News from Florida shows perfect unanimity in the State for secession, and the enthusiasm is increasing daily.

Lincoln was burnt in effigy at Fernandina on Friday last.

Lincoln left Springfield on February 11; he would not return alive. An old friend and neighbor—the Illinois Journal—related it the next day, Lincoln's birthday, February 12, 1861.

DEPARTURE OF MR. LINCOLN—PARTING ADDRESS

Long before the hour appointed for the departure of the special train provided for Mr. Lincoln and suit, hundreds of his friends and fellow-citizens, without distinction of party, had assembled at the station of the Great Western Railway to tender him their respects, grasp once more that honest hand, and bid him God speed on his eventful journey. A subdued and respectful demeanor characterized the vast assemblage. All seemed to feel that they were about to witness an event which, in its relations to the future, was of no ordinary interest.

At precisely five minutes before eight o'clock, Mr. Lincoln, preceded by Mr. Wood, of New York, slowly made his way from his room in the station, through the expectant masses which respectfully parted right and left at his approach to the car provided for his use. At each step of his progress towards the car, friendly hands were extended for a last greeting. On reaching the platform of the car, Mr. Lincoln turned toward the people, removed his hat, paused for several seconds, till he could control his emotions, and then slowly, impressively, and with profound emotion, uttered the following words:

"Friends, no one who has never been placed in a like position, can understand my feelings at this hour, nor the oppressive sadness I feel at this parting. For more than a quarter of a century I have lived among you, and during all that time I have received nothing but kindness at your hands. Here I have lived from my youth until now I am an old man. Here the most sacred ties of earth were assumed; here all my children were born; and here one of them lies buried. To you, dear friends, I owe all that I have, all that I am. All the strange, chequered past seems to crowd now upon my mind. To-day I leave you; I go to assume a task more difficult than that which devolved upon General Washington. Unless the great God who assisted him, shall be with and aid me, I must fail. But if the same omniscient mind, and the same Almighty arm that directed and protected him, shall guide and support me, I shall not fail, I shall succeed. Let us all pray that the God of our fathers may not forsake us now. To him I commend you all—permit me to ask that with equal sincerity and faith, you all will invoke His wisdom and guidance for me. With these few words I must leave you—for how long I know not. Friends, one and all, I must now bid you an affectionate farewell."

It was a most impressive scene. We have known Mr. Lincoln for many years; we have heard him speak upon a hundred different occasions; but we never saw him so profoundly affected, nor did he ever utter an address, which seemed to us as full of simple and touching eloquence, so exactly adopted to the occasion, so worthy of the man and the hour. Although it was raining fast when he began to speak, every hat was lifted, and every head bent forward to catch the last words of the departing chief. When he said, with the earnestness of a sudden inspiration of feeling, that *with God's help he should not fail*, there was an uncontrollable burst of applause.

At precisely eight o'clock, city time, the train moved off, bearing our honored townsman, our noble chief, ABRAHAM LINCOLN to the scenes of his future labors, and, as we firmly believe, of his glorious triumph. God bless honest ABRAHAM LINCOLN!

He was on the way, from the depot of the Great Western Railway in Springfield, on through cities in Indiana, Ohio, Pennsylvania, New York, Maryland, and many whistle stops en route. The leading voice of Secession in the South, the Charleston Mercury, dominated by fanatical Robert Barnwell Rhett, reported correspondence from Cincinnati. From the Mercury, Feb. 26, 1861.

Our Cincinnati Correspondence

———

CINCINNATI, February 13, 1861.

The Progress of Abraham—A Tame Reception—Abolitionism All Talk—An Indiana Duel—Dull Times in the Great West—The Foray Upon the South, &c, &c.

Old ABE, with a retinue of office seekers, whose name is legion, arrived here yesterday. Mrs. ABE, and several young ABES, formed a part of the select party. For several days prior to his advent, the Abolition papers of the city (and they are all of that dark hue, save one), were industriously at work with a view to raise as great an amount of enthusiasm as possible in behalf of the quondam rail-splitter and flat-boat commander whether or not deserving.

The reception, however, was tame; and the military appeared with awfully thin ranks (and here let me add that none of the Irish companies paraded to do honor to the Abolition President). ABE's speech at Indianapolis shadows forth the programme of his administration. Coercion is to be the order of the day.

Mrs. ABE flourished extensively while en route, and evidently was desirous of getting up some capital on her own hook. To a gentleman who entered the royal train while on its way to this city, and who saluted her, she replied: "How do you flourish, 'old boy?'" "Have you got a paper?" "What do they say about us?" In attendance upon this Right Worshipful President of the abolition party were Col. [Edwin V.] SUMNER and Major [David] Hunter, of the Army, detailed as a military escort by "Hasty Plate of Soup," in order that [Virginia's] Governor [Henry A.] WISE should not capture them with his cohorts while on their way to the Federal Capital.

The "ancient rail-splitter" was dined and wined here by the faithful, and to-day left for Columbus.

Cincinnati can boast of being as rank an abolition city as there is upon the continent. "Niggerdom" triumphs in every quarter.

A few days ago I chanced to hear a conversation between a highly respectable citizen and a more respectable negro. The white citizen regretted that there was not a "LOUIS NAPOLEON at the head of the government, who would send down South a million of men to whip the rascals into their senses, and allow the darkey to have his just rights; he would give 'em h-ll," said the white citizen. "Well," said the black citizen, "I don't know, bos; if the people who make such a fuss about us would only let us alone, I think that we could get along much better by ourselves; but they talk about the black man and what they are going to do, but it is all talk."

Business is very dull in this burg. Thousands of mechanics walk the streets out of employment, and there is much suffering among the poor. Recently a free soup house has been established to supply the poor with food, a thing unknown here before. The South is said to be the cause of all the trouble. No one suspects that the election of a Black Republican President has anything to do with producing the misery and destitution that is apparent everywhere. Poor South, "how many sins are laid at your door!"

I do not think that many battalions from this State, however, are likely to volunteer to make a "foray upon the South" in carrying out the "irrepressible conflict." They will prefer to stay at home, as Old Kentucky may have something to say about such a demonstration.

SOUTH.

The Lincoln-hating New York World of the Civil War, edited by Manton Marble, to be suppressed temporarily later, played it fairly straight in relating the story of Mr. Lincoln and the young girl who asked him to grow a beard. From the World, Feb. 19, 1861.

MR. LINCOLN'S JOURNEY
CLEVELAND TO BUFFALO
From Our Own Correspondent

BUFFALO, Feb. 16.

The train bearing the President and suite left Cleveland this morning at 9 o'clock. Quite a large crowd was assembled at the depot and along the line of the track for some distance. The train consisted of one baggage car and three passenger cars, one of the latter beautifully carpeted, curtained, and upholstered for the occupancy of the President's party.

At Euclid, a station near Cleveland, a man was injured by the premature discharge of a cannon. A telegraphic report of his death, received at the next station, was subsequently contradicted. At Wickliffe, Willoughby, Painesville, and other small stations, clusters of people, gathered from the adjacent country, were assembled, ranged along platforms, swarming upon adjoining roofs, clinging upon posts and fences, and exhibiting the heartiest enthusiasm. At Westfield an interesting incident occurred. Shortly after his nomination Mr. Lincoln had received from that place a letter from a little girl, who urged him, as a means of improving his personal appearance, to wear whiskers. Mr. Lincoln at the time replied, stating that although he was obliged by the suggestion, he feared his habits of life were too fixed to admit of even so slight a change as that which letting his beard grow involved. To-day, on reaching the place, he related the incident, and said that if that young lady was in the crowd he should be glad to see her. There was a momentary commotion, in the midst of which an old man, struggling through the crowd, approached, leading his daughter, a girl of apparently twelve or thirteen years of age, whom he introduced to Mr. Lincoln as his Westfield correspondent. Mr. Lincoln stooped down and kissed the child, and talked with her for some minutes. Her advice has not been thrown away upon the rugged chieftain. A beard of several months' growth covers (perhaps adorns) the lower part of his face. The young girl's peachy cheek must have been tickled with a stiff whisker, for the growth of which she was herself responsible.

At Girard, a station near Erie, a profound sensation was created by the sudden appearance of Mr. Horace Greeley. He wore that mysteriously durable garment, the white coat, and carried in his hand a yellow bag, labelled with his name and address, in characters which might be read across Lake Erie. He had, it was said, mistaken the special for the general train, and was a good deal embarrassed on finding himself so suddenly cheek by jowl with the chief of the great and triumphant party which he had so large a hand in establishing, and of which he is one of the most powerful and least judicious supporters. He at first made an incursion into the reporters' car, where he was captured, and marched off in triumph, by Mr. Secretary Nicolay, to the President's car. Here he was introduced for the first time to Mrs. Lincoln. At the next stopping place Greeley suddenly disappeared. His arrival and departure were altogether so unexpected, so mysterious, so comical, that they supplied an amusing topic of conversation during the rest of the journey.

At Dunkirk, at the conclusion of a brief speech, Mr. Lincoln, placing his hand upon a flag-staff from which the stars and stripes waved, said, "I stand by the flag of the Union, and all I ask of you is that you stand by me as long as I stand by it." It is impossible to describe the applause and the acclamation with which this Jacksonian peroration was greeted. The arches of the depot echoed and re-echoed with the ring of countless cheers. Men swung their hats wildly, women waved their handkerchiefs, and, as the train moved on, the crowd, animated by a common impulse, followed, as if they intended to keep it company to the next station. Inside the car the enthusiasm created by the conclusion of the speech was scarcely less than the outside assemblage had exhibited. The company evinced a general disposition to intone hurrahs and sing patriotic songs out of tune.

In the journey to Washington there could be some light moments, though for Lincoln it was long hours and many short speeches. Vanity Fair, whose Charles F. Browne ("Artemus Ward") reached the President's funny bone often, found some humor in the journey. Reprinted in The Crisis, *Columbus, Ohio, March 7, 1861.*

From *Vanity Fair*

PROGRESS OF MR. LINCOLN

Myself, Abe, and the rest, have encountered a rapid succession of large things, in the oration way, since I last wrote you.

Abe is becoming more grave. He don't construct as many jokes as he did. He fears that he will get things mixed up if he don't look out and sincerely as I regard myself competent to fill the Consulship of Liverpool, I fear he will. "I am not so much a Washington as I was," he touchingly remarked to me this morning. "No," I replied, "George is dead."

We made a short stop at Cleveland, Painesville, and Erie, but passed Buffalo, in consequence of Gen. Scroggs being absent. It was also deemed not worth while to stop at Rochester, as I. Butts was out of town.

At Albany we were not "recepted," until sometime after our arrival, on account of our inability to find Gov. Morgan. We all went off to find the old Governor, and finally Weed and I discovered him in the colored tier of the theater, in company with Horace Greeley. They came down and "recepted" us. "Got any tobacker in your trowses, Horace?" says I. "No," he replied, looking sternly at Thurlow, "the Weed don't agree with me."

On entering the Capitol, Mr. Lincoln remarked to Gov. Morgan, that he believed the other Penitentiary was located at Auburn. It was a painful error. Mr. Lincoln apologized immediately, on discovering his mistake.

Col. Ellsworth is with us. Old Scott is to resign in favor of Col. Ellsworth, immediately on our arrival at Washington. We all think that Scott is played out, and are in favor of Col. Ellsworth. Scott is very old. Dear, me, yes! Col. Ellsworth is only thirteen years of age.

It is to be deeply regretted that the hotels along our route thus far have not been properly conducted. Although my connection with *Vanity Fair* was well kown, not a single hotel dead-headed me. I was compelled, indeed, to pay for my beverage. You will thus see why I studiously refrain from making the slightest allusion to the Delevan House at Albany, or the Ashton House in this city. Neither of these hotels has "gentlemanly clerks."

A pleasing incident occurred at Hudson. Several young ladies came into the cars, and the President elect folded them rapturously to his throbbing bosom. They said "don't" which induced the President to believe that they liked it.

The dailies have told you of our reception in the Metropolis. Henry

Ward Beecher told me, as we were getting some coffee and cakes in Chatham street, Wednesday evening, that it was indeed an extensive thing.

It is popularly believed that Mr. Lincoln is not classically educated, which belief had somewhat obtained among our party; but at the dinner at the Astor, where the bills of fare are printed in French, Mr. Lincoln unhesitatingly called for a *sine quanon* of beans and an *Ipsdixit* of pork, thus showing his thorough familiarity with deceased languages.

Mr. Lincoln says that New York and Philadelphia are larger places than Springfield, being more thickly settled.

Mr. Lincoln has abstained from facetiously designating hotel napkins as towels, since Gen. Nye, whose winning ways and polite deportment are strikingly similar to those of the late Lord Chesterfield, joined the party.

Mr. Lincoln continues to measure with all tall men who present themselves, and in various other dignified ways presents a full understanding of the grave duties which will shortly surround him. The assertion that he dare not let his measures be known is a weak invention of the enemy. He measures with every man who wants him to.

Yours, in haste,   C. AUGUSTUS.

Detective Allan Pinkerton's spies discovered a plot against the President-elect in Baltimore. Pinkerton reported, "We have come to know, Mr. Lincoln, and beyond the shadow of a doubt, that there exists a plot to assassinate you. The attempt will be made on your way through Baltimore, day after tomorrow." Lincoln's schedule was changed and he arrived in the capital secretly. The New York Tribune, Feb. 25, 1861, had this to say about the last stage of the journey to Washington.

THE REIGN OF RUFFIANISM

We take it for granted, in the absence of positive, official information, that President Lincoln, in resorting to so extraordinary a step as to travel in disguise and enter *incognito* into the Federal Capital, did so for sufficient reasons. We take it for granted that Mr. Lincoln is not wanting in personal courage, for we know that whenever in the course of his life he has been called upon to exercise that quality it has never failed him, whether for aggression or defense. We take it for granted, therefore, that the peril which threatened him was imminent and great, and that it was one against which personal courage could avail nothing. The danger, no doubt, was one that did not concern him alone; it was not, probably, secret assassination or public murder in some preconcerted riot of which so old and so brave a soldier as Gen. Scott warned him to beware. As the measures resorted to to escape it were extraordinary, so also, without doubt, was the peril itself. What was it? We no more know than our readers. But this we do know—that it is the only instance recorded in history in which the recognized head of a nation—head, whether by choice or inheritance—has been compelled, for fear of his life, to enter the capital in disguise. Tyrants have fled from their palaces under false names and assumed characters, when the exasperated people have compelled them to abdicate their thrones; dethroned monarchs have escaped in the garb of common men at the approach of a foreign enemy; pretenders to royal seats to which they had no right have sought from secret hiding-places and with feigned names and purposes to rally the discontented into open rebellion; but never before among a civilized people has King or President been reduced by the circumstances of the times to such an extremity for protection, where his right to govern was unquestioned and unquestionable. What, then, is the conclusion? Simply that one section of this country is only semi-civilized. It may call itself republican; it may profess the abstract faith of Christianity; it may possess, to a certain limited degree, the arts of a cultivated people; it may live under some of the forms of enlightened society; but it wants that inherent moral sense, that accurate conception of social law, that intelligent submission to the purpose of civil government which mark the highest civilization. It is merely semi-barbarous in its spirit, savage in its instincts, reckless of human life and human rights, faithless in everything but brute force, unintelligent in its aims, and unscrupulous in the means with which it seeks to attain them. In a society so constituted, it is not strange there should be found many persons who could conceive and execute some diabolical plot of slaughter, sparing neither sex, nor age, nor numbers—such as the destruction of a railroad train—that the death of one man might be compassed, in the hope of accomplishing thereby the overthrow of a popular Constitutional Government. Against such designs, formed among a people possessed of the vices and forces of civilization without its virtues and restraints, personal courage, or character, or position, may avail nothing, and there is no defense but evasion. It seems probable that had not Mr. Lincoln resorted to this method of escape, neither he nor any of his party would have ever reached Washington alive.

Four years ago the reign of ruffianism was openly instituted at the

South. The popular intelligence and morality of that region knew no higher method wherewith to meet the progress of opinion and the growth of events. How many men and women were banished and killed in the year 1856 at the South for believing that Slavery is not the best form of human society it is impossible to say, or even to know. We have counted at least a score recorded in a single newspaper within a brief period, and those, of course, were but a fraction of the whole. When, four years later, it is evident that the hostility to Slavery is becoming still more universally diffused, and it so far successfully asserts itself as to forbid its extension into the Territories, then ruffianism becomes still more rampant, and men are imprisoned, banished or killed not by scores, but by hundreds. When this state of things goes not only unpunished but almost unrebuked by the country at large, and it assumes even an organic form in the plunder of public property, the seizure of public forts, and the defiance of the supreme law of the land, what reason have we for expecting that the fierce and brutal spirit which rules the society where such ruffianism grows will stop at anything which seems to dim its intelligence likely to aid in the accomplishment of its ends? The attempted assassination of Mr. Van Wyck at Washington, the proposed plan to get rid of Mr. Lincoln, whatever it was, and at whatever expense of the lives of others, even of women and children, are merely new developments of Southern and slaveholding barbarism, the only way in which innate ruffians can meet the new exigencies of the moment. And these will be followed by acts with more certain results, unless, in the mean time, the supremacy of law shall be asserted in obedience to Northern civilization, and by other means than persuasive words.

The venomous Rhett of South Carolina, stoking trouble whenever and wherever he could, lit the fire for the Secessionist elements. Before the inauguration he talked up not merely independence from the Union but war—dispatches such as these greeted Lincoln as he arrived in Washington. From the Charleston Mercury, Feb. 26, 1861.

Our Washington Correspondence

WASHINGTON, February 21, 1861.
Uncle Sam's Soldiers Don't Want to Fight the South.—Abe's Cabinet Still Doubtful.—Botts' Place.—Foggy Discussion About Future Territory in the Peace Congress.—Lincoln's Course.—Arkansas and Missouri Elections.— War on Northern Soil.—Yankees Waking up to the Fact.—Border States Can't Get Out of the Way.—They Must Take a Hand on One Side or the Other.—March Winds, etc., etc.

Those in the middle classes, who have access to the soldiers now quartered here, and are on intimate terms with them, assure me that they are just as anxious as the citizens themselves that matters should be amicably adjusted. Many of them, some say a majority, affirm that when the worst comes to the worst they will not fight against the South. Those who can resign, will do so; those who cannot, will desert.

Some uncertainty exists as to LINCOLN's future course, WEED and SEWARD claim to have possession of him; and so do GREELEY, SUMNER and the Coercionists generally. While his speeches have been more guarded lately, one can still detect a vein of coercion running through them. If he can do so, he will certainly play the ANDREW JACKSON. If the rag-money scheme becomes a law, and the Treasury gets pretty full, the rail-splitter will infallibly throw the bloody spear. For in the body of LINCOLN the spirit of JOHN BROWN "still lives.". . .

The returns from Arkansas and Missouri are very encouraging to the Republicans, who now, more than ever, are convinced that the Border States "can't be kicked out." They are not far wrong. Certainly nothing short of steady kicking can do it. If the Border States are to be saved, LINCOLN will be their saviour. The natural desire of an ignorant man to atone for mental deficiency by assuming an immense amount of moral firmness, may lead him into acts of great folly and oppression. And his so-called conservative Cabinet will join him, heart and hand, as soon as the reins of power are fairly within their grasp.

Northern men are slowly waking up to the fact that, when war begins, it will be waged on Northern soil; and even they who have urged the border States to remain in the Union as a barrier between the combatants, begin to think that this barrier will not only give way to the advance of the Southern army, but actually join it. When men get to fighting with revolvers, it is not usual for persons, even of the largest size, to stand in the way of the bullets. They step aside very quickly, and, if they happen to be so situated that they can't do that, they join one party or the other, as a matter of security and self-defence.

One week in advance, March, true to its character, "comes in like a lion." So fierce is the wind, and so dense and suffocating the clouds of dust, that the attractions of the Capital fail to draw the usual attendance. Even the hacks and carriages are forced to seek the wet side streets to avoid the terrible dust on Pennsylvania Avenue.

SEVEN.

Our Washington Despatches.

WASHINGTON, February 23.—ABRAHAM LINCOLN, President elect of the Northern States, crept into Washington most unexpectedly by the daylight train from Baltimore. It is well understood that he was in dread of an attack on the way. To guard against this, he gave out that he would arrive by to-night's train, and, in the meantime, he took measures to come *incognito* twelve hours earlier. Everybody here is disgusted at this cowardly and undignified entry.

A telegram was received to-day by Secretary TOUCEY, from the South, which created intense excitement in semi-official circles, as the rumor flew round that it reported an attack on Fort Pickens. I have reason to know that the telegram referred to subjects entirely different.

A despatch announcing the arrival of President DAVIS in Charleston filled President BUCHANAN with alarm, and he hastened to Mr. TYLER's hotel to inquire what it meant. Mr. TYLER assured Mr. BUCHANAN that the mission of President DAVIS was one of peace and not of war—that no attack would be made on Fort Sumter until the character of LINCOLN's inaugural was known. If its tone should be pacific, no attack, he said, would be made. If warlike, the attack would begin immediately.

Chapter 6

President at War

MARCH 1861–APRIL 1862

March 4, 1861, the day of inauguration. For Lincoln, four years, one month, ten days to April 15, 1865. Thirty-four States were in the Union; but seven declaring themselves out. Rumblings came from Fort Sumter; here Major Robert Anderson would not be allowed to buy fresh supplies in Charleston for the Federal garrison he commanded. Lincoln waited at Willard's Hotel, waiting to be sworn in at the Capitol, and friends brought counsel and rumour. The political bosses were trying to call in obligations; and every Cabinet post already a center of discontent. To future Secretary of State Seward, Lincoln had written a few months before regarding patronage: "Justice to all." Instead it began to be a little for all, divided justice, and an imminent and constant balancing of politics, principles and public opinion.

There was much cordiality in Lincoln's manner on the surface but below lay a bedrock of principle. Between election and inauguration, on the burning issue, Lincoln had said: "Let there be no compromise on the question of extending slavery. If there be, all our labor is lost, and, ere long, must be done again." His position was in the record, people had heard it, if they cared to listen, since 1854.

The country was aflame with anticipation of what he would say. Editors North and South were kept busy telling the President-elect what he should say. The language of this self-educated man now was all-important. Language could be the lanyard.

Lincoln worked over the words with utmost care. The first draft in Springfield was changed as events altered from week to week. But the bedrock would not be changed. Before the inauguration the Louis-

ville Daily Courier said, "Never has greater responsibility devolved on one man." In the North, James Gordon Bennett's *New York Herald*, March 4, 1861, reflected the doubts and brewing anti-Lincoln sentiments.

THE INAUGURAL OF MR. LINCOLN

This day is the 4th of March—a day which has been looked forward to with intense anxiety by the country. It is the day of inauguration, when the President elect becomes President *de facto*. The ceremony will take place at twelve o'clock, and Mr. Lincoln, like Mr. Buchanan, will deliver his inaugural before taking the oath of office. Never since the formation of the government was an inauguration day invested with so much of gloom. There is no longer any apprehension of disturbance at the capital; but the little cloud "the size of a man's hand" which appeared in the Southern horizon on the morning after the 6th of November has grown and spread and become darker and darker, till now the whole Southern heavens are overcast, and tempest seems almost inevitable. The clouds at the North, too, have been ever since gathering and growing blacker, and moving forward in dense masses charged with electricity. It only needs a word and a blow from one man to produce a collision and make the theory of the irrepressible conflict a fearful practical reality. A word alone may be sufficient to precipitate the antagonistic elements upon each other, but, followed up by a blow, the result is certain.

No President of the United States has ever been inaugurated under such circumstances before. It is a new era in the history of the country— an unprecedented result of a Presidential election. It is the first time that a party organized on an issue involving a controverted question of morals and religion—a party organized moreover on a purely sectional issue, in opposition to the institutions of fifteen States, divided by a geographical line from the other States—was enabled to elect its candidate to rule over the whole Union, including those fifteen Southern States, not one of which gave him a vote. Upon this dangerous issue, therefore, Mr. Lincoln has been borne into power by a party whose principles are antagonistic to the principles of the people—whose combined opposition stands recorded in the ratio of three and a half to one. The popular vote for Mr. Lincoln was 1,865,840. The whole vote was 4,739,982. The official vote against him was thus 2,874,142. If from those who voted for him we deduct the whigs and conservatives, who merely desired a change, and did not intend to endorse the Chicago platform, and who if they had to vote now would

This newly discovered drawing of Lincoln was made by Pierre Morand, a French business agent and artist who spent much time in and out of Washington during the war. "In life Mr. Lincoln's features and movements impressed me so vividly," he said, after making the President's acquaintance, "that I made several good sketches of him in various attitudes in June, 1864." This one is labeled: "Abraham Lincoln, elaborated from a rough sketch in possession of Colonel D. H. Strother, without date. Probably at Soldiers' Home. Lincoln in summer dress." The President had a cottage at the Soldiers' Home, three miles from the White House. This drawing, reprinted here for the first time since it came to light in 1953, is reproduced from the original held by the Missouri Historical Society.

Der erste Brief.

Two scenes from Lincoln's youth—reading his first letter, and working as a flatboatman—visualized in a German biography, "Abraham Lincoln," by Dr. Max Lange, printed in Leipzig, 1866.

Die Floßfahrt.

Lincoln's earliest photograph was taken by a daguerreotypist, probably in 1846. It is believed to have been made by N. H. Shepherd, soon after the photographic process was invented.

The Lincoln-Douglas debates.

Lincoln on the day he spoke at Cooper Union, New York, Feb. 27, 1860. This was the first portrait made of Lincoln by Mathew Brady.

This campaign poster made by Currier & Ives, the most popular printmakers of the time, was used by the Republicans a month after the convention. The lithograph copied a photograph of an ambrotype made in 1858.

HON. ABRAHAM LINCOLN.
OF ILLINOIS.
NATIONAL REPUBLICAN CANDIDATE FOR SIXTEENTH PRESIDENT OF THE UNITED STATES.

ne month after Lincoln was nominated for President, Henry Louis Stephens designed this cartoon for Vanity Fair, June 9, 1860. Lincoln carries a Negro baby over a rotting rail while Horace Greeley in the background shouts advice, "Don't drop the carpet bag." The reference to Blondin in the accompanying caption and the explanation of Lincoln in his costume is that Charles Blondin, French acrobat, had crossed Niagara Falls on a tightrope in 1859 and, in the summer when this cartoon appeared, was touring the country.

SHAKY.

DARING TRANSIT ON THE PERILOUS RAIL.   .   .   .   Mr. Abraham Blondin De Lave Lincoln.

HARPER'S WEEKLY.
A JOURNAL OF CIVILIZATION

VOL. IV.—No. 202.]   NEW YORK, SATURDAY, NOVEMBER 10, 1860.   [PRICE FIVE CENTS.

Entered according to Act of Congress, in the Year 1860, by Harper & Brothers, in the Clerk's Office of the District Court for the Southern District of New York.

HON. ABRAHAM LINCOLN, BORN IN KENTUCKY, FEBRUARY 12, 1809.—[PHOTOGRAPHED BY BRADY.]

The President-elect, in an engraving adapted from a photograph by Brady, as he appeared on the front page of Harper's Weekly. In at least one Southern city, when this issue of Harper's came by mail, it went undelivered because of Lincoln's picture.

OF ILLINOIS, THE PRESIDENTIAL CANDIDATE FOR THE REPUBLICAN PARTY.—PHOTOGRAPHED BY BRADY.—SEE PAGE 659.

A more flattering version of the Brady first photograph of Lincoln as it was engraved for Frank Leslie's Illustrated Weekly, Oct. 20, 1860.

PROF. LINCOLN IN HIS GREAT FEAT OF BALANCING.

At the time of inauguration, the "great feat of balancing" was peace or war, reconciliation or the challenge of Fort Sumter. Secretary of State Seward here is ringmaster; on the left in the audience sits a caricature of Horace Greeley. This cartoon by Henry L. Stephens appeared in Vanity Fair, March 23, 1861.

Le Message de M. Lincoln.

Nous avons publié hier les principaux passages du Message extraordinaire de M. Lincoln, et nos lecteurs ont pu se faire une idée de ce document. Le moindre de ses défauts est la prolixité. Dans notre vieille Europe, une demande d'hommes et d'argent, nécessitée par des circonstances analogues, se formulerait en termes clairs et concis. Les choses se traitent différemment dans le Nouveau-Monde. L'Américain aime les longs bilans; rien ne doit être omis ni

Le Message de M. Lincoln.

"Yesterday we published the principal passages of Mr. Lincoln's extraordinary message, and our readers were able to formulate some idea of this document. The least of its faults is prolixity. In our old Europe, an appeal for men and money, necessitated by similar circumstances, would be couched in clear, concise terms. Things are done differently in the New World . . . ."

From La Patrie, July 21, 1861

ONE GOOD TURN DESERVES ANOTHER.

Old Abe: "WHY I DU DECLARE IT'S MY DEAR OLD FRIEND SAMBO! COURSE YOU'LL FIGHT FOR US, SAMBO. LEND US A HAND, OLD HOSS, DU!"

A British view of the motive behind emancipation. This drawing from Punch, or the London Charivari, appeared Aug. 9, 1862. It was drawn by John Tenniel, the magazine's noted artist, whose initials appear in the lower right corner. The British drawing served the purpose — with some alterations — of the Southern Illustrated News, Richmond.

ONE GOOD TURN DESERVES ANOTHER.

Old Abe: "WHY I DU DECLARE IT'S MY DEAR OLD FRIEND SAMBO! COURSE YOU'LL FIGHT FOR US, SAMBO. LEND US A HAND, OLD HOSS, DU!"—London Punch.

The Tenniel drawing for London Punch was copied seven months later by the Southern Illustrated News, Richmond, on March 14, 1863. Some small changes were made. Lincoln's hat in the South became a Scotch cap —a reference to his supposed headgear when he went from Baltimore to Washington in disguise. The face of the Negro in the Richmond redrawing lost much of its strength.

ABE LINCOLN'S LAST CARD; OR, ROUGE-ET-NOIR.

This Punch drawing by John Tenniel appeared on Oct. 18, 1862, following the use of The London Times idea that freeing the slaves was a desperate last-trump card. Lincoln faces Jefferson Davis and plays a black spade which bears the countenance of a Negro.

MASKS AND FACES.

With the fatal day of full freedom less than two months away, the Southern Illustrated News, Nov. 8, 1862, published this drawing of Lincoln. This Richmond weekly was one of the few illustrated publications in the South.

King Abraham before and after issuing the EMANCIPATION PROCLAMATION.

This drawing by A. R. Waud, from Harper's Weekly, May 2, 1863, is captioned: "The President, General Hooker, and their staffs at a review in the Army of the Potomac."

SCHOOLMASTER LINCOLN AND HIS BOYS.—*Lincoln*—Waal, boys, what's the matter with yer; you haint been hurt, hev yer? *McClellan.*—Them fellers that run away has been beatin' us. *Lincoln.*—What fellers? *McClellan.*—Bob Lee and Jeb Stuart and them. *Lincoln.*—I sent you out to fetch them same fellers back, so's I could wallop 'em. *McClellan.*—Yes, but Bob Lee took and bunged me in the eye. *Pope.*—And Stunwall Jackson he kicked me in the rear until he broke my arm. *Banks.*—Yes, and that same feller gouged me and run me until I run my leg off and hev to wear a wooden one. *Burnside.*—All of 'em, Bob Lee, Stunwall and Stuart, jumped on me at Fredericksburg and give me fits; that's the reason my jaw is tied up, to keep my teeth from chatterin', for I've had a fit of the ager ever since. *Lincoln.*—You are a worthless set, all of you. You haint no spunk. I'm agoin' to spank every one of yer. Come up here.

The Southern Illustrated News, Richmond, Jan. 31, 1863, comments on Lincoln's troubles with his generals.

THE GREAT "CANNON GAME."

ABE LINCOLN (aside). "DARN'D IF HE AIN'T SCORED AG'IN!—WISH I COULD MAKE A FEW *WINNING* HAZARDS FOR A CHANGE.

This drawing by John Tenniel appeared in Punch, May 9, 1863. The same issue of the London satirical weekly contained an article called **The Great American Billiard Match**, explaining that between the players, Lincoln and Jefferson Davis, Lincoln so far had been **outgeneraled.**

BRUTUS AND CÆSAR

FROM THE AMERICAN EDITION OF SHAKSPEARE.

The Tent of Brutus (LINCOLN.)   *Night.   Enter the Ghost of* CÆSAR.

Brutus. Wall, now! Do tell! Who's you!

Cæsar. I am dy ebil genius, massa LINKING
Dis child am awful Inimpressional.

This portrayal of Lincoln as Brutus originally appeared in Punch, London, Aug. 15, 1863, where it was drawn by John Tenniel. The Southern Illustrated News, as it did several times with anti-Lincoln cartoons, had its own artist recopy the drawing crudely. It reappeared Oct. 31, 1863, with accompanying playlet.

BROWNLOW'S KNOXVILLE WHIG,
AND REBEL VENTILATOR.

VOLUME I.   KNOXVILLE, TENN., WEDNESDAY, NOVEMBER 11, 1863.   NUMBER 1.

This is a section of Volume I, Number 1, of what was one of the unique publications of the Civil War—and surely the most daringly named. The editor was Parson W. G. Brownlow, who said that his was "the last and only Union paper left in the eleven seceded states." It was subsequently shut down for two years, but reappeared on Nov. 11, 1863, when the Union forces entered East Tennessee.

Lincoln as he appeared in Washington in 1864. This drawing from life was made by the French artist and business agent, Pierre Morand, and is reproduced for the first time since his Civil War drawings were discovered by the Missouri Historical Society in 1953.

DON'T SWAP HORSES.

JOHN BULL. "Why don't you ride the other Horse a bit? He's the best Animal."
BROTHER JONATHAN. "Well, that may be; but the fact is, OLD ABE is just where I can put my finger on him; and as for the other—though they say he's some when out in the scrub yonder—I never know where to find him."

In this campaign drawing General McClellan, the Democratic candidate nominated at Chicago, looks on as Britain's John Bull tries to persuade Brother Jonathan, one of Uncle Sam's citizens, to dismount from "Old Abe." From Harper's Weekly, Nov. 12, 1864.

This grotesque characterization of Lincoln by John Tenniel appeared in Punch, Dec. 3, 1864. It was to be regretted the following April; in December it was a comment on re-election.

THE FEDERAL PHŒNIX.

ABRAHAM LINCOLN AT HOME.

This engraving, which appeared in Harper's Monthly in early 1865, shows the President and Tad. It was adapted from an early Brady photograph, popular around the country.

BRITANNIA SYMPATHISES WITH COLUMBIA.

England's reaction to Lincoln's death — Punch on May 6, 1865, made amends for its wartime series of cartoons against Lincoln. John Tenniel's drawing, Britannia Lays a Wreath on Lincoln's Bier, includes the figure of an unshackled Negro slave. The same issue of Punch included a poem that was both tribute and apology.

Reaction to Lincoln's death in Italy — Page 1 news on May 3, 1865, in the Gazzetta di Firenze, which reprinted La Perseveranza di Milano.

La *Perseveranza* di Milano dice :

La tragica fine di Lincoln e l' incerta aspettativa su quello che sta per accadere agli Stati Uniti, sotto l' impressione di quel fatto e col nuovo governo , dà grande interesse a quell' atto del defunto presidente che fu l' ultimo suo , cioè al discorso da lui pronunciato nel giorno 13 aprile dopo la capitolazione di Lee; nel qual discorso manifestava in embrione le sue idee circa al futuro ordinamento della Unione.

Leggendo il discorso , che facciamo seguire qui sotto, non possiamo a meno d' ammirare una volta di più la semplicità, la schiettezza, il buon senso, la sapienza che deriva dalla rettitudine del cuore e dalla fermezza di carattere di quest' uomo raro. Voi vedete in quest' uomo, che si è educato

throw their suffrages in a very different direction, the strictly republican vote was about one million, against upwards of 3,700,000 opposed to the Chicago platform. Yet it has been claimed, ever since the election, that the small republican minority have a right to enforce their policy over the large majority, to the overthrow of the constitution, to the disruption of the confederacy, and even to civil war. . . .

In consequence of the soothing tone of the speeches of Mr. Seward, who, it was known, was to be Premier in Mr. Lincoln's Cabinet, expectations of moderation were formed which are now dashed to earth by Mr. Seward's recent votes. And Mr. Lincoln himself, who had remained silent at Springfield when the people demanded his voice to still the rising storm, has lately spoken in words not calculated to reassure the country or disperse the clouds of war sweeping overhead. According to our best information, he persists in the revolutionary doctrines of the Chicago platform as the practical policy of his administration, and will neither make nor advise concessions. The radical wing of the republican party appears to have prevailed over the moderates, as the Jacobins in the French Revolution prevailed over the Girondists of the party, and from the inaugural, therefore, to-day, nothing conciliatory is to be expected.

Now, if the tone of this official manifesto should turn out to be of the nature indicated by all our intelligence from Washington—holding out the sword and not the olive branch—and if that be the real expression of the new President's sentiments and the veritable programme of his policy, and not merely a bait to gain some point from the ultras of his own party, which would be playing an extremely foolish part, the ceremony to-day will be not only the inauguration of a President, but the inauguration of civil war, and it will give birth to a new conservative party at the North which will utterly rout and destroy the republican party, horse, foot and artillery. Mr. Lincoln had a glorious game in his hands, but we fear he has lost it forever. He might have saved the country and become second only to Washington in the hearts of the people; a few hours will tell whether he is the man for the occasion.

Taking the oath, Lincoln said: "One section of our country believes slavery is right, and ought to be extended, while the other believes it is wrong, and ought not to be extended. This is the only substantial dispute." And further: "We are not enemies, but friends." The language was conciliatory, yet firm enough to please Greeley's New York Tribune, March 6, 1861.

MR. LINCOLN'S ADDRESS

The almost universal satisfaction with which the Inaugural Address of President Lincoln is received is the strongest evidence of the anxiety with which it was waited for, as well as of the high character of the document itself. For nearly four months the people of this country, strong in the power of self-government to which our institutions have bred them, have sustained themselves, as no other nation could have done, virtually without a central government, and while all the evil elements in the discontented and vicious of the community were appealed to by an apparently successful rebellion. Undoubtedly we have been drifting fast into anarchy; the reign of scoundrelism was impending, and might have already overwhelmed us but for the patient forbearance of the people with an effete and expiring government, and the patient waiting for the government to come, on which all hopes and all fears were centered. But had it been evident that the incoming Administration was to be a mere continuation of the imbecile policy of the last three months, the country sustained no longer by the hope of something better to come, would have fallen presently into general wreck and ruin, at least for a season, incapable of holding together even by that powerful cohesion of popular government, which is at once the result and the test of the excellence of our Republican system. The feeling then would necessarily be one of great relief were the Address merely an assurance of some positive firmness on the part of the new Administration.

But how much more must it gratify the public expectation when the address is found to be marked by a sagacity as striking as its courage, and by an absence of all passion as remarkable as its keen division of the line of duty, its unequivocal statement of the issues at stake, and uncompromising admissions of their precise value. Upon the question of Slavery the President frankly acknowledges all that the Constitution requires, as the Republican party has done before him, and proclaims the duty of fulfiling those requirements. So there is no hypocritical profession of a hasty alacrity at performing what is the exceptional duty under a free government, and he is careful to characterize it as held by the majority of the people as strictly a "dry legal obligation." The question of Slavery in the Territories, inasmuch as the Constitution is silent in relation to it, he holds must be settled by the majority and their decision acquiesced in by the minority. Nor does he submit on this point to the *dictum* of the Supreme Court. In a few pregnant sentences, worthy the charge of a Chief Justice to a jury, and containing more sound law than is often found in charges twenty times its length, he clears away all the assumed settlement of the question by the Dred Scott decision. To the binding character of such decisions in private suits he assents, but he considers that the people would practically cease to be their own masters and resign the right of self-government into the hands of that tribunal, if they acknowledge that the policy of the Government is to be irrevocably fixed by the decisions of the Supreme Court, to which the Constitution gives no political power. And this is as sound common sense as it is good law, and sweeps away at a dash all the cobwebs of sophistry that have been woven over the public mind by the judgment in the case of Dred Scott.

But it is in the admirable treatment of the Secession question that Mr. Lincoln is most entitled to the gratitude of the country, and must certainly, it seems to us, command the support of all good citizens. The duty of the head of the Government to assert the rights of the Government itself is so self-evident a truth that the truth of the corollary is no less so—that those will be guilty of commencing civil war, if any shall arise, who shall attempt to hinder the Federal Government from occupying its own property. The avowal of his purpose, in this regard, is unequivocal, unhesitating, firm, and earnest. One thing only can be understood from it—he means to execute the laws. But as there is no hesitation, so there is no haste; and the firmness of his purpose is tempered by mercy. He means evidently to provoke no unnecessary hostilities, and only where his duty is perfectly clear to protect the rights of the whole will he assert the authority of the Federal Government. If in the interior of the Southern States foolish people will not permit the presence of Federal officers, they will be permitted to do without them, as they only are the losers; but where revenue is to be collected which belongs to the whole people, or where forts are to be reoccupied which no more belong to the section where they happen to be than they do to the people of the most distant corner of the Union, then the laws must be executed, and the power of the Federal Government asserted. But time, no doubt, will be given to the unhappy people, betrayed by an imbecile Government into excesses which four-months ago they never contemplated, to return to their allegiance, and restore the property of which they have possessed themselves under a lamentable delusion.

The clearness with which the President states his position on this point is as remarkable as its firmness, and so persuaded will the country be that it is a wise plan, and that it is a plan which must confine all further disturbances to a few localities in settling the difference with the South, and that no disastrous consequences will follow it to any of the interests of the country, that we predict that the people will now turn to their several affairs, the mechanic to his craft, the farmer to his plow, the merchant to his merchandise, all men to their usual callings, satisfied that they may safely leave the question in the hands of one perfectly able to manage it, who will bring order out of seeming chaos, reason out of folly, safety out of danger, and that in so doing he will not sacrifice the national honor or jeopard any of the national interests.

If the seccessionists opinion-makers wanted to probe, they could find the words they were looking for in the Inaugural Address: "The power confided to me, will be used to hold, occupy, and possess the property, and places belonging to the government, and to collect the duties and imposts." The rest of that sentence could be ignored—as in this editorial from the Richmond Whig—when Lincoln continued, "but beyond what may be necessary for these objects, there will be no invasion—no using of force against, or among the people anywhere." Reprinted in the Charleston Mercury, March 9, 1861.

COERCIVE POLICY OF THE INAUGURAL
From the Richmond Whig

We desire to repeat what we said on yesterday, that the coercive policy, foreshadowed in President Lincoln's Inaugural, towards the seceding States, will meet with the stern and unyielding resistance of a united South. The declaration contained in that document to the effect that the Federal Government intend "to hold, occupy and possess the property and places belonging to the Government, and to collect the duties and imposts," necessarily involves war; and war, as remarked by Mr. Dorman in his speech in Convention on yesterday, involves a total and permanent disruption of the Union.

It is too late now to discuss the rightfulness or the wrongfulness of the abstract doctrine of secession. Six or seven States have already proclaimed themselves independent of the Union, and have organized a Provisional Government, and are now in the act of discharging all the functions of a separate nationality. It is the part of wise and practical men, and it is especially the duty of the Federal Administration at Washington, to look facts in the face—to meet and accept facts as they find them, and dispose of them with a view to the interests of peace and harmony. Let Lincoln carry out the policy indicated in his Inaugural, and civil war will be inaugurated forthwith throughout the length and breadth of the land. The Gulf States, in our judgment, have acted rashly, unneighborly, and improperly; but, considering them erring sisters, entitled to our sympathies and our aid in an emergency, Virginia can never consent, and will never consent, for the Federal Government to employ coercive measures towards them. And the stupendous folly of such a policy is perfectly apparent. For, as we have said, it would lead to certain and inevitable war, and to the complete and eternal destruction of the Union. It would ultimately force all the Border States to make common cause with the Gulf States, and what would the Federal Government gain by such an operation? The thing is inadmissible—it is utterly absurd and ridiculous; and if Lincoln and his advisers wish to avoid serious trouble, and save the peace of the country, they will abandon their coercion policy, and take their stand on the broad platform of common-sense and common justice. "To hold, occupy, and possess the property and places belonging to the Government," within the limits of the seceded States, is a thing that can't be done—it is impracticable, and an attempt in that direction would be followed by an immediate collision between the State and Federal authorities, which would lead, in the end, to a general and disastrous civil war between the North and the South. Let President Lincoln reconsider his determination, and let him address himself to a peaceful solution of our national difficulties, and the Union may yet be restored in all its pristine dimensions, strength and glory.

In the Convention on yesterday the coercive doctrine of the Inaugural was the subject of extended debate. Many resolutions were offered in regard to it, all of which deprecated and denounced it in the strongest terms, and asserted the duty of Virginia to resist such policy by all the means at her command. It is manifest that the tone and language of the Inaugural on this point have created considerable excitement and indignation among the people of the State, and have aroused a spirit of resistance which will not tamely submit to see that policy carried into effect towards the seceding States. We are clearly of the opinion that the Convention should promptly and explicitly define the position of the State on this subject of coercion, and make it known to Lincoln and his Administration that any employment of force against the seceding States will be met by Virginians with instant and determined resistance. Let such formal and solemn declaration be unanimously made by the Convention, to-day, in the name of the people and the Commonwealth, and we feel sure it will exert the desired effect upon the Cabinet Councils at Washington. Let this declaration, too, be coupled with the earnest request, on the part of the State, that instead of "holding, occupying and

possessing the property and places belonging to the Government," within
the limits of the seceding States, the Federal Government should forthwith give them all up, as the only hope of preserving peace, preventing
civil war and reconstructing the Union.

In conclusion, we express the earnest hope that President Lincoln
and his advisers will perceive the impracticability and folly of attempting
to carry out the coercive policy indicated in the Inaugural, and that they
will forthwith abandon it, and forthwith announce to the country that it
has been abandoned. For, let it be distinctly understood at Washington
that, upon the abandonment of that unwise and insane policy depends
the adherence of Virginia and the other Border States to the Union, and,
consequently, the hope of a reconstruction of the Union and the preven-
tion of civil war.

*Rhett's Charleston Mercury would also ignore the moderate
language of the Inaugural and concentrate on the sentence about possessing the places belonging to the Federal Government. In its psy-
chopathic drive toward war, the Mercury on March 9, 1861, found in
the words of the Inaugural by "King Lincoln" an "honest declaration
of war."*

THE ABOLITION REGIME

Our Washington Correspondence

WASHINGTON, March 5, 1861.
*The Inaugural—A Declaration of War—The Hour has Come—Cabinet not
yet Made Up—John Bell Probably Going In—Civil War in Virginia and
Tennessee—Crowd Thinned Out—Office-Seekers Hanging On—Dust and
Wind, etc., etc., etc.*

President ABRAHAM LINCOLN reigns over all but six of the late
United States. In the Inaugural Address which his Excellency (?) vouch-
safed to deliver on yesterday, he manifested no disposition to relinquish
the pleasure of reigning over all the States. He said plainly as a man could
say anything, that the Union was intended to be, and should be, perpetual, and that his purpose was to "hold, occupy and possess," or in
other words to hold, take and retain all the forts and arsenals that ever
belonged to the late government, and to do this by force of arms, unless
"the people, his masters," refuse to sustain him with men, money and
munitions of war. When he uttered this fiat of war in an emphatic tone,

a great and prolonged shout rose up from all the people, one half of whom could not hear him. Evidently he had a *claque* around him.

He will also "collect the duties and imposts." Beyond the power which may be necessary for these objects, there will be no invasion, no using of force. So there *will* be *invasion*, there *will* be *force*. But not in "interior localities." In plain terms, then, the navy will be used on the seacoasts and against the rebellious ports; but the army will be reserved as yet. People of Charleston *prenez garde!* Sumter will be reinforced, if possible. Men of Pensacola, keep a sleepless eye on Pickens. I confess that this honest declaration of war is what I had not expected of LINCOLN. Under SEWARD's adroit handling, I thought coercion would have been buttered over much more thickly. And it cannot be denied that sweet and suasive phrases are not wanting in the address; but the naked truth is none the less apparent and unmistakable for all that. King LINCOLN— Rail Splitter ABRAHAM—Imperator! We thank thee for this. It is the tocsin of battle, but it is the signal of our freedom. Quickly, oh quickly begin the fray. Haste to levy tribute. "Enforce the laws" with all possible speed! We have no money to pay, but we have treasure enough—liquid wealth, redder than any gold and infinitely more precious. Be sure, be very sure, O! low-born, despicable tyrant, that the price of liberty will be paid—good measure, heaped up, shaken down, running over, in hot streams fresh from hearts that will not, cannot beat in the breasts of slaves. Then shall we hear the thunder from Sumter, and the fierce reply from Moultrie and from Cumming's Point.

ABRAHAM still staggers to and fro like a drunken man under the intoxication of his new position, and the pressure of opposing forces. Such has been the strain upon the poor creature's nerves by the partizans of CHASE and CAMERON, that a day or two ago he burst into tears and oaths, and cried, "My God! Gentlemen, what shall I do? How can I decide?" Unhappy being!

It is now tolerably certain that JOHN BELL, of Tennessee, will get a seat in the Cabinet. He has taken time by the forelock, in announcing his willingness to accept before any offer was made. While the place has not been distinctly tendered, I am well persuaded he was *sent* for. The value of such a man in the Cabinet is perfectly well understood by that arch wire-worker, SEWARD. When BELL is in, the chains will be riveted on the Border States. This involves a sad necessity. Civil War begins in Virginia and Tennessee. We had hoped to avoid so terrible a calamity, but it has been forced on us. It has taken some time for the resistance party to make up its mind to the dire necessity but "what must be, will be."

They were Tories and traitors to vanquish in '76. Our fathers took up arms against all comers. Shall we be less valiant? Heaven forbid!

Already the city is much emptied of its surplus population. The carpet-bag horde of place-hunters hang on, and will continue to do so until the offices are disposed of. Resignations come in slowly. Congressmen have taken the wings of the morning, and are off. Many of them will go to Montgomery. The rattle of drums may be heard all day long. Washington is henceforth a fortified stronghold. What, with streets as dry as the desert of Sahara, and the wind blowing great guns and driving dense clouds of impalpable dust before it, we are having a horrid time.

SEVEN.

Charleston, because of Fort Sumter, was flammable for the torch of war. What the Charleston Mercury, March 9, 1861, had to say was closely followed in Washington as an indication of attitudes toward Major Anderson and his garrison. Here Lincoln acquired a new name to add to his growing list, "Jackson the Deuce."

Our Washington Correspondence

WASHINGTON, March 6, 1861.

Waiting for War to Begin—Opinions of the Inaugural—The Bluster and Back-Down States—Le Pays, Lyons and Mercier—Commissioners from the Confederate States—Lincoln's Personal Appearance—King Stork and King Log, etc., etc., etc.

"Turn, fortune, turn thy wheel," is now the prayer of all true Southern men. The declaration of war has been spoken: let it be made good in deeds. That is the sincere wish of every lover of civil liberty, who is willing to anticipate the evil hour that must soon come, and does not count the cost of freedom from Abolition tyranny. As yet, the Ourang-Outang at the White House has not issued his orders for the collection of the revenue and for the reinforcement of the forts. On the contrary, a dispatch is inserted, by official authority doubtless, to the effect that Major ANDERSON "considers himself safe," and thinks that "reinforcements had better not be sent to him!" Wise Major, or rather wise Republican War Department, which speaks for the Major.

The Abolition-Republican papers are delighted with the Inaugural. With cruel admiration, they call it a "State paper." The *Tribune* pushes its irony to an extreme, and speaks about "Mr. LINCOLN's statesmanlike talent for silence." Whew! He displayed it on the road with a vengeance. Of all the opinions yet given, none is so complete a summing up of the whole Inaugural in a single sentence as the following from this same *Tribune:*

> But Mr. Lincoln, while dwelling upon the folly of the South in seeking in disunion a remedy for their supposed ills, holds out to her no promise of any new guaranty of her rights.

That is the whole thing in a nut-shell.

How do the Border States relish this little joke of denying their rights *in toto?* I saw last night a number of dispatches from various points in the Confederate and Border States, which were intended for the New York papers and do not appear in our city journals. The dry contentment expressed in that from Charleston was delicious. Wilmington also seemed well pleased with coercion. At other places, like Raleigh and Richmond, much indignation had been stirred up by the Inaugural. It will amount to nothing, unless actual force is used. Mr. EDMUND RUFFIN has taught us in four words—"bluster and back down"—the whole secret of Union-loving wrath.

The *Herald* republishes a significant article from NAPOLEON's organ, *Le Pays,* which places the South in its true position as oppressed and assailed by "Northern pretension." Some think that Mr. FAULKNER must have indoctrinated the editor with just views of the long quarrel which has been pending between the two sections. If we add to the opinion of *Le Pays* the statement which appears this morning, that Lord LYONS and M. MERCIER have notified the Abolition Government that "a paper blockade" will not be recognised by France and England, we may feel sure that the Cotton States did not "reckon without their host" when they counted on the power of the "King" to secure their independence.

Hon. M. J. CRAWFORD, Commissioner from the Confederate States to treat with the Abolition Emperor, is here. The other Commissioners are momently expected, and may have arrived early this morning. There has been no interview, so far as I can yearn. Coercionists of the worst sort talk of arresting these gentlemen and hanging them for treason. Bosh! JACKSON the DEUCE will have to split several millions more rails before his nerves get strong enough for that.

A Senator, who sat within a few feet of LINCOLN while he was in the Senate Chamber on the day of the Inauguration, says his face is enough of itself to hang him, if he happened to be in a California mining district while any stealing was going on, and the thief was not known, but only suspected. He is very awkward, and made three or four attempts to sit down before he succeeded. Then, allowing no one to catch his deep-sunken eye, he sat motionless, save when his chest heaved every minute or two, showing the suppressed emotion and excitement within. One can't help feeling pity for him. I fear he cannot live long. The cares of State, the constant dread of unknown evils, and the incessant annoyance of place hunters, will go far towards destroying him, as they did HARRISON and TAYLOR.

We are told that the military escort to BUCHANAN, yesterday, was "spontaneous." Perhaps. Objectionable as he may have been, the people must feel his vast superiority to his successor. King Stork has come in place of King Log. Let us do all honor to departing Log.

The weather continues chilly and cheerless. I shall play Micawber one day longer, and then, whether anything "turns up" or not, I shall make my congé to the readers of THE MERCURY.

SEVEN.

In Kansas, too, a "Southron" correspondent found that the In-augural address meant war. An interesting piece of news comes out— the Indian tribes in Kansas "are all slaveholders" and will go with the South. From the Charleston Mercury, March 19, 1861.

THE CRISIS IN KANSAS
Our Leavenworth Correspondence

LEAVENWORTH, KAN., March 5, 1861.

Lincoln's Inaugural—What is Thought of it in the Far West—The Feeling in Missouri—Kansas as Bad as Ever—A Plan of Subjugating the South-west—The Indians Sympathise with the South—Military Preparations— A Reign of Terror, etc., etc., etc.

LINCOLN's Inaugural was received here last night. It means coercion —war. Holding, occupying and possessing government property means quartering an army of occupation throughout the Southern Confederacy; holding forts on Southern soil *vi et armis*; reinforcing Forts Sumter and Pickens, and re-taking Fort Moultrie and all other posts now in possession of the South. Collecting revenue means blockade of Southern ports, and levying tribute upon Southern commerce at the cannon's mouth. War is inevitable.

As long as it was reasonable to indulge in the hope that our difficulties could be adjusted without conflict of arms, we clung to the delusion; but the bloody intent of this foreshadowing manifesto, illy concealed by equivocal verbiage, knocks the last plank from under us, and we must fight or yield. No concession is to be granted; no compromise offered; no settlement proposed. The solemn act of seven sovereign States, dissolving allegiance with a government no longer entitled to their fealty and respect, and erecting themselves into a free and independent nation, is treated as mere child's play. ABRAHAM LINCOLN says to the South: "You can amuse yourself with a mock government, but you must obey my government; you can raise a revenue of your own, but you must pay mine; you can have mail facilitiies by paying for them—if you don't accept those which I extend, you shall have none other; you can build forts, but those now on your soil are mine—you shall not have them—I will retake them, hold them, and shell your towns and cities if you resist me; you can raise your armies, but mine shall be there to watch them, and, if necessary to carry out my despotic reign, to conquer them. The South is called upon to submit to the yoke. She will never do it. She does not court war, but she will not shrink from it.

Would the thousands who read THE MERCURY like to hear how the fight is going on upon the frontier? I will tell them. Missouri is acting coolly and deliberately. She has had no thoughts of secession, yet entertains a strong sympathy for her Southern sisters. Her Convention, now in session, will not pass a secession ordinance, but they will speak out and tell ABRAHAM LINCOLN that when he proposes to coerce the South he must include Missouri in his calculations. Missouri is loyal to Southern institutions, and will prove it when the proper time arrves.

Now, about ths God-forsaken, famine-stricken, nigger-thief-ridden State of Kansas. Those who think the deadly hatred of the South which once burnt so fiercely upon these prairies, is well nigh extinct, were never more mistaken. This devilish hostility is only slumbering—not even dormant—for ever and anon its activity is seen in raids upon Missouri. Like a frozen viper warmed to life by the fire, it is at this moment coiling itself to strike.

The Chocktaw Indians have lately passed resolutions to go with the South. The Cherokees will follow suit. They are all slaveholders, and hard fighters; and, in conjunction with an army of Arkansans, will be a terror to the Abolition invaders. The occupation of Texas will not be a bloodless one. BEN McCULLOUGH's Rangers will want no better pastime than a shy at LINCOLN's cohorts. While the Kansas militia are jointing in the fray, they had better watch the *pirates of the plains*. Let them once leave the borders of their own State, and the Kiowa, Sioux and Pawnee Indians can exterminate the whites from Pike's Peak to Missouri river. Extensive military preparations are going on all over the State, but principally in the southeast, bordering on the thinly settled counties of Missouri. The militia will be organized at the sitting of the State Legislature on the 2t6h instant. MONTGOMERY, the notorious cut-throat of Southern Kansas, will be a Brigadier-General, and JENNISON, his partner in crime, will also hold a commission. Secret associations are rapidly forming among Republicans. Men are being "spotted," and the names of pro-slavery men taken down and marked with a sign.

I believe the first gun fired at Sumter will put the bloody ball in motion here.

SOUTHRON.

At the beginning of Lincoln's first term, Punch, the satirical English weekly, supported the United States. Thereafter it was vitriolic. London Punch, March 30, 1861.

THE COMMINUTED STATES

Who can say where Secession will stop? That is a question which is raised by MR. LINCOLN, in a part of his inaugural address, directed to enforce upon fools and madmen the necessity of acquiescence by minorities in the decision of majorities. The President tells the frantic portion of his fellow countrymen that:—

"There is no alternative for continuing the Government but acquiescence on one side or the other. If a minority in such a case will secede rather than acquiesce, they make a precedent which in turn will ruin and divide them, for a minority of their own will secede from them whenever a majority refuses to be controlled by such a minority. For instance, why may not any portion of a new confederacy, a year or two hence, arbitrarily secede again, precisely as portions of the present Union now claim to secede from it? All who cherish disunion sentiments are now being educated to the exact temper of doing this."

The force of this simple reasoning will be seen by the lunatics to whom it is addressed, during their lucid intervals, if they have any. It may even be hoped that some of them may recover the use of their reflecting faculties so far as to be enabled to follow out PRESIDENT LINCOLN's argument, and their own folly, into ultimate consequences and conclusions. Then they will see what is likely to be the end of Secession, for it is not quite true that there is no end to Secession, and the end of Secession will be for the Secessionists an end of everything. Seceders will go on seceding and subseceding, until at last every citizen will secede from every other citizen, and each individual will be a sovereign state in himself, self-government personified, a walking autonomy, a lone star, doing business and supporting itself off its own hook.

In France note was taken of the conflicting views of the Northern press on Lincoln's Inaugural Address, and the difficulties in general which faced the Federal Government in any attempt to bring back the Confederate States into the Union. From La Patrie, Paris, March 29, 1861, which maintained a correspondent in New York.

LE DISCOURS DE M. LINCOLN
[Mr. Lincoln's Speech.]

What are we to think of Mr. Lincoln's speech? In view of the divergent opinions expressed in the United States, we in Europe have the right to put this question. Whereas on the one hand *The* [New York] *Times, The Courier and Enquirer,* and *The* [New York] *Tribune* approve unreservedly of the new president, and speak of his "calm, inflexible courage in the face of any eventuality," of his "ability," of his "prudent wisdom," of his conciliating tone"; on the other hand, *The* [New York] *Herald, The Express, The Journal of Commerce,* and *The United States Courier* declare that "Mr. Lincoln's language is neither candid nor worthy of a statesman"; that "he betrays at once both indecision and a strong tendency toward coercive measures." And whereas in the Senate Mssrs. Dixon and Douglas are asking that this speech be broadcast throughout the country in order to calm the people's spirits, Mr. Clingman answers that the tenor of this document could bring on civil war.

Anyone who has read the presidential document will easily understand these contradictory judgments. Irresolution fairly shines forth in every one of Mr. Lincoln's acts—in Chicago as in Cincinnati, as in the White House. Just when people are looking to him for a frank, clear statement, he finds nothing more explicit to say to the waiting nation than that he will do his duty, but, he adds prudently, "in so far as that will be possible." "The power which has been vested in me," he says, "will be used to hold, to occupy, and to possess the properties and the territories which belong to the government, and to collect taxes." Then he declares that there will be no invasion, no use of force. And he indicates a means of solving this difficult problem. "To make the mystic chords of memory vibrate to the touch of the good angels of the country—chords which resound from our battlefields upon every heart which beats, in every home of this vast country."

Will this means, more poetic than practical, suffice to bring the Confederate States back into the Union? Will it restore the forts and the arsenals, the ships of the nation which the Confederates have seized or which have been handed over to them? Mr. Lincoln speaks of "holding, occupying, possessing the properties of the government." But these properties are in the hands of a power which up to the present has given proof of only skill and energy, which in six weeks has raised 50,000 militiamen and organized a small regular army. This army, just as we had foreseen, has been trained by those Southern officers who have abandoned the old Federal government: among others, General Twiggs, with nearly all the troops of Texas and New Mexico, Adjutant General Cooper, Assistant General Withers, and Major T. Beauregard of the Engineers Corps, who is to lead the attacks against Fort Sumter.

To oppose such adversaries, General Scott has gathered together in Washington 633 men from all the troops, but according to a report made to the Congress we now know that it will take *two months* to bring this corps up to 4,000 men. Assuming that this "army" is assembled, it will have to be transported to the South. Now, it takes eight days just to go from New York to New Orleans by rail, then there are forests and gigantic rivers to be crossed. These alone will offer almost insurmountable obstacles to military operations, and if and when these obstacles have been overcome, the Northern troops will arrive in the South just when the yellow fever is raging.

The Federal government, it is true, has ordered ships at distant stations to join forces at New York immediately, because Mr. Lincoln is depending on the fleet to blockade the Southern ports. But as we have already said, the loyalty of the Navy is in doubt, and it seems odd to see the Northern States attempting to blockade the Confederate States whose coastline is three or four times more extensive than their own. Furthermore, the President should not lose sight of the principle of European maritime law proclaimed by the Congress of Paris: "In order to be obligatory blockades must be effective, that is, they must be maintained by a force sufficient to prevent access to the enemy city." (Supplementary declaration of April 16, 1856.) The least powerful of nations, by virtue of this declaration, will be able to spurn the claims of Mr. Lincoln, who with a fleet of 86 on paper, the weakness of which has been revealed by the Americans themselves, will never be able to blockade effectively nearly 1,500 leagues of coastline!

Confronted with such a situation, Mr. Lincoln's irresolution becomes more excusable, but in view of this, what is the purpose of the boasts which he has sown throughout this speech? Does he hope to deceive the Confederates of the South? We do not think so; especially after having read the vigorous reply of one of his opponents in a letter dated March 5 [1861] which has just been published. "We will never pay tribute to the United States. The only hope for a peaceful solution is the immediate abandonment of any idea of the collection of revenue by the United States, and the evacuation of all forts in the Confederacy.

"The only practical course for the Northern conservatives is to insist on a peaceful separation, or energetically to combat the Northern radicals in order to win the spring elections, then to dissolve the Union and to join our fresh, vigorous, liberal, and expanding republic. A rebuilding of the old edifice under Lincoln is a material absurdity."

There is a great gulf between this clear-cut program and that of the White House. To close it would require nothing less than reconciling the claims of the Democrats and the Republicans, the abolitionists and the advocates of slavery, the champions of free trade and the protectionists.

Lincoln's two constant friends in the New York press—William Cullen Bryant of the New York Post and Henry J. Raymond of the New York Times—were not above lending advice to the President when they felt the need, or his need. In the stumbling days and weeks after the Inauguration, the North called for action. The Times, April 3, 1861, spoke up in this now-famous editorial.

WANTED—A POLICY

The Washington correspondent of one of our morning contemporaries says:

"The point of embarrassment concerning Fort Sumpter, in the President's mind, as announced with entire candor, is, that if it be yielded, and the Federal authority be thus withdrawn under real or supposed necessity, similar reasons may be urged as to Fort Pickens and other points, which are not considered in the same category."

We should be very sorry to think that the President's mind was embarrassed, or his action controlled, in any degree by such considerations at this late day. Undoubtedly in themselves they deserve serious and grave attention. But they should have been weighed and disposed of long ago. It is by no means a new discovery that much may be said on both sides of every question;—and persons who have nothing better to do may amuse themselves by such carefully balanced dialectics. But President LINCOLN has duties and responsibilities on his hands which forbid his indulgence of such tastes. He is required to act,—and action requires decision. Certainly it is a momentous question whether Fort Sumpter should be evacuated or not:—there are many reasons to be urged for it and many against it. But Mr. LINCOLN is under the necessity, after full consideration of both sides, to adopt one course or the other;—and when adopted he should act as if no objections had ever been urged against it. If he has decided to evacuate Fort Sumpter, he should do it frankly,—not with apologies or useless "embarrassments." The effect of such a step should have been considered long ago.

It is idle to conceal the fact that the Administration thus far has not met public expectation. The country feels no more assurance as to the future,—knows nothing more of the probable results of the secession movement,—than it did on the day Mr. BUCHANAN left Washington. It sees no indications of an administrative policy adequate to the emergency, —or, indeed, of any policy beyond that of listless waiting to see what may "turn up." There are times when such a policy may be wise;—but not in presence of an active, resolute, and determined enemy. . . .

The fact is, our Government has done absolutely *nothing*, towards carrying the country through the tremendous crisis which is so rapidly and so steadily settling down upon us. It allows everything to *drift*,—to float along without guidance or impulse of any kind. This might be well enough, if the Southern States were pursuing the same policy. But while we are idle, they are active. While we leave everything at loose ends, they make everything tight and snug for the coming storm. Such a course can have but one result. The President must adopt some clear and distinct policy in regard to secession, or the Union will not only be severed, but the country will be disgraced. No great community can *drift* into ruin, without losing character as well as prosperity. It must, at least, make an effort at self-preservation, if it would avoid the contempt inseparable from imbecility. A nation may be overcome by outward force, or destroyed by internal treachery;—but if it struggles nobly and gallantly against its enemies, whatever else it may lose, it preserves the respect of the world, as well as its own. We are in danger of losing everything—even honor. The public sentiment is already demoralized,—the heart of the people is deadened,—and the patriotism of the country is already paralyzed, to a degree which a year ago we should not have thought possible in any contingency. Rebellion in the popular judgment has ceased to be a crime. Treason has become respectable. Men throughout the North think and talk of the revolution which is crushing the best Constitution the world ever saw,—which is sweeping away a Government which has done more for popular rights and popular interests than any other the earth has ever known, as they would talk of a partisan canvass for control of a village corporation. Deeds of infamy, compared with which ARNOLD's treason shines bright as the sun at noonday, excite scarcely a passing remark, and the fate of the great Republic of the Western World—the great Republic of human history—excites scarcely as much interest as the fluctuations of the Stock market, or the ups and downs of a local canvass. . . .

It is the high, the imperative duty of President LINCOLN, in this solemn crisis of the nation's fate, to give the American people this guidance and leadership. He was perfectly right in saying at Springfield that upon his shoulders rests a responsibility more weighty than has ever fallen upon any one of his predecessors. That responsibility is not met by supervising the distribution of office. Mr. LINCOLN should reserve his thoughts and his strength for nobler duties than presiding over the wranglings of hungry and selfish hunters for patronage and place. He wastes powers that belong to the nation,—he squanders opportunities which millions upon millions of gold will never bring back, for rescuing the nation from the most fearful perils. We shall not be suspected of any but the most friendly sentiments towards the President of the United States, when we tell him, what the courtiers who hang upon his favor will not dare to whisper,— that he must go up to a higher level than he has yet reached, before he can see and realize the high duties to which he has been called. He has spent time and strength in feeding rapacious and selfish partisans, which should have been bestowed upon saving the Union and maintaining the authority of the Constitution he has solemnly sworn to defend. He has not done what he was expected to do as soon as he should assume the reins of power—summon back, by word and act, the loyalty of the American people to the flag and the Government of their common country. The Union is weaker now than it was a month ago. Its foes have gained courage, and its friends have lost heart. Step by step the new Confederacy marches forward towards solid and secure foundations,—and day by day the bright hopes of the lovers of the Union fade and die away.

The Administration *must have a policy of action,*—clear and definite in the end it aims at, wise and resolute in the means employed, and proclaimed to the people as the standard around which they can rally. What it should be, it is not for us to say. That is a matter requiring wise and careful deliberation on the part of those who are responsible; but it should be *decided* upon promptly, and then carried into effect with steady and dauntless resolution.

The President has to decide whether he will *enforce the law* at the hazard of civil war,—or whether he will waive the execution of the law, and *appeal to the people* of the seceded States on behalf of the Union. One or other of these courses he should lose no time in adopting,—simply because every day lost renders less possible the success of either. If he decides to enforce the laws, let him call Congress together and demand the means of doing it. If he decides upon Peace, let him proclaim his purpose,—and seek at once the confidence and favor of the people whom he desires to win. Let him first disarm the fears of War which now unite, by outward pressure, the Southern people,—and then let him proceed to organize a Union Party in every Southern State, and to strengthen and encourage it by all the legitimate means at his disposal. Why has SAM HOUSTON, of Texas, been left to fight the battle of the Union alone,— without a word of encouragement, or promise of a man or a dollar from the Government at Washington? Why have the Union men in Louisiana been abandoned without an effort, to the despotism of the minority which has usurped control of their affairs? Why have the noble-hearted champions of the Union and the Constitution in Virginia and Tennessee and Kentucky, been ignored utterly in the use of the Executive patronage and in all the public action of the Federal Government? Simply, in our judgment, because the Administration has decided upon no means of meeting the secession movement,—because it has no POLICY. It is going on blindly,—living from hand to mouth,—trusting in the chances of the future for deliverance from present and impending perils.

We trust this period of indecision, of inaction, of fatal indifference, will have a speedy end. Unless it does, we may bid farewell to all hope of saving the Union from destruction and the country from anarchy. A mariner might as well face the tempest without compass or helm, as an Administration put to sea amid such storms as now darken our skies, without a clear and definite plan of public conduct. The country looks eagerly to President LINCOLN for the dispersion of the dark mystery that hangs over our public affairs. The people want *something* to be decided on—some standard raised—some policy put forward, which shall serve as a rallying point for the abundant but discouraged loyalty of the American heart. In a great crisis like this, there is no policy so fatal as that of having no policy at all.

The New York Evening Day-Book—Van Evrie, Horton & Olney, editors and proprietors—strongly against the Abolitionist sentiment in parts of the East, talked in language that sounded remarkably similar to that heard in the Southern press. Later on, when the war intensified, this newspaper was barred from the mails in some areas. On April 6, 1861, the Day-Book fostered one of the small tales with sex overtones about Lincoln; these popped up in the hostile press occasionally.

THE WARLIKE ASPECT.—There is a remarkable bustle going on, both in the army and navy, by the orders of our negro-Republican Administration, which looks as if some savage and slaughterous design were in the wind. The Washington correspondents, for nearly all the papers, agree in ascribing these warlike preparations to a determination on the part of Lincoln and his Cabinet to blockade the southern ports. Did we not consider the party in power a set of madmen, we should, at once, pronounce such rumors false. Blockading the ports would be an act of war, and the Executive Department of the government has no power to declare war— that has been wisely reserved to Congress alone. We believe the revolutionary Abolitionists, who are now in possession of the government, capable of usurping any power that they could hope to maintain; but even they are not mad enough to suppose that the city of Washington would be in their possession six weeks after the people should understand that they had usurped authority for the purpose of making war upon the South. It is probable that the present movement is with the design of making a demonstration of the federal power at Fort Pickins. But, whatever the plan is, it is designed for effect, to give the red-hot Republicans something to talk about, while the administration perfects its main business of dividing the plunder to which it has fallen heir. The South, however, it seems is ready to receive their "friends." We shall soon see, at any rate, whether, Lincoln is determined to plunge the country in the irremidiable horrors of civil war.

ALL SORTS OF ITEMS

The great Black Republican "Wigwam," in which Abe Lincoln was nominated for President, was to have been sold at auction on Saturday last. The country under his administration is rapidly "going" the same way.

———

Some of the newspapers mention with agreeable surprise the fact that the President has appointed a young man, keeper of some light house, on the sole recommendation of his sweetheart. Old Abe has an eye for a pretty girl, and why should he not have an ear too? Did he not refuse, while at the City Hall in this city, to shake hands with a young man, but said, "if your sister was here, I would shake hands with her."

In New England, where abolition sentiment flowered and found articulate voices, the Democratic organs sided in some instances with the Secessionists. In Maine, several months after this editorial appeared, pro-Administration townfolk raided the offices of the Democrat in Bangor and burned its printing equipment in the public square. This editorial from the Bangor Democrat is reprinted in the New York Evening Day-Book, April 18, 1861.

OPPOSITION TO CIVIL WAR
From the Bangor Democrat

A VOICE FROM MAINE

Throughout the broad land of the fair South, the rising sun is no longer welcomed with the cheerful song of the husbandman wending his way to the toil of his peaceful field, but is greeted with the drum-beat that summons to arms the gathering hosts of war. From Carolina to the Rio Grande all is hasty preparation for a fearful conflict of arms. There, to-day, are no peaceful, happy and quiet homes, for the invader is on their soil, and the government which was created to protect and defend them, has ruthlessly turned its guns against their altars and firesides. Gray-headed fathers, stout-hearted husbands, and fair-cheeked youths, are taking a tearful adieu of their wives, their children, their mothers and their sisters, and buckling on their armor, and hastening away to battle-fields from which many, many may never return to gladden their homes again. This, reader, is no fanciful picture; it is a stern reality. To-morrow, in thousands of homes, wives, mothers, daughters and little children will gather in mournful silence around the family board no longer cheered by the presence of their natural guardians and protectors.

Why is all this? It is because that old Tory party, which under a multitude of names and disguises, first resisted the independence of America, and after its Government had become an established fact, has been unceasing in its efforts to get possession of it, and after having gained possession of it, by hypocritically assuming the sacred garb of freedom, it has undertaken to convert that Government into an instrument of tyranny, and to use all its powers to overturn the very bulwarks of liberty itself—the Sovereignty of the States. Yes, Abraham Lincoln, a Tory from his birth, is putting forth all the powers of Government to crush out the spirit of American liberty. Surrounded by gleaming swords and glistening bayonets at Washington, he sends forth fleets and armies to overawe and subdue that gallant little State which was the first to raise its voice and arm against British oppression.

DEMOCRATS OF MAINE! The loyal sons of the South have gathered around Charleston as your fathers of old gathered about Boston, in defense of the same sacred principles of liberty—principles which you have ever upheld and defended with your vote, your voice and your strong right arm. Your sympathies are with the defenders of the truth and the right. Those who have inaugurated this unholy and unjustifiable war are no friends of yours—no friends of Democratic Liberty. Will you aid them in their work of subjugation and tyranny.

When the Government at Washington calls for volunteers or recruits to carry on their work of subjugation and tyranny under the specious phrases of "enforcing the laws," "retaking and protecting the public property," and "collecting the revenue," let every Democrat fold his arms and bid the minions of tory despotism do a tory despot's work. Say to them fearlessly and boldly in the language of England's great Lord, the Earl of Chatham, whose bold words in behalf of the struggling Colonies of America in the dark hours of the revolution, have enshrined his name in the heart of every friend of freedom, and immortalized his fame wherever the name of liberty is known—say in his thrilling language: "If I were a southerner, as I am a northerner, while a foreign troop was landed in my country, I would never lay down my arms—never, NEVER, NEVER."

After the bombardment and evacuation of Fort Sumter, Lincoln issued a proclamation on April 15, 1861, calling forth the militia of the several states of the Union "to the aggregate number of seventy-five thousand, in order to suppress said combinations [of unlawful elements in the States of South Carolina, Georgia, Alabama, Florida, Mississippi,

Louisiana and Texas]." One of these states reacted with bravado, as noted in the Daily Picayune, New Orleans, April 18, 1861.

LINCOLN'S PROCLAMATION

THE RIOT ACT

The most insolent part of the proclamation of the Military Dictator at Washington is in its command to the people of those States which have embraced the cause of Southern independence, as vulgar disturbers of the peace, "to disperse" within twenty days.

It is the form of proclamation against disorderly mobs, and shows in its use how little his comprehension has been able to reach of the true character of the Southern movements and the true nature of the laws under which he takes such enormous powers.

The statute of 1795, from which Lincoln extracts the pretext for his action, was framed expressly and singly for enabling the President to aid civil magistrates in the executing the laws. The authority given by the act is, to use the militia, in any number, at his discretion, to execute the laws, whenever they shall be obstructed by "combinations too powerful to be suppressed by the ordinary course of judicial proceedings, or by the powers vested in the Marshals." The single purpose, distinctly alleged, for the use of this authority, is to execute that which the courts in their ordinary course should have failed to perform. Mr. Lincoln showed his sense of the force of this deduction by changing the words of the statute, and reciting in the proclamation that the laws could not be executed in the ordinary "way," suppressing the recital of the law that the ordinary way was the course of civil proceedings first, and their failure as the contingency for having resort to the soldiery. Without the previous exhaustion of civil processes, the power to use militia does not vest at all. Mr. Lincoln's Government has neither courts nor officers within the Confederate States, and there can therefore be no civil remedy to try. But this would create other lines of duty than the assumption by an Executive of the powers of a Military Dictator without law.

Having taken the power, with or without law, he proceeds to go through the forms as though there were a case of disorderly riot, but in a manner which shows that he does not appreciate the meaning of the law which he is wresting from its true character to the purposes of despotism and warfare.

That same statute provides as follows for the course to be pursued when the President comes to use the forces he is authorized to call out:

Whenever it shall be necessary, in the judgment of the President, to use the military force hereby directed to be called forth, the President shall forthwith, by proclamation, command such insurgents to disperse, and retire peaceably to their respective abodes, within a limited time. [Act of 1795, sec. 2.]

The most obtuse mind, not employed in searching for a pretext for using extraordinary powers, could not fail to see in this section unerring corroborative proof of the intent of the law to be auxiliary to a previous civil process, and to be aimed against mere mob violence. After calling out troops, and before using them, the President is required to command the insurgents, by proclamation, peaceably to disperse. The simple direction of the law is, that he is not to fire upon a mob which he finds engaged in obstructing a law, without first giving them time to disperse peaceably. In the popular language, which we borrow from the English vocabulary, he must "read the riot act" before he gives the order to fire. It is very slender authority and a most extraordinary construction on which to issue a command to a whole people, combined in one unanimous act of revolution, describing them as a mob of insurgents to be scattered by a discharge of musketry, if they do not instantly disband.

The formula of reading the riot act to the people of the South, the governments of seven States, and the common government at Montgomery, to scatter before a paper manifesto, is a piece of sublime impudence, which would be perfectly ludicrous if it were not so wicked and mischievous in its bearings upon interests of transcendent magnitude. The brutal party chief, who in his grasping at the power of a despot to institute a bloody civil war, transcends and perverts the very law from which he derives his pretext for usurpation, becomes an object of detestation.

And who are these "insurgents" whom the imperious edict commands to disband and disperse within twenty days from that of the announcement of his will? What are the "combinations" which have so far extinguished all civil jurisdiction by the United States, that Mr. Lincoln abandons all thought of attempting to have recourse to it, and begins by subjecting them to the menace of subjugation by the Northern militia?

The most conspicuous of the "combination" of "insurgents" is the orderly and perfected government at Montgomery, holding the delegated power of the seven States, and wielding with their unanimous consent their whole physical force, disbursing their means and directing their armies. To them first is the Lincoln command to disperse within twenty days specially directed.

Next to them, as constituent elements of that combination, is the series of organized combinations against the denunciation at Washington of the seven political communities, the people of which, each in its special capacity as an integral State assembled in conventions, and binding all their citizens to each other and to the State by all the sanction of sovereignty, to unanimous action in resistance to Federal authority. Every State is, therefore, another combination to obstruct and forbid the exercise within their limits of any Federal authority. Here are seven more "combinations," powerful ones, too, which are summoned to disband.

Every legislative body within each of these States is another body living under the Presidential definition of insurgent combinations. Every court of justice, in every State, is sworn to the same allegiance, and is another organized combination to expel Federal jurisdiction. There are, moreover, to be specially noted by Mr. Lincoln as objects of particular solicitude in his programme of dispersion, by proclamation, considerable armies, well officered and equipped, and ready for battle, under the direction of the Confederate Government, and every State has its particular army and every city and town its local guards, and behind, and around, and encircling all, three millions of people, pledged by every consideration of honor, pride, patriotism, self-respect and self-protection, to maintain them and each other in this quarrel, with life and fortune, with all they have and all they hope for.

These are the "combinations" against which Mr. Lincoln has fulminated his proclamation, ordering them, in the words of the statute, which he attempts to follow, but suppresses the command, quite as imperative as the other, that shall "retire peaceably to their respective abodes." He reads the riot act to the Confederate Government, and the seven State Governments, executive officers, their courts, their soldiery, and their people, to dissolve their combinations immediately, and prepare to receive his government quietly, or expect to be overrun, occupied, and held subject by the hordes of shouting Wide Awakes from the North!

Is it possible for the frenzy of faction to go a step farther in insolence of purpose, heedless of law and right, and daring wickedness of purposes? The sounding manifesto may not be followed by a vigor equal to the inveterate malice of the purpose. It is not safe to underrate the capacity of an enemy for mischief, and the absurd gasconade of the proclamation may be followed by acts as insensate.

The militia may perhaps be hired to come down this way for the purpose of the proclamation; but if they ever get across the Potomac or the Ohio, we venture, without imitating the Lincoln style of braggery, to say that they will be made thankful for permission "to disperse and retire peaceably to their respective abodes."

The line followed by the Copperhead as well as the Secessionist press was that the Lincoln Administration failed to respect the Constitution—the same Constitution Lincoln reasoned in his Inaugural he was sworn to defend so that he could pass on to a successor a country intact in its laws and boundaries. The New York Evening Day-Book, April 18, 1861, took the line.

HOW MR. LINCOLN MAY RESTORE PEACE TO THE COUNTRY

Mr. Lincoln is evidently a believer in the savageries of old Europe, and thinks that the only way to "save the Union" is to resort to the bayonet, just as Louis Napoleon "saves" society in France! But he is behind the times, behind 1776, when the great and immortal truth that *governments must rest on the consent of the governed, was instituted for the benefit of all coming generations of men.*

But, it is asked, how is he to carry on the government—to fulfil his his Constitutional duty—to make good his oath to enforce the laws, &c., when the people of seven States are in open and avowed hostility to him, and those of eight more are in a position of armed neutrality, and ready at the "drop of the hat" to join their seceding neighbors, and set him at defiance?

Well, at first sight, this does look bad, certainly, but then as an American who should have taken in the truth with his mother's milk, that this is a government of opinion and cannot be worked an hour on the old world system of physical force, Mr. Lincoln should see and must see that no outward pressure of the bayonet can, by any possibility whatever, "save the Union." Furthermore, he should see that there is a grand mistake somewhere, for, as Mr. Jefferson declared in the immortal Declaration of Independence, all experience proves that mankind are averse to Revolution, and it is only when the causes for such a terrible necessity become insupportable that they resort to it, and therefore that the people of the South, who are now in open hostility to a government that for eighty years has conferred on them such boundless blessings, must be impelled by an awful necessity, indeed, to separate from such government.

True, it may seem to him that they are very foolish. He may even believe that a policy instituted at Washington, which shall ultimately end in the "abolition of slavery," would really be a great good to the people of the South, but he should also see that they should be more competent to judge of their wants, their welfare or otherwise, in this respect, than he possibly can be. And we repeat, when he sees them willing to forego the almost boundless blessings of the Union, rather than have such a policy instituted, then he certainly should mistrust his own views; indeed, as we have said, should be perfectly convinced that there was an awful mistake in this matter somewhere.

But leaving all this out of view, we can suggest a course to Mr. Lincoln which, if faithfully, and truly, and patriotically adopted, will enable him to heal the wounds of the nation, and restore peace, fraternity and prosperity to the whole people. If he will stand fair and square by the Constitution, as interpreted by the Supreme Court, its legitimate expounder, all will soon be well. That court has decided that this is a government of white men, based on equal rights, and, as a neccessary corrolary, that all American citizens are entitled to an equal protection for their persons and property within federal jurisdiction. If Mr. Lincoln will issue a proclamation or manifesto to the country declaring that he accepts this decision of the Supreme Court, and will faithfully act upon it, and at once proceed to change the personel of his official assistants in accord with it, he will find no difficulty whatever in enforcing the laws or otherwise in fulfilling his executive functions.

But will Mr. Lincoln do this? Will he thus stand by the Constitution of his country as that glorious instrument is interpreted by the Supreme Court—the sole legitimate organ of interpretation? Will he abandon the Chicago platform, which pledges him to the violation of the Constitution, and places him in an attitude of deadly hostility to the people of fifteen States, and thus restore peace and fraternity to the nation, or will he go on in his mad delusion after "impartial freedom" for negroes, and thus ruin his country? Strange and wonderful madness, indeed! If the end or object aimed at by his frantic and benighted followers could be accomplished, they would inflict evils on American civilization that would require centuries to recover from, and the destruction of the Union, in comparison, would really be of trifling importance!

In poem and prose, Lincoln became the personification of Northern evil. From the Charleston Mercury, May 18, 1861, gloating about Fort Sumter.

FORT SUMTER

———

A HEROIC POEM, IN THREE CANTOS

———

By CHARLES EDWARD LEVERETT, JR.

———

CANTO I.

Now glory be to Uncle Abe, and Scott, his lion pet,
And Seward, the righteous pontifex, who rules the Cabinet;
And glory to the mighty fleet that stood off Charleston Bar,
And left the dauntless Anderson to bear the brunt of war.

The Patriarch in Washington had summoned to his side
His squad of Solons, brilliant men, the rabble's joy and pride,
And some were looking very black, and some were looking blue,
The nation was at loggerheads, and none knew what to do,
And little light had yet been thrown upon the States' affairs,
For Abe, tho' good at splitting rails, was bad at splitting hairs.
Then up arose that valiant man, Lieutenant-General Scott,
And drew his sword, like Philip's son, and cut the Gordian knot.
"Now, by this waxed moustache, he said, and looked around the group,
And by these lips that tasted once a 'hasty plate of soup,'
I raise my voice for horrid war, 'tis just the thing for me,
Too long it is since I have had a military spree,
With all our gallant peddlars, our knack at making clocks,
Our taste for wooden nutmegs, and glorious Plymouth Rocks,
Our reverence for a Higher Law, our Godly pulpit rant,
With all the talents which in Yankee land are now extant,
A generalissimo, like me would find it no great thing
To gallop through the South, and whip the Chivalry, by Jing!"
He said, the hero whose chief joy was hearing bullets whiz,
And drew a red bandana forth, and wiped his warlike phiz,
Around the room a stifled buzz of admiration went,
When on his trembling knees arose the doughty President.
"Now, by old Andrew Jackson's shade, and by the oaths he swore,
And by his hickory stick, and by the thunder of his snore,

And by the proud contempt he showed for Carolina gents,
And English grammar," quoth old Abe, "them's jist my sentiments.
Great Seward shall gull the Southrons, like a wily diplomat,
With promises and flummery, with 'bother, this and that;
And I will launch a squadron forth, in secret, on the seas,
And reinforce Fort Sumter with 'old horse,' and bread and cheese;
Poor Doubleday, that wretched man, whose appetite ne'er fails,
Has been obliged, for three weeks now, to eat his finger nails,
While underneath his very nose, the rebels sit and cram
Their throats with beef, and turtle-soup, and English peas, and lamb.
Ho! then, for Carolina, my veterans brave and true,
'Tis high time that the Chivalry should learn a thing or two;
I swear my hungry soger boys shall soon have meat and drink,
I, gallant spouse of Mrs. Abe, and Pa of Bobby Link!"

So spake the "old man eloquent," and hushed he there and then,
The Cabinet all looked devout, and answered him Amen. . . .

CANTO III.

A telegram is flying North, 'tis pithy, sharp and curt—
"Fort Sumter's taken—tell Old Abe that no-bod-y is hurt."

A panic strikes the Cabinet, they wriggle in their chairs,
Seward mutters "curses deep, not loud"—Welles tries to say his prayers;
Old Uncle Abe, their royal liege, grows pallid at the news,
Uneasy twitch the nimble feet within his nimble shoes,
All downward through his spindle shanks a nervous tremor flows,
And fast the courage oozes from the hero's valiant toes;
His hair begins to stand on end, his eyes are full of dread,
Already in the streets he hears the Southern cohorts tread,
Already through the White House gates he sees the legions pour,
Already dreams their battle-axe is thundering at his door,
Already feels fierce cow-hide boots assail him in the rear,
And finds, alas, the seat of war uncomfortably near!
"Now if," he cries, "my councillors, ye are inclined to flee,
(For 'tis not every one who'd like to face the Chivalry),
And if the prospect of a fray should fill you with alarm,
If ye demand a Captain who will lead you out of harm,
Pack up your spoils, and while the Gin'ral keeps the foe at bay,

Put ye you trust in Providence, and set your legs in play,
And follow where this soger-cloak, all streaming in my flight
Is like a streak of lightning seen dissolving from the sight.
Ho, ho! for Illinois, my braves! hip, hip hurrah, away;
Do what you choose—for me—why, *I'll be hanged if I will stay!"*

Now glory be to Uncle Abe, and Scott, his bully pet,
And Seward, the cook and bottle-washer of the Cabinet;
And glory to the mighty fleet that stood off Charleston Bar,
And left the dauntless Anderson to bear the brunt of war!

*By perverse reasoning, reiterated more than once editorially, some
Southern opinion compared the North to the Tories of '76. This fairly
harmless poem took aim at Lincoln and the Yankee Doodles. From
the Charleston Mercury, June 4, 1861.*

THE OLD RIFLEMAN

SOUTHERN ARMY

Now bring me out my buckskin suit!
  My pouch and powder, too!
We'll see if seventy-six can shoot
  As sixteen used to do.

Old Bess! We've kept our barrels bright!
  Our trigger quick and true!
As far, if not as fine a sight,
  As long ago, we drew!

And pick me out a trusty fling!
  A real white and blue,
Perhaps 't will win the *other* tint,
  Before the hunt is through!

Give boys your brass percussion caps!
  Old "shut pan" suits as well!

265

There's something in the sparks; perhaps
There's something in the smell!

We've seen the red-coat Britain bleed!
The red-skin Indian, too!
We never thought to draw a bead
On Yankee-doodle-doo!

But, Bessie! bless your dear old heart!
Those days are mostly done;
And now we must revive the art
Of shooting on the run!

If Doodle must be meddling, why,
There's only this to do:
Select the black spot in his eye
And let the daylight through!

And if he doesn't like the way
That Bess presents the view,
He'll may be, change his mind and stay
Where the good Doodles do!

Where Lincoln lives. The man, you know,
Who kissed the Testament:
To keep the Constitution? No?
To keep the Government?

We'll hunt for Lincoln, Bess! old tool,
And take him half and half;
We'll aim to hit him, if a fool,
And miss him if a calf!

We'll teach these shot gun boys the tricks
By which a war is won:
Especially how seventy-six
Took tories on the run.

Lincoln called a special session of Congress on July 4, 1861, to review his first four months in office and share information about Fort

Sumter and other matters. The measured words of the Inaugural now gave way to blunt language—"such will be a great lesson of peace; teaching men that what they cannot take by an election, neither can they take it by a war—teaching all, the folly of being the beginners of a war." A daily newspaper, The South, published in Baltimore, edited by Thos. W. Hall, Jr., was suspended two months after this editorial appeared. The South, July 8, 1861, referring to Lincoln "in his insanity."

LINCOLN AND HIS WANTS

So exalted and so responsible is the office of President of the United States that, to a properly regulated mind, it is difficult to treat with contempt or disrespect, its incumbent. Notwithstanding the daily behaviour of President Lincoln, we cannot altogether rid ourselves of this old-fashioned notion, and, therefore, have been disposed to view his most extraordinary message to Congress in the most charitable light.

We confess ourselves at loss to know how to treat it. We have carefully read and re-read it, to possess ourselves of its true "purpose" and meaning. Some parts of it lead us to believe that, in utter forgetfulness of the high and solemn obligations imposed upon him, Mr. Lincoln has, in keeping with his reputed habit, dealt with the present horrible state of public affairs, in the spirit of a joker! It is hard, if not impossible, to tell the precise meaning of the following language:

> "It is now recommended that you give the legal means for making this contest a short and decisive one; that you place at the control of Government for the work at least four hundred thousand men and four hundred millions of dollars. That number of men is about one-tenth of those proper ages within the regions where apparently all are willing to engage, and the sum is less than the twenty-third part of the money value owned by the men who seem ready to devote the whole."

Does he gravely mean to call for FOUR HUNDRED THOUSAND MEN, AND FOUR HUNDRED MILLIONS OF DOLLARS? Or, does he merely design to hit a back-handed lick at the hypocrites and blusterers of the Northern press and cities, who, whilst they cry, "havoc," cowardly remain out of harm's way? The language will justify either construction. If intended as a joke, he has shown himself simply to be a disgusting fool, and if by it is meant in seriousness to ask, that such immense and unexampled means be placed at his uncontrolled disposal, he is worse than a fool; he is the equal, in despotic wickedness, of Nero or any of the other tyrants who have polluted this earth.

There have been occasions in the history of this country when it was believed to be necessary to place at the disposal of its Executive Magistrate, means to defend its honor, and shield it from a *foreign* invasion; but never, until this calamitous period, has any one been audacious enough to propose or advise the bestowal on the President, of such gigantic powers as Lincoln asks may be conferred on himself. That truly great man and pure patriot, Andrew Jackson, when treaty obligations had been repudiated by France, and the property of our people threatened by that power with confiscation, asked that the sum of *three* millions of dollars might be put at his disposal to vindicate the national character and ensure protection to our coast. But so great and unusual was the demand then considered—so great an augmentation of the power of the Executive, and so dangerous a precedent—that Daniel Webster openly declared in the Senate Chamber, that sooner than make such a grant of power to the President, "he would prefer the walls of the Capitol should be battered down by the cannon of the enemy." A similar unwillingness was manifested in the conduct of Mr. Calhoun during the Mexican War. He declared that he would rather plant a dagger in his own heart, than place *ten* millions of money at the discretion of the President for the prosecution of the war; and this declaration he accompanied with the most positive assurance of his entire faith in the honesty and patriotism of President Polk, of whose administration he was a decided supporter.

We repeat that we are at a loss to understand whether Lincoln intended by the language we have quoted from his message, only to play the buffoon, or whether in his insanity he hopes to subjugate a free people and overturn their Constitution, by the enormous *"subsidies"* which he demands of Congress. It has been well said that "fools rush in where angels fear to tread"; Abraham Lincoln hesitates not to ask for *hundreds* of millions to enslave his own countrymen, although the most enlightened of statesmen refused to allow stern and well approved patriots to have within their discretion the expenditure of but a few millions, the country being in imminent danger of, or actually involved in, war with foreign nations. Sadly indeed have men and the times changed.

Lincoln had used straight talk in his extraordinary message to Congress on July 4, 1861, pinning the blame of secession on the South-

ern States. *As in Charleston, there were poets, too, in Baltimore. From* *The South, July 19, 1861.*

MESSAGE OF PRESIDENT LINCOLN, TO THE FEDERAL CONGRESS, 4TH JULY, 1861

Once more, Representatives, Senators, all,
You come to my Capitol, swift at my call.
'Tis well: for you've something important to do
In this most disagreeable national stew;
For since I came hither to run the machine,
Disguised in Scotch Cap and in full Lincoln green,
There's the devil to pay in the whole d——d concern,
As from Cameron, Seward and Chase you will learn;
Yet, though everything here of a burst-up gives warning,
I'm certain you'll put it all right in the morning:
So to do as I tell you, be on the alert,
For the panic's fictitious and nobody's hurt.

I have started no war of invasion, you know,
Let who will, pretend to deny it—that's so;
But I saw from the White House an impudent rag,
Which they told me was known as Jeff Davis' flag,
A waving above Alexandria high,
Insulting my Government, flouting the sky;
Above my Alexandria (isn't it Bates?
Retrocession's a humbug; what rights have the States?)
So I ordered young Ellsworth to take the rag down,
Mrs. Lincoln, she craved it to make a new gown;
But young Ellsworth, he kinder got shot in the race,
And came back in a galvanized burial case;
But then Jackson, the scoundrel, he got his desert;
The panic's fictitious and nobody's hurt.

It is true I sent steamers which tried for a week
To silence the rebels down there at the Creek;
But they had at Game Point about fifty or more
Rifled cannon set up in a line on the shore,

And six thousand Confederates practised to fire 'em,
(Confound these Virginians, we never can tire 'em!)
Who made game of our shooting and crippled our fleet,
So we prudently ordered a hasty retreat;
With decks full of passengers, dead heads, indeed,
For whom of fresh coffins these straightway was need.
And still later at Gresham's they killed Captain Ward
In command of the *Freeborn*, 'twas devilish hard;
But in spite of all this, the rebellion's a spurt;
The panic's fictitious and nobody's hurt.

Herewith I beg leave to submit the report
Of Butler, the General, concerning the sport
They had at Great Bethel, near Fortress Monroe,
With Hill and Magruder some four weeks ago;
And here let me say a more reckless intruder
I never have known than this Colonel Magruder;
He has taken the Comfort away from Old Point,
And thrown our peninsular plans out of joint;
While in matters of warfare to him Gen'l Butler
Would scarce be thought worthy to act as a sutler,
And the insolent rebels *will* call to our faces
The flight at Great Bethel the "New Market Races;"
Then supersede Butler at once with whoever
Can drive this Magruder clean into the river;
And I shall be confident still to assert,
That the panic's fictitious and nobody's hurt!

'Tis my province, perhaps, herein briefly to state
The state of my provinces, surly of late,
Missouri and Maryland—one has the paw
Of my Lyon upon her, and one has the law,
Called martial, proclaimed through her borders and cities;
Both are crushed, a Big Thing, I make bold to say, *it* is.
St. Louis is silent and Baltimore dumb,
They hear but the monotone roll of my drum.
In the latter vile sea-port I ordered Cadwallader
To manacle Freedom, and though the crowd followed her,
Locked up in McHenry, she's safe, it is plain,
With Merryman, Habeas Corpus and Kane.

And as for that crabbed old dotard, Judge Taney,
For much I would put him on board of the Pawnee,
And make his decisions a little more curt;
For the panic's fictitious and nobody's hurt!

And now I'll just say what I'd have you to do
In order to put your new President through—
First, four hundred millions is wanted by Chase,
He cannot run longer the Government's face;
And Cameron wants, for the use of old Scott,
Some three hundred thousand more men than he's got.
Then sixty new iron-plate ships to stand shells
Are loudly demanded (must have 'em) by Welles;
For England, the bully, won't stand our blockade,
And insists that we shall not embarrass her trade;
But who fears the British? I'll speedily tune 'em
As sure as my name is *E Pluribus Unum*,
For I am myself the whole United States,
Constitution and Laws, (if you doubt it, ask Bates.)
The Star Spangled Banner's my holiday shirt—
Hurrah for Abe Lincoln, there's nobody hurt!

That this civil war in the New World would erupt seemed apparent to the French "in our Old Europe," according to the correspondent of *La Patrie* of Paris, *July 21, 1861*, commenting on the President's extraordinary message to Congress, and somewhat puzzled by Mr. Lincoln's legalistic interpretation of the South's obligations.

LE MESSAGE DE M. LINCOLN
[Mr. Lincoln's Message.]

Yesterday we published the principal passages of Mr. Lincoln's extraordinary message, and our readers were able to formulate some idea of this document. The least of its faults is prolixity. In our old Europe, an appeal for men and money, necessitated by similar circumstances, would be couched in clear, concise terms. Things are done differently in the New World. The American loves long balance sheets; nothing may be omitted or skimmed over lightly. Everything has to be put before his eyes, totalled, signed and countersigned *ne varietur*: in a word, he must have his reckoning. In this respect, we may say that Mr. Lincoln has served his people to their hearts' content; his accounts are in perfect order.

It would be of no interest to us to examine these accounts here. Our readers are familiar with the events leading to the secession of the Southern states and with subsequent events. The details into which the President of the United States goes, and the discussion upon which he embarks, will not tell them anything new about these matters. We want to point out, however, a very keen preoccupation of the message relative to the sharing of the Federal debt. Mr. Lincoln reproaches the Southern states for moving out without paying their rent; this is an item which he cannot make up his mind to put down to "profit and loss."

"The nation," he says, "has paid in money for the territory from which several of these states were formed; is it just that they withdraw without permission and without restitution? All in all, the nation has paid great sums of money—nearly 100 million dollars, I believe, to wrest Florida from its aboriginal tribes; is it just that she now leave the Union without consent, without making payment in return? The nation is now in debt because of loans made for the benefit of the so-called seceded states as well as of the others; is it just that creditors lose their money, or that the remaining states pay for everything? Part of the present national debt was contracted to pay off the old debts of Texas; is it just that this state secede and not pay any part of these debts itself? And when we shall all have seceded there will be no one left to pay the debts; is this just to the creditors?"

We can see by the emphasis he places on it that Mr. Lincoln is counting on this argument to decide the vote in favor of the 400,000 men and 400 million dollars. The Southern states have not only seceded from the Union, they are threatening to bankrupt it. This situation gives pause, and the people may well resign themselves to sacrifices in order to avert such an extremity. Such is the meaning, if we are not mistaken, of his remarks.

Perhaps it could be objected that the question of the debt is a separate question, that there will be time enough to consider it after the solution of the political question. Yet in recognizing the fact that the measures proposed by Mr. Lincoln are in part intended to put the Union in a position to take precautionary steps toward the sharing of the debt by the seceded states, it must be agreed that these measures have been strangely chosen. In one stroke the debt is being increased by 400 million dollars—that is, 2 billion francs. If the Union is victorious, will she make the seceded states pay this? That would be tantamount to ruining the South.

Will the South then become a financial burden to all the other states? In spite of having been shared, the damages would be no less considerable. Mr. Lincoln does not seem to doubt that this sum will be voted by the Congress and raised by public subscription. We certainly hope it will be, although the awesomeness of the figure could cause some hesitation. But what is going to happen? The Southern states, inspired by the example, will in turn make a supreme financial effort, and no matter which side is victorious, it will, in the long run, go into the most ruinous liquidation.

In order to make the struggle short as well as decisive, the President of the United States is asking for no fewer than 400,000 men. This, too, is an enormous figure. But what will he do with these 400,000 men when he has gotten them? Is he going to transform them into soldiers in two weeks, in a month, or even in three months? As we all know, the Americans are not a military nation. All the branches of military service are, in a sense, yet to be created. Before these 400,000 men can be properly trained, time will pass, much more time than they think; the war will spread and will inevitably become long-drawn.

Much blood spilled and immense sums expended only to achieve, in the end, a negative result! This is the prospect which the American conflict offers us today. No matter what she may do, the Union is completely dissolved and, in our opinion, can never be restored if the South should fall. In being forced back into the Union, the South would be submitting to a situation against which her sentiment and her interest would protest. The law of the strong has never been union with the stronger. To think that this is being considered seriously in Washington!

The South of Baltimore—established in April of '61 with the avowed intention of furthering the Confederate cause—was suspended in September. J. M. Mills & Co. then became publishers, in a leader saying, "We intend to make 'The South' a news paper." The tune changed on Oct. 14, 1861.

CHARACTERISTIC

The editor of the Philadelphia *Journal* narrates the following joke, perpetrated by Mr. Lincoln upon an unfortunate office seeker. The jest is so much in the President's well known style, that no one can doubt its authenticity. We are only surprised that one of his friends should have seen fit to give it to the world:

Mr. Lincoln, for weeks, at intervals, had been visited by a Philadelphia politician, who claimed a certain office, on account of some peculiar services which he had rendered the "good cause." Whenever our modest Philadelphian got a good chance, he invariably talked to "Honest Old Abe," and poured into his listening ear, the vast amount of service he had rendered him in the campaign of "Wide Awakes," lanterns and pa-patriotic banners.

Mr. Lincoln always listens with that quiet good humor which so pre-eminently distinguishes him, and, in every "boring" interview, with all the frankness of a "backwoodsman," thanked the Philadelphia patriot for his inestimable services. Still the applicant made no seeming progress, and, in the third week of his "boring" expedition, seemed to be no nearer the attainment of the desired office than on the first day of his advent at Washington, the Grand Mecca of all hungry politicians. Our friend had spent his last dollar at the "late Willard's" Hotel. He had become desperate, and had made up his mind to go home and pick up "odds and ends" there, although it gave him nothing but potatoes and milk to live on.—So, for the last time, he determined to call on Mr. Lincoln, and ascertain from him whether or not he should receive the office he sought. He caught the President alone, and began to importune him. He stated his claims—what he had done—his primeval claims for the office, declaring at the same time that if he did not receive the office, the effects would be most disastrous to the general administration.

Lincoln took him aside, and the politician thought his day of triumph had arrived, and that he would go home with his commission. But, the President merely said to him, My dear sir, before I left Springfield, Illinois, I had in my pig sty a little bit of a pig, that made a terrible commotion—do you know why? Because the old sow had just one more little pig than she had teats, and the little porker that got no teat made a terrible squealing.

The Philadelphia politician took the hint, collapsed, and the next day went home to pick up the odds and ends of his business, which had terribly suffered in his absence and search for office.

NEW DIVORCE REGULATION
From the Richmond Despatch, Oct. 10

PROCLAMATION EXTRAORDINARY.—It is rumored that Lincoln is about to issue a proclamation declaring all matrimonial relations existing between his loyal subjects, male or female, and Secession enemies, male or female, to be null, void, and thenceforth dissolved, the parties divorced being at liberty to contract new marriage relations as shall please them so to do, so that their new spouses be good and loyal persons.

On this subject the *Enquirer* says that Mr. Lincoln will induce the next Congress to pass a divorce act, to divorce wives residing within the jurisdiction of Abraham, where husbands have left them with the intention of aiding the fortunes of the South.

John C. Frémont commanded the Union forces in Missouri; Lincoln in '56 came close to running as his Vice President when Frémont led the Republican ticket. Lincoln sought to hold the wavering States in the Union. When Frémont on his own issued a proclamation that would punish Confederate sympathizers and free their slaves, Lincoln reminded him of the consequences. Comment on the delicate matter appeared in the New York Tribune, Oct. 22, 1861.

HOW TO PARALYZE AN ARMY

The *Herald* of yesterday, in its special dispatch from Washington, had the following:

> "No doubt is now entertained of the speedy removal of Gen. Fremont from the command in Missouri. There is some hesitation on the part of a portion of the Administration in reference to this movement, but it is attributable altogether to a feeling of delicacy, or political considerations, all of which must eventually yield to the requirements of the public service, which, after investigation, seem imperatively to demand the removal of Fremont."

—What must be the effect of such statements not only on the fine army under Gen. Fremont's immediate command, but on the vast and important Military Department over which he presides? How can he enforce obedience from and infuse energy into his numerous subordinates while they are led to expect from day to day his ignominious dismissal from his post? For this paragraph was no doubt promptly telegraphed to St. Louis, to Jefferson City, and beyond, by Gen. Fremont's eager and implacable enemies.

Abraham Lincoln is the commander-in-chief of the Army and Navy of the United States. It was he who assigned Gen. Fremont to the command of the Department of Missouri. It was a great and arduous trust, considering Gen. Fremont's limited military experience. That he has committed mistakes and errors in the discharge of that trust, we think more than possible. That he has been deficient in zeal or loyalty, no human being believes. That a more experienced soldier might have done better is by no means improbable. Had we been one of Mr. Lincoln's advisers, and been asked by him whether to assign to Gen. Fremont the command second in importance in the National service, we should probably have said "No—give him the command of a division in active service, but place the department in charge of some veteran like Hunter or Sumner or Sigel." But to Gen. Fremont was assigned the more trying position; and we have done what we could to have him properly sustained and enabled to prosecute his campaign with some chance of success. Should the Executive see fit to supersede him, we shall defer to that act as one clearly within the President's official discretion. The suggestion that the latter is jealous of Gen. F., or afraid of his bearing off the laurels of the contest, is utterly contemptible. He may misjudge; but Abraham Lincoln will never displace Gen. Fremont except upon a clear conviction that the success of the National arms will thereby be promoted. Let the President never hesitate to place and displace military officers as he shall from time to time deem most conducive to the public good, and never fear that he will not be sustained in so doing, even by those whose judgment may differ from his own.

At the beginning of December, 1861, Lincoln sent his first annual message to Congress. It was businesslike—concerned with judicial reform, Indian affairs, and other domestic subjects, including an oft-quoted comment on labor: "Labor is prior to, and independent of, capital. Capital is only the fruit of labor, and could never have existed if labor had not first existed. Labor is the superior of capital, and deserves much higher consideration." The New York Tribune, Dec. 4, 1861, made these remarks.

THE PRESIDENT'S MESSAGE

The country and the world will not fail to mark the contrast between the Message just transmitted to Congress by President Lincoln and that so recently addressed to the rival rebel conclave by Jefferson Davis. The latter is quite commonly presumed the abler of the two; he is certainly the better grammarian; and he knows how to use the English language with decided perspicuity and force. But the spirit of his manifesto is truculent, sanguinary, demoniac; he "clothes himself with curses as with a garment;" and he does not scruple to assert the most atrocious false-hoods with regard to the aims and impulses of the Federal Government and of the loyal States. Yet, while boastful, defiant, and savage, talking as though his resources were boundless and his career as a rebel chief had been an uninterrupted succession of victories, his voice rings hollow and empty; you feel that his confidence is assumed, and his lying vaunts and accusations the last efforts of despair.

President Lincoln, on the other hand, is not moved even by this unseemly display of rage and malignity, to one harsh inculpation. He very properly lays stress on the truth that the Southern rebellion is a war upon the proper dignity of labor and upon the political franchises of the poor; he strongly deprecates such a retrograde as the leading rebels clearly contemplate toward the Dark Ages wherein Despotism and Aristocracy ruled the masses with a rod of iron; but he breathes not an unkind impulse toward even the authors and promoters of this giant wickedness, which has already brought death to thousands and wretchedness to hundreds of thousands. They have plunged the nation into an abyss of carnage and devastation, with no more reason than could be assigned for commencing a war upon the sun which gives light and heat to all; they must be vanquished and put down: but he would do them no harm beyond what the good of the country and their own crimes render indispensable. He deals in no railing accusations; he indulges in no boasts of victories already won or certain soon to be achieved; but he cherishes an undying faith in the American People, and a confidence in the benignity of God. Thus strengthened and assured, the President looks calmly on the momentous drama now being enacted by our distracted countrymen in the sight of an astonished world, believing that Reason must yet resume her sway, and the integrity of the Union be fully vindicated and confirmed.

We make no synopsis of the doctrines and topics of the Message, because its commendable brevity and its intrinsic interest will insure its universal and intent perusal. Comparatively brief as it is, it touches on a great variety of topics, and its exposition of our National condition will be found satisfactory and reassuring. On the paramount question of the attitude which the Nation shall maintain with regard to slaves and Slavery, the President says:

"In considering the policy to be adopted for suppressing the insurrection, I have been anxious and careful that the inevitable conflict for this purpose shall not degenerate into a violent and remorse-less revolutionary struggle. I have, therefore, in every case, thought it proper to keep the integrity of the Union prominent as the primary object of the contest on our part, leaving all questions which are not of vital military importance to the more deliberate action of the Legislature. In the exercise of my best discretion, I have adhered to the blockade of the ports held by the insurgents, instead of putting in force by proclamation the law of Congress enacted at the late session for closing those ports. So also, obeying the dictates of prudence as well as the obligations of law, instead of transcending, I have adhered to the act of Congress to confiscate property used for insurrectionary purposes. If a new law upon the same subject shall be proposed, its propriety will be duly considered. *The Union must be preserved,* and hence all indispensable means must be employed. We should not be in haste to determine that radical and extreme measures, which may reach the loyal as well as the disloyal, are indispensable."

—The spirit of this is admirable, and will command general approval. It is right and proper that the President of the whole Union should labor and hope for the restoration of the Union with the least possible sacrifice of pre-existing ties and interests. Mr. Lincoln places the duty of preserving the Union above all conflicting considerations; and therein he is clearly right. He defers to the judgment of Congress, and will doubtless abide by that judgment. It is a very open secret that he was utterly averse to the Confiscation Act, and signed it with great reluctance; but he now intimates no lingering doubt of the policy or justice of that act. He may be late to realize the necessity of still sterner measures aimed at the source and mainspring of the rebellion; but he will not defeat the will of the loyal people, as embodied and expressed by their representatives. Hand in hand the Executive and the masses have entered upon this tremendous struggle, and they will not, they must not, fall out by the way to its triumphant conclusion.

That the integrity of the Union should be the paramount object of loyal Americans in this contest, is on all hands conceded. The practical question is—Can this end be promoted by further deference to and bolstering up of Slavery? While rebel corsairs are sinking and burning our unarmed merchant vessels on the ocean, shall we recognize and uphold the claim of rebels to property in human beings? We say, No—it is dangerous, fatal to do so: it is giving a factious and unjust strength to the public enemy; it is cherishing the viper which has its fangs now fastened in the National breast. Notify the slaveholders frankly that they may have thirty or sixty days more in which to lay down their arms and return to loyalty; but if they shall continue to defy the National authority and menace the National existence after the expiration of that term, their slaves shall, as a matter of inexorable public policy—nay, as a means of saving the National life at a cost less than ruinous—be proclaimed free, and invited to make their way to the Union lines, and there be recognized and treated as freemen. Such is the policy which we believe most effective and most merciful, and we trust it will yet receive the President's hearty concurrence.

The Trent Affair—the seizure by the U.S. Navy sloop San Jacinto of Confederate Commissioners to Britain and France, James M. Mason and John Slidell, from the Royal Mail Packet Trent—thrust Lincoln into a major foreign policy decision. The London Morning Chronicle said, "Abraham Lincoln, whose accession to power was generally welcomed on this side of the Atlantic, has proved himself a feeble, confused and little-minded mediocrity . . . the navies of England will blow out of the water [Lincoln's] blockading squadrons." When this editorial appeared in The Times, of London, Dec. 17, 1861, Lincoln's silence in his message to Congress nettled Britain. The Confederate Commissioners, however, were allowed to continue their interrupted trip to Europe.

The style of the American PRESIDENT has fallen with the fortunes of the Republic. Instead of the jolly, rollicking periods of former days, each of which seemed to suggest at its close a stave of "Hail, Columbia," we have now got a discursive and colloquial essay, ill arranged and worse expressed. Nor does the matter redeem the style. It is really wonderful, when we consider the present state of the American Republic, how any one placed in the position of Mr. LINCOLN could have taken the trouble to produce so strange a medley, so incomposite a rhapsody. There are several subjects on which we earnestly desire information, and on no one is it afforded. Above all things, we want to know what view the American Cabinet takes of the affair of the Trent, what advice it has received from its legal counsellors, and with what feelings it approaches the coming controversy. On this point there is not a word. Then, we should like to hear a little of the financial measures by which the equilibrium between revenue and expenditure is to be preserved in the face of so vast an outlay. We should like to know what measures the PRESIDENT proposes to adopt with regard to the slave population of the Southern States; whether, with one-half of his Cabinet, he is for emancipation, or, with the other half of his Cabinet, for a maintenance of the rights of the slaveowner. On all these points our oracle is silent. But, if he tells us very little that we want to know, he amply indemnifies us by telling us a great many things in which we have no interest. He has a plan for readjusting the circuits of the judges and for the codification of the statute law. He is very minute on the receipts and disbursements of the Post-office and the Patent-office. He is anxious to extend the district of Columbia into Virginia. He has something to say on the Exhibition of 1862. He has, in common with most of his predecessors, a plan for getting rid of free Negroes by a system of colonization, and has room for an argument to show, not, as he wishes, that labour is independent of capital, but how little progress the most ordinary doctrines of political economy have made in the higher circles of American politicians.

It is not easy to see why Mr. LINCOLN should have omitted from his speech all notice of the case of the Trent. If he means to give up the persons illegally seized, one would have thought it no unwise precaution to prepare the public mind for such a decision. If he means to keep them, we cannot understand why he does not grasp at all the popularity that is to be had in exchange for present war and future ruin, instead of allowing it to be picked up by obscure Members of Congress embarking in a contest whether the transcendent merits of Commodore WILKES [commander of the San Jacinto] would be best rewarded by thanks or by a gold medal. Possibly the simple solution may be that the PRESIDENT has as yet arrived at no conclusion at all, and that, perplexed by the divisions of his Cabinet, he has been content to let the matter alone till events shall determine for him that which he is unable or unwilling to determine for himself. He will not have long to wait. Each successive mail brings us the report of some fresh instance in which the American nation is step by step committing itself to a war policy with England, till, when challenged for its final decision, it will probably find that it has gone too far to have any power of retractation. The Government has received the prisoners, the Admiralty has thanked Commodore WILKES, and Congress has now given the seal of its approbation to a proceeding so deeply offensive to Great Britain. It is hardly possible to imagine a Government sunk so far below its duties and responsibilities as to allow all this to go on and make no sign either of assent or dissent. The PRESIDENT is bound to lend his aid in guiding the Legislature to a true decision on a matter so nearly touching the duties and the character of the Executive. He ought to set before it the principles involved in the question, and to give it every opportunity in his power of arriving at a conclusion conformable to the real interests of the country. But he has done nothing of all this, and has abandoned the vessel of the State to drift helpless before the gale of popular clamour. The PRESIDENT has given us, instead of the information we desire, his opinion on the real cause of the present war. The North, he says, are fighting for the integrity of the Union—that is, as Lord RUSSELL [British Secretary for Foreign Affairs] said, for empire, to compel the South, by force of arms, to live under a Government which they detest. The South, on the other hand, are fighting against the rights of the people—that is, against the rights of the people of the North to govern them against their consent. This description ought to put an end to the statement, so often repeated, that Slavery is the main matter in dispute. But the South have done still worse, and, not content with questioning the right of the North to govern them, they have even gone to the extent of questioning the wisdom of certain Northern institutions. Thus persons are actually found to wish for a restriction of the suffrage; to contend, in spite of the evidence afforded by the North of the purity of election, and the high moral and intellectual qualities secured by such a process, that it is better election should be confined to legislators, and not extended to magistrates; and some have even been heard to pronounce the horrible name of "MONARCHY." No wonder that Mr. LINCOLN, luxuriating in the Paradise to which the will of an unbridled democracy has introduced him, and looking forward to a desperate struggle with England, brought about apparently by the same cause, should feel a pious horror of those who venture to think such experience not conclusive, and the existing constitution of the United States a little short of perfection! We have nothing to say for Slavery, but if Mr. LINCOLN's description of the South is indeed true, —if she is fighting to emancipate herself from the blind tyranny of a degraded mob, from elective judges and elective governors,—he has given his antagonists a better title to European sympathy than they have hitherto possessed, and thrown upon his Government the stigma of fighting to impose upon others institutions which have already brought it to the verge of ruin.

But the most remarkable part of Mr. LINCOLN's speech is that in which he touches the relations of his Government with foreign countries. The fact seems, on his own showing, to be, that all foreign countries have hitherto preserved a strict neutrality; that they have resisted all applications from the South to make common cause with it against the North; and that they have quietly submitted to a blockade which grievously injures their commerce and manufactures. These facts would have called forth from the chief of any other Government in the world, Republican or Monarchical, a gracious and courteous acknowledgment of the respect and forbearance with which a nation, not remarkable for carrying either of these qualities to excess, has been treated by all other nations in its hour of trial. Nothing can be more ungracious, more contrary to the usual conditions of international courtesy, than the language with which President LINCOLN repays the consideration extended to him. "These nations," he says, "appear as yet not to have seen their way to their objects"—that is, the restoration of commerce—"more directly or clearly through the destruction than through the preservation of the Union." This is a broad insinuation that foreign nations are actuated by the meanest and most selfish motives, and Mr. LINCOLN is content, as he cannot deny that we have hitherto done right, to express a suspicion that we did so for reasons we cannot avow without shame. It is not wonderful that a notice of foreign relations begun in this spirit should end with the exhortation with which we are already familiar in the circular of Mr. SEWARD, to fortify the seacoast, the great lakes, and rivers. After all, says Mr. LINCOLN "the safety and stability of the Republic depend, not on foreign nations, but upon ourselves." That is perfectly true at this moment, because foreign nations earnestly desire peace and to avoid all occasion of quarrel, but it will cease to be true the moment that America has forced us into a war, for one of the many evils of war is that a nation is deprived by it of the control of its own destinies, and forced to shape its course, not by its own will, but by the decision of war itself.

Lincoln's Secretary of State, in the view of the South, was a Premier to a King. The feeling persisted that Seward and the abolitionist press of New York were without scruples; the fact that the Confederate Commissioners were surrendered was interpreted as a loss of honor. The Richmond Daily Dispatch, Jan. 8, 1862.

TRY A GENTLEMAN.—We really think it would be worth while for the North—that is, to use its own favorite vernacular, it would pay to offer a premium for a gentleman as the next Premier of the United States. As to the President, it matters not much, as experience has shown, whether he be a philosopher or an ass. In point of fact, the two animals, in political positions, differ not much, except in the length of their ears. Nor is it very important whether the President is a high-minded statesman or a vulgar demagogue. If he is the first, the people will desert him, and if he is the last, he will desert the people. A gentleman in the Presidency would give mortal offense to the magnificent vulgar. It is the theory of the United States that the People are Kings, that the Plug Ugly or Dead Rabbit is as much a monarch as "Gentleman George," and every attempt of the President, who is but the upper servant of the people, to put on airs, wear a clean shirt, and behave himself with decency, dignity and ceremony, like George Washington, would naturally excite the suspicion of the populace and make them jealous of an attempt to usurp their sovereignty and introduce the One King Power into America. But the Premier, who, according to the American theory, is only "a servant of servants," and, in the case of Lincoln's Premier, is literally, a "slave of the Devil," might be a gentleman, without detriment to the public weal, however injurious it might be to his individual prospects. At all events, it would be worth while to try the experiment.—If Lincoln had appointed a Secretary of State who was a gentleman, this civil war would not now be raging in America. Seward began his career by pandering to anti-Masonry, and wound up with Abolitionism, showing himself from first to last a cunning and unprincipled demagogue, capable of descending to any moral and political abyss, for the purpose of advancing his individual fortunes. Since he has been Premier, he has lied—that is the only word which describes his deceptions—in the meanest and basest manner. He lied in inducing the Southern Commissioners to believe that Fort Sumter would be evacuated, and he has just lied with great preciseness, and in the most formal and deliberate manner, to Lord Lyons, in denying that the outrage perpetrated by Commander Wilkes was authorized by the Government. Now, it is impossible for a man to be at the same time a gentleman and a liar, and the fact that the North is represented in its relations with foreign countries by the most shameless liar in the world, will cause its reputation to stink in the nostrils of all Christendom. The foreign nations have some strong prejudices on the subject of having gentlemen at the head of Government, and as the office of Secretary of State brings him directly in contact with the outside world, it is highly important that he should not be a blackguard. We therefore recommend the North to offer a large reward for the discovery of a gentleman to succeed Wm. H. Seward in his present office.

Time was when it would not have been difficult for them to find a proper person. In the old days before universal suffrage had demoralized the whole race, there were such men in the North as DeWitt Clinton, and the Livingstons, Van Rensealaers, Van Nesses, and other worthy Knickerbackers, who possessed every attribute of a gentleman, and who consequently would have cut off their right hands before being guilty of falsehood, or sacrificing the national honor, as Seward has done in the surrender of the Southern Commissioners upon compulsion. But a man who has no sense of personal honor can have no sense of national honor. He is incapable of conceiving what it is, and thinks it sentimental and foolish. Dollars and cents are his only standard of propriety. Let the North, if it can, find a man who has sucked in elevated ideas with his mother's milk, and it may yet retrieve its reputation.

"Mas Linkum" is a character in this poem—so is "old mammy." The poem is a caricature of classic prejudice in its naïveté. From the Richmond Dispatch, Jan. 16, 1862.

A SOUTHERN SCENE

"Oh! mammy, have you heard the news?"
Thus spake a Southern child.
As to the aged nurse's face
She upward glanced and smiled.

"What news you mean, my little one?
It must be mighty fine,
To make my darling's face so red,
Her sunny blue eyes shine."

"Why Abram Lincoln, don't you know,
The Yankee President,
Whose ugly picture once we saw
When up to town we went.

"Well he is going to free you all,
And make you rich and grand.
And you'll be dressed in silk and gold
Like the proudest in the land.

"A gilded coach shall carry you
Where'er you wish to ride;
And, mammy, all your work shall be
Forever laid aside."

The eager speaker paused for breath,
And then the old nurse said,
While closer to her swarthy cheek
She pressed the golden head:

"My little missus stop and res—
You're talking mighty fas;
Jes look up dere, and tell me what
You see in yonder glass?

"You sees o'd mammy's wrinkly face,
As black as any coal;
And underneath her handkerchief
Whole heaps of knotty wool,

"My darlin's face is red and white
Her skin is soff and fine,
And on her pretty little head,
De yaller ringlets shine.

"My chile, who made dis difference
Twixt mammy and twixt you?
You reads de dear Lord's blessed book,
And you kin tell me true.

"De dear Lord says it must be so;
And, honey, I for one,
Wid tankful heart will always say,
His holy will be done.

"I thanks mas Linkum all de same,
But when I wants for free,
I'll ask de Lord of glory
Not poor buckra man like he.

"Come, little missus, say your prayers,
Let old mas Linkum 'lone.
The debil knows what b'longs to him,
And he'll take care of his own!"

The North, too, put "Abe" to use in poem and song. Between the lines of such "songs" as this one from the *New York Tribune* of March 7, 1862, were the importunements of those who felt the time was near to strike for the abolition of slavery.

A SONG TO ABE.

Up and bear the sway, Abe, Up and bear the sway,

Let Trea-son know she has a foe, And

Freedom has a stay, Abe! You're the pride of all, Abe,

You're the pride of all, Abe, You're the pride of

all the braves, Now ready at your call, Abe!

I.

Up and bear the sway, Abe,
Up and bear the sway;
Let Treason know she has a foe,
And Freedom has a stay, Abe.
You're the pride of all, Abe,
You're the pride of all, Abe,
You're the pride of all the Braves
Now ready at you call, Abe.

II.

Up and bear the sway, Abe, &c.
Thousands sigh and weep, Abe,

Thousands sigh and weep, Abe,
Thousands sigh and weep and cry
To enter Freedom's Gate, Abe.

III.

Up and bear the sway, Abe, &c.
Thousands in their might, Abe,
Thousands in their might, Abe,
Will ready march at your command,
And die for Freedom's Right, Abe.

IV.

Up and bear the sway, Abe, &c.
You're the pride of all, Abe,
You're the pride of all, Abe;
E'en Traitors yet will bow the knee,
And own your honored call, Abe. W. B.

Chapter 7

The Emancipator

APRIL 1862–JANUARY 1863

When Lincoln was twenty-eight years of age and a Representative in the Illinois General Assembly, resolutions were passed by the strongly pro-Southern legislators saying that "the right of property in slaves, is sacred to the slave-holding states by the Federal Constitution, and that they cannot be deprived of that right without their consent." Only two legislators dissented—"Dan Stone and A. Lincoln, Representatives from the county of Sangamon." They said: "[We] believe that the institution of slavery is founded on both injustice and bad policy; but that the promulgation of abolition doctrines tends rather to increase than to abate its evils." Thus Lincoln, in 1837, speaking out qualifiedly against slavery.

During his first Inaugural he repeated a statement made during the great debates with Senator Douglas: "I have no purpose, directly or indirectly, to interfere with the institution of slavery in the states where it exists. I believe I have no lawful right to do so, and I have no inclination to do so." The main goal then was the Union and the Constitution, and it remained so as the Civil War unfolded. Lincoln could draw a distinction between his personal feelings against slavery and his public actions, which he construed as moderate under the Constitution.

But now events moved toward emancipation. Abolitionist opinion hammered at the White House. European opinion was a factor, and it surely could not find disfavor with freedom. From a military viewpoint, the slaves could be a source of manpower. Southern publications ran columns of advertisements offering rewards for the return of runaway slaves (one in a Richmond paper said the man's identifying marks were whip welts across the back); runaways who came to Union camps could be of service.

Against this background Lincoln sent a special message to Congress on March 6, 1862, calling for a resolution "that the United States ought to coöperate with any state which may adopt gradual abolishment of slavery, giving to such state pecuniary aid, to be used by such state in its discretion, to compensate for the inconveniences public and private, produced by such change of system." He hoped such a resolution would "lead to important practical results."

The idea of compensated emancipation received strong approval in the New York press; at least the emancipation part did. To Henry J. Raymond, Lincoln wrote privately, "I am grateful to the New York journals, and not less so to The Times than to others, for their kind notices of the late special message to Congress," and asked for another article in The Times, which had said compensated emancipation would be too expensive. (The talk was of $400 for each slave.) The following editorial appeared in the New York Tribune, March 7, 1862.

THE PRESIDENT FOR FREEDOM

We never printed a State paper with more satisfaction than we feel in giving to our readers the Special Message of President LINCOLN to Congress yesterday, by which he recommends the passage of a joint resolve proffering National coöperation and pecuniary aid to each and every State which shall see fit to inaugurate the Abolition of Slavery within its borders. This Message constitutes of itself an epoch in the history of our country. It has no precedent; we trust it may have many consequents. It is the day-star of a new National dawn. Even if it were no more than a barren avowal by the Chief Magistrate of the Nation that IT IS HIGHLY DESIRABLE THAT THE UNION BE PURGED OF SLAVERY, it would be a great fact, of far weightier import than many battles. But it is not destined to remain unfruitful. Congress will be more than ready to welcome and act upon it. It will lead to practical results, and these the most important and beneficent. The 6th of March will yet be celebrated as a day which initiated the Nation's deliverance from the most stupendous wrong, curse and shame of the Nineteenth Century. Years may elapse before the object boldly contemplated in this Message shall be fully attained; but let us never harbor a doubt that it will ultimate in a glorious fruition.

—We believe our neighbor of The Herald lately suggested the re-election of Abraham Lincoln as President of the United States. We heartily second the motion. Mr. Counselor Brady, likewise, at a recent Tammany festival, predicted that Mr. Lincoln would prove himself a good Democrat before the expiration of his present term. We congratulate the Counselor on the speedy fulfillment of his prophecy. The world does move!

The transmission of this Message to Europe by to-morrow's steamer seals the fate of the Rebellion in every Christian land. Dahomey is the last hope of the traitors in their eager quest of recognition and of allies. No civilized nation will think of entering into alliance with Jeffdom in view of this glorious demonstration that "Union and Liberty" are indeed "one and inseparable." Long live the American Republic!

Greeley's New York Tribune, in the forefront of the fight to abolish slavery, found much good in the President's message, and took to task Bennett's Herald and Raymond's Times for failure of enthusiasm. The Tribune, March 8, 1862.

THE MESSAGE OF FREEDOM

The wisdom of the measure proposed by Mr. Lincoln in his message to Congress, published yesterday, impresses us, as we presume it will the country, more and more, the more we consider it. The thing proposed to be done, the way in which it is proposed to do that thing, and the time chosen for the proposal, commend themselves to us as evidences of a very careful observation and study of the present aspect of affairs, a large foresight, and a calm confidence in the conclusions reached. The *Herald* strikes a blow at the President by considering and affecting to praise the message in the same article that it gives unbounded commendation to one of the most malicious pro-slavery speeches ever made in Congress—Mr. Cowan's; The *Times* doubts that its purpose will ever be gained, while it asks for it a fair discussion; but we do not, of course, like the first, believe it to be a cheat and a sham, nor, like the last, hold it as a mistake. It is not merely a vigorous State paper, honest, wise, forcible; but one of those few great scriptures that live in history and mark an epoch in the lives of nations and of races. The first era of the supremacy of the rights of man in this country dates from the Declaration of Independence; the second began on the 6th of March, 1862, with the Emancipation Message of President Lincoln.

The time was chosen wisely for its promulgation. Had it been earlier it would have been premature. All Europe, and especially England, has taunted us for months that the Government had no policy, and especially that it was not carrying on war for the Abolition of Slavery. Its policy has been and is the suppression of insurrection, and it chooses to deal with Slavery only as Slavery comes in its way. To have announced what might or what might not be our future relations to that question would have, at least, seemed a weak compliance with a foreign clamor. To have indicated in the months past, when disaster and gloom overwhelmed or menaced us, all that Mr. Lincoln announces now might have been construed into a threat, to be disregarded because extorted from our fears. Of the future, indeed, we know nothing, but even a few weeks hence that which is an honorable proposition now, would perhaps, then, seem an ungenerous mockery of an offer of a choice from the victor to the vanquished. But the moment chosen is open to none of these objections. Europe holds her peace, and pretends no longer either to dictate or deride; the clouds of dismay and doubt have rolled away, and left a clear horizon bright with the fire of victories; but the war is not yet over, and we appeal to an enemy who has not yet laid down his arms. We neither humiliate ourselves nor wound his pride in proposing now a plan whereby a burden shall be equally divided for the common good, at the same time he is gently but firmly told that that burden is to be taken from our shoulders, at any rate, when we find we can bear it no longer.

The Message ought, and we think will, unite all parties. The conservative who abhors rash measures, and dreads innovation, will approve a measure which proposes to get rid of the cause of rebellion, to give the country permanent peace and not periodical panic, and to do this gradually and with as little injustice as is possible in so great a social revolution. The radical will not withhold his approbation from a proposal that promises to the eye of faith so much. It may be that some of the Border Slave States will gladly avail themselves of the offer of Mr. Lincoln, and if they do the North will as gladly accept its share of so great an act. But if they do not, though there is, so far as that particular proposition is concerned, as Mr. Lincoln says, an end, yet the end, nevertheless, is not yet as to the subject. And nobody, it is manifest, sees this more clearly than the President. His is one of those minds that work, not quickly nor brilliantly, but exhaustively. Through this matter he has looked to the final conclusion. He sees that, however often rebellion may be suppressed at the South, it will never be ended so long as Slavery has an assured existence. The continuation of Slavery as a permanent institution on which no inroad has been made is the continuation of war, for resistance to the Federal Government must be permanently suppressed, and resistance brings war. Whatever is indispensable to this end must be done, and Slavery, therefore, must fall either in one way or the other. Let the slaveholders begin the reform, and we will give them our hearty aid; if they will not, then we must do it without them, as a necessary step toward the establishment of permanent peace and the supremacy of the Union; for Slavery is Rebellion. The South has the choice—of beginning the work with the help of the whole country, and the system thus to be left to gradually disappear, from natural but inevitable causes; or she may refuse, and resent the offer, and take the consequences of continued resistance. This is clearly Mr. Lincoln's meaning, and his convictions are of a character that do not proclaim themselves merely in words. Taking no counsel of flesh and blood in this matter, but remembering his responsibility as the Head of a great nation whose very existence is threatened, he goes straight to the root of the disease, when he sees the time has come, and determines upon its eradication. There is nothing violent in his remedy; it outrages none of the professed doctors who have proposed its treatment, but it must commend itself to the common sense of everybody else. It may be quick or it may be slow, according to circumstances; but, at any rate, it will be certain. For our part, we thank God that Abraham Lincoln is President of the United States, and the whole country, we cannot doubt, will be thankful that we have at such a time so wise a ruler.

Some of Lincoln's generals tried to jump the gun on emancipation. General Hunter, commanding at Port Royal, S.C., declared that slaves in South Carolina, Georgia and Florida were "forever free." Lincoln reacted quickly, reserving for himself the right to decide where and when and how. The New York Tribune, May 20, 1862, showed the prevailing disappointment.

GEN. HUNTER OVERRULED

The President has decided to rescind or modify Gen. [David] Hunter's Order setting free all the slaves in his Military Department. It was his right to do so, and we bow to his decision. We cannot doubt that Gen. Hunter judged wisely and acted nobly so far as the prosperity of the Union cause in his own District was concerned. We do not believe the President holds a different opinion. But it is *his* duty to survey the whole ground, to determine what is best not for three States only, but to insure the triumph of the Union cause everywhere. And from his decision there is no appeal.

But we entreat the President now to consider and act upon the manifest necessity of having a definite, unvarying, clearly understood policy with regard to this subject. On behalf of the whole People we demand an unequivocal official answer to these questions—"What shall be the future condition of the slave of a Rebel who escapes from the dominions of Jeff. Davis and comes within the lines of our armies?" "What of those slaves who are abandoned by their Rebel masters fleeing before the advancing hosts of the Union?" "What of the slave whose Rebel master remains with him until both are enveloped by the Union forces?"

These questions are eminently and urgently practical. They are inevitably passed upon daily by commanders of departments, of divisions, of posts. And there are about as many variant answers as decisions. One commander welcomes all that come to him, treats them as men, and gets the best work he can out of them. Another (until Congress peremptorily forbade it) sent them back to their Rebel masters! A third refuses them admission to his lines at all. No matter how important, how essential, may be the information they bring, the service they are eager to perform, he orders them back to the Rebels. Had Gen. [Henry] Halleck instead of Gen. Hunter been in command at Port Royal last week, the heroic negroes who brought the Rebel-owned dispatch steamboat Planter away from Charleston wharf, piloted her through the Rebel vessels and under the guns of their forts with the Confederate and Palmetto flags flying, and finally hoisted a white flag and thus bore down on the blockading fleet, handing her over a good prize, with six capital cannon on board, would have to be thrust back into Slavery, with their women and children. Mr. Lincoln cannot intend this; yet this is the drift of Gen. Halleck's Order, which stands unrevoked, unmodified to-day. True, there are no Democrats nor Border-State men to raise a clamor against it; but it is no less shameful and damaging than if there were.

—Let no one be discouraged nor alienated because of this Presidential step. Mr. Lincoln only reserves to himself as Commander-in-Chief, the power to proclaim the abolition of Slavery. It is not without purpose that he refers to the "definite solemn proposal" made by himself to the Border States on the 6th of March, and adopted by large majorities in both Houses of Congress. He "beseeches" them to accept that proposal, warns them not to be "blind to the signs of the times." If they are deaf to his earnest words they and the whole country may know what to expect. "The

Stars in their courses fight against" Slavery, and its doom is sure. Every gun fired in this struggle, no matter on which side, no matter what else it hits or misses, lodges a ball in the carcase of the writhing monster. Man may hesitate or vacillate, but the judgment of God is sure, and under that judgment Slavery reels to its certain downfall.

Lincoln's firmness in revoking General Hunter's own emancipation proclamation brought forth praise from California, which saw Lincoln not as an indecisive Chief Executive—the frequent accusation of the Eastern opinion makers—but as a "Jacksonian President." From the Daily Alta California, San Francisco, June 17, 1862.

A JACKSONIAN PRESIDENT

By the steamer which arrived yesterday, we have the text of the proclamation issued by the President, revoking the proclamation of Gen. Hunter, declaring the slaves in his Department, consisting of South Carolina, Georgia, and Florida free. Said the General: "Slavery and martial law in a free country are altogether incompatible. The persons in these three States—Georgia, South Carolina, and Florida—heretofore held as slaves, are, therefore, declared forever free." It is undoubtedly true that slavery and martial law, in a free country, are incompatible. For that matter, slavery and any kind of law in a free country could not exist together. The trouble was that Georgia, South Carolina, and Florida do not constitute what may be termed a free country. In them, or, more properly speaking, in Georgia and South Carolina, slavery has been the rule since the Constitution of the United States was framed.

It is true that the States in question are in rebellion, but we believe that rebellion has not the sympathy of all the citizens there resident. It is the theory of the Government, that Secession was planned by restless politicians, and not by the people themselves, and that when reason reässerts her sway, loyalty will again flourish in these regions as luxuriantly as of old.

The proclamation of Gen. Hunter excited the more surprise from the fact, that he was sent to take charge of the Department of the South, under the belief that he was not at all biased by sectionalism. The controversy which he had a short time before, with Jim Lane in Kansas, furnished grounds for the formation of such an opinion. The fulmination, therefore, to which reference is made, came upon the country like a clap of thunder in a clear sky. It created such excitement that the President considered it to be his duty to disavow it, though not officially informed of the fact, and, whether genuine or false, to declare it void and of no effect. Ever since Mr. Lincoln assumed the reins of government, he has in every act shown that he knows, as the old political phrase goes, "no North, no South, no East, no West," and, furthermore, that he is never afraid to take the responsibility when occasion requires it. Few men in his position could have summoned up courage enough to remove Fremont six months ago; but Mr. Lincoln, as soon as necessity required it, did take that momentous step, and the country sustained him. The Hunter escapade presented almost equal difficulties, but Mr. Lincoln hesitated not for a moment. The war in which the country is engaged is one for the restoration of the Union and not of subjugation. If emancipation were the policy of the Government, subjugation would be the result of the conflict.

Not only has the President disavowed Hunter's proclamation, but he has taken occasion to prevent, for the future, all such unwarrantable proceedings. "I further make known," he says, "that whether it be competent for me, as Commander-in-Chief of the Army and Navy, to declare the slaves of any State or States free, and whether at any time, or in any case, it shall have become a necessity indispensable to the maintenance of the Government to exercise such supposed power, are questions which, under my responsibility, I reserve to myself, and which I cannot feel justified in leaving to the decision of commanders in the field. These are totally different questions from those of police regulations in armies and camps."

The firmness of Jackson is admired to the present day. We doubt very much if the hero of the Hermitage ever gave utterance to a more vigorous sentiment. It has about it the genuine Hickory ring. It was high time that the proclamation mania of our generals should be crushed. It was rapidly becoming a positive nuisance; for at one time every general thought he ought to set up for himself, the moment he received a command. The Government has a policy, and our generals are only the agents selected to carry it out, and nothing else. If they were allowed to give expression to their own views at every point at which they might happen to be stationed, soon it would be difficult to make out what we are fighting about.

Mr. Lincoln was elected the President of the United States, and it is evident that President he is determined to be. He has not and will not divide up the Executive power, like poor old Buchanan, and leave himself nothing but a puppet in the hands of designing men.

The Emancipator APRIL 1862–JANUARY 1863

The Crisis of Columbus, Ohio, was one of the leading Copperhead papers. It was edited by a fanatically hostile Democratic wheelhorse, Samuel Medary, who printed hateful anti-Lincoln and proslavery stories, and took delight in reprinting reports such as this one, July 2, 1862. Its source was Edward Dicey, who wrote for English periodicals and spent six months in the North; this description of Lincoln was widely reprinted by the anti-Lincoln press.

HOW ABE LOOKS

An English magazine writer gives the following description of the President:

To say he is ugly is nothing; to add that his figure is grotesque is to convey no adequate impression. Fancy a man about six feet high, and thin in proportion, with long bony arms and legs, which somehow seem always to be in the way; with great rugged furrowed hands, which grasp you like a vice when shaking yours; with a long scraggy neck and a chest too narrow for the great arms at his side. Add to this figure a head, coconut shaped and somewhat too small for such a statue, covered with rough, uncombed hair, that stands out in every direction at once; a face furrowed, wrinkled, and indented as though it has been scarred by vitriol; a high narrow forehead, sunk beneath bushy eyebrows, two bright, somewhat dreamy eyes, that seem to gaze through you without looking at you; a few irregular blotches of black bristly hair, in the place where beard and whiskers ought to grow; a close-set thin-lipped, stern mouth, with two rows of large white teeth, and a nose and ears which have been taken by mistake from a head twice the size. Clothe this figure then in a long, tight, badly-fitting suit of black, creased, soiled, and puckered up at every salient point of the figure (and every point of this figure is salient,) put on large, ill-fitting boots, gloves too long for the long bony fingers, and a puffy hat covered to the top with dusty puffy crape, and then add to all this an air of strength, physical as well as moral, and a strange look of dignity coupled with all the grotesqueness, and you will have the impression left upon me by Abraham Lincoln.

A by-product of a declaration freeing the slaves, argued abolitionists as the war looked grim for the North, would be starvation for the Confederates. The National Intelligencer of Washington, D.C., wavered a good deal on the subject of slavery. To the New York

Tribune, it could be "treasonous"; to more moderate eyes it appeared friendly to Lincoln. William W. Seaton served as editor of the Intelligencer, which had first printed Lincoln's name back in the days when he was a Congressman. Lincoln read the Intelligencer faithfully for many years including, undoubtedly, this editorial on July 31, 1862.

HOW TO END THE WAR

We have more than once been called during the past week or two to express our regret at the lamentable fact that at the present time, when all loyal journals should be directing their best and undivided energies to the promotion of enlistments, a small class of malcontents should be seeking to divert public attention from this most immediate duty by engaging in discussions extrinsic to the paramount issue, and by especially inveighing against the President because he has not issued a certain proclamation under the confiscation and emancipation act. For ourselves we have to repeat, what we said on Saturday last, that since the terms of this act, in its ninth section, declaring the circumstances under which slaves of rebels are free, do not depend at all for their force on a public proclamation by the President, we cannot see the necessity for any such step on the part of the Executive, who, it is to be presumed, has taken care that our commanders in the field should be officially apprized through the War Department of the will of Congress in the premises. At the same time, as we have heretofore said, we see no objection to a reduction by the President of the terms of the ninth section of this act into the shape of a proclamation, whether meant for the instruction of our Generals or for the enlightenment of slaves in the revolted States. Indeed there is one aspect of the question which rather inclines us to wish that the President might find it compatible with his convictions of public duty to issue some such paper as these complainants ask at his hands. We are well assured that it would prove brutum fulmen, but its demonstrated inefficiency might perhaps open the eyes of amiable and sanguine philanthropists, who, until the experiment is tried, will continue to credit such representations as the following, contributed to the New York Evening Post by a corespondent who has lived in Virginia; and who writes after having, as he says, "conversed with an old Virginia acquaintance, a recent refugee from Richmond, who for the last year has been a member of the rebel General Longstreet's family, and who, though a man of color, seems to understand the condition of affairs at the South much better than some of our Generals":

"How strange that our great men and rulers should not see that the stomach is the weak point of the enemy! He will have little stomach to fight the bad fight of rebellion on an empty stomach. When the great words of liberty and freedom shall be sounded from the high places of power like a trumpet through the land, the knell of the rebellion will be tolled.

"But we are asked how the negroes on the plantations are to be informed of such a decree of the Government. How little do those who ask such questions know of the negro character! The negroes are familiar with every swamp and mountain pass, through glen and forest, and at night, guided by the stars, the gospel of freedom would be circulated from cabin to cabin almost with telegraphic swiftness. *The plough would stand still in the furrow, the ripened grain would remain unharvested, the cows would not be milked, the dinners would not be cooked,* but one universal hallelujah of glory to God, echoed from every valley and hill-top of rebeldom, would sound the speedy doom of treason."

Certainly, if all this can be accomplished by a Presidential proclamation of the ninth section of the confiscation and emancipation act, we say let us have it by all means, and the sooner the better. If the "stomach is the weak point of the rebels," and if a proclamation of freedom is going to put an end to all culinary operations in the "Confederate States," we shall conquer a peace none the less signal for being bloodless. What would this be but bringing the blockade home to every rebel's business and bowels? When it was hoped by Mr. Perceval to bring the French to reason by keeping them without rhubarb and calomel, Sydney Smith remarked on the sublime spectacle suggested by the thought that no purge could be taken between the Weser and Garoane, and that in consequence of the British Orders in Council the bowels of mankind were locked up for fourteen degrees of latitude. Without castor-oil he thought the French might for some months, to be sure, carry on a lingering war, but what could they do without bark? Would a people live under a Government where antimonial powders could not be procured? Would they bear the loss of mercury, or persist in a war which laid an embargo on Godfrey's cordial?

But Mr. Perceval's plan of conquest and constipation was nothing as compared with that now commended to the adoption of the President. At his word the plough, we are told, would stand still in the Southern furrow; the ripened grain (except that already garnered for the want of a proclamation to prevent) would remain unharvested; the vaccine udders throughout the South would, for lack of ebon hands to tend the cowpen, be doomed to stay their lacteal streams—a thought affecting, it may be, to all humane friends of the bovine creation, but not without its military suggestions every where outside of Africa, that *arida nutrix leonum;* and, finally, *no more dinners would be cooked in all* "rebeldom." This last consideration is not only final but conclusive. It is plain that without "dinners" the rebels cannot long protract the war. Even the most determined "fire-eater" must eventually succumb, with nothing more substantial to sustain his ardor than the igneous diet on which he would be left to regale in the absence of the "loyal blacks" who erst were wont to cater for his *cuisine.* He may, if he will, mix gunpowder with his whiskey, but can he hope to keep his courage up without bacon and greens? If hominy be wanting can the Southern Confederacy expect to thrive? If the "corn dodger" be taken away must not General Jefferson Davis sue for a speedy peace? In view of such decisive results how can the President justify himself in withholding the proclamation? Is this a time to be tender towards Southern "stomachs" when the "vitals" of the country are being pierced by Southern bayonets? Is it of more importance that the rebels should have "dinners" than that the Union should be saved?

On Aug. 20, 1862, Horace Greeley wrote an open letter to President Lincoln called "The Prayer of Twenty Millions." Greeley, presuming himself the voice of the masses, said: "What an immense majority of the loyal millions of your countrymen require of you is a frank, declared, unqualified, ungrudging execution of the laws of the land, more especially of the Confiscation Act. That act gives freedom to the slaves of rebels coming within our lines, or whom those lines may at any time enclose—we ask you to render it due obedience by publicly requiring all your subordinates to recognize and obey it." Lincoln chose the National Intelligencer of Aug. 23, 1862, as his forum for an open reply—which the whole country, North, South, East and West, read and thought over.

A LETTER FROM THE PRESIDENT

EXECUTIVE MANSION,
Washington, August 22, 1862.

Hon. HORACE GREELEY:

DEAR SIR: I have just read yours of the 19th, addressed to myself through the New York Tribune. If there be in it any statements, or assumptions of fact, which I may know to be erroneous, I do not now and here controvert them. If there be in it any inferences which I may believe to be falsely drawn, I do not now and here argue against them. If there be perceptible in it an impatient and dictatorial tone, I waive it in deference to an old friend whose heart I have always supposed to be right.

As to the policy I "seem to be pursuing," as you say, I have not meant to leave any one in doubt.

I would save the Union. I would save it the shortest way under the Constitution. The sooner the national authority can be restored the nearer the Union will be "the Union as it was." If there be those who would not save the Union unless they could at the same time save slavery, I do not agree with them. If there be those who would not save the Union unless they could at the same time destroy slavery, I do not agree with them. My paramount object in this struggle is to save the Union, and is not either to save or to destroy slavery. If I could save the Union without freeing any slave I would do it, and if I could save it by freeing all the slaves I would do it; and if I could save it by freeing some and leaving others alone, I would also do that. What I do about slavery and the colored race, I do because I believe it helps to save this Union; and what I forbear, I forbear because I do not believe it would help to save the Union. I shall do less whenever I shall believe what I am doing hurts the cause, and I shall do more whenever I shall believe doing more will help the cause. I shall try to correct errors when shown to be errors; and I shall adopt new views so fast as they shall appear to be true views.

I have here stated my purpose according to my view of official duty; and I intend no modification of my oft-expressed *personal* wish that all men everywhere could be free. Yours,

A. LINCOLN.

THE PRESIDENT'S LETTER

When the very original idea of addressing in the columns of the New York Tribune a letter to President Lincoln, in the name and by the authority of "twenty millions" of the American people, entered the head of Mr. Horace Greeley, we suppose he had little idea that his communication, if ever reaching the eye of his distinguished correspondent, would receive from that correspondent the honor of a response. Still less could he have expected or wished that the response should be of a nature to give so much more satisfaction to the "twenty millions" of loyal men in whose behalf he assumed to speak, than he, their self-elected organ, is likely to find in it. We hope, however, that when Mr. Greeley has duly pondered the pithy sentences of the President's letter he will be able to rejoin, if he proposes to continue the "correspondence," in a spirit which shall be slightly less arrogant, dictatorial, and acrimonious. "Twenty millions" of his countrymen have a right to claim this at his hands, in deference to the high office whose incumbent he ventures to arraign before the bar of public opinion in their name.

Lincoln issued his preliminary Emancipation Proclamation on Sept. 22, 1862. In it he declared that the following January, all slaves in the rebellious States "shall be then, thenceforward, and forever free." Lincoln measured the reaction himself in a note to Vice President Hamlin, ". . . commendation in newspapers and by distinguished individuals is all that a vain man could wish." The National Intelligencer on Sept. 23, 1862, was not sanguine about the proclamation.

PROCLAMATION OF THE PRESIDENT

The reader will find in another part of to-day's Intelligencer a Proclamation of the President of the United States, declaring prospectively the emancipation of slaves in the Insurgent States on the first of January next, unless, in the meantime, the people of these States shall so far return to their constitutional relations as to send Representatives to Congress.

With our well-known and oft-repeated views respecting the inutility of such proclamations, it can hardly be necessary for us to say that, where we expect no good, we shall be only too happy to find that no harm has been done by the present declaration of the Executive.

This new proclamation with regard to the contingent emancipation of slaves in the insurgent States not being self-enforcing any more than the proclamation of Gen. Hunter in regard to the immediate emancipation of slaves in the States of South Carolina, Georgia, and Florida, the only difference between the two papers resides in the signatures respectively attached to them. And as, in themselves considered, they are likely to prove equally void of practical effect, we are not without the suspicion that the President has taken this method to convince the only class of persons likely to be pleased with this proclamation of the utter fallacy of the hopes they have founded upon it. This opinion, we may add, derives confirmation from the fact that he suspends for some months the enforcement of so much of his declaration as denounces the emancipation of slaves in punishment for contumacy on the part of the Insurgent

States, while he gives immediate force and effect, so far as force and effect result from proclamations, to the regulations prescribed by the new article of war and the provisions of the confiscation act in the matter of slaves. On any other theory than this the proclamation may be said to open issues too tremendous, and to be fraught with consequences too undeveloped, to admit of calculation or forecast by any intelligence we can command.

An old enemy from the West was heard from—the Chicago Times, Sept. 24, 1862, which had fought Lincoln and the rival Chicago Tribune all during the great debates of '58. Speaking for the conservatives and Democrats, the Democratic organ protested against the proclamation.

THE EMANCIPATION PROCLAMATION

Two days ago the President was wonderfully strong in the confidence of the country, not because of his military conduct of the war, for, in the opinion of all men, that had been disastrous, but because he had steadily manifested an apparently inflexible determination to adhere faithfully to the constitution in the political management of the war and in the general administration of the government. It was the merit of this adherence that, in the minds of all good and right-thinking men, covered his multitude of sins in the military conduct of the war. So long as he seemed to be fast-anchored to the constitution, good and right-thinking men never ceased to hope and believe that experience would teach him to correct and overcome his military mistakes, and that finally the government of the constitution would prevail over rebellion, and that THE UNION would be re-established.

Now that he has cut loose from the constitution—now that he has resorted to the same higher law than the constitution for the professed purpose of suppressing the rebellion by which the rebellion justifies itself —good and right-thinking men know not what to think or believe, or whither to turn for anchorage. They are smitten with a sense of alarm and dismay. They feel that the foundations of the government are unsettled, if not broken up—that the ship is adrift without master, compass or rudder, and that the chances of wreck are vastly greater than of safety.

If the policy of the proclamation were any more defensible than the President's constitutional power to issue it, the shadows which it has cast over the land would not be so impenetrable. It is an act of as bad faith to every conservative man in the North as it is a terrible blow to the Union men of the border slave States. The President has himself apprehended that it might drive fifty thousand Union soldiers, belonging to the border slave States, from the Union armies! We trust and pray that it will not, but that it will not work a most injurious revolution in the sentiment of those States we dare not hope; and as to Kentucky and Tennessee, what a time is this to hazard such a revolution! We await intelligence of its effect in those States with the most painful anxiety.

If we desired more conclusive arguments against the mere policy of the proclamation than any we have elsewhere seen, we should seek them in the answer of the President to the memorial of the religious fanatics of this city, contained in our yesterday's issue. "What good," asked he, "would a proclamation of emancipation from me do, especially as we are now situated? I do not want to issue a document that the whole world will see must necessarily be inoperative, like the Pope's bull against the comet. Would my word free the slaves, when I cannot even enforce the constitution in the rebel States? Is there a single court or magistrate or individual that would be influenced by it there? And what reason is there to think it would have any greater effect upon the slaves than the late law of Congress, which I approved, and which offers protection and freedom to the slaves of rebel masters who come within our lines. Yet I cannot learn that that law has caused a single slave to come over to us. And suppose they could be induced, by a proclamation of freedom from me, to throw themselves upon us, what should we do with them? How can we feed and care for such a multitude? General Butler wrote me, a few days since, that he was issuing more rations to the slaves who have rushed to him than to all the white troops under his command. They eat and that is all." Before the President issued the proclamation he would have done well to publicly answer these objections to the policy of it.

If utter desperation had not before seized the people of the rebel States, as a consequence of the abolition and confiscation measures of the Congress at Washington, it will seize them now. The war hereafter, on their part, will be a contest for existence as communities and individuals.

We protest against the proclamation, in the name of the constitution, in behalf of good faith to the conservative millions of the northern and border States, and for the sake of the only means by which it has at any time been possible to restore the Union. We protest against it as a monstrous usurpation, a criminal wrong, and an act of national suicide.

Nevertheless, democrats and other conservative people will not withdraw from the war. They will fight in it and support it as before, not to preserve the government, for that is subverted, but to maintain a government. To do otherwise is to invite internal revolution, anarchy and confusion, and to sink into disgrace as a people in the eyes of Christendom. The southern rebellion is not a whit more tolerable because of this most untoward proclamation. That must be resisted, whatever shall come; and as to what shall come, we can only watch and wait.

The Republican Chicago Tribune picked up the "atrocious sentiment" of the Democratic Chicago Times and condemned its old rival with traditional gusto for failure to "support the Government." From the Chicago Tribune of Sept. 24, 1862, which also reminded readers that Stephen Douglas, dead for more than a year, had supported Lincoln's Administration.

SUPPORT THE GOVERNMENT

During all the time that we have labored for the overthrow of slavery in the revolted States, as at once the cause and support of the rebellion, we have been charged by the opposite party with "opposing the government." The charge was untrue, and known to be so by those who made it, for our columns have borne daily testimony for eighteen months to our zeal in forwarding every measure, in field or council, for the most vigorous prosecution of the war, for the largest armies, for the heaviest taxes—in a word, for "the most stupendous preparations" for crushing armed traitors, that Stephen A. Douglas counselled with his latest breath. All this we have done with an eye single to the glory of the Union, and the perpetuity of its free institutions. We have not hesitated to urge what we deemed the proper policy to be pursued in regard to slavery, but when we have found that our ideas were not adopted by those to whom the destinies of the nation were lawfully entrusted, we have not abated a jot or tittle of our unfaltering support of the government in all its efforts to crush the rebellion, and preserve the priceless treasures committed to its hands.

Now we ask of those, who have heretofore chided us in no measured terms, *that they too shall support the government.* We intend to give it the same unconditional aid and encouragement that it has always received at our hands, and we shall hope to make it the more effective, as we believe that liberty is the life-giving spirit of the Union, and slavery its deadly poison. Is it unreasonable that we ask those who have differed from us, as patriots and lovers of their country, to give the government their support, now that emancipation is to be proclaimed as the last weapon wherewith to strike down the rebellion? We speak only to true men and patriots. To those who love slavery better than their country and their country's flag, and who echo the atrocious sentiment of the Chicago *Times*, that "the Government, by the act of the President, is itself in rebellion," we have only to say that the sooner they shoulder muskets and step into the ranks of Jeff. Davis the sooner will they take their true places and act out the real sentiments of their hearts. But the great body of the people, Democrats as well as Republicans, will come up as one man to the support of the government in its faithful efforts to preserve the Union. Upon the heaven defying traitors who have drawn the sword against their country rests the responsibility of the act. They can even now prevent its taking effect by laying down their arms and returning to their allegiance. If *they* choose that the blow shall fall let it fall, and let all the people say Amen!

In Lincoln's Springfield, the hometown paper, the Illinois State Journal, saw the Proclamation as only second in importance to the Declaration of Independence. From the Journal, Sept. 24, 1862.

THE BOLT FALLEN

President Lincoln has at last hurled against rebellion the bolt which he has so long held suspended. The act is the most important and the most memorable of his official career—no event in the history of this country since the Declaration of Independence itself has excited so profound attention either at home or abroad.

While its justice is indisputable, we may well suppose that the step has been taken reluctantly. A people waging a causeless and unholy war against a mild and just Government have forfeited the right to protection by that Government. No principle is clearer. Yet the President has repeatedly warned the people of the rebellious States to return to their allegiance without effect. He now employs the power with which Congress and the Constitution have clothed him. There can be but one opinion among all true friends of the country. *The President must and will be sustained.* That extremists will condemn—one class because emancipation is not immediate and unconditional: the other because it is proclaimed even prospectively, is to be expected. But those who refuse to support the Government in the exercise of its necessary and just authority are traitors and should be so treated, whatever name they may wear. True patriots of every name rally around the President, determined that the Union shall be preserved and the laws enforced.

On the Pacific Coast, the *Alta California* of San Francisco, Sept. 25, 1862, one of the largest newspapers physically in the country, stood by the President and indeed found reason to believe that "Danes on the island of San Croix" had a method of dealing with Negroes that could be copied.

THE LAST PROCLAMATION

The late proclamation of the President on the subject of slavery, so far, seems to have been well received on the other side of the mountains. The invasion of Maryland by the rebels has given rise to different views altogether on the subject of the war. So long as the fighting was confined to the heart of Virginia the alternative was only the recognition and independence of the South. If our armies were defeated at all points and the loyal States were so exhausted that they could put no more men in the field, the worst it was thought that could happen would be separation. Lee's advance to the frontiers of Pennsylvania gave rise to an entirely new set of ideas. It then became apparent that the independence of the rebel States was not the only issue involved. The war at once assumed a higher and more important aspect. It was this: that if we do not conquer the rebel States, the rebel States will conquer us.

From that stand point the contest has been and is now viewed by all thoughtful men. The rebels, to be sure, have been driven back, but the character which the movement imparted to the struggle was none the less marked and significant, and demolished every consideration which has for a year and more stayed the hand of the Administration in its dealings with this most atrocious rebellion. We have borne and forborne enough for the "loyal men of the South." They have afforded us no assistance in our efforts to crush the rebellion, and it is the manifest duty, therefore, of the people of the loyal States to waste no more blood and treasure for them, but to seek the shortest and most decisive path of ending the war. . . .

The proclamation of the President is based upon military necessity, and success is the only consequence for which military necessity cares. Farther than that we need not go at present. By and by, however, political questions, connected with this great revolution in the labor system of the South, will have to be considered. Immediate and absolute emancipation would benefit neither whites nor blacks. To be a blessing instead of a curse it must be gradual in its operation. The first duty of the Government will be to teach the negroes self-reliance, and that can only be done by a gradual slackening of the reins. The Danes on the island of San Croix have elaborated a system of dealing with them which might with advantage be copied.

The military effects of the proposed emancipation appeared to be a handy rationalization for friends as well as lukewarm foes of the President's "new policy." It was expected that Negroes, North and South, would spring to the Union cause; so said the abolitionists. The Washington National Intelligencer, Sept. 26, 1862, said "we have reason to know that [Lincoln's] own faith is weak on this point."

PRELIMINARY TESTS OF THE "NEW POLICY"

We have already sufficiently indicated our opinion of the "new policy" which President LINCOLN threatens to enforce with the army and navy of the United States after the first of January next, in case, at that date, any State or parts of States should fail to be represented in Congress. At the same time we have placed on record our augury of the consequences likely to flow from this proposed attempt to make emancipation part and parcel of our plan of military operations for the restoration of the Union.

As the policy which the President proposes to enforce in this matter is appointed to take effect only after the first of January next, we are not yet called to consider it in any other than its theoretical aspects, or its contingent results, so far as these are already descried by different classes of observers. To these we may have occasion to refer at some length on a future day.

At present we desire to remind the friends and patrons of this "new policy" that the President, in yielding to a "pressure" from which he long sought to "relieve the country," has now a right to look to them for a confirmation of all the promises that have been made and all the predictions that have been uttered in the hope of extorting from him this reluctant proclamation. The President says, (as well he may say,) in some remarks which will be found in another column, as addressed to an assemblage of the people of this city, that he has issued this proclamation "under a very heavy and solemn sense of his responsibility." He says he is still, in his position, "environed with difficulties," and therefore he has a right to claim that the confidence he has placed in the advisers who have so vehemently urged this step shall not be shown to have been misplaced.

We will at present designate only two things which he must expect to see speedily realized, as the condition of putting any trust in the policy which, after long "deliberation," he has finally adopted.

In the first place, the President, by introducing into his proclamation the promise of freedom to all slaves escaping into our army lines, has evidently determined to test at once the sagacity of the men who have confidently predicted that this simple declaration would put an end to the rebellion. He therefore makes this part of his edict *immediate* in its application, so that during the next three months he will have a good opportunity of proving the value of proclamations and testing the wisdom of his accepted counsellors. What he has a right to expect may be read in the following prediction of the Chicago Tribune, made a few weeks ago, when it was clamoring for just such a paper as it has now got:

> "But hark! Massa Lincoln, the great supreme law-giver in the Union, proclaims them free men and women. The law which has bound the chains on their limbs is itself broken, swept away, or submerged by the higher and more authoritative edict of the President of the whole Union, who pronounces them emancipated by virtue of an act of the Nation's Legislature. The voice of the President would sound throughout Secessia louder than the seven thunders. In the ears and hearts of four millions of slaves it would carry with it the weight and authority of the voice of Jehovah speaking from the Mount to the children of Israel in the wilderness. In the mind of the negro, all State laws, local customs, and masters' orders would be null and void and not binding upon his conscience or conduct. To hold him longer in slavery could only be done by brute force, which would speedily prove to be impracticable."

If there be any wisdom, therefore, in the anti-slavery astrologers, and if there be any virtue in proclamations, Mr. Lincoln expects in a few weeks to see such a stampede of "loyal blacks" deserting their rebel masters as has not occurred for centuries in the history of popular migrations. We have reason to know that his own faith is weak on this point, and therefore he will the more hope to find the judgment of his advisers approved by the event. What his own opinion in the matter is was candidly stated to a committee who a few days ago waited upon him from Chicago soliciting a proclamation, and to whose report, to be found in another column, we invite the particular attention of our readers, as in that report they will find a summary of the pithy and forcible arguments with which

Mr. Lincoln has exploded the whole theory of paper proclamations as a means of war or of emancipation.

It remains to be seen whether the President or his advisers have been the more sagacious in their anticipations under this head. He has left the latter without excuse or occasion for fault-finding, if the "loyal blacks" do not now fly to our standards "like doves to the windows."

The second thing which the President has a right not only to expect, but to demand, at the hands of his rejoicing and delighted friends, is that the ranks of the army shall be instantly filled to overflowing with eager and valiant recruits, asking to be led against the enemy and to fire at his "magazine." On this point the President has not been left to trust in mere hap-hazard promises. In an official letter, addressed to the Secretary of War under date of last May 19th, the Governor of Massachusetts expressed a doubt whether on a sudden call he could succeed in raising three regiments to fight for the Union and the Constitution under the war policy that then prevailed. But he said that if the President would let "the Massachusetts boys" "fire at the enemy's magazine," and if the President would recognize "black men as legally capable of loyalty," why, then, "the roads would swarm, if need be, with multitudes whom New England would pour out to obey his call" to fight "with God and human nature on their side.". . .

As under the original war policy Massachusetts has not yet filled her quota of the drafted militia men, and as there has been some resistance to the draft in Connecticut, (where, as in Massachusetts, it has seemed a "heavy draft on their patriotism,") it is to be understood that the effect of the President's proclamation in those quarters will be magical. "The roads will swarm" with volunteers. No draft will now be necessary in all New England. To doubt it would be to question the sagacity of Governor [John A.] Andrew and to do discredit to the willingness of New England's sons to fight "with God and human nature on their side." For ourselves, we shall watch the result with much interest, because on the success of the preliminary experiment which the President is trying with proclamations will obviously depend the degree of his confidence in the advantages of the "new policy" he has concluded to adopt.

Lincoln moved gradually before the public on emancipation, conducting something of a debate in the open to weigh all sentiments. The anti-slavery forces seemed to be in control after the preliminary Emancipation Proclamation in September of '62. To a public meeting of religious leaders favoring freedom, Lincoln had declared: "Would my word free the slaves, when I cannot even enforce the Constitution in the rebel states? . . . I have not decided against a proclamation of liberty to the slaves, but hold the matter under advisement." The New York Herald, Sept. 27, 1862, voiced the Democratic line on the subject.

THE PRESIDENT'S EMANCIPATION ANTI-SLAVERY PROCLAMATION—"THE POPE'S BULL AGAINST THE COMET"

The special deputation which recently waited upon President Lincoln, with a memorial from an abolition meeting in Chicago in favor of national emancipation, have rendered no small service to the country in procuring in advance of its issue, the President's sensible views of his late comprehensive proclamation on the subject. Thus the truth is made manifest that this proclamation, beyond the enforcement of the Confiscation act, is only a tub to the abolition whale, the President regarding it as "necessarily inoperative, like the Pope's bull against the comet."

He very pointedly and properly asked of this aforesaid committee, "What good would a proclamation of emancipation from me do, especially as we now stand? Would my word free the slaves when I cannot even enforce the constitution in the rebel States? Is there a single court, or magistrate, or individual, that would be influenced by it there? And what reason is there to think it would have any greater effect upon the slaves than the late act of Congress (Confiscation), which I approved, and which offers protection and freedom to the slaves of rebel masters who come within our lines? And suppose they could be induced by a proclamation of freedom from me to throw themselves upon us, what should we do with them? How can we feed and care for such a multitude? General Butler wrote me a few days since that he was issuing more rations to the slaves who have rushed to him than to all the white troops under his command. They eat, and that is all; though it is true that General Butler is feeding the whites also by the thousands; for it nearly amounts to a famine there." These remarks of President Lincoln clearly show that he has no faith in the miracles which his Chicago committee so eloquently assured him would finish up this rebellion with a proclamation of emancipation.

But to silence the clamors of our shrieking and howling abolition faction, and to put them to the test of their promises, including a new batch of nine hundred thousand volunteers for the war, President Lincoln has issued his proclamation of emancipation. He declares that after the first day of January next all the slaves in every State, or in any designated part thereof, which shall be then in rebellion against the Union, shall be "then, thenceforward and forever free." There, good people, is your proclamation. It practically signifies nothing; but much is gained if you will only stop this intolerable clamor. Very true, in the interval to the 1st of January, the armies of the rebellion may be pushed down into the cotton States, and then, with the advance of our forces, our abolition fanatics may anticipate the practical work of a sweeping emancipation. But there is no occasion for sensible men to apprehend any such thing. With the northern frontier line of the rebel armies pushed down into the cotton States, there will be an end of the rebellion. Further resistance in the exhausted cotton States, when placed between our victorious armies on the land side and our iron-clad gunboats on the sea side, will be madness, and those States, with their institution of slavery, will be saved by a seasonable capitulation.

Such are doubtless the expectations of the President, and hence these three months grace which he allows to the States involved in this rebellion to save themselves and their domestic institutions. Slavery, as a local affair in the loyal border slave States, remains untouched and respected, and it will be respected in every rebellious State which shall have returned to its allegiance and be represented in Congress by the 1st of January. The President thus expects to reclaim, and not to destroy, the people of our rebellious States. He has, we dare say, not the remotest idea that this conditional proclamation of emancipation will go into practical effect. He expects this rebellion to be suppressed before the expiration of the present year, and that thus the question of slavery under the constitution will be restored to the absolute control of each of the States directly concerned in the maintenance or removal of the institution.

These three months grace to our rebellious States have secured to the President, let us hope, a three months armistice from our besotted abolitionists. And if, during this interval, they in good faith cease to embarrass and torment him, and cease to intermeddle with the plans and movements of our armies, we have no doubt that Honest Abraham Lincoln's great object of restoring the Union in its integrity will be consumated before the end of the year.

The Preliminary Emancipation Proclamation—with its provision for full emancipation by the end of 1862—was closely watched for its effects in the Border States. One of the arguments all along against emancipation was that the loyal states on the border of Civil War would be pushed South if slaves were set free. The reactions in Kentucky and Maryland were noted in the Louisville Journal and Baltimore American, both reprinted in the National Intelligencer, Washington, Oct. 8, 1862.

From the Louisville Journal

It is evidently an arbitrary act of the President as Commander-in-Chief of the army and navy of the Union. In short, it is a naked stroke of military necessity. We shall not stop now to discuss the character and tendency of this measure. Both are manifest. The one is as unwarrantable as the other is mischievous. The measure is wholly unauthorized and wholly pernicious. Though it cannot be executed in fact, and though its execution probably will never be seriously attempted, its moral influence will be decided, and purely hurtful. So far as its own purpose is concerned, it is a mere *brutum fulmen*, but it will prove only too effectual for the purposes of the enemy. It is a gigantic usurpation, unrelieved by the promise of a solitary advantage, however minute and faint, but on the contrary aggravated by the menace of great and unmixed evil.

Kentucky cannot and will not acquiesce in this measure. Never! As little will she allow it to chill her devotion to the cause thus cruelly imperilled anew. The Government our fathers framed is one thing, and a thing above price; Abraham Lincoln, the temporary occupant of the Executive chair, is another thing and a thing of comparatively little worth. The one is an individual, the sands of whose official existence are running fast, and who, when his official existence shall end, will be no more or less than any other individual. The other is a grand political structure, in which is contained the treasures and the energies of civilization, and upon whose lofty and shining dome, seen from the shores of all climes, centre the eager hopes of mankind. What Abraham Lincoln, as President, does or fails to do may exalt or lower our estimate of himself, but not of the great and beneficient Government of which he is but the temporary servant. The temple is not the less sacred and precious because the priest lays an unlawful sacrifice upon the altar. The loyalty of Kentucky is not to be shaken by any mad act of the President. If necessary she will resist the act, and aid in holding the actor to a just and lawful accountability, but she will never lift her own hand against the glorious fabric because he has blindly or criminally smitten it. She cannot be so false to herself as this. She is incapable of such guilt and folly.

———

From the Baltimore American

And as to its effects upon the institution in the Border States, it is not at all problematical. If Virginia or North Carolina become Free States by the terms of the proclamation, the exemption resulting to Maryland is of no practical value whatever. With Free States on both sides of her, who would care to own negroes here? and what possible advantage would we have over those obnoxious to the terms of the President's manifesto in other States? As the matter stands even at present negro property here has become so uncertain in its tenure that in many portions of our Commonwealth they are as good as free already.

As to the effects of the proclamation in the most disloyal States, they will amount to little or nothing so far as any hopes of bringing them to terms are concerned. They will be exasperated, it is true; but not to the point of accomplishing any more against the Government than they would do otherwise, because it would seem impossible to add to the rancor they at present exhibit. The State, of all others, where perhaps certain injury may be done by the proclamation is Kentucky; and if there is danger of alienating or dividing the Union sentiment there, it would certainly have been better—even as a mere matter of policy—that it should not have appeared.

That slavery should expect any quarter to be shown it any where after what has occurred, is not the least of the marvels of the times. Exulting in its power in the outset to wage a war of *aggression* against those disposed to "Let it alone," if it would let them alone, let it not be surprised, on failing, to find its antagonists determined to cripple it to that extent that it will never plague the nation more.

But even slavery in the perilous predicament in which it is placed may comfort itself with the reflection that paper proclamations will not overcome its artillery and other means of making war. The proclamation is little to the purpose if the Government finds itself unable to give effect to its provisions and so in the yet untouched strongholds of the institution it may bid—for a yet considerable period—utter defiance to its assailants. It is the practical that must decide its fate at last, since military necessity is apt to bear down all before it when men are foolish enough to invite revolution to their aid for any particular purpose to find at the last that they are unable to control it.

In the South anger ran red at the preliminary Emancipation Proclamation. The Richmond Enquirer said, "What shall we call him?

Coward, assassin, savage, murderer of women and babies? Or shall we consider them all as embodied in the word fiend, and call him Lincoln, the Fiend?" The Richmond Dispatch, Oct. 2, 1862, found that a new resistance would develop.

THE TWIN PROCLAMATIONS

Not content with proclaiming all the negroes of the South free, and inviting them to engage in a war with their masters, the ruler of Yankeedom has issued another proclamation declaring martial law throughout all that interesting region of country. The object of this proclamation it is easy to perceive. The Democratic party has been making powerful demonstrations of late throughout the Yankee States. The signs indicate a desperate struggle with the Abolitionists proper, who now have the entire control of the Government, and the possible subversion of the power which they have hitherto wielded so mercilessly and so disastrously to the cause of humanity and free government. There was but one way to suppress them so thoroughly as to render their success henceforth and forever a matter of utter impossibility. That way was by the sword. The people of Yankeedom are consequently as absolutely the slaves of a military despotism as the Russians or Austrians. For them there is no law but the law military. They are learning, in its full force, the meaning of Julius Caesar's terrible saying, *"inter arma silent leges,"* ("in time of war the laws are silent.") The law, indeed, has no more voice in Yankeedom at this moment than it had in Rome when the whole republic was writhing in the iron grasp of the great Dictator. The courts had as well be closed, if they are not already; for the voice of its victims cannot be heard beyond the walls of the military prison. Lincoln has effected a complete triumph over the Yankee nation. He has set aside its laws and trampled its boasted Constitution under foot. Those who were once his fellow citizens, are now his timid and abject slaves. They scarcely dare whisper opposition to their nearest and dearest friends. John Quincy Adams said, many years ago, that he could drive a wagon through the seams of the Constitution. Lincoln scorns to seek its destruction by any process so slow and so liable to opposition. He annihilates the whole at a blow.—Security to life, security to limb, security to property, the freedom of speech, the liberty of the press—all that renders life worth preserving—all that the fathers of the Revolution thought they had guaranteed by the Constitution—all, all, are swept into nonentity by the mere dash of his pen. History does not record a usurpation so bold, so open, so thoroughly successful. Caesar,

Cromwell, or Bonaparte never attempted a revolution so astounding. Yet Caesar, Cromwell and Bonaparte were among the greatest men that ever lived, and Lincoln is one of the smallest.

It is not difficult to understand the causes which lay at the bottom of Lincoln's unparalleled success. Not Rome, when it had been the sport of contending factions for two hundred years; not England, when it had been the victim of Puritan government for ten years; not France, after it had been successively the foot-ball of a debased nobility and corrupt priesthood, of scheming philosophers and blood-thirsty Jacobins, was half so corrupt as the universal Yankee nation when Lincoln was called to preside over its destinies.—A venal press, and a representation both in Congress and in the State Legislatures that scarcely affected the virtue of common honesty, indicated a people corrupt to the core. An intense love of money pervading all classes had long since stifled all the finer feelings of humanity. As in the days that preceded the French revolution, infidelity had become a part of the national creed. A cold materialism, that acknowledged no worship but the worship of the almighty dollar, had usurped the place of all religion. Added to all this was a hatred of the Southern people, their opposites in every particular, who had always held them in the utmost scorn, and had never been scrupulous in expressing what they felt. They knew their absolute dependence upon the South; they knew that their prosperity, of which they perpetually boasted, was derived entirely from Southern labor. The Union secured to them the fruits of that labor; hence their avarice taught them to value it for what it brought. For the same reason they very naturally opposed the separation of the South, and instigated, in addition, by their hatred, they were prepared to go any lengths to gratify their two ruling passions of avarice and revenge. It is by ministering to these that Lincoln has succeeded so completely in destroying the liberty of that people.

These two proclamations indicate two things which the South ought to bear in mind. The proclamation of martial law removes all difficulty in the way of raising troops. Lincoln, we are told, has signified his determination to swell his ranks to a million. The abolition proclamation means a determination to make a San Domingo of the South. We have this advantage over the inhabitants of that island—they were taken, by surprise; we have had ample warning.

Two "foreign" journals of opinion in the United States—the French Courrier des États-Unis and the British New York Albion—

found the President's emancipation plan contradictory. *Reprinted in the National Intelligencer, Washington, Oct. 8, 1862.*

From the Courrier des Etats-Unis [French organ]

Did Mr. Lincoln really believe that this proclamation would bring back the owners of slaves into the Union by re-assuring to them their property if they return to their allegiance, or by showing them, on the contrary, that their property would be lost if they persist in the idea of a separation? Such must have been his thought, for it seems to be at least the only favorable explanation of which his manifesto admits. In this case we must take into consideration his good intention, without, however, for that reason extenuating the fault he has committed. By whatever name it may be characterized, and whatever point of departure may be assigned to it, the rebellion of the South has now passed far beyond the period when we could hope to see it yield either to a promise or to any menace whatsoever. The Confederacy will simply await the 1st of January without being in any degree moved by the decree of abolition just announced; or rather, in the progress of ideas which the South henceforth will hold, the perspective of this decree will inspire her with redoubled ardor and animosity. In this view, consequently, the Presidential proclamation is either a sword plunged in water or oil cast on the flames. It is therefore impolitic, like every act involving great danger without being counterbalanced by a manifest utility. Will it be pretended that this utility may be sought for in the powerful co-operation which abolition will bring to the Federal arms?

Does the Government at Washington mean to say that from January 1st it will call for a servile war to aid it in the conquest of the South? We refuse to admit so odious a supposition, one which would at the same time be so signal an avowal of impotency. We refuse, above all, to believe Mr. Lincoln and his advisers so blind as not to see that a servile war would prepare for them an issue of two contests instead of one; for, after making the Southern Confederacy swim in the blood of the whites shed by the hands of the slaves, it would be necessary to drown the negro revolt in the blood of the slaves themselves. Madmen may look this double barbarity in the face without horror, but the chief of Executive power, who proclaims each day that his sole object is the re-establishment of the Constitution and the salvation of the country, cannot surely dream of the reconstruction of the Union upon such a pedestal of ruin and dead bodies.

Nevertheless, in rejecting this fearful explanation, we seek in vain any other reason for the measure announced by Mr. Lincoln. It is evidently not an absolute principle which inspires him, since, far from striking at the root of the institution of slavery, he, on the contrary, reaffirms its constitutional legitimacy. He goes even further; he offers the protection of the Government as bounty and recompense to all slaveholders who will range themselves under his flag. He admits slavery wherever it will abide under the shadow of the starry banner; he only menaces it when met under the folds of another standard. It is, then, clearly a means of war which he seeks; and abolitionism in his hands is not the proclamation of human liberty; it is simply a weapon to which he has recourse against his enemies. We do not know whether the idea of influencing the mind of Europe in favor of the Federal cause may have had some weight in the drawing up of this fatal manifesto; but, if so, the error has been great, and great will be the deception.

The men in Europe who still hold to the famous axiom, "perish the country, rather than a principle," would perhaps blindly applaud a general and radical decree of abolition, but they would be the first to stigmatize a partial emancipation inspired solely by the need of seeking amongst the liberated slaves auxiliaries in a work of blood. If Mr. Lincoln wished to act on principle, he should repudiate the institution of slavery wherever it exists; if he wished to act with policy, he should abstain from menacing it at all. In trying to steer between these two inflexible alternatives he has committed an act which is neither that of a man of solid conviction nor of a statesman. Once more he has allowed himself to be led astray by the sad habit which the contests of party have made a second nature with him, and which consists in bringing to the government of the whole country the same expedients for keeping an equilibrium as suffice for the management of an electoral convention.

God grant that this error may not produce new convulsions ten times more terrible still than those which already rend the country!

From the N.Y. Albion [British organ]

This is general emancipation held in *terrorem* over the South, if it does not return to its allegiance before New Year's day, with a broad hint to the negroes that they are at liberty to cut their masters' or mistresses' throats, if there be any hesitation about the matter.

As for Europe, it is a ludicrous delusion to imagine that any sentimental effect will be produced by the tardy adoption of a sliding scale principle. It does not need the sarcasm of a Times, or the malignity of a Saturday Review, to point out the hollowness of a policy that is made contingent on dates. If the South be beaten and submit in ninety-eight days, slavery is the law of the land; if the operation requires ninety-nine days to effect it throroughly, emancipation takes its place! Again, if from the sentimentality of Exeter Hall you turn to the interested views predominant at the Tuileries, what follows? Is intervention rendered less probable, inasmuch as, to difficulty in procuring cotton, might succeed a total cessation in producing it? Is the universal confusion which would ensue upon sudden emancipation, and the consequent abandonment of all hopes of a supply, a very tempting prospect for those who are looking anxiously for the hour when peace—not anarchy—shall be proclaimed? Never believe it.

We will hold that nothing can or will induce British intervention; but if Great Britain were ruled and moved to action by the principles attributed to her by most American writers of to-day, the receipt of President Lincoln's emancipation edict would be the signal for an abandonment of neutrality.

The Times of London thundered against Lincoln's proclamation for what it considered too hasty action. "We do not think that even now, when Mr. Lincoln plays his last card, it will prove to be a trump," said The Times, Oct. 7, 1862—an analogy which Punch, the British satirical weekly, made the subject of a drawing and poem.

It is rarely that a man can be found to balance accurately mischief to another against advantage to himself. President LINCOLN is, as the world says, a good-tempered man, neither better nor worse than the mass of his kind—neither a fool nor a sage, neither a villain nor a saint, but a piece of that common useful clay out of which it delights the American democracy to make great Republican personages. Yet President LINCOLN has declared that from the 1st of January next to come every State that is in rebellion shall be in the eye of Mr. LINCOLN a Free State. After that date Mr. LINCOLN proposes to enact that every slave in a rebel State shall be for ever after free, and he promises that neither he, nor his army, nor his navy will do anything to repress any efforts which the negroes in such rebel States may make for the recovery of their freedom. This means, of course, that Mr. LINCOLN will, on the 1st of next January, do his best to excite a servile war in the States which he cannot occupy with his arms. He will run up the rivers in his gunboats; he will seek out the places which are left but slightly guarded, and where the women and children have been trusted to the fidelity of coloured domestics. He will appeal to the black blood of the African; he will whisper of the pleasures of spoil and of the gratification of yet fiercer instincts; and when blood begins to flow and shrieks come piercing through the darkness, Mr. LINCOLN will wait till the rising flames tell that all is consummated, and then he will rub his hands and think that revenge is sweet. This is what Mr. LINCOLN avows before the world that he is about to do. Now, we are in Europe thoroughly convinced that the death of slavery must follow as necessarily upon the success of the Confederates in this war as the dispersion of darkness occurs upon the rising of the sun; but sudden and forcible emancipation resulting from "the efforts the negroes may make for their actual freedom" can only be effected by massacre and utter destruction. Mr. LINCOLN avows, therefore, that he proposes to excite the negroes of the Southern plantations to murder the families of their masters while these are engaged in the war. The conception of such a crime is horrible. The employment of Indians sinks to a level with civilized warfare in comparison with it; the most detestable doctrines of MAZZINI are almost less atrocious; even Mr. LINCOLN's own recent achievements of burning by gunboats the defenceless villages on the Mississippi are dwarfed by this gigantic wickedness. The single thing to be said for it is that it is a wickedness that holds his head high and scorns hypocrisy. It does not pretend to attack slavery as slavery. It launches this threat of a servile rebellion as a means of war against certain States, and accompanies it with a declaration of general protection to all other slavery.

Where he has no power Mr. LINCOLN will set the negroes free; where he regains power he will consider them as slaves. "Come to me," he cries to the insurgent planters, "and I will preserve your rights as slaveholders; but set me still at defiance, and I will wrap myself in virtue and take the sword of freedom in my hand, and, instead of aiding you to oppress, I will champion the rights of humanity. Here are whips for you who are loyal; go forth and flog or sell your black chattels as you please. Here are torches and knives for employment against you who are disloyal; I will press them into every black hand, and teach their use." Little Delaware, with her 2,000 slaves, shall still be protected in her loyal tyranny. Maryland, with her 90,000 slaves, shall "freely accept or freely reject" any project for either gradual or immediate abolition; but if Mississippi and

South Carolina, where the slaves rather outnumber the masters, do not repent, and receive from Mr. LINCOLN a licence to trade in human flesh, that human flesh shall be adopted by Mr. LINCOLN as the agent of his vengeance. The position is peculiar for a mere layman. Mr. LINCOLN, by this proclamation, constitutes himself a sort of moral American Pope. He claims to sell indulgences to own votaries, and he offers them with full hands to all who will fall down and worship him. It is his to bind, and it is his to loose. His decree of emancipation is to go into remote States, where his temporal power cannot be made manifest, and where no stars and stripes are to be seen; and in those distant swamps he is, by a sort of Yankee excommunication, to lay the land under a slavery interdict.

What will the South think of this? The South will answer with a hiss of scorn. But what will the North think of it? What will Pennsylvania say—Pennsylvania, which is already unquiet under the loss of her best customers, and not easy under the absolute despotism of the present Government at Washington? What Boston may say or think is not, perhaps, of much consequence. But what will New York say? It would not answer the purpose of any of these cities to have the South made a howling wilderness. They want the handling of the millions which are produced by the labour of the black man. Pennsylvania desires to sell her manufactures in the South; New York wishes to be again broker, banker, and merchant to the South. This is what the Union means to these cities. They would rather have a live independent State to deal with than a dead dependency where nothing could be earnt. To these practical persons President LINCOLN would be, after his black revolution had succeeded, like a dogstealer who should present the anxious owner with the head of his favourite pointer. They want the useful creature alive. The South without its cotton and its sugar and its tobacco would be of small use to New York, or even to Philadelphia; and the South without the produce of its rice and cotton, and its sugar and tobacco, would be but a sorry gain, even if it could be obtained. If President LINCOLN wants such a conquest as this, the North is, perhaps, yet strong enough to conquer Hayti. A few fanatics, of course, will shout, but we cannot think that, except in utter desperation and vindictiveness, any real party in the North will applaud this nefarious resolution to light up a servile war in the distant homesteads of the South.

As a proof of what the leaders of the North, in their passion and their despair, would do if they could, this is a very sad document. As a proof of the hopelessness and recklessness which prompt their actions, it is a very instructive document. But it is not a formidable document. We gather from it that Mr. LINCOLN has lost all hope of preserving the Union, and is now willing to let any quack try his nostrum. As an act of policy it is, if possible, more contemptible than it is wicked. It may possibly produce some partial risings, for let any armed power publish an exhortation to the labouring class of any community to plunder and murder, and there will be some response. It might happen in London, or Paris, or New York. That Mr. LINCOLN's emancipation decrees will have any general effect bearing upon the issue of the war we do not, however, believe. The negroes have already abundantly discovered that the tender mercies of the Northerners are cruelties. The freedom which is associated with labour in the trenches, military discipline, and frank avowals of personal abhorrence momentarily repeated does not commend itself to the negro nature. General BUTLER could, if he pleased, tell strange stories of the ill success of his tamperings with the negroes about New Orleans. We do not think that even now, when Mr. LINCOLN plays his last card, it will prove to be a trump. Powerful malignity is a dreadful reality, but impotent malignity is apt to be a very contemptible spectacle. Here is a would-be conqueror and a would-be extirpator who is not quite safe in his seat of government, who is reduced to such straits that he accepts a defeat as a glorious escape, a capitulation of 8,000 men as an unimportant event, a drawn battle as a glorious victory, and the retreat of an invading army which retires laden with plunder and rich in stores as a deliverance. Here is a President who has just, against his will, supplied his antagonists with a hundred and twenty guns and millions of stores, and who is trembling for the very ground on which he stands. Yet, if we judged only by his pompous proclamations, we should believe that he had a garrison in every city of the South. This is more like a Chinaman beating his two swords together to frighten his enemy than like an earnest man pressing on his cause in steadfastness and truth.

Some sages in Britain were saying that people in one lifetime would be able to see both the Revolution and dissolution of the United States. Punch, Oct. 18, 1862, rubbed it in gleefully in this poem accompanying the Tenniel drawing, "Abe Lincoln's Last Card."

ABE'S LAST CARD; OR, ROUGE-ET-NOIR

BRAG's our game: and awful losers
We've been on the Red.
Under and above the table,

Awfully we've bled.
Ne'er a stake have we adventured,
    But we've lost it still,
From Bull's Run and mad Manassas,
    Down to Sharpsburg Hill.

When luck's desperate, desperate venture
    Still may bring it back:
So I'll chance it—neck or nothing—
    Here I lead THE BLACK!
If I win, the South must pay for't,
    Pay in fire and gore:
If I lose, I'm ne'er a dollar
    Worse off than before.

From the Slaves of Southern rebels
    Thus I strike the chain:
But the slaves of loyal owners
    Still shall slaves remain.
If their owners like to wop 'em,
    They to wop are masters;
Or if they prefer to swop 'em,
    Here are our shin-plasters!

There! If that 'ere Proclamation
    Does its holy work.
Rebeldom's annihilation
    It did oughter work:
Back to Union, and you're welcome
    Each to wop his nigger:
If not at White let slip darky
    Guess I call that vigour!

The Atlantic Monthly, November 1862 issue, ran an unsigned
article called "The President's Proclamation." The author was Ralph
Waldo Emerson, whose essays helped to form the thought of literary
America. The Atlantic Monthly was founded in Boston in 1857 and
named by Oliver Wendell Holmes. Emerson's name appeared in the
Table of Contents. His essay reflected the favorable attitude of The
Atlantic toward Lincoln's acts.

THE PRESIDENT'S PROCLAMATION
[BY RALPH WALDO EMERSON]

In so many arid forms which States incrust themselves with, once in a century, if so often, a poetic act and record occur. These are the jets of thought into affairs, when, roused by danger or inspired by genius, the political leaders of the day break the else insurmountable routine of class and local legislation, and take a step forward in the direction of catholic and universal interests. Every step in the history of political liberty is a sally of the human mind into the untried future, and has the interest of genius, and is fruitful in heroic anecdotes. Liberty is a slow fruit. It comes, like religion, for short periods, and in rare conditions, as if awaiting a culture of the race whch shall make it organic and permanent. Such moments of expansion in modern history were the Confession of Augsburg, the plantation of America, the English Commonwealth of 1648, the Declaration of American Independence in 1776, the British emancipation of slaves in the West Indies, the passage of the Reform Bill, the repeal of the Corn-Laws, the Magnetic Ocean-Telegraph, though yet imperfect, the passage of the Homestead Bill in the last Congress, and now, eminently, President Lincoln's Proclamation on the twenty-second of September. These are acts of great scope, working on a long future, and on permanent interests, and honoring alike those who initiate and those who receive them. These measures provoke no noisy joy, but are received into a sympathy so deep as to apprise us that mankind are greater and better than we know. At such times it appears as if a new public were created to greet the new event. It is as when an orator, having ended the compliments and pleasantries with which he conciliated attention, and having run over the superficial fitness and commodities of the measure he urges, suddenly, lending himself to some happy inspiration, announces with vibrating voice the grand human principles involved,—the bravoes and wits who greeted him loudly thus far are surprised and overawed; a new audience is found in the heart of the assembly,—an audience hitherto passive and unconcerned, now at last so searched and kindled that they come forward, every one a representative of mankind, standing for all nationalities.

The extreme moderation with which the President advanced to his design,—his long-avowed expectant policy, as if he chose to be strictly the executive of the best public sentiment of the country, waiting only till it should be unmistakably pronounced,—so fair a mind that none ever listened so patiently to such extreme variations of opinion,—so reticent that his decision has taken all parties by surprise, whilst yet it is the just sequel of his prior acts,—the firm tone in which he announces it, without inflation or surplusage,—all these have bespoken such favor to the act, that, great as the popularity of the President has been, we are beginning to think that we have underestimated the capacity and virtue which the Divine Providence has made an instrument of benefit so vast. He has been permitted to do more for America than any other American man. He is well entitled to the most indulgent construction. Forget all that we thought shortcomings, every mistake, every delay. In the extreme embarrassments of his part, call these endurance, wisdom, magnanimity, illuminated, as they now are, by this dazzling success.

When we consider the immense opposition that has been neutralized or converted by the progress of the war, (for it is not long since the President anticipated the resignation of a large number of officers in the army, and the secession of three States, on the promulgation of this policy,)—when we see how the great stake which foreign nations hold in our affairs has recently brought every European power as a client into this court, and it became every day more apparent what gigantic and what remote interests were to be affected by the decision of the President,—one can hardly say the deliberation was too long. Against all timorous counsels he had the courage to seize the moment; and such was his position, and such the felicity attending the action, that he has replaced Government in the good graces of mankind. "Better is virtue in the sovereign than plenty in the season," say the Chinese. 'T is wonderful what power is, and how ill it is used, and how its ill use makes life mean, and the sunshine dark. Life in America had lost much of its attraction in the later years. The virtues of a good magistrate undo a world of mischief, and, because Nature works with rectitude, seem vastly more potent than the acts of bad governors, which are ever tempered by the good-nature in the people, and the incessant resistance which fraud and violence encounter. The acts of good governors work at a geometrical ratio, as one midsummer day seems to repair the damage of a year of war.

A day which most of us dared not hope to see, an event worth the dreadful war, worth its costs and uncertainties, seems now to be close before us. October, November, December will have passed over beating hearts and plotting brains: then the hour will strike, and all men of African descent who have faculty enough to find their way to our lines are assured of the protection of American law.

It is by no means necessary that this measure should be suddenly marked by any signal results on the negroes or on the Rebel masters. The force of the act is that it commits the country to this justice,—that it compels the innumerable officers, civil, military, naval, of the Republic to range themselves on the line of this equity. It draws the fashion to this side. It is not a measure that admits of being taken back. Done, it cannot be undone by a new Administration. For slavery overpowers the disgust of the moral sentiment only through immemorial usage. It cannot be introduced as an improvement of the nineteenth century. This act makes that the lives of our heroes have not been sacrificed in vain. It makes a victory of our defeats. Our hurts are healed; the health of the nation is repaired. With a victory like this, we can stand many disasters. It does not promise the redemption of the black race: that lies not with us: but it relieves it of our opposition. The President by this act has paroled all the slaves in America; they will no more fight against us; and it relieves our race once for all of its crime and false position. The first condition of success is secured in putting ourselves right. We have recovered ourselves from our false position, and planted ourselves on a law of Nature.

> "If that fail,
> The pillared firmament is rottenness,
> And earth's base built on stubble."

The Government has assured itself of the best constituency in the world: every spark of intellect, every virtuous feeling, every religious heart, every man of honor, every poet, every philosopher, the generosity of the cities, the health of the country, the strong arms of the mechanics, the endurance of farmers, the passionate conscience of women, the sympathy of distant nations,—all rally to its support.

Of course, we are assuming the firmness of the policy thus declared. It must not be a paper proclamation. We confide that Mr. Lincoln is in earnest, and, as he has been slow in making up his mind, has resisted the importunacy of parties and of events to the latest moment, he will be as absolute in his adhesion. Not only will he repeat and follow up his stroke, but the nation will add its irresistible strength. If the ruler has duties, so has the citizen. In times like these, when the nation is imperilled, what man can, without shame, receive good news from day to day, without giving good news of himself? What right has any one to read in the journals tidings of victories, if he has not bought them by his own valor, treasure, personal sacrifice, or by service as good in his own department? With this blot removed from our national honor, this heavy load lifted off the national heart, we shall not fear henceforward to show our faces among mankind. We shall cease to be hypocrites and pretenders, but what we have styled our free institutions will be such. . . . Whilst we have pointed out the opportuneness of the Proclamation, it remains to be said that the President had no choice. He might look wistfully for what variety of courses lay open to him: every line but one was closed up with fire. This one, too, bristled with danger, but through it was the sole safety. The measure he has adopted was imperative. It is wonderful to see the unseasonable senility of what is called the Peace party, through all its masks, blinding their eyes to the main feature of the war, namely, its inevitableness. The war existed long before the cannonade of Sumter, and could not be postponed. It might have begun otherwise or elsewhere, but war was in the minds and bones of the combatants, it was written on the iron leaf, and you might as easily dodge gravitation. If we had consented to a peaceable secession of the Rebels, the divided sentiment of the Border States made peaceable secession impossible, the insatiable temper of the South made it impossible, and the slaves on the border, wherever the border might be, were an incessant fuel to rekindle the fire. Give the Confederacy New Orleans, Charleston, and Richmond, and they would have demanded St. Louis and Baltimore. Give them these, and they would have insisted on Washington. Give them Washington, and they would have assumed the army and navy, and, through these, Philadelphia, New York, and Boston. It looks as if the battle-field would have been at least as large in that event as it is now. The war was formidable, but could not be avoided. The war was and is an immense mischief, but brought with it the immense benefit of drawing a line, and rallying the Free States to fix it impassably,—preventing the whole force of Southern connection and influence throughout the North from distracting every city with endless confusion, detaching that force and reducing it to handfuls, and, in the progress of hostilities, disinfecting us of our habitual proclivity, throuh the affection of trade, and the traditions of the Democratic party, to follow Southern leading. . . .

. . . And the aim of the war on our part is indicated by the aim of the President's Proclamation, namely, to break up the false combination of Southern society, to destroy the piratic feature in it which makes it our enemy only as it is the enemy of the human race, and so allow its reconstruction on a just and healthful basis. Then new affinities will act, the old repulsions will cease, and, the cause of war being removed, Nature and trade may be trusted to establish a lasting peace.

We think we cannot overstate the wisdom and benefit of this act of the Government. The malignant cry of the Secession press within the

Free States, and the recent action of the Confederate Congress, are decisive as to its efficiency and correctness of aim. Not less so is the silent joy which has greeted it in all generous hearts, and the new hope it has breathed into the world. It was well to delay the steamers at the wharves, until this edict could be put on board. It will be an insurance to the ship as it goes plunging through the sea with glad tidings to all people. Happy are the young who find the pestilence cleansed out of the earth, leaving open to them an honest career. Happy the old, who see Nature purified before they depart. Do not let the dying die: hold them back to this world, until you have charged their ear and heart with this message to other spiritual societies, announcing the melioration of our planet.

"Incertainties now crown themselves assured,
And Peace proclaims olives of endless age."

Meantime that ill-fated, much-injured race which the Proclamation respects will lose somewhat of the dejection sculptured for ages in their bronzed countenance, uttered in the wailing of their plaintive music,— a race naturally benevolent, joyous, docile, industrious, and whose very miseries sprang from their great talent for usefulness, which, in a more moral age, will not only defend their independence, but will give them a rank among nations.

Lincoln's annual December message to Congress came a month before the scheduled time for full emancipation. He still nurtured his "legal" plan of compensated emancipation, but he was not adamant. "In giving freedom to the slave," he said in the message, "we assure freedom to the free—honorable alike in what we give, and what we preserve." The National Intelligencer of Washington, Dec. 2, 1862, found the President's address moderate.

THE PRESIDENT'S MESSAGE

The reader will find in another part of to-day's Intelligencer the Message of the President of the United States, which was yesterday communicated to Congress.

Never has such a paper been delivered to the National Legislature under auspices so grave, and rarely, if ever, has one been awaited with equal solicitude by the people of the country, who are in the habit of looking to these Presidential expositions for a forecast of the purposes and policy which will guide the Executive Department of the Government. And such expositions, if interesting at all times, become greatly more important at the present day, when, in the conduct of a Titanic war, the President is called to deal with problems and to discharge duties which give to his functions such an enlarged sphere of activity and such an increase of power.

It will not be expected that we should enter to-day upon any detailed analysis, still less upon any critical appreciation of the Message. These we reserve for another day, when we shall have had opportunity to weigh more carefully the views of the President, which, it will be perceived, are expressed with a deliberation, and at the same time with an earnestness, which bespeak the presence of strong convictions.

We cannot omit to state, however, that the document, in the cursory perusal we have been able to give it, has left upon our minds no other than a favorable impression, especially if regard be had to the spirit and temper in which it is conceived, and in these respects it is safe to say that the paper, by its admirable prudence, must equally disappoint the wishes and the fears that have been entertained by different classes of citizens in advance of its publication.

No reader can fail to be struck with the force of the geographical argument, as stated by the President, against the policy or the possibility of any permanent separation of the States now embraced in the Union. And the conservative power—a power especially conservative of the Union—which he finds in the position and the economical necessities of the great mediterranean region of our continent, must give new heart and hope to all who, amid the agitations of the present time, refuse to believe in other than "one country, one Constitution, and one destiny" for the people of our distracted land.

The chief interest of the Message will naturally be found by every reader in that portion which treats on the relations of slavery. To this the President has evidently given a consideration at once elaborate and earnest. The merely incidental manner in which he refers to the Proclamation of last September 22d, especially when taken in connexion with the expansion he has given to his favorite project for "compensated emancipation," sufficiently indicates the direction in which he looks for a beneficent melioration in the condition of the African race now held in bondage. It is impossible to read what he has written under this head without feeling respect for his candor and his patriotic inspirations, however much the

329

reader may dissent from the practicability of the plan which he urges upon the adoption of Congress and the acceptance of the country. But if no immediate good is destined to result from the recommendation of the President's plan for ending the war by providing for the peaceful and gradual extinction of slavery, the tolerant and conciliatory spirit in which he discusses its details cannot be regarded as other than an omen of good by the friends of the Union, among whom, as the President says, "there is a great diversity of sentiment and policy in regard to slavery." In seeking to arbitrate among these diversities of honest convictions he gives a proof of practical statesmanship, which, in the spirit it manifests, is hopeful beyond the letter of the plan he expounds. And if it be true, as the President says, that, because of these diversities, we waste much strength in struggles among ourselves, he has certainly, by his example, invited the patriotic of all opinions to practise that "mutual concession" by which "we should harmonize and act together." This, he adds, "would be compromise, but it would be compromise among the friends and not with the enemies of the Union." We hope that the censorious and exacting of every class will learn to emulate the President's moderation in this respect.

Lincoln issued the Emancipation Proclamation on Jan. 1, 1863, true to his promise. "I do order and declare that all persons held as slaves within said designated States, and parts of States, are, and henceforward shall be free," Lincoln said. "And upon this act, sincerely believed to be an act of justice, warranted by the Constitution, upon military necessity, I invoke the considerate judgment of mankind, and the gracious favor of Almighty God." In Lincoln's Springfield, the Illinois Journal on Jan. 6, 1863, commented: "This great man, whom it is not extravagant to say is God-like in his moral attributes, child-like in the simplicity and purity of his character, and yet manly and self-relying in his high and patriotic purpose—this man who takes no step backward— let him consummate the grandest achievement ever allotted to man, the destruction of American slavery." Abroad, the London Times, Jan. 15, 1863, argued—diplomatically but ambiguously—for emancipation, yet against Lincoln.

It would seem that in the interval which has elapsed between the battle of Fredericksburg and the commencement of the new year the advocates of more conciliatory and more violent counsels have fairly fought their battle out, and that victory has declared in favour of the latter. Mr. LINCOLN has finally adhered to the policy from which he showed at one moment some inclination to draw back. He has kept his promise to the very letter; he has declared the negroes in the States now at open war with the North free, except within certain districts occupied by the Federal forces, and has pledged the Government of the United States to recognize and support the freedom so granted by their naval and military force. From this Proclamation Missouri, Tennessee, Kentucky, and Maryland are exempt; so that it would seem to be the policy of the PRESIDENT to interpose an isthmus of slavery between the two masses of free States which are to extend to the North and South of it. Pronounced under other circumstances, by another person, and at another time, such a Proclamation might well excite once more the enthusiasm which penetrated the whole mind of England in the days of WILBERFORCE and CLARKSON. We should most unfeignedly rejoice were the words to which the PRESIDENT has given utterance capable of carrying with them their own fulfilment. To slavery we have ever entertained the most rooted aversion. Not all the valour, not all the success of the South, has ever blinded us to this black spot on their fair escocheon. But even tainted as they are with this foul stain they have commanded our admiration and our sympathy from the gallantry with which they have maintained their cause, and from the obvious truth that the struggle was for separation on the one part and compulsory retention on the other, the emancipation or continued slavery of the negro being only used as means to forward the ends of the North. While it was supposed that the South could be brought back by giving every security for the continuance of slavery, the North never dreamt of emancipation. When it was found that no such conciliation was possible, the North, as a weapon of war, and not as a concession to principle, has finally decided on emancipation. That this measure is no homage to principle or conviction, but merely a means of raising up a domestic enemy against the Southerners in the midst of the Southern States, is abundantly proved from the fact that slavery, so odious in Alabama, is tolerated in Kentucky. Its abolition is a punishment to rebels; its retention is a reward to patriots; it is not the accursed thing to be rooted out at all hazards. Its abolition is the punishment of rebellion; its retention is the reward of adherence to the Union.

Still, though there is little homage to principle in the PRESIDENT's Proclamation, any attempt on the part of the American Government, however tardily, reluctantly, and partially made, to emancipate any portion of the negro race, must have an effect on the opinion of mankind, and tend to what we have never doubted would in some way or other be the final result of this war, the abolition of slavery. But our exultation is by no means without misgivings. The PRESIDENT has proclaimed freedom, but he is without power to enforce his Proclamation. Except in the neighbourhood of New Orleans, where General BUTLER has already done all that is possible to create a servile war, the PRESIDENT of the United States has no power whatever to enforce his Proclamation. If the blacks are to obtain the freedom he promises them, it must be by their own hands. They must rise upon a more numerous, more intelligent, better armed, and braver community of whites, and exterminate them, their wives, and children, by fire and sword. The PRESIDENT of the United States may summon them to this act, but he is powerless to assist them in its execution. Nay, this is the very reason why they are summoned. The armies of the South have gained a clear superiority over the armies of the North, and it is to redress this balance that the negro, burning, ravishing, massacring, and destroying, is summoned to the conflict. If these things are not done at all, there will be, for the present at least, no emancipation; if they are done, they will provoke retaliatory action, which is but too likely to end in the extermination of their perpetrators. In neither case has the friend of humanity any cause to rejoice. It must also be remembered that this act of the PRESIDENT, if it purposed to strike off the fetters of one race, is a flagrant attack on the liberties of another. The attempt to free the blacks is a flagrant attack on the liberties of the whites. Nothing can be more unconstitutional, more illegal, more entirely subversive of the compact on which the American Confederacy rests, than the claim set up by the PRESIDENT to interfere with the laws of individual States by his Proclamation, unless, indeed, it be the attempt of Congress to dismember the ancient State of Virginia, and create a new State upon its ruins. It is preposterous to say that war gives these powers; they are the purest usurpation, and, though now used against the enemies of the Union, are full of evil presage for the liberties of the States that still adhere to it. It is true that the PRESIDENT advises the negroes to abstain from all violence except in self-defence, and to labour for reasonable wages. But the PRESIDENT well knows that not a slaveholder in the South will obey his Proclamation, that it can only be enforced by violence, and that if the negroes obtain freedom it will be by the utter destruction of their masters. In such a state of society to speak of wages—that is, of a contract between master and servant—is a cruel mockery. In the South the negro can only exist apart from his master by a return to the savage state—a state in which, amid blood and anarchy and desolation, he may frequently regret the fetters he has broken, and even the master whom he has destroyed. He cannot hope for a better situation than that of his race in the North—

a situation of degradation, humiliation, and destitution which leaves the slave very little to envy. Mr. LINCOLN bases his act on military necessity, and invokes the considerate judgment of mankind and the judgment of ALMIGHTY GOD. He has characterized his own act; mankind will be slow to believe that an act avowedly the result of military considerations has been dictated by a sincere desire for the benefit of those who, under the semblance of emancipation, are thus marked out for destruction, and HE who made man in His own image can scarcely, we may presume to think, look with approbation on a measure which, under the pretence of emancipation, intends to reduce the South to the frightful condition of St. Domingo.

In the meanwhile the PRESIDENT, who is thus lavish of the lives and fortunes of blacks and whites, seems to find no release from the ill-success which for the last eight months has so unremittingly pursued his arms. Affairs in the South-west are assuming an aspect more and more serious every day. The operation which we anticipated a few days ago—that of a movement by the Confederates at Fredericksburg on the right flank of the Federal forces—has taken place, and the indefatigable General STUART has seized on the telegraph, and intercepted valuable information by that means from the War Department at Washington. A desperate battle has taken place between the two armies in Tennessee, the account of which bears a very ominous resemblance to a Federal defeat. The Federals have been repulsed in several attacks on the fortress of Vicksburg, on the Mississippi. Surely these things should be enough to make the PRESIDENT reflect on the desperate course he is pursuing. In the midst of violent party divisions, in ostentatious contempt of the Constitution, with the most signal ill-success in war, he is persisting in the attempt to conquer a nation, to escape whose victorious arms is the only triumph which his Generals seem capable of gaining. Every consideration of patriotism and policy calls upon him to put an end to the hopeless contest, but he considers the ruin is not deep enough nor the bloodshed plentiful enough, and so he calls to his aid the execrable expedient of a servile insurrection. Egypt is destroyed, but his heart is hardened, and he will not let the people go.

Chapter 8

Commander-in-Chief

JANUARY 1863–JUNE 1864

Between the Emancipation Proclamation on Jan. 1, 1863, and his renomination for a second term on June 8, 1864, Lincoln exercised his Constitutionally given duty of Commander-in-Chief—to a greater degree than any other President. "McClellan has the slows," Lincoln put it quaintly while waiting for the egotistical commander of the Army of the Potomac to get cracking. The search for a general who would fight with audacity and without excuses continued into 1864 until Lincoln finally found his man in Grant.

The Emancipation and its effects were intertwined with the military situation. Lincoln called early for the use of colored troops in spite of the prejudices against the Negro in many quarters—the Cabinet, the Generals, the Copperhead press. Between Emancipation and the end of the war 180,000 Negroes enlisted and fought under the Union flag—"brave in action, patient under dangerous and heavy labors, and cheerful amid hardships and privations." Grant supported Lincoln on the use of colored troops: "By arming the Negro," he wrote to Lincoln, "we have added a powerful ally. They will make good soldiers, and taking them from the enemy weakens him in the same proportion they strengthen us."

For Lincoln and the Union troops high moments were to come. Lee was repulsed at Gettysburg, and the day was to be consecrated in a few appropriate remarks. Contrary to legend, the Gettysburg address, said The New York Times, was followed by "long continued applause." The military draft, amnesty and reconstruction and the Union Army turning the tide—these affairs commanded the attention of the President before renomination.

In the South, the Commander in Chief of the United States was called the "Dictator" who ruled "Doodle-land." There were forebodings of decisive military actions in the summer and fall. This editorial appeared in the Southern Illustrated News, Richmond, March 14, 1863.

THE TIMES

March, true to its reputation, comes in like a lion, literally and politically. Lincoln is made Dictator of all the North, and vested with full power of the purse and the sword. Loud are the blusterings of Yankee papers over this downfall of the last vestige of American liberty. With three millions of men and billions of "greenbacks," the Great Rebellion is to be not only crushed, but "pulverized." Pulverized is a very terrible word—equal to the rattling of the largest Chinese gong—but it may not be inadmissible to remark, that a people who have stood two years of crushing, are just the people to relish two or more years of pulverizing. From Europe the breezes blow as coldly as from the North. The English Parliament has assembled, the Queen's Address has been read, and all the great guns have spoken, and all, even our so-called special friend, Lord Derby, unite in the determination to adhere to England's policy of strict neutrality. The effect of this unanimous expression of British sentiment upon France remains to be seen. It will probably delay action on the part of the Emperor, and postpone indefinitely our recognition. Yankeedom will be delighted beyond bounds; the work of·pulverizing will go on with renewed vigor, and—we shall have to whip our way out of the vast network of difficulties that surrounds us. . . .

Next in importance to the news from Doodle-land and from Europe, is the unpleasant tidings which comes to us from all parts of the Confederacy in regard to the scarcity of food. Beyond a doubt, we shall be at a loss for meats before the year is over. Bread, the staff of life, we shall have, and in a few months Spring vegetables will come in freely; but looking to the future, we foresee that unless our farmers and planters put forth their utmost endeavors, there will be something like a famine in the land. It is strange that legislation should be needed in a case like this. None would be if there were no impressments, and no Yankee souls in Southern bodies. The question is very simple. We are to be exterminated or made the slaves of the most loathesome of the human species, or we are to conquer and become the wealthiest and best of modern nations. Five or ten times our number of infuriated Yankees are to be hurled against us during the coming Summer and Fall, our own slaves are to be turned against us, and in all the world there is no genuine sympathy and aid for us; yet in this dreadful hour, when every atom of physical force in the Confederacy is needed, and every man of sense knows there can be no human force without adequate food, men are found mean enough to debate whether they ought or ought not to plant cotton and tobacco. If Mr. Davis were, like Lincoln, a Dictator, such men would be hanged instantly; but we being a free people, and intending to remain free alike of Davis and Lincoln, have one only certain recourse, and that is to make food as remunerative to the farmer, or more so, than cotton or tobacco. But wherever a patriot or a true lover of his liberty and rights is found, there will be no need for an appeal to the sordid impulses of cupidity. All such will strain every nerve to supply the deficiency of food—impelled thereto partly by the common sense which teaches them that the sustenance of the army is the maintenance of liberty, but mainly by the warm impulse of the heart, which needs not the instruction of self-interest. He alone is patriot in this gloomy hour, who discards all thoughts of present pecuniary emolument in the grand and noble hope of supplying those sinews of war, which, in God's good time, will bring what wealth can never buy—the proud inheritance of freedom, and the unconquerable love of freedom to ourselves, our children and our children's children.

Yankee papers report that the famous "cut-off" opposite Vicksburg is complete, that the gun-boats have all passed through, and that hob is to be played generally in the vicinity of Port Hudson. On the same authority we learn that our privateers, the Florida and the Retribution, have been gobbling up Yankee merchantmen at a frightful rate. A whaler that had the temerity to attack the Retribution is said to have been sunk with all on board. We also learn that Dictator Lincoln has begun his career of supreme power by seizing all the arms, private and public, in New York city—a good beginning, which we trust will have a bad ending. Peace movements and speeches are reported in this and that Yankee State, but they are all bosh. Such attempts to disturb the tyranny at Washington will end ignominiously, unless we of the South back them up with a number of truly great victories.

The welfare of the Indians and their position during the Civil War occupied Lincoln's attention in all four of his annual messages to Congress. In his third annual Lincoln said, "Sound policy and our imperative duty to these [Indian] wards of the government demand our anxious and constant attention to their material well-being, to their progress in the arts of civilization." The Lawrence Republican, Kansas, April 9, 1863, reprinted the Missouri Democrat on an Indian delegation visiting Lincoln.

"BIG INJUNS" AT THE WHITE HOUSE

The delegation of Indian chiefs which passed through here a few weeks ago, toward Washington, have had an interview with the President, which the correspondent of the *Missouri Democrat* thus describes:

The delegations of Indian chiefs from the Western plains, under the charge of Commissioner Dole, were introduced to the President at the White House yesterday. The Cheyennes were represented by Lean Bear, War Bonnet and Standing Water; the Kiowas by Yellow Buffalo, Lone Wolf, Yellow Wolf, White Bull and Little Heart; the Arapahoes by Spotted Wolf and Nevah; the Comanches by Pricked Forehead and Ten Bears; the Apaches by Poor Bear, and the Caddoes by Jacob. As the interpreter called out their names they each successively advanced and gave the President a hearty shake of the hand. This through, the President informed them that if they had anything to say he would be pleased to hear them. Lean Bear, the Chief orator, then essayed to make a speech, but not being able to bear the unaccustomed sight of majesty, he was compelled to lean on a chair for support to his trembling knees. He made loud protestations of friendship for the whites, after he got going, in true Indian style, and delicately reminded the "Great Chief of the White People" that being very rich and Indian very poor, he would be able to do something handsome for them, and especially to send them back home as soon as possible. Others followed in the same strain. The President then replied: "You have all spoken of the strange sights you see here among your pale-faced brethren; the great number of the people you see; the big wigwams; the difference between our people and your own. But you have seen only a small part of the pale-faced people. There are those here who have come from countries a great deal further off than you have come. We think this world is a great round ball, and we have people here who have come from almost the other side of it, to hold council with us as you have done."

The President, evidently desirous of improving the occasion by "diffusing knowledge among men" then had a globe brought in, and alluding to Prof. Henry, of the Smithsonian Institute, told the Chiefs that one of our learned men would now give them an explanation of our ideas of this great ball we live on. Prof. Henry then proceeded to develope the doctrine of the spheres and sundry geographical points, no doubt to the edification of the unclothed representatives of the Rocky Mountains, who listened with becoming gravity. After a few further remarks from the President, the interview terminated.

There was as usual an indefatigable photographer present, who, cornering the Chiefs and a number of visitors in the White House Conservatory, "took their mugs."

DEATH OF AN INDIAN CHIEF

WASHINGTON, April 6.

The leading Indian Chief, "Yellow Wolf," of the Kiowa tribe, from Colorado, here at the head of the Indian delegation, died at one of our hotels last night, of pneumonia, and was buried to-day in the Congressional Cemetery. He was their principle spokesman in the late interview with the President. His last advice to his companion chiefs was to remain at peace with the whites.

When this article appeared (accompanied by the Tenniel drawing "The Great 'Cannon Game'"), decisive military battles were in the offing. The British weekly, Punch, May 9, 1863, while professing neutrality, leaned toward the South.

THE GREAT AMERICAN BILLIARD MATCH

Considerable excitement has been caused in sporting circles by this long protracted match, which, owing to the style of play adopted by the parties, appears to make but very little progress toward a finish. The largeness of the stakes depending on the contest might be supposed to make the players careful in their strokes, but few expected that the game would last so long as it has done, and no one now dare prophesy when it will be finished. It having been resolved to play the cannon game, some anxiety at first was not unreasonably felt among the backers of Jeff Davis, the crack player for the South; but the knowing ones, who knew their man, made no attempt to hedge, notwithstanding what was said about his being out of play and, in the cannon game especially, somewhat overmatched. It is needless to remark here that the first strokes which he made quite justified their confidence, and, indeed, throughout the game he has done nothing yet to shake it, so that if he have but a fair amount of luck, his backers feel assured that he won't easily be beaten, and an extra fluke or two might make him win the match.

As for old Abe Lincoln, the champion player of the North, his backers, we believe, are as confident as ever that he is the best man, although at times his play has not appeared to prove it. There is no doubt that he has more strength at his command, but strength is of small use without knowing how to use it. Abe Lincoln may have skill, but he has not yet shown much of it; and certainly he more than once has shown himself outgeneralled. His backers say he purposely is playing a slow game, just to draw out his opponent and see what he can do. In ninety days, they say, he is cocksure of a victory, but this is an old boast, and nobody except themselves now places any faith in it. Abe's famous Bull Run stroke was a bad start to begin with, and his Charleston break has ended in his having to screw back, and thus slip into balk to save himself from mischief.

How the game will end we won't pretend to prophesy. There are plenty of good judges, who still appear inclined to bet in favor of the South and longish odds are offered that the game will be a drawn one. Abe's attempt to pot the niggers some put down as a foul stroke, but whether foul or not, it added little to his score. Upon the whole we think his play has not been much admired, although his backers have been vehement in superlatively praising it. There is more sympathy for the South, as being the weaker side—a fact which Jeff's supporters indignantly deny, and which certainly the North has not done much as yet toward proving. Without ourselves inclining one way or the other, we may express a neutral hope that the best player may win; and we certainly shall echo the desire of all who watch the game if we add that the sooner it is now played out the better.

To the Negroes about to be liberated, the Union forces meant Lincoln—or "Linkum." This poem appeared in the Lawrence Republican, Lawrence, Kansas, May 21, 1863.

THE LINKUM GUNBOATS

SONG OF THE BEAUFORT NEGROES

Say, darkies, have you seen the massa
Wid the muf'stach on his face,

Go long de street sometime dis mornin',
    Like he gwine to leabe de place?
He seen a smoke way up de ribber,
    Where de Linkum gumboats lay,
He took his hat and left berry sudden,
    An' I spec' he's run away.
      De massa run, ha ha,
        De darkey stay, ho, ho!
    It must be now de kingdom am akoming,
    And de year ob jubilo.

He six foot one way, two foot tudder,
    An' he way tree hundred poun',
His coat so big he couldn't pay de tailor,
    An' it won't go half way round;
He drill so much dey call him cap'n,
    An' he gets so dreadful tann'd,
I spec' he'll try and fool dem Yankees
    For to tink he's contraband.
               Chorus.

De darkeys feel so lonesome libbin'
    In de log house on de lawn,
Dey move dere tings in massa's parlor
    For to keep it while he's gone;
Dere's wine an' cider in de cellar,
    An' de darkey's dey'll hab some,
I spec' dey'll all be confiscated
    When de Linkum gumboats come.
               Chorus.

De oberseer he gib us trouble,
    An' he dribe us round a spell,
So we lock him up in de smoke-house cellar,
    Wid de key trown in de well;
De whip is lost and de handcuff broken,
    But de massa 'll get no pay;
He's ole enough, big enough, ort to know better
    Dan to went and run away.
               Chorus.

This "Lincoln Catechism" was widely reprinted throughout the South. It appeared in the Southern Illustrated News, Richmond, on May 22, 1863.

THE LINCOLN CATECHISM

Question.   What is the Constitution?
Answer.   A league with hell—now obsolete.
Q.   What is the Government?
A.   Abraham Lincoln, Charles Sumner and Owen Lovejoy.
Q.   What is the President?
A.   A general agent for negroes.
Q.   What is Congress?
A.   A body organized for the purpose of appropriating funds to buy Africans, and to make laws to protect the President from being punished for any violations of law he may be guilty of.
Q.   What is an army?
A.   A provost guard to arrest white men and set negroes free.
Q.   Whom are members of Congress supposed to represent?
A.   The President and his Cabinet.
Q.   What is understood by coining money?
A.   Printing green paper.
Q.   What does the Constitution mean by "freedom of the press?"
A.   The suppression of Conservative newspapers.
Q.   What is the meaning of the word "liberty?"
A.   Incarceration in a bastile.
Q.   What is a Secretary of War?
A.   A man who arrests people by telegraph.
Q.   What are the duties of a Secretary of the Navy?
A.   To build and sink gunboats.
Q.   What is the business of a Secretary of the Treasury?
A.   To destroy State Banks, and fill the pockets of the people with irredeemable U.S. shinplasters.
Q.   What is the meaning of the word "patriot?"
A.   A man who loves his country less and the negro more.
Q.   What is the meaning of the word "traitor?"
A.   One who is a stickler for the Constitution and laws.
Q.   What are the particular duties of a Commander-in-Chief?
A.   To disgrace any General who does not believe that the negro is better than a white man.

Q. What is the meaning of the word "law?"
A. The will of the President.
Q. How were the States formed?
A. By the United States.
Q. Is the United States Government older than the States which made it?
A. It is.
Q. Have the States any rights?
A. None whatever, except what the General Government bestows.
Q. Have the people any rights?
A. None, except what the President gives.
Q. What is the *habeas corpus?*
A. It is the power of the President to imprison whom he pleases.
Q. Who is the greatest martyr of history?
A. John Brown.
Q. Who is the wisest man?
A. Abraham Lincoln.
Q. Who is Jeff Davis?
A. The Devil.

Amid all the difficulties about generalship of the Army of the Potomac, the correspondence between McClellan and Lincoln was brought to light. The war dragged on into the summer and Lincoln sent instructions to General Hooker on how to maneuver the Union forces—documents showing Lincoln to be a military strategist. The Chicago Tribune, edited by Lincoln's friends, came right out and said that he should take personal command of the army. The suggestion was reprinted in the Lawrence Republican, Kansas, June 4, 1863.

THE PRESIDENT AS GENERAL

Of all the men in and about Washington, Abraham Lincoln is the best fitted to take command of the army in the vicinity of that city; because he has a nicer, more comprehensive and accurat idea of the difficulties to be overcome and the value of the material at his disposal, than any one of his advisors, civil or military. His correspondence with McClellan, not long since printed, shows, that had his ideas prevailed, the Peninsula campaign, which cost a multitude of men, never would have been undertaken; that, after the battle of Malverin Hills, Richmond would have fallen; and that, after Antietam, the rebel army would have been cut to pieces and destroyed, and the war virtually ended. And now, with a staff well up in the details of the military art, each of whom would be willing to do his duty for his country, forgetting for a while the jealousies and animosities of the profession, he would, in Hooker's place, do what no other General has accomplished. We say this with the more confidence because we know that he is thoroughly acquainted with the topography of Eastern Virginia—every path, road, defile, mountain, stream and wood is accurately fixed in his mind, as well as the military relation and the value of one to the others; and because whenever his notions of what should or should not be, have been departed from, our armies have, just to the extent of the departure, been overtaken with disaster. Our only apprehension would be, that, just at the moment of victory, his kindness, of heart would impel him to call a halt, lest the enemy should get hurt; but this risk should be assumed; and in spite of it, we propose that Old Abe takes the reins into his own hands; and being in himself President, General-in-Chief, and Secretary of War, lead our armies to victory. We sincerely believe he can do it. If he does not, who will?

—*Chicago Tribune.*

The Fourth of July, 1863, and scheduled ceremonies in Washington became the occasion for this editorial in the Southern Illustrated News, June 20, 1863.

FREEDOM, AND THE FOURTH OF JULY

The approaching Fourth of July is to be celebrated with great pomp in Washington, and signalized by the elevation to its pedestal—on the topmost point of the great dome of the Capitol—of the colossal statue of FREEDOM, the last work of Crawford. A picture of this statue has long ornamented the Five Dollar bills of the Yankee Treasury, and as all "E. Pluribus Unum" is flooded with greenbacks, the people of the United States are, perhaps, more familiar with it than with any other work of art in the world. Indeed, their familiarity with the picture of Freedom may be said to have increased just as their practical acquaintance with the goddess herself has declined, the inflation of Mr. Chase's currency, and the circulation of his "promises to pay," being in exact correspondence, running *pari passu* with the establishment of an absolute despotism over the country. It is well, therefore, that the image of FREEDOM should be removed from the walks of men, since her spirit has long ago fled the land; and the top of the new dome being the highest and most inaccessible point yet artificially raised on the continent, it is the most appropriate that could be selected for the reception of this image.

Mr. Lincoln is learning his lessons in the art of enslavement very well. Some one remarked of some very bad government, (we are sorry to confess we do not recollect who said it, whether Talleyrand, or Madame De Stael, or other celebrity of their time, or of what government it was said, whether Napoleon's or that of the Bourbons, but no matter;) that it was a "despotism tempered with epigrams," and it is well known that all tyrants seek to amuse or captivate by shows and spectacles the people whom they would enslave. The gladiatorial combats of old Rome kept the populace entertained while the Caesars plundered the treasury and ran riot in their palaces; and in our own days, the Bonapartes have beguiled the French nation with fetes and fire-works, while they were rivetting the chains which should bind the people from the Channel to the Pyranees. Old Abe, under instruction of Seward, is beginning to profit by the lessons of history, and this Freedom celebration in Washington is intended to delight the Yankees, from whom Freedom has taken her everlasting flight.

In one of the most beautiful of the lighter poems of Mr. Tennyson, he tells us how Freedom became an inhabitant of the earth; that it was by slow advances and partial revelations that she came to make herself known to men, and that her ancient habitation was afar off—

> Of old sat Freedom on the heights,
>   The thunders breaking at her feet—
> Above her shook the starry lights,
>   She heard the torrents meet.
>
> From age to age she did rejoice,
>   Self-gathered in her prophet mind,
> But fragments of her mighty voice
>   Came rolling on the wind.
>
> *   *   *
>
> *Then stept she down through town and field*
>   *To mingle with the human race,*
> And part by part to men revealed
>   The fullness of her face.

The Yankee nation, or rather their master, Mr. Lincoln, seems determined to drive her back again to her cold seat in the clouds, and so he places her statue, not in the vestibule of the capitol, where men would approach it every day—not in the halls of Congress, where Freedom has no sort of business—but most appropriately upon the spot which the Devil once chose for a purpose of his own, "on the highest pinnacle of the temple," where it will be in nobody's way, and will never more be thought of by a degraded and disfranchised race.

"Mr. Lincoln at least rejects all compromises, and slips the leash of interminable war." At last the Union had taken the initiative, first in the defense of Gettysburg, then in the capture of Vicksburg. The President prodded his generals not just to defend or repulse or capture enemy cities; nothing would do but the surrender of Lee's army. Grudgingly, the London Times, Sept. 18, 1863, saw Lincoln's leadership as a sign of both firmness and obstinacy.

It must be confessed that Mr. LINCOLN possesses at least the quality of perseverance, guided by little wisdom, it is true, and perhaps it deserves a less honourable name, but still in all his published documents one traces a certain natural pertinacity which carries an air of honesty, if not of statesmanship. He has but one cry, —"the maintenance of the "Union." He seems able to see no other object possible to him, and he measures every measure solely by its relation to this purpose. The letter which we published on Wednesday at length is a curious illustration of this feeling of his mind. He seems unable to discuss any question without relation to it. The justice or injustice of the Emancipation Proclamation he can only discuss in his capacity as a Commander-in-Chief coercing rebellious States by all the means in his power. The employment of negroes in the army has for him no other importance than the value they may be to the operations of his Generals. Whatever wishes and hopes he may have about emancipation he postpones to his duty as President, which in this case resolves itself into his duty as Commander-in-Chief. Whether or no there is, as some people have asserted, a settled design in a political party in America to break down the rights of individual States for the purpose of forming a compact Federal organization, it is impossible to attribute this design to President LINCOLN. He does not show himself capable of any such organized policy. He may be used by cleverer and more designing men for their own purposes, but he himself is a man of only one idea. The circumstances of the time of his election gave him a hobby, and he is fairly carried away by it. The horse goes a great deal too fast for him, and hurries him on with it. He has no time to dismount, and if the hobby-horse should gallop towards a precipice Mr. LINCOLN will certainly go over with it.

This helpless and blind pertinacity would be excusable and harmless in Mr. LINCOLN, but it is inexcusable and disastrous in the President of the United States. It makes him useless, and worse than useless, for that which ought to be his great purpose, the guiding and controlling the vast forces of passion and interest and ideas which sway the unsettled nation he presides over. No one can have failed to observe that the Americans act almost entirely under the influence of impulses, and never with the calm decision which protracts and steadies our contests in Europe. Into whatever party they throw themselves, they maintain its platform with a wild fanaticism which has no regard to consequences, either to themselves or to others. The Abolitionists agitate for emancipation without a thought of how it is to be attained, or the consequences to the South or themselves, and the Union party will have the Union maintained at any risk of "blood and treasure." We wonder at a free people submitting to outrages on the freedom of the subject, the liberty of the press, and the rights of property, which would have raised a revolution at any time in the history of this country; but the truth is the Americans do not think about the matter, they are possessed by a wild madness for a particular object, whether attainable or not, and they will dash themselves against any obstructions to reach it. The great work of a President of so excitable a people ought to be to direct these uneducated and fanatic impulses, and to control them into an ordinary and reasonable path. But the PRESIDENT is as much possessed as the rest. He gives no thought to the results of his policy, he has no plan for a compromise with the South; he identifies himself with one of the great parties of the State, and is carried away with them, he knows not where.

The consequence is that every passion and every madness surges unchecked over the vast territory of the States. Men are let loose by the PRESIDENT's own example from all obligations but that of gaining their object, and they regard neither justice nor humanity in pursuing it. If passion and reason in union constitute a perfect character, the Americans may be best described as creatures of passion, without reason, or only that lower acuteness of understanding which enables them to adapt means to their immediate ends. We are led to these remarks by two or three incidents in the American intelligence which we published yesterday. A Senator of the United States, speaking in the peaceful State of Maine, boasts that "there are forty-four regiments in New York to help the Government to enforce the draught, and there is not one of them who would not sooner shoot a Copperhead, put a bullet through his brain, than he would shoot a rebel;" and the assertion was repeated twice for greater distinctness. Let our readers try to imagine language like this used by an English statesman of note in an address to his constituents, and they may be able to form some idea of the anarchy of passion which possesses the Americans. It displays a blind and senseless ferocity emancipated from all regard to law and order by what the PRESIDENT considers the necessity of war. Such language, no doubt, says a great deal more than it means; but words react on the heart and head, and it does not want much more such talking as this to transform the United States into a sort of Mexico, a mere stage for lawless violence and selfish ferocity. . . .

Every impulse of passion and fanaticism seems to be set free to work its will, and for all we can see at present the fiery elements will fight out their fearful struggles until they are tired into exhausted quiet. Mr. LINCOLN at least rejects all compromises, and slips the leash of interminable war.

This playlet, portraying Lincoln as Brutus, turned up (from London's Punch, Aug. 15, 1863 issue) in the Southern Illustrated News, Richmond, Oct. 31, 1863. An indication of Britain's general favoritism toward the Confederacy was the frequent reprinting of anti-Lincoln cartoons and articles in the Southern press.

[From the London Punch.]
BRUTUS AND CAESAR
——
(From the American Edition of Shakespeare.)
——

The Tent of Brutus (LINCOLN). Night. Enter an
        Ethiopian Serenader with a Banjo.
    Serenader.   You sent for me, my lord?
    Brutus.   Jerusalem!
I calculate, Siree, I did that same.
    Canst thou hold up thy heavy eyes awhile,
    And touch thine instrument a strain or two?
    Serenader.   Ay, my lord, an't please you
    Brutus.   It does, my b'hoy.
I trouble thee too much, but thou art willing.
Sing me a soothing song, yet sensible.
        SERENADER Sings.

Bold MASSA LEE, him coming after we,
    Whack, jack, crack, jibble obble lack
Brave MASSA MEADE, him berry strong indeed,
    Whack, jack, crack, jibble obble lack.
       &c., &c., &c.
           [SERENADER *falls asleep.*
Brutus. 'Tis a sweet tune, yet sleepy. He is fast,
I will not do him so much wrong to wake him.
I'll rather read. Where is the noble work
Whence I cull anecdotes and jocund jests
Wherewith to ornament my statesmanship,
Making smooth SEWARD smile, stiff STANTON
    scowl?
O, JOSEPH MILLER, thou art mighty yet.
Where was I? Ha! "A lawyer met a clown.
               [*He reads.*
Driving a pig to market, and observed,
'Why, thereby hangs a tail,' to which, "—By
    gosh,
This darned eternal moderator burns
As badly as——
        Enter the Ghost of CAESAR.
        Wall, now! Do tell! Who's you?
Caesar. I am dy ebil genus, massa LINKING.
Dis child am awful Impressional,
As massa did obserb.
    Brutus.   I never did.
My word was Irrepressible, base nigger.
    Caesar. All de same, massa, in one hundred
    year.
    Brutus. Be off, black spectre. How I hate
    thy looks!
Thou art the cause of all my allfire bother:
Would every Black were deep in the Black Sea,
Or every son of HAM were cut so thin
That I could eat him up in sangwidges.
    Caesar. More bother yet for massa, for dis
    child
Stick close to him like wax, eh, golly, iss.
    Brutus. Begone, I say.

Caesar.   Massa am not polite;
Him call him up, him call him man and brudder,
Him give him Mancipation, and a gun
To shoot at massa DAVY.
      Brutus.   DAVIS, fool.
DAVIS's Straits are not as great as mine,
But DAVY—would thou wert in Davy's Locker.
      Caesar. Him 'tick to massa.
      Brutus.   Tick.   Thou may'st say that.
How's massa to get tick?   (That's none so bad.)
      Caesar. Dat massa's business. For one little
            time
Dis child be off, but soon him come again,
And play de Debbil looking over LINCOLN.
      Brutus. Vamoose! Go! Slope to him whom
            thou hast named,
And whom I've raised in this here blessed war.
Away, black cuss!   [CAESAR *vanishes.*
            SERENADER *Awakes, and Sings.*
MASSA BENNETT GORDON 'fraid to stick a sword on,
      Whack, jack, crack, jibble obble lack,
MASSA HORACE GREELEY look a little mealy,
      Whack, jack, crack, jibble obble lack,—
            [BRUTUS *gives him a violent kick, which sends*
                  him flying out of the tent.
      Brutus.   Darn thy brute jargon!   (*laughs.*)—
            HOOKER fled not quicker.
Rebellion's dead, or ought to be.   Let's liquor.
                        [*Exit.*

   Nearly a year after the Emancipation Proclamation, the "tyrant
Lincoln" was being condemned. The Southern Illustrated News, Oct.
31, 1863, expressed the resentment in a poem "By a Rebel."

LINES ON THE PROCLAMATION
Issued by the Tyrant Lincoln, April 1st, 1863.

———

BY A REBEL.

———

"Are there no stones in heaven but what serve for the
            thunder, precious villain?"

We have read the tyrant's order
And the signet to the rule,
And thought the kingly jester meant
To make an April fool,
For we knew that nothing better
Than a joke in such a strain
Could e'er be made to emanate
From his degraded brain;
For he orders every man and child,
In palace or in cot,
To fast and pray on such a day—
To fast and pray for what?

* * * * * * * * * *

To ask Almighty God to bless
A despot's roll of crime;
To ask that he will bring distress
On a more Christian clime;
To ask that murder, rapine, blood,
May meet with more success;
That the noblest, fairest land on earth,
Be made a wilderness—
To ask the pure and holy God
To bless his guilty plans,
And with approval sanctify
The tyrant's blood-washed hands.

Pray that a mother's prayer be lost
When dragged from home in chains;
The orphan's cry ascend unheard,
When weeping it complains;
Pray that the tyrant's iron bands
May rust on maiden forms,
And that his galling manacles
May bruise their fair white arms;
Pray that their tender voices die,
Their tears in torrents pour,
And that their bleaching bones may strew
The gloomy dungeon's floor.

Pray for a rack, a guillotine,
    On which to lash the free,
That the music of their torture
    And their cries of agony,
May mingle with the stifled sob
    Of woman's broken heart,
To sate the maniac-tyrant's soul,
    And blunt remorse's dart;
Pray for more women searching,
    With their coward hireling band,
To degrade a helpless people,
    And insult a fallen land.

* * * * * * * * * *

Oh, God! to thee thy people cry—
    The God in whom they trust—
That thou wilt aid them in their need,
    And raise them from the dust;
And in thy vengeance, mighty God,
    Thy lightning dagger thrust
Into the shameless tyrant's heart,
    And drain its sordid lust;
Hurl down his broken sceptre,
    And break his blood-stained throne,
And applauding worlds shall clap their hands
    To drown the tyrant's groan!

Unequivocally, Parson Brownlow and his Knoxville Whig and
Rebel Ventilator stood behind Lincoln. Brownlow, a Union voice in
the Upper South—"when the Secessionists go to Washington to de-
throne Lincoln," he said, he would seize a bayonet in defense—risked
his life (though he was not an Abolitionist) to keep the light burning
for Lincoln in Tennessee. His newspaper flaunted the Stars and Stripes
until it was suspended; upon its reappearance on Nov. 11, 1863, Brownlow came out full blast for Lincoln.

OUR COURSE OF POLICY

In assuming the editorial control and publication of this paper, after
our long absence, and since the occupation of East Tennessee by the

Union army, it may not be out of place for us to state in brief, but unmistakable terms, what our course will be. We understand that some solicitude is manifested upon this question in certain rebel quarters. Those who know us, as all East Tennesseans do, need not be enlightened on this subject, but those who have forgotten us, as most rebels have, are entitled to the information they seek.

We are not here to excuse this or that act of the Washington Government, nor yet to censure President Lincoln for what he has done, or to wish that he had done otherwise. We indorse all he has done, and we find fault with him for not having done more of the same sort! The Federal Government has been too lenient, and too slow to punish rebels, and to crush out this most abominable, wicked and uncalled for rebellion, from its very commencement.

The mediation we shall advocate, is that of the cannon and the sword, and our motto is—no armistice on sea or land, until all, ALL the rebels, both front and rear, in arms, and in ambush, are subjugated or exterminated! And then we are for visiting condign punishment upon the leaders in the rebellion, who may survive the struggle, in the unholy crusade against civilization. It is not enough to say that certain prominent characters acknowledge that the rebellion has failed, and that having lived under the United States in former days, they will try to do so again. Let them submit to the laws and Constitution of the Federal Government, and cease to find fault with it, or pack up their effects and leave the country. Let them speedily, and without any mental reservation, learn to behave themselves, and render a willing obedience to law and order, or let them quit the country. And none but loyal men are to be heard in the casting up of the accounts of men who have done the amount of mischief those leading rebels have!

A portrait of the President appeared in Wisconsin that looked upon Lincoln as a man and symbol in the midst of crisis. The Galesville Transcript, Nov. 13, 1863, was published in Trempealeau County, Wisc., with this interesting footnote to its Republicanism noted in an early issue: "In order to succeed, a county paper must have advertising. To obtain this, our Republican friends, who have the patronage in their hands, require that our paper be made an organ of that party; a requisition which we find the majority of both parties concede to be just. . . . we accept Republican principles as the method of removing from our county that curse and outrage on humanity, Human Slavery." The Home Journal is credited in this Wisconsin editorial.

PRESIDENT LINCOLN

Since Abraham Lincoln has occupied the Presidential chair, editors abroad and many at home have appeared to consider it an especial study to prove that he (the President) possesses very ordinary capacities. Even his best friends have only been able to put in a word edgewise, suggesting he is honest and good. In the first place, it is claimed that Nature is at fault in his physical construction, giving him a homely face and unequal limbs; placing him in bad grace with the ladies at the out set.—Then it is claimed that little amends were made in making up his intellect or in its cultivation. In short our fifth-rate journals whose paragraphs abound with inaccuracies, have made it a point to criticize his language and logic. Although Mr. Lincoln has been pretty thoroughly criticised and abused, we believe the time is coming—that it is really at hand when justice will be done one of the best men who has been honored with the highest office in the gift of the Republic.

A writer in the *Home Journal* contrary to the general rule, thus speaks of Mr. Lincoln:

> . . . Mr. Lincoln is a *man* and vindicates his claim to the title of *gentleman* by his obvious desire and determination "to do good and not evil all the days of his life," even though he bear the reproach of some little want of that outward varnish of manners, which even in this advanced stage of the world's civilization and enlightenment, imposes upon many of the admirers of the old *regime* at Washington.
>
> . . . His straight forward honesty and courage, expressed in such language as becomes such qualities, have long been a puzzle and a vexation to those who believe that language was intended to conceal our thoughts. How can an old wily diplomatist, accustomed to wrap up his worldly and selfish ends in a sugared mist of words, get along with our President's short, incisive sentences and simple truthfulness? No man could find two meanings in them, and they have therefore the gift of silencing at once all who would gladly use them for evil purposes. The very fact that Mr. Lincoln's thoughts came to us in such English that pleases Heaven, bears witness to his courage and honesty; for he has choice English in his power, nay at his very elbow! if he chose to wear any sort of mask, even that of elegance. We have had enough in times past, of artfully constructed periods and "glittering generalities," and we have long enough worshipped mere intellect without principle or adroitness without

high purpose. Our President is teaching us to value things above words, integrity rather than cunning goodliness before courtliness. . . .

Absolute truth, stern resolution, clear insight, solemn faithfulness, courage that cannot be daunted, hopefulness that cannot be dashed—these are qualities that go a long way to make up a hero, whatever side the possessor of them may take in any lawful conflict. *And it wouldn't be easy to dispute Mr. Lincoln's claim to all of these.* He has never given up a good servant or a sound principle. He has never shut his eyes to facts, or remained in ignorance of them. *He has never hesitated to do his work, or faltered in doing it.* No resolution has remained *in nubibus* with him because it was a strong one. No measure has been adopted merely because 'Something must be done.' The exigencies of a fanatical war have never betrayed him into fanaticism; and the sharp stings of satire have never drawn from him an exclamation of ill humor, or even an imprudent rejoinder.

On November 19, 1863, the National Cemetery at Gettysburg was dedicated. This is how the New York Times reported the day in its issue of Nov. 20, 1863. The "long continued applause" comment belies the legend that Lincoln's audience was stunned into silence.

THE HEROES OF JULY.

A Solemn and Imposing Event.

Dedication of the National Cemetery at Gettysburgh.

IMMENSE NUMBERS OF VISITORS.

Oration by Hon. Edward Everett—Speeches of President Lincoln, Mr. Seward and Governor Seymour.

THE PROGRAMME SUCCESSFULLY CARRIED OUT

The ceremonies attending the dedication of the National Cemetery commenced this morning by a grand military and civic display, under

355

command of Maj.-Gen. COUCH. The line of march was taken up at 10 o'clock, and the procession marched through the principal streets to the cemetery, where the military formed in line and saluted the President. At 11½ the head of the procession arrived at the main stand. The President and members of the Cabinet, together with the chief military and civic dignitaries, took position on the stand. The President seated himself between Mr. SEWARD and Mr. EVERETT after a reception marked with the respect and perfect silence due to the solemnity of the occasion, every man in the immense gathering uncovering on his appearance.

The military were formed in line extending around the stand, the area between the stand and military being occupied by civilians, comprising about 15,000 people and including men, women and children. The attendance of ladies was quite large. The military escort comprised one squadron of cavalry, two batteries of artillery and a regiment of infantry, which constitutes the regular funeral escort of honor for the highest officer in the service.

After the performance of a funeral dirge, by BIROFIELD, by the band, an eloquent prayer was delivered by Rev. Mr. STOCKTON. . . .

Mr. EVERETT then commenced the delivery of his oration, which was listened to with marked attention throughout. . . .

Although a heavy fog clouded the heavens in the morning during the procession, the sun broke out in all its brilliancy during the Rev. Mr. STOCKTON's prayer and shone upon the magnificent spectacle. The assemblage was of great magnitude, and was gathered within a circle of great extent around the stand, which was located on the highest point of ground on which the battle was fought. A long line of military surrounded the position taken by the immense multitude of people.

The Marshal took up a position on the left of the stand. Numerous flags and banners, suitably draped, were exhibited on the stand among the audience. The entire scene was one of grandeur due to the importance of the occasion. So quiet were the people that every word uttered by the orator of the day must have been heard by them all, notwithstanding the immensity of the concours. . . .

PRESIDENT LINCOLN'S ADDRESS

The President then delivered the following dedicatory speech:

Fourscore and seven years ago our Fathers brought forth upon this Continent a new nation, conceived in liberty and dedicated to the proposition that all men are created equal. [Applause.] Now we are engaged in a great civil war, testing whether that nation, or any nation so conceived and so dedicated, can long endure. We are met on a great battle-field of that war. We are met to dedicate a portion of it as the final resting-place of those who here gave their lives that that nation might live. It is altogether fitting and proper that we should do this. But in a larger sense we cannot dedicate. We cannot consecrate, we cannot hallow this ground. The brave men, living and dead, who struggled here have consecrated it far above our power to add or detract. [Applause.] The world will little note nor long remember, what we say here, but it can never forget what they did here. [Applause.] It is for us, the living, rather to be dedicated here to the refinished work that they have thus so far nobly carried on. [Applause.] It is rather for us to be here dedicated to the great task remaining before us, that from these honored dead we take increased devotion to that cause for which they here gave the last full measure of devotion; that we here highly resolve that the dead shall not have died in vain; [applause.] that the Nation shall under God have a new birth of freedom, and that Governments of the people, by the people and for the people, shall not perish from the earth. [Long continued applause.]

Three cheers were then given for the President and the Governors of the States.

After the delivery of the addresses, the dirge and the benediction closed the exercises, and the immense assemblage separated at about 4 o'clock.

A subscription of $280 was made by the Marshals attending these ceremonies, to be devoted to the relief of the Richmond prisoners.

In the afternoon, the Lieutenant-Governor elect of Ohio, Col. ANDERSON, delivered an oration at the Presbyterian Church.

The President and party returned to Washington at 6 o'clock this evening, followed by the Governors' trains. Thousands of persons were gathered at the depot, anxiously awaiting transportation to their homes, but they will probably be confined to the meagre accommodations of Gettysburgh till to-morrow.

The Gettysburg celebration was again the subject of a report in the New York Times of Nov. 21, 1863, which told how the people saw Lincoln that day.

THE GETTYSBURGH CELEBRATION

From our Special Correspondent

GETTYSBURGH, Penn.,
Thursday Evening, Nov. 19, 1863

All the noteworthy incidents of the celebration here to-day have already been sent off to you by telegraph, and it would have gratified your correspondent exceedingly if he could also have got off, but fate, combined with the miserable railroad arrangements, has ordained that he should spend another night in this over-crowded village. The only train that has been permitted to leave here, to-day, was the special train bearing the President and his party, which left at 6 o'clock this evening. Even the mail train, which should have left at 8 o'clock this morning, was detained for fear it would come in collision with some of the numerous trains that have been following each other in rapid succession from Hanover Junction, bringing visitors to the Dedication. How they are all to sleep here to-night it is difficult to imagine. All the hotels as well as the private houses were filled to overflowing last night. Every housekeeper in Gettysburgh has opened a temporary hotel, and extends unbounded hospitality to strangers—for a consideration. People from all parts of the country seem to have taken this opportunity to pay a visit to the battle-fields which are hereafter to make the name of Gettysburgh immortal. The Dedication ceremonies were apparently a minor consideration, for even while Mr. EVERETT was delivering his splendid oration, there were as many people wandering about the fields, made memorable by the fierce struggles of July, as stood around the stand listening to his eloquent periods. They seem to have considered, with President LINCOLN, that it was not what was *said* here, but what was *done* here, that deserved their attention. During the last three days, the scenes of the late battles have been visited by thousands of persons from every loyal State in the Union, and there is probably not a foot of the grounds that has not been trodden over and over again by reverential feet. But little over four months have passed away since the champions of Slavery and Freedom met here in deadly strife, and already the name of Gettysburgh has become historical, and its soil is classic ground. This, too, while the contest is yet undecided, and the camp-fires of the contending armies still illumine the Southern sky. If the people of the North can thus forestall history, it is because the manifest justice of their cause enables them to see the future in the present, and to behold in the fresh made graves of their fallen sons the shining monuments of their glory in ages to come. . . .

After the dedication ceremonies were over, the President returned to the residence of Mr. WILLS, whose guest he has been since he arrived here, and from thence walked to the church on Baltimore-street, to listen to an oration by Lieut.-Gov. ANDERSON, of Ohio. He walked up to the church arm in arm with the famous TOM BURNS, the only man in Gettysburgh who had patriotism or pluck enough to take a gun on his shoulder and help the Union army defend his town.

Soon after the arrival of the President at Gettysburgh last evening, he was serenaded by a Baltimore band, and after numerous calls for "the President," "Old ABE," "Uncle ABE," "Father ABRAHAM," "the next President," &c., &c., was induced to make his appearance at the door. He said he was tired, and did not feel like speaking, and as a man who did not feel like talking was apt to say foolish things, he begged to be excused from making a speech. The audience cheered the sentiment, and the President, taking it for granted he was excused, retired to his room.

The Chicago Times saw the whole Gettysburg Address in conflict with the Constitution and so reasoned in an editorial on Nov. 23, 1863. (The Chicago Times, strongly anti-Lincoln, had been suspended for one day by General Burnside the previous June and then reinstated by order of President Lincoln, following widespread opposition to a violation of press freedom in spite of Editor Wilbur Storey's Copperheadism.) The erroneous reporting of Lincoln's words at Gettysburg seemed to support the accusations made against the Chicago Times's accuracy by Lincoln proponents during the debates with Douglas way back in '58.

THE PRESIDENT AT GETTYSBURG

It is not supposed by any one, we believe, that Mr. Lincoln is possessed of much polish in manners or conversation. His adherents, however, claim for him an average amount of common sense, and more than an ordinarily kind and generous heart. We have failed to distinguish his pre-eminence in the latter, and apprehend the former to be somewhat mythical, but imagine that his deficiencies herein being less palpable than in other qualities constituting a statesman have led his admirers greatly to overestimate him in these regards. These qualities are unfailing guides to appropriateness of speech and action in mising with the world, however slight may have been the opportunities afforded their possessor for becoming acquainted with the usages of society.

The introduction of Dawdleism in a funeral sermon is an innovation upon established conventionalities, which, a year or two ago, would have been regarded with scorn by all who thought custom should, to a greater or less extent, be consulted in determining social and public proprieties. And the custom which forbids its introduction is founded on the propriety which grows out of the fitness of things, and is not therefore merely arbitrary, or confined to special localities, but has suggested to all nations the exclusion of political partianship in funeral discourses. Common sense, then, should have taught Mr. Lincoln that its intrusion upon such an occasion was an offensive exhibition of boorishness and vulgarity. An Indian in eulogizing the memories of warriors who had fallen in battle would avoid allusion to differences in the tribe which had no connection with the prevailing circumstances, and which he knew would excite unnecessarily the bitter prejudices of his hearers. Is Mr. Lincoln less refined than a savage?

But aside from the ignorant rudeness manifest in the President's exhibition of Dawdleism at Gettysburg,—and which was an insult at least to the memories of a part of the dead, whom he was there professedly to honor,—in its misstatement of the cause for which they died, it was a perversion of history so flagrant that the most extended charity cannot regard it as otherwise than willful. That, if we do him injustice, our readers may make the needed correction, we append a portion of his eulogy on the dead at Gettysburg:

> "Four score and ten [sic] years ago our fathers brought forth upon this continent a nation consecrated [sic] to liberty and dedicated to the proposition that all men are created equal. [Cheers.] Now we are engaged in a great civil war, testing whether that nation or any other [sic] nation so consecrated [sic] and so dedicated can long endure."

As a refutation of this statement, we copy certain clauses in the Federal constitution:

> "Representatives and direct taxes shall be apportioned among the several States which may be included in this Union, according to their respective numbers, which shall be determined by adding to the whole number of free persons, including those bound to ser-

vice for a term of years, and excluding Indians not taxed, three-fifths of all other persons."

"The migration or importation of such persons as any of the States now existing shall think proper to admit shall not be prohibited by the Congress prior to the year 1808, but a tax or duty may be imposed on such importation, not exceeding ten dollars for each person."

"No amendment to the constitution, made prior to 1808, shall affect the preceding clause."

"No person held to service or labor in one State under the laws thereof, escaping into another, shall, in consequence of any law or regulation therein, be discharged from such service or labor, but shall be delivered up on claim of the party to whom such service or labor may be due."

Do these provisions in the constitution dedicate the nation to "the proposition that all men are created equal"? Mr. Lincoln occupies his present position by virtue of this constitution, and is sworn to the maintenance and enforcement of these provisions. It was to uphold this constitution, and the Union created by it, that our officers and soldiers gave their lives at Gettysburg. How dared he, then, standing on their graves, misstate the cause for which they died, and libel the statesmen who founded the government? They were men possessing too much self-respect to declare that negroes were their equals, or were entitled to equal privileges.

In England the Gettysburg Address was drowned out by the windy speech of Edward Everett that day and a talk by Henry Ward Beecher in Brooklyn. The London Times, Dec. 4, 1863, was no different than most American publications which ignored or overlooked Lincoln's famous battlefield words.

THE CIVIL WAR IN AMERICA
From Our Own Correspondent
NEW YORK, Nov. 20.

The papers of to-day are almost entirely filled up by two speeches delivered by two orators as unlike each other as it might well be possible for this Western world to produce—Mr. Everett's inaugural oration at Gettysburg, and Mr. Beecher's "Impressions of the feeling in Europe with respect to the American War," spoken at the Brooklyn Academy of Music.

The inauguration of the cemetery at Gettysburg was an imposing ceremony, only rendered somewhat flat by the nature of Mr. Everett's lecture, and ludicrous by some of the luckless sallies of that poor President Lincoln, who seems determined to play in this great American Union the part of the famous Governor of the Isle of Barataria. Honest old Abe arrived at Gettysburg on Wednesday evening, and after supper was serenaded by the band of the 5th New York Artillery. There was a loud call for the President. He appeared, and was loudly cheered, when he opened his mouth and said:—

"I appear before you, fellow-citizens, merely to thank you for this compliment. The inference is a very fair one that you would hear me for a little while at least were I to commence to make a speech. I do not appear before you for the purpose of doing so, and for several substantial reasons. The most substantial of these is that I have no speech to make. (Laughter.) In my position it is somewhat important that I should not say any foolish things. (A voice.—'If you can help it.') It very often happens that the only way to help it is to say nothing at all. (Laughter.) Believing that it is my present condition this evening, I must beg of you to excuse me from addressing you further."

Mr. Seward soon afterwards spoke rather more to the purpose, urging that the cause of the war was slavery, and that the war would end in the removal of its cause. He had hoped to see slavery die by peaceful means, but he was destined to see it die by the fates of war. The after-supper speeches of Wednesday, however, were hardly to be looked upon as a prelude of the great sayings and doings of the ensuing day. Yesterday the proceedings were opened by the Rev. Mr. Stockton with a long and impressive prayer, followed up by the dedicatory address by the President, got up in a somewhat different style from his extempore effusion of the eve, when at last the time came for the orator of the day to open his MS.

The Hon. Edward Everett is a lady's orator. I remember conversing with fair enthusiasts who sat under that gentleman's pulpit on his début as a Unitarian minister in Boston, and who had not, after many years, recovered from their rapture at the "solemn, handsome, inspired countenance," the "stately bearing," the "deep, mellow voice" of the youthful preacher, and especially at the "graceful wave of the dazzling white hand," as it followed the cadence of his well-rounded periods. On all occasions where words are wanted—not thoughts—where feelings are to be tickled —not roused—nothing can be more refreshing or pleasing than to hear and see Mr. Everett. Here, however, mere rhetoric was out of place, and whatever effect the lecture may have had on the feminine part of the audience, which mustered rather strong on the spot, there is no doubt that it reads tame beyond belief, and is such a performance as would scarcely win the prize for composition over the common run of undergraduates. Mr. Everett begins by high-sounding allusions to Athens and Marathon; he gives a very minute description, or say circumstantial and more than technical report, of the three great battle-days of July, 1863; then launches forth into an inquiry into the causes of the war, proving that "the kettle began it," that the rebels are rebels, and rebellion the most hideous crime man can be guilty of when it aims at the overturn of the best of all possible Governments. He added that division had always been the bane of all communities, but that the wounds inflicted by political dissensions soon healed, and the very scars were effaced by time, and instanced the case of England, the wars of the Roses, the rebellion and revolution, and those of Germany, Italy, France, &c. Anything more dull and commonplace, anything less calculated to call forth deep or lively or lasting emotions, it would not be easy by the most fastidious taste, the most unwearied industry, and the most consummate scholarship without a soul to it to produce. Mr. Ward Beecher's address was something different. It is not his first appearance before a Brooklyn audience since the popular preacher got home; but he was awfully sea-sick during his voyage, and his qualmish efforts to speak before his full recovery must not be taken into account. Last evening he was in the vein, and being addressed by a brother preacher, Mr. Storrs, who praised him for "having literally taken the British lion by the ears, and drawing it with so dexterous a gentleness, and so wise a firmness, that the Royal beast roared in approbation of the treatment," Mr. Beecher answered, modestly enough, that, "he put no immoderate estimate on his services," though "he believed he did some good wherever he spoke. The object of his speech was to point out to his countrymen which classes and parties of the English public were in favour of the Northern cause and which were against it. He was sure of the middle and lower classes—of the heart of the English people;" "the upper-class, as they are called, are on the side of the South." The reasons by which these latter are actuated are "commercial interest and rivalry therein, class power and fear of contagion of American ideas; the fact that the Americans are too large and strong a nation." For the rest, the cause of the Union numbered many friends in England among the members of the Government—the Queen and the late Prince Consort first and foremost,

—many organs of the Press, and a number of worthy and influential persons, of whom he gave the names in the midst of the applause of his delighted audience. Mr. Beecher's style of eloquence is now familiar to most people in England, and needs no remark on my part. Only it seems that he last evening addressed his audience with a kind of home feeling, and that the certainty of success bore him up so as to render his triumph more brilliant than any achieved by him on former occasions.

Lincoln's third annual message to Congress was accompanied by a Proclamation of Amnesty and Reconstruction on Dec. 8, 1863. The President set one matter straight: "While I remain in my present position I shall not attempt to retract or modify the Emancipation Proclamation; nor shall I return to slavery any person who is free by the terms of that proclamation." The Richmond Examiner commented: "In proposing these utterly infamous terms, this Yankee monster of inhumanity and falsehood, had the audacity to declare that in some of the Confederate States the elements of reconstruction were ready for action." The New York Tribune, Dec. 10, 1863, saw the message and amnesty having good effect here and abroad.

THE PRESIDENT'S MESSAGE

The plan presented by President Lincoln in his Annual Message for the restoration of the insurgent States to the authority and rights abdicated by their rebellion, will attract the widest attention both in this country and in Europe. Hitherto the attorneys of treason on the stump and in the journals of the loyal States have urged the uselessness of desisting from rebellion as an excuse for persistence therein. "If they should withdraw their support from the rebel leaders and return to loyalty and fidelity, you will nevertheless confiscate all their property and divest them of every civil and political right: so why should they? What is to be their motive—their inducement?" The President has answered the question and silenced the cavil. Every person now within the territory of the Rebellion, with the exception of two or three thousand of its more conspicuous and determined chiefs, may secure a full pardon to-morrow, and be restored to all his former privileges as a loyal citizen of the United States, with his property intact (save that which may have already been confiscated and sold), on the easy condition of his swearing allegiance to the United States, and to abide by and aquiesce in the acts of Congress and Executive Proclamations affecting the status of slaves, "so long and so far as not repealed, modified, or declared void by Congress, or by a decision of the Supreme Court." Here is required no assumption of the universal efficiency and irrevocable validity of those acts and proclamations, but a simple agreement to respect and abide by them, and each of them, until the same shall be invalidated either by Congress or the Supreme Court of the United States. How can any one who means to be loyal at all, object to these conditions? Ninety of every hundred Rebels may be restored to every right to-morrow without sacrificing or relinquishing any particle of their property; while nine-tenths of the residue are required to relinquish nothing but their right to oppress and sell their fellow men. We believe Tennessee, Louisiana and Arkansas may be re-organized and restored to the Union on this basis at an early day, and that the residue will gradually follow.

Henceforth, it can neither be truthfully nor plausibly said that those who have once been Rebels have no inducement to return to loyalty, no hope but in the triumph of Disunion. They may come back to-morrow and enjoy every political or social privilege and advantage enjoyed or claimed by any of us. We proffer them equality with ourselves. Should not that suffice and content them?

The country must now realize that naught but Slavery obstructs the way to Peace and Reunion. In no metaphoric or poetic sense, the Union and Liberty are henceforth inseparable. They will either rejoice in a common deliverance and triumph or fill the same bloody grave.

Of course, the master-spirits of the revolt will not be conciliated. They have staked their all upòn the cast, and must stand the hazard of the die. But what possible motive will a non-slaveholder have for persisting in rebellion after receiving due notice of the issuing of this Proclamation? Merciless bands may still scour the region cursed by the revolt, and drag every man and youth into the Rebel camps—often by the help of bloodhounds: but to what end shall the non-slaveholding conscripts remain and fight? What they risk and lose by contumacy is obvious: where is the counterbalancing gain? Depend on it, this Proclamation, if seconded and sustained in the loyal States, will go far to break the back of the Rebellion.

In Europe, it will be even more generally efficient. The fiendish malevolence betrayed by the Secession oracles is rarely or never exhibited in Europe through quotations from the Rebel journals; yet none can fail to realize the regretful tenderness and kindly charity wherewith the Rebel masses are contemplated by the President. Though his official term of service has been rendered anxious and troubled by their treason, he has never ceased to regard them as deceived and misled, and to desire their speedy return to loyalty and peace. The more influential British and French journals conceal this, so far as possible, from their readers; yet the truth gradually makes itself known and respected. But when the loyal North, through the President, proffers amnesty and restoration on the single condition of acquiescence in Universal Freedom until Congress or the Supreme Court shall decide that this is a condition which the President had no right to impose, why should any stand out? And how can Liberal Europe withhold her ardent, active sympathy from the cause that asks nothing of its deadly enemies but that they let the oppressed go free? *The Times* will misrepresent and *The Saturday Review* defame us as usual; the aristocracy may still frown or sneer; but the masses of Europe, already instinctively our friends, will be impelled by this proffer to a more general and hearty enthusiasm in behalf of that Union which now represents, even more emphatically than hitherto, the aspirations of bowed and struggling Labor throughout the civilized world. Thanks, then, to our President, for the wise humanity and generous impulses which prompted the issue of his Proclamation of amnesty! It must be that in this sign we shall conquer!

> *The President's amnesty message brought no words of approbation from The Times, London, Dec. 22, 1863, which found, with odd reasoning, praise for the slaveholders who had stood up for the rebellion "with a readiness unsurpassed in history."*

As the Confederacy has copied the practice of the Union as regards the meeting of Congress, we receive at the same time the Messages of the rival American Presidents. Mr. LINCOLN has not been prevented by a dangerous illness from addressing the Federal Legislature in terms that will satisfy the most extreme zealot of the Republican party, and Mr. DAVIS, on the other hand, declares the unfaltering determination of his Government to persist in the war, although former victories have not been able to save the Confederacy from calamities inflicted by the superior numbers of the enemy. But the Message of the more powerful magistrate is the document which has the greater interest for Europe. Mr. LINCOLN is now possessed of an authority within what may be called his dominions greater than has ever been known even during his high-handed Presidency.

A year ago the Democratic party was still formidable. The city and to a great extent the State of New York were opposed to the Government, if not to the war. Pennsylvania and Ohio were hostile; the Western States, with Illinois at their head, were wavering between a peace policy and the relentless theories of the Republicans. The PRESIDENT had not yet been able to abandon the system of espionage and summary imprisonment which he had established soon after his accession. The forts which were the objects of such indignation to the Democrats continued to receive their unwilling inmates; and in some of the larger cities it was doubtful whether a majority of the inhabitants were not as treasonable in thought as those who were immured in any Federal prison. Mr. LINCOLN's position is now more secure, and the tone of his Message shows the effect of the last year's success, both political and military. Last year he was about to issue his edict of emancipation amid the doubts and disapprobation of the greater part of the Northern people. This year he has no such thunderbolt to launch, and consequently need not use defiant or deprecatory language to those who are to judge his policy. But he thinks that the successes on the Mississippi and in Tennessee are sufficient to authorize a Proclamation of another kind.

The most striking feature of the present Message is the amnesty which Mr. LINCOLN thinks fit to proclaim to the Southern people. If the obstinate and fierce-tempered population who have been resisting his armies for two years and a half will now abandon the PRESIDENT they have elected, the politicians who administer their Government, the representatives whom they have sent to Congress, the Generals who lead their armies, the naval officers who have defended their seaports and commanded their cruisers, then they will be allowed to return under the protection of the United States, with such property as may remain to them when their slaves are set free. We know not what effect Mr. LINCOLN anticipates from this Proclamation. A year ago he was prepared with one which was expected speedily to bring the Confederate Government to ruin. A year ago the more sanguine politicians at Washington actually looked upon the war as nearer its end than they do now. A grant of freedom to four millions of slaves must, in their opinion, produce consequences so momentous that the Southern Confederacy would be unable to stand the shock. All, indeed, that the Federals have gained by the capture of Vicksburg and Chattanooga does not equal what the more ardent Republicans hoped for from the Proclamation of January. But that edict produced no perceivable effect upon the Southern people, except to make them more stubborn in their resistance than before. We think it doubtful whether there is any district of the Confederacy where the present Proclamation will have a more powerful effect than the last.

In places that are occupied by Federal troops it may be that some of the proprietors will make their submission in order to save their estates from the grasp of military commanders and the adventurers who follow in their train; but, in spite of the hardships the Southern people have undergone, the diminution of their numbers, the wretched state of their finances, and the loss of some of the most important regions of the Confederacy, there is, we think, little chance that they will accept the offers made to them. When a race of men have been subjected to the trials and excited by the passions of such a war as this, considerations of interest and prudence have little weight. The whole man is changed, the temper is made savage, and the antipathies engendered by a furious struggle make the prospect of returning to the companionship of civil life with the enemy more hateful than the utmost which he can inflict. If the Southern people had not been urged on by animosities stronger than any which we Englishmen have ever felt for a foe, they would undoubtedly have come back to the Union when they first found the North resolute in the conduct of the war, and the European Powers unwilling to interfere. It is now eighteen months at least since they must have been convinced that they would have to struggle against the whole power of the Northern States, without any help from France or England, except at the most an empty recognition, and with the Northern PRESIDENT determined to use, if necessary, the arms of the negro against them. They knew that they must undergo a long and doubtful contest, and that even if they succeeded in achieving their independence, it must be at the cost of frightful private calamities, and probably the ruin of that social system which they seceded and took up arms to maintain. Yet, though towards the close of last year they might have returned to the Union almost in triumph, with the glories of the Chickahominy still bright, and with LEE and JACKSON the most popular heroes of a reconstructed Union, they repelled all the advances of the Democrats, saw without wavering the renewed ascendancy of the party at the North most hostile to themselves, and obeyed a stringent Conscription Act with a readiness unsurpassed in history.

The class of men, too, who are excepted from the amnesty are precisely those who are all-powerful in the Confederate States. If the old men and the women and children were desirous of ending their privations by reunion, their wishes would avail little as long as the country is governed directly by the army, and the army is under the control of the statesmen and Generals whom Mr. LINCOLN requires to be left to his mercy. The trials of the army may be great, but soldiers have seldom a strong desire for the termination of a war, unless, indeed, they are engaged in monotonous garrison duties far from the scene of strife. The excitement of the campaign and the quickening rivalries which it engenders are enough to keep troops in the proper war spirit, as long as they are not depressed by want or exhausted by defeats and fatigue. The Confederate soldiers probably suffer less from the privations of the country than any class of the citizens, for, according to all accounts, every district is put under contribution for them, and the defence of the Republic is made paramount to every private interest. These considerations can hardly fail to have been present to Mr. LINCOLN's mind, since they have been obvious to the Northern press, and present themselves at once to us. We may, then, presume that his amnesty is rather intended as a demonstration of confidence in Federal success than a measure likely to have practical consequences.

Amnesty and the oath of allegiance brought forth anguished cries from the New York Daily News, owned and edited by the treacherous Benjamin Wood, Democratic Congressman and brother of the Tammany mayor, Fernando Wood. This publication, which carried a slogan "Devoted to Peace and Constitutional Liberty," in reality stood for appeasement and slavery by Constitutional fiat. In anti-Lincolnism, it matched any Southern newspaper. This editorial, "Mr. Lincoln's Treachery," appeared on Jan. 10, 1864.

MR. LINCOLN'S TREACHERY

The masses, generally, are slow to reflect upon their actual political condition. Absorbed in the occupations that yield them subsistence, they have often no leisure, and oftener no inclination to study the gradual changes that are being wrought in their system of government. They take a superficial glance at passing events, condemn or approve according to their hasty conceptions, but in most cases shrink from the labor of a thorough analysis, and avoid the responsibility of taking an active and conspicuous part in opposition or support of the theories and measures adopted by those in power. Sometimes, upon the eve of an important election, they shake off their apathy, and give way to brief spasms of excitement; but rarely does the citizen take the trouble to explore the labyrinths of party action, or weigh in an exact balance the sometimes ruinous consequences of legislative or executive conduct. He reads in the public prints that his fellow-countrymen have been dragged off to prison or sent into exile; he hears of the suspension of judicial writs; he is conscious that the Constitution and the law have been repeatedly violated by men in office, and understands that his form of government is undergoing some mysterious process of mutation; but, until the foot of tyranny is at his own threshold, until his own fireside is invaded, and injustice and oppression made him their victim, he fails to appreciate the extent of the wrong, the imminence of the danger, the necessity for his individual exertions in behalf of the common weal. At last, when despotism has completed its net, the masses awaken to the consciousness that they are in the meshes. Too late then to interrupt the action of the loom that weaves those tangles around Liberty; or if interrupted, it must be by the application of the strong hand. The engine must be shattered, the web rent asunder by the last terrible agency of political change, and armed revolution. When the people have endured beyond their patience, they appeal to that awful vindicator, and are either confirmed in bondage or disenthralled.

When Mr. Lincoln commenced his official career as the Federal Executive, he was particularly careful to avoid startling the masses with the shadow of the coming policy. To have given even an intimation of the Abolition-disunion purpose that has since been developed would then have aroused a popular resistance that would have been fatal to the realization of the scheme. The design, undoubtedly already conceived, was vailed from public view by the most unequivocal assurances of an opposite intention. In his inaugural address Mr. Lincoln said: "I have no purpose directly or indirectly to interfere with the institution of slavery in the States where it exists. I believe I have no lawful authority to do so. I have no inclination to do so."

Compare those lines with the conditions of the Amnesty Proclamation, and mark the contrast and the contradiction. And again he alludes to "a proposed amendment to the Constitution, to the effect that the Federal Government shall never interfere with the domestic institutions of the States, including that of persons held to service," and says: "I depart from my purpose to say that holding such a provision *to now be implied constitutional law*, I have no objection to its being made express and irrevocable." Well, in the face of that "implied constitutional law," then acknowledged, the Administration, chiefly by Executive proclamation, constitutionally the weakest but by usurpation the most powerful element of our Government, have not only "interfered with the domestic institutions of the States," but have assumed for the Federal authority the control of the very existence of the institution of slavery. That institution, too, which has hitherto been held sacred under the name of the elective franchise has been tampered with in the North till its virtue is gone, and in the South, according to the intent of the Amnesty, has been withdrawn from the body of the people, and given exclusively to a few thousand Federal retainers, sworn to the Abolition creed. It is even claimed by the partisans of the Administration that the terms of the "Amnesty" give the slaves themselves the privilege to reconstruct the State Governments according to their wishes; witness the following extract from a speech delivered, on Monday last, at the Freedman's Celebration at the Cooper's Institute: "I hope that the Amnesty Proclamation will be so construed as that any ten thousand black men may organize and demand and obtain a republican form of government." Yet this Executive, who now proclaims that no Southerner shall enjoy the elective franchise except upon taking an oath to vote for the destruction of slavery, and who designs, according to the interpretation of his adherents, to include the negroes of the South in that one-tenth of the population to whom the right of suffrage is confined, asserted at his inauguration that he had "no purpose, directly or indirectly, to interfere with the institution of slavery," and believed that he had "no lawful authority to do so." What change has been made in the Constitution that now gives him the authority which he then disavowed? What power abrogated that "implied constitutional law," which he then admitted forbade Federal interference with slavery? This is the explanation: Mr. Lincoln in the first place appreciated the necessity of deceiving the people, because then he was unsupported in despotism by armies drilled into perfect subordination to his will. He deceived them by protesting his innocence of Abolition purposes; he deceived them by quoting the true spirit of the Constitution, and afterward acting in direct opposition to his own interpretation; he deceived them by luring them to arms with the battle cry of Union, and having reduced some half million of them to the condition of automatons by the restraints of military discipline, he renounces the old battle cry and boldly unfurls the flag of Abolitionism.

Meanwhile, while their kindred perish to serve the purpose of fanaticism, the masses of the North are witnessing the transformation of their Government to an absolutism. Their liberties vanish, their rights are ignored; the weapons bequeathed to them to keep tyranny aloof are snatched from their hands and turned against them; the ballot box itself, intended for their protection, is made the instrument of their destruction. Therefore, we say, the masses are slow to reflect upon their actual political condition; or ere this they would have understood their peril, and have interposed the shield of popular moral resistance, without awaiting to be goaded to the sterner remedy of revolution.

Parson Brownlow's Knoxville Whig and Rebel Ventilator, blending religion and radicalism, was a strong friend of Lincoln—in its editor's own peculiar manner. It was the Parson who had said from Tennessee that he would fight the rebels "until Hell freezes over and then fight them on the ice." In 1865, he was to become Governor of Tennessee, and later a U.S. Senator. In these two editorials, from the "Ventilator" of Jan. 23, 1864, he talks about Lincoln the Radical and the war.

WHAT IS A RADICAL?

There are radicals in politics, in religion, in science, in war, in trade, and in all that engages the attention of man: But the word radical, for a few years past, has been the worst abused word in the English language. In the South it is hissed from the mouths of Secessionists against Union men—in the North, it is hissed from the mouth of every "Copperhead" against loyal men. It is an epithet of contempt on the lips of all old maids and fossils, who oppose the spirit of progress. These fossils, had they lived in the days of Hampden, Sydney, Hancock, Washington, Jefferson, and Patrick Henry, would have denounced these men as most hateful radicals. Noah was a radical for attempting to launch his ark and open up a new communication with heaven. Galileo was a radical; and persecuted Luther, whom the whole Protestant world worship, was a radical of the first water. Even the great Fulton, when he began to experiment with steam, was sneered and mocked at, as a crazy radical.—In a word, had it not been for these radicals, the world would now be standing where it was six thousand years ago!

A. Lincoln, Esq., is a radical, and will, during a reign of four years, crush out the largest rebellion known to the world! Thanks to God for the gift of such a radical!

WHO ORIGINATED THE WAR

Among ignorant and uninformed persons, there is a great howl made, on the part of traitors to the United States Government, because Lincoln precipitated the war by sending reinforcements to Fort Sumter, thereby provoking hostilities. Why, this whole statement, acquiesced in by loyal men until all hands agree that it is true, is palpably false. We were battling for the Union, then, at the head of our press in Knoxville, and we claim to know all about the facts in the case. We repeat, the whole story is false, manufactured by traitors and circulated by bad men to influence ignorant minds. No reinforcements were sent—nothing but some provisions to keep the gallant Major ANDERSON and about eighty men from starving, who were surrounded and threatened by 6,000 rebels, with their floating batteries. Pryor, of Virginia, was there—made a speech in Charleston, and urged the rebels to fire upon the Fort—said Virginia would not vote out until some blood was spilt. They took Pryor at his word—they fired—they crushed out ANDERSON and his gallant band with a storm of fire, and, for the first time in the life of our nation, brought our flag down in disgrace. This was done by *Rebels*, and their tory sheets in every Rebel State boasted of the infamous achievement, and of the cowardice of the Lincoln Government.

The United States Government built that Fort and owned it, and not South Carolina, or a mob Government organized at Montgomery. Lincoln sends food there to a starving garrison of less than one hundred men. That miserable old dotard, that corrupt old traitor, *James Buchanan*, refused to do it, said he had no power to do it, and thus he left his successor to do his *sworn* duty. The epitaph of Buchanan is written on every door facing, at every cross-roads, on every rock overhanging a navigable river, and on every tree and wall—it flames forth with living fire, and with a serpent's hiss—*Traitor!* TRAITOR!! TRAITOR!!!

The first great attempt made to destroy this Government was made by Aaron Burr, the last great effort was by the Southern disciples of *Burr*, under the lead of a baser man and a greater fool, *Jeff. Davis*.

Around the world the names of two Americans were known: Abraham Lincoln and Harriet Beecher Stowe. They had met at the White House. Lincoln said, "So you're the little woman who wrote the book that made this great war." They talked with understanding. Early in 1864 she wrote a biographical appraisal for the religious journal, The Watchman and Reflector, reprinted in another Boston publication, Littell's Living Age, Feb. 6, 1864. She quotes him here as telling her, "Whichever way it ends, I have the impression that I sha'n't last long after it's over."

From the Watchman and Reflector

ABRAHAM LINCOLN

BY MRS. HARRIET BEECHER STOWE

The revolution through which the American nation is passing is not a mere local convulsion. It is a war for a principle which concerns all mankind. It is THE WAR for the rights of the working classes of mankind, as against the usurpation of privileged aristocracies. You can make nothing else of it. That is the reason why, like a shaft of light in the judgment-day, it has gone through all nations, dividing to the right and the left the multitudes. For us and our cause, all the common working classes of Europe—all that toil and sweat and are oppressed. Against us, all privileged classes, nobles, princes, bankers, and great manufacturers, and all who live at ease. A silent instinct, piercing to the dividing of soul and spirit, joints and marrow, has gone through the earth, and sent every soul with instinctive certainty where it belongs. The poor laborers of Birmingham and Manchester, the poor silk weavers of Lyons, to whom our conflict has been present starvation and lingering death, have stood bravely for us. No sophistries could blind or deceive *them;* they knew that our cause was *their* cause, and they have suffered their part heroically, as if fighting by our side, because they knew that our victory was to be their victory. On the other side, all aristocrats and holders of exclusive privileges have felt the instinct of opposition, and the sympathy with a struggling aristocracy, for they, too, feel that our victory will be their doom.

This great contest has visibly been held in the hands of Almighty God, and is a fulfilment of the solemn prophecies with which the Bible is sown thick as stars, that he would spare the soul of the needy, and judge the cause of the poor. It was he who chose the instrument for this work, and he chose him with a visible reference to the rights and interests of the great majority of mankind, for which he stands.

Abraham Lincoln is in the strictest sense *a man of the working classes.* All his advantages and abilities are those of a man of the working classes; all his disadvantages and disabilities are those of a man of the working classes; and his position now at the head of one of the most powerful nations of the earth, is a sign to all who live by labor that their day is coming. Lincoln was born to the inheritance of hard work as truly as the poorest laborer's son that digs in our fields. At seven years of age he was set to work, axe in hand, to clear up a farm in a Western forest. Until he was seventeen his life was that of a simple farm laborer, with only such intervals of schooling as farm laborers get. Probably the school instruction of his whole life would not amount to more than one year. At nineteen he made a trip to New Orleans as a hired hand on a flat boat, and on his return he split the rails for a log cabin and built it, and enclosed ten acres of land with a rail fence of his own handiwork. The next year he hired himself for twelve dollars a month to build a flat boat and take her to New Orleans; and any one who knows what the life of a Mississippi boatman was in those days, must know that it involved every kind of labor. In 1832, in the Black Hawk Indian War, the hardy boatman volunteered to fight for his country, and was unanimously elected a captain, and served with honor for a season in frontier military life. After this, while serving as a postmaster, he began his law studies, borrowing the law books he was too poor to buy, and studying by the light of his evening fire. He acquired a name in the country about as a man of resources and shrewdness; he was one that people looked to for counsel in exigencies, and to whom they were ready to depute almost any enterprise which needed skill and energy. The surveyor of Sangamon County being driven with work, came to him to take the survey of a tract off from his hands. True, he had never studied surveying—but what of that? He accepted the "job," procured a chain, a treatise on surveying, and *did the work*. Do we not see in this a parable of the wider wilderness which in later years he has undertaken to survey and fit for human habitation *without* chart or surveyor's chain?

In 1836 our backwoodsman, flat-boat hand, captain, surveyor, obtained a license to practise law, and, as might be expected, rose rapidly.

His honesty, shrewdness, energy, and keen practical insight into men and things soon made him the most influential man in his State. He became the reputed leader of the Whig party, and canvassed the State as stump speaker in time of Henry Clay, and in 1846 was elected representative to Congress. Here he met the grinding of the great question of the day—the upper and nether millstone of slavery and freedom revolving against each other. Lincoln's whole nature inclined him to be a harmonizer of conflicting parties rather than a committed combatant on either side. He was firmly and from principle an enemy to slavery—but the ground he occupied in Congress was in some respects a middle one between the advance guard of the anti-slavery and the spears of the fire-eaters. He voted with John Quincy Adams for the receipt of anti-slavery petitions; he voted with Giddings for a committee of inquiry into the constitutionality of slavery in the District of Columbia, and the expediency of abolishing slavery in that District; he voted for the various resolutions prohibiting slavery in the territories to be acquired from Mexico, and he voted forty-two times for the Wilmot Proviso. In Jan. 16, 1849, he offered a plan for abolishing slavery in the District of Columbia, by compensation from the national treasury, with the consent of a majority of the citizens. He opposed the annexation of Texas, but voted for the bill to pay the expenses of the war.

But at the time of the repeal of the Missouri Compromise he took the field, heart and soul, against the plot to betray our territories to slavery. It was mainly owing to his exertions that at this critical period a Republican Senator was elected from Illinois, when a Republican Senator in the trembling national scales, of the conflict was worth a thousand times his weight in gold.

Little did the Convention that nominated Abraham Lincoln for President know what they were doing. Little did the honest, fatherly, patriotic man, who stood in his simplicity on the platform at Springfield, asking the prayers of his townsmen and receiving their pledges to remember him, foresee how awfully he was to need those prayers, the prayers of all this nation, and the prayers of all the working, suffering common people throughout the world. God's hand was upon him with a visible protection, saving first from the danger of assassination at Baltimore and bringing him safely to our national capital. Then the world has seen and wondered at the greatest sign and marvel of our day, to wit: a plain working man of the people, with no more culture, instruction, or education than any such working man may obtain for himself, called on to conduct the passage of a great people through a crisis involving the destinies of the whole world. The eyes of princes, nobles, aristocrats, of dukes, earls, scholars, statesmen, warriors, all turned on the plain backwoodsman, with his simple sense, his imperturbable simplicity, his determined self-reliance, his impracticable and incorruptible honesty, as he sat amid the war of conflicting elements, with unpretending steadiness, striving to guide the national ship through a channel at whose perils the world's oldest statesmen stood aghast. The brilliant courts of Europe levelled their opera-glasses at the phenomenon. Fair ladies saw that he had horny hands and disdained white gloves. Dapper diplomatists were shocked at his system of etiquette; but old statesmen, who knew the terrors of that passage, were wiser than court ladies and dandy diplomatists, and watched him with a fearful curiosity, simply asking, "Will that awkward old backwoodsman really get that ship through? If he does, it will be time for us to look about us."

Sooth to say, our own politicians were somewhat shocked with his state-papers at first. Why not let us make them a little more conventional, and file them to a classified pattern? "No," was his reply, "I shall write them myself. *The people will understand them.*" "But this or that form of expression is not elegant, not classical." "*The people will understand it,*" has been his invariable reply. And whatever may be said of his state-papers, as compared with the classic standards, it has been a fact that they have always been wonderfully well understood by the people, and that since the time of Washington, the state-papers of no President have more controlled the popular mind. And one reason for this is, that they have been informal and undiplomatic. They have more resembled a father's talks to his children than a state-paper. And they have had that relish and smack of the soil, that appeal to the simple human heart and head, which is a greater power in writing than the most artful devices of rhetoric. Lincoln might well say with the apostle, "But though I be rude in speech yet not in knowledge, but we have been thoroughly made manifest among you in all things." His rejection of what is called fine writing was as deliberate as St. Paul's, and for the same reason—because he felt that he was speaking on a subject which must be made clear to the lowest intellect, though it should fail to captivate the highest. But we say of Lincoln's writing, that for all true, manly purposes of writing, there are passages in his state-papers that could not be better put; they are absolutely perfect. They are brief, condensed, intense, and with a power of insight and expression which make them worthy to be inscribed in letters of gold. Such are some passages of the celebrated Springfield letter, especially that masterly one where he compares the conduct of the patriotic and loyal blacks with that of the treacherous and disloyal whites. No one can read this letter without feeling the influence of a mind both strong and generous.

Lincoln is a strong man, but his strength is of a peculiar kind: it is not aggressive so much as passive, and among passive things, it is like the strength not so much of a stone buttress as of a wire cable. It is strength swaying to every influence, yielding on this side and on that to popular needs, yet tenaciously and inflexibly bound to carry its great end; and probably by no other kind of strength could our national ship have been drawn safely thus far during the tossings and tempests which beset her way.

Surrounded by all sorts of conflicting claims, by traitors, by half-hearted, timid men, by Border States men, and Free States men, by radical Abolitionists and Conservatives, he has listened to all, weighed the words of all, waited, observed, yielded now here and now there, but in the main kept one inflexible, honest purpose, and drawn the national ship through.

In times of our trouble Abraham Lincoln has had his turn of being the best abused man of our nation. Like Moses leading his Israel through the wilderness, he has seen the day when every man seemed ready to stone him, and yet, with simple, wiry, steady perseverance, he has held on, conscious of honest intentions, and looking to God for help. All the nation have felt, in the increasing solemnity of his proclamations and papers, how deep an education was being wrought in his mind by this simple faith in God, the ruler of nations, and this humble willingness to learn the awful lessons of his providence.

We do not mean to give the impression that Lincoln is a religious man in the sense in which that term is popularly applied. We believe he has never made any such profession, but we see evidence in passing through this dreadful national crisis he has been forced by the very anguish of the struggle to look upward, where any rational creature must look for support. No man in this agony has suffered more and deeper, albeit with a dry, weary, patient pain, that seemed to some like insensibility. "Whichever way it ends," he said to the writer, "I have the impresion that *I* sha'n't last long after it's over." After the dreadful repulse of Fredericksburg, his heavy eyes and worn and weary air told how our reverses wore upon him, and yet there was a never-failing fund of patience at bottom that sometimes rose to the surface in some droll, quaint saying, or story, that forced a laugh even from himself.

There have been times with many, of impetuous impatience, when our national ship seemed to lie water-logged and we have called aloud for a deliverer of another fashion,—a brilliant general, a dashing, fearless statesman, a man who could dare and do, who would stake all on a die, and win or lose by a brilliant *coup de main*. It may comfort our minds that since He who ruleth in the armies of nations set no such man to this work, that perhaps He saw in the man whom He did send some peculiar fitness and aptitudes therefor.

Slow and careful in coming to resolutions, willing to talk with every person who has anything to show on any side of a disputed subject, long in weighing and pondering, attached to constitutional limits and time-honored landmarks, Lincoln certainly was the *safest* leader a nation could have at a time when the *habeas corpus* must be suspended, and all the constitutional and minor rights of citizens be thrown into the hands of their military leader. A reckless, bold, theorizing, dashing man of genius might have wrecked our Constitution and ended us in a splendid military despotism.

Among the many accusations which in hours of ill-luck have been thrown out upon Lincoln, it is remarkable that he has never been called self-seeking, or selfish. When we were troubled and sat in darkness, and looked doubtfully towards the presidential chair, it was never that we doubted the good-will of our pilot—only the clearness of his eyesight. But Almighty God has granted to him that clearness of vision which he gives to the true-hearted, and enabled him to set his honest foot in that promised land of freedom which is to be the patrimony of all men, black and white—and from henceforth nations shall rise up to call him blessed.

With the nominating convention for President less than four months away, the Copperhead New York Daily News began to see ulterior motives behind all of "Dictator" Lincoln's decisions. From the Daily News, Feb. 15, 1864.

HE CAN'T DO IT

By whom and when was Abraham Lincoln made dictator in this country? We are aware of no solemn vote of Congress declaring the Republic to be in danger, and the necessity for its salvation of suspending temporarily the normal function of the Constitution and the laws, that Abraham Lincoln may be invested with an absolute dictatorship. How, then, shall we qualify numerous acts of the President during the last three years, notoriously without the sphere of his executive duties, and some of them involving the highest legislative as well as executive powers, such as could be properly performed only by one invested with dictatorial authority. We must qualify such acts as sheer usurpation—audacious, criminal, perjured usurpation. President Lincoln has been guilty of usurpations, which if the dictatorial powers assumed were not used for his protection, would certainly subject him to impeachment and condign punishment.

Pretermitting all other arbitrary acts, we have now to do with one, than which none more high-handed, despotical and atrocious can be found in the history of usurpers; and we signalize it to the reprobation of his countrymen and the astonishment of the world. We allude to the recent annihilation by a stroke of his pen and the proclamation of a military lieutenant, of the sovereignty of Louisiana. No other authority than that possessed as President of the United States is alleged for this act. The proclamation begins: "I, Abraham Lincoln, President of the United States, do," &c., and the only "whereas" precedent to the enacting clause and justificatory of this annulment of the Constitution and laws of Louisiana, and the institution of a new government for that State is in these words: "And whereas, it is now desired by some persons heretofore engaged in said rebellion to resume their allegiance to the United States, and to reinaugurate loyal State governments within, and for their respective States; therefore," &c.

In this cavalier way is it that President Lincoln deals with State sovereignty! Louisiana and Arkansas have thus fallen beneath his pen. Texas, Alabama, and Tennessee, Georgia, Florida, and the two Carolinas will soon follow. President Lincoln is in great haste now to make "loyal" States of these erring sisters, and to "restore the Union." Having been unable to effect it by force of arms and proclamations, during three years (those pestilent Southerners partaking in a provokingly slight degree of the nature of the spaniel that licks the hand which strikes him), the President is now getting up a trick of political hocus-pocus, by which, in the course of a few months, he hopes to make those now "rebelious" States seem to march in file harmoniously with these "loyal" States, exhibiting to astonished and admiring Europe the charming spectacle of a "restored Union." He therefore "proclaims, declares, and makes known" that whenever in any of those now "rebellious" States a number of persons, not less than one-tenth in number of the votes cast in such States at the Presidential election of 1860, and having taken a certain "oath" prescribed, and not having violated it, &c., and "excluding all others," shall re-establish a State Government which shall be Republican—Black —(?)—and "in no wise contravening said oath," such "shall be recognized as the true Government of the State." The farce!

But why this crying anxiety, the curious may ask, to have those "rebellious" States made "loyal," and the "Union restored" in the course of a very few months from this current February? The Presidential election comes on next Autumn. President Lincoln means to be a candidate for re-election; and he hopes that the Electoral Colleges in those thus-to-be-recovered and thus-to-be-"loyal" States will, out of pure gratitude to him who has treated them so kindly these three years, aided by such military and functionary influence as perhaps he may be able to bring to bear upon them, cast their votes unanimously for him, and thus assure his re-election.

We say to President Lincoln that if he counts to foist himself in this manner upon the country for a second term he will be grievously disappointed. The people see through this game, and will not permit it to be successfully played. If he should venture, on the 4th of March, 1865, to reseat himself in the Presidential chair by virtue of an election secured by such shallow trick, we tell him plainly he cannot succeed. There will either be forcible resistance, or, as his first and legal election caused secession South, his second illegal election will cause secession North and West, and break up utterly this Union. The North and West have borne much; but they would not stand such impudent jugglery.

Greeley fired a round for effect before rolling up his anti-Lincoln artillery for the '64 Presidential nomination. He smarted under real and imagined slights by the President; Henry Raymond of The New York Times, Greeley's newspaper enemy, had become Lincoln's confidant—"my Lieutenant-General in politics," Lincoln called Raymond. This rankled Greeley. From the New York Tribune, Feb. 23, 1864.

OPENING THE PRESIDENTIAL CANVASS FOR 1864

It has been our earnest desire that all public discussion of Presidential preferences should be forborne to the latest possible period—at least, so as to await the result of the Spring campaign against the Rebellion. We may be deceived, as we often have been; but we cherish sanguine hopes that the just authority of the Union will be practically reëstablished by the 4th of July next. We heartily wish that the impending Presidential contest could be banished from every loyal mind until that period, while every energy, every effort, should be devoted to the one paramount object of suppressing the Rebellion and restoring Peace to our distracted country. If our hopes should be realized, we should all be better prepared to judge, four or five months hence, who had deserved best of our country, and who had proved himself most competent and best calculated to grapple with the great and difficult problems which must be developed by the progress of "reconstruction." But others have cherished and acted on views radically diverse from ours; so we find the country plunged into a Presidential campaign, simultaneously with that which, we trust, is to seal the fate of the Rebellion. The Democratic National Committee some time since called a National Convention of their party, to assemble at Chicago on the 4th of July, to nominate candidates for President and Vice-President. Gen. McClellan has been sedulously commended as a Democratic candidate for President for some two years past, and the pertinacity and zeal of his personal backers seem likely to be rewarded with a formal nomination. In fact, the sad remains of the late Bell-Everett party gave him a sort of one some weeks ago. Yesterday, the Republican National Committee met in Washington and agreed to hold a kindred Convention of the supporters of the Union War at Baltimore on the 6th day of June. The canvass is therefore fairly opened, in defiance of our wishes. And the renomination of President LINCOLN has already been urged by the Legislatures and Conventions of several States; while some movements in favor of Gen. FREMONT and Gov. CHASE respectively have more recently solicited public attention. We give a synopsis of all these in another part of this paper, and shall here give, as a commentary thereon, a synopsis of the reasons which seem to us to dictate the nomination of another than Mr. Lincoln on the part of those who have sustained his Administration and the War for the Union.

Let us premise that, while each has a perfect and undoubted right to his preference and its free and full expression, great care must be used that our discussions do not become heated and exasperating, and so divide us into factions so alienated and embittered as to prevent our cordial, efficient, coöperation in the great struggle before us. We propose in due time to set forth our own preference, freely and decisively, and seek a nomination in accordance therewith; but, whether our choice or another be ratified, we propose to do our utmost for the candidates who shall be agreed on by those with whom we have battled for the preservation of the Union, the vindication of the rightful authority, and the enforcement of its laws. We may and should confer, and discuss: we must not be divided and arrayed against each other. Let each be careful to say or do nothing that will render coöperation impracticable, or even difficult, in the support of the good and true men who will be nominated, be their names what they may.

We propose here to consider briefly the main reasons urged in the State resolves and letters herewith given for renominating Mr. LINCOLN. They will be found substantially as follows:

I. *Mr. Lincoln has well discharged the responsibilities of his exalted station.*

This is true. We are among those who worked hard to elect Mr. Lincoln, and we are satisfied with the manner in which his public duties have been discharged. He has been patriotic, honest, and faithful. He has done his utmost to serve and save the country. True, he has sometimes erred in judgment, and made mistakes: who has not? He is not infallible—not a genius—not one of those rare great men who mold their age into the similitude of their own high character, massive abilities and lofty aims. But, considering his antecedents and his experience of public affairs— considering that few or none of us anticipated the terrible War which he has been compelled to wage and the treasonable factiousness which has confronted and resisted him even in the loyal States, we are sure the verdict of History in his case will be, 'Well done, good and faithful servant!' The luster of his many good deeds will far outlive the memory of his mistakes and faults. To this extent, then, we agree with the Legislatures and Conventions that have presented him as their favorite for reëlection.

II. *He is the first choice, for the next Presidential term, of a large majority of those who have thus far supported his Administration and the War.*—We consider this, also, quite true. It would be strange indeed if he were not. In the fearful ordeal through which we have passed, his place has necessarily and uniformly been first in the thoughts of the loyal Millions; his name first, after God's in their prayers. To say that, knowing far more, they think more of and feel a warmer attachment to him than to any other living man, is only saying that he has not proved an utter disappointment and failure.

But we dissent altogether from the deduction that Mr. Lincoln ought to be renominated because the loyal masses—not having begun seriously to think of the prospective Presidential contest—have not yet fixed upon some one else to succeed him in his high position. And we consider the signatures of members of Legislatures to letters to the President commending his official course and asking him to run again, as anything but decisive indications of an unbiased choice.

No doubt, a great majority of those who together triumphed as Unionists in the State Elections of 1863, if required to vote for President to-morrow, would vote for Mr. Lincoln. They would have no fair opportunity to make another choice. But so the great body of the Federalists of 1800 undoubtedly preferred John Adams for President; yet running him defeated and broke down their party; when, had they supported John Jay instead, they would have triumphed, and had before them long years of power and usefulness. So a great majority of the National Republicans of 1828 preferred John Quincy Adams for a second term; but they were beaten with him nevertheless more disastrously than they could have been had he given place to Henry Clay. So Martin Van Buren was the undoubted first choice of the great body of the Democrats in 1840; while Gen. Harrison was not the first choice of the Whigs; yet Harrison beat Van Buren more overwhelmingly than Clay could have done. The party that gratified its preference was routed; the party that sacrificed its preference was sweepingly triumphant. And so in the elections respectively of Polk and Pierce. But we need not pursue these illustrations.

III. It has been settled—we think, well settled—by the deliberate action of both political parties, that a President in office is not to be reëlected unless under the pressure of extraordinary circumstances. It was for over forty years the general rule to elect for a second term: for the last thirty years, no President has been rechosen. An amendment of the Constitution, making a President ineligible for a second term, has been often urged—we think not wisely. Better leave the matter where it is—

in the hands of the People. They will, at long intervals, decide that a necessity for reëlection exists; when none such is obvious and pressing, they will decline to reëlect. We do not see how this could be improved.

—The practical question, then, is this—Has Mr. Lincoln proved so transcendently able and admirable a President that all consideration of the merits, abilities, and services of others should be postponed or forborne in favor of his reelection? This is a question whereon, pending the definitive selection of our candidates, there should be the utmost freedom of opinion and expression. We answer it in the negative. Heartily agreeing that Mr. Lincoln has done well, we do not regard it as at all demonstrated that Gov. Chase, Gen. Fremont, Gen. Butler, or Gen. Grant, cannot do as well. We freely admit Mr. Lincoln's merits; but we insist that they are not such as to eclipse and obscure those of all the statesmen and soldiers who have aided in the great work of saving the country from disruption and overthrow. And, if others have done as well in their respective spheres, then we hold that the genius of our institutions, the salutary One Term principle, which has been established by the concurrence of each of our great parties, and by the action of the people, over-ruling either in turn, counsels the choice of another from among our eminent Unionists for President from and after March 4, 1865.

Such are our convictions. We place them before our readers in company with those of the Legislatures and Conventions which have indicated an opposite conclusion, and ask that judgment be rendered in accord with the preponderance, not of authority, but of reasons.

A reasoned editorial on the President and the next Presidential election appeared in Harper's Weekly, March 5, 1864, which was the antithesis of Greeley's reasoning in the Tribune—it found love and growth and a humanity in the President.

THE PRESIDENT

The pamphlet entitled "The next Presidential Election," which is being widely distributed under Congressional franks, announces that the political campaign of 1864 has opened. And now that it has begun, it is desirable in every view, that it be ended as soon as possible by the nomination. The Union men of the country will naturally wish to know at the earliest moment who is to carry their standard, that they may be able to devote all their time and force to the prosecution of the war and the restoration of the Union, instead of wasting them in personal squabbles among themselves.

Obviously in the midst of a war which, begun amidst the sneers and skepticism of foreign governments, and the sad doubt and fear of true men at home, has yet advanced to a near prospect of final victory, it would be a great moral advantage to retain, before all the world, the same general front; to say, on the one hand, to the rebels that the terrible experience of the three years past will be the experience of the four or five to come, if they do not yield, and to the world at large that the people of the United States are steadily bent upon the original purpose of the war, and by every legitimate means whatever, inflexibly mean to restore the Union and maintain the Government. If, indeed, the condition of public affairs were different; if our military lines were marked by disasters; if the rebellion had evidently strengthened itself; if there were a reasonable expectation that the Government might be overthrown; if trade were prostrated or industry paralyzed; if we had been overtaken by crushing financial calamity; if there were no fair prospect of recruiting our armies with veterans and the best of new men; if the measures of the Government at home had been such as to create a powerful and threatening opposition, or had been unfaithful to human liberty; in a word, if there were not a general conviction deep down in the heart of the people that, allowing for all faults and mistakes, and weaknesses, from which no men and no administration can be free; yet, under all the circumstances, military, social, and political, public affairs have been upon the whole, and certainly so far as the President is concerned, sagaciously and honestly conducted, then a change in the head of the Government would be not only wise, but it would be inevitable. . . .

The pamphlet in question urges its plea upon the ground that if a President be eligible for more than one term he will use the enormous patronage of his office to secure another nomination. But it is very clear that to limit the term is not to prevent his corrupt use of patronage. He will, in that case, if inclined to abuse his power, merely turn his energies to securing the succession to the favorite of his party. And the objection lies against vesting patronage in any office whatever, because, if a President may use his patronage to secure a renomination, a Secretary may use his to defeat the President. Take, for instance, the case of two conspicuous public men at this moment, upon the honorable character of each of whom no aspersion had been cast, even by implication, before the appearance of this pamphlet—we mean Mr. Lincoln, the President, and Mr. Chase, the Secretary of the Treasury. Each of them wields enormous patronage. The President, according to the pamphlet, should not be eligible for two terms lest he should misuse his patronage. Very well. And the Secretary of the Treasury—? If the reasoning be sound, he should not be eligible at all lest he should misuse his. Is it proposed that no officer who commands patronage shall be eligible to the Presidency?

As a fact, however, the President is eligible for two terms; and this pamphlet—wisely anonymous—therefore suggests that, if Mr. Lincoln can so wield his patronage at this time as to secure his re-election, it will be much easier for him, with half a million of soldiers and enormous treasures at his command, to have himself re-elected from term to term through his natural life! The author has spared us the necessity of the *reductio ad absurdum*. For he is speaking of Mr. Lincoln; and unless we have entirely misapprehended the impression he has made upon the people, it would be as easy to persuade them to elect Mr. Vallandigham President as to believe Mr. Lincoln to be a new Aaron Burr.

The other argument against the renomination of the President is not theoretical, but practical; it is, that the people are mortified, humbled, and disappointed by the duration of the war, for which, says the pamphlet, nothing but the vacillating policy of the President is responsible. Yet, whoever will deliberately picture to himself the condition of the country and of the public mind at the beginning of the war; the utter lack of general belief that there was to be a war; the want of an army and a navy; the indifference and doubt of the great Democratic opposition at the North; the want of a sentiment of nationality; the question as to the coercive power of the Government; the political and social sympathy with the rebels; the hatred of abolitionism, and the careful excuse of men who said that they were willing to maintain the Union but not to touch slavery; the empty treasury; the universal scorn and jealousy of the Western European Powers; the long demoralization of the public mind, which had been carefully wrought by Calhoun and his political school, which had so long controlled the Government, and so successfully that some men now in high office were willing to let the South go—whoever will recall all this will probably agree that the President had before him a task which required infinite sagacity, patience, and moderation. His success would depend upon his ability to interpret the real popular sentiment, and to distinguish between enthusiasm and conviction. If he lagged, or went too fast, he would equally fail. Every step he took must seem wise to the great public mind, whether it pleased or displeased the ardent van of thinkers and talkers, who are the educators, but not the representatives, of public opinion. Elected as a Republican, known as the author of the saying in reference to slavery and freedom in this country, "A house divided against itself can not stand," supposed (as he was supposed at that time) to be ruled by the Secretary of State, who had declared the existence of the irrepressible conflict, Mr. Lincoln knew that whatever might be the love of the Union—and even that was to be proved—the hate of abolitionism was practically universal. His object was, it must have been, to have a party to sustain the Government, and that party must be, so far as practicable, the undivided North. Senator Yulee, of Florida, had openly said in Washington what every body feared: "The North will have enough to do to take care of itself." Franklin Pierce had written to Jefferson Davis that the war would be at the North. Had the President made a mistake, Yulee and Pierce would have been true prophets. Had the President said on the 15th April, 1861, "Slavery has attacked the Union, slavery is abolished," the suspicious jealousy of the Opposition would have burst into full cry: "There! we knew it. He takes advantage of a riot in South Carolina to overthrow the Union and plunge us into civil war." But the President, equal to his great office in the most solemn crisis of our history, said, simply, "The Union and Government must be maintained by force;" and the country, with its party-spirit paralyzed, cried, "Amen!"

The President knew, what every thinking man knew, that the terrible light of war would illuminate the whole question of its origin and scope. He knew that every gun and rifle and pistol was a more persuasive anti-slavery orator than had ever been heard; that every drop of the blood of sons and brothers and friends would wash clear a thousand eyes that had been blinded, and that before long public opinion would justify and demand measures which some men then saw to be inevitable, but for which the country was not yet ready. Therefore, when General Frémont, one of those men, issued this order, the President said, "No, not yet. The policy must be general when it is adopted, and I must be the judge of the time and the way." So to General Hunter he said in substance: "I do not deny that it may become necessary to do what you have done, but I am the person to order it." There were many faithful men who, when they heard his words, said, sadly, "He does not understand the case, and we are lost." There were many faithless men who thought, "The rebellion is sure of success." If you say that he ought to have trusted the popular enthusiasm, which would have supported the extremest measures, at least you confess that it is only a question of relative sagacity between you and the President. You think the people were ready. He thought they were not. And observe that now, more than two years afterward, the Senate of the United States, almost purged of secessionists, can not make up its mind to pay colored soldiers, who have most bravely fought for the flag, the wages which the Government expressly agreed to pay them. Do you suppose they would debate the point a quarter of an hour if these soldiers were white? The President can not rightfully do what he honestly thinks the people ought to wish, but what he honestly thinks they do wish, because only what they do wish will stand. There were men enough who said, when General Frémont's order came, "Certainly; arm the slaves, and they will make short work of rebels." But within six months these same men were sighing for well-stocked plantations. The sagacity which distinguishes between the furious but evanescent gust of excitement and enthusiasm and the steady trade-wind of principle is the very quality to be desired in a chief magistrate at this time; and among all the prominent men in our history from the beginning none have ever shown the power of understanding the popular mind so accurately as Mr. Lincoln. Nothing is more natural and more common than that an ardent man should in one breath declare that the people wish this or that course to be pursued, and in the next sneer at the President because he yields only to a pressure of the people. What should he yield to? And did Mr. Lincoln ever resist it? Did he ever lag behind it? The President can not treat the nation as a general does an army, and make it subject to his arbitrary will; and although the Constitution wisely intrusts during war the most important powers to his discretion, that discretion consists in his wise estimate of the conviction and desire of the public mind as to their exercise.

From the beginning of his term the President has evidently been persuaded that this was a people's war: that, if the people were wise and brave enough, they would save the Union and the Government; and if they were not, then that no leader could or ought to save them. Twenty months ago he was without a party. The Copperheads hated him; the "Conservative Republicans" thought him too fast; the "Radical Republicans" thought him too slow; the War Democrats were looking for the chance of a return to political power. He held steadily upon his way. As he thought the country ready he took each advancing step. He issued the preparatory proclamation. He followed it with the New Year's decree. He wrote the Greeley letter, the Vallandigham letter, the Springfield letter, simple, plain, direct; letters which the heart of every man in the land interpreted, and, unlike any other instance in our political annals, every letter he wrote, every speech he made, brought him nearer to the popular heart; so that now it is a little too late to call him "well-meaning," "incompetent," "a mere joker," because it is the general conviction that he is no man's puppet; that he listens respectfully to his Cabinet and then acts from his own convictions; that by his calm and cheerful temperament, by his shrewd insight, his practical sagacity, his undaunted patience, his profound faith in the people and their cause, he is peculiarly fitted for his solemn and responsible office. Nor is it likely that the people who elected him when he was comparatively unknown will discard him because, in the fierce light of war which tries every quality and exposes every defect, he has steadily grown in popular love and confidence.

Lincoln had at last found his Potomac commander. On March 9, 1864, he told Grant, "The nation's appreciation of what you have done, and its reliance upon you for what remains to do, in the existing great struggle, are now presented with this commission, constituting you Lieutenant General in the Army of the United States." It had been the President's decision, but Bennett's New York Herald, April 2, 1864, twisted the appointment in this editorial—an example of one of New York's "newspaper Generals" on the attack.

GENERAL GRANT, THE WAR DEPARTMENT AND THE PRESIDENT

General Grant was made commander of all the United States armies by the friends of the administration in Congress because they had no faith in the military abilities of General Halleck, and because they believed that it was necessary for the safety of the country that the President should have better military advice than any that General Halleck had been able to give. They saw how completely our military operations had failed of their object in the East, and, in common with the whole country, they believed that the fault lay, not in the want of any proper quality in our troops, but solely between the President and General Halleck. Consequently they desired to replace the President's mediocre adviser by an able soldier; they desired that a technical strategist, a martinet and a Marplot, should not occupy the highest place in our armies while there was a man of genius to fill it; they desired that General Halleck's influence should no longer be felt in the operations of our armies, and that General Grant should be supreme in that his proper sphere. And these men are naturally dissatisfied at the manner in which the President has failed to carry out, and has even thwarted, their wishes. In the persistent retention of General Halleck near to the President's person they see an inevitable source of future trouble—the seeds of an evil that cannot but cost the country a bitter price in honor, in blood, in money. As General Halleck—fairly on trial for nearly two years—had not the ability to originate the great plans that are to crush the rebellion, it is hardly to be expected that he will appreciate the great plans of another; and it is believed that he will be but too ready to criticise and carp at these plans—as Thersites was never without his sneer at Achilles—and will thus be a source of discord in our councils. Nor is it to be expected that a man of Halleck's calibre will have the moral elevation and greatness of soul to cordially co-operate with one who, being his subordinate in the West, has come forward so rapidly, and finally pushed him from his "pride of place," as Grant has.

Apparently the friends of the administration in Congress have not made their wishes sufficiently plain to the President even yet, and the evidence of this is that there has been no change in his conduct. Metternich, sent to Paris at a critical period in the history of Europe, to study the Emperor Napoleon in the interest of those who desired peace, wrote of him the three words, "He is unaltered." Europe was to be swept again with the hurricane of war. And the President, after so many fearful lessons, and after the withering rebuke of Grant's promotion, is still unaltered, and is going on in the same old way. He keeps his Marplot at his elbow, and under the Marplot's advice manipulates our armies as he pleases. He ignores Grant as he did Scott and McClellan, and we are likely to have reproduced in this summer the tragedies which resulted from the fact that while the generals in the field were carrying on the war in their way the President was carrying on the war in quite another way, and doing more to defeat our armies than the enemy could possibly do. Recently very important changes have been made in the Army of the Potomac, by which two army corps have been put out of existence, and by which the most sweeping changes have been made in the organization of that army and in its corps and division commanders. A measure of such vital consequence to the efficiency of that army certainly called for very ample deliberation on the subject; and it is without precedent in military history that such a measure should be undertaken and carried through without the sanction of the general who is to lead the army in battle. Yet it is positively certain that the whole change in the Army of the Potomac, made after Grant was appointed commander of all our armies, was made without his advice being asked upon the subject, and without his knowledge. It was done entirely by the President and by General Halleck and General Meade. From this, as the first result of the retention of General

Halleck near to the President, Congress may see that its work is only half done. It was not enough to elevate General Grant: General Halleck must be put out of the way; and until that is done there is no hope that the conduct of the war will be different in the future from what it has been in the past.

With the army in new hands, it was thought that the war would take a new and vigorous start, and that the President would relinquish his Presidential intrigues and assist in every way in his power to end this great struggle. But he is unaltered in all respects. In the same manner as he continues his plans against the generals he continues his intrigues in the State Legislatures, and in the little, dirty political conventions all over the country. But he will find that Congress will be firmer and more decided with him on this point than on that of the generals. Unless he shall very soon make his position positive on this point it will be made positive without his assistance. If he does not soon broadly and distinctly declare that he will not accept a nomination, and will not be a candidate for re-election, it is somewhat more than probable that both houses of Congress will make a declaration on this point that will equally astonish both the President and the country.

The political sides lined up as the convention neared. A National Union mass meeting came out for Lincoln. A Cleveland convention of "radical Republicans" was called prior to the Baltimore convention of regular Republicans. The radicals would nominate General Frémont. Bennett's Herald in New York thought in terms of General Grant. In spite of this vicious editorial which appeared on May 20, 1864, in the New York Herald, by election day Bennett was persuaded to support Lincoln.

THE RECENT LINCOLN MEETING—A GATHERING OF THE GHOULS

The Lincoln meeting at the Cooper Institute last Friday evening was one of the most disgraceful exhibitions of human depravity ever witnessed in this wicked world. It was a gathering of ghouls, vultures, hyenas and other feeders upon carrion, for the purpose of surfeiting themselves upon the slaughter of the recent battles. We remember nothing like it in the history of politics. The great ghoul at Washington, who authorized the meeting, and the little ghouls and vultures who conducted it, have succeeded in completely disgusting the people of this country, and have damaged themselves irretrievably.

In the midst of the terrible conflicts of the past three weeks, while thousands of lives were being sacrificed for the national cause, and while every patriotic man was watching with intense and anxious interest the painful progress of events, these ghouls thought only of Lincoln's renomination, the control of the Baltimore Convention and their own chances for petty offices. At the sound of the cannon which was to decide the fate of the country these ghouls hurried down from the mountains, these vultures flocked from the plains, these hyenas sneaked out of their holes, to feast upon the bodies of the slain and gorge themselves with the best blood of the land. They met in horrible conclave in the Cooper Institute, and proceeded to dig up the graves of our soldiers, to tear open the wounds of the wounded, to riot amid carnage and make themselves fat with gore.

There was Clay Smith, the Kentucky ghoul, and Oglesby, the military ghoul, and Arnold, the Congressional ghoul, and Spencer, the legal ghoul. These were the orators of the meeting and they all devoted themselves to praising Lincoln, the great Presidential ghoul, and advocating his renomination and re-election. Their arguments were corpses. Their rhetoric was blood. Their similes were drawn from death and wounds. Their logic was, that because Lincoln had killed so many men he ought to be allowed another term to kill as many more. They cared nothing for the country, for the nation, for the Union; but they rejoiced in carnage, because they hoped it would advance their fortunes, and they gloated over the red river of blood, because they hoped that it would float them into power again. We repeat that so disgraceful and disgusting an exhibition is nowhere chronicled in the history of politics before. It is without a parallel or comparison, and we lack words to stigmatize it as it deserves.

If Lincoln's re-election were not impossible; if the blunders he has committed and the criminalities for which he is responsible had not placed him out of the Presidential ring; if the people had not long ago decided that General Grant is to be our next President, this ghoul-like meeting would alone destroy his chances and render his defeat a foregone conclusion. The trick of claiming credit for carnage and trying to make capital out of wholesale slaughter was too transparent and too boldly played. In ancient times the ghouls stole slyly to their abominable festivals at midnight, by the pale glimmer of the sickly moon; but these modern ghouls parade themselves in open day, advertise their purpose in the daily papers, and gather publicly in a hall lit with the blaze of gaslights, as if anxious to be universally abhorred and despised. The head ghoul at Washington had not sense enough to forbid the meeting. The ghouls and vultures here had not sense enough to postpone it. With brazen faces they confronted an audience whose friends and relatives they were about to devour, and begged for a longer lease of power. Could the force of unblushing depravity much further go?

We anticipate that this meeting of political ghouls will alienate from Lincoln every honest man who has hitherto been deluded into supporting him. Through the action of the Cleveland Convention it will completely extinguish the proposed convention at Baltimore. The nominee of the Cleveland Convention has been already selected, not by politicians, but by events. General Grant, who has hitherto saved the country, is the only man who can govern it for the next four years, and settle all the vexed questions which surround the permanent suppression of the rebellion. For this work Lincoln has shown himself as incompetent, during the present administration, as he has shown himself destitute of any sentiment, any feeling, any judgment, by indulging in vulgar jokes at the most solemn crisis of our history, and countenancing a gathering of political vultures while our armies were actually engaged with those of Jeff. Davis in the most desperate and decisive battles of the war. We hope to see at Cleveland an immense assemblage of the people of all political creeds, actuated by one patriotic impulse. Many of the leading republicans in the State will be there. All the anti-Weed republicans will attend in a body. The democrats will be represented by their best and purest leaders, and by thousands of the rank and file. Indeed, there seems to be a strong disposition among democrats to make Grant their candidate. Now is the time for Tammany Hall to fulfil her pledges. Let democrats and republicans unite upon some such ticket as Grant and Fremont, and Lincoln and his ghouls will be annihilated in advance of an election.

The French newspapers, taking a leaf from the British, saw political motives behind the campaign of the Union Army against Richmond prior to the nomination convention. This fantasy—that Lincoln wanted to see Grant defeated in battle and thus eliminate him as a popular candidate—followed the Copperhead line of illogic. (The journalistic slang in this editorial is literally translated—for example, "bit the dust" is from "mordu la poussière.") From La Patrie, Paris, May 25, 1864.

LA CINQUIÈME CAMPAGNE DES FÉDÉRAUX

CONTRE RICHMOND

[THE FIFTH FEDERAL CAMPAIGN AGAINST RICHMOND]

Yesterday's dispatches bring us news of the Union Army's fifth march on Richmond, which has just ended.

It is curious to see to what extent the commanding general, Grant, has adopted the plan followed last year by his predecessor, Hooker. He sets out at the same time of year, in the same month, fords the Confederate Rubicon at the same place, advances directly on Richmond, crossing the battlefield where twelve months before so many of his compatriots bit the dust, and on almost exactly a year to the day of Hooker's defeat, is in turn beaten by Lee and his generals, the human ramparts of Richmond.

The people of the North must be dismayed by this defeat, which no one expected. There was such great confidence everywhere in the military talents of General Grant; he had "tanned the hides of the rebels" so thoroughly in the West (Grant was head of a leather manufacturing concern before the war)—at Vicksburg, Chattanooga, etc. that the Yankees counted on seeing him follow the same procedure against General Lee. But they forgot one thing—that in the West Grant had to confront only second-rate generals and armies numerically very weak.

Only President Lincoln understood the situation, and as Grant was his greatest rival for the presidency next November, he should not be sorry to be rid of this candidate whose defeat will finish him in public opinion. This is what the present enemies of the President have always hinted at, and now that the disaster is a reality, they will not fail to accuse Mr. Lincoln, as always, of not having helped General Grant as much as he could have.

Nothing could be more unjust than such an accusation. On May 4 [1864], when the Union Army set out, the press was filled with dithyrambs in honor of this invincible army, which, well-fed and well-equipped (better than any in the world) surged into battle with the cry of "On to Richmond!" But of what avail is brute force, badly led, when it must contend against intelligent men, led by a great military chief, who are defending their independence?

The impending Republican nominating convention in Baltimore appeared assured for Lincoln, following the opposition Republican convention in Cleveland. Lincoln's firmest supporter, The New York

*Times, saw the "expediency of a second Presidential term" in this
editorial on May 28, 1864, ten days before the convention.*

THE RECENT STATE CONVENTIONS—MOVEMENTS
FOR PRESIDENT LINCOLN

The great States of New-York, Ohio, and Illinois have just held
their Union State Convention, and have all unanimously declared for
the renomination of President LINCOLN. This action completes the com-
mittal of the Union party through all the loyal States, save Missouri, to
the policy of making no change in the Executive chair. It is now made
certain that the National Convention will be substantially a unit on this
momentous question. ABRAHAM LINCOLN will be renominated by acclamation.

The little squad of bolters, we believe, persist in their intention to
hold an opposition convention, in Cleveland, next week. We like this.
A political campaign with a foregone conclusion would naturally be a
dull one. Something to lighten it up is needed; and this convention
promised to be as good as a play. The only capacity in which these people
meet is that of malcontents. They are simply dissatisfied with the policy
of President LINCOLN; but will find it impossible to agree upon any positive policy of their own. The predominent element in this body, will,
doubtless, be radical, so-called, but this appellation is a mere generality.
The gradations of radicalism are almost infinite—from that which contents itself with the complete extirpation of Slavery, to that which will
stop short of nothing but out-and-out practical "miscegenation," with
the abolition of every distinction, political and social, between the races.
FRED. DOUGLASS demands that the convention shall come up to this latter
mark. Of course the majority of the convention will not be prepared
for this; and yet they will find it impossible to make any substantial issue
with the Administration on any other ground. The same unyielding, impracticable spirit which impels these men away from Baltimore will
necessarily have full sweep in Cleveland, and we are sure of one of the
funniest of hurly-burlies. No practical result can come from it, and the
country will have an excellent laugh for nothing.

That thorough good sense of the American people was never more
clearly exhibited than in the concurrence of the immense majority of
loyal men everywhere in the expediency of electing ABRAHAM LINCOLN to
a second Presidential term. Presidential reëlections have of late years been
utterly discarded. A popular sentiment had set in against them which al-

most had the force of constitutional law. The last instance of the kind was that of ANDREW JACKSON, a generation ago; and but for such a national crisis as this rebellion, it would probably never again have happened. But this settled popular persuasion that Presidents ought never to be tempted with the hopes of a reëlection readily yields to such an exigency as the present, and that, too, by spontaneous movement. No nominating convention ever met which was so little the product of party machinery, so directly the emanation of the popular will, as that which will soon assemble in Baltimore. The resolutions which have been passed by Legislatures, and other representative bodies of the people, have not come from any management of politicians. The pretence that they owe their existence to wire-pulling and intrigue is too absurd to impose upon anybody. Intrigue, doubtless, in some circumstances, can do much to shape party action, but however dextrous its application, it never secures unanimity. The bare fact that intrigue is necessary pre-supposes variance of opinion; and, instead of producing concurrence, it stimulates opposition to work by counter intrigue, and a strife which shall get the advantage inevitably follows. Unanimity at the preliminary stage can come only from a spontaneous community of feeling. Chicanery never generates it. So far as regards the accomplishment of unselfish ends, many politicians, doubtless, would have found their account in a new Administration, which would have gone into a general re-distribution of the offices. Had there been anything like a good prospect for effecting a change, the mere lovers of the loaves and fishes we may be sure, would have brought into play the extremest resources of intrigue against the Administration. To a slight extent it was attempted; but its hopelessness soon became so apparent that the attempt was abandoned, and the uncontrollable will of the people was submitted to with the best grace possible. Political intriguers, party managers, have found their avocation gone. They have had no alternative but to fall in with the great popular current, whose single impulse is the necessity of sweeping down the rebellion.

This irresistible popular sentiment is the more extraordinary in view of the unexampled abuse which has been poured upon the Administration for the last two years. No living man was ever charged with political crimes of such multiplicity and such enormity as ABRAHAM LINCOLN. He has been denounced without end as a perjurer, a usurper, a tyrant, a subverter of the Constitution, a destroyer of the liberties of his country, a reckless desperado, a heartless trifler over the last agonies of an expiring nation. Had that which has been said of him been true there is no circle in DANTE's Inferno full enough of torment to expiate his iniquities. Yet

the American people are to confer upon him an honor which this generation has not before witnessed. Their answer to all this horrible stream of
blackest crimination will be his re-elevation to the highest office in their
gift; and that, too, by a majority never before known to our political
history.

Now, what does all this evince? Are we to suppose that the people
have deliberately struck a league with all the powers of wickedness, or
that they have been smitten with an incapacity to distinguish right from
wrong? Either one of these, or else the guilt rests not with ABRAHAM LIN-
COLN, but with his railers. Either the people have themselves become
traitors or idiots, or all this Copperhead vituperation has a common
source with the rebel vituperation, whose virulence has hardly exceeded it.

Chapter 9

The Second Term

JUNE 1864–APRIL 14, 1865

The party splitters went to work in '64—as they had maneuvered against the Rail Splitter candidate in '60. There were enough disgruntled Generals around to choose from, some with only half their reputations shot away. Even in the Cabinet a candidate worked for the nomination; but Mr. Chase of Treasury had been tripped by too flagrant politicking on his own behalf. The Republican wheelhorses moved obliquely this time for their candidate was a President who, to the public eye, watched the war more closely than the political arena.

Way back in 1846 Lincoln had taken notice of the divisive actions of political parties: "It is certain that struggles between candidates do not strengthen a party; but who are most responsible for these struggles, those who are willing to live and let live, or those who are resolved, at all hazards, to take care of 'No. 1'?" Lincoln now gave the party politicians no comfort, "letting the thing run itself." Meanwhile, before the regular Republicans met, New Yorkers calling themselves War Democrats spoke up for General Grant. At the Cleveland convention of the Radical Democracy, General Frémont was nominated for President on a platform of a one-term Presidency, with reconstruction of the States to be left up to Congress—a strange convention mainly united in its desire not to see Lincoln attain a second term. Frémont, for whom Lincoln had campaigned in '56, in accepting declared that he did so to obviate Lincoln's nomination.

On June 7, 1864, the Republicans met in Baltimore. The temporary chairman was Robert J. Breckinridge, Kentucky. "Does any man doubt," he said, "that Abraham Lincoln shall be the nominee?" The

399

delegates roared their approval. Henry J. Raymond of *The New York Times* served as chairman of the convention's platform committee. The roll call showed 484 votes for Lincoln, 22 for Grant (the Missouri delegation). *The New York Tribune*, June 9, 1864, "bowed to the decision" of the convention.

THE BALTIMORE NOMINATIONS

The Union National Convention yesterday presented, with entire unanimity, the name of ABRAHAM LINCOLN as a candidate for reëlection to the Presidency of the United States. This nomination is in unquestionable accord with public sentiment and all its manifestations. A great majority of the Unionists believe and feel that Mr. Lincoln ought to be recognized and deferred to as President in every part of our country. They feel that rebellion in a republic adds perfidy to treason—that it is a repudiation of the most sacred voluntary engagements, as well as infidelity to country and to liberty. Hence they urge that the reëstablishment of the National authority would be imperfect if the chief magistrate whose election was made the pretext for revolt were to be set aside, and the Rebels permitted to cover their retreat from their untenable position by a pretense that Lincoln's supersedure had obviated their chief objection to recognizing and obeying the National authority. Millions have doubtless felt that to set Mr. Lincoln aside, and elect another President in his stead, would be plausibly accounted an admission that the Secessionists had some excuse for their treason.

We admit the force of this consideration; but it seems to us far outweighed by one that points to a different choice, and which we will here briefly indicate:

The life of the Republic is still in imminent peril. Its foes are of its own household; proverbially the bitterest and least relenting. Apart from the outright Secessionists, who are fighting for Disunion, pure and simple, with the fury of fiends, there is a large and formidable party, even in the loyal States, who are at heart enemies to the National cause. They are not Secessionists; they do not favor permanent Disunion; but they are devotees of the Slave Power, and hope for "reconstruction" through its triumph. In spite of ample demonstration, they will not believe that the Rebels hate them as they do us, while despising them far more; and they say to themselves, and privately to each other, "Let the War break down; let the Government be forced, through defeat and bankruptcy, to make peace with the Rebels on their own terms; that will upset the party now in power and put us in their places; and we can easily restore the Union: for, if the Rebels won't come to us, we'll go to them—adopt their Constitution, obtain admission, State after State, into their Confederacy (leaving out New-England as incorrigibly 'fanatical,') and thus restore the Union on a sound 'conservative' basis, silencing or banishing all 'agitators' and advocates of 'isms,' and live in fraternal peace and harmony evermore, glutting the markets of the world with Cotton and Tobacco, importing no end of Fabrics, Wares and Liquors, and all getting rich and enjoying ourselves. Why not?"

Now, these men are really and bitterly hostile to the Government, in its struggle for the National life; but they make their assaults under cover of hostility to the Administration. And the renomination of Mr. Lincoln will inevitably intensify their efforts and rebarb their arrows. A Presidential Election implies dissent, difference, discussion, criticism—nay, license, assault, and open hostility. You cannot punish as seditious or suppress as disloyal assaults which wear the guise of partisan disparagement and electioneering slang. It will be false as falsehood can be that the President does not wish the Rebellion put down—wants the War to go on indefinitely—does not support our Generals in the field, but leaves this or that command to be sacrificed—makes campaigns subordinate to carrying this or that State, &c., &c.—but unprincipled knaves will persistently assert all these and far more, and ill-informed, hot-headed partisans will believe them. Charges that would be utterly forborne, or would fall powerless and harmless, will not be rëiterated and widely credited, because the President at whom they are aimed is also a candidate for rëelection. These charges will often convert passive into active and efficient hostility to the prosecution of the War; and it will never do to put their authors and disseminators into Fort Lafayette; for that would be deemed a palpable interference with the freedom of elections. And thus, at a time when the sore trials of the Republic should be nearly over, we feel that some of their worst phases are just before us.

That the President has made grave mistakes in the prosecution of our great struggle, all are aware: that he has *meant* to do wrong, no one really believes. Loathing bloodshed and scarcely crediting the possibility of its occurrence, he yet gave fair and full notice that, from the taking of his inauguration oath, he should hold himself under the most solemn obligation to enforce, to the extent of the power reposed in him, the laws of the United States throughout the geographical area of our country. But, before he had struck a blow in accordance with this conviction, the Rebels commenced open war by the bombardment of Fort Sumter; and from that hour he has done his best to perform his duty. If another's best would have been better still, that is not his fault but his misfortune. And there lives no man who could have assumed the Presidency when he did without encountering, and seeming to deserve, severe criticism. Had he called out a million men at the start, and crushed the Rebellion forthwith by sheer weight of numbers, he would have been accused of spending vast sums needlessly and inordinately deranging the National industry under the impulse of partisan hate and selfish ostentation. He erred in the opposite direction; but there was no course possible whereby he could have avoided calumny and silenced detraction. And now all the hates and spites and slights and disappointments of a four years' momentous struggle are to be conjured up against him; and against not him only, but against all who battle with him for the overthrow of the Rebellion.

We cannot but feel that it would have been wiser and safer to spike the most serviceable guns of our adversaries by nominating another for President, and thus dispelling all motive, save that of naked disloyalty, for further warfare upon this Administration. We believe the Rebellion would have lost something of its cohesion and venom from the hour in which it was known that a new President would surely be inaugurated on the 4th of March next; and that hostility in the loyal States to the National cause must have sensibly abated or been deprived of its readiest, most dangerous weapons from the moment that all were brought to realize that the President, having no more to expect or hope, could henceforth be impelled by no conceivable motive but a desire to serve and save his country, and thus win for himself an enviable and enduring fame.

All this is of the past. The will of a great majority of the Unionists has been heard, and it says, "Let us have Abraham Lincoln as our President for another term!" We bow to their decision, and ardently hope that the result may vindicate their sagacity and prove our apprehensions unfounded.

Lincoln, notified of his nomination, said, "I will neither conceal my gratification, nor restrain the expression of my gratitude, that the Union people, through their convention, in their continued effort to advance the nation, have deemed me not unworthy to remain in my present position." A report in the New York World, June 18, 1864, was of a hostile enough nature to indicate that the campaign was on.

The Second Term JUNE 1864–APRIL 14, 1865

MR. LINCOLN IN PHILADELPHIA

What the President Did and Said at the Great Sanitary Fair.
He makes a Little Speech, Cracks a Little Joke, and
Drinks a Little Cold Water

RAILSPLITTING ORATORY DESCRIBED

How Old Abe Walks and Talks and Shakes Hands.

From Our Own Correspondent

PHILADELPHIA, June 16, [1864].

To-day your correspondent has belonged for a brief moment to that happy-go-lucky class of whom Shakespeare says that they "have greatness thrust upon them"—that is, reflected greatness, derived from the presence of the great. I have been face to face with, shaken hands, and conversed with the President of these United States, and now attempt to give you a brief description of some of my impressions of the "Second Washington."

I was at Baltimore at the time Mr. Lincoln went through that city of risks on his way to the inauguration, but his passage was accomplished with so much celerity, and under cover of a costume so irregular, that I was unable to obtain a view of his illustrious countenance, and had not, until to-day, even had a "square look" at the man whose fame has been by accident rendered immortal. I came; I saw to-day; I am satisfied.

WHY MR. LINCOLN CAME TO THE FAIR.

It was given out here, some time before the opening of the Sanitary Fair, that Mr. Lincoln would, in the gratification of his desire for "inaugurations," grace with his presence the initial ceremonies of the great exhibition. But for the duties of his position, what with the capture of Richmond, the manufacture and manipulation of his convention at Baltimore, the process of renominating himself, and the minor but perplexing matter of conducting the affairs of the government, he found his hands full, and was compelled to forego attendance at the fair until after it had made several days' progress. It can hardly be said of him, however, he "came a day after the fair."

403

"GOING TO THE FAIR."

At a quarter past four Mr. Lincoln entered a barouche and four and was conveyed to the fair, escorted by various military organizations, and flanked by the inevitable rag, tag and bobtail. At five o'clock the President arrived at the entrance on Eighteenth Street, and after considerable squeezing was passed into the building, the police being scarcely able to keep off the crowd. I could not help thinking how the boisterous mass would surge back before a few determined Metropolitans; but then, this is Philadelphia, and we can't expect everything in these rural villages.

Mr. Lincoln, with great difficulty, reached the reception room of the executive committee. Here he gave wings to one of those terse, clear-cut and original expressions which so mark the man. "I'd like," said he, "I'd like a little cold water." Memorable words! . . .

Shortly after this solemn passage in a great man's life, Mrs. Lincoln was announced. She speedily passed into the ladies' room. The President's wife looks as robust as ever. Her maternal graces bloom so brilliantly as when she left her rural home, wondering what "they say of us," and floated toward Washington. Time does not attenuate her substantial form, and evidently sits lightly on her plac'd brow. Her walk is not less queenly than when she played in the prairie state the charming role of the "pretty maid milking her cow;" and while possibly greater amplitude of skirt is necessary than of yore, yet she still shows traces of her youthful *ensemble*.

The President spent about an hour in making the tour of the fair, and finally brought up at the "collection room," where a well-prepared table was arranged. Your reporter was not near enough to catch the President's first words upon entering the banquet hall, but is informed that he whispered to a companion on the left flank, "This is a right smart get-out."

HOW HE SHAKES HANDS.

Mr. Lincoln passed some time in shaking hands. This salutation is with him a peculiarity. It is not the pump-handle "shake," nor a twist, nor a spasmodic motion from side to side, nor yet a reach toward the knee and a squeeze at arm's length. When Mr. Lincoln performs this rite, it becomes a solemnity. A ghastly smile overspreads his peculiar countenance, then, after an instant's pause, he suddenly thrusts his "flapper" at you as a sword is thrust in tierce; you feel your hand enveloped as in a fleshy vice, a cold clamminess overspreads your unfortunate digits; a corkscrew burrows its way from your finger nails to your shoulder, the smile disappears, and you know that you are unshackled. You carefully count your fingers to see that none of them are missing, or that they have not become assimilated in a common mass, and wonder why Mr. Lincoln does not put that "hand" on the throat of the rebellion, instead of employing it in writing proclamations.

ABRAHAM'S PERSONNEL.

Mr. Lincoln does not grow handsomer as he grows older. He never was a very pretty man. He is large, but not voluptuous. Had he been (alas! that he was not) born a woman, he never would have been mistaken for the model of the Paphian Venus. But writing proclamations and suppressing newspapers evidently is less congenial to him than poleing flatboats or splitting rails. Indeed, the martial port which he obtained in his many and sanguinary wars with the heathen savages of the Western wilds, has entirely left him. Still, he is evidently cultivating "characteristics." He may not desire to imitate the philosopher of Spruce street, but his neck-tie is an outrage, and the manner in which he wears it a still greater atrocity. Why should he allow an unseemly knot to show itself under his left ear? It gives rise to unpleasant thoughts in the minds of the faithful and wicked comparisons among his numerous enemies.

BUT FEW JOKES.

"The Second Washington" did not, on this occasion, that I can learn, crack many jokes—smutty or otherwise. Whether the solemnity of the occasion overpowered him, or whether he felt billious, I am uninformed. It is said that when he began the work of filling himself up with the good things of the table, he exclaimed: "I'll fight it out on this line if it takes all summer." I hope this is not true. The expression is not as new as it might be; and really I'm afraid it will become general if it's repeated a few hundred thousand times more.

LAST AND TOP OF ALL.

But all things have an end, and it is time this letter followed the universal rule. I will barely mention how the shoddy people roared them-

selves hoarse, how the gushing Loyal Leaguers invited him to their headquarters, how he made another Demosthenic oration there, how he addressed the loyalists outside in a two-minute speech, and how, afterward,
he made a last appearance as a public speaker in response to the calls of
the National Union Club, and how, finally, he retired to his hotel,
wrapped the drapery of his couch about him, and laid down to sleep and
(possibly) to pleasant dreams.

*The fact that Lincoln had put himself on the voting block a
second time meant his end—so believed the Democratic organ and
longtime foe in Springfield, the* Illinois State Register, *Aug. 7, 1864.*

THE END OF LINCOLN

The country has reason to be thankful that Abraham Lincoln's ambition and arrogance had become so great that he was induced to use the
power of his patronage to secure the republican nomination for another
term. It was the one thing needed to secure the utter overthrow of the
party that has brought all this misery upon the republic. The danger was
that some one would be brought forward who would plead an exemption
from all responsibility for the blunders and crimes of the present administration, and that the people would overlook the fact that their trials
arose not so much from the men in power as from the principles of the
party which has sustained them. But now, with the candidature of Mr.
Lincoln, there is no dodging the issue. Republican principles, as demonstrated by the administration of affairs during the last three years, must
be approved or disapproved at the ballot box. We rejoice that the issue
is presented in this naked, undisguised form. The administration, of
which Mr. Lincoln is the chief, tricked the country into a war, which it
has proved itself incapable of prosecuting successfully or concluding hon-
orably. It has violated the rights of the people, in a manner, which, in any
other country, would have provoked a revolution. The most powerful
monarchy in Europe would not dare commit the outrages which have
been put upon us by the Lincoln administration. But the people have
discovered that the delusion under which they have labored for three
years, that they could afford to surrender their own liberty to secure
territorial unity, is a monstrous fallacy, and they are now settling down
to the determination that whether the Union is saved or not, *constitutional liberty must be preserved!* The surrender of personal rights, and
the establishment of an erratic, irresponsible despotism, does not help

the cause of the Union a particle, and the people are becoming convinced of the fact. The doom of Lincoln and black republicanism is sealed. Corruption and the bayonet are impotent to save them. The sovereign people have willed it, and the would be despots at Washington must succumb to their fate. Long live the republic!

After a summer of heavy fighting, General Sherman's field forces captured Atlanta and all saw military victory as a factor in Lincoln's political favor. The South, too, realized "all this in the interest of Lincoln and of the party which is to profit by his election; or, which is the same thing, by the continuance of this war." The Richmond Dispatch, Sept. 14, 1864.

The Lincoln party in Yankeedom are making precisely such a use of the capture of Atlanta as we foresaw and foretold they would. Bells are rung, cannon are fired, processions are ordered, orations delivered, and the whole land called upon to rejoice and be glad, for that the rebellion, so often slain and buried before, is slain and buried yet once again.— Lincoln, to intensify the deception and add as much as practicable to his own chances of re-election, orders a day of thanksgiving to be set apart for the mighty triumph at Atlanta—a triumph which consisted in the infliction of a loss of fifteen hundred men upon General Hardee—with quite an equal loss on the part of the Yankees—and the occupation, without resistance, of Atlanta, which our forces had already held many weeks longer than they expected to hold it. The object of all this parade and flourish of trumpets is too palpable to be mistaken. It is done to make the Yankee nation forget the innumerable bloody defeats its armies have sustained since last May—the one hundred and fifty thousand that Grant has lost to slaughter or captivity in Virginia—the seventy or eighty thousand that have been slain, wounded, or taken under Sherman—the entire expulsion of their troops from Texas—the disgraceful defeat of Banks in Western Louisiana and the almost entire loss of that State—the recovery of Arkansas almost entirely by the Confederates—the inauguration of a furious war in Kentucky—the defeat in Florida—making altogether a series of disasters such as rarely ever befel a modern army in so short a space of time. And it has succeeded. The little success at Atlanta, swelled and exaggerated by the most infamously mendacious press that the world ever beheld, into a mighty achievement, commanding the most momentous results, has already made the Yankee nation forget its defeats and humiliations—has run them mad with exultation, and has roused once more the cry for blood. Incapable of being taught by experience, the people of Yankeedom—as we knew they would—trust implicitly to their lying oracles, as though they had never deceived them before, when they tell them for the fiftieth time that the rebellion is on its last legs, and that they need only an expenditure of a hundred thousand more lives to crush it forever. And all this in the interest of Lincoln and of the party which is to profit by his election; or, which is the same thing, by the continuance of this war. They play for a high stake, and their "dice are human bones."

Such form a portion of the devices by which the Yankee nation is to be seduced into a continual support of Lincoln and the war; but these are not all. The interesting people whom it is proposed to amuse in this manner, love war and glory; but it is always with a proviso that they come in for a share of the glory only. They do not greatly desire to take any of the hard knocks that precede the glory and are necessary to its acquisition. They have a peculiar horror of the draft, and there is great danger that the enforcement of it may turn to the disadvantage of the war candidate. It is unfortunate, certainly, for the prospects of Lincoln that it should come on just at this particular moment. Especially is the great city of New York, which has already shown symptoms of a determination to resist, a subject of intense anxiety to the war candidate and his party. Accordingly, a device, so transparent that it could deceive no other people on the face of the earth, has been adopted to keep quiet the multitude of Gotham. They are told that there will be no draft amongst them—that their prodigious patriotism has already gone far ahead of the requisitions of the Government—that they will be credited with a number of men fully equal to the whole number that they will be assessed with. Other portions of the country are dangerous likewise, for they have votes, and may give them against Lincoln if he presses the draft. This head of the Cerberus must also be gratified with a sop, and Stanton throws it to them. He tells them there will be no draft anywhere for five or six weeks, and so they may go about their business for the present. Indeed, he thinks if they will only send Grant one hundred thousand more men, he is sure that not more than three hundred thousand will be required, and two-thirds of these will only be required to keep open roads and rivers, restore commerce, and settle other matters appertaining to conquest, Grant having by this time done all the fighting that is to be done. Last of all, to lull the whole nation to rest, Seward tells them that there will be no draft at all—that no draft is necessary—that volunteers enough have been found to fill up the ranks to the required extent—that is, to the extent of five hundred thousand!!! We hope to be excused for marking this passage with three notes of admiration. It is so wonderful, that nothing short of three could properly express our amazement.

These proceedings indicate one thing, at least, very clearly. It is that Lincoln and his followers have a mortal fear of this draft, and that they dare not at this time attempt to enforce it. Yet that it will be enforced, at the point of the bayonet if necessary, is as clear as that the sun rises in the east and sets in the west. Let Lincoln be first assured of success, and then we shall see how speedily he will dispose of all objections, and what disposition he will make of those who urge them. How completely soever he may succeed in blinding his own people to his intentions, it does not become the people of these Confederate States to be equally blind. That the draft will be executed, and that completely and thoroughly, we repeat we hold to be absolutely certain. That Grant will be heavily reinforced, although for the present he may not be able to obtain the full hundred thousand that he calls for, we likewise consider a certainty. We state our belief with no view of depressing the spirits of our people, which, however cast down for the moment, have always risen to the full height of every emergency whenever it has been presented to them. We are fully able to meet and to master all the circumstances of the crisis which is about to present itself to us, and our object is to prepare our people for doing so.

The Democratic National Convention nominated General Mc-Clellan in Chicago, as expected. Abroad, the London Times, Sept. 22, 1864, saw the military situation as a leading factor in the election.

General M'CLELLAN's acceptance of the Chicago nomination completes the preparations for the Presidential contest. The lists are now open, the champions produced, the issue is declared, and the battle inevitable. Mr. LINCOLN's friends fought hard against assumptions so unfavourable to their own prospects. They first argued that there could be no unanimity at Chicago, and that the strength of the Democratic party would be destroyed by division; but these hopes were dashed to the ground by a political accord and union unexpected, probably, by the Democrats themselves. Since the nomination of General M'CLELLAN under circumstances so promising. they have speculated anxiously on his refusal of the offer. Many of the Republican journals have overwhelmed him with compliments only to remind him that by his acceptance of such a proposal he would forfeit all his numerous claims to popular respect, and ruin himself in the estimation of the country. But this chance of escape is now lost also. General M'CLELLAN accepts the nomination and consents to stand. Thus the match is made, and the game must be played out. Desperate, too, in the extreme will be the grapple between the combatants, for the champions and the parties are the most formidable that could be pitted against each other. Mr. LINCOLN can no longer hope to slip into a second term of office, either unopposed or with only a contemptible opposition. The great party of the Democrats have coalesced in perfect unanimity against him, and they have secured as their willing candidate the very man whose name would bring the greatest strength to their cause.

From this time, therefore, the prospect is clearly and sharply defined. The gladiators have stepped into the political arena, and they must fight according to the laws of the strife. They are not ill-matched. If the Democrats, when fairly united, are not the more powerful party of the two, Europe has been greatly misinformed of the state of opinions in America; but the Republicans have the advantage of possession, a firmer and less equivocal policy than their adversaries, and the chances of support from military success. We have already been assured that SHERMAN's victory in Georgia proved immediately favourable to Mr. LINCOLN's cause, though the measure of that success is now given in the General's own report. On the day following the battle he advanced with his army only to find his enemy impregnably posted just six miles off. So securely was the Confederate General intrenched, and so strong was his force, that SHERMAN declined to attack him, and prudently retired. Yet the victory which pushed a Southern army this short distance in retreat, but left it still in a plight to defy the conquerors, sufficed for the moment to send LINCOLN up and M'CLELLAN down, and the not improbable capture of Mobile may perhaps contribute to the depression of the Democratic cause. On the other hand, a great military disaster would assist Mr. LINCOLN's opponents, so that the ordinary political calculations are liable to incessant disturbance from the incidents of war. . . .

General M'CLELLAN wishes to consult the susceptibilities of the War Democrats, and to catch the votes of stray Republicans, and so he professes to uphold the Union "at all hazards"—that is, even, if necessary, at the cost of continued war. President LINCOLN wishes to catch the votes of stray Democrats, and so his SECRETARY [of State Seward] throws over the Slavery question, and all other questions, save that of Union, that might stand in the way of peace. In short, the ostensible "platforms" of the two candidates are identical, except that one is turned upside down. Mr. LINCOLN cannot forego the Union, and so must keep on fighting, but he will make peace, if the Union is preserved, as unconditionally as anybody. General M'CLELLAN cannot forego the Union, but, instead of going on with the war, he puts the peace experiment first, and reserves the fighting for afterwards. We have repeatedly expressed our opinion that the policy of the War Democrats is logically untenable, for it means pacific war, or warlike peace. The Republican policy is more consistent— "peace when you please, and on the terms you know, but war till then." It would be hard, however, to say that the inconsistent policy is not a judicious one. If the Americans themselves do not know their own minds, or, knowing them, dare not speak them, the Democratic policy is skilfully adapted to their uncertainties or fears. It bridges the space between them and the object which they desire. That object is peace, and the Democrats put peace in the foreground. At present, they couple it with conditions which save the national pride, but are probably quite incompatible with the object itself. A short time hence, the conditions may be dropped while the object is kept in view, and the nation, after enjoying a respite from the trials of war, and tasting the blessings of peace once more, may gradually resolve on retaining these blessings, even at the expense of what would now be thought an impossible surrender.

The prisoners of war became a political issue. There were charges and countercharges of ill treatment, of failure to exchange and of Lincoln making Union prisoners whose military service had expired languish in jail. Of this, the Richmond Sentinel, Sept. 22, 1864, advised—advice from a strange quarter indeed—McClellan orators to make political capital.

LINCOLN AND HIS PRISONERS OF WAR

"Resolved, That the shameful disregard of the Administration
to its duty in respect to our fellow-citizens, who now, and long have
been, prisoners of war, in a suffering condition, deserves the severest
reprobation on the score alike of public and common humanity."

The above is one of the resolutions of the Chicago platform. It condemns the conduct of the Washington authorities in reference to the exchange of prisoners of war, in language strong and severe, but more than justified by the occasion. We trust that the course pursued by LINCOLN, through his Commissioners of Exchange, will now be fully canvassed before his people, and their judgment invited thereon. And, indeed, it is but reasonable to suppose that those who are arraigning LINCOLN for alleged misdeeds and deficiencies, will be sure to visit him with thorough exposure on a point so vulnerable, and so nearly touching the sympathies and sensibilities of the people. We know of no more damaging weapon of assault, in the hands of a fearless orator, than the simple story of the neglect, abandonment, and immolation, which LINCOLN's soldiers have experienced at his hands, when overtaken by the severities of fortune. At the very time when the sympathies of their rulers should be most exercised, those who have periled life and limb in battle, who have endured toil and exposure in the camp and on the march, are cast off, without pity, and abandoned to the horrors of imprisonment in crowded quarters and remote regions. It is, indeed, "a shameful disregard" of duty to his unfortunate soldiers; and well deserves "the severest reprobation" of his own people and of the world.

If any proof be needed of the brutal inhumanity that marks the course of the enemy in this matter—if any aggravation be possible of an offence disgraceful in the extreme—they are found in the allegations of the criminals themselves. As if not content with the odium of abandoning their soldiers to an indefinite captivity, in a climate to which they are unaccustomed, and to them unwholesome, they take great pains to declare that these prisoners endure not only the horrors inseparable from such a condition, but the most terrible additions thereto. Not only the discomfort, the filth, the disease of a crowded camp, and the intolerable tedium of confinement, but *starvation* is a part of their lot. This, which they falsely bring as a charge against us, is a real condemnation of themselves; for we are bound to give them credit for believing what they say.

The sum is this, therefore: LINCOLN leaves some forty or fifty thousand of his soldiers in captivity. They are undoubtedly very miserable, as prisoners must necessarily be, and he believes that they are suffering the pangs of starvation; dying by inches of the pinchings of hunger and destitution. He leaves them in this condition voluntarily and deliberately; against his agreement with us, and under the severest reprobation alike of public and private humanity. This vast multitude he leaves to pine, and to suffer, and to die, when in a day he could secure their liberty by any fair and equal exchange. This he refuses—refuses, because he deliberately rejects an exchange, refuses, because he prefers that his men remain in such captivity as he alleges they suffer. We do not believe that any people on earth can be found who would sustain their rulers in such a course. We do not believe that the people of the United States can be induced, even by their violent hatred of us, to consent to this wanton, unnecessary, barbarous, diabolical sacrifice of their own sons and brothers and friends.

A new feature of wickedness has been added to the record which LINCOLN and his agents have made, concerning the captive Federals. Occasionally, a few have gained their liberty on each side, by a sort of special exchange. But SHERMAN, in some late negotiations for such an object, has revealed the policy that rules at Washington, touching a large class of the Federal prisoners.—It was obvious before, but had not been avowed. LINCOLN specially and peculiarly abandons those captives whose terms of service have expired! He made them fight in some cases up to the last day of their service, exposing them to death and to capture; but, when captured, he utterly forsakes them. They are not to be exchanged, even when others may. . . .

It should be added, too, that many supplications have gone up from the prison houses to the throne in Washington, for relief.—Deputations have been permitted by us to utter their prayers in person. Their petitions have been slighted, and in answer to their prayers, LINCOLN has put new bars and bolts on their prison doors. If the McCLELLAN orators cannot arouse the people by proclaiming this story, and exposing the conduct of the Administration touching their prisoners, it will be because they have stocks and stones for auditors.

"For an hundred years to come historians will be engaged in placing in their true light the events which are now transpiring"—so wrote a Chicago Tribune editorialist, Sept. 28, 1864, prophetically. This old newspaper friend of Illinois days printed this historic editorial as a campaign boost for Lincoln.

OUR COUNTRY'S FUTURE

The spectacle of our reunited country, resuming its onward march to material prosperity and empire, after the interruption caused by the war, with the Union maintained, the Government disenthralled and regenerated, and Slavery, the sole cause of dissension, obliterated, dedicating our whole land to freedom and our whole people to enlightenment, civilization and christianity, without a stain on our flag, or a foe to our unity, is one well calculated to fill our hearts with hope, and to reconcile us to the fierce ordeal through which we are passing. Heretofore the practice of slaveholding in half the country has made it the antagonist of the other in every respect. There labor has been degraded, the laborer left untaught, and the doctrine that capital should own, sell, lash, and if resisted shoot or burn labor, has put on the livery of "Democracy" thus converting half the Union into a charnal house of despotism, without a free religion, free speech, free press or free schools. There despots, who could not brook rivalry or equality, but who looked upon freedom as a reproach, upon christianity as an accusation, and upon competition as an encroachment, have been bred;—their gospel—force, their argument with their inferiors the whip, with equals and superiors the pistol, sword or bowie knife. In the regenerated Union the poor man will everywhere feel that his toil is honorable and his position as a citizen as respectable as that of the capitalist. In the restored Union the free school, a free press, and free speech will be enjoyed by all without asking the leave of some adjacent owner of a thousand slaves. . . .

For an hundred years to come historians will be engaged in placing in their true light the events which are now transpiring. What wonder that many of the present day do not rightly comprehend a march of events which will form a study for future ages—as have the periods of Themistocles, Caesar, Cromwell and Napoleon, for those which followed them? For a century to come military skill will consist in a knowledge of the changes in military science now being wrought: Republican statesmanship will consist in a thorough acquaintance with the principles of government now being contended for and settled in battle. The fame of orators will be founded upon their ability to portray in glowing terms of eulogy the heroism of our people and to connect their success with the principles of truth, and liberty. The reputations of artists will be made by immortalizing on canvas the fields of Donelson, Vicksburg and Mission Ridge, and the still more imposing scene yet to be witnessed of the capture of Charleston and the surrender of Richmond. But of one fact we may rest assured. While the present age looks at it mainly as a struggle for Union and nationality, the future will regard as equally important what we regard as but an incident, viz: the regeneration of the Republic and the vindication of true democracy and of the rights of labor, by the abolition of slavery. Not willingly, even for a future or a fame so glorious, would the people of the free North have entered upon the present contest. But driven into it reluctantly, and accepting so great an issue as the total abolition of American slavery, only when such a policy offered our last and best hope of success, we may still look through the stormy present into the near and bright future, borrowing of the provision which there awaits us. These hopes sustain us. We are living in times that try men's souls. Half a century hence to have lived in this age will be fame. To have served it well will be immortality. Think of this, and when you cast your vote in November, vote for the unity of the republic, for the rights of man and for the only candidates who represent them—Abraham Lincoln, of Illinois and Andrew Johnson, of Tennessee.

Before the voters of the United States went to the polls, the South reasoned that the "Ape" would exercise his "dictatorial" powers to insure victory. All along the newspapers of the Confederacy pictured Lincoln in the language of the Copperhead press when it came to political affairs. From the Richmond Dispatch, Nov. 7, 1864.

LINCOLN'S MANAGEMENT—HIS ELECTION

When Lincoln told the snivelling committee from Tennessee that he meant to manage his "side" of the Presidential election in his "own way," it was readily understood that he meant to do just what he would have done without such announcement, namely: employ all the means in his power—his officers, his detectives, his bribes, his military power, and his uncontrolled and irresponsible authority over all Yankeedom—to assure his own election and defeat McClellan. He has been true to his promise. He has been wide awake, and his machinery has worked beautifully. Never was there a display of more cunning manoeuvring or more artful management. He has driven little Mac already from his defences, but he has no gunboats to "cower under" as he had when General Lee drove him from his defences near Richmond. Lincoln—whilst his own followers are the most dishonest and most unscrupulous body of men on this earth, whilst their organization is reeking with the foulest corruptions —has contrived to fasten upon the McClellan party election frauds that would do credit to his own supporters. This is the richest joke ever perpetrated by the Ape. The frauds are proved, and two of their perpetrators have been sentenced to imprisonment for life! A prominent New Yorker, one Colonel North, now stands charged with similar frauds, and the military court exhibits a determination to try his case without delay, of course, that it may bear upon the election. One Judge Parker, of New York, and others, had, by commission from Governor Seymour, come on to Washington to assist North in his difficulty. Judge Parker took high ground at first; but finding that the odds were terribly against him, moderated his views; in the language of a Yankee letter-writer, "roosted lower!" North is understood to have been an agent of Governor Seymour to attend to the army vote and see fair play—at least, we suppose, in the New York regiments. He walked into Lincoln's trap, and the Ape will take especial delight in "keel-hauling" him. He has a grudge against Seymour, and will be most grateful to him for affording him such a chance for a little revenge. North has by this time "gone up," (Yankee,) under order of his military judges.

A notable feature in these developments is the several confessions made by parties, whose testimony convicted themselves and others. No one, we suppose, imagines that these confessions were the result of anything like remorse or repentance; men in Yankeedom are not in the habit of repenting until their frauds are either discovered of fail altogether. No; they were induced by bribery, and nothing else. It is not even certain that the rascals were guilty of all they confessed, though, in the general, men do not confess crime of which they are innocent; a Yankee never, unless he can make money by assuming guilt when innocent, as may have been the case with these confessors to Father Abraham.

It is amusing to see with what holy horror the Union and Abolition men and the corrupt Lincoln press affect to regard these frauds of the McClellanites. Such virtue has been witnessed never before! The *Tribune* tells the world, with triumph, that a batch of one hundred and ninety fraudulent votes, since sold to the McClellan party, had been "offered to Mr. Boardman, the Union candidate for Congress in the Seventh District" (New York), "for a dollar and ninety cents apiece." That virtuous paper adds: "The traffic was indignantly scouted!" No doubt of it. It deserved to be so scouted by any New York politician, because of its contemptible, small retail character. The vendor underrated his man—a few thousand votes would have met with a much more respectful reception!

Poor McClellan stands, in effect, convicted before the world, and is as much to be pitied as that poor ass which was, by the beasts in council, condemned to death for nibbling a few blades of grass in the parsonage, while the killing of a score of lambs, by the lion, was pronounced by the prosecutor, the fox, as no offence at all; since lambs, very sheepish and cravenly animals at best, were occasionally necessary for the health and digestion of his royal highness, the king of the forest! So will the beastly supporters of the Ape tone down and excuse his monstrous outrages and magnify and denounce the short-comings and peccadilloes of his competitor, who has not the stamina to perpetrate any great frauds, and has not the opportunity to do so if he had. Lincoln will take care of that.

In short, Lincoln is managing his side of the election in his most approved style. He will be "sent on" for another term triumphantly. He is to be still further tried. He is our best man. His defeat would be the signal for the agitations of conventions and truces at the South that would produce divisions of an injurious character amongst us, in the midst of which that enemy who meditates our ruin and abasement might gain immense advantages over us. Give us Lincoln with his brutalities—those inhuman measures and persecutions which have united our people, given vigor to our resistance, and must finally establish our independence.

Lincoln won. He carried every state but Kentucky, Deleware and New Jersey. "But the rebellion continues," Lincoln said, "and now that the election is over, may not all, having a common interest, re-unite in a common effort, to save our common country?" The Richmond Dispatch, Nov. 9, 1864, could only wonder at the reason why the Yankee nation voted as it did.

Yesterday will be long remembered in the annals of mankind. On yesterday, twenty millions of human beings, but four years ago esteemed the freest population on earth, met at various points of assemblage for the purpose of making a formal surrender of their liberties—not to a great military conquerer; not to a renowned statesman; not to a fell-citizen who has done the State services that cannot be estimated in worldly wealth; not to one who has preserved the State from foreign tyranny, or increased its glory and its greatness at home; not to a Caesar or a Napoleon, the glory of whose achievements might be pleaded as an apology for the abject submission of the multitude; but to a vulgar tyrant, who has never seen a shot fired in anger; who has no more idea of statesmanship than as a means of making money; whose career has been one of unlimited and unmitigated disaster; whose personal qualities are those of a low buffoon, and whose most noteworthy conversation is a medley of profane jests and obscene anecdotes—a creature who has squandered the lives of millions without remorse and without even the decency of pretending to feel for their misfortunes; who still cries for blood and for money in the pursuit of his atrocious designs. To such a man, yesterday, the people of the so-called United States surrendered their lives, their liberties, their persons, and their purses, to have and to hold the same for at least four years, and for so much longer as he shall choose. For it is plain that, if he so will it, he may hold on for his natural life, and transmit the sceptre to his descendants. There is nothing in the world to prevent him, should he feel so disposed, and there is no reason to think that thus disposed he will not be. It seems strange to us that he should have condescended to submit to an election at all; and we are convinced he would never have done so, had he not been convinced beforehand that it would result in his favor. How McClellan could ever have been so infatuated as to thrust himself in his way, we are unable to conceive. The light punishment he had to expect, was to be crushed, for he might have felt assured that, even had he been elected, he would not have been allowed to take his seat. All the preparations of Lincoln indicate a determination to take possession of the Government by force—his military arrangements; the stationing of soldiers about the polls; the arrest of the New York commissioners; the prohibition against any tickets but his own in the fleet; his jealous supervision of the voting in the army—all these indicate a determination to conquer by the ballot-box if possible, but, in any event, to conquer. How could McClellan expect to weather such a storm as his adversary had it in his power to raise at any moment of the day? Even the grand resort of tyranny in all ages has not been overlooked in this case. Huge conspiracies are discovered; designs to burn whole cities; to overthrow the best Government under the sun; to shoot Lincoln; to stuff the ballot-box; to assist the Confederate arms; to do everything that is awful; and just in the very nick of time—just in time to imprison influential friends of McClellan, and to keep the body of his supporters from going to the polls. And this farce is to be called an election; and Lincoln, seated upon his throne at Washington by the bayonets of his troops as decidedly as the First Napoleon was seated upon the imperial throne of France by the military power of the nation, still retains the title of President, and adheres to the forms of a republic, as Augustus and Tiberius had themselves regularly elected consuls and tribunes long after they had concentrated all power in their own persons.

We are prone to believe that every nation enjoys the exact proportion of freedom to which it is entitled. If the Yankees have lost their liberties, therefore, we think it self-evident that it is because they never deserved to have them. If they are slaves, it is because they are fit for the situation.— Slaves they have been for years to all the base passions that are indicative of a profligate and degenerate race; and when nations advance to that point, the transition to material bondage costs but a single step.

Surely, the surrender which the Yankees made on yesterday of their liberties to the Jack Pudding, Abraham Lincoln, is in its way the most remarkable event of which history makes mention. Surely, the Yankee nation, if not the greatest, is, at least, the most interesting of all existing nations.

418

In the North, the election was hailed as a Constitutional victory and a personal triumph and vindication of Lincoln. Lincoln himself saw it as a good test for the Government that it could have an election in the midst of a war. From Harper's Weekly, Nov. 19, 1864.

THE ELECTION

ABRAHAM LINCOLN AND ANDREW JOHNSON have been elected, by enormous and universal majorities in almost all the States, President and Vice-President of the United States for the next four years. This result is the proclamation of the American people that they are not conquered; that the rebellion is not successful; and that, deeply as they deplore war and its inevitable suffering and loss, yet they have no choice between war and national ruin, and must therefore fight on. In an unfortunate moment for himself General M'CLELLAN permitted his name to be used as the symbol of the cowardice and subjugation of his fellow-citizens, and from that moment his defeat was a foregone conclusion.

The moral effect of the election both at home and abroad will be of the most impressive character. It shows our foreign enemies that they have nothing to hope from the divisions of this country, while the rebels will see in it the withering and invincible purpose of their loyal fellow-citizens, who ask of them nothing but obedience to the Constitution of the United States, and the laws and acts made in pursuance of it. Whenever they shall choose to overthrow the military despotism that holds them fast—whenever they shall see that no great section of this country can, under equal and respected laws, have any permanent and profound interest different from all the rest—then they will find that the loyal men of the country are longing to throw down their arms and cement a Union that shall be eternal.

But the lesson of the election is, that every constitutional act and law must be absolutely respected. There must be no threats, no revolts, and no hope of extorting terms by arms. The Constitution is the sole condition of the Government; and if citizens differ as to what is constitutional, that difference must be peacefully and constitutionally settled. This is what the people have declared by four years of war, and this is what they confirm by the re-election of Mr. LINCOLN. In himself, notwithstanding his unwearied patience, perfect fidelity, and remarkable sagacity, he is unimportant; but as the representative of the feeling and purpose of the American people he is the most important fact in the world.

One other of the most significant lessons of the election is, that the people are conscious of the power and force of their own Government. They expect the utmost vigor in the prosecution of the war by every legitimate method, and they naturally require that the authority of the Government, which is to be established by the continuance of the war, shall not be endangered by its end. When the authority of any Government is openly and forcibly defied it must be maintained unconditionally by arms. When that authority is established and unquestioned, every wise Government will be friendly, patient, conciliatory but firm and just.

Yet the grandest lesson of the result is its vindication of the American system of free popular government. No system in history was ever exposed to such a strain directly along the fibre as that which ours has endured in the war and the political campaign, and no other could possibly have endured it successfully. The result is due to the general intelligence of the people, and to the security of perfectly free discussion. Let that be maintained and jealously defended by all parties in the land, at every country cross-road, and in every city and State, and the Union and the Government are forever secure. They have been maintained by the authority of the Government itself, and we see the result. Thank God and the people, we are a nation which comprehends its priceless importance to human progress and civilization, and which recognizes that law is the indispensable condition of Liberty.

England saw the election of Lincoln to a second term as but an interruption in a larger struggle—the conduct of the war of the rebellion. From the London Times, Nov. 25, 1864.

In America all other topics have been forgotten for a time in the excitement of the Presidential Election. The Republican party are extreme in their rejoicing, for they have been completely victorious. It is stated that Mr. LINCOLN has 213 electoral votes, against 21 for General M'CLELLAN, and a popular majority of nearly 400,000. It is also announced that the votes of Tennessee, Louisiana, and Arkansas will, probably, not be taken, as the majority in the rest of the Union will allow them to be disregarded without any change in the result. The speeches of the PRESIDENT and of his principal advisers indicate sufficiently how it is purposed to employ the new lease of power. The war will begin again in the ensuing spring with fresh vigour. The policy of emancipation will probably receive the formal sanction of Congress. The confiscation of rebel property will be strictly enforced. Proclamation will succeed proclamation, and draught will follow draught so long as it is necessary to keep up to their present standard the immense armies of the Republic. In all this the dominant party is no doubt sincere. The nation has accepted Mr. LINCOLN's plan of "pegging away," and has no other idea than to continue the war in the style of the last four years, by sending three or four different armies into the heart of the Confederacy to occupy some unimportant town, or linger in front of the enemy's earthworks. The hope of the Federals is that one, two, three, or four years—for they are not oversanguine now—will find the Confederacy exhausted of men, or its people shaken in resolution. Through all the speeches of the Northern politicians there is a vagueness of plan and an avoiding of military details which show how puzzled they are to reconcile even the last campaign with the speedy conquest of the South. But there is a blind confidence that the conquest is to be achieved somehow, and a belief that the re-election of Mr. LINCOLN has removed one of the greatest difficulties from their path. So much are the Republicans elated that they begin to be good-natured to their opponents. The Democrats are informed that the victorious party bear them no ill-will, and would gladly see all Americans unite for the salvation of the country. They are bidden to take notice of their own weakness, of the completeness of their defeat, and the impossibility of their making any effectual opposition to Mr. LINCOLN during his second term of power. The country has heard the worst that can be said against the PRESIDENT; it knows of his arbitrary arrests, his Emancipation edicts, his appointment of military dictators, his ceaseless demand for men, and the depreciation of the currency which has accompanied his campaigns. But everything has been—to use the American expression—endorsed by the popular vote. The PRESIDENT may conduct the war as he pleases for four years more, and fill the fortresses with his political enemies. He may bring down the value of the dollar to a few pence, and fill every household with mourning for those carried away to perish by disease or fall before the Confederate rifles. No political party will be able to make head against him; no single State of importance will any longer question his authority. Even New York has elected a Republican Governor, and Mr. SEYMOUR will cease to influence events by his half-hearted opposition. The Democrats are invited to consider these things and to desist from their useless endeavours. Their answer has not yet been given, for they have at present scarcely recovered from their great defeat. But many of them will, no doubt, be content for a time to forego opposition. The main body of the party will, of course, shape their course according to the fortunes of the war, for a political party in America has too enduring an organization, and is kept together by too attractive prospects of place and power, to accept a defeat as final, and submit in mass to the enemy. . . .

The Confederates will trust to the power of the Government and of public opinion to bring to the army the great number of men who still remain unemployed. From this source they expect to obtain as many as will place their armies in a position to defend the chief points of their territory during the ensuing year; but should these not be enough, there can be little doubt that a levy of negroes will be made. The people are ready for it, the Governors have assented to it, and President DAVIS can effect it when he pleases. This seems to be felt at the North, for the expectation of a speedy peace has not accompanied the re-election of Mr. LINCOLN. The political event which has filled the Republican party with exultation was no sooner certain than the price of gold, reduced by the fall of Atlanta, began to rise once more—a sure sign that those whose trade teaches them to observe events most closely see as yet no end to their country's troubles.

This poem, following the re-election of Lincoln, appeared in London's Punch, Dec. 3, 1864, accompanying the "Federal Phoenix" drawing by Tenniel.

THE FEDERAL PHOENIX

WHEN HERODOTUS, surnamed "The Father of History"
    (We are not informed who was History's mother),
Went a travelling to Egypt, that region of mystery,
    Where each step presented some marvel or other,

In a great city there, called (in Greek) Heliopolis,
    The priests put him up to a strange story—rather—
Of a bird, who came up to that priestly metropolis,
    Once in five hundred years, to inter its own father.

When to filial feeling apparently callous,
    Not a plume ruffled (as we should say, not a nair rent),
In a *pot-pourri* made of sweet-spice, myrrh, and aloes,
    He flagrantly, burnt, after burying, his parent.

But POMPONIUS MELA has managed to gather
    Of this curious story a modified version,

In which the bird burns up itself, not its father,
And soars to new life from its fiery immersion.

This bird has oft figured in emblems and prophecies—
And though SNYDERS ne'er painted its picture, nor WEENIX
Its portraits on plates of a well-known fire-office is,
Which, after this bird's name, is christened the Phœnix.

Henceforth a new Phœnix, from o'er the Atlantic,
Our old fire-office friend from his brass-plate displaces;
With a plumage of greenbacks, all ruffled, and antic
In OLD ABE's rueful phiz and OLD ABE's shambling graces.

As the bird of Arabia wrought resurrection
By a flame all whose virtues grew out of what fed it,
So the Federal Phœnix has earned re-election
By a holocaust huge of rights, commerce, and credit.

One day in December—"by way of a joke"—President Lincoln wrote a news article. He gave it to the Daily Chronicle, Washington, D.C., for Dec. 7, 1864. The pro-Lincoln paper in Washington was established in 1862 by Lincoln's friend and political confidant, John Forney, who also published the Press in Philadelphia. The article ran with "A. LINCOLN" as author.

THE PRESIDENT'S LAST, SHORTEST, AND BEST SPEECH

On Thursday of last week two ladies from Tennessee came before the President asking the release of their husbands held as prisoners of war at Johnson's Island. They were put off till Friday, when they came again; and were again put off to Saturday. At each of the interviews one of the ladies urged that her husband was a religious man. On Saturday the President ordered the release of the prisoners, and then said to this lady, "You say your husband is a religious man; tell him when you meet him, that I say I am not much of a judge of religion, but that, in my opinion, the religion that sets men to rebel and fight against their government, because, as they think, that government does not sufficiently help some men to eat their bread on the sweat of other men's faces, is not the sort of religion upon which people can get to heaven!"

A. LINCOLN

423

For the last time, Lincoln sent his annual message to Congress. In it Lincoln said, "In presenting the abandonment of armed resistance to the national authority on the part of the insurgents, as the only indispensable condition to ending the war on the part of the government, I retract nothing heretofore said as to slavery. . . . In stating a single condition of peace, I mean simply to say that the war will cease on the part of the government, whenever it shall have ceased on the part of those who began it." The New York Tribune, Dec. 7, 1864, commented on the message.

THE PRESIDENT'S MESSAGE

The Message of the President, which was yesterday delivered to both Houses of Congress, is, as all Mr. Lincoln's state papers are, a straightforward and business-like document. It gives to Congress and the country a condensed but methodical statement of our National affairs in all their foreign and domestic relations, and in a style so plain and brief that it is certain to be universally read and universally understood.

In our foreign relations there is nothing to cause the slightest apprehension for the future, nor is any change intimated, except in relation to the Treaty with Great Britain as to the increase of our naval armament upon the Lakes. But the necessity for the stipulated notice for the termination of the Treaty arises, not from any hostility in the attitude of Great Britain, but to guard our own border more effectually from hostile incursions, in that direction, from Southern Rebels.

But the Message is mainly and necessarily taken up with a comprehensive review of our domestic affairs, and, considering that we are carrying on a war inevitably expensive in human life, in national prosperity, and in national wealth, the statement is eminently satisfactory. The condition of our national finances can hardly be given in fewer words than those of the President. . . .

The announcement of the future policy of the President in regard to the war and to Slavery, has been looked for with anxiety and will be read with eager interest. In reviewing the result of the late election, he considers it as simply "an additional element to be considered," inasmuch as it is "the voice of the people now for the first time heard upon the question" of the war. To "maintain the integrity of the Union" he accepts as the firm and "nearly unanimous purpose" of the people—the purpose not only of all who voted the Union ticket, but of the great majority of those who did not, inasmuch as no candidate "ventured to seek votes on the avowal that he was for giving up the Union." Therefore, in obedience to the will of the people, as well as his own convictions, the President will never give up the Union. Until it is restored in all its integrity he will continue the war. With the leader of the insurgents he can enter into no negotiations for peace, because that leader will listen to no terms but the independence of the Southern Confederacy. But with his followers the President is ready to enter upon the question of peace, on the condition that they lay down their arms and submit to the National authority under the Constitution. Some of them, he knows, already desire peace and reunion, and their number may increase. This is the only hope of peace held out in the Message, except by victory in war, and the President accepts the election as his justification by the people of this determination.

He recommends the present Congress to abolish Slavery by Constitutional amendment. If it fails to do so, as it has once already, he asserts it to be only an act postponed, as it is certain to be done by the Congress elect. For himself he retracts nothing he has ever said or done in regard to Slavery. He will not retract or modify the Emancipation Proclamation, nor will he ever return to bondage a human being freed by that Proclamation or by acts of Congress. He says emphatically that if the people make such an act an executive duty they must find somebody else to perform it.

Such are the important points of the Message, and not even the most violent opponent of Mr. Lincoln can complain that his policy has an uncertainty about it, or that it is not as thoroughly radical as his warmest admirer would have it. Peace by the submission or conquest of Rebels, and the total abolition of Slavery, will be the determined purpose of the new Administration. The country has sanctioned and will accept the policy.

Before the Second Inaugural Address, Punch on Dec. 10, 1864, published a burlesque of what they thought Lincoln would say. It was brutally clever and published long enough in advance of the actual inaugural the following March for Lincoln to see it, and for readers to wonder what he thought as he read it.

PRESIDENT LINCOLN'S INAUGURAL SPEECH
(By Ultramarine Telegraph)

Well, we've done it, gentlemen. Bully for us. Cowhided the Copperheads considerable. *Non nobis*, of course, but still I reckon we have had a hand in the glory, some. That reminds me of the Old World story about the Hand of Glory, which I take to have been the limb of a gentleman who had been justified on the gallows, and which the witches turned into a patent moderator lamp, as would lead a burglar safe into any domicile which he might wish to plunder. We ain't burglars, quite t'other, but I fancy that if ULY GRANT could get hold of that kind and description of thing to help him into Richmond, he'd not be so un-Christian proud as to refuse the hand of a malefactor. (*Right, right!*) Well, right or left hand, that's no odds, gentlemen. (*Laughter.*) Now I am sovereign of the sovereign people of this great and united republic for four years next ensuing the date hereof, as I used to say when I was a lawyer. (*You are! Bully for you!*) Yes, gentlemen, but you must do something more than bully for me, you must fight for me, if you please, and whether you please or not. As the old·joke says, there's no compulsion, only you must. Must is for the King, they say in the rotten Old world. Well, I'm King, and you shall be Viceroys over me. But I tell you again, and in fact I repeat it, that there's man's work to do to beat these rebels. They may run away, no doubt. As the Irishman says, pigs may fly, but they're darned onlikely birds to do it. They must be well whipped, gentlemen, and I must trouble you for the whipcord. (*You shall have it!*) Rebellion is a wicked thing, gentlemen, an awful wicked thing, and the mere nomenclating thereof would make my hair stand on end, if it could be more standonender than it is. (*Laughter.*) Truly awful, that is when it is performed against mild, free, constitutional sway like that of the White House, but of course right and glorious when perpetrated against ferocious, cruel, bloodthirsty old tyrants like GEORGE THE THIRD. We must punish these rebels for their own good, and to teach them the blessings of this mighty and transcendental Union. (*We will, we will!*) All very tall talking, gentlemen, but talking won't take Richmond. If it would, and there had been six Richmonds in the field, we should long since have took them all. If Richmond would fall like Jericho, by every man blowing of his own trumpet, we've brass enough in our band for that little feat in acoustics. But when a cow sticks, as GRANT does, in the mud, how then? (*Great laughter.*) Incontestably, gentlemen, this great and mighty nation must give her a shove on. Shove for Richmond, gentlemen. (*That's the talk!*) Now about these eternal blacks, you expect me to say something touching them, though I suppose we're none of us too fond of touching them, for reasons in that case made and provided, as I used to say. Well, listen. We've got them on our hands, that's a fact, and it reminds me of a nigger story. Two of these blacks met, and one had a fine new hat. "Where you got dat hat, SAMBO?"

says t'other. "Out ob a shop, nigger," says SAMBO. " 'Spex so," says t'other, "and what might be the price ob dat hat?" "Can't say, zactly, nigger, the shopkeeper didn't happen to be on the premises." (*Laughter.*) Well, we've got the niggers, and I can't exactly say—or at least I don't think you'd like to hear—what might be the price of those articles. But we must utilise our hats, gentlemen. We must make them dig and fight, that's a fact. There's no shame in digging, I suppose. Adam digged, and he is a gentleman of older line than any of the bloated and slavish aristocracies of Europe. And as for fighting, they must feel honoured at doing that for the glorious old flag that has braved for eighty-nine years and a-half, be the same little more or less, the battle and the breeze. (*Cheers.*) Yes, and when the rebellion's put down, we'll see what's to be done with them. Perhaps if the naughty boys down South get uncommon contrite hearts, we may make them a little present of the blacks, not as slaves, of course, but as legal apprentices with undefined salaries determinable on misconduct. (*Cheers.*) Meantime, gentlemen, I won't deny that the niggers are useful in the way of moral support. They give this here war a holy character, and we can call it a crusade for freedom. A man may call his house an island if he likes, as has been said by one of those fiendish British writers who abuse our hospitality by not cracking us up. (*War with England!*) Well, all in good time, gentlemen. Let our generals learn their business first. I don't blame them, mind you, that they haven't learned it yet, for when a man has kept a whiskey-store, or a bar, or an oyster-cellar, or an old-clothes' shop for years, he can't be expected, merely because he puts on a uniform, to become a Hannibal or a Napoleon, or even a Marlborough or a Wellington. Likewise, they must learn to keep reasonable sober. Friends at a distance will please accept this intimation. (*Roars of Laughter.*) When that's done, and the rebels are whipped, and we are in want of more fighting, we'll see whether Richmond in England, where the QUEEN's palace of Windsor Castle is situate lying and being, is a harder nut to crack than Richmond nearer us. (*Cheers.*) Gentlemen, one thing more. Did you ever hear the story of the farmer who had been insulted by an exciseman? "He wur so rude," said the farmer, "that I wur obliged to remonstrate with him." "And to what effect did you remonstrate?" asked a friend. "Well I don't know about effect, but I bent the poker so that I was obliged to get a hammer to straighten it." Gentlemen, we must straighten this glorious Union, and the hammer is taxes. (*Laughter.*) You may laugh, but you must pay. I don't mean to be hard upon this mighty nation, and our friend MR. COBDEN (*cheers*) has already indirectly informed the besotted masses of British slaves that we intend to repudiate our greenbacks, except to the amount they may be worth in the market when redeemed. But the poker wants a deal of hammering, nevertheless, and you must pay up. You'll hear more about this from a friend of mine in the Government, so I only give you the hint, as the man said when he kicked his uncle down-stairs. (*Laughter.*) I believe that's about all I had to say, and this almighty Union will be conserved to shine through the countless ages an ineffable beacon and symbol of blessed and everlasting light and glory if you will only mind the proverb of Sancho Panza, which says, "Pray to God devoutly, and hammer on stoutly." (*Laughter, cheers, and cries of "Bully for you!"*)

The British press analyzed the President's message and found it warlike. They also pointed out that Mr. Lincoln was "safely seated till March, 1869." From the London Times, Dec. 19, 1864.

The summary of Mr. LINCOLN's Message to Congress received by the Asia contains little from which the people of the North can derive encouragement or consolation. If, indeed, they have altogether forgotten the past, and resolutely close their eyes to the future, they may find it pleasant to listen again to the repetition of the old style of address. It is the fourth year of the war, and the position of the Government, military and financial, is rapidly growing worse; yet the predictions so often made, and always falsified by the event, are again hazarded with as much confidence as ever. The North must continue to fight, and must succeed at last. The resources of the nation are unexhausted, and "are believed to be inexhaustible." The question between the South and North is one that can be tried only by war, and decided only by victory. The question, therefore, must remain in dispute till the arbitrator gives the decision, which must be in favour of the strongest. On this point the North never had the slightest doubt. But, even while taking such complacent views of the terrible conflict in which they are engaged, it must sometimes perplex them that the triumph they are always told awaits them should be delayed so long.

The Message effectually destroys any expectations that may have been formed by the advocates of peace. After the recent speech of General BUTLER at New York, there was an impression that Mr. LINCOLN would intimate to Congress the possibility of coming to some terms of accommodation with the South. BUTLER, it was supposed, spoke by official inspiration, and there were rumours that the opening of the second term of Mr. LINCOLN's Presidency would find the war suspended by an armistice. The Message proves conclusively that General BUTLER was not the oracle the public supposed. The offers to the South he spoke of turn out to be only the old terms of surrender and submission. These terms, totally inconsistent with the object with which the South commenced the war, it might have accepted long ago. But it refused them when Mr. LINCOLN offered to "the loyal" the reward of a permission to retain their slaves, while those of "rebels" were emancipated by proclamation. They refused them equally when promised an amnesty, and when threatened with forfeiture of their estates. The Southerners are, by Mr. LINCOLN's Message, offered precisely the same terms now, with more emphasis laid on the penalties that may be incurred by refusing them. He intimates that the decrees relating to "forfeitures" may be sharpened, and that slavery, now abolished only by proclamation, may be abolished by an Act of Congress. But to these old measures of coercion attaches the old difficulty that has hitherto deprived the threats of the Northern Government of any appreciable effect. To put them into execution the South must be conquered, and again brought under one authority. The proclamation that Mr. LINCOLN himself ridiculed as resembling "a Pope's Bull against the comet" never liberated a single slave. The Federal armies have, by force of arms, released thousands. The bayonet was the emancipator, not the proclamation. . . .

But while the tenour of the Message is decidedly warlike, proving that Mr. LINCOLN's re-election has in no degree affected the policy of the Government, Mr. LINCOLN himself seems to anticipate a great change in the public opinion of the South on the termination of Mr. JEFFERSON DAVIS's Presidency. It would be very unsafe to make any prediction as to what may be the state of affairs North or South two years hence. Mr. DAVIS retains his authority till the end of 1866, and cannot be re-elected. Mr. LINCOLN is safely seated till March 1869, and he appears to be speculating on his official survivorship. He thinks that the South, when released from the government of Mr. DAVIS, will be, not more disposed, but more able to listen to conditions. He assumes that the population have revolted "on compulsion," and that there are many better disposed, and ready on the first good opportunity to return to their allegiance and the Union. This also seems to be a repetition of an old assertion. The first armed expedition into Southern territory was intended to discover and liberate Northern opinion. The experiment was not successful, nor have any of the more recent invasions had a more favourable result. Equally fruitless have been the attempts to discover this friendly feeling by the destruction of all property on the Federal lines of march. But it is still a firm conviction in the North that its friends in the South are compelled to conceal their sympathy, which they will in due time manifest. Mr. LINCOLN fixes the end of Mr. DAVIS's Presidency as the opportunity. Till then, we presume, the war will certainly continue.

Peace feelers floated up in the air; some returned to earth. The Confederate peace commissioners came through the lines for a talk. Lincoln wrote to Grant, "Let nothing which is transpiring change, hinder, or delay your military movements or plans." The New York World, Feb. 3, 1865, reported the peace meeting in its own peculiar anti-Lincoln way.

PRESIDENT LINCOLN AND THE PEACE CONFERENCE

If President LINCOLN resembled any other statesman who ever held so high an office, his going half way to meet in person the confederate commissioners would electrify the country. But his sense of dignity is of an odd and peculiar sort, and he is so prone to do unexpected things that it is not safe to interpret his conduct by the rules of official etiquette. When the French Emperor was uncivil to the Austrian minister at a New-Year's reception, every statesman and publicist at once foreboded a troubling of the peace of Europe; and the event justified the inference. But it will not do to reason from analogy, and conclude that the momentous issues of peace and war can be descried in the personal demeanor of President LINCOLN. He is the same chief magistrate of a great nation who wrote a labored letter to HORACE GREELEY in reply to a newspaper criticism; who made a flying visit to West Point to consult General SCOTT; who is in the frequent practice of doing quaint things which show nature and naivete, but not a high and studied official bearing. When, therefore, he surprises the country by suddenly flitting down to Fortress Monroe to hold an interview with the agents of JEFFERSON DAVIS, it would not be safe to attach much political consequence to so extraordinary an exhibition of official condescension.

A meeting at Fortress Monroe between President LINCOLN and Mr. DAVIS himself, would be more in accordance with the proprieties of that kind of intercourse; for although our government cannot recognize Mr. DAVIS as the head of a state, he has a quasi rank as such; and, at any rate, is more nearly the official equal of Mr. LINCOLN than his envoys. In their military capacity each is commander-in-chief of one of the belligerent armies; and, as military commanders, they might meet and confer without compromising the dignity of either. If the country could learn that Mr. DAVIS left Richmond yesterday as suddenly as Mr. LINCOLN left Washington, and that the belligerent chiefs are now in conference at Fortress Monroe, it would gratify feelings infinitely deeper than a sense of wondering curiosity.

GOD forbid that we should impute it to President LINCOLN as a fault that he condescends to this extraordinary act of courtesy, and goes so far to meet the mere agents of what he is bound to regard as a spurious and usurping government. Probably he has not troubled himself with the question of etiquette at all; or if he has, he may regard all rebel functionaries as holding the same official rank—that is to say, no official rank at all. Regarding them all as mere insurgents or rebels, he may think that no such comparisons can properly have place; and that it is no abdication of dignity for him to imitate the example of WASHINGTON in the Whisky Insurrection, when, to prevent the effusion of blood, he made a long journey to confer with its leaders. Any steps taken by Mr. LINCOLN which really conduce to peace, will be approved by all right-thinking men.

Our readers must pardon us for these references to the mere frippery of the negotiations. If we had any authentic knowledge of their substance, we would gladly discuss it.

All questions of form aside, the visit of the President and Secretary of State is a good deal of a riddle. The rebel commissioners set out for Washington; why then did not Messrs. LINCOLN and SEWARD consult their own convenience and receive them at Washington? It is evident that, for some reason, their presence in Washington is not desired. Most assuredly it is not regard for the dignity of the government that stops them on the way; for it is a greater concession for the President to go and meet than it would be to stay and receive them. It is not, then, a question of dignity, but of expediency. The only thing that can be accomplished by excluding them from the capital, is, to prevent their having intercourse with other people than the President and Secretary. If permitted to come to Washington, they could hardly be immured there as prisoners. Men of standing and influence would call on them; and it may be feared that other persons than the officers of the government would influence the negotiations. The same reasons which prevent, and by our laws punish as a crime, unauthorized intercourse between the two hostile sections, are perhaps equally strong against an interchange of sentiments and information between the rebel commissioners and persons who would seek interviews with them in Washington. If nothing comes of the negotiations,

Mr. LINCOLN may not wish the rebels to have the advantage of such information as their agents might extract from general conversation. They were permitted to pass the lines merely to confer with the government; that is to say, with its chief officers. The purpose of their mission neither contemplates nor requires any other intercourse. But it could not very well be avoided, considering the intense and excited curiosity which prevails, except by the course which has been taken, of meeting them at a place from which all intruders can be excluded without violating courtesy or resisting importunities.

The excess of courtesy and condescension practiced toward these envoys is probably, therefore, a politic maneuver of the government to retain that monopoly of this kind of intercourse which justly, and by the laws of Congress, belongs to it. If this conjecture is well-founded, all the sanguine inferences drawn from the extraordinary course of the President and Secretary are of little account.

A Southern view of the peace negotiations saw Lincoln trying to make capital of the move to close the war for his own esteem. This attitude was an insult, according to the Richmond Sentinel, Feb. 15, 1865.

MR. LINCOLN'S STATEMENT

The statement of President LINCOLN of his connection with the late negotiations, reflects a deeper discredit upon him than the report of our own Commissioners. It confesses that the interview which he took so much pains to invite, he afterwards took equal pains to obstruct, and to render abortive; as if Yankee perfidy, worse than Punic faith, must be displayed on this, as upon every other possible occasion.

That the meeting was held at all, is due only to accident and Gen. GRANT.—When our Commissioners arrived opposite to the hostile lines, General GRANT was away. General ORD, commanding the army of the James, unwilling to assume the responsibility of receiving the gentlemen, referred the matter to Washington. Thence a messenger was promptly dispatched to General ORD's headquarters, with instructions that amounted to an exclusion of the Confederate deputies. They were required to yield everything in issue, as a preliminary to a conference for a settlement! History furnishes no parallel to such a proceeding.

Meantime Gen. GRANT returned to his headquarters before Mr. LINCOLN's messenger arrived there; and acting on his own responsibility, he at once received the Confederates, and notified his superiors in Washington. Mr. LINCOLN now modified his instructions for holding our Commissioners at bay on the picket lines, so far as to direct their detention at GRANT's headquarters, until the messenger should arrive with the test that was to repel them. This messenger, a Maj. ECKERT, seems to have performed the part assigned him with fidelity and success. He arrived at GRANT's headquarters at 4 P.M. and that same evening notified Mr. LINCOLN that he had put a period to the progress of the Confederates, their answer being "not satisfactory."

At this second critical period, Gen. GRANT comes again to the rescue. Just one hour after Major ECKERT had telegraphed to Mr. LINCOLN that he had arrested the Confederate embassy, Gen. GRANT, at 10:30 P.M. telegraphed Mr. LINCOLN "confidentially, but not officially, to become a matter of record." Mr. LINCOLN has not treated the message either as confidential or unofficial. He has both told it and placed it on the record, and we have thus learned its contents. He stated to Mr. LINCOLN the favorable prepossessions he had derived from conversation with two of the commissioners, the fears he had that their repulse without an interview would "have a bad influence," and his desire that Mr. LINCOLN should himself hold a conference with them.

This instantly changed Mr. LINCOLN's purpose again, and he set out immediately for Fortress Monroe. Whether he expected to find the Commissioners in the tractable mood which Gen. GRANT supposed, or whether he, too, had been brought to fear the "bad influence," of a refusal to receive them at all, we need not stop to conjecture. It is sufficient to know that when he received them he demanded terms that he knew to be utterly inadmissable, and which were intended to be so; terms which no people, worthy of being associated with by persons who respect themselves, ever did or ever could accept.

It is a curious inquiry whether Mr. LINCOLN, when he dispatched Mr. BLAIR to the Confederate capital, intended the *role* which he has since played. We scarcely suppose he did. The explanation of his deeply perfidious and dishonorable conduct is probably to be found in the party necessities that press upon him. We pass over the quibble, the diplomatic prevarication, the Pickwickian denial, with which he attempts to disconnect himself with Mr. BLAIR's mission here. Such nonsense will impose on no one.—Let the next man who wishes to "go South and return" apply for a "pass" to Mr. LINCOLN, and see whether he will be gratified, as he tells us Mr. BLAIR was, without any intimation of his object, or of what he proposed to "say or do!" Mr. BLAIR was as much an agent here as Messrs. STEPHENS, HUNTER and CAMPBELL were our agents; informal, the whole of them, but yet agents the whole of them.

The news of what was transpiring had meanwhile, given great dissatisfaction to that portion of Mr. LINCOLN's party which is hostile to him, and which numbers a very large majority in the United States Senate, besides being extremely formidable in the House. These "radicals" so-called, of which SUMNER and WADE are types, were horrified at the thought of peace. Their hyena instincts are yet unappeased. They love to sit in their safe places, and bid blood flow.—Hence an assault was prepared upon Mr. LINCOLN in connection with this BLAIR-peace negotiation, from which he recoiled. It was thus, we believe, that he was deterred from his first purpose, and hence set about repelling the conference which he had invited, and of conciliating the wrath of his Congress by fresh indignities to the Confederates. It mattered not that he was enacting a deed than which no other could be more disgraceful to the head of a nation.— Actaeon was being bayed by his own hounds—and he essayed to appease them by opening up a fresh prospect of blood.

Mr. LINCOLN has been successful only in part. He has stirred the depths of Confederate resentments by the insult which he has offered us, but he has given but indifferent satisfaction to his irate Senators. The explanation which they demanded of him, they received in sullen silence. In the House some applause was heard from his partisans; but his household adversaries give him no credit, and proffer him no truce.

On March 4, 1865, Lincoln was sworn in for a second term that would expire in 1869. In Washington the cannon boomed and the crowds cheered. Victory was in the wind. In Springfield, Lincoln's oldest friend among the opinion makers, the Illinois State Journal, March 4, 1865, said, "May he live to see the nation under his Administration at peace. . . ."

THE INAUGURATION

At noon, to-day, Abraham Lincoln takes the oath of office for another four years term as President of the United States. In the light of the history of the past four years the event is one of deep interest and peculiar significance.

Four years ago President Lincoln stood where he will stand to-day, and, for the first time took the oath of office. Washington was full of traitors—they thronged the Capitol—had the ear of an imbecile President—and even filled the Government offices. The President elect had been forced to pass through Baltimore in disguise to escape assassination. Seven States had already declared themselves out of the Union, and had inaugurated an insurgent government at Montgomery, Ala., with Jeff. Davis at its head. Traitors were confident and defiant, regarding the possession of the soil of all the then Slave States, including Maryland, Kentucky and Missouri, and even the Capital itself, as a mere question of time. Our navy had been dispersed over foreign waters; our armies was scattered and its ranks thinned and feeble; a majority of its principal officers were in the interest of treason; our arsenals were plundered and empty; the treasury had been robbed and was bankrupt. Throughout the South the wildest excitement reigned; forts, mints, custom-houses, vessels and other public property were being seized by the insurgents professing to act under State authority; while in the North there was almost universal distrust and alarm.

Surrounded by these circumstances, President Lincoln first assumed the cares of State. Around him stood such men as Taney, Douglas, Wigfall, Wade, Breckinridge, Chase, Crittenden, Buchanan—friends and foes, patriots and traitors, mingled in the same group. The gifted and the eloquent Baker introduced the President elect to the vast concourse, when he proceeded to read his inaugural address, than which no words proceeding from human lips were ever listened to with more intense interest. That address contained these significant utterances:

"I hold that in the contemplation of international law and of the Constitution, the Union of these States is perpetual. * * * I shall take care, as the Constitution itself expressly enjoins on me, that the laws of the Union be faithfully executed in all the States. * * * The power confided to me will be to hold, occupy and possess the property belonging to the Government, and to collect the duties on imports; but beyond what may be necessary for these objects—no using of force against or among any people anywhere. * * * You have no oath registered in heaven to destroy the Government, while *I* have the most solemn one to 'preserve, protect and defend it.' "

Four years have passed, but to these principles sublimely enunciated, President Lincoln has been true. In that time what changes have occured. Baker has yielded up his life at Ball's Bluff in defense of the cause which he so eloquently maintained in the councils of the nation. Douglas has expired with the words of a generous patriotism ringing upon his lips. Crittenden and Taney are no more. Others of that group have gone into the ranks of the enemies of that Union, for the preservation of which thousands of the brave and true have sacrificed their lives. We have had four years of sanguinary strife; the whole land has resounded with the cries of mourning; our country's map is dotted all over with battle fields; but the Government to-day stands stronger than ever before. Instead of shivering on the brink of a civil war of unknown length, the nation to-day rests in the assurance that the war is almost at an end. The forts and other property of the United States have been "re-occupied and re-possessed," the national flag floats again in triumph over the soil of every seceded State; by the voluntary act of the people, slavery, the pretext and cause of the war, has been abolished in five States and will soon disappear in all the others by virtue of the Proclamation of Emancipation and an amended Constitution; and our victorious armies are gathering around the rebel capital for the last act in the grand drama. Such are the changed aspects which four years have wrought. All honor to Abraham Lincoln through whose honesty, fidelity and patriotism, these glorious results have been achieved. May he live to see the nation under his Administration at peace and all the more prosperous because in the past he has been true to Freedom and Union.

In the South, Lincoln's inauguration day was different from that of his predecessors—"not one of whom ever stood up in that Eastern portico with hands red with the slaughter of his fellow-beings." From the Daily Express, Petersburg, Va., March 4, 1865.

INAUGURATION DAY

This is a great day in Yankeedom. Emperor Abraham's coronation is to come off in the Capitol at 12 o'clock, and on the august occasion solemnities and gayeties will be blended, and there will be a great parade. In other words, Lincoln will be inaugurated in the customary form, President of the United States (such of them as remain united) for four years from to-day. The ceremony will be an imposing one in more than a single sense. It will be distinguished for a display of all the attractions and extravagancies which so much charm the Yankee eye. A tremendous crowd will be upon the Capitol grounds, and fortunate will be the individual who has not half a dozen of his ribs stove in by the surgings and heavings of such an immense mass of living human flesh swayed to and fro by the excitements of the hour. There will be countless flags and streamers with the "Stars and Stripes" resplendently conspicuous—a spectacle that will throw all hearts into spasms of ecstacy. There will be music from thousands of instruments.—The drum and fife, the trumpet, the bassoon, and all its band accompaniments, will peal forth their varied sounds in chorus and fill the ear with tumultuous delight. The cannon, too, will roar forth their rude and boisterous harmony and remind the gaping and exhilerated sight-seers of the scenes which are being enacted in War's drama in the beautiful land stretching away from the opposite bank of the Potomac to the Mississippi. But why need we enter any further into the details of ostentatious pageantry which make up the programme of a Yankee Inauguration day?—They are sufficiently familiar to thousands in every State of the Confederacy, who in the days of the old Union—the palmy days of the late Great Republic—used to flock to Washington on the fourth of March, every four years, for the purpose of witnessing and participating in the celebration of this then highly honored day. Very different was it in character and significancy from what it now is. With Buchanan's Inauguration closed the long list of those celebrations of the day which used to inspire even Southern breasts with joy and pride. A new era was introduced by Lincoln—an era which is separated by a line as broad and as distinct as any that ever divided two chapters of a narrative, from the scenes that characterized the preceding era of Inaugural observances.—The Lincoln style of doing this sort of business is in sad contrast to that which marked the demonstrations on the part of the people in the days of his predecessors—not one of whom ever stood up in that Eastern portico with hands red with the slaughter of his fellow-beings—with a soul loaded down with the guilt of wholesale murder, robbery and arson. Lincoln has the supreme gratification of associating in his mind, while he is taking for the second time the oath of Chief Magistrate, the greatest and blackest catalogue of offences against his God, his country and humanity, that ever one man on the American continent could present for the world's abhorrence.

But what do he and his people care about this? What is it to him or them that war devours its hecatombs of victims? Did not Nero fiddle whilst Rome was burning? And will not Lincoln be as jubilant to-day as if his skirts were as unstained with blood as the vesture of an infant? He swore publicly four years ago to support the Constitution, and no sooner was his oath registered in Heaven than he coolly and deliberately commenced a series of systematic violations of it, which have been continued down to the present time. Again will he to-day repeat the same oath, and to-morrow will witness the same contemptuous disregard of it. The universal Yankee nation will shout and clap their hands over his inaugural utterances and hail him as their ruler with acclamations louder—far louder, than they did four years ago. They will feast, sing and dance to-night. The banquet and the ball will be gloriously enjoyed and mirth and merriment will hold high carnival in the voluptuous saloons of Washington and the other cities of the North.

Bennett's New York Herald, which had finally come out for Lincoln after being among his severest critics, now found him "the unquestioned master of the situation in reference to American affairs, at home and abroad." From the Herald, March 4, 1865.

PRESIDENT LINCOLN'S SECOND TERM—HIS CABINET AND HIS POLICY

The second term of Abraham Lincoln as President of the United States, commences to-day. He is our first President who has had a second inauguration since that of General Jackson, in 1833—thirty-two years ago. From Jackson to Lincoln we have had a lot of one term Presidents; and, excepting General Harrison and General Taylor—both prematurely cut off—they have been of the order of temporizing and trading politicians. Through all the batch we look in vain for the marks of a statesman. We find them, without exceptions, the mere creatures of juggling conventions and corrupting bargains, going on from bad to worse, from Van Buren down to Buchanan. Nor were the arts by which these men were advanced to power more demoralizing than their base devices to retain it. The consequences are before us in the armed legions of this terrible civil war.

Abraham Lincoln himself, in 1860, like Polk, Pierce and Buchanan, was adopted only as a one term compromise by the various cliques of his party wrangling and scheming for the nomination. In this view his very obscurity and apparently unambitious mediocrity made him preferable to more prominent men among the quarrelling politicians concerned. The republican wirepullers, like the democrats, after the reign of Jackson, were looking for a convenient instrument, when they picked up their master in that good-natured, uncouth, ungainly and unpretending Illinois railsplitter, Abraham Lincoln. It is said that the College of Cardinals at Rome, in their elections of the Pope, on several occasions, in resorting to the same expedient, have been cheated in the same way. We are sure that Honest Old Abe was nominated at Chicago without the remotest idea of his becoming a candidate for a re-election, but with a deliberate calculation from Seward men, Chase men and others that he was the very man to be moulded to their purposes for the succession.

Nor were the events of the first three years of Mr. Lincoln in the White House such as to suggest the probability of his renomination. The magnates of his party laughed at the proposition when first thrown out by the HERALD. It was as amusing as one of Old Abe's jokes. But with the approach of the Baltimore Convention the radical dignitaries of the party began to discover their mistake. They were outwitted and outgeneralled completely. They became mutinous; they threatened secession; they tried it in a feeble experiment or two, but they were subdued—from Chase and Fremont, Wade and Winter Davis, down to Bryant and Greeley. We need not repeat the story. Old Abe was renominated and re-elected, and he enters upon his second term of office to-day.

What line of policy will he now pursue? What changes will he make in his Cabinet? To the first question we shall probably have a satisfactory answer in his inaugural address to-day—and perhaps not. To the second inquiry no very elaborate answer is needed. Excepting the appointment of Mr. McCulloch to the Treasury, and a change in the Interior Department, we expect no Cabinet changes; and under Old Abe's system of discipline no further changes are necessary. He is the master, and the members of his Cabinet are his chief clerks. He consults them, he hears them, and then tells them what to do. He indulges Mr. SEWARD in his diplomatic correspondence by the volume, but his theories and arguments touching our foreign policy and domestic relations stand merely as the opinions of Mr. Seward. Old Abe is not bound by them. It is hardly possible that he has ever read or heard a tenth part of the voluminous writings of his inexhaustible Premier. In short, it matters little whether Mr. Lincoln's chief advisers are Tom, Dick and Harry or Sam, Bob and Peter, so long as they are subject to his opinions as their supreme law. He has told me that his course has been shaped by the logic of events, and we presume that this will continue to be his policy. Meantime Greeley and the other anti-Seward radicals may point as much as they like to the broad hints of the Baltimore platform in reference to the Secretary of State; it is all moonshine to Old Abe.

He is a most remarkable man. He may seem to be the most credulous, docile and pliable of backwoodsmen, and yet when he "puts his foot down he puts it down firmly," and cannot be budged. He has proved himself, in his quiet way, the keenest of politicians, and more than a match for his wiliest antagonists in the arts of diplomacy. He upsets, without an effort, the most formidable obstacles of caucuses and congresses, and seems to enjoy as a huge joke the astonishment of his friends and enemies. Plain common sense, a kindly disposition, a straightforward purpose, and

439

a shrewd perception of the ins and outs of poor weak human nature, have enabled him to master difficulties which would have swamped almost any other man. Thus to-day, with the most cheering prospects before him, this extraordinary railsplitter enters upon his second term the unquestioned master of the situation in reference to American affairs, at home and abroad.

Let us hope that in his general policy through the four years to come all the budget of blunders of the four years that are past will be completely effaced and forgotten, or that they will only serve to brighten the crowning glories of a successful administration.

Lincoln's Second Inaugural—"with malice toward none; with charity for all"—is ranked with the great documents of American history. Lincoln himself said of it, "I expect [it] to wear as well as—perhaps better than—anything I have produced." An old enemy, the Chicago Times, March 6, 1865, true to form, was unmoved.

THE INAUGURAL ADDRESS

The inaugural addresses of the past presidents of the United States are among the best of our state papers. Profound in their comprehension of the principles of the government; exalted in their aspirations; magnificent in their patriotism; broad, liberal, catholic in their nationality; elevated in their literary style,—they will stand forever as the grandest monuments of American statesmanship. They were consonant with the national character. They were the natural product of the glorious years in which the republic grew from its revolutionary birth to be the most powerful nation on the face of the earth.

Contrast with these the inaugural address of Abraham Lincoln, delivered in the city of Washington on Saturday, and printed in these columns this morning! "What a fall was there, my countrymen." Was there ever such a coming out of the little end of the horn? Was ever a nation, once great, so belittled? Is such another descent of record in the history of any people?

We had looked for something thoroughly Lincolnian, but we did not forsee a thing so much more Lincolnian than anything that has gone before it. We did not conceive it possible that even Mr. Lincoln could produce a paper so slip shod, so loose-joined, so puerile, not alone in literary construction, but in its ideas, its sentiments, its grasp. He has outdone himself. He has literally come out of the little end of his own horn. By the side of it, mediocrity is superb.

Let us trust in Heaven that it is not typical of our national degeneracy. Great, indeed, is our fall if the distance be so far as this performance of yesterday is beneath the statesmanship of former times.

Its appearance did not excite the slightest public interest in this city. It fell as if still-born. There would seem to have been some popular premonition of what was coming. The opportunity was a grand one to withdraw for a moment the earnest gaze of the country from the passing stupendous events in the military field, and attract it to the central figure which has power to direct those events. How incompetent was Mr. Lincoln to embrace that opportunity we do most painfully behold.

The religious tone of the Second Inaugural, annoying cynics North and South, struck Americans then and there as a humble and magnanimous address above the sounds of battle. Lincoln said of the speech to Thurlow Weed, "Men are not flattered by being shown that there has been a difference of purpose between the Almighty and them." The National Intelligencer, Washington, March 6, 1865, said the final paragraph of the Inaugural deserved "to be printed in gold."

All that we find space to say this morning on the Inaugural Address of the President is to speak well of it, as we are forced to interpret the few and fitly expressed words which compose the practical part of the document. Mr. LINCOLN re-affirms his former Inaugural, and all his former and familiar declarations of sentiment and policy with reference to the war. He thus utters anew the conservative features of his Inaugural Address of 1861; also, the views which he declared in his noted letter to Mr. Greeley; so he thus repeats his various proclamations of amnesty offered to the South; likewise the terse exposition made in his last annual message of the relation of the rebel States to their constitutional rights; and he avows anew the spirit which he manifested by his personal conference with the Peace Commissioners sent from Richmond.

We have a word to say about the sentimental and religious views embodied in this Address, which, solemnly entertained and conscientiously and reverently spoken as we have no doubt, may be subject nevertheless by the prejudiced and careless to that sort of criticism which objects that the written laws which men enact for their government shall be construed according to the consciences and religious theories of those temporarily entrusted with their protection and execution. Woe to the nation that shall fall into the hands of ungodly rulers; and equal woe to the people whose rights and interests shall be involved and torn in the whirlpool created by jarring theological sects. Whatever good men may think of the providence of GOD in human affairs, (and none more devoutly than ourselves believe that there is such interference,) nevertheless he may well beware who undertakes to say that in the sight of GOD he is without sin, and that his adversary should be burned as a heretic. Mr. LINCOLN cannot intend to convey any such self-righteous dogma. He is merely regarding the war in its obstinacy and causelessness on the part of the rebels; he is contemplating the unlooked-for magnitude of, and great social results which have unexpectedly sprung from the rebellion, and the continued perverseness of the reckless and straightened South, when he ventures the hypothesis that the rebels, judicially blind, may be doomed to greatly protracted punishment because of the offence of slavery. He certainly does not design to affirm the narrow opinion that the chastisement of Heaven which has fallen upon this nation is to be regarded by the North with the pharisaical pride which shall say, WE are *without sin*. The rebellion out of the question, our offences in the sight of Heaven, as a people who, amid luxury and pride and political corruption, have forgotten the Almighty, are too manifold and rank to admit of such impious audacity. In conclusion, we desire no better words from the President for our platform than compose the concluding paragraph of his Inaugural Address. They are equally distinguished for patriotism, statesmanship, and benevolence, and deserve to be printed in gold:

> With *malice* towards *none*; with CHARITY for all; with *firmness*
> in the *right*, as God gives us to see the right, let us strive on to finish
> the work we are in; to BIND UP THE NATION'S WOUNDS; to care for him
> who shall have borne the battle, and for his widow and his orphan
> —to do ALL which may *achieve* and CHERISH a just and a *lasting*
> PEACE, among ourselves, and with all nations.

That Lincoln should appeal to a Divinity appeared puzzling to the South, which had regarded him as an ogre. Was not this the Lincoln who had said nearly twenty years ago, "That I am not a member of any Christian church is true . . . ?" The Daily Express, Petersburg, Va., March 9, 1865.

LINCOLN'S INAUGURAL NO. 2

This is a queer sort of document, being a compound of philanthropy, fanaticism and scriptural morality.—On the subject of the war, he would have the world to believe that his bosom is overflowing with the most distressing emotions in contemplating its horrors, and that he used all his efforts and influence to prevent its breaking out. But "somehow" or other the "slave interest" forced it upon him, and he had to choose between the alternatives of letting the nation survive or seeing it perish.—It is sufficient to say there were no such alternatives presented to him. The only alternatives were for him to leave eleven sovereign States to the peaceful enjoyment of their rights, or to draw the sword and compel them to live the slaves of a Union which abolitionism and the lusts of commerce had converted into an engine of oppression and impoverishment to them. He chose to draw the sword, but by a dirty trick succeeded in throwing upon the South the *seeming* blame of firing "the first gun." He was afraid to fire it himself, and resorted to craft and perfidy to get, what he considered, the advantage of a provocation that, in the eyes of his people, would justify his resort to open and active hostilities. Everybody knows that the bombardment of Fort Sumter was brought about by a gross breach of faith by Lincoln, and that, in fact, he was just as guilty of inaugurating this war, as if he had sent an armed squadron into Charleston Harbor with orders to fire upon the city, before a gun was fired by the Confederates. He has made a good deal of history, but none that will disgrace him more in the eyes of future generations than the part he acted in the Fort Sumter affair, by which he managed to precipitate hostilities without *technically* incurring the odium of having struck "the first blow." But let this pass.

The most curious portion of his Inaugural is the latter half of it, where he enacts the character of a saintly devotee. His allusions to Almighty Power and his citations from the scriptures might well become a Preacher of Righteousness. He seems to be thoroughly imbued with reverence for the Gospel of peace and with faith in Divine revelations. One would suppose that his knees were almost lacerated by his prayers and that his heart was the abode of all the Christian graces—that his whole time, except when his public duties forced him into carnal performances, were spent in prayer, and supplication, and that it was the supreme delight of his life to meditate upon Heavenly things. It is not for us to know any human heart, and still less such a heart as Lincoln's. God is the great searcher of this deceitful and most desperately wicked organ, and He alone knows whether it is always what the lips of its owner would represent it to be. So just here we will refrain from expressing our opinion, saying with Lincoln, who borrowed the idea and most of the words from our Saviour's sermon on the Mount: "Let us judge not, that we be not judged"—and so we take our leave of his Inaugural.

After the Second Inaugural, an American General wondered, "What will Europe think of this utterance of the rude ruler, of whom they have nourished so lofty a contempt? Not a prince or minister in all Europe could have risen to such an equality with the occasion." The London Times, March 17, 1865, was complimentary about the brevity of the speech but suspicious of Lincoln's motives.

For the first time since the days of General JACKSON's immense popularity an American President has been inaugurated for the second time. The circumstances under which Mr. LINCOLN assumes office for another term of four years are so strange and impressive that they may justify an address full of a kind of Cromwellian diction and breathing a spirit very different from the usual un-earnest utterances of successful politicians. This short inaugural speech reveals the disposition and the opinions of the Federal Magistrate more completely than many of the verbose compositions which have proceeded from his predecessors. We cannot but see that the PRESIDENT, placed in the most important position to which a statesman can aspire, invested with a power greater than that of most Monarchs, fulfils the duties which destiny has imposed on him with firmness and conscientiousness, but without any feeling of exhilaration at success or sanguine anticipation of coming prosperity. The brief allusion to the expectations of the two parties during the early days of the war shows what is passing through the mind of the Chief Magistrate when he looks back to four years of slaughter, and turns round to gaze into the black darkness which shrouds the future. All dreaded the war, all sought to avoid it. When the last inaugural address was delivered Secession was but half accomplished. Virginian officers attended President LINCOLN for two months after his installation, and many of them left the Federal capital with unwilling hearts to fight in the cause to which they felt themselves bound. This war was not a thing that came suddenly or without deliberation. Everything that could be said for it or against it was freely uttered before the first great armies were in the field. President BUCHANAN thought it impossible to restrain the action of a State. On the other hand, there had never been wanting men who told the North that they must keep no terms with slaveowners and traitors. The mass of the people went into war unwillingly, and yet with but little knowledge of what was before them. "Neither party," says Mr. LINCOLN, "expected the magnitude or duration which it has already attained; neither anticipated that the cause of the conflict might cease even before the conflict itself should cease. Each looked for an easier triumph and a result less fundamental and astonishing." Mr. LINCOLN anticipates that this result will be in favour of his section of the Union, but, warned by experience, he does not venture to predict an early term for the great settlement. In his Message of a few months since he gave his opinion that the war would last at least as long as Mr. JEFFERSON DAVIS remained at the head of the Southern people. This opinion, so far from being changed by the successes the Federals have since gained, is expressed in even stronger terms on the present occasion. In a tone of mingled resolution and despondency he prays that the scourge of war may pass away, but professes himself resigned to the infliction of the present evils "until the wealth piled by bondsmen during 250 years of unrequited toil shall be sunk, and until every drop of blood drawn with the lash shall be paid by another drawn with the sword."

Such language is not unbecoming a man who has been continued in power avowedly that he may persist in a devastating war. Mr. LINCOLN has no doubt made up his mind to carry through to the letter the policy which has been indicated in his Proclamations and Messages. For this he laboured during his first term of office; for this, in the worst days of Federal ill-success, he issued his decree for the abolition of slavery. It was in consequence of his steadfastness on these points that he was re-elected by a great majority, and he could not, if he would, shrink from doing all that he has promised, and which his party expect. But even after fortune has favoured the Northern arms so abundantly and continuously the PRESIDENT abstains from any of those predictions which were rife in the early part of the war. He knows too well the difficulties of the task which still lies before his Government, he thinks of the armies which must be kept up, the debts that must be incurred, the derangement of political and social relations which must be endured before the States of the old Union return to their former condition. His address appears to be intended to repress the more sanguine expectations of the Northern people, and to intimate to them that fresh exertions and sacrifices will be necessary for the attainment of their object. The re-action caused by disappointed hope is often dangerous, and if the Federals should imagine that the present summer will bring the end of the war, and should then be deceived in their expectations, a feeling of discouragement akin to that of last autumn might possibly supervene. Mr. LINCOLN, therefore, like a prudent statesman, conceals his own hopes, if he cherishes any, and bids the people, in effect, to make up their minds for another considerable term of fighting.

Some light penetrated through the British cloak of prejudice against Lincoln and his Administration. The Second Inaugural revealed a greatness that could not easily be distorted. *The Spectator*, London, regarded the address as "by far the noblest which any American President has yet uttered." *The Spectator's* article, "Mr. Lincoln," appeared on March 25, 1865, and posthumously in *Littell's Living Age*, Boston, April 22, 1865.

From the Spectator, 25th March

MR. LINCOLN

We all remember the animated eulogium on General Washington which Lord Macaulay passed parenthetically in his essay on Hampden. "It was when to the sullen tyranny of Laud and Charles had succeeded the fierce conflict of sects and factions ambitious of ascendency or burning for revenge, it was when the vices and ignorance which the old tyranny had engendered threatened the new freedom with destruction, that England missed the sobriety, the self-command, the perfect soundness of judgment, the perfect rectitude of intention to which the history of revolutions furnishes no parallel, or furnishes a parallel in Washington alone." If that high eulogium was fully earned, as it was, by the first great President of the United States, we doubt if it has not been as well earned by the Illinois peasant-proprietor and "village lawyer" whom, by some divine inspiration, or providence the Republican Caucus of 1860 substituted for Mr. Seward as their nominee for the President's chair. No doubt he has in many ways had a lighter task than Washington, for he had not at least to produce a Government out of chaos, but only to express and execute the purposes of a people far more highly organized for political life than that with which Washington had to deal. But without the advantages of Washington's education or training, Mr. Lincoln was called from a humble station at the opening of a mighty civil war to form a Government out of a party in which the habits and traditions of official life did not exist. Finding himself the object of Southern abuse so fierce and so foul that in any man less passionless it would long ago have stirred up an implacable animosity, mockèd at for his official awkwardness, and denounced for his steadfast policy by all the democratic section of the loyal States, tried by years of failure before that policy achieved a single great success, further tried by a series of successes so rapid and brilliant that they would have puffed up a smaller mind and overset its balance, embarrassed by the boastfulness of his people and of his subordinates, no less than by his own inexperience in his relations with foreign States, beset by fanatics of principle on one side who would pay no attention to his obligations as a constitutional ruler, and by fanatics of caste on the other who were not only deaf to the claims of justice but would hear of no policy large enough for a revolutionary emergency, Mr. Lincoln has persevered through all without ever giving way to anger, or despondency, or exultation, or popular arrogance, or sectarian fanaticism, or caste prejudice, visibly growing in force of character, in self-possession, and in magnanimity, till in his last short Message to Congress on the 4th of March we can detect no longer the rude and illiterate mould of a village lawyer's thought, but find it replaced by a grasp of principle, a dignity of manner, and a solemnity of purpose, which would have been unworthy neither of Hampden nor of Cromwell, while his gentleness and generosity of feeling toward his foes are almost greater than we should expect from either of them. It seems to us, we confess, a discreditable and hardly intelligible thing that the pro-Southern English journals which are exulting with such vehement delight over the squalid vulgarity of the new Vice-President's drunken inaugural—forgetting that both the squalor and the vulgarity of thought are the legacy left by the southern slaveholders to the "mean whites" of the border States, of whom Mr. Johnson, journeyman tailor of Tennessee, is the representative,—should not recognize the calm and grand impartiality displayed, even though it be by a foe, in the President's recent weighty address,—by far the noblest which any American President has yet uttered to an American Congress. Yet the fact is that its finest sentences have been deliberately distorted from their true and obvious meaning into the expression of a bloodthirsty spirit, the farthest possible from their real tenor. After confessing candidly the complicity of the North in the guilt of slavery, and the righteousness of the judgment by which North and South alike suffer its retribution, Mr. Lincoln went on to say, "Fondly do we hope, fervently do we pray, that this mighty scourge of war may speedily pass away. Yet, if God wills that it continue till all the wealth piled by the bondsman's two hundred and fifty years of unrequited toil shall be sunk, and until every drop of blood drawn with the lash shall be paid by another drawn with the sword, as was said three thousand years ago so still it must be said, that the judgments of the Lord are true and righteous altogether." Will it be believed that English journals have garbled this sentence by citing out of it the hypothetical clause, "Yet if it [the war] continues until the wealth piled by bondsmen by 250 years' unrequited toil be sunk, and until every *drop of blood* drawn by the *lash* shall be paid with *another* drawn by the *sword*," without either the introductory or the final words,—decapitated and mutilated of its conclusion,—simply in order to prove Mr. Lincoln's bloodthirstiness?

They might almost as fairly cite from the psalm the words, "If I forget thee, O Jerusalem!" minus the clause, "let my right hand forget her cunning," to prove that the Psalmist was deliberately contemplating the renunciation of his patriotic duties and ties. But these are the critics who do not wish to understand Mr. Lincoln, who wish indeed to misunderstand him. . . .

The war once declared by his opponents, our readers know how he treated the slavery question,—not from any doubt that slavery was the root of the whole struggle, but from a profound doubt whether he was justified in anticipating the divine moment for its extinction. He was not placed there as God's instrument to put down slavery, but as His instrument for administering the Government of the United States "on the basis of the constitution," and the question might settle itself far better than he could settle it. Slowly he was forced, bit by bit, to see that the one duty was involved in the other, and as he saw he accepted it; but even then his only fear was lest he should interfere too much in the great forces which were working out their own end. He was chosen, as men usually are, to do that which he was most fearful of doing,—not because he did not see that it was a great work,—but because he only very gradually opened his eyes to its being a work in which he, with his defined duties, had any right to meddle. And now he speaks of it in just the same spirit as a great natural process, not entrusted to him or dependent on him, of which no one can foresee the course and the exact issue. Both North and South, he says, were equally confident in the justice of their cause, and appealed to God to justify that confidence. He has not justified either of them wholly. "The prayers of both could not be answered, that of neither has been answered fully. The Almighty has His own purposes."

Mr. Lincoln presents more powerfully than any man that quality in the American mind which, though in weak men it becomes boastfulness, is not really this in root, but a strange, an almost humiliated trust in the structural power of that political Nature which, without any statesman's co-operation, is slowly building up a free nation or free nations on that great continent, with an advance as steady as that of the rivers or the tides. It is the phase of political thought most opposite to, though it is sometimes compared with, the Caesarism that is growing upon the European side of the Atlantic.

The Emperor of the French thinks the Imperial organ of the nation almost greater than the nation,—certainly an essential part of it. It is men like Mr. Lincoln who really believe devoutly, indeed too passively, in the "logic of events," but then they think the logic of events the Word of

God. The Caesar thinks also of the logic of events, but he regards himself not as its servant but its prophet. He makes events when the logic would not appear complete without his aid, points the slow logic of the Almighty with epigrams, fits the unrolling history with showy, rhetorical dénouements, cuts the knot of ravelled providences, and stills the birth-throes of revolution with the chloroform of despotism. Mr. Lincoln is a much stupider and slower sort of politician, but we doubt if any politician has ever shown less personal ambition and a larger power of trust.

The close of the war seemed at hand. Grant and Sherman at the end of March, 1865, met with Lincoln at City Point, Va., to deliver the final blows. Once again Horace Greeley offered advice on peace, though a previous mission had failed. Speaking for himself rather than for "twenty million" this time, Greeley outlined what the President should do in the New York Tribune, March 22, 1865.

THE TIME HAS COME

There are those pretty high in authority who say, "There is no use in offering terms to the Rebels, for their leaders will never submit to the authority of the Union, and they only negotiate to gain time." We do not believe this; but, if we did, it would not at all weaken our faith that the President should promptly and frankly appeal to the insurgents in deprecation of the further prosecution of their hopeless struggle, giving them substantial reasons for desisting forthwith. Whatever may be the malignity or desperation of the leaders, it is clear that the masses do not share it. Davis's persistent efforts, and more emphatically his recent elaborate endeavor, to prove our Government implacably averse to negotiation, and immovably resolved on universal confiscation and devastation, indicate beyond mistake the drift of opinion in Dixie toward submission and peace. What use in showing, to people inflexibly resolved on independence, that our Government would grant no conditions? What motive for the recent attempt to open negotiations with Gen. Grant, if it were not deemed necessary at least to make a feint of negotiating on a lower plane than that of 1861?

We fully credit our recent information from Richmond that Lee has confidentially apprised Davis that he cannot hold out against the hosts now gathering for his overthrow.We believe what is left of the Rebellion can and will be crushed any how; but we are utterly averse to the needless shedding of one drop of human blood. So long as War is essential to the life of the Republic, let War rage, though it whelm cities in blood and cover the land with ruins and ashes; but let peace be secured at the very first moment compatible with the unity of the Nation and the freedom of all her people. As we have shown the Old World how a free people lavish their money and their blood when the existence of their country is at stake, so let us give her rulers a lesson in magnanimity and clemency to vanquished insurgents. Let not the victory of the Republic be stained by a single act of vengeance—by one wanton infliction of pain. Blood has flowed in rivers—let it flow on if the necessity shall be found still to exist; but let not the National ensign be stained by one drop shed to punish rather than to save.

What we would have President Lincoln do is simply to set lucidly and briefly before the Rebels the terms on which he would have them lay down their arms and submit to the National authority. These terms should convey his ultimatum on the following points:

    I. Union—Disunion.
    II. Amnesty—Treason.
    III. Confiscation—Property.
    IV. Emancipation—Slavery.
    V. Reconstruction—State subversion.
    VI. Representation in Congress.

It may be urged that some of these topics lie without the sphere of the Executive; but this is rather specious and technical than practical and vital. In matters of War and Peace, the President stands for the People, and may count with confidence on their ratification of his acts. Jefferson knew and avowed that he exceeded his constitutional powers in purchasing Louisiana, but he was eminently justified in taking the responsibility. So let the President proffer such terms as he thinks proper, and never doubt that he will be sustained in so doing. The country sighs for an honorable and lasting Peace, and such seems now within reach. Woe to the hesitancy or perverse counsel which shall prevent its realization!

—"But suppose the Rebel Chiefs are still obdurate?"

We answer, They can damage nobody but themselves. Let President Lincoln now make a specific, circumstantial, magnanimous public overture, and the great body of the Southern Whites will insist on its acceptance. They have long enough submitted to famine, nakedness, misery and death, at the beck of unchastened ambition. Proffer them an alternative, and they will be dragged or pushed no further in this wretched course. Only give them "a place whereon to stand," and they will speedily compel the leaders to submit or maintain the struggle unaided. Half the insurgents would come over at once: what could the rest do without them?

Once more we exhort the President to offer terms to the insurgents without delay. We do not mean to suggest or hint at any bases of pacification, since we desire that the conditions proffered shall be emphatically the President's own. We know that his heart is right, and we are confident that the terms it will prompt him to offer are such as the insurgents ought to accept—such as a large majority of them will choose to accept. Let not another day of carnage anticipate a proffer which is morally certain to paralyze the arm of Treason and quench the torch of Rapine. Let this long devastated land speedily rejoice in the unspeakable blessings of Peace!

At 8:15 on the morning of April 3, 1865, Richmond fell. The next day Lincoln visited the capital of the Confederacy. This straight account appeared in The New York Times, *April 8, 1865.*

FROM RICHMOND

Visit of President Lincoln to Richmond—his interview with prominent citizens—immense enthusiasm of the colored population—the City perfectly tranquil.

Headquarters, Army of the James
RICHMOND, Tuesday, April 4, 1865.

The most interesting fact to be recorded to-day is the visit of the President to Richmond.

Mr. Lincoln, accompanied by his young son and Admiral Porter, arrived at the Rocketts at 2 P.M., in the *Malvern*, and proceeded at once to the mansion of Ex-President Davis, now the headquarters of Maj.-Gen. Weitzel.

The arrival of the President soon got noised abroad, and the colored population turned out in great force, and for a time blockaded the quarters of the President, cheering vociferously.

It was to be expected, that a population that three days since were in slavery, should evince a strong desire to look upon the man whose edict had struck forever the manacles from their limbs. A considerable number of the white population cheered the President heartily, and but for the order of the Provost-Marshal, issued yesterday, ordering them to remain within their homes quietly for a few days, without doubt there would have been a large addition to the numbers present. After a short interval the President held a levee—Gen. Devins introducing all the officers present. The President shook hands with each, and received the hearty congratulations of all.

The Presidential party, attended by Gens. Weitzel, Devins, Shepley, and a brilliant staff of officers, then made a tour round the city—drove rapidly round the capitol—stopping for a few moments to admire Crawford's magnificent statue of Washington, in the grounds of the capitol, and returned to Gen. Weitzel's headquarters at 5:30.

The President and party left Richmond at 6:30 P.M.

In Richmond the President said to swarming Negroes: "Don't kneel to me. You must kneel to God only and thank him for your freedom." A colorful report of how the liberated Negro first saw "Marse Linkum" appeared in the Boston Journal, reprinted in Littell's Living Age, Boston, April 22, 1865.

Correspondence of the Boston Journal

THE PRESIDENT'S ENTRY INTO RICHMOND

I was standing upon the bank of the river, viewing the scene of desolation, when a boat pulled by twelve sailors came up stream. It contained President Lincoln and his son, Admiral Porter, Capt. Penrose of the army, Captain A. H. Adams of the navy, Lieut. W. W. Clemens of the signal corps. Somehow the negroes on the bank of the river ascertained that the tall man wearing a black hat was President Lincoln. There was a sudden shout. An officer who had just picked up fifty negroes to do work on the dock, found himself alone. They left work, and crowded round the President. As he approached I said to a coloured woman,—

"There is the man who made you free."

"What, massa?"

"That is President Lincoln."

"Dat President Linkum?"

"Yes."

She gazed at him a moment, clapped her hands, and jumped straight up and down, shouting "Glory, glory, glory!" till her voice was lost in the universal cheer.

There was no carriage near, so the President, leading his son, walked three-quarters of a mile up to Gen. Weitzel's headquarters—Jeff Davis's mansion. What a spectacle it was! Such a hurly-burly—such wild, indescribable ecstatic joy I never witnessed. A coloured man acted as guide. Six sailors, wearing their round blue caps and short jackets and bagging pants, with navy carbines, was the advance guard. Then came the President and Admiral Porter, flanked by the officers accompanying him, and the correspondent of *The Journal*, then six more sailors with carbines— twenty of us all told—amid a surging mass of men, women and children, black, white, and yellow, running, shouting, dancing, swinging their caps, bonnets and handkerchiefs. The soldiers saw him and swelled the crowd, cheering in wild enthusiasm. All could see him, he was so tall, so conspicuous.

One coloured woman, standing in a doorway, as the President passed along the sidewalk, shouted, "Thank you, dear Jesus, for this! thank you, Jesus!" Another standing by her side was clapping her hands and shouting, "Bless de Lord!"

A coloured woman snatched her bonnet from her head whirled it in the air, screaming with all her might, "God bless you, Massa Linkum!"

A few white women looking out from the houses waved their handkerchief. One lady in a large and elegant building looked awhile, and then turned away her head as if it was a disgusting sight.

President Lincoln walked in silence, acknowledging the salutes of officers and soldiers and of the citizens, black and white! It was the man of the people among the people. It was the great deliverer, meeting the delivered. Yesterday morning the majority of the thousands who crowded the streets and hindered our advance were slaves. Now they were free, and beheld him who had given them their liberty. Gen. Shepley met the President in the street, and escorted him to Gen. Weitzel's quarters. Major Stevens, hearing that the President was on his way, suddenly summoned a detachment of the Massachusetts 4th Cavalry, and cleared the way.

After a tedious walk, the mansion of Jeff Davis was reached. The immense crowd swept round the corner of the street and packed the space in front. Gen. Weitzel received the President at the door. Cheer upon cheer went up from the excited multitude, two-thirds of whom were coloured.

The officers who had assembled were presented to the President in the reception room of the mansion.

Judge Campbell, once on the Supreme bench of the United States, who became a traitor, came in and had a brief private interview with the

President in the drawing-room. Other citizens called—those who have been for the Union through all the war.

The President then took a ride through the city, accompanied by Admiral Porter, Gens. Shepley, Weitzel, and other officers. Such is the simple narrative of this momentous event; but no written page or illuminated canvas can give the reality of the event—the enthusiastic bearing of the people—the blacks and poor whites who have suffered untold horrors during the war, their demonstrations of pleasure, the shouting, dancing, the thanksgivings to God, the mention of the name of Jesus—as if President Lincoln were next to the son of God in their affections—the jubilant cries, the countenances beaming with unspeakable joy, the tossing up of caps, the swinging of arms of a motley crowd—some in rags, some barefoot, some wearing pants of Union blue, and coats of Confederate gray, ragamuffins in dress, through the hardships of war, but yet of stately bearing—men in heart and soul—free men henceforth and forever, their bonds cut asunder in an hour—men from whose limbs the chains fell yesterday morning, men who through many weary years have prayed for deliverance—who have asked sometimes if God were dead—who, when their children were taken from them and sent to the swamps of South Carolina and the cane brakes of Louisiana, cried to God for help and cried in vain; who told their sorrows to Jesus and asked for help, but who had no helper—men who have been whipped, scourged, robbed, imprisoned, for no crime. All of these things must be kept in remembrance if we would have the picture complete.

No wonder that President Lincoln who has a child's heart, felt his soul stirred; that the tears almost came to his eyes as he heard the thanksgivings to God and Jesus, and the blessings uttered for him from thankful hearts. They were true, earnest, and heart-felt expressions of gratitude to God. There are thousands of men in Richmond to-night who would lay down their lives for President Lincoln—their great deliverer, their best friend on earth. He came among them unheralded, without pomp or parade. He walked through the streets as if he were only a private citizen, and not the head of a mighty nation. He came not as a conqueror, not with bitterness in his heart, but with kindness. He came as a friend, to alleviate sorrow and suffering—to rebuild what has been destroyed.

CARLETON.

In captured Richmond, the tide of anger began to subside. They had seen Lincoln; had seen him as he shook hands with the wounded, Union and Confederate. Four days after his visit there, the Evening

Whig, Richmond, April 8, 1865, told the people of a Lincoln—"by this time"—they had not heard of for years.

Everybody knows, by this time, what sort of a man President Lincoln is: but it is not wrong, under present circumstances, to reproduce the brief description of His Excellency, given by Hon. Wm. L. Goggin in the Virginia Convention, in 1861, during his two days' speech on "Federal Relations."

Mr. Goggin said that he knew Mr. Lncoln well during twelve years previous. "I am, perhaps, the only member in this hall, or the only person in the sound of my voice, who does know him well. It was my chance as it was my duty to serve with him in Congress upon the same committee for two years. There is not a gentleman within the sound of my voice —a member of this or any other deliberative body—who does not know that from the kind of intercourse which exists between the members of a committee of any legislative assembly each is able to judge somewhat, not only of the strength of intellect, but of the character, and qualities of mind which those associated with him may possess. Well, sir, I say—and I think it is due to him that I should say it—that I regarded Mr. Lincoln as industrious and attentive to his duties—that there was no man upon that committee who worked with more diligence, or who more faithfully discharged his duties, and he argued with *great ability* many of the complicated questions which arose for discussion."

The impartial world will sustain Mr. Goggin's estimate of the Chief Magistrate of the Union. His fidelity to duty is only surpassed by his diligence, and whatever may be said of his pleasantries and cogent phraseology, no unprejudiced person will dispute the assertion that he can argue "complicated questions" with "great ability."

While Lincoln lived, his enemies were alive. He made his last public address on April 11, 1865, talking not in sorrow but in gladness of heart about reconstruction: "Let us all join in doing the acts necessary to restoring the proper practical relations between these states and the Union; and each forever after, innocently indulge his own opinion whether, in doing the acts, he brought the states from without, into the Union, or only gave them proper assistance, they never having been out of it." The New York World, April 13, 1865, found that "Mr. Lincoln gropes, in his speech, like a traveler in an unknown country without a map."

PRESIDENT LINCOLN'S SPEECH
OF RECONSTRUCTION

The vagueness, indecision, and, we will venture to add, emptiness of the speech which we published yesterday, cannot be attributed to the haste of a sudden extemporaneous effort, for there is evidence that it was prepared with unusual care and deliberation. On the evening previous to its delivery, Mr. LINCOLN declined to hazard any expressions on the reconstruction question on the ground that he was to speak on that subject the next night, and wished to weigh his language. It is stated in a Washington dispatch that the speech was written out beforehand and read from a manuscript. Considering how little it contains, this precaution is evidence not only of care, but of timidity. The President was so afraid of misconstruction or criticism that he said nothing, or what comes so near to nothing that he might as well have not broken silence at all. As if conscious of the vacuity of his speech, he closed it by intimating that he might make proclamation to the South, and was meditating its substance.

And yet this speech, vague and vacillating as it is, stirred up the ire of the radicals; and this, too, not for its halting negation of purpose, but its assumed hostility to their policy. The Washington telegrams to the [New York] *Tribune* foam over with rage. The speech is, in the main, a mere apologetic defense of Mr. LINCOLN's policy in Louisiana; but as the radicals have made that policy a special ground of attack, his faltering adherence to it is regarded as a declaration of hostility to them.

Mr. LINCOLN ought to learn, from the fruits of this experiment, how little he has to gain by shirking the questions which it is his duty to meet with a statesmanlike boldness. By a speech anviously composed to deprecate the wrath of the radicals, he has incurred as strong expressions of their censure, as he could have done by the distinct avowal of a decided policy. He has let the radicals see that he fears them; and has thereby given them fresh encouragement to bully him. It is true that they have a great advantage over him in their predominance in Congress; but Congress cannot meet until December, unless he calls them together, and, meanwhile, the military *eclat* of our generals will cause the popular current to flow in the President's favor, and float any sound and reasonable policy which he espouses with courage, and supports by weight of his great position. Before December, he may carry forward the work of reconstruction to so advanced a stage that Congress will not dare to face public odium and undo his work. But if he allows himself to be cowed by the radicals, he will drift like a hull without a helm till Congress meets, and then be driven at the mercy of the storm.

Mr. LINCOLN gropes, in his speech, like a traveler in an unknown country without a map. And in the excess of that timidity which fears to make any committals as to the route he will take, he declares that the lines drawn on maps are "mere pernicious abstractions—good for nothing at all." Chief among these "pernicious abstractions," which, according to Mr. LINCOLN, can have "no effect other than the mischievous one of dividing our friends," is the question whether the states which passed ordinances of secession are in, or out of, the Union. He dares not pronounce on this question for fear of dividing his party, and so calls it a "pernicious abstraction." But, in truth, it lies at the roots of the great problem of reconstruction; the restoration of the Union, *in any manner,* being impossible without taking a position on it on one side or the other. . . .

The National Intelligencer of Washington, D.C., which had been read once by a New Salem postmaster, had recorded the name of a new Congressman from Illinois, had been a Whig organ and had broken with the President on the emancipation issue, found Lincoln's last public address "this great and good speech." From the Intelligencer, April 13, 1865.

The country has indeed cause for congratulation in the speech of the President, reported in yesterday's INTELLIGENCER. This remarkable speech is wise in sentiment; it is pervaded by the logic of the heart; while the keeness and clearness of perception and grasp of thought which distinguish it, considering the magnitude and complications of the intricate problem which he handles, are certainly remarkable. The simple and fit and familiar words in which he clothes his propositions and suggestions, and what of argument he advances, confirm the best opinions which have been entertained of the elevated character of the mind of the Chief Magistrate.

The first and great thought of the President is, *to welcome the States to their* PLACES *in the Union.* He wishes to consider the States "AT HOME" within the Union; and he does not desire to hear any discussion as to whether or not they have been out of the sisterhood. He does not even recognize that they have seceded; he speaks of them as the "so-called" seceded States. This is entirely in accord with the position which the INTELLIGENCER has always ascribed to the President, and is as broad and liberal a platform, as soulful and generous an intimation, as the mind and heart of man could extend, in the matter of greeting and assurance to the disordered South. We use the phrase "disordered South" in reference to the main point made by the President in the words, "Let all join in doing the acts necessary to RESTORING the proper practical relations between these States and the Union." Jostled out of their orbits, the President would not, therefore, create another constellation; he would "restore" the old field, with every star exactly as heretofore.

The practical statesmanship of the speech lies in what the President says about the establishment and protection of civil governments in the South, and which he enforces by the illustration of Louisiana. This proposition has already been advanced and maintained in these columns, in support of the President's mode of restoration. This plan is the best which the President can see; and he will adhere to it until more wisely advised. In our judgment, the wit of man can do nothing better than adopt the simple process of the working of the old State machinery. It will soon grow if favorably fostered, and adjust itself to its former proportions. Assuming the theory of the Union to be unchanged, and its substance to be the same as before the war, then the Union, in contemplation of law, is intact. Shall we destroy the vine because it needs pruning? Or, to adopt the apt figure of the President, can we have the fowl if we smash the egg?

On all doubtful and involved questions, pertinent to a future day, and which are essentially secondary, the President expresses no opinion and deals in no intimations. He disposes of such obscurities as only a practical statesman can. To use his own admirable language, "An exclusive and inflexible PLAN would surely become a new entanglement. Important principles may and must be inflexible."

An eminent sense of justice characterizes this speech; it is from a lofty stand-point; it soars away above party; it is paternal as well as fraternal; it is Christian, and its spirit will be hailed with delight and responded to by almost the unanimous voice of the masses of the people, South as well as North. If any man says that he should have said more; that he should have obtruded opinions on the relations between Federal and State authority, as hereafter to be defined: that he should have talked dogmatically about the political future of the blacks; that he should have asserted something in behalf of Federal power and prerogative; in other words, that he should have ventured a coup d'état or practical dictatorship, then we respond, that the nation has just reason to thank GOD that ABRAHAM LINCOLN, as disclosed thus far to us, is no such man! His aim appears to be to find and to do the right, within the limits of the Constitution and the laws. And high evidence of this is found in the fact that he is not disposed to accept the questionable argument which asserts that no more than three-fourths of the States are necessary to ratify the constitutional amendment which abolishes slavery. "I do not commit myself against this (the President remarks) further than to say that such a ratification would be questionable, and sure to be persistently questioned; while a ratification of three-fourths of all the States would be unquestioned and unquestionable." This is as far above the partisan, the "radical," the "fanatic," as the highest statesmanship is above the lowest demagogism.

We breathe freely since reading this great and good speech, which seems also to reflect the present spirit of the more influential among the Republican newspapers; of those of that class of the press which have been esteemed as "radical." We cordially thank the President for the stand he has so nobly taken, notwithstanding the embarrassments that surround him, growing out of the weight of the questions which press upon him, and encountering, as he is compelled to do, great discordance of opinion among those who claim to be his especial friends. He has opened wide the gate to restoration; and thus far, he has grandly performed his part. "There all the *honor* lies."

> "One self-approving hour whole years outweigh
> Of stupid starers, and of loud huzzas."

Chapter 10

As They Saw Him

APRIL 15–MAY, 1865

A light rain fell in Springfield.

"My friends," he had said that day, leaving his neighbors, going to Washington as the President-elect, "no one, not in my situation, can appreciate my feeling of sadness at this parting. To this place, and the kindness of these people, I owe everything. Here I have lived a quarter of a century, and have passed from a young to an old man. Here my children have been born, and one is buried. I now leave, not knowing when, or whether ever, I may return. . . ."

Now, four years later, after another American Revolution, they returned him to Springfield.

Now they saw him. The printers took the one-point column rules and turned them downside up into six-point shrouds of black. The poets groped in the language that he had used with such deceptive simplicity and found that simple words could not fully explain him. The preachers and the politicians, those who knew him and those who had followed him, North, South, East, West, in Europe, spoke mightily. And the people who didn't speak and couldn't find the proper expressions, they saw him. The people, who couldn't be fooled, had an instinct.

In his own time, his truths came through, with the help of the opinion makers and in spite of them. It had been his revolution, too; he had rebelled for independence and human freedom. Somehow they saw him. He was history.

In the good columns of the Daily State Journal, Springfield, Sangamon County, Illinois, the hometown paper, the Sangamo Journal—

which had once carried a letter to the editor from a twenty-three-year-old New Salem youth who signed himself, "Your friend and fellow-citizen, A. Lincoln"—the news was reported on Monday, April 17, 1865.

THE GREAT NATIONAL CALAMITY

ABRAHAM LINCOLN IS DEAD! These portentious words, as they sped over the wires throughout the length and breadth of the land on Saturday morning last sent a thrill of agony through millions of loyal hearts and shrouded a nation, so lately rejoicing in the hour of victory, in the deepest sorrow. The blow came at a moment so unexpected and was so sudden and staggering—the crime by which he fell was so atrocious and the manner of it so revolting, that men were unable to realize the fact that one of the purest of citizens, the noblest of patriots, the most beloved and honored of Presidents, and the most forbearing and magnanimous of rulers had perished at the hands of an assassin. The horrifying details recalled only the scenes of blood which have disgraced barbaric ages. People were unwilling to believe that, in our own time, there could be found men capable of a crime so utterly fiendish and brutal. One of the assassins, in a crowded theater, stealthily approaches a man against whom he could have no just cause of enmity; a man so tender in his feelings and sympathies that all his errors were on the side of mercy; a man who had been twice elected to the highest office in the gift of a great people—and without giving any notice of his presence, while his victim, with his wife sitting by his side, is wholly unconscious of danger, deliberately discharges a pistol from behind, piercing the head of the President with the fatal ball, then availing himself of the bewilderment of the audience, leaps upon the stage, and makes his escape. The other assassin, at nearly the same moment, obtrudes himself into the sick chamber of a man who, but a few days before, had narrowly escaped death by being thrown from his carriage, whose life is hardly yet free from danger, and commences a murderous assault upon his prostrate and helpless victim, and the unarmed attendants. It is impossible to conceive anything more fiend-like and diabolical. And yet, this is called "chivalry!"—and the perpertrators profess to be influenced by the love of liberty. It is the "chivalry" of the desperado, and the love of liberty which controls the highwayman and the enemy of humanity.

The nation is bereaved. Every loyal man and woman mourns the loss of one whose unswerving justice, whose pure and unsullied honor and incorruptible integrity, whose magnanimity of character and mercifulness towards his enemies had won the respect even of those enemies themselves. All but traitors mourn him as a personal friend. At such an hour as this and in sight of the fearful crime that has been committed, the spirit of mere partisanship is disarmed and its voice silenced. Nothing but the most uncontrollable and demoniac treason dares to assail a man so foully dealt with, or gloat over the "deep damnation of his taking off."

President Lincoln died at the hand of *Slavery*. It was Slavery that conceived the fearful deed; it was Slavery that sought and found the willing instrument and sped the fatal ball; it is Slaverd alone that will justify the act. Henceforth men will look upon slavery as indeed "the sum of all villainies," the fruitful parent of all crime. This murder was an assault upon the principles of free Government, inasmuch as he was the choice of a large majority of the nation for the office which he filled. He has fallen in the very hour of victory, when constitutional free Government was being vindicated, and when peace seemed just ready to return to a land torn and distracted by civil war. Despite the calumnies of his enemies, his fame is now secure. History and posterity will do him justice. His memory will be a rich inheritance to our nation, attracting to his tomb the lovers of freedom from all lands, and dividing with that of Washington the admiration of the world. With a slight change of phraseology, the closing lines of the magnificent lyric will apply to the death of ABRAHAM LINCOLN:

"As Christ died to make men holy, HE DIED to make men free,
"While God is marching on."

In Springfield, too, was the "Douglas paper," the Illinois State Register, which had once cautioned Lincoln about his "assumed clownishness" and had maligned him as a political enemy frequently. The nuances of the April 15, 1865, editorial were interesting—"We realize that the great Douglas has now a companion in immortality . . ."

THE NATIONAL CALAMITY

To-day, the nation mourns the loss of our Chief Magistrate. President Lincoln is no more.

Just in the hour when the crowning triumph of his life awaited him; when the result for which he had labored and prayed for four years with incessant toil, stood almost accomplished; when he could begin clearly to see the promised land of his longings—the restored Union—even as Moses, from the top of Pisgah, looked forth upon the Canaan he had, for forty years, been striving to attain, the assassin's hand at once puts a rude period to his life and to his hopes. As Moses of old, who had led God's people through the gloom and danger of the wilderness, died when on the eve of realizing all this his hopes had pictured, so Lincoln is cut off just as the white wing of peace begins to reflect its silvery radiance over the red billows of war. It is hard for a great man to die, but doubly cruel that he should be cut off after such a career as that of him we to-day mourn.

Under the frown of the death-angel all evil passions, and all party strife disappear. It is the president of the United States that is suddenly cut down; it is the whole people of the nation who are now bereaved. We forget the points of difference of the four years past, and think only of Abraham Lincoln, the kindly and indulgent man, beloved of his neighbors, and of the chief magistrate who has honestly followed the path that seemed to him best for the welfare of the people. We seek in vain the motives which actuated the perpetrator of this hideous crime. If a rebel, where will rebels look for a man who will judge them with more leniency, whose treatment will be more kindly, or who will receive them with a more catholic and forgiving spirit? Where, now, will the man be found, able to grasp the reins of government, just fallen from those stiff and nerveless hands? What living brain so thoroughly comprehends the present state of affairs, and is so well prepared for future exigencies, as that which the bullet of the murderer has forever stilled? Conjecture is vain for motives to prompt this monstrous deed. It seems to us they can only be found in private, personal revenge.

Abraham Lincoln was born in Hardin county, Kentucky, on the 12th of February, 1809; he was accordingly in his 57th year at the time of his assassination. He removed, with his father, to Indiana in 1816, where he received a limited education; he spent two years at school in Stafford County, Va.; taught school and studied law for a time in Culpeper county, of that state, and removed to Illinois in 1830. He served as a captain of volunteers in the Black Hawk war, was at one time post master of a small country village in this state; served four years in the Illinois legislature, during which time he again turned his attention to the study of law, and settled in this city in its practice. He was a member of the whig national convention in 1840, that nominated Gen. Taylor for the presidency; was a representative in congress from 1847 to 1849, and his career, since the renowned canvass of Illinois by himself and Mr. Douglas, is fresh in the minds of everyone.

The effect of this terrible blow cannot, now, be estimated. Just when the nation seemed about to emerge from the gloom and disorder which have encompassed it for four dreadful years—on the very anniversary of the day which commenced the civil war, we are suddenly plunged into chaos again. We need not inquire whether another hand may at once be found to grasp the helm, and steer the ship of state steadily and safely through the dangers that again thicken about her prow; we all know that to no eye save his was the chart he had mapped out in his own mind so clear, to no hands, however tried can skillful, can the management of our national vessel be thus suddenly entrusted with undoubting confidence. Lincoln had piloted her through the fiercest fury of the storm; no new pilot can now guide the ark of our hopes so clearly, even through the smooth waters of approaching peace.

No national calamity so serious as his death could have befallen us. The bitterest and most radical opponent of his administration cannot fail to recognize, in the mere political bearing of the event, the terrible solemnity of the blow we have received. While we mourn the loss of the genial and kindly neighbor we once knew so well, and mingle our tears and sympathies with those of his bereaved family, we all feel alike keenly the fresh perils to which the nation is subjected.

But tears and regrets are alike unavailing, and the crushing sense of this great sorrow is all that we can now distinctly feel. We realize that the great Douglas has now a companion in immortality, and that when the roll of statesmen whose genius has left its impress upon the destiny of the country shall be complete, no names will stand higher, or shine with purer lustre, than the two which blaze upon the escutcheon of Illinois.

In New York, base of the "newspaper Generals," the second guessers and advisors, who courted and were courted by Lincoln, whose columns influenced the national and foreign press, Bennett's respected New York Herald, April 17, 1865, said that even a "hundred years hence" (the year 1965) historians would still be surprised by his greatness.

THE GREAT CRIME—ABRAHAM LINCOLN'S PLACE IN HISTORY

Abraham Lincoln, in the full fruition of his glorious work, has been struck from the roll of living men by the pistol shot of an assassin. That is the unwelcome news which has, for the last two days, filled every loyal heart with sadness, horror and a burning thirst for retribution. That is the news which has swept away from the public mind every sentiment of leniency or conciliation towards the conquered brigands of the South, and in whose lurid light, as by the phosphorescent flames recently enkindled in the crowded hotels of this city by men with rebel commissions in their pockets, we are again terribly reminded of the absolute barbarity and utter devilishness of the foemen we have now tightly clutched in our victorious grasp. The kindliest and purest nature, the bravest and most honest will, the temper of highest geniality, and the spirit of largest practical beneficence in our public life, has fallen a victim to the insane ferocity of a bad and mad vagabond, who had been educated up to this height of crime by the teachings of our "copperhead" oracles, and by the ambition of fulfilling those instructions which he received "from Richmond." Of him, however, and the bitter fruits to the South and to all Southern sympathizers which must follow his act as inevitably as the thunder storm follows the lightning flash, we do not care in this moment of benumbing regret and overwhelming excitement to allow ourselves to speak. The deliberations of justice must be held in some calmer hour; while, for the present, we can but throw out some few hurried reflections on the character of the giant who has been lost to our Israel, and the glorious place in history his name is destined to occupy.

Whatever judgment may have been formed by those who were opposed to him as to the calibre of our deceased Chief Magistrate, or the place he is destined to occupy in history, all men of undisturbed observation must have recognized in Mr. Lincoln a quaintness, originality, courage, honesty, magnanimity and popular force of character such as have never heretofore, in the annals of the human family, had the advantage of so eminent a stage for their display. He was essentially a mixed product of the agricultural, forensic and frontier life of this continent—as indigenous to our soil as the cranberry crop, and as American in his fibre as the granite foundations of the Apalachian range. He may not have been, and perhaps was not, our most perfect product in any one branch of mental or moral education; but, taking him for all in all, the very noblest impulses, peculiarities and aspirations of our whole people—what may be called our continental idiosyncracies—were more collectively and vividly reproduced in his genial and yet unswerving nature than in that of any other public man of whom our chronicles bear record. . . .

This estimate of the place inevitably to be occupied in the world's history by the great National Chief whose loss we mourn may not prove either a familiar or pleasant idea for the mere partisans of the present day to contemplate; but it will be found none the less a true and philosophical estimate. In the retrospective glance of history the "accidents," as they are called, of his elevation will all have faded out of sight; and the pen of the historian will only chronicle some such record as the following:— From the very humblest position in a family subsisting by agricultural labor, and himself toiling for daily bread in his early youth, this extraordinary man, by the gifts of self-education, absolute honesty of purpose, perfect sympathy with the popular heart and great natural endowments, first rose to eminence as a lawyer; then graduated in Congress; was next heard of as the powerful though unsuccessful rival for national Senatorial honors of the democratic candidate for the Presidency, over whom he subsequently triumphed in 1860; and four years later we find him, in the midst of overwhelming financial embarrassments, and during the uncertain progress of the bloodiest and most desolating civil war ever waged, so completely retaining the confidence of the American people as to be triumphantly re-elected to the first office in their gift. They will claim for him all the moral influences, which—acting through material forces and agencies—have led to the abolition of slavery, and the permanent enthroning of popular institutions on this continent; and, in their general summing up of this now unappreciated age in which we have our feverish being, and in their pictures of those events wherein the clamorous partisans of the past week were prone to urge that Mr. Lincoln had been but a passive instrument, his name and figure will be brought forward in glowing colors on their canvass, as the chief impelling power and central organizer of the vast results which cannot fail to follow our vindication of the popular form of government.

And surely some hundred years hence, when the staid and scholarly disciples of the historic Muse, bring their grave eyes to scan and their brief tapelines to measure the altitude and attitude, properties and proportions of our deceased Chief Magistrate, their surprise—taking them to be historians of the present type—will be intense beyond expression. It has been for centuries the tradition of their tribe to model every public character after the style of the heroic antique. Their nation-founders, warriors and lawmakers have been invariably clad in flowing togas, crowned with laurel or oak wreaths, and carrying papyrus rolls or the batons of empire in their out-stretched hands. How can men so educated—these poor, dwarfed ransackers of the past, who have always regarded greatness in this illusory aspect—ever be brought to comprehend the genius of a character so externally uncouth, so pathetically simple, so unfathomably penetrating, so irresolute and yet so irresistible, so *bizarre*, grotesque, droll, wise and perfectly beneficent in all its developments as was that of the great original thinker and statesman for whose death the whole land, even in the midst of victories unparalleled, is to-day draped in mourning? It will require an altogether new breed and school of historians to begin doing justice to this type-man of the world's last political evangel. No ponderously eloquent George Bancroft can properly rehearse those inimitable stories by which, in the light form of allegory, our martyred President has so frequently and so wisely decided the knottiest controversies of his Cabinet; nor can even the genius of a Washington Irving or Edward Everett in some future age elocutionize into the formal dignity of a Greek statue the kindly but powerful face of Mr. Lincoln, seamed in circles by humorous thoughts and furrowed crosswise by mighty anxieties. It will take a new school of historians to do justice to this eccentric addition to the world's gallery of heroes; for while other men as interesting and original may have held equal power previously in other countries, it is only in the present age of steam, telegraphs and prying newspaper reporters that a subject so eminent, both by genius and position, could have been placed under the eternal microscope of critical examination. . . .

. . . while we all must mourn with sad and sickened hearts the success of the great crime which has removed our beloved and trusted President from the final scenes of the contest he had thus far conducted to a triumphant issue, let us not forget that by the circumstance of death the seal of immortality has been stamped upon his fame; nor is it any longer in the power of changing fortune to take away from him, as might have happened had he lived, one of the most solid, brilliant and stainless reputations of which in the world's annals any record can be found—its only peer existing in the memory of George Washington.

The brilliance of Mr. Greeley and yet the independence of expression—which Lincoln had never, in generosity, confused with enmity—emerged in the New York Tribune's editorial of April 19, 1865. It included the fascinating thought that Andrew Johnson should have been the President during the Civil War and Lincoln the President to pacify the country in the Reconstruction years.

MR. LINCOLN'S FAME

Without the least desire to join in the race of heaping extravagant and preposterous laudations on our dead President as the wisest and greatest man who ever lived, we feel sure that the discerning and considerate of all parties will concur in our judgment that Mr. Lincoln's reputation will stand higher with posterity than with the mass of his contemporaries—that distance, whether in time or space, while dwarfing and obscuring so many, must place him in a fairer light—that future generations will deem him undervalued by those for and with whom he labored, and be puzzled by the bitter fierceness of the personal assaults by which his temper was tested.

One reason for this is doubtless to be found in the external, superficial, non-essential tests by which we are accustomed to gauge contemporary merit. A king without his crown and purple robes is, to the vulgar apprehension, a solecism, an impossibility. A coarsely clad, travel-stained, barefoot Jesus, could get no hearing in our fashionable synagogues, though his every discourse were a Sermon on the Mount. And Mr. Lincoln was so essentially, unchangeably a commoner—among embassadors and grandees in the White House the identical "Old Abe" that many of us had shaken by both hands at Western barbecues—his homely, pungent anecdotes so like those we had heard him relate from political stumps and by log-cabin firesides—that the masses thought of him but as one with whom they had been splitting rails on a pleasant Spring day or making a prosperous voyage down the Mississippi on an Illinois flat-boat, and had found him a downright good fellow. We have had Presidents before him sprung from the loins of poverty and obscurity, but never one who remained to the last so simply, absolutely, alike in heart and manner, one of the People. No one who approached him, whether as minister or messenger, felt impelled either to stoop or to strut in his presence. He was neither awed by assumption nor disgusted by vulgarity. He was never constrained nor uneasy in whatever presence, and he imposed no constraint nor ceremony on others. Every one found him easy of access, yet no one felt encouraged to take undue liberties. Mr. Everett, one of the best bred, most refined and fastidious of our countrymen, after observing his bearing among the cabinet and foreign ministers, the governors, senators, generals, and other notables, collected at the Gettysburg celebration, pronounced him the peer in deportment of any one present. Presuming that to be the fact, it is probably due to the circumstance that he alone never thought of manners, nor how he nor any one else was appearing to others. His mind was intent on matters of wider and more enduring consequence.

Mr. Lincoln has suffered in the judgment of his immediate contemporaries from the fact that, of all things that he might have been required to do, the conduct of a great war was that for which he was least fitted. For War requires the utmost celerity of comprehension, decision, action;

and Mr. Lincoln's mind was essentially of the "slow and sure" order. It was pretty certain to be right in the end; but in War to be right a little too late is equivalent to being wrong altogether. Besides, War sometimes requires sternness; and he was at heart tender and merciful as a woman. He might have saved many lives by prompt severity toward a few of the active traitors who thronged Baltimore and Washington directly after the fall of Sumter, and openly, ostentatiously exulted over our disaster at Bull Run. That extreme lenity which befits the close of a civil war was most unluckily evinced by him at the beginning of ours, giving every coward to understand that, while there was peril in steadfast loyalty, it was perfectly safe to be a Rebel. To human apprehension, Andrew Johnson should have been the man to grapple with and crush the Rebellion, with Abraham Lincoln to pacify the country at its close and heal the gaping wounds opened by four years of desperate, bloody conflict: but it was otherwise decreed.

There was never an hour when the strength, the resources of the Republic were not ample for the direct and signal overthrow of Slaveholding Treason; but the imbecility, incapacity, and lack of purpose, so common among our high Military officers in the early stages of our struggle—disqualifications which our Commander-in-Chief should have promptly overcome, even though it had been requisite to shoot a General daily for two or three months—long rendered our success at best doubtful. Hence, foreigners, who noted the effect without a knowledge of the cause —confidently, and not unreasonably, predicted our ultimate failure. It was a perfectly natural, though happily ill-grounded, deduction that a Government that could lose such a battle as that of Bull Run, when it had superabundant means to win it, would never put down a gigantic Rebellion. But our President was like our horse Eclipse, in the great Northern and Southern match race of 1824, wherein the North was badly beaten on the first heat, but won the second and third.

As Premier of a Government like the British, where the position requires skill and tact in debate while the duties of administration are divided, Mr. Lincoln would have been far more happily placed and would have done better service than in our Presidential chair, whereof the incumbent must mainly speak and act through others. His forte lay mainly in debate, or rather in the elucidation of profound truths, so that they can hardly evade the dullest apprehension. No other man ever so successfully confronted, before a prejudiced, negro-despising audience, the plausible fallacies of Senator Douglas's vaunted "Popular Sovereignty." His familiar exposition of that doctrine in his Springfield speech opening the Senatorial canvass of 1858—"If A. wants to make B. a slave, C. *shall not interfere*"—was only paralleled in that passage of one of his replies to his great antagonist, which reads:

> My distinguished friend says it is an insult to the emigrants of Kansas and Nebraska to suppose that they cannot govern themselves. We must not slur over an argument of this kind because it happens to tickle the ear. I admit that the emigrant to Kansas or Nebraska is competent to govern himself; *but I deny his right to govern any other person without that person's consent.*

Men of greater talent have made Republican speeches in this City; but Mr. Lincoln's Cooper Institute address of March, 1860, remains to this day the most, lucid, cogent, convincing argument of them all. So at the consecration of the Gettysburg National Cemetery (Nov. 19th, 1863) where Edward Everett made an elaborate and graceful oration, and others spoke fitly and well, the only address which the world will remember was that of the President, who simply said:

> Fourscore and seven years ago our fathers brought forth upon this continent a new nation, conceived in liberty, and dedicated to the proposition that all men are created equal. Now we are engaged in a great civil war, testing whether that nation, or any nation so conceived and so dedicated can long endure. We are met on a great battle-field of that war. We have come to dedicate a portion of that field as a final resting-place for those who here gave their lives that that nation might live. It is altogether fitting and proper that we should do this. But in a larger sense we cannot dedicate, we cannot consecrate, we cannot hallow this ground. The brave men, living and dead, who struggled here, have consecrated it far above our power to add or detract. The world will little note, nor long remember, what we say here, but it can never forget what they did here. It is for us, the living, rather to be dedicated here to the unfinished work which they who fought here have thus far so nobly advanced. It is rather for us to be here dedicated to the great task remaining before us, that from these honored dead we take increased devotion to that cause for which they gave the last full measure of devotion; that we here highly resolve that those dead shall not have died in vain; that this nation under God, shall have a new birth of freedom, and that government of the people, by the people, and for the people, shall not perish from the earth.

—"I have not assumed to control events—events have controlled me," said Mr. Lincoln, in answer to a Kentucky complaint that he was more radical in 1864–5 than he had been in 1861–2. That was the simple truth, naively and tersely expressed; and in that truth is exhibited both the weakness and the strength of the utterer. He was not the man of transcendent genius, of rare insight, of resistless force of character, who bends everything to his will: On the contrary, he was one of those who have awaited opportunity, and thought long and patiently, before venturing on an important step, hearkening intently for that "voice of the people" which was to him, in most cases, "the voice of God." He hesitated to put down his foot, feeling the ground carefully, deliberately; but, once down, it was hard to make him take it up again. A striking and honored exemplar of some of the best points in our National character, he sleeps the sleep of the honored and just, and there are few graves which will be more extensively, persistently visited, or bedewed with the tears of a people's prouder, fonder affection, than that of Abraham Lincoln.

In The New York Times, whose Henry Raymond had campaigned so intently for the re-election of Lincoln, the Second Inaugural was remembered as the address which soared above all others. From The Times, April 17, 1865.

THE LAST ADDRESS OF THE PRESIDENT TO THE COUNTRY

Probably all men in all quarters of the world, who read President Lincoln's last Inaugural Address, were impressed by the evident tone of solemnity in it, and the want of any expression of personal exultation. There he stood, after four years of such trial, and exposed to such hate and obloquy as no other great leader in modern history has experienced, successful, reëlected, his policy approved by the people and by the greater test of events, the terrible rebellion evidently coming to its end, and he himself now certain of his grand position in the eyes of history—and yet not a word escaped him of triumph, or personal glory, or even of much hopefulness. We all expected more confidence—words promising the close of the war and speaking of the end of our difficulties. Many hoped for some definite line of policy to be laid out in this address. But instead, we heard a voice as if from some prophet, looking with solemn gaze down over the centuries, seeing that both sides in the great contest had their errors and sins, that no speedy victory could be looked for, and yet that the great Judge of the world would certainly give success to right and justice. The feeling for the bondmen and the sense of the great wrong done to them, with its inevitable punishment, seemed to rest with such solemn earnestness on his soul, that to the surprise of all and the derision of the flippant, an official speech became clothed in the language of the Bible. The English and French critics all observed this peculiar religious tone of the Inaugural, and nearly all sensible persons felt it not unsuited to the grandeur and momentous character of the events accompanying it. Many pronounced it a Cromwellian speech; but it had one peculiarity, which Cromwell's speeches never possessed—a tone of perfect kindness and good-will to all, whether enemies or political opponents.

"With charity to all and malice for none," President Lincoln made his last speech to the world. Men will reperuse that solemn address with ever increasing interest and emotion, as if the shadow of his own tragic fate and the near and unseen dangers to the country, rested unconsciously on its words. It will seem natural that no expression of exultation or personal triumph escaped the great leader of this revolution, but that his mind was filled with the impressive religious lessons of the times. It will be thought characteristic of his sense of justice and his sincere humanity, that his last public address to the country was most of all occupied by the wrongs done to the helpless race, whose friend and emancipator he had been. And it will seem but a part of his wonderful spirit of good-will to all, that not a syllable of bitterness toward the enemies of his country, to the traitors at home, or his personal revilers, passed his lips.

It is such a speech to the world as a Christian statesman would gladly have his last—earnest, humane, truly but not technically religious, filled with forgiveness and good will.

When generations have passed away, and the unhappy wounds of this war are healed, and the whole nation is united on a basis of universal liberty, our posterity will read the dying words of the great Emancipator and the leader of the people with new sympathy and reverence, thanking God that so honest and so pure a man, so true a friend of the oppressed, and so genuine a patriot, guided the nation in the time of its trial, and prepared the final triumph which he was never allowed to see.

Along the edges of the Confederacy that was, in the Frankfort Commonwealth, Frankfort, Ky., April 18, 1865, they spoke this way about a native son who was born near Hodgenville, Kentucky: "when Abraham Lincoln fell, the South lost its best and truest friend."

PRESIDENT LINCOLN

A terrible blow has fallen upon our nation, a deed of horror has been enacted that has filled us all with dread. We cannot yet realize that such a wicked, cruel act has been committed in our land—appalled by its cruelty and enormity we could not give credence to the report. But the fact is established now—Abraham Lincoln, our noble and beloved President, is dead, stricken down, unarmed, defenceless, and unwarned, by the hand of a rebel assassin.

LINCOLN IS DEAD. How hard it is to pen these words, how heart-rending is the thought to which they give birth, of the irreparable loss which the nation has sustained in the death of him who loved it and had given himself wholly to the work of effecting its salvation. For in the midst of his usefulness a good man has fallen, a true and pure patriot; a President who had done his duty well, with a conscience void of offense toward God and man, and who had ruled his people as a loving father, always tempering justice with mercy and always ready to succor and forgive.

LINCOLN IS DEAD. The awful fact which these few words convey has filled the land with mourning. How suddenly had it turned our joy to sadness, our gladness to grief. In the very midst of our rejoicing over the late triumph of the Union over the rebellion, of our joy in view of the ending of our civil strife, and of our thoughts and purposes of love towards those who have brought all these troubles upon us at whose hands we have so greatly suffered, this crushing blow has come upon us, turning the light to darkness, our happiness to misery, our laughter to tears. God in mercy grant it may not, too, turn our thoughts of peace and love towards our enemies into purposes of deadly hate and implacable revenge.

LINCOLN IS DEAD. They have conspired against his life, have sought and taken it, towards whom he had not one thought of hate, to whom he had again and again made most gracious offers of peace and pardon, and for whose kind and merciful reception back to their old places in the Union, his last thoughts and work were given. Truly they knew not what they did—when Abraham Lincoln fell, the South lost its best and truest friend.

LINCOLN IS DEAD. He has fallen at his post, working for the restoration of the Union to its old harmony and prosperity. And in this work there was an earnest desire to serve his whole country. In his heart there was no hate of the rebellious South, no feeling of revenge on account of the terrible wrongs it had inflicted upon our happy land, no bitterness of spirit towards those who continually maligned and traduced him. By the bands of love he would draw back those of rebellion to their old allegiance. Thus have they rewarded him.

LINCOLN IS DEAD. He has given his life a sacrifice for ours. That the Union might be preserved and the enjoyment of life, liberty and property be insured to us and our posterity, he called the people to arms after the blow struck at Sumter. For that, and for all that he has done well and wisely for the suppression of the rebellion, he has incurred the hatred of rebels in arms and their sympathizers in our midst. This hatred has bred vengeance, and vengeance has done its base, cowardly work in the assassination of our President. Thus he has laid down his life for ours— he has fallen a martyr to his country's cause, and in his country's memory his praise shall ever live.

LINCOLN IS DEAD. The nation lives. Our Government will still survive. He had led it safely through the dangers which threatened its existence and already every loyal heart has sung its "Hallelujah" for the happy deliverance and the bright prospect of peace. But our President, like Moses of old, was only permitted a glimpse of the promised day of peace and union, and then died. Now we sorrow, but not as those which have no hope. Our hope and faith, which have so long upheld the nation, yet remain;—the hope of peace which shall be enduring and true, faith in the justice of our cause and the permanency of the Union. So we shall live to bless the memory of him who saved his country and established it on foundations that can never be destroyed. Future generations will call him blessed.

LINCOLN IS DEAD. Sad and terrible words! Gloom has settled down upon our hearts, sorrow is deep and unfeigned; we have all lost a father and a friend. This truth all will yet learn and coupled with the remembrance of our country's trouble will always be the name of her deliverer, never spoken but with emotions of deepest love and tenderest regard— the name of Abraham Lincoln.

In the capital of the rebellion, where earlier in the month Lincoln had walked the streets with his son Tad while Negroes fell to their knees, the Richmond Whig spoke of the assassination as a blow to the South. The Richmond Whig editorial was reprinted on Page 1 of the Louisville Journal, Ky., April 27, 1865.

THE DEATH OF THE PRESIDENT

Assassination of President Lincoln.—The heaviest blow which has ever fallen upon the people of the South has descended, Abraham Lincoln, the President of the United States, has been assassinated! The decease of the Chief Magistrate of the nation, at any period is an event which profoundly affects the public mind, but the time, manner, and circumstances of President Lincoln's death render it the most momentous, the most appalling, the most deplorable calamity which has ever befallen the people of the United States.

The thoughtless and vicious may effect to derive satisfaction from the sudden and tragic close of the President's career; but every reflecting person will deplore the awful event. Just as everything was happily conspiring to a restoration of tranquility, under the benignant and magnanimous policy of Mr. Lincoln, comes this terrible blow. God grant that it may not rekindle excitement or inflame passion again.

That a war, almost fratricidal, should give rise to bitter feelings and bloody deeds in the field was to be expected, but that the assassin's knife and bullet should follow the great and best loved of the nation in their daily walk, and reach them when surrounded by their friends, is an atrocity which will shock and appall every honorable man and woman in the land.

The secrecy with which the assassin or assassins pursued their victims indicates that there were but few accomplices in this inhuman crime. The abhorrence with which it is regarded on all sides will, it is hoped, deter insane and malignant men from the emulation of the infamy which attaches to this infernal deed.

We cannot pursue this subject further. We contemplate too deeply and painfully the terrible aspects of this calamity to comment upon it further.

From Texas came horrible reactions. They were slow to catch on, still fighting the war—and Lincoln as the personification of Yankee evil. A newspaper in Dallas, the Herald, said, "God almighty ordered this event or it could never have taken place." And in the Tri-Weekly Telegraph, in Houston, edited and owned by E. H. Cushing, on April 25, 1865, appeared these shocking words.

From now until God's judgment day, the minds of men will not cease to thrill at the killing of Abraham Lincoln, by the hand of Booth, the actor, in the theatre at Washington, on the night of April 14th, 1865. It goes upon that high judgment roll for nations and for universal man, with the slaying of Tarquin, of Caesar, of Charles I, of Louis XVI, of Marat. Variously, most oppositely will men judge it. Some will regard it with all the horror of the most wicked assassination, others will feel it to be that righteous retribution which descends direct from the hand of God upon the destroyer of human liberty, and the oppressor of a free people. Ours should not have been the hand for the deed. Nor does our conscience yield approval to it. But whilst we often condemn the human instrumentality, the death it inflicts is recognized to be a doom of that awful Nemesis which avenges wrong in dark and cruel fate. Mr. Lincoln was, it is true, the lawful head of the government of the United States. It may be that his own sense of right has gone along with all his acts in that high place. He has impressed us as natively a kindly, genial man. We do not suppose a love of oppression, or tendency to wrong, any part of his original disposition. We believe he thought at the beginning, that the great movement of the Southern people for self-government was a mere passionate outbreak, caused by designing leaders, and that the hearts of the great mass of the people would soon return to the Union. In good faith, he thought "nobody hurt," and very few likely to be hurt. He thought that the "fire-eaters" who had been warning and threatening in words so long at Washington, had even carried secession to the extent of a practical joke. No doubt he expected the Union soon to be re-established, and an era of good feeling to prevail. Even when the war had assumed serious proportions, he professed that its only object was to enable the loyal majority of the South to re-assert their rights; he disclaimed the right of the Northern people to avail themselves of the pretext of the common government in order to subjugate and rule the South; and owned that they had made a most monstrous and wicked mistake, for which they deserved the condemnation of mankind, if that loyal Southern people did not exist, and it proved to be a war of North against South.

Fully embarked, however, in the war, the change came upon Mr. Lincoln, which has ever come upon the souls of men over which any great end of ambition or fanaticism obtains control, and settles into fixed purpose. Robespierre, a tender young philanthropist, resigned a judgeship in his native village of Arras rather than pass the death sentence of the law on a malefactor, believing that human life should never be taken even by a judicial tribunal. He went up to Paris, and becoming involved in the revolution, and seeing in its triumph the great and eternal good of France;

destruction of life, the blood of the best and noblest in torrents, seemed to him God's appointed way to reach it, and a grimmer monster than he was, although always "neatly dressed," "fond of flowers," and known by the titles of "the just" and "the incorruptible," and as "the great man of the republic," does not disfigure the world's annals. And so Abraham Lincoln came to think that the one great and supreme object—it may be he thought it the object of real and ultimate good to mankind—was the complete and unresisted re-establishment of the power of the government of the United States by the arms of the Northern people, and by the arms of foreign mercenaries from every land, and even by the arms of our own domestic slaves, over the people of the Southern States. No constitution, no law, no right, no humanity stood in the way of this end. Treasure was nothing, human life was nothing, old and cardinal principles of liberty and sentiments of right were nothing, in order to effect it. We saw successively in his public documents how superruling became his purpose, and how callous to all the usual motives of humanity he grew. 75,000 men, 300,000 men, 500,000 men—men—victims without number. Our slaves to be freed and armed against our lives, our cities burned, our fields ravaged, all that would sustain life, wasted and destroyed. In one of his messages he said, with grim and terrible satisfaction, that *under all circumstances our land would remain.* Where the fierce Attilla, calling himself "the curse of God," swept with his barbaric hordes, the historian records as the marks of his terrible wrath, that "he left only the sky and the earth remaining." Attilla, perhaps, joyed in the devastation. Abraham Lincoln, doubtless, did not. He may have felt pity, but no remorse; and to fasten despotism upon a people free as himself, entitled to life and liberty and the pursuit of happiness like himself, he would have stood unmoved and inflexible, and with no eye turned to heaven, would have seen them swept from the earth, and *only the land remaining,* and felt himself a great Republican President, and one of the world's heroes. And so he is recognized and applauded by the people of the North to-day, and his name fills cathedral and church, and the public places, and the voices of all, and many of them name it above the name of Washington. . . .

What sacrifices, by flame and sword, by insult, confiscation, exile and death, and by all the wrongs which make oppression bitter, shall be required of us as the expiation, we know not. All of them we defy. Not a soldier, nor a woman, an old man nor a lisping child with true heart to this Southern land but feels the thrill, electric, divine, at this sudden fall in his own blood of the chief of our oppressors. Monomaniac, assassin, villain, may have been the hand. We approve it not. Open, fair and honorable shall be all our own acts, and those we shall ever advise or uphold. But we stand still before the Providences of God. And with that deep, ineffaceable, eternal feeling which led the great souled patriots of noble old Virginia to inscribe as her motto upon her shield, "Sic Semper Tyrannis," so say we, a thousand and a thousand times, "Sic Semper Tyrannis. Not in fair fight merely, not on the field of honorable battle, not by the law's formal sentence, but every where and by all means, Sic Semper Tyrannis. Whoever would impose the fate of servitude and slavery on these Confederate States, whatever fatal Providence of God shall lay him low, we say, and say it gladly, God's will be done. These are feelings for which we are ready to stand at His judgment bar! Our prayer to Him, like that of the great French patriot is, "whoever may perish, may our country be free."

On the Pacific Coast, the anger of the people swelled at the news of the President's death. How word was first received and the thoughtful comment that followed came out in the Daily Alta California, San Francisco, April 16, 1865.

THE EFFECT IN SAN FRANCISCO

The news of the terrible tragedy which has just been enacted at the Capital of the Nation was first received here with doubt and hesitation. There were few who could bring themselves to believe that a crime so unspeakably atrocious could have been committed, but soon proof upon proof began to accumulate.

The extras issued from the offices of the ALTA and *Bulletin* furnished the details of the terrible event with such circumstantiality that nothing was left upon which a hope might be based either of exaggeration or mistake. At once the shops were everywhere closed. All business was suspended. The bells tolled, and the emblems of mourning were everywhere displayed.

Then the public wrath began to kindle, soon it burst forth into a consuming conflagration, threatening the destruction of everything treasonable in its path. The offices of certain obnoxious publications were entered and their types and presses thrown into the street. In the building in which the ALTA CALIFORNIA is published is also the office of the *Echo du Pacifique*, a French paper. The idea was inculcated that it was a secession paper, and the excited populace were determined to serve it in the same way; but as they could not reach it without passing through our part of the building, and as under such terrible excitement there would not be much chance for the distinguishment of one room from another—one set of types from the other—we were obliged to bar the doors and prevent admission.

And there was reason for the excitement—cause ample and sufficient for the phrenzy which had seized upon the public mind. The news which we had received from the other side was enough to heat the blood and madden the brain of the most cool and phlegmatic. It was more than human nature could stand, and especially that hot, impulsive nature which flourishes here. It was, indeed, more than men could bear.

The type and material of the *Echo du Pacifique* were taken military possession of last night, by the forces under General McDowell, and are now in his custody.

THE UNITED STATES IN MOURNING

Never did a nation mourn more deeply for its dead Chief than does the American Union to-day for Abraham Lincoln. The flags at half-mast, the drapery of black, the tolling bells, the stoppage of business, are not the mere demonstrations of ceremonious respect for a dead President; the sad faces, the sad hearts, the general expression of sorrow show the popular love for, and trust in, the man who had led his country through the great trials of the last four years, and who, having been crowned with success, was about to achieve a second triumph in healing the wounds that remain after the victory.

But it was not to be so. The hand of the assassin interfered. Treason has been crushed, and nothing was left but assassination. The attempt at the life of the nation having failed, the life of its representative was taken. A fitting termination for the work commenced four years ago. Rebellion, war, rapine, ruin and assassination—these are the principles and practices which form the glories of the chivalry of slavery.

And our President is gone—the man of our choice—the man in whom all had supreme confidence, who had been true to us, who would be kind to our enemies, who would yield nothing to weak friend or strong foe, who, in the most trying circumstances had shown no sign of weakness, no vacillation, no excitability, no despair, no unseemly anger, no meanness, no dishonesty, no stain of any kind upon his honesty or his honor. Such a man as the nation needed, such a man was Abraham Lincoln. He had his eccentricities, but they did not affect his moral character.

Years will elapse before the vast importance of the struggle for Union and Liberty in the nation which occupies the vanguard of human progress, will be properly estimated; but when that time comes, and when the peculiar moderation and firmness of Lincoln are fully appreciated, he will probably be placed with those most eminent examples of conscientious statesmen—Aristides and Washington.

For Abraham Lincoln, the nation mourns as a mother for her first-born. The great leader whom it has so long followed with a confidence which knew no abatement, is no more. He had performed all his duties in a becoming manner. He had done a great work. He had secured for himself an immortal and an honorable place in the pantheon of history. His martyrdom crowns his heroic life, and gives to his virtues a higher lustre, and to his name a more brilliant eminence. The words written by Willis on the death of Harrison, may be appropriately applied to Lincoln:

> "The first mourner to-day
> Is the Nation, whose Father is taken away!
> Wife, children and neighbor may mourn on his knell:
> He was lover and friend to his country as well!
> For the stars on our banner, grown suddenly dim,
> Let us weep, in our darkness, but weep not for him!
> Not for him who, departing, leaves millions in tears!
> Not for him who has died full of honors and years!
> Not for him who ascended Fame's ladder so high
> From the round at the top he has stepped to the sky!

We lament a nation that has lost its Father, and in its orphanhood knows not where to look for consolation or safety. Him we knew, in him we trusted; in his hands we knew that all was safe, but now what is to become of us? Our national troubles against which we had fought so stubbornly, and with so much sacrifice, appeared to be subdued; the dawn of peace, quiet, prosperity and good feeling was already lighting up the sky and bringing gladness to all hearts, and in the midst of all comes this vile, demoniac assassination to destroy the man to whom all sides looked as their best friend and most powerful protector.

When the cortege reached New York, Greeley's Tribune, April 24, 1865, got in a final and rather strange comment. Reconstruction was in the forefront and Lincoln's inaction and silence seemed eminently right—a concession on the part of the Tribune, which had always prodded Lincoln to be more forthright.

WHAT HE DID NOT SAY

The earthly remains of our late President will this morning reach our City on their way to their final rest, and will remain with us till to-morrow afternoon. It seems, then, a fit moment for recalling attention to the wisdom and patriotism evinced by our loved and lost leader in his reserve and silence—in what he took care *not* to say or do during his occupancy of the Presidential chair. For many a fool has the credit of clever or smart sayings—perhaps justly: but to refrain from follies that are current and popular, steadfastly refusing to lend them any countenance whatever, evinces a profound and invincible sagacity rare among even the ablest of public men.

I. Mr. Lincoln, throughout his arduous term of service of President —in fact, throughout his entire public career—utterly, stubbornly refused to utter a word calculated to embroil us in a contest with any foreign power. "ONE WAR AT A TIME"—the words with which he decided the Trent case—were the key-note of his entire official career. He never pro-posed the idea, once so popular, of getting out of our domestic struggle by plunging into one with a European power. None of the bogus "Monroe doctrine" bravado, which so tickles the ears of most groundlings, ever escaped his lips. He was of course annoyed and embarrassed by the French invasion of Mexico, and he never concealed his dislike to that Napoleonic blunder; but he felt that it ill became the chief of a great nation to indulge in warnings and menaces which he was notoriously unable, during our Civil War, to back by material persuasions. It would have been easy and popular to plunge the country into a great foreign war; but that would have been to ensure its permanent disruption and overthrow. Mr. Lincoln saw the right from the outset, and had the courage and patriotism to pursue it.

II. He never talked vindictively, nor threatened to hang or shoot men who were not in his power. He probably had as clear and keen a per-ception of the wickedness of the Slaveholders' Rebellion as any other man could have; but he said little about it, and never barked at those who were not within reach of his bite. Mrs. Glass's initial direction for hare-cooking —"First, catch your hare"—he was never tempted to violate. And if wrath and bitterness, with a fearful looking-for of judgment, now pervade the Rebel breast, it was not incited by anything ever uttered by President Lincoln.

III. He always kept us clear as might be of the tangle of premature "Reconstruction." He instinctively saw from the start, in this as in other respects, the folly of quarreling over the disposition of the fox's skin while the fox was still uncaught. First, break the back of the Rebellion before you undertake to pass sentence on the Rebel chiefs; vanquish and disperse the Rebel armies before you quarrel about the terms of rëadmitting to our counsels States not yet ready to come back on any terms. To settle questions as they severally arise, and not to divide the loyal strength on topics not yet in order, were among the maxims by which President Lincoln's course was steadily guided. When "Reconstruction" became practical, he was ready to act on it, and not before. His refusal to approve the Wade-Davis bill of last year was based avowedly on this principle. And his successor will find *his* task lighter in consequence.

Our country has had greater statesmen, abler speakers or writers, more efficient administrators, than Abraham Lincoln; but which of them ever evinced such a talent for silence where speech was perilous and the events of to-morrow very likely to overset the wisest judgment of to-day? While his wise and noble acts are duly honored, let not his equally beneficent hesitations and reticences be forgotten.

In Great Britain most of the press had to about-face quickly. They did so in many instances by deploring at some length the means of death before saying some kind words. Not every publication recanted; the Tory London Standard, April 21, 1865, said: "He was not a hero while he lived, and therefore his cruel murder does not make him a martyr." The London Morning Post that day expressed the general shock.

The startling intelligence which has reached us from America will excite but one sentiment in the minds of all, no matter what their political predilections. Northerner and Southerner, European and American, slaveholder and abolitionist, must equally concur in reprobating the dastardly crime which has just been consummated. The President of the United States of America has, in the moment of what he at least considered to be victory, and at the very instant when he had reason to believe that the gigantic enterprize to which he devoted himself was on the point of being crowned with success, fallen by the hand of an assassin. The event is so astounding that it is with difficulty we can bring ourselves to realize its occurrence, much less to estimate its consequences. It is but a few short days since the great and crowning events of the civil war took place, since Richmond was evacuated, and the army of Virginia laid down its arms, and since Mr. Lincoln, boasting once more to be not only *de jure* but *de facto* President of the entire American Republic, proclaimed it to the civilized world, and appointed a day of general thanksgiving to inaugurate the commencement of a new and happier era. On Sunday, the 9th of the present month, General Lee capitulated; on the following day Mr. Lincoln congratulated his fellow-citizens on the happy issue of the arduous struggle in which they had been so long engaged, and besought their co-operation in that no less arduous work of reconstruction to which he purposed devoting the second period of his official career and on the Friday following he was brutally murdered. In the annals of history there are to be found but too many instances in which the chief magistrate of a State has fallen by the assassin's hand, but we doubt if there is one which, by its surrounding circumstances, will retain a deeper hold on the memory of posterity than the murder of the American President. What Mr. Lincoln might have been, and what he might have accomplished, must always remain matters of speculation; but that he should have been arrested midway in his career, and that the wishes of a great nation should be frustrated by the will of a rabid fanatic, points a moral of the futility of all human projects, which, however trite, is not uninstructive. At the very time when most persons would have concurred in approving the policy of the Northern States in again electing Mr. Lincoln to the Presidential office, and would have gladly seen him endeavour to reconstruct the edifice which has been so cruelly shaken, he is suddenly carried from the scene. 'The king is dead. God save the king.' As it is in monarchies, so it is in republics.

> *The Times of London, pattern-maker of opinion in Britain and on the Continent, which had maintained a haughty and hostile attitude toward Lincoln, slowly, ever so slowly, changed. On April 28, 1865, it predicted that Lincoln would be the "last citizen President."*

The assassination of President LINCOLN will nowhere—we will venture to say not even in the United States—excite so much horror as in this country. We have long since repudiated the creed of the assassin, and the leaders of each House were never more emphatically the exponents of public opinion than when they gave notice last night of an address to the CROWN expressing the sympathy of Parliament with the Government and people of the United States. There is no opinion or sentiment in this country that can palliate this crime and deaden its shock. Besides our national abhorrence of assassinations we have also a profound respect for rulers, by whatever way they came to their high place. President LINCOLN ranked in our minds with Kings and Emperors, and was as much "the LORD's anointed" to simple English loyalty as any crowned head in Europe. There might have been reasons which, in the great distance and greater differences that divide us, might have tended to lessen our sympathy with the PRESIDENT. There are American statesmen of much higher abilities, and more educated for rule, who have done all they can to repel our sympathies, and have to some extent succeeded. But no American of Mr. LINCOLN's vigorous character, resolution, earnestness, and free humour has ever been so simple and inoffensive towards this country. While we could not but regard the selection of such a man to be the ruler of some thirty-five millions, a third of them on the eve of secession, as highly characteristic of Republican institutions, we yet all wondered to see him there. We wondered all the more because he did not personally illustrate any principle upon which either Union could be enforced or Separation justified. President LINCOLN was a man evidently anxious to do his duty, and prepared, with what most Englishmen would think recklessness, to undertake any post. He was anxious to keep well with everybody, and have not a foe in the world. So far he was a type of Union. But he wished, also, to keep things as they were. He brought no policy to a position of almost absolute power and fearful responsibility except a stubborn determination worthy of an old English Conservative. We must suppose one of our old-fashioned county members raised by some caprice of fortune or of politics to the government of this country before we can fully appreciate the case of Mr. LINCOLN four years ago. He gave himself up to the one instinct of keeping together the Union at any cost. Whether he was right or wrong we know not; the cost we do know—at least, some of the cost, for the account is not yet closed, and in it the PRESIDENT and, we fear, his Secretary of STATE are the last sad victims.

No experience, no calculation, can ever prepare us for the sudden blow which cuts short a living power and extinguishes a future which our anticipations have created. But the other day we were all asking, with excusable impatience, what President LINCOLN might do in his hour of triumph, what he had said or done, what he would do, what he ought to do. Four years more he seemed to have in his quiver, and how would he use them? Death has yet been tender of the modest term to which the Union has restricted the concession of supreme power, and in no instance has he come in this terrible form. Our own statesmen have not been so highly favoured. For the four coming years there is work to fill the most inventive mind, and we felt there was a strong hand and a good will to do all that could be done. All at once this mainstay of our speculations is gone, and we search in vain for a ruling will or a living guide. Of course we remember the lessons we learnt at school, and then took as a matter of course—that a great cause must have its martyr, a reconciliation must be with sacrifice, and even the first in a line of Emperors must consecrate with his blood the throne of his successors. We have lately been reading an elaborate pleading by an Imperial author to this effect, urged afresh with modern instances, and with the satisfactory conclusion that, so far as regards a neighbouring Empire, the victim has been offered and the rite all duly done. All the analogies, however, point to one moral. It is that President LINCOLN is the last citizen President. His successor will be a man with guards, with a dagger's point or a muzzle always turning towards him wherever he goes, and unable to visit a theatre without sentries posted in every doorway, every corridor, every staircase, as we have seen at Naples. The new PRESIDENT will be only as like the old PRESIDENT as the Black Prince is like NELSON's old flagship the Victory. Thence comes the fearful question,—How is it possible to secure a man from his foes, and strengthen his hands for good, without making him too strong and too secure, like the strong place of which we have lost the key, and which we can no longer open ourselves? The assassin who shortens the term of power also lengthens it, and when we resolve to overcome him we may perhaps end by justifying him. Such are the turns of that dreadful game of one might against another might and that measuring of conclusions which we in this island avoid and keep at a safe distance, by all manner of means, more or less producible before Parliaments and defensible in speeches, but yet necessary, so we think, if they do but answer this purpose.

It was fondly thought that open and regular war would stop, and indeed had already stopped, the personal encounters which had heretofore made life hideous in a great part of the Union. That hope is extinguished, for it is impossible not to fear that the late sad example will be followed. Here, then, is that national vice in which so many races have spent their best energies, and put the finishing stroke to their fortunes. The cause that takes to assassination ruins itself and extends the reign of oppression. We can only warn the Southern States most solemnly against taking that course and committing themselves to that groove, whence experience shows it will be impossible to retrace their steps. They have appealed to war bravely, and on the whole fairly, and, as it appears, they have been overwhelmed by superior numbers and resources. If the appeal was right, they ought to abide it, and not betake themselves to another and far lower arbitrament. Hitherto they have enjoyed a large share in the sympathies of the British people, who saw in their struggle for independence only a repetition of that fought and won ninety years ago on the same ground, and of many another trial of manhood fought by their common ancestors ages ago in these islands. The British people have given vent to their feelings for the weaker side, with perhaps excessive warmth and dangerous candour. It is what they always have done, and always will do, whatever the consequences, and the Americans take after them in this respect. We see with pleasure that Mr. MASON, the informal representative of the Southern States, repudiates this crime, and if the Southern States themselves do not utterly and even more emphatically renounce it and its authors they will forfeit all the sympathy which remains as the solace of their misfortunes. They will drive the whole British public into rapid and strong adhesion to the Federal cause, which will become under these circumstances the only symbol of order and security in that part of the world. They may or may not value our respect, but even when all else is gone honour has its value.

In stinging prose and vicious cartoons, London Punch castigated Lincoln during the war. The satirical weekly was an important journal of opinion not only in Britain but in the North and South, where its items and drawings were reprinted. In the May 6, 1865, issue, Punch made a full confession for its anti-Lincolnism, first, in a John Tenniel drawing "Britannia Sympathizes With Columbia," second, in this poem by Tom Taylor.

ABRAHAM LINCOLN

Foully Assassinated April, 14, 1865

You lay a wreath on murdered Lincoln's bier,
    You, who with mocking pencil wont to trace
Broad for the self-complacent British sneer
    His length of shambling limb, his furrowed face,

His gaunt, gnarled hands, his unkempt, bristling hair,
    His garb uncouth, his bearing ill at ease;
His lack of all we prize as debonair,
    Of power or will to shine, of art to please.

You, whose smart pen backed up the pencil's laugh,
    Judging each step, as though the way were plain;

Reckless, so it could point its paragraph
    Of chief's perplexity or people's pain.

Beside this corps, that beats for winding sheet
    The Stars and Stripes he lived to rear anew,
Between the mourners at his head and feet,
    Say, scurril-jester, is there room for you?

Yes, he had lived to shame me from my sneer,
    To lame my pencil, and confute my pen—
To make me own this hind of princes peer,
    This rail-splitter a true-born king of men.

My shallow judgment I had learnt to rue,
    Noting how to occasion's height he rose,
How his quaint wit made home-truth seem more true,
    How, iron-like, his temper grew by blows.

How humble yet how hopeful he could be;
    How in good fortune and in ill the same;
Nor bitter in success, nor boastful he,
    Thirsty for gold, nor feverish for fame.

He went about his work—such works as few
    Ever had laid on head and heart and hand—
As one who knows where there's a task to do
    Man's honest will must heaven's good grace command:

Who trusts the strength will with the burden grow,
    That God makes instruments to work his will,
If but that will we can arrive to know,
    Nor tamper with the weights of good and ill.

So he went forth to battle on the side
    That he felt clear was liberty's and right's,
As in his peasant boyhood he had plied
    His warfare with rude nature's thwarting mights—

The uncleared forest, the unbroken soil,
    The iron back, that turns the lumberer's axe;

As They Saw Him APRIL 15–MAY 1865

The rapid, that o'erbears the boatman's toil,
    The prairie, hiding the mazed wanderer's tracks.

The ambushed Indian, and the prowling bear—
    Such were the needs that helped his youth to train:
Rough culture—but such trees large fruit may bear
    If but their stocks be of right girth and grain.

So he grew up, a destined work to do,
    And lived to do it; four long-suffering years'
Ill-fate, ill-feeling, ill-report lived through,
    And then he heard the hisses change to cheers,

The taunts to tribute, the abuse to praise,
    And took both with the same unwavering mood:
Till, as he came on light from darkling days
    And seemed to touch the goal from where he stood,

A felon hand, between the goal and him,
    Reached from behind his back, a trigger prest—
And those perplexed and patient eyes were dim,
    Those gaunt, long-laboring limbs were laid to rest.

The words of mercy were upon his lips,
    Forgiveness in his heart and on his pen,
When this vile murderer brought swift eclipse
    To thoughts of peace on earth, good will to men.

The Old World and the New, from sea to sea,
    Utter one voice of sympathy and shame!
Sore heart, so stopped when it at last beat high,
    Sad life, cut short just as its triumph came.

A deed accurst! Strokes have been struck before
    By the assassin's hand, whereof men doubt
If more of horror or disgrace they bore;
    But thy foul crime, like Cain's, stands darkly out.

Vile hand, that brandest murder on a strife,
    Whate'er its grounds, stoutly and nobly striven;

And with the martyr's crown crownest a life
With much to praise, little to be forgiven!

France, like Britannia, showed sympathy. They contrasted Lincoln and his regime with the despotism of the French Emperor. An ode by J. H. Serment, inspired before the assassination by a picture of a fugitive slave being caught by bloodhounds, went: "O Lincoln! O justum et tenacem, ô toi/Qui soutins sans plier, et d'une âme indomptable,/Le fardeau le plus lourd et le plus redoubtable/Qu'ait jamais supporté tribun, sénat ou roi;/Ton nom seul suffirait, ô vengeur de la loi!/Pour racheter l'honneur d'une ère méprisable." In La Patrie, April 28, 1865, Paris, an editorial talked of Lincoln's true nobility in a country so long ruled by nobles.

LA MORT DE M. LINCOLN
[Mr. Lincoln's Death]

The violent death of Mr. Lincoln has stunned and dejected the whole world. Yet we cannot but think of the assassin who has created new complications in the American problem. We do not dare believe that this crime is the work of a political faction, and we hesitate to own that any personal vengeance could have thus enveloped two statesmen [Lincoln and Seward] in its fury, the two true heads of the government of the North!

This fatality weighs heavily on the unhappy country which, after being devastated for four years by an iniquitous war, is suddenly cast down again into the most mournful of states at the very moment when peace seemed possible!

Perhaps the first feeling which such an event arouses is horror. Whatever may have been the assassin's motive, there is too much cowardice in the act to stem the indignation of all Europe. The greatest indignation rises at the thought of the trouble that the death of Mr. Lincoln and his Secretary may cause in the North as well as the South.

The results of the victories gained by the Union Army may now all be nullified!—that is, from the political point of view. The hopes which the South had taken from Mr. Lincoln's first declarations may now all be disappointed forever. These hopes were alive, and you have seen how gladly we hailed them. But Mr. Lincoln's death came at a time propitious to the glorification of his memory. He died at a time when he was preaching reconciliation and the forgetting of the past, when he was nobly repressing the blameworthy exultation of the victorious faction.

Is it not possible that the assassin may have arisen from the ranks of this very faction, foiled in its dreadful schemes? Who knows? One may well wonder. Civil wars have this horrible aspect—that they bring to the surface from the very depths of society creatures whose unleashed passions know no limit whatever. The re-establishment of peace in America meant the ruin of those newly created generals, of those agents whose powers, augmented even more by the suspension of the *habeas corpus*, had brought about such excesses.

It is, perhaps, in the ranks of the victims of these excesses that American justice will find the culprits. One word dropped by Mr. Lincoln's assassin reveals a fanaticism which would probably place on the President's own shoulders the responsibility for the acts of the Butlers, the MacNeils, the Turchins—those guilty proconsuls who obtained official sanction for their crimes, and then bloodied Washington politics with the murder of the Southern officer Beale. It is, unfortunately, not unlikely that the grief of a parent or a friend gave birth to two assassins!

Horrible war, which began in 1861 with the double suicide of Jackson and Ellsworth, each accusing the other of tyranny, and which, toward the end, armed the brothers Booth! . . .

This crime is a double misfortune for America! It will reawaken bloodthirsty passions, and perhaps pave the way for terrible reprisals, all at a moment when Mr. Lincoln was exerting himself to repair the past, and wanted to be an instrument of peace! His death is of no avail, and can be of no avail to the South, but it gives rise to the danger of enfeebling the North through factionism.

Now it is an open war between the majority which has applauded Mr. Lincoln's spirit of reconciliation—we called attention to them yesterday—and that zealous minority which has protested against the terms accorded the vanquished. The blow which struck Mr. Lincoln and Mr. Seward seems to have threatened General Grant too. Do they want then to do honor to the Federal commander for the surrender of Lee?

In consequence of the regular functioning of the Constitution the minority from which violence may be feared today has one of its partisans in power. We recall that six months ago, at the time of the elections, the moderate press exclaimed: "What would become of the Republic in the event of Mr. Lincoln's death, when Mr. Johnson should exercise supreme authority?" It is as if these papers had had a presentiment of the sorrowful news which was to strike America.

It is known that Mr. Johnson is a former member of the slave party. Carried along in the course of events from the workshops of a master tailor to the platforms of public meetings, later named military governor of Tennessee (after having disavowed his early convictions) he became the fiery representative of that extreme faction, the "black Republicans," against which Mr. Lincoln has so long fought. It is he who, reduced to the sole role of President of the Senate, presented there on March 4 last the sad spectacle of the most degraded drunkenness.

Dispatches inform us, it is true, that his first words issued from the White House have revived public confidence. Let us hope that this confidence will not be disappointed; let us hope it for all America, North and South. But we shall not conceal our anxiety. It is great, because everything is disposed to nurture it: this crime which we should not have dared to forsee, the state of irritability which recent events have caused among some men, the hope that the death of a leader can inspire in his vanquished enemies, and finally the disorder, the moral and political disorder which a four-year-long civil war must inevitably bring about in a country where society, in a constant state of ferment, knows no law other than human passion! . . . ERNEST DRÉOLLE.

The French historian Henri Martin predicted that Lincoln "will stand out in the traditions of his country and the world as an incarnation of the people and of modern democracy itself." M. Martin had been one of the signers of a document from "friends of America" in France, distinguished Frenchmen who called themselves abolitionists and supported Lincoln during the war. This comment on the man the French saw as a libertarian appeared in Le Siècle, April 29, 1865, Paris.

Slavery, before expiring, has gathered up the remnants of its strength and rage to strike a coward blow at its conqueror. The Satanic pride of that perverted society could not resign itself to defeat; it did not care to fall with honour, as all causes fall which are destined to rise again; it dies as it has lived, violating all laws, divine and human. In this we have the spirit, and perhaps the work of that famous secret association, the Golden Circle, which after preparing the great rebellion for twenty years, and spreading its accomplices throughout the West and North, around the seat of the Presidency, gave the signal for this impious war on the day when the public conscience finally snatched from the slaveholders the government of the United States. The day on which the excellent man whom they had just made a martyr was raised to power, they appealed to force, to realize what treason had prepared. They have failed. They did not succeed in overthrowing Lincoln from power by war; they have done so by assassination. The plot appears to have been well arranged. By striking down with the President his two principal ministers, one of whom they reached, and the General-in-Chief, who was saved by an accidental occurrence, the murderers expected to disorganize the Government of the Republic and give fresh life to the rebellion. Their hopes will be frustrated. These sanguinary fanatics, whose cause has fallen not so much by the material superiority as the moral power of democracy have become incapable of understanding the effects of the free institutions which their fathers gloriously aided in establishing. A fresh illustration will be seen of what those institutions can produce. The indignation of the people will not exhaust itself in a momentary outburst; it will concentrate and embody itself in the unanimous, persevering, invincible action of the universal will; whoever may be the agents, the instruments of the work, that work, we may rest assured, will be finished. The event will show that it did not depend upon the life of one man or of several men. The work will be completed after Lincoln as if finished by him; but Lincoln will remain the austere and sacred personification of a great epoch, the most faithful expression of democracy. This simple and upright man, prudent and strong, elevated step by step from the artizan's bench to the command of a great nation, and always without parade and without effort at the height of his position, executing without precipitation, without flourish, and with invincible good sense, the most colossal acts, giving to the world this decisive example of the civil power in a republic, directing a gigantic war, without free institutions being for an instant compromised or threatened by military usurpation, dying finally at the moment in which, after conquering, he was intent on pacification—and may God grant that the atrocious madmen who killed him have not killed clemency with him, and determined instead of the peace he wished, pacification by force—this man will stand out in the traditions of his country and the world as an incarnation of the people and of modern democracy itself. The great work of emancipation had to be sealed, therefore, with the blood of the just even as it was inaugurated with the blood of the just. The tragic history of the abolition of slavery which opened with the gibbet of John Brown, will close with the assassination of Lincoln. And now let him rest by the side of Washington, as the second founder of the great republic. European democracy is present in spirit at his funeral, as it voted in its heart for his re-election, and applauded the victory in the midst of which he passes away. It will wish with one accord to associate itself with the monument that America will raise to him upon the capital of prostrate slavery.

In Italy republican liberals had reached out to Lincoln all during the rebellion. Garibaldi, in the midst of the war, had signed an address to Lincoln, "Emancipator of the Slaves of the American Republic," saying, "Heir of the aspirations of Christ and of John Brown, you will pass to posterity with the name of the Emancipator; more enviable than any crown or any human treasure." The Perseverance of Milan, reported in the Gazzetta di Firenze, May 3, 1865, Florence, reprinted Lincoln's last speech on reconstruction and made these perceptive comments.

The Perseverance of Milan reports:

The tragic end of Lincoln, and the uncertain expectation that is to befall the United States, under the impact of that occurrence and of the new government, gives great interest to the defunct president's last act, that is, to his discourse given on April 13, after Lee's capitulation; in which discourse he displayed in embryo his ideas about the future order of the Union.

Reading this discourse, which we append below, we cannot but once more admire the simplicity, the sincerity, the good sense, the wisdom that springs from this unique man's righteousness of heart and firmness of character. You see in this man, who is self-educated, and who sallied to the Republic's top position, and who was re-elected because his country had to realize in him the most difficult task of conquering such an extraordinary crisis; you see in him that sense of justice, of moderation, of unaffected patriotism and awareness of proper responsibility that reminds one of those great characters of history who must leave imprints of themselves to a nation and era, because they are their measures.

Lincoln does not wish to impose his opinion upon a nation that governs itself by the dictates of the majority; he is humble, he counsels but does not command; he entreats with a certain placid affection and does not pretend to conduct himself with the magniloquence of one who even would have the right to trumpet services rendered to the fatherland; and yet, how much authority in those words so modest, so serene in the awareness of willing good to his own and no other nation; so certain even when beset by doubts that necessarily rise in the mind of a man who comprehends how to speak to a people in the exercise of liberty!

How much wisdom in that allusion to the good, aptly worthy of him who schooled himself in the eternal book of the Bible and of nature, in which is said it must please you to hatch an egg instead of breaking it before it yields a chick! What a lesson he gives to his compatriots and to all, to us ourselves, on the expediency of cultivating with affection the seeds of the good and to understand things as they are, and not to see them as one would wish they were, in order to attain the best possible in given circumstances! What a difference between this republican, who loves foremost his nation, who respects the opinions of others, who tolerates adverse opinions without disdain, who stands in the camp of facts, and certain other ambitious ones of authority, intolerant of others' opinions, perpetual self-adulators, deprecators of him who does not praise them, ready to substitute their fancies for reality!

We do not wish to comment singly on Lincoln's discourse; but we are certain that righteous souls and logical minds, if they have a knowledge of American facts and are not opinionated, will, like us, judge this discourse, this historical document, for him whom it well fits. It is the testament of a great and honest statesman, of whom it will be said that he wished to restore the dignity of man in the poor and the scorned Negro race, and that he died a martyr for a sacred cause, that of humanity and true Christianity.

Of all the journalists and confidants who seemed to hold passkeys to Lincoln's time, one man especially stood out as a respected newsman and, above all, friend. He was Noah Brooks, who had heard Lincoln speak on the Illinois prairie, had covered his Cooper Union address, had reported Lincoln's daily life and actions under the name of "Castine" for the Sacramento Union, of California, had been slated to be Lincoln's private secretary—finally, was almost a guest of the President that night in Ford's Theatre. In Harper's Monthly Magazine, May 1865 issue, Noah Brooks summed up a life for contemporary readers and told some of the little stories of the great man as he saw him.

PERSONAL RECOLLECTIONS
OF ABRAHAM LINCOLN
[By Noah Brooks]

It is natural that friends should tenderly and frequently talk of the loved and lost, descanting upon their virtues, narrating the little incidents of a life ended, and dwelling with minute particularity upon traits of character which, under other circumstances, might have remained unnoted and be forgotten, but are invested now with a mournful interest which fixes them in the memory. This, and the general desire to know more of the man ABRAHAM LINCOLN, is the only excuse offered for the following simple sketch of some parts of the character of our beloved Chief Magistrate, now passed from earth.

All persons agree that the most marked characteristic of Mr. Lincoln's manners was his simplicity and artlessness; this immediately impressed itself upon the observation of those who met him for the first time, and each successive interview deepened the impression. People seemed delighted to find in the ruler of the nation freedom from pomposity and affectation, mingled with a certain simple dignity which never forsook him. Though oppressed with the weight of responsibility resting upon him as President of the United States, he shrank from assuming any of the honors, or even the titles, of the position. After years of intimate acquaintance with Mr. Lincoln the writer can not now recall a single instance in which he spoke of himself as President, or used that title for himself, except when acting in an official capacity. He always spoke of his position and office vaguely, as "this place," "here," or other modest phrase. Once, speaking of the room in the Capitol used by the Presidents of the United States during the close of a session of Congress, he said, "That room, you know, that they call"—dropping his voice and hesitating —"the President's room." To an intimate friend who addressed him always by his own proper title he said, "Now call me Lincoln, and I'll promise not to tell of the breach of etiquette—if you won't—and I shall have a resting-spell from 'Mister President.'"

With all his simplicity and unacquaintance with courtly manners, his native dignity never forsook him in the presence of critical or polished strangers; but mixed with his angularities and bonhomie was something which spoke the fine fibre of the man; and, while his sovereign disregard of courtly conventionalities was somewhat ludicrous, his native sweetness and straightforwardness of manner served to disarm criticism and impress the visitor that he was before a man pure, self-poised, collected, and strong in unconscious strength. Of him an accomplished foreigner, whose knowledge of the courts was more perfect than that of the English language, said, "He seems to me one grand gentilhomme in disguise."

In his eagerness to acquire knowledge of common things he sometimes surprised his distinguished visitors by inquiries about matters that they were supposed to be acquainted with, and those who came to scrutinize went away with a vague sense of having been unconsciously pumped by the man whom they expected to pump. One Sunday evening last winter, while sitting alone with the President, the cards of Professor Agassiz and a friend were sent in. The President had never met Agassiz at that time, I believe, and said, "I would like to talk with that man; he is a good man, I do believe; don't you think so?" But one answer could be returned to the query, and soon after the visitors were shown in, the President first whispering, "Now sit still and see what we can pick up that's new." To my surprise, however, no questions were asked about the Old Silurian, the Glacial Theory, or the Great Snow-storm, but, introductions being over, the President said: "I never knew how to properly pronounce your name: won't you give me a little lesson at that, please?" Then he asked if it were of French or Swiss derivation, to which the Professor replied that it was partly of each. That led to a discussion of different languages, the President speaking of several words in different languages which had the same root as similar words in our own tongue; then he illustrated that by one or two anecdotes, one of which he borrowed from Hood's "Up the Rhine." But he soon returned to his gentle cross-examination of Agassiz, and found out how the Professor studied, how he composed, and how he delivered his lectures; how he found different tastes in his audiences in different portions of the country. When afterward asked why he put such questions to his learned visitor he said, "Why, what we got from him isn't printed in the books; the other things are."

At this interview, it may be remarked in passing, the President said that many years ago, when the custom of lecture-going was more common than since, he was induced to try his hand at composing a literary lecture—something which he thought entirely out of his line. The subject, he said, was not defined, but his purpose was to analyze inventions and discoveries—"to get at the bottom of things"—and to show when, where, how, and why such things were invented or discovered; and, so far as possible, to find where the first mention is made of some of our common things. The Bible, he said, he found to be the richest storehouse for such knowledge; and he then gave one or two illustrations, which were new to his hearers. The lecture was never finished, and was left among his loose papers at Springfield when he came to Washington.

The simplicity of manner which shone out in all such interviews as that here noticed was marked in his total lack of consideration of what was due his exalted station. He had an almost morbid dread of what he called "a scene"—that is, a demonstration of applause such as always greeted his appearance in public. The first sign of a cheer sobered him;

he appeared sad and oppressed, suspended conversation, and looked out into vacancy; and when it was over resumed the conversation just where it was interrupted, with an obvious feeling of relief. Of the relations of a senator to him he said, "I think that Senator ——'s manner is more cordial to me than before." The truth was that the senator had been looking for a sign of cordiality from his superior, but the President had reversed their relative positions. At another time, speaking of an early acquaintance, who was an applicant for an office which he thought him hardly qualified to fill, the President said, "Well, now, I never thought M—— had any more than average ability when we were young men together; really I did not"—a pause.—"But then, I suppose he thought just the same about me; he had reason to, and—here I am!"

The simple habits of Mr. Lincoln were so well known that it is a subject for surprise that watchful and malignant treason did not sooner take that precious life which he seemed to hold so lightly. He had an almost morbid dislike for an escort, or guard, and daily exposed himself to the deadly aim of an assassin. One summer morning, passing by the White House at an early hour, I saw the President standing at the gateway, looking anxiously down the street; and, in reply to a salutation, he said, "Good-morning, good-morning! I am looking for a news-boy; when you get to that corner I wish you would start one up this way." There are American citizens who consider such things beneath the dignity of an official in high place.

In reply to the remonstrances of friends, who were afraid of his constant exposure to danger, he had but one answer: "If they kill me, the next man will be just as bad for them; and in a country like this, where our habits are simple, and must be, assassination is always possible, and will come if they are determined upon it." A cavalry guard was once placed at the gate of the White House for a while, and he said, privately, that he "worried until he got rid of it." While the President's family were at their summer-house, near Washington, he rode into town of a morning, or out at night, attended by a mounted escort; but if he returned to town for a while after dark, he rode in unguarded, and often alone, in his open carriage. On more than one occasion the writer has gone through the streets of Washington at a late hour of the night with the President, without escort, or even the company of a servant, walking all of the way, going and returning.

Considering the many open and secret threats to take his life, it is not surprising that Mr. Lincoln had many thoughts about his coming to a sudden and violent end. He once said that he felt the force of the expression, "To take one's life in his hand;" but that he would not like to face death suddenly. He said that he thought himself a great coward physically, and was sure that he should make a poor soldier, for, unless there was something in the excitement of a battle, he was sure that he would drop his gun and run at the first symptom of danger. That was said sportively, and he added, "Moral cowardice is something which I think I never had." ...

If Mr. Lincoln's critics may be trusted, he had too much goodness of heart to make a good magistrate. Certain it is that his continually-widening charity for all, and softness of heart, pardoned offenders and mitigated punishments when the strict requirements of justice would have dealt more severely with the criminal. It was a standing order of his office that persons on matters involving the issue of life and death should have immediate precedence. Nor was his kindness confined to affairs of state; his servants, and all persons in his personal service, were the objects of his peculiar care and solicitude. They bore no burdens or hardships which he could relieve them of; and if he carried this virtue to an extreme, and carried labors which others should have borne, it was because he thought he could not help it.

He was often waylaid by soldiers importunate to get their back-pay, or a furlough, or a discharge; and if the case was not too complicated, would attend to it then and there. Going out of the main-door of the White House one morning, he met an old lady who was pulling vigorously at the door-bell, and asked her what she wanted. She said that she wanted to see "Abraham the Second." The President, amused, asked who Abraham the First might be, if there was a second? The old lady replied, "Why Lor' bless you! we read about the first Abraham in the Bible, and Abraham the Second is our President." She was told that the President was not in his office then, and when she asked where he was, she was told, "Here he is!" Nearly petrified with surprise, the old lady managed to tell her errand, and was told to come next morning at nine o'clock, when she was received and kindly cared for by the President. At another time, hearing of a young man who had determined to enter the navy as a landsman, after three years of service in the army, he said to the writer, "Now do you go over to the Navy Department and mouse out what he is fit for, and he shall have it, if it's to be had, for that's the kind of men I like to hear of." The place was duly "moused out," with the assistance of the kind-hearted Assistant-Secretary of the Navy; and the young officer, who may read these lines on his solitary post off the mouth of the Yazoo River, was appointed upon the recommendation of the

President of the United States. Of an application for office by an old friend, not fit for the place he sought, he said, "I had rather resign my place and go away from here than refuse him, if I consulted only my personal feelings; but refuse him I must." And he did.

This same gentleness, mixed with firmness, characterized all of Mr. Lincoln's dealings with public men. Often bitterly assailed and abused, he never appeared to recognize the fact that he had political enemies; and if his attention was called to unkind speeches or remarks, he would turn the conversation of his indignant friends by a judicious story, or the remark, "I guess we won't talk about that now." He has himself put it on record that he never read attacks upon himself, and if they were brought persistently before him he had some ready excuse for their authors. Of a virulent personal attack upon his official conduct he mildly said that it was ill-timed; and of one of his most bitter political enemies he said: "I've been told that insanity is hereditary in his family, and I think we will admit the plea in his case." It was noticeable that Mr. Lincoln's keenest critics and bitter opponents studiously avoided his presence; it seemed as though no man could be familiar with his homely, heart-lighted features, his single-hearted directness and manly kindliness, and remain long an enemy, or be any thing but his friend. It was this warm frankness of Mr. Lincoln's manner that made a hard-headed old "hunker" once leave the hustings where Lincoln was speaking, in 1856, saying, "I won't hear him, for I don't like a man that makes me believe in him in spite of myself."

"Honest Old Abe" has passed into the language of our time and country as a synonym for all that is just and honest in man. Yet thousands of instances, unknown to the world, might be added to those already told of Mr. Lincoln's great and crowning virtue. He disliked innuendoes, concealments, and subterfuges; and no sort of approach at official "jobbing" ever had any encouragement from him. With him the question was not, "Is it convenient? Is it expedient?" but, "Is it right?" He steadily discountenanced all practices of government officers using any part of the public funds for temporary purposes; and he loved to tell of his own experience when he was saved from embarrassment by his rigid adherence to a good rule. He had been postmaster at Salem, Illinois, during Jackson's administration, William T. Barry being then Postmaster-General, and resigning his office, removed to Springfield, having sent a statement of account to the Department at Washington. No notice was taken of his account, which showed a balance due the Government of over one hundred and fifty dollars, until three or four years after, when, Amos Kendall being Postmaster-General, he was presented with a draft for the amount due. Some of Mr. Lincoln's friends, who knew that he was in straitened circumstances then, as he had always been, heard of the draft and offered to help him out with a loan; but he told them not to worry, and producing from his trunk an old pocket, tied up and marked, counted out in six-pences, shillings, and quarters, the exact sum required of him, in the identical coin received by him while in office years before. . . .

Just after the last presidential election he said: "Being only mortal, after all, I should have been a little mortified if I had been beaten in this canvass before the people; but that sting would have been more than compensated by the thought that the people had notified me that all my official responsibilities were soon to be lifted off my back." In reply to the remark that he might remember that in all these cares he was daily re-membered by those who prayed, not to be heard of men, as no man had ever before been remembered, he caught at the homely phrase and said: "Yes, I like that phrase, 'not to be heard of men,' and guess it's generally true, as you say; at least I have been told so, and I have been a good deal helped by just that thought." Then he solemnly and slowly added: "I should be the most presumptuous block-head upon this footstool if I for one day thought that I could discharge the duties which have come upon me since I came into this place without the aid and enlightenment of One who is wiser and stronger than all others."

At another time he said, cheerfully, "I am very sure that if I do not go away from here a wiser man, I shall go away a better man, for having learned here what a very poor sort of a man I am." Afterward, referring to what he called a change of heart, he said that he did not remember any precise time when he passed through any special change of purpose or of heart; but he would say that his own election to office, and the crisis im-mediately following, influentially determined him in what he called "a process of crystallization," then going on in his mind. Reticent as he was, and shy of discoursing much of his own mental exercises, these few utterances now have a value with those who knew him which his dying words would scarcely have possessed.

No man but Mr. Lincoln ever knew how great was the load of care which he bore, nor the amount of mental labor which he daily accom-plished. With the usual perplexities of the office—greatly increased by the unusual multiplication of places in his gift—he carried the burdens of the civil war, which he always called "This great trouble." Though the intellectual man had greatly grown meantime, few persons would recog-nize the hearty, blithesome, genial, and wiry Abraham Lincoln of earlier days in the sixteenth President of the United States, with his stooping figure, dull eyes, care-worn face, and languid frame. The old, clear laugh never came back; the even temper was sometimes disturbed; and his natural charity for all was often turned into an unwonted suspicion of the motives of men, whose selfishness cost him so much wear of mind. Once he said, "Sitting here, where all the avenues to public patronage seem to come together in a knot, it does seem to me that our people are fast approaching the point where it can be said that seven-eighths of them were trying to find how to live at the expense of the other eighth."

It was this incessant demand upon his time, by men who sought place or endeavored to shape his policy, that broke down his courage and his temper, as well as exhausted his strength. Speaking of the "great floodgates" which his doors daily opened upon him, he said, "I suppose I ought not to blame the aggregate, for each abstract man or woman thinks his or her case a peculiar one, and must be attended to, though all others be left out; but I can see this thing growing every day." And at another time, speaking of the exhaustive demands upon him, which left him in no condition for more important duties, he said, "I sometimes fancy that every one of the numerous grist ground through here daily, from a Senator seeking a war with France down to a poor woman after a place in the Treasury Department, darted at me with thumb and finger, picked out their especial piece of my vitality, and carried it off. When I get through with such a day's work there is only one word which can express my condition, and that is—*flabbiness*." There are some public men who can now remember, with self-reproaches, having increased with long evening debates that reducing "flabbiness" of the much-enduring President.

Mr. Lincoln visited the Army of the Potomac in the spring of 1863, and, free from the annoyances of office, was considerably refreshed and rested; but even there the mental anxieties which never forsook him seemed to cast him down, at times, with a great weight. We left Washington late in the afternoon, and a snowstorm soon after coming on, the steamer was anchored for the night off Indian Head, on the Maryland shore of the Potomac. The President left the little knot in the cabin, and sitting alone in a corner, seemed absorbed in the saddest reflections for a time; then, beckoning a companion to him, said, "What will you wager that half our iron-clads are at the bottom of Charleston Harbor?" This being the first intimation which the other had had of Dupont's attack, which was then begun, hesitated to reply, when the President added, "The people will expect big things when they hear of this; but it is too late—*too late!*"

During that little voyage the captain of the steamer, a frank, modest old sailor, was so much affected by the care-worn appearance of the President, that he came to the writer and confessed that he had received the same impression of the Chief Magistrate that many had; hearing of his "little stories" and his humor, he had supposed him to have no cares or sadness; but a sight of that anxious and sad face had undeceived him, and he wanted to tell the President how much he had unintentionally wronged him, feeling that he had committed upon him a personal wrong. The captain was duly introduced to the President, who talked with him privately for a space, being touched as well as amused at what he called "Captain M——'s freeing his mind."

The following week, spent in riding about and seeing the army, appeared to revive Mr. Lincoln's spirits and to rest his body. A friend present observed as much to him, and he replied, "Well, yes, I do feel some better, I think; but, somehow, it don't appear to touch the tired spot, which can't be got at." And that, by-the-way, reminded him of a little story of his having once used that word, spot, a great many times in the course of a speech in Congress, years ago, so that some of his fellow-members called him "spot Lincoln," but he believed that the nickname did not stick. Another reminiscence of his early life, which he recalled during the trip, was one concerning his experience in rail-splitting. We were driving through an open clearing, where the Virginia forest had been felled by the soldiers, when Mr. Lincoln observed, looking at the stumps, "That's a good job of felling; they have got some good axemen in this army, I see." The conversation turning upon his knowledge of rail-splitting, he said, "Now let me tell you about that. I am not a bit anxious about my reputation in that line of business; but if there is any thing in this world that I am a judge of, it is of good felling of timber, but I don't remember having worked by myself at splitting rails for one whole day in my life." Upon surprise being expressed that his national reputation as a rail-splitter should have so slight a foundation, he said, "I recollect that, some time during the canvass for the office I now hold, there was a great mass meeting, where I was present, and with a great flourish several rails were brought into the meeting, and being informed where they came from, I was asked to identify them, which I did, with some qualms of conscience, having helped my father to split rails, as at other odd jobs. I said if there were any rails which I had split, I shouldn't wonder if those were the rails." Those who may be disappointed to learn of Mr. Lincoln's limited experience in splitting rails, may be relieved to know that he was evidently proud of his knowledge of the art of cutting timber, and explained minutely how a good job differed from a poor one, giving illustrations from the ugly stumps on either side.

An amusing yet touching instance of the President's preoccupation of mind occurred at one of his levees, when he was shaking hands with a host of visitors, passing him in a continuous stream. An intimate acquaintance received the usual conventional hand-shake and salutation; but, perceiving that he was not recognized, kept his ground, instead of moving on, and spoke again; when the President, roused by a dim consciousness that something unusual had happened, perceived who stood before him, and seizing his friend's hand, shook it again heartily, saying, "How do you do? How do you do? Excuse me for not noticing you at first; the fact is, I was thinking of a man down South." He afterward privately acknowledged that the "man down South" was Sherman, then on his march to the sea.

Mr. Lincoln had not a hopeful temperament, and, though he looked at the bright side of things, was always prepared for disaster and defeat. With his wonderful faculty for discerning results he often saw success where others saw disaster, but oftener perceived a failure when others were elated with victory, or were temporarily deceived by appearances. Of a great cavalry raid, which filled the newspapers with glowing exultation, but failed to cut the communications which it had been designed to destroy, he briefly said: "That was good circus-riding; it will do to fill a column in the newspapers; but I don't see that it has brought any thing else to pass." He often said that the worst feature about newspapers was that they were so sure to be "ahead of the hounds," out-running events, and exciting expectations which were sure to be disappointed. One of the worst effects of a victory, he said, was to lead people to expect that the war was about over in consequence of it; but he was never weary of commending the patience of the American people, which he thought something matchless and touching. I have seen him shed tears when speaking of the cheerful sacrifice of the light and strength of so many happy homes throughout the land. His own patience was marvelous; and never crushed at defeat or unduly excited by success, his demeanor under both was an example for all men. Once he said the keenest blow of all the war was at an early stage, when the disaster of Ball's Bluff and the death of his beloved [Edward D.] Baker smote upon him like a whirlwind from a desert.

It is generally agreed that Mr. Lincoln's slowness was a prominent trait of his character; but it is too early, perhaps, to say how much of our safety and success we owe to his slowness. It may be said, however, that he is to-day admired and beloved as much for what he did not do as for what he did. He was well aware of the popular opinion concerning his slowness, but was only sorry that such a quality of mind should sometimes be coupled with weakness and vacillation. Such an accusation he thought to be unjust. Acknowledging that he was slow in arriving at conclusions, he said that he could not help that; but he believed that when he did arrive at conclusions they were clear and "stuck by." He was a profound believer in his own fixity of purpose, and took pride in saying that his long deliberations made it possible for him to stand by his own acts when they were once resolved upon. It would have been a relief to the country at one time in our history if this trait of the President's character had been better understood. There was no time, probably, during the last administration, when any of the so-called radical measures were in any danger of being qualified or recalled. The simple explanation of the doubt which often hung over his purposes may be found in the fact that it was a habit of his mind to put forward all of the objections of other people and of his own to any given proposition, to see what arguments or counter-statements could be brought against them. While his own mind might be perfectly clear upon the subject, it gave him real pleasure to state objections for others to combat or attempt to set aside.

His practice of being controlled by events is well known. He often said that it was wise to wait for the developments of Providence; and the Scriptural phrase that "the stars in their courses fought aaginst Sisera" to him had a depth of meaning. Then, too, he liked to feel that he was the attorney of the people, not their ruler; and I believe that this idea was generally uppermost in his mind. Speaking of the probability of his second nomination, about two years ago, he said: "If the people think that I have managed their case for them well enough to trust me to carry up to the next term, I am sure that I shall be glad to take it."

He liked to provide for his friends, who were often remembered gratefully for services given him in his early struggles in life. Sometimes he would "break the slate," as he called it, of those who were making up a list of appointments, that he might insert the name of some old acquaintance who had befriended him in days when friends were few. He was not deceived by outside appearances, but took the measure of those he met, and few men were worth any more or any less than the value which Abraham Lincoln set upon them.

Upon being told that a gentleman upon whom he was about to confere a valuable appointment had been bitterly opposed to his renomination, he said: "I suppose that Judge ——, having been disappointed before, did behave pretty ugly; but that wouldn't make him any less fit for this place, and I have a Scriptural authority for appointing him. You recollect that while the Lord on Mount Sinai was getting out a commission for Aaron, that same Aaron was at the foot of the mountain making a false god, a golden calf, for the people to worship; yet Aaron got his commission, you know." At another time, when remonstrated with upon the appointment to place of one of his former opponents, he said: "Nobody will deny that he is a first-rate man for the place, and I am bound to see that his opposition to me personally shall not interfere with my giving the people a good officer."

The world will never hear the last of the "little stories" with which the President garnished or illustrated his conversation and his early stump speeches. He said, however, that as near as he could reckon, about one-sixth of those which were credited to him were old acquaintances; all of the rest were the productions of other and better story-tellers than himself. Said he: "I do generally remember a good story when I hear it, but I never did invent any thing original; I am only a retail dealer." His anecdotes were seldom told for the sake of the telling, but because they fitted in just where they came, and shed a light on the argument that nothing else could. He was not witty, but brimful of humor; and though he was quick to appreciate a good pun, I never knew of his making but one, which was on the Christian name of a friend, to whom he said: "You have yet to be elected to the place I hold; but Noah's *reign* was before Abraham." He thought that the chief characteristic of American humor was its grotesqueness and extravagance; and the story of the man who was so tall that he was "laid out" in a rope-walk, the soprano voice so high that it had to be climbed over by a ladder, and the Dutchman's expression of "somebody tying his dog loose," all made a permanent lodgment in his mind. . . .

Latterly Mr. Lincoln's reading was with the humorous writers. He liked to repeat from memory whole chapters from these books; and on such occasions he always preserved his own gravity though his auditors might be convulsed with laughter. He said that he had a dread of people who could not appreciate the fun of such things; and he once instanced a member of his own Cabinet, of whom he quoted the saying of Sydney Smith, "that it required a surgical operation to get a joke into his head." The light trifles spoken of diverted his mind, or, as he said of his theatre-going, gave him refuge from himself and his weariness. But he also was a lover of many philosophical books, and particularly liked Butler's Analogy of Religion, Stuart Mill on Liberty, and he always hoped to get at President Edwards on the Will. These ponderous writers found a queer companionship in the chronicler of the Mackerel Brigade, Parson Nasby, and Private Miles O'Reilly. The Bible was a very familiar study with the President, whole chapters of Isaiah, the New Testament, and the Psalms being fixed in his memory, and he would sometimes correct a misquotation of Scripture, giving generally the chapter and verse where it could be found. He liked the Old Testament best, and dwelt on the simple beauty of the historical books. Once, speaking of his own age and strength, he quoted with admiration that passage, "His eye was not dim, nor his natural force abated." I do not know that he thought then how, like that Moses of old, he was to stand on Pisgah and see a peaceful land which he was not to enter.

Of the poets the President appeared to prefer Hood and Holmes, the mixture and pathos in their writings being attractive to him beyond any thing else which he read. Of the former author he liked best the last part of "Miss Kilmansegg and her Golden Leg," "Faithless Sally Brown," and one or two others not generally so popular as those which are called Hood's best poems. Holmes's "September Gale," "Last Leaf," "Chambered Nautilus," and "Ballad of an Oysterman" were among his very few favorite poems. Longfellow's "Psalm of Life" and "Birds of Killingworth" were the only productions of that auther he ever mentioned with praise, the latter of which he picked up somewhere in a newspaper, cut out, and carried it in his vest pocket until it was committed to memory. James Russell Lowell he only knew as "Hosea Biglow," every one of whose effusions he knew. He sometimes repeated, word for word, the whole of "John P. Robinson, he," giving the unceasing refrain with great unction and enjoyment. He once said that originality and daring impudence were sublimed in this stanza of Lowell's:

> "Ef you take a sword and dror it,
> An' stick a feller creatur thru,
> Gov'ment hain't to answer for it,
> God'll send the bill to you."

Mr. Lincoln's love of music was something passionate, but his tastes were simple and uncultivated, his choice being old airs, songs, and ballads, among which the plaintive Scotch songs were best liked. "Annie Laurie," "Mary of Argyle," and especially "Auld Robin Gray," never lost their charm for him; and all songs which had for their theme the rapid flight of time, decay, the recollections of early days, were sure to make a deep impression. The song which he liked best, above all others, was one called

"Twenty Years Ago"—a simple air, the words to which are supposed to be uttered by a man who revisits the play-ground of his youth. He greatly desired to find music for his favorite poem, "Oh, why should the spirit of mortal be proud?" and said once, when told that the newspapers had credited him with the authorship of the piece, "I should not care much for the reputation of having written that, but would be glad if I could compose music as fit to convey the sentiment as the words now do."

He wrote slowly, and with the greatest deliberation, and liked to take his time; yet some of his dispatches, written without any corrections, are models of compactness and finish. His private correspondence was extensive, and he preferred writing his letters with his own hand, making copies himself frequently, and filing every thing away in a set of pigeon-holes in his office. When asked why he did not have a letter-book and copying-press, he said, "A letter-book might be easily carried off, but that stock of filed letters would be a back-load." He conscientiously attended to his enormous correspondence, and read every thing that appeared to demand his own attention. He said that he read with great regularity the letters of an old friend who lived on the Pacific coast until he received a letter of *seventy pages* of letter paper, when he broke down, and never read another. . . .

His thoughtfulness for those who bore the brunt of the battles, his harmonious family relations, his absorbing love for his children, his anxiety for the well-being and conduct of the emancipated colored people, his unwavering faith in the hastening doom of human slavery, his affectionate regard for "the simple people," his patience, his endurance, his mental sufferings, and what he did for the Nation and for Humanity and Liberty—these all must be left to the systematic and enduring labors of the historian. Though he is dead, his immortal virtues are the rich possession of the nation; his fame shall grow with our young Republic; and as years roll on brighter lustre will adorn the name of Abraham Lincoln.

. . . *and as years roll on brighter lustre will adorn the name of Abraham Lincoln.*

Index

Index

Courier, Norwich [Conn.], 144
Courrier des États-Unis [U.S.], 316, 317
Covode, John, 180
Cowan, Edgar, 291
Crawford, M. J., 245
Crawford, Thomas, 187–88, 452
Crisis [Columbus, Ohio], 228, 297
Critic, London [England], 193
Crittenden, John J., 53, 112, 113, 184, 185, 196, 435
Cross, J. L. H., 51
Cushing, E. H., 476
Cushman, William H. H., 108

Daily Advertiser, Boston, 60
Daily Alta California [San Francisco], xv, 295, 479
Daily Chronicle [Washington, D. C.], 423
Daily Commercial, Cincinnati, xv, 136, 163, 173
Daily Courier, Louisville [Ky.], 235–36
Daily Dispatch, Richmond [Va.], 282
Daily Express [Petersburg, Va.], 436, 442
Daily News, New York, xiv, 369, 379
Daily Picayune [New Orleans, La.], 194, 258
Daily State Journal [Springfield, Ill.], 461
Daily Times, Chicago, 92
Dallas Herald [Texas], 219, 476
Danville Sun [Illinois], 75
Davidson, Jim, 124
Davidson, William H., 27
Davis, Jefferson, 52, 53, 234, 269, 276, 294, 300, 306, 337, 339–40, 343, 366, 373, 387, 393, 422, 429–30, 431, 435, 445, 449, 451–53
Davis, Winter, 439
Dawson, John, 11, 13

Day-Book, New York Evening, 255–56, 261
Dayton, William L., 78–82, 169, 172
Delano, Columbus, 169
Delta, New Orleans, 98, 99
Democrat, Bangor [Me.], 256
Democrat, Free [Galesburg, Ill.], 123
Democrat, Independent [Concord, N. H.], 126
Democrat, Missouri, 338
Democratic Press, Peoria [Ill.], 58
Democratic Review, 27
Democrat, St. Louis [Mo.], 211
Derby, Lord, 336
Detroit Advertiser, 186
Devens, Charles, 452
Dewey, Chester P., 105
Dicey, Edward, 297
Dispatch, Richmond [Va.], 274, 282, 284, 315, 407, 415, 417
Dix, John A., 53
Dixon, James, 249
Dodge [Abram R.], 25
Dole, William P., 338
Doubleday, Abner, 264
Dougherty [John], 22
Douglas, Stephen Arnold, 15–18, 27, 53, 68, 70–73, 82–94, 96–119, 122–143, 150–53, 156, 159–61, 177, 181, 184–87, 189–91, 193, 199, 203, 205, 207, 217–18, 249, 289, 305, 359, 435, 463–65, 470
Douglass, Fred (erick), 395
Draper, Simeon, 203, 214
Dreolle, Ernest, 492
Dudley, Thomas H., 169
Duer, William, 53
Duncan, Governor [Ill.], 26, 27
Dunn, George G., 54
Dupont, Samuel F. [Admiral], 502

Early [Jacob M.], Dr., 9, 10
Echo du Pacifique [San Francisco], 479, 480

Eckert [Thomas T.], Major, 433
Edwards, Cyrus, 21
Edwards [Ninian W.], 9, 13, 21
Eggleston, Benjamin, 140
Elkin, G., 12
Elkin, Thomas C., 14
Elkin, Col. William F., 13
Ellsworth [Elmer], Colonel, 229, 269, 491
Elwell, George, 123
Embree, Elisha, 54
Emerson, Ralph Waldo, xv, 323, 324 ff.
English [R. W.], Dr., 32, 40, 41, 42
Enquirer, Cincinnati [Ohio], xv, 137
Enquirer, Richmond [Va.], 275, 314
Evansville Journal [Indiana], 187
Evarts, William M., 168, 172
Evening Day-Book, New York, 255, 256, 261
Everett, Edward, 186, 187, 210, 355 356, 358, 361, 362, 363, 381, 468, 469, 471
Ewing, William Lee D., 32, 40, 41, 43
Examiner and Herald, Lancaster [Pa.], 143
Examiner, Richmond [Va.], 364
Express, Daily [Petersburg, Va.], 436, 442

Felch, Alpheus, 53
Fell, Jesse W., 145, 146
Fessenden, William P., 164
Fillmore, Millard, 66, 68, 184
Firenze, Gazzetta di [Florence, Italy], 494
Fish, F. S., 51
Fletcher [Job], 11, 13
Folsom, Abby, 99
Foote [Henry S.], 53
Ford, Allen N., 49
Ford [Thomas], 40
Forney, John, 423

Forum, Rockford [Ill.], 54
Francis, Simeon, 3, 11, 23, 24
Frankfort Commonwealth [Ky.], 473
Franklin, Benjamin, 87, 156
Free Democrat [Galesburg, Ill.], 123
Fremont, John C., xiv, 78, 79, 80, 81, 155, 197, 275, 276, 296, 381, 384, 387–88, 391, 393, 399, 439
Frost, T. G., 124
Fulton [Robert], 372
Fulton Telegraph [Ill.], 26, 27

Galesville Transcript [Wisconsin], 353
Garibaldi, xvi, 494
Garrison [William L.], 99, 117
Gazette, Cincinnati, 141, 187
Gazette, Illinois [Lacon, Ill.], 49, 74, 129
Gazzetta di Firenze [Florence, Italy], 494
Giddings [Joshua], 71, 375
Gilman, George S., 160
Goggin, William L., 196, 455
Gott, Representative [Conn.], 189
Graves, E. C., 51
Grant, U. S., 335, 384, 389–94, 399, 400, 407–09, 426, 430, 432–33, 449, 491
Greeley, Horace, xii, xiii, 50, 52, 54, 59, 110, 131, 167, 176, 178, 180–81, 198, 228–29, 233, 237, 291, 300–01, 381, 384, 388, 430, 439, 441, 449, 468, 481
Green, Bowling, 14, 16
Green [Peter], 22
Gregory, D. S., 53
Grimshaw, Jackson, 183

Hale, John P., 53
Halleck, Henry [General], 294, 389–91
Hall, N. K., 53

Index

Index